CW00501207

TYLER'S FAMILY PROVISION

Third edition

TYLER'S FAMILY PROVISION

THIRD EDITION

Richard D Oughton MA (Cantab), LL M (Pennsylvania)
of Lincoln's Inn and the Northern Circuit, Barrister-at-Law; Hollins & Bridge Street Chambers, Manchester

CONSULTING EDITOR
ELG Tyler, MA (Oxon)
of Lincoln's Inn, Barrister-at-Law; Barrister and Solicitor of the High Court and Federal Courts of Australia and of the Supreme Court of Tasmania

Butterworths
London, Edinburgh, Dublin
1997

United Kingdom	Butterworths a Division of Reed Elsevier (UK) Ltd, Halsbury House, 35 Chancery Lane, LONDON WC2A 1EL and 4 Hill Street, EDINBURGH EH2 3JZ
Australia	Butterworths, SYDNEY, ADELAIDE, BRISBANE, CANBERRA, MELBOURNE and PERTH,
Canada	Butterworths Canada Ltd, TORONTO and VANCOUVER
Ireland	Butterworth (Ireland) Ltd, DUBLIN
Malaysia	Malayan Law Journal Sdn Bhd, KUALA LUMPUR
New Zealand	Butterworths of New Zealand Ltd, WELLINGTON and AUCKLAND
Singapore	Reed Elsevier (Singapore) Pte Ltd, SINGAPORE
South Africa	Butterworths Publishers (Pty) Ltd, DURBAN
USA	Michie, CHARLOTTESVILLE, Virginia

A CIP Catalogue record for this book is available from the British Library.

First edition 1971
Second edition 1984

Printed and bound in Great Britain by Clays Ltd, St Ives PLC

Preface to the third edition

The principal aim of this book remains as stated in the preface to the Second Edition, namely to answer two questions: firstly the practical question whether a particular applicant is entitled to be awarded provision by the Court, and if so, how much, and secondly, the theoretical question of why such an award is made. It remains my belief that only by answering the latter question can the former question be properly answered. If I have not always arrived at the correct solution to the many problems in this area of the law, I hope that I have at least illuminated some of the relevant arguments.

I would like at this point to thank the two university teachers who first introduced me to family provision, namely the late John Hall at St John's College, Cambridge and Professor Martin Aronstein at the University of Pennsylvania Law School. I suspect that ultimately John Hall and I would have disagreed on many aspects of family provision. However I remain indebted to him for giving me a thorough grasp of family law, without which I, as a Chancery practitioner, would not have been able to attempt this book. There must be very many others who are similarly grateful for his excellent teaching. Professor Aronstein introduced me to a more critical analysis of the law of succession, some of which has found its way into this book.

Edward Tyler has continued, from the other side of the world, to assist me as consulting editor.

I am grateful for Miss Joy Brereton supplying me with a copy of her thesis for her Master of Laws degree and to Miss Paula Fallows who has guided me through the minefield of pensions on divorce.

The permission of Her Majesty's Stationery Office to reprint the table of public opinion on page 34A is gratefully acknowledged.

I am grateful for the indulgence of my publishers in permitting me to include in the Appendices material not generally available.

The law is stated at 1 August 1997, although later developments have been noted where possible.

R D Oughton
Hollins & Bridge Street Chambers,
Manchester.

Contents

ABBREVIATIONS

ALBERY	Albery, *The Inheritance (Family Provision) Act 1938* (1950)
CRETNEY	Cretney and Masson, *Principles of Family Law* (6th edn, 1997)
DE GROOT AND NICKEL	De Groot and Nickel, *Family Provision in Australia and New Zealand* (1993)
DICKEY	Dickey, *Family Provision after Death* (1992)
first edition	Tyler, *Family Provision* (1st edn, 1971)
GILCHRIST SMITH	Gilchrist Smith, *Intestacy and Family Provision* (1952)
JACKSON AND DAVIES	*Jackson's Matrimonial Finance and Taxation* (6th edn, 1996)
LAW COM	Law Commission Report No 61 – Family Law: Second Report on Family Property: Family Provision on Death (1974)
RAYDEN	*Rayden and Jackson on Divorce and Family Matters* (16th edn, 1991)
ROSS	Ross, *Inheritance Act Claims: Law and Practice* (1993)
ROSS MARTYN	Ross Martyn, *Family Provision:Law and Practice* (2nd edn, 1985)
second edition	*Tyler's Family Provision* (2nd edn, 1984)
WORKING PAPER	Law Commission Working Paper No 42 – Family Law: Family Property Law (1974)
WRIGHT	Wright, *Testator's Family Maintenance in Australia and New Zealand* (3rd edn, 1974)
the 1938 Act	The Inheritance (Family Provision) Act 1938
the 1965 Act	The Matrimonial Causes Act 1965
the 1975 Act	The Inheritance (Provision for Family and Dependants) Act 1975

TABLE OF STATUTES

References in **bold** type indicate where the section of an Act is set out in part or in full.

TABLE OF STATUTORY INSTRUMENTS

References in **bold** type indicate where the section of an Act is set out in part or in full.

TABLE OF CASES

A

B

E

PAGE

H

M

PAGE

Chapter 1

HISTORICAL INTRODUCTION

Testamentary Freedom

Testamentary freedom means that a person may dispose of his or her property by will as he or she wishes. It means, for example, that a married man may disinherit his wife and children and leave all his property to his mistress, or vice versa. It involves the principle of disherison. This principle survives in few, if any, countries in the world today.[1] It does not survive in many jurisdictions today because the rights of a testator to control his property after his death are thought to be of less importance than the testator's duties to members of his family and the state, which require that property be given to certain members of the testator's family in preference to other members of the testator's family or outsiders. The nature of these duties to the family and to the state are discussed in Chapter 2. There are three general techniques for restricting testamentary freedom.

First, the testamentary power may be restricted to a proportion only of the estate. The surviving spouse or children of a deceased may automatically be entitled to a specified proportion of the deceased's estate, so that the deceased's testamentary freedom only applies to the remainder. This is sometimes called the forced share or *legitim* system. This is the position under French Law, for example, where a proportion of a deceased man's estate – called *'la réserve (héréditaire)'* – automatically passes to certain near relatives (but these do not include the widow). The part of his estate of which he can dispose is called '*le (quotité) disponsible*'. The size of the '*réserve*' depends on the number of claimants, but is not less than one-third or more than three-quarters of the estate.[2] And under Scots law a wife is automatically entitled to 'the wife's part' of her husband's movable property and the children to 'the bairn's part'. The wife is entitled to one-third of the estate if there are surviving children, or one-half if there are no children. The child or children is or are entitled to one-third if there is a surviving widow, or one-half

1. See Dainow, 'Unrestricted Testation in Quebec' (1935–36)10 Tulane L Rev 400.
2. For French law see Amos and Walton, *Introduction to French Law* (3rd edn 1967), Ch 12 and p 333 *et seq.*

if there is not. The deceased is only free to dispose of the rest of his movable property. A husband is similarly entitled to a part of his deceased wife's movable estate.[3]

A second or alternative method of forced share system by which duties to members of the deceased's family may be enforced is where certain relatives are given the right to set aside the will, if it provides less than a specified portion of the estate for the relative. The difference between an automatic fixed share and an elective share is that the latter requires the disinherited relative to take positive steps to enforce his rights. The elective share was adopted in post-classical Roman Law. Certain near relatives of the deceased might impeach the will on the ground that they had been unjustly deprived of the share of the inheritance to which they were entitled. That share was the share to which they were entitled on intestacy. The testator's children were entitled under Justinian's legislation to one-third of the estate, or, if there were five or more of them one-half. Certain other relatives were entitled to one-quarter. The claimants did not have an automatic right to the appropriate part of the estate but had to claim it by action – the *querela inofficiosi testamenti*. In proper circumstances they might be justly disinherited. A widow had no right to bring the *querela*. On her husband's death she was entitled to recover her dowry. Later, a widow without a dowry was given the right to claim one-quarter of her husband's estate. A husband could keep his deceased wife's dowry. If she had none, he was entitled, subject to certain restrictions, to claim one-quarter of the estate.[4]

The elective share approach has also been adopted in most American jurisdictions, where a surviving spouse is entitled to set aside a will in so far as it does not give a minimum portion of the estate of the deceased spouse.[5] The existence of an elective forced share regime rather than an automatic forced share regime in both Roman and American law is probably due to the prior existence of testamentary freedom upon which the elective share regime was subsequently imposed.

3. For Scots law see MacDonald, *An Introduction to the Scots Law of Succession*; Meston, *The Succession (Scotland) Act 1964* (4th edn). Much of the law is set out in the Succession (Scotland) Act 1964.
4. For Roman law see Thomas, *Textbook of Roman Law*, Chs XLVII, XLVIII.
5. A typical elective share provision is contained in the Uniform Probate Code s 2-201–2-207. This gives the spouse a right to one-third of the estate (2-201(a)), provided an election is made within six months of the grant of probate (2-205(a)). On 31 August 1975 the Uniform Probate Code had been enacted in Alaska, Arkansas, Colorado, Idaho, Minnesota, Montana, Nebraska, New Mexico, North Dakota, South Dakota and Utah. The Republic of Ireland has adopted an elective share system for spouses, but a discretionary system for children, see Part IX of the Succession Act 1965; Brady, *Succession Law in Ireland*, Ch 7.

The third method, which is adopted by English law and certain Commonwealth jurisdictions, is the system of judicial discretion. Under this system complete testamentary freedom exists, but the courts are given power to reform the will of a testator to the extent of making reasonable provision for his dependants. It resembles the second system in so far as the will stands until impeached, but differs from that system in so far as the claimant is not entitled to a fixed share.

The persons who benefit from limits on disinheritance vary considerably. Under French Law the blood relatives of the deceased benefit from the restrictions, the deceased's spouse is protected not by any restriction on testation, but by the matrimonial property regime. In contrast the beneficiary of the restraints on testation in American jurisdictions (except Louisiana) are spouses of the deceased; infant children of the deceased benefit to only a minor extent[6] and adult children not at all.

Testamentary Freedom in English Law[7]

English law has only recognised *absolute* testamentary freedom for the comparatively short period from 1891 when the Mortmain and Charitable Uses Act of that year removed all restrictions from testamentary gifts to charities to 1938 when the Inheritance (Family Provision) Act was passed. However, substantial testamentary freedom did exist in England during the eighteenth and nineteenth centuries. This testamentary freedom was a direct reversal of the law in medieval times.

For a while after the Norman Conquest there may have been testamentary freedom. But as regards the personal property of a deceased by the twelfth century his widow and children were automatically entitled to fixed proportions of his estate; one-third of the estate respectively, if the deceased left both widow and children; or one-half of the estate, where the deceased left either a widow or children. The *writ de rationabili parte bonorum* lay against the executors for the enforcement of these rights. But more often the rights were asserted in the ecclesiastical courts. The deceased

6. Eg Uniform Probate Code s 2-403 (Family Allowance).
7. Pollock and Maitland, *History of English Law* (2nd edn) Vol III, p 348 *et seq*; Holdsworth, *History of English Law* (5th edn) Vol III, pp 550–556; (3rd edn) Vol IV, pp 438–439, 464–466, Plunknett, *A Concise History of the Common Law* (5th edn), pp 735–745; Keeton and Gower, 'Freedom of Testation in English Law' (1935) 20 Iowa L Rev 326; Dainow, 'Limitations on Testamentary Freedom in England' (1940) 25 Corn L Q 337.

was only free to dispose of the remaining proportion of his estate. If he left neither widow nor heir he could dispose of his property as he wished. These restrictions had ceased in most parts of the country by the fourteenth century but they continued in the Province of York, Wales and London until abolished by statutes in 1692, 1696 and 1724 respectively. Section 3 of the Wills Act 1837 provided that a person was entitled to dispose by will of all his personal estate.

On the other hand as regards realty it was clear by Bracton's time (circa 1257) that freehold could not be devised, save where there was a local custom, such as gravelkind, to the contrary. This restriction was linked with the doctrine of tenure and the services and incidents thereof. The principle of primogeniture and the importance of the incidents such as wardship involved the property passing automatically to the heir, so that there was no place for testamentary freedom. Nevertheless the restriction was avoided by conveying land to feoffees to uses to the use of the feoffor until his death and thereafter to the uses declared by his will. The desire to have what was in effect a power to devise was, perhaps, one of the main reasons for the popularity of uses. The Statute of Uses 1535 was intended to put an end to this practice. This resulted in the rebellion in 1536 known as the 'Pilgrimage of Grace' which led to the Statute of Wills 1540. The Statute of Wills (as amended in 1542) allowed landowners to devise two-thirds of the land held by them in Knight's Service and all the land held in socage. But devises under the Statute of Wills did not avoid feudal dues, for which those taking under the devise were thereby made liable. Subsequently testators took advantage of the Statute of Uses and, by employing a combination of an executed use and a power of appointment, contrived to create a transaction which served the same function as a devise but avoided liability for feudal dues.[8] The Tenures Abolition Act 1660 converted Knight's Service into socage and thereby implemented the Statute of Wills – since feudal dues were abolished there was no longer any need to make a devise other than under the power given by that Statute.

As regards the power of married women to dispose of property by will it is only comparatively recently that they have had such power and eventual full equality of power of testamentary disposition between the sexes was only effected by the Married Woman's Property Act 1893.

Although a man had testamentary freedom in respect of realty after 1660 this was subject to a wife's right of dower. This was the

8. See Simpson, *An Introduction to the History of Land Law*, pp 179–180.

right of a widow to a life-interest in one-third of the freehold estates of inheritance of her husband of which he was seised during the marriage (otherwise than as a joint tenant) and which issue of the marriage, if any, were capable of inheriting.[9] Until the Dower Act 1833 the widow's right could not be overridden by any disposition made by the husband. However, the right could be avoided by making substantial provision for her before marriage by way of jointure or thereafter by various conveyancing devices which employed uses. The Dower Act 1833 enabled a husband to defeat his widow's right to dower either by alienation, *inter vivos* or by will, or by a declaration to that effect in a deed or his will. Dower was abolished, save for an exceptional case, by the Administration of Estates Act 1925.[10]

A widower was given the somewhat similar interest of courtesy in his deceased wife's realty.[11] The widower's right of courtesy was a life interest in the whole of the wife's real estate subject to certain conditions being satisfied. After the Married Women's Property Act 1882, a wife could defeat her husband's right.[12] Courtesy was abolished by the Administration of Estates Act 1925, save for two exceptional cases.[10]

So from 1833 onwards a man could dispose of all his property, except for limitations on gifts to charities repealed in 1891, without having to make provision for his widow or children. The nadir of state intervention in the disposition of a deceased's estate was reached in 1925 when the rules for the distribution of property on intestacy ceased to be based upon any particular social policy, such as the policy against sub-division of holdings and in favour of the perpetuation of a dynasty which led to male primogeniture, but were based upon the average provision of a sample of wills.[13] As the enactment of the Inheritance (Family Provision) Act 1938 was to demonstrate, support for testamentary freedom was as a principle

9. See Megarry and Wade, *The Law of Real Property* (5th edn), pp 544–546. For a surprisingly rosy view of dower and courtesy, see MacFarlane, *Marriage and Love in England 1300-1840*, p 282.
10. Administration of Estates Act 1925, ss 45(1) and 51(2); Law of Property Act 1925, s 130(4).
11. See Megarry and Wade, *The Law of Real Property* (5th edn), pp 543–544.
12. Before 1882 she could only defeat her husband's right if the property had been conveyed to her separate use.
13. See Wolstenholme and Cherry, *Conveyancing Statutes* (12th edn) Vol II, p 1398. See also Report of the Committee on the Law of Intestate Succession (1951) Cmd 8310, para 17. Law Commission Report No 187 'Family Law: Distribution on Intestacy' (1989) espoused value judgments as to the form of the law, but supported its conclusions by public opinion surveys.

not as strong as a mere chronicle of legislation would indicate. The triumph of testamentary freedom in the eighteenth and nineteenth centuries was not necessarily the result of great support for the idea of testamentary freedom as such, although such support was not lacking,[14] but the result of an accidental coincidence of interests which all found freedom of testation convenient and desirable. The landed families supported freedom of testation because wills enabled settlements to be created which even more than the canons of descent for land ensured that land remained in the family and because wills ameliorated some of the consequences of male primogeniture by permitting the creation of jointures for widows and portions for younger sons and daughters.[15] The opponents of male primogeniture supported freedom of testation as a means of avoiding the canons of descent for the devolution of land. There was little support for institutions such as dower, which could in any event be avoided, since they complicated title to land and made the transfer of land more expensive, a matter on which the supporters and opponents of the system of settled land were united in opposition.[16] Restricting testamentary freedom was only to be seriously advanced after the rules on intestacy became coherent and acceptable to the feminist lobby.

Twentieth Century Limitations on Freedom of Testation in the United States

In most of the common law jurisdictions in the United States dower never became as easily barred as in England[17] and thus testamentary freedom never became as absolute as in England. While dower was regarded as archaic, being both inefficient in protecting a widow's interest in that it only applied to land and could to a certain extent be avoided and a serious obstacle to the marketability of land, its

14. For supporters of freedom of testation see pp 35–37, *post.*
15. For the landed families' methods of holding land in settlement see Spring, 'Nineteenth Century Land Settlements' (1964) 8 Am Jo Legal History 209. For a discussion of how females adapted to and benefited from freedom of testation and the rules of intestacy, see Spring, *Law, Land & Family*.
16. For the attitudes of the landed classes to land law reform in the nineteeth century, see Spring, 'Landowners, Lawyers and Land Law Reform in Nineteenth-Century England' (1977) 22 Am Jo Legal History 40 and for the radical demands for 'Free Trade in Land', see Thompson, 'Land and Politics in England in the Nineteenth Century', 5th series, 15 Trans Roy Hist Soc.
17. Powell, *The Law of Real Property* (1974), s 209 [2].

objects were widely supported. During the twentieth century many states replaced dower with a system whereby a spouse was entitled, upon her election, to a minimum share, usually expressed as a proportion, and typically one-third, of the deceased's estate.[18]

The Birth of Family Provision in New Zealand[19]

Most British colonies received English law in the nineteenth century, which gave a deceased total freedom of testation. Indeed freedom of testation was even imposed upon Quebec after its capture by the British,[20] although it otherwise retained the civil law.

At the turn of the century attempts were made to limit freedom of testation in New Zealand. After the rejection of an earlier attempt to introduce the Scottish system of fixed shares,[1] the New Zealand Parliament passed in 1900 the Testators Family Maintenance Act. This enabled the widow, widower or child, of any age, whether married or unmarried, to apply to the court for provision out of the deceased's estate if the testator's will[2] made inadequate provision for the 'proper maintenance and support' of the applicant. The Act, described as 'unquestionably one of the great and original contributions of New Zealand to modern law',[3] broke new ground in that rights to the succession of a person's estate could be altered by the court in the exercise of a wide discretion. The choice of a discretionary system was partly influenced by the prior enactment of a similar statute for Maori land,[4] partly by analogy with the Destitute Persons Act, which enabled a child or spouse to claim maintenance against a person while alive rather than depend upon the state for support and partly, no doubt, as a political compromise between the supporters and opponents of testamentary freedom. The discretionary system acted as a curb upon the worst excesses

18. See fn 5, p 3, *ante*.
19. The best account of the beginnings of family provision in New Zealand is Robson, *The British Commonwealth: The Development of its Laws and Constitutions Vol 4 New Zealand* (2nd edn), pp 471–475. See also Stephens, *The Law Relating to Family Provision in New Zealand* (2nd edn); Wiren, 'Testators' Family Maintenance in New Zealand' (1929) 45 LQR 378; Dainow, 'Restricted Testation in New Zealand, Australia and Canada' (1938) 36 Mich L Rev 1107, 1108–1109; DE GROOT AND NICKEL, para 104.
20. Dainow, 'Unrestricted Testation in Quebec' (1935–36) 10 Tulane L Rev 400.
1. Robson, *The British Commonwealth: The Development of Its Laws and Constitutions Vol 4 New Zealand* (2nd edn), p 471.
2. The Act only applied where the deceased died testate.
3. Prof Laufer quoted in *Robson*, op cit, p 472.
4. Native Land Court Act 1894, s 46.

of an unfettered power of testation, without abolishing the power where public policy did not demand that a deceased leave his property to certain relatives. The discretionary system is an attempt at a more individualised justice, rejecting any uniform solution for the whole variety of human relations. Although primarily promoted as a measure to alleviate a burden on the public purse, the jurisdiction was invoked substantially to alter private rights.[5]

The original statute was re-enacted in a consolidating measure in 1908.[6] The New Zealand courts developed the 'moral duty' test in exercising the jurisdiction. Provision would only be ordered in favour of an applicant if the testator failed in his 'moral duty' to the applicant. The 'moral duty' test has two aspects. Firstly, it demonstrates that an applicant must show something more than that he comes within the class of applicants who may apply before a court will exercise its powers. Secondly, its emphasis on a moral duty diverts attention from any actual dependence upon the deceased by the applicant or the existence of a legal duty to maintain the applicant owed by the deceased. The general approach of the New Zealand courts was laid down by the New Zealand Court of Appeal in *Allardice v Allardice*,[7] which decision and general approach were approved in a cursory manner by the Privy Council.[8] The applicants in *Allardice v Allardice* were three married adult daughters and two adult sons of the deceased by a first marriage. The deceased died possessed of a large estate, which by his will he left to his second wife and the issue of that union. The sons were able-bodied and were not dependent upon the deceased prior to his death. The daughters were supported by their husbands, who earned only small wages, and were not dependent upon the deceased prior to his death. The applicants' claim was dismissed at first instance, but the Court of Appeal allowed an appeal by the daughters, but not the sons, and awarded the daughters annuities of either £40 or £60 each. The Privy Council dismissed an appeal by the executors of the deceased. In allowing the appeal of the daughters, the Court of Appeal

5. *Robson*, op cit, pp 473–474.
6. Family Protection Act 1908, printed in Tillard, *Family Inheritance* (1st edn), pp 251–253.
7. *Sub nom Re Allardice* (1910) 29 NZLR 959.
8. [1911] AC 730. The Board only required argument from the unsuccessful appellants and the matter was only argued for less than a full day, since part of the day was spent upon hearing *Samaradiwakara v De Saram* [1911] AC 753. Two of the members of the Board (Lord Shaw of Dunfermline and Lord De Villiers) came from jurisdictions and traditions where *legitim* existed. The advice of the Board, given by Lord Robson, takes up less than two full pages of the law reports and strongly emphasises that a court sitting in London should not interfere with the discretion of a lower court sitting locally.

enunciated the following principles,[9] which were expressly approved by the Privy Council.[10]

(a) The legislation is something more than a statute to extend the Destitute Persons Act.[11]
(b) The legislation is not a statute to empower the Court to make a new will for the estate.
(c) The legislation allows the Court only so far as necessary to provide for the proper maintenance and support of any applicant where adequate provision has not been made for their maintenance and support by the will of the testator.
(d) In the case of a widow, at all events, if not in the case of a widower, the Court will make more ample provision than in the case of children, if the children are physically and mentally able to maintain and support themselves.

The New Zealand system of family provision proved to be politically acceptable and was quite widely used by applicants.[12] It was copied with local variations by all the Australian jurisdictions before the Second World War[13] and by most of the Canadian Provinces before and after the Second World War.[14]

Viscount Astor's *Motion* in 1928

In England restrictions on testamentary freedom were only seriously proposed in 1928 when Viscount Astor initiated a debate in the

9. (1910) 29 NZLR 959 at 968, per Stout CJ.
10. [1911] AC 730 at 734.
11. As to the Destitute Persons Act, see p 7, *ante*.
12. Gold, Note, (1938) 1 Mod L Rev 299 states that in the five years preceding 1938 applications under the New Zealand legislation represented 1.75% of the number of grants of representation made. This would seem to be a remarkably large proportion considering that the purpose of most wills is to increase a spouse's intestate share rather than reduce it (see Dunham, 'The Method, Process and Frequency of Wealth Transmission on Death' (1962) 30 UChi L Rev 241) and the number of applications in England and Wales (See Appendix A).
13. For the Australian and New Zealand legislation in 1993 see DE GROOT AND NICKEL, Appendix III.
14. Dainow, 'Restricted Testation in New Zealand, Australia and Canada' (1938) 36 Mich L Rev 1107; Laskin, 'Dependants' Relief Legislation' (1939) 17 Can Bar Rev 181; Gray, 'Dependants' Relief Legislation' (1939) 17 Can Bar Rev 233; Brown, 'Dependants' Reliefs Acts' (1940) 18 Can Bar Rev 261; Bale, 'Limitation of Testamentary Disposition in Canada' (1964) 42 Can Bar Rev 367.

House of Lords. Although, as votes upon the various Inheritance Bills in the House of Commons during the 1930s were to demonstrate, the idea of restricting absolute freedom of testation was popular, the public and members of both Houses of Parliament were essentially apathetic about freedom of testation. Therefore to effect any change in the law, it was necessary for a pressure group to bring the issue before the public and Parliament. Such a pressure group was the feminist 'National Union of Societies for Equal Citizenship', whose secretary was Mrs Hubbock and whose president was Miss Eleanor Rathbone, the Independent MP for the Combined English Universities. It was Mrs Hubbock's achievement that the question of freedom of testation was brought before Parliament. Once the matter was brought before Parliament, it soon became apparent that the only substantial opposition to a limitation on absolute freedom of testation came from a small section of the Conservative Party and the legal establishment.

The matter first came before Parliament in 1928 when Viscount Astor moved a motion in the House of Lords to set up a select committee to investigate whether the law of inheritance should be changed in the light of the experience of Scotland, Australia and other parts of the Empire.[15] Viscount Astor was fully briefed by the National Union of Societies for Equal Citizenship before moving the motion. His Lordship stated that while what he regarded as 'unjust wills' were exceptional, they were sufficiently numerous to cause concern.[16] He suggested that wives, children (of any age) and 'other dependants of the deceased' should have certain rights to challenge the testamentary disposition of the deceased.[17] Lord Astor was somewhat ill served in the major example of the unfairness of freedom of testation he used before the House of Lords. The example was of a man who died possessed of an estate of £1,500,000 and who left his estranged wife and legitimate children only £30,000 and the remainder of his estate to his mistress and illegitimate children.[18] Lord Astor specifically suggested that the discretionary New Zealand system should be adopted.[19]

Viscount Astor's motion was strongly opposed by Viscount Haldane, the Liberal turned Labour former Lord Chancellor. Lord Haldane regarded a discretionary system as unworkable and courts as an unsuitable tribunal to vary wills.[20] He was not impressed either

15. 71 HL Parl Deb, col 37 (16 May 1928).
16. 71 HL Parl Deb, cols 39–40.
17. 71 HL Parl Deb, col 38.
18. 71 HL Parl Deb, cols 39–40.
19. 71 HL Parl Deb, cols 42–43, 45.
20. 71 HL Parl Deb, cols 46–47.

by the idea of reasoning from a few 'hard cases' or by the particular facts of the 'hard cases' given by Viscount Astor. He thought that a testator would be the best judge of his own will and that the only alternative to complete freedom of testation was wills made by the state and that accordingly no middle way was possible.[1] Lord Buckmaster was more favourable to the aims of the motion, but he was 'unmoved' by Viscount Astor's hard cases and considered that a widow who was left £30,000 was more than adequately provided for.[2] He thought that a system of fixed shares was preferable to a discretionary system.[3]

The government, speaking through Viscount Hailsham, the Lord Chancellor, opposed Viscount Astor's motion. Viscount Hailsham was implacably opposed to any restriction on freedom of testation.[4] The government was specifically opposed to a select committee because of the pressure of government business and the lack of public interest in the subject.[5] Lord Merrivale, the President of the Probate, Divorce and Admiralty Division, opposed any substantial limitation on freedom of testation, but thought that the jurisdiction of magistrates to order husbands to support their wives should be extended to support after the death of the husband.[6] In the light of the lack of support from fellow peers and the opposition from the Woolsack, Viscount Astor did not press his motion.[7]

Undaunted by this failure, Mrs Hubbock continued to lobby for some protection for wives and infant children. The National Union published a pamphlet called 'Unjust Wills', highlighting particular injustices of absolute freedom of testation.[8] This contained 18 particular cases of hardship, somewhat better examples than those used by Viscount Astor in the House of Lords debate. These 18 'hard cases' were obtained by inserting an advertisement in a newspaper, but no investigation of any claim was made.[9] Viscount Astor had a bill drafted which had a first reading in the House of Lords on 1 August 1928.[10] The bill permitted any 'spouse, child, remoter issue or any dependant' to apply to the court for provision (clause 1(1), but only if they were actually dependent upon the

1. 71 HL Parl Deb, col 47.
2. 71 HL Parl Deb, col 51.
3. 71 HL Parl Deb, col 52.
4. 71 HL Parl Deb, cols 53–56.
5. 71 HL Parl Deb, col 57.
6. 71 HL Parl Deb, col 60.
7. 71 HL Parl Deb, col 60.
8. Originally published as an article in *Fortnightly Review* April 1929.
9. Report of the Joint Committee on the Wills and Intestacies (Family Maintenance) Bill, 17 June 1931, Evidence of Mrs Hubbock, para 37.
10. Wills and Intestacies (Family Maintenance) Bill, PRO LCO 2/1185.

deceased (clause 1(8)). An applicant could only apply to the court for provision if the will and any *inter vivos* advances did not give the applicant a certain minimum provision – in the case of a spouse the income of one-third of the estate or an annuity of £3,000 (clause 2). Viscount Astor's Bill was supported by a conference of women's organisations held by the National Union on 27 November 1928. Organisations supporting the measure included the British Federation of the University Women, the Catholic Women's League, the College of Nursing, the Conservative Women's Reform Association, the Mothers' Union, the National Council of Women and the Women's National Liberal Federation.[11]

The debate in the House of Lords stimulated an article to appear in the *Law Quarterly Review* explaining the New Zealand system.[12] The Lord Chancellor's Department consulted Sir Benjamin Cherry, the draftsman of the 1925 legislation, who acted as an unofficial adviser to the Department on all matters of property law. He advised against a system of fixed shares, but thought that the New Zealand system was both workable and likely to be politically acceptable.[13]

A second Bill was presented by Viscount Astor on 6 March 1929,[14] but could not be discussed because of the General Election of 1929. This election brought new hope to the proponents of some limitation on absolute freedom of testation. Both Ramsay MacDonald and Lloyd George in answer to a questionnaire from Mrs Hubbock expressed general support for Viscount Astor's Bill. Pointedly Stanley Baldwin did not reply to the questionnaire.[15] Viscount Sankey, the new Lord Chancellor, was quite favourable to Viscount Astor's Bill, as was Viscount Parmoor, an influential left-leaning Law Lord.[16]

1930 and 1933 Bills

In the session 1930–31, the Wills and Intestacies (Family Maintenance) Bill was introduced as a private member's Bill by Miss Eleanor Rathbone MP.[17] The Bill's supporters included Dr Burgin

11. Memorandum, PRO LCO 2/1185.
12. Wiren, 'Testators' Family Maintenance in New Zealand' (1929) 45 LQR 378.
13. Memorandum, 7 May 1928 (this probably was used by the Lord Chancellor in drafting his speech); Letter from Cherry to Sir Claud Schuster, 10 May 1928, PRO LCO 2/1185.
14. Draft Bill, PRO LCO 2/1185.
15. Answers to questionnaire, PRO LCO 2/1185.
16. Letter from Viscount Sankey to Viscount Astor, 10 October 1929; Letter from Lord Parmoor to Viscount Sankey, 16 October 1929; PRO LCO 2/1185.
17. The First Reading was on 31 October 1930.

MP, a leading Conservative solicitor, Sir John Withers MP, a leading London solicitor and the Conservative MP for Cambridge University, Viscountess Astor MP, and Miss Ellen Wilkinson MP. The Bill, probably drafted by Sir Benjamin Cherry,[18] elaborated Viscount Astor's Bills of 1928 and 1929. However, the Bill departed from its predecessors in that it proposed fixed shares, which could be ignored with the approval of the court. The administrative machinery adopted was of considerable complexity and placed upon the executors, in the first instance, the duty of deciding whether provision was inadequate and that therefore, proceedings should be commenced. The only applicants would be spouses and infant children, all maintenance for children ceasing at age 23. Prior to the second reading of the Bill on 20 February 1931, the National Union circularised all MPs and re-issued their pamphlet 'Unjust Wills' in a second edition.[19]

During the second reading debate the Bill was promoted by Miss Rathbone with the arguments that it would alleviate many hard cases and that the obligations of marriage should not end on death.[20] The measure was supported from the Labour benches,[1] but was the subject of considerable criticism from the Conservative backbenches.[2] This criticism took two forms, a general objection to any restriction of freedom of testation and a particular objection to the complicated system of fixed shares tempered with judicial discretion which would apply to all wills, most of which were unobjectionable. Several of these objectors expressed a preference for the New Zealand system, which was less over-inclusive. These objections were summed up by Sir Dennis Herbert MP:

> It is a paternal and grandmotherly scheme for managing the affairs of everyone, on the assumption that everyone, or 99 out of 100, do not know how to, or will not have the decency to manage their affairs properly.[3]

The government view, given by Sir Stafford Cripps, the Solicitor-General, was non-committal, but very cautious.[4] At the

18. Letter from Schuster to Bowker, Law Officers' Department, 16 February 1931, PRO LCO 2/1187.
19. Circular and Pamphlet, PRO LCO 2/1187.
20. 248 HC Parl Deb, cols 1641–1651.
1. 248 HC Parl Deb, cols 1651–1653 (Mr A Henderson).
2. 248 HC Parl Deb, cols 1653–1656 (Capt Bourne), 1657 (Sir Samuel Roberts), 1661–1665 (Mr Llewellyn-Jones), 1668–1670 (Sir Cooper Rawson), 1673–1674 (Major Llewellyn), 1693–1698 (Sir Dennis Herbert).
3. 248 HC Parl Deb, col 1696.
4. 248 HC Parl Deb, cols 1686–1691.

end of the debate the Bill was given a second reading by a majority of 149 votes for, with 28 votes against. As agreed beforehand with the Lord Chancellor, the matter was referred to a joint committee of both Houses chaired by Lord Thankerton. The Committee heard evidence from Mrs Hubbock, who stressed that a widow should have a share in her late husband's estate by right and not merely a right to apply for charity from the court.[5] Mrs Hubbock specifically opposed any right to maintenance for adult children.[6] The committee were very impressed by the evidence of the Public Trustee and the Law Society that the Bill, with its partial system of fixed shares, upset and varied very many wills which were entirely unobjectionable.[7] The Chancery Judges through Bennett J sent a memorandum to the Committee, which read:

> The conclusion at which they (the Chancery Judges) arrived was that there are so many grave objections to the Bill in its present form that they would regret to see it passed into law …
>
> The judges of the Chancery Division do not think that there would be any real objection to a measure which enabled a Court in a case where no adequate provision had been made for a spouse or infant children to order proper provision to be made for them out of the deceased's estate having regard to all the circumstances.[8]

There is reason to believe that in private the Chancery Judges viewed the New Zealand system as both unworkable as a matter of practice and wrong in principle, but expressed support for the New Zealand system as the lesser of two evils.[9]

In the light of this unanimous objection from knowledgeable parties to the form of the Bill, the Committee by a majority of 8–3 reported against the Bill in its present form or any system of fixed shares. The Committee did acknowledge that in a small, but not negligible number of cases, freedom of testation did result in injustice to spouses and infant children.[10] The Committee did report in general terms in favour of a scheme whereby a surviving spouse

5. Report of the Joint Committee on the Wills and Intestacies (Family Maintenance) Bill, 17 June 1931, Evidence of Mrs Hubbock.
6. Op cit, para 79.
7. Op cit, evidence of Mr Charles May, Mr Leonard Holmes, Sir Oswald Simpkin, Public Trustee; Letter from Law Society, 5 June 1931.
8. Op cit, letter of 21 May 1931.
9. See memorandum of Sir Thomas Inskip A-G, 2 March 1934 (extract in fn 19, p 16, *post*) and memorandum of Chancery Judges, 2 November 1937 (set out at p 18, *post*).
10. Report of the Joint Committee on the Wills and Intestacies (Family Maintenance) Bill, 17 June 1931, para 3.

or infant child could apply to the Court for maintenance from the deceased's estate.[11] With this Report and the General Election of 1931 Miss Rathbone's Bill failed.

1934 Bill

The 1931 General Election returned a very large Conservative majority, which was probably more in favour of, or rather more interested in,[12] some restriction of absolute freedom of testation than the Labour Party. The Report of the Joint Select Committee appeared to give a green light to legislation on the New Zealand model. The first chance which the new Parliament had to discuss any measure restricting absolute freedom of testation was in the 1933–34 session when Sir John Wardlow-Milne MP, a Conservative back-bencher, won a high place in the ballot for private members' Bills. Sir John Wardlow-Milne introduced a Power of Disinheritance Bill, under which spouses and children of any age could apply to the Court for provision out of the deceased's estate. Among the Bill's supporters on the first reading was the newly elected MP for Crewe, Donald Somervell KC.[13] The Bill met little opposition on the floor of the House of Commons, the second reading being unopposed,[14] and the Committee Stage being only eventful for the defeat of an amendment moved by the Attorney-General excluding County Courts from jurisdiction under the Act.[15] While there was little overt opposition to the Bill in Parliament, there was considerable opposition to it in the Government. While Viscount Sankey, the Lord Chancellor, was still a supporter of the Bill's aims, Inskip, the Attorney-General, disliked the Bill, but not sufficiently to oppose it openly, and wished to water down its provisions by amendment and perhaps 'talk the Bill out'.[16] Viscount Hailsham, now Secretary

11. Op cit, para 7.
12. See the remarks of Mr Rhys Davies MP that the Bill was 'Only concerned with a quarrel between the rich people of this country' at 288 HC Parl Deb, col 2044 (27 April 1934) and see remarks of Schuster in a letter to Bowker, Law Officers' Department, 16 February 1931, '... the Bill excites a good deal of interest among that wing of the professional feminists who belong to the upper and middle classes. I should not have thought that the ordinary working woman could feel much enthusiasm about it ...', PRO LCO 2/1187.
13. 283 HC Parl Deb, col 404.
14. 284 HC Parl Deb, col 1082 (18 December 1933).
15. 1933–34 Report of Standing Committee A, Inheritance (Family Provision) Bill, 20 March 1934.
16. Letter, Sir Claud Schuster to Graham-Harrison, Parliamentary Draftsman, 29 December 1933, PRO LCO 2/1188.

of State for War, remained as opposed to the measure as he was when it was first mooted six years before and regarded it as an error of the Whips that the Bill ever obtained an unopposed Second Reading.[17] Sir Claud Schuster, the Permanent Secretary to the Lord Chancellor, regarded the Report of the Joint Select Committee in 1931 as more a rejection of the complicated system of fixed shares proposed in Miss Rathbone's Bill than an endorsement of the New Zealand system. He regarded the merits of the New Zealand system as unproven, thought that its adoption would lead to a great deal of litigation and observed presciently that the New Zealand system still had not decided whether 'excluded relatives have a right to be protected against destitution, or a right to the kind of maintenance to which they have been accustomed'.[18] Several of the Chancery Judges appear to have changed their opinion of the discretionary system since their memorandum to the Joint Select Committee in 1931 and were now very hostile to the Bill.[19] The result of this opposition was that the Bill was deliberately talked out by the Attorney-General and Conservative backbenchers during the Report Stage and consequently died.[20]

1935 Bills

Two private members' Bills on the lines of Sir John Wardlow-Milne's Bill were introduced in the 1935–36 session, but neither was sufficiently well placed in the Ballot to stand any chance of becoming law.[1]

17. Letter, Viscount Hailsham to Sir Claud Schuster, 28 February 1934, PRO LCO 2/1188.
18. Letter, Sir Claud Schuster to Sir Maurice Gwyer, 19 February 1934, PRO LCO 2/1188.
19. Memorandum of Sir Thomas Inskip A-G, 2 March 1934: 'I find the Bill is regarded with great anxiety – I may also say hostility by such Chancery Judges as I have consulted informally, Luxmoore and Bennett among them. I also mentioned it to Tomlin last night and he takes great objection to the proposal to give a Chancery Judge carte blanche in the manner set forth in the Bill.' PRO LCO 2/1186.
20. 2888 HC Parl Deb, cols 2029–2095 (27 April 1934). The letter of Mr Galbreath MP to Sir Claud Schuster, 30 April 1934, makes it clear that the talking out of the Bill was deliberate, PRO LCO 2/1188.

1. The Inheritance (Family Provision) (No 1) Bill introduced by Mr Gardner MP, was withdrawn, 310 HC Parl Deb, col 45 (16 March 1936). The Inheritance (Family Provision) (No 2) Bill introduced by Miss Rathbone MP failed to obtain a Second Reading because of inadequate time on 20 March 1936, 310 HC Parl Deb, cols 849–852.

1936 and 1937 Bills

A further attempt at legislating on the lines of the 1934 Bill in the 1936–37 session again failed because the promoter did not gain a sufficiently high place in the Ballot for Private Members' Bills.[2] Although there was some opposition to the Bill on its Second Reading, the Bill obtained its Second Reading without a division,[3] the Government officially – through Sir Terence O'Connor, the Solicitor-General – taking a neutral position.[4] After an uneventful Committee Stage, the Bill's low position in the Ballot ensured, despite a petition from about 200 MPs requesting the Government to provide extra time,[5] that it was easily talked out during the Report Stage.[6]

However, the supporters of the Bill were much luckier during the next session when Mr Holmes, the backbench Conservative Member for Harwich came first in the Ballot for Private Members' Bills and chose to introduce essentially the same Bill which had been talked out five months previously. The Second Reading Debate was considerably livelier than the debates in previous years, with considerable opposition from the Conservative backbenches. The Bill was attacked for the lack of precision in its guidelines as to how the Court should exercise its discretion,[7] for being likely to cause a considerable amount of litigation,[8] and for infringing a valuable freedom.[9] The undesirable effects of guaranteeing an inheritance for adult children were noted.[10] Despite this strenuous opposition, the Bill was given a Second Reading with a majority of 159 votes for, 29 votes against,[11] those voting in favour including the future Lord Chancellor, David Maxwell-Fyfe MP.

The Second Reading of the Bill brought matters to a head. The Cabinet, while agreeing that the Law Officers' public position of

2. 317 HC Parl Deb, col 391.
3. 319 HC Parl Deb, cols 512–536 (22 January 1937).
4. 319 HC Parl Deb, col 533.
5. 325 HC Parl Deb, col 1759 (Miss E Rathbone) (28 June 1937).
6. 325 HC Parl Deb, cols 1757–1762.
7. 328 HCParl Deb, cols 1296–1297, 1299 (Lt Col Heneage), 1302 (Major Dower), 1313 (Sir Patrick Spens KC), (Sir Donald Somervell A-G), 1364 (Mr Lewis).
8. 328 HC Parl Deb, col 1302 (Major Dower), 1314 (Sir Patrick Spens KC).
9. 328 HC Parl Deb, cols 1323–33 (Major Sir George Davies). Sir A Soutby at cols 1332–1333 called the Bill, 'a blackmailing weapon' and at col 1334 stated, 'It seems to me that the Bill has been brought in more on sentimental grounds than any other'.
10. 328 HC Parl Deb, col 1305 (Major Dower), 1343 (Mr Pethick-Lawrence).
11. 328 HC Parl Deb, col 1371 (5 November 1937).

neutrality was correct, wished the Bill to be talked out.[12] However, the amount of time available and its support in the House of Commons made this appear a remote possibility. The Chancery Judges expressed their views on the Bill in a memorandum submitted to the Lord Chancellor three days before the Bill had its Second Reading. This *private* memorandum shows a different attitude on the desirability of the Bill to the attitude shown *publicly* in their memorandum to the Joint Select Committee. The Judges submitted:

> ... the Judges of the Chancery Division consider [that the jurisdiction] can be exercised without any indispensible difficulty. They think it however desirable to suggest that the power to make provision for a widow should be confined to widowhood.
>
> Five of the Judges of the Chancery Division are of the opinion that the fundamental objection in principle to interference with testamentary disposition outweighs any advantage which might be expected from the proposed Bill.
>
> One of the Judges of the Chancery Division (Clauson J) feels compelled to differ from his brethren and takes the view that if it be made clear that the maintenance is to be confined to widowhood, and in the case of children, minority, the Bill will prove a useful extension of the powers of the Court.[13]

Viscount Hailsham, now returned to the Woolsack, was as opposed to the Bill as ever, but realised that public opposition might be impolitic[14] and that the Bill might very likely pass in its present form. He agreed with Sir Donald Somervell, the Attorney-General, who was essentially a supporter of the Bill,[15] that the best course would be to seek to amend the Bill.[16] The amendments which the Attorney-General sought were:

(a) the Bill to be limited to the principle of maintenance only;
(b) no provision for adult children;
(c) no County Court jurisdiction;
(d) an upper limit to the amount of provision.

12. Cabinet Meeting Minute, 2 November 1937, PRO LCO 2/1189.
13. Memorandum of Chancery Judges, 2 November 1937, PRO LCO 2/1189.
14. Letter from the Private Secretary to the Lord Chancellor to the Private Secretary to the Attorney General, 11 November 1936, PRO LCO 2/1189.
15. See Somervell's support for the 1934 Bill and letter from Sir Donald Somervell A-G to Home Secretary, 1 December 1936, PRO LCO 2/1189.
16. Letter from Sir Terence O'Connor S-G to Viscount Hailsham, LC, recording conversation with Sir Donald Somervell A-G, 18 November 1937, PRO LCO 2/1189. See also remarks of Mr Holmes at 335 HC Parl Deb, col 477.

The Lord Chancellor was particularly opposed to the County Court having jurisdiction; in a pencil note, he wrote, 'County Court should be excluded – Testators won't know where they are'.[17] These amendments were readily accepted by Mr Holmes, the promoter of the Bill, except that he insisted that adult unmarried daughters should be able to apply.[18] In return for this agreement the Government promised a smooth passage through the remaining stages of the Bill and the assistance of Parliamentary Counsel.

The amendments were introduced during the Committee Stage.[19] The Bill was given a Third Reading on 29 April 1939.[20] Although Mr Holmes, the promoter of the Bill, was quite willing to accept the amendments proposed by the Law Officers, Miss Rathbone MP, the originator of such legislation in the House of Commons, expressed her regret that the Bill as it would eventually become law was a much more limited measure than she had originally intended.[1] The Bill was taken uneventfully through its stages in the House of Lords by Lord Russell of Killowen.[2] Eventually, over a decade since Viscount Astor first raised the matter in Parliament, the Inheritance (Family Provision) Act 1938 was given the Royal Assent on 13 July 1938.

The 1938 Act

The Act came into effect for the estates of persons dying after 13 July 1939.[3] Jurisdiction was limited to the High Court and the Palatine Courts[4] and the Act only applied if the deceased died testate.[5] The only persons who could apply were spouses of the deceased, an infant son, an unmarried daughter and an adult son or married daughter who by reason of some mental or physical disability were incapable of maintaining themselves.[6] Provision could

17. Pencil Note of Lord Chancellor, 18 November 1937, PRO LCO 2/1189.
18. Memorandum to Viscount Hailsham LC, 19 November 1937, PRO LCO 2/1189.
19. 1937–38 Report of Standing Committee A, Inheritance (Family Provision) Bill.
20. 335 HC Parl Deb, cols 459–488.
1. 335 HC Parl Deb, col 482.
2. 108 HL Parl Deb, col 709 (First Reading, 2 May 1938); 109 HL Parl Deb, cols 799–803 (Second Reading, 31 May 1938); 110 HL Parl Deb, cols 245–255 (Committee Stage, 23 June 1938); col 436 (Report Stage, 30 June 1938); col 616 (Third Reading, 7 July 1938).
3. S 6(2).
4. S 5(1).
5. S 1(1).
6. S 1(1).

only be by way of periodic payments,[7] unless the estate was under £2,000 when capital payments could be made.[8] Complicated provisions prohibited the Court from ordering maintenance where the surviving spouse was given by the will two-thirds of the income of the net estate and there were no children of another marriage of the deceased eligible to apply[9] and restricted the amount of provision which could be ordered to a maximum of two-thirds of the income of the net estate.[10] These provisions were to give rise to considerable problems of interpretation.[11]

There were about 200 cases a year commenced in the first 12 years of the Act's operation.[12] The reported cases demonstrate that the Court used its powers cautiously and that the Court saw its powers essentially as a power of review to be exercised in exceptional cases, rather than as a licence to rewrite the testamentary dispositions of the deceased. While widowers were only exceptionally awarded provision,[13] widows were usually successful, although in line with the statutory restrictions on quantum, the amount of such provision was generally modest.

The absence of a great flood of litigation, as had been predicted by opponents of the 1938 Act, is a reflection that 'unjust wills' were the exception rather than the rule. No doubt some applicants were unable to commence proceedings because of the cost of High Court proceedings and the absence of legal aid and because of the Court's reluctance to order any kind of provision in cases of small estates.[14] Although many major problems of detail were unresolved after the jurisdiction had existed for ten years,[15] the Judges of the Chancery Division had developed a reasonably consistent approach to applications. Such consistency owes much to the fact that the jurisdiction was exercised essentially by six judges who were in close contact with each other. It is doubtful whether such consistency could have been obtained if the jurisdiction were to be exercised by a large and disparate number of County Court judges, even subject to energetic control by the Court of Appeal.

7. S 1(2).
8. S 1(4).
9. S 1(1) proviso.
10. S 1(3).
11. ALBERY, 6–7, 13–18.
12. Crane, 'Family Provision on Death in English Law' (1960) 35 NYUL Rev 984,1000; Appendix A.
13. *Re Sylvester* [1941] Ch 87, [1940] 4 All ER 269; *Re Styler* [1942] Ch 387, [1942] 2 All ER 201; *Re Pointer* [1941] Ch 60, [1940] 4 All ER 372; *Re Lawes* (1946) 62 TLR 231.
14. *Re Vrint* [1940] Ch 920, [1940] 3 All ER 470.
15. See ALBERY.

That the 1938 Act after its first decade was believed to be working well and performing a useful function was demonstrated by the Report of the Committee on the Law of Intestate Succession which reported in 1951.[16] This committee was set up principally to consider whether the spouse's statutory legacy should be increased. The committee was chaired by Lord Morton of Henryton and included Michael Albery, the author of a recent book on the 1938 Act, and Sir John Foster KC MP. The committee's report, accurately described in the House of Commons as 'brief, lucid and unanimous',[17] recommended that the statutory legacy where a deceased leaves a child and a spouse should be increased from £1,000 to £5,000. While this recommendation was thought to be the correct solution in most cases, it could possibly work injustice where the surviving spouse was a survivor of a second marriage and there were infant children of a prior marriage of the deceased.[18] In such cases it was thought proper that the infant children should have the right to apply to the Court under the 1938 Act. Accordingly the report recommended that the 1938 Act be extended to cover cases of total intestacy.[19] The committee considered that the 1938 Act did not need significant amendment but did consider that the restrictions on awarding capital sums and on the amount of provision might be examined.[20] The recommendations of the Morton Committee which permitted applications to be made under the 1938 Act when the deceased died intestate and permitted widows and widowers to be awarded the whole of the income of the net estate and increased the limit for lump sums to £5,000 were carried into effect by the Intestates' Estates Act 1952 which had a smooth and relatively quick passage through Parliament.

A further significant extension of family provision legislation took place in 1958,[1] when divorced spouses were allowed to apply for provision out of the deceased's estate. The Royal Commission on Marriage and Divorce, whose chairman was Lord Morton of

16. Cmd 8310. For a delightful discussion of the Report of the Committee and the enactment of the Intestates' Estates Act 1952, see Cretney, 'Intestacy Reforms – The Way Things Were, 1952' [1994] Denning L Rev 35.
17. 4498 HC Parl Deb, col 1081 (28 March 1952, Mr Hylton-Foster).
18. Cmd 8310, paras 19, 45–47.
19. Cmd 8310, para 45.
20. Cmd 8310, para 49.
1. The Act was preceded in 1957 by a measure enabling maintenance agreements which were enforceable against a deceased's estate to be varied after the death of the covenantor – Maintenance Agreements Act 1957, s 2, subsequently re-enacted as Matrimonial Causes Act 1965, s 25; Matrimonial Proceedings and Property Act 1970, s 15; Matrimonial Causes Act 1973, s 36. This jurisdiction was and is not greatly used; see Appendix A .

Henryton, recommended that a divorced spouse should be entitled to apply for maintenance against the estate of the deceased spouse in a similar manner to applications under the 1938 Act.[2] This recommendation was carried into effect by the Matrimonial Causes (Property and Maintenance) Act 1958, section 3.[3] Although formally promoted as a private members' Bill, the legislation was in effect a Government measure.[4] The Cabinet specifically insisted that the legislation should enable husbands as well as wives to apply.[5] During the drafting of the legislation there was a disagreement between the Parliamentary Counsel (traditionally recruited from the Chancery Bar) and the Registrars of the Probate Divorce and Admiralty Division as to how far the legislation should follow the scheme of the 1938 Act as opposed to the machinery of divorce legislation.[6]

The Bill had a relatively uneventful passage through Parliament, being expressly welcomed by Lord Merriman, the President of the Probate, Divorce and Admiralty Division.[7] The only significant opposition came from Conservative backbenchers, led by Mr P Ingress-Bell QC, a Chancery barrister, who objected to the absence of an express prohibition on claims by guilty parties in divorce proceedings.[8] The Act, instead of merely amending the 1938 Act by adding a new class of dependants, set up a separate statutory regime, similar to, but not the same as, the 1938 Act to be administered in the Probate, Divorce and Admiralty Division. This jurisdiction was used by surprisingly few applicants when compared with the number of applications under the 1938 Act,[9] and bearing

2. Royal Commission on Marriage and Divorce (1957) Cmd 9678, para 524.
3. Subsequently re-enacted by Matrimonial Causes Act 1965, s 26.
4. Papers in PRO LCO2/6152.
5. Papers in PRO LCO2/6152.
6. Papers in PRO LCO2/6152.
7. 209 HL Parl Deb, col 777 (20 May 1958). The Bill was piloted through the House of Lords by Lord Meston, whose son was to make an important speech during the passage of the Law Reform (Succession) Act 1995, see p 105, *post*.
8. 587 HC Parl Deb, col 811 (Mr P Ingress Bell QC, 2 May 1958); 588 HC Parl Deb, cols 785–790 (Mr P Ingress Bell QC), cols 790–792 (Mr S McAdden), col 801 (Major Hicks-Beach) (16 May 1958).The comment of Sir Hugh Lucas-Tooth MP in a letter dated 5 May 1857 to D W Dobson of the Lord Chancellor's Department, 'I think that Mr Bell's real objection is a general dislike of legislation' (PRO LCO2/6152) is a grossly unfair criticism of a man who had deep religious reservations about divorce. Sir Hugh Lucas-Tooth MP sponsored the Bill in the House of Commons ; he had originally been intended to sponsor the Intestates' Estates Act 1952 through the House of Commons, see Cretney, 'Intestacy Reforms – The Way Things Were, 1952' [1994] Denning L Rev 35, at 48, footnote 106.
9. See Appendix A

in mind that relations between divorced spouses are likely to be far more acrimonious than relations between spouses merely separated by death.

Family Provision Comes of Age – The Family Provision Act 1966

The most radical change in the family provision legislation came in 1966, with the enactment of the Family Provision Act 1966.[10] While the 1966 Act was promoted as essentially dealing with only technical amendments, it represented a substantial extension of the jurisdiction and was an endorsement by Parliament of the principle of varying testamentary disposition by judicial discretion. The 1966 Act was not preceded by a report of a learned committee, but was occasioned by the decision of the Court of Appeal in *Re Gale*.[11] *Re Gale* had shown that the restrictions on the amount of provision which could be awarded under the 1938 Act[12] went further than had been thought previously and threatened to invalidate a considerable number of orders made prior to it. The 1966 Act removed all restrictions upon the amount of provision which could be ordered[13] and reversed *Re Gale* retrospectively.[14] The restriction upon applications where the surviving spouse had been left two-thirds of the estate was removed.[15] The Court was empowered to award lump sums,[16] in estates of whatever size, which gave the Court power to award the entire estate to a dependant. The Court was further empowered to award interim provision[17] and the rules on applications out of time were assimilated for the 1938 Act and section 26 of the Matrimonial Causes Act 1965, which had replaced section 3 of the Matrimonial Causes (Property and Maintenance) Act 1958.[18] Additionally the County Court was given jurisdiction under the 1938 Act and section 26 of the Matrimonial Causes Act

10. In February 1997 no documents had been deposited at the Public Record Office concerning the Family Provision Act 1966.
11. [1966] Ch 236, [1966] 1 All ER 945.
12. S 1(3), 1938 Act.
13. Family Provision Act 1966, s 3(1).
14. Family Provision Act 1966, s 3(1).
15. Family Provision Act 1966, s 2(1).
16. Family Provision Act 1966, s 4(1).
17. Family Provision Act 1966, s 6(1), overruling *Re Ferrar's Application* [1966] P 126, [1966] 3 All ER 78, CA.
18. Family Provision Act 1966, s 5(1).

1965 where the estate did not exceed £5,000,[19] the then limit on equity proceedings in the County Court being £500. The net result of the Family Provision Act 1966 was to remove most of the concessions extracted by the Attorney-General prior to the passing of the 1938 Act. With only one opposing voice,[20] the 1966 Bill had an easy passage through Parliament.

While the 1966 Act considerably enlarged the powers of the Court, it did not affect the general approach of the Court to the exercise of its powers. Considerable use was made of the powers to award greater provision, particularly the enlarged power to award lump sums. On occasions the Court awarded surviving widows of happy marriages the whole of the estate.[1]

In 1970 during the discussion of the Administration of Justice Bill which reorganised the Divisions of the High Court an attempt by a divorce barrister[2] to transfer jurisdiction under the 1938 Act from the Chancery Division to the new Family Division of the High Court was defeated in the House of Commons.[3]

Reform in the 1970s

One of the major successes of the Law Commission, set up in 1965, was the substantial reform and codification of divorce law and property and support rights arising upon divorce effected by the early 1970s. The Law Commission wished to continue the reform and codification of the law of family property by examining succession rights and the ownership of matrimonial property, principally the matrimonial home, during the continuance of the marriage. In fulfilment of these aims the Law Commission published a substantial Working Paper in 1972 which dealt with, inter alia, family provision and the possibility of introducing a system of fixed inheritance rights.[4]

The Working Paper was not merely motivated by a general desire for reform and to tidy up the law on family provision, but was particularly concerned with the paradox which had resulted

19. Family Provision Act 1966, s 7(1), following the suggestion of Ungoed-Thomas J in *Re Clayton* [1966] 2 All ER 370, [1966] 1 WLR 969.
20. 735 HC Parl Deb, cols 928–930 (Mr C Fletcher-Cooke, 4 November 1966).
1. *Re Carter* (1968) 112 Sol Jo 136, Buckley J; *Re Parkinson* (1975) Times, 4 October, CA; *Bayliss v Lloyds Bank Ltd* (9 December 1977, unreported), CA.
2. Mr Bruce Campbell QC.
3. 801 HC Parl Deb, cols 109–117 (4 May 1970).
4. Law Commission Working Paper No 42 on Family Property Law ('WORKING PAPER').

from the very wide powers being given to the Court to vary and transfer property rights upon divorce, whereby a divorced wife would be better protected than a widow.[5] The Working Paper recommended that the statutory provisions be consolidated and the jurisdiction be administered in one Division of the High Court only, which would be the Family Division.[6] The Law Commission in its analysis of family provision for spouses stressed the theoretical differences between rights of support and property rights, although it acknowledged that the two rights were complementary and in many cases overlapped.[7] For instance a person who is awarded a house by the Court is given both a valuable piece of property and considerable support for his day to day needs. After characterising the 1938 Act as only affording rights of support, the Law Commission, rather surprisingly in the light of its emphasis upon the comparison of the spouse's rights on divorce and death, tentatively decided against extending the family provision jurisdiction to enable the survivor of a marriage to claim a 'fair share' in the estate of the other.[8] The reason given for this conclusion was the fear of litigation if any spouse could apply to the Court if the deceased's will awarded him or her less than his or her entitlement on intestacy.[9] It must be noted that despite the theoretical differences in approach between the 1938 Act and the jurisdiction to vary property rights upon divorce, since 1966 and with the exception of very large estates, in practice a spouse would be unlikely to be awarded more on divorce than upon an application under the 1938 Act.[10]

The Law Commission considered at some length the matters which should guide the exercise of the Court's discretion, but failed to set out any really useful criteria.[11] The Working Paper suggested that the Court's powers to settle property or order specific property to be awarded to applicants available in divorce proceedings should also be available in family provision proceedings.[12] The Law Commission discussed whether remarriage should determine a spouse's right to maintenance and noting that a spouse's life-interest in an intestacy did not determine on remarriage and that it was

5. WORKING PAPER, para 0.21.
6. WORKING PAPER, paras 3.4–3.45.
7. WORKING PAPER, para 3.1.
8. WORKING PAPER, para 3.9.
9. WORKING PAPER, paras 3.8, 3.9, 3.11.
10. See the cases of *Re Carter* (1968) 112 Sol Jo 136: *Re Parkinson* (1975) Times, 4 October; *Bayliss v Lloyds Bank Ltd* (9 December 1977, unreported), CA, where widows were awarded the entire net estate of their deceased husbands.
11. WORKING PAPER, paras 3.16–3.22.
12. WORKING PAPER, paras 3.24–3.31.

becoming less common for testators to leave property to spouses for their widowhood, recommended that a spouse's remarriage should not *automatically* determine an award of maintenance.[13]

The Law Commission recommended that adult children should be able to apply, but considered that the Court would only award provision in a relatively few cases in situations not dissimilar to the situations of adult children who could apply under the 1938 Act.[14] A further extension of the class of applicants was proposed by permitting any person who was dependent upon the deceased immediately prior to his death to apply.[15]

Many other detailed changes in the working of the system were recommended including the enlargement of the 'net estate' out of which provision could be ordered to prevent avoidance.[16]

Additionally the Law Commission examined a system of fixed shares on death as an alternative or an addition to a system of family provision. The actual system proposed by the Law Commission as being the most suitable for adoption in England and Wales, was essentially a variant of the spouse's elective share as widely employed in many of the jurisdictions in the United States.[17] The Law Commission's general preference for the discretionary system of family provision over a system of fixed shares appeared to be based upon the view that family provision worked, being an individualised system of justice and having the minimum interference with testamentary freedom. The Law Commission was no doubt mindful that the extra advantages to be gained from a more substantial reform of succession rights might not be compensated for by the delays in getting such controversial legislation enacted as compared with the relative case of enacting more modest, technical changes in the law.

The Law Commission received a large number of representations on the tentative conclusions of the Working Paper, but only in one respect did the representations cause the Law Commission materially to alter its proposals. As part of its reform of matrimonial property law the Law Commission commissioned a survey of how married couples actually held property, their views as to how matrimonial property should be held and their views on succession rights.[18] The survey was published in 1972 after the

13. WORKING PAPER, para 3.32.
14. WORKING PAPER, paras 3.39–3.43. For detailed consideration of applications by adult children, see Chapter 6, Part 3, *post*.
15. WORKING PAPER, para 3.47. For detailed consideration of the class of 'other dependants', see pp 78–103, *post*.
16. WORKING PAPER, paras 3.70–3.71.
17. WORKING PAPER, Part 4.
18. Todd and Jones, *Matrimonial Property*.

Working Paper had been published. The results of the survey on people's attitudes to testamentary freedom are set out at the end of this chapter. A significant majority of the people sampled thought that a deceased should be obliged to make provision for the surviving spouse in his will.[19] This was interpreted by the Law Commission to indicate public support for extending family provision for spouses from the principle of support only to awarding the surviving spouse a 'just share' in the deceased's estate.[20] An examination of the question asked in the survey demonstrates considerable support for some restriction of testamentary freedom in favour of a surviving spouse, but reveals no preference for any particular standard of provision. What the survey did reveal was a preference for a system of fixed shares rather than judicial discretion as the machinery for effecting the restriction on testamentary freedom.[1] The survey also revealed a large majority against restricting freedom of testation to benefit children.[2]

The Law Commission's Report and Draft Bill published in 1974[3] substantially followed the recommendations of the Working Paper, save in regard to the standard of provision for spouses. The new proposal was that the family provision was to be a device whereby a surviving spouse could gain a 'just share' in the deceased's estate. The Law Commission stated that its change of mind was heavily influenced by the results of the survey, but its eventual conclusion seemed inexorably to follow from the desire to assimilate property rights on death and divorce and the actual experience of the courts' exercise of their powers under the Matrimonial Causes Act 1973 to give spouses a 'just share' as well as maintenance upon divorce.[4] The Draft Bill put forward a complete statutory code for the law of family provision.

19. Op cit, paras 8.1, 11.3.
20. LAW COM, para 13.
1. Todd and Jones, *Matrimonial Property*, para 8.1. 57% of husbands and 59% of wives preferred a system of fixed shares to a system of judicial discretion. Similar results both in the cases of spouses and adult children were obtained by a similar survey in Greater Cleveland, Ohio, USA in the middle 1960s, Sussman, Cates and Smith, *The Family and the Inheritance*, pp 209–210. Broadly similar conclusions were drawn by a Public Opinion Survey undertaken in 1988 for the Law Commission in its Report Family Law: Distribution on Intestacy (No 187). Strictly the questions related to intestacy, but the thrust of the responses was clearly to elevate spouses and to be uninterested in succession rights for children.
2. Para 8.2.
3. Report No 61, Second Report on Family Property: Family Provision on Death ('LAW COM').
4. The Law Commission specifically refers to this at para 14 and cites *Wachtel v Wachtel* [1973] Fam 72, [1973] 1 All ER 829, CA; *Trippas v Trippas* [1973] Fam 134, [1973] 2 All ER 1, CA; *Harnett v Harnett* [1974] 1 All ER 764, [1974] 1 WLR 219, CA.

The Bill was introduced in the 1974–75 Parliamentary Session as a Government Bill. Although the Bill was enacted without any substantial amendment, the discussion of both its overall aims and detailed provisions was the most lively and intelligent discussion of the principles of restricting freedom of testation since the original attempts at legislation in the 1930s.[5] The Bill was introduced by Lord Elwyn-Jones, the Lord Chancellor, in the House of Lords in the Spring of 1975. Although the Bill had an unopposed second reading,[6] the debate was notable for three speeches. Lord Simon of Glaisdale, a former President of the Family Division, was very much in favour of the Bill and largely opposed to any kind of testamentary freedom. At one point in his speech he seemed to favour a system of *legitim* for adult children.[7] He asked unsuccessfully for an assurance from the Lord Chancellor that the Rules of Court made under the Act would assign the jurisdiction solely to the Family Division.[8] He was particularly pleased with the larger standard of provision awarded to spouses and saw it as a means of correcting an unjust system of holding matrimonial property, whereby the wife who could not work because she brought up the children of the marriage was often deprived of a share in her husband's income and wealth, income only made possible by the wife agreeing to look after the children.[9] He stated:

> My Lords, a functional division of co-operative labour of that sort calls in justice for the sharing of the rewards of the labour. The breadwinner is morally bound to share the loaf he has been free to gain. He is bound during his life-time and he is bound if he makes accumulation after his death.

The Earl of Mansfield, a Conservative peer, opposed strongly the extension of the class of applicants to include all adult children.[10] Considerable scepticism of the Bill and the whole family provision jurisdiction was evinced by Lord Wilberforce, the senior Chancery Lord of Appeal.[11] A large part of his speech is worth setting out in full:

5. The discussion of s 1(1)(e) in Parliament is not dealt with in this Chapter, but at pp 81–84, *post*.
6. First Reading, 356 HL Parl Deb, col 1423 (13 February 1975); Second Reading, 358 HL Parl Deb, cols 917–935 (20 March 1975).
7. 358 HL Parl Deb, col 926.
8. 358 HL Parl Deb, cols 926–927.
9. 358 HL Parl Deb, cols 925–926, 927–928. See also Lord Simon of Glaisdale's remarks in *Schaefer v Schuhmann* [1972] AC 572 at 595G–596E, [1972] 1 All ER 621 at 635g-636e, PC. Similar sentiments were expressed by Lord Denning MR in *Wachtel v Wachtel* [1973] Fam 72 at 92E–H, [1973] 1 All ER 829 at 837g–828b, CA quoting the Royal Commission on Marriage and Divorce (Cmd 9678), para 652 and Sir Jocelyn Simon P in (1965) 62 LS Gaz 345.
10. 358 HL Parl Deb, col 923.

> I am speaking as one – I think the only one here – who has actually administered the 1938 Act, and who sat in court to decide cases under it. It really is a very difficult jurisdiction. In the first place, it has the disadvantage that it places a premium upon those who can go to good legal advisers, prepare a good legal case and make a good presentation before the court. It certainly encourages disputes between families. It is also a very difficult jurisdiction for the judge to exercise.
>
> We are given in Clause 3 of this Bill a whole list of considerations which are meant to guide the judge. But I can assure your Lordships that when one is sitting there and trying to make up one's mind what is fair and right for a particular man, of whose life history one knows little, what is fair and right to do as regards his divorced wife, his widow, a possible mistress, illegitimate children – to decide how to distribute the merits and demerits between these people is painful and exceedingly difficult. I am by no means certain that one is able in many cases to reach the right result. All one can do is to do one's best and hope that the result is what it should be. But it is not an ideal solution. It is not made ideal by using words such as 'fair', 'reasonable', 'just' and so on. The difficulty of bringing about a good result remains intense.[12]

The Committee Stage of the Bill was essentially concerned with a series of amendments which would restrict the scope of the Bill proposed by the Earl of Mansfield and opposed by Lord Simon of Glaisdale. Unfortunately Lord Wilberforce was unable to attend the detailed discussion of the Bill because of illness. Lord Mansfield claimed that he had Lord Wilberforce's support for his amendments.[13] The most important amendment was to restrict the classes of children who could apply to infant children or children who were physically or mentally disabled from supporting themselves.[14] Lord Mansfield noted that maintenance for a child under the divorce jurisdiction ended at 18 and that the Law Commission envisaged that applications by adult children would be successful only rarely, and thought that it was wrong for persons whose applications would only rarely, if ever, succeed should have a right to apply.[15]

The amendment was strongly attacked by Lord Simon of Glaisdale who described it as a 'wrecking amendment'.[16] In his

11. 358 HL Parl Deb, cols 932–925. Significantly Lord Simon of Glaisdale dissented in *Schaefer v Schuhmann*[1972] AC 572, [1972] 1 All ER 621, whereas Lord Wilberforce was part of the majority.
12. 358 HL Parl Deb, col 933.
13. 358 HL Parl Deb, col 1065 (24 April 1975).
14. 359 HL Parl Deb, col 1064.
15. 359 HL Parl Deb, cols 1064–1067.
16. 359 HL Parl Deb, col 1068.

speech Lord Simon stressed the importance of the family and family ties for the security of society, but made no attempt to distinguish between different members of the family. Lord Simon stated that it was an aim of the Act to do what the testator had intended to do, but failed to do, which would include making provision for adult children.[17] Lord Simon further drew the House's attention to the jurisdiction under the 1938 Act to award provision to an adult, unmarried daughter, the Divorce Court's power to order maintenance for a child beyond 18 years, where the child was engaged in full-time education, the absence of age limits in Commonwealth jurisdictions and the need to protect a child who sacrificed much to look after an ageing parent.[18] Lord Simon's speech, which does not deserve the praise of the Lord Chancellor who described it as 'one of the most devastating speeches in destruction of an amendment that in 30 years in two Houses of Parliament [he has heard]',[19] is underlain by a belief that adult children should, by virtue only of the relationship of parent and child be entitled to a share in their deceased parent's estate – a belief rejected by the Law Commission[20] and by public opinion[1] and unlikely to obtain a majority in the House of Commons.[2] Further opposition to the amendment came from Lady Ward of North Tyneside who thought that a daughter who looked after a parent should be able to claim,[3] and from the Lord Chancellor who also made the point that provision should be made for children who continued full-time education after the age of 18.[4] Lord Leatherland opposed the amendment as it would deprive the court of jurisdiction to award an eldest son provision to take over the family business.[5] In the light of this unanimous opposition the amendment was withdrawn.[6] It is interesting to speculate whether had Lord Wilberforce been fit and had the amendment been worded less restrictively it would have been passed.

17. 359 HL Parl Deb, col 1069; compare *Re Christie* [1979] Ch 168, [1979] 1 All ER 546.
18. 359 HL Parl Deb, cols 1069–1071.
19. 359 HL Parl Deb, col 1072.
20. LAW COM, paras 73–79.
1. See the table of results of the survey of public opinion on p 34A.
2. Some clue to Lord Simon of Glaisdale's approach can be gleaned from his introductory remarks about the place of 'the family' in British politics, 359 HL Parl Deb, cols 1067–1068. And see also his remarks that anti-avoidance provisions are 'absolutely necessary' (col 1086).
3. 359 HL Parl Deb, cols 1071–1072.
4. 359 HL Parl Deb, col 1074.
5. 359 HL Parl Deb, cols 1077–1078.
6. 359 HL Parl Deb, col 1079.

During the Committee Stage a further attempt by Lord Simon of Glaisdale to commit the Lord Chancellor to assigning the jurisdiction to the Family Division failed.[7] A further six amendments restricting the scope of the Bill were proposed by the Earl of Mansfield and withdrawn after opposition from the Lord Chancellor and Lord Simon of Glaisdale,[8] including an amendment to require that costs should always follow the event and that the Legal Aid Fund should always be liable for the costs of a losing legally aided applicant.[9] Displaying a view contrary to that held by most practitioners, Lord Simon of Glaisdale in response to that amendment stated that the existing practice as to costs and to legal aid worked well.[10] The further progress of the Bill through the House of Lords was uneventful.[11]

The Bill was guided through the House of Commons by the Solicitor-General and was given an unopposed Second Reading with only a little adverse comment.[12] In introducing the Bill the Solicitor-General announced that the Government had decided to preserve the concurrent jurisdiction of the Chancery and Family Divisions of the High Court and that the applicant would normally have the choice of forum.[13] During the Committee Stage there was extensive discussion on the definition of clause 1(1)(e) which permitted any person actually dependent upon the deceased to apply – this is discussed in Chapter 4 on Applicants. Little else of substance was discussed during the Committee Stage or the Report Stage.[14]

Only during the Third Reading Debate was any substantial attack made upon the Bill's principal aim of further restricting testamentary freedom and then by a solitary Conservative MP.[15] One Labour solicitor MP stated that 'malicious wills' were frequent and

7. 359 HL Parl Deb, cols 1079–1080 (Lord Simon of Glaisdale), col 1080 (Lord Elwyn-Jones LC). The Earl of Mansfield (who had previously practised in the Queen's Bench Division) had earlier stated that he found himself 'in the middle ... of a first class dispute between the Chancery Division and the Family Division' (col 1078).
8. 359 HL Parl Deb, cols 1080–1108.
9. 359 HL Parl Deb, col 1099.
10. 359 HL Parl Deb, cols 1099–1100.
11. 360 HL Parl Deb, cols 532–535 (Report Stage, 12 May 1975); col 943 (Third Reading adjourned, 15 May 1975); 361 HL Parl Deb, cols 1377–1380 (Third Reading, 24 June 1975).
12. 895 HC Parl Deb, col 337 (8 July 1975); cols 1681–1694 (16 July 1975); col 1910 (17 July 1975).
13. 895 HC Parl Deb, col 1685.
14. 1974–75 HC Parl Deb Standing Committees, Vol IV, cols 3–32 (Committee Stage, 29 July 1975); 898 HC Parl Deb, cols 169–181 (Report Stage, 29 October 1975).
15. 898 HC Parl Deb, cols 183–186 (Mr Banks).

wondered whether the class of applicants could be extended to cover employees of the deceased.[16] Despite these late objections to the principle of the Bill, it was given an unopposed Third Reading.[17]

The Inheritance (Provision for Family and Dependants) Act 1975

The Bill received the Royal Assent on 12 November 1975 and came into effect during the next year. While the detailed provisions of the Act dealing with machinery, in so far as they have been used, have worked well, considerable uncertainty remained about some of the more fundamental changes brought about by the Act. After one false start,[18] the courts have approached the enhanced standard of provisionfor surviving spouse sensibly. While the Courts have refused to award adult children provision in all but the most extreme circumstances, no coherent principle has been evinced for distinguishing between adult children who have been awarded provision and those who have not. Both the definition of class (e) applicants – other persons actually dependent upon the deceased – and the quantum of provision to be awarded to such applicants has caused a great deal of trouble for the courts and eventually led to amending legislation in the form of the Law Reform (Succession) Act 1995.

The Law Reform (Succession) Act 1995 enabled 'cohabitees' as such to apply and arose as an almost unforeseen byproduct of the Law Commission's consideration of the law of intestacy. The detailed history of the work of the Law Commission and the passage of the legislation through Parliament are dealt with in Chapter 4.[19] From the point of view of a historian, two significant matters about the the Law Reform (Succession) Act 1995 may be noted. Firstly, the Law Commission completely failed to address the problems with the 1975 Act, such as the position of adult children and section 1(1)(e). Surely it would have been better to have the new class of cohabitant as replacing 'other dependents' within section 1(1)(e) rather than merely as an additional class of applicant. Further, the Law Commission gave no consideration to introducing Testamentary Promises legislation on the New Zealand model,[20]

16. 898 HC Parl Deb, cols 191–192 (Mr Douglas-Mann).
17. 898 HC Parl Deb, cols 182–201 (29 October 1975).
18. *Re Besterman* [1984] Ch 458, [1984] 2 All ER 656; see further pp 172–179, *post*.
19. See pp 104–106, *post*.
20. See fn 9, p 103, *post*.

surely the best answer to many 'hard cases' in this area of the law. Secondly, the Law Reform (Succession) Act 1995 passed the House of Commons without any discussion whatsoever,[1] a remarkable commentary on the political acceptablity of family provision legislation. It appears that as inherited wealth has become more widely spread in England and Wales, the legislative treatment of such wealth has excited less political interest.

In 1991 under the provisions of the Courts and Legal Services Act 1990 the County Court was given unlimited jurisdiction under the 1975 Act.[2] While this represents a downgrading in status of family provision claims, it has not led to a wholesale abandonment of the High Court as a forum for applications under the 1975 Act.

A historian of family provision would have also noted that the 1990s have been characterised by increasingly sure-footed and confident judicial decisions, particularly at the level of the Court of Appeal. A typical decision of the Court of Appeal under the 1975 Act before 1990 was hesitant, generally given on a narrow basis and emphasised the limits of interference by the Court of Appeal.[3] After 1990 there was a series of reported cases where the Court of Appeal displayed a remarkable confidence and command of the legislation and took refuge in neither technicality nor the limits of appellate review.[4] This may be due to members of the Court of Appeal having had more experience of the 1975 Act both at first instance and in the Court of Appeal. Further, there has at last been considerable cross-fertilisation of ideas between the Chancery and Family Divisions of the High Court.[5] This has continued with the judgment

1. HC Parl Deb Vol 261, col 811; Vol 265, col 199.
2. S 25 of the County Courts Act 1984 as inserted by The High Court and County Courts Jurisdiction Order 1991, SI 1991/724.
3. Compare the judgment of Oliver J in *Re Coventry* [1980] Ch 461, [1979]2 All ER 408 with the judgments of the Court of Appeal in the same case, [1980] Ch 461, [1979] 3 All ER 815. In fairness to the Court of Appeal the reported case law on family provision from 1960 to 1975 was remarably anodyne and technical in its approach, and the Court of Appeal contained many more judges who dealt with family provision cases less frequently than did the Chancery Division when the 1938 Act came into force.
4. *Moody v Stevenson*[1992] Ch 486, [1992] 2 All ER 524; *Re Jennings*[1994] Ch 286, [1994] 3 All ER 27; *Cameron v Treasury Solicitor* [1997] 1 FCR 188, [1996] 2 FLR 716; *Re Krubert* [1997] Ch 97, [1996] 3 FCR 281. The decision of the Court of Appeal in *Goodchild v Goodchild* [1997] 3 All ER 63 can be regarded as a retrograde step.
5. Eg the Court of Appeal in the divorce case of *Dart v Dart* [1996] 2 FLR 286 at 298B–H corrected errors in the Court of Appeal's decision under the 1975 Act in *Re Besterman* [1984] Ch 458, [1984] 2 All ER 656. In *Cameron v Treasury Solicitor* [1997] 1 FCR 188, [1996] 2 FLR 716 the Court of Appeal (Butler-Sloss, Peter Gibson and Thorpe LJJ, all of whom gave reasoned judgments) elegantly used both *Re Coventry* and divorce principles to reach its decision.

of Thorpe LJ in *Wells v Wells* who stated that compensation for loss of income should be worked out according to the same principles, whether they were being assessed by the Queen's Bench Division in a personal injuries or Fatal Accidents Act case, by the Family Division on divorce or by the Chancery and Family Divisions under the 1975 Act.[6] Family provision is ceasing to be an oddity and is becoming part of the mainstream of the private law of obligations.[7]

The coming into force of the 1975 Act led to a significant increase in applications for family provision. However, in so far as the Judicial Statistics deal with applications under the 1975 Act and can be relied upon, there has been relatively little growth in the number of applications since about 1980.[8] This is surprising as cohabitation outside marriage (and hence outside the ambit of the rules of intestacy) and owner occupation have all significantly increased[9] and there has been a continuing high level of divorce. The lack of any substantial increase in the number of applications might be explained by the modern habit of unhappy marriages ending in divorce before death, rather than the parties living apart but legally married at the date of death, and the prevalence of 'clean break' orders on divorce. Indeed due to 'clean break' and section 15 orders,[10] the number of former spouses applying under the 1975 Act is rapidly declining. Furthermore, in many cases, particularly with cohabitees, the passing of property by survivorship and the making of discretionary payments or nominated payments under pension schemes removes any need to alter dispositions effected by a will or an intestacy.

6. [1997] 1 All ER 673 at 705c-d, [1997] 1 WLR 652 at 686D, CA. The House of Lords has granted leave to appeal [1997] 1 WLR 870.
7. The author's principal recollection of being taught family provision as an undergraduate in 1974–75 is a list of technical distinctions between the 1938 Act and the jurisdiction for former spouses and no discussion of any wider principle. It is the author's view that the analysis of Fuller and Perdue, 'The Reliance Interest in Contract Damages' (1936) 46 Yale LJ 52 and the work of Professor Atiyah on the basis of contractual obligations are both highly relevant to understanding family provision.
8. See Appendix A. The anecdotal evidence of the author and his immediate professional colleagues is to the same effect.
9. For a study of owner occupied houses as inherited wealth, see Hamnett, Harmer and Williams, *Safe As Houses:Housing Inheritance in Britain.*
10. For s 15, see pp 271–274, *post*.

1971 Survey of Popular Attitudes to Inheritance Rights

"When a married man makes a will do you think that he should be entirely free to distribute his possessions as he wishes or should he be made by law to include his wife in the will?"

When a married man	Husbands %	Wives %
Entirely free	34	31
Made to include wife	55	59
Qualified Answer	11	10

			Divorced or separated	
When a married man	Widowers %	Widows %	Men %	Women %
Entirely free	36	18	63	21
Made to include wife	56	68	27	67
Qualified answer	8	14	10	12
When a married woman				
Entirely free	45	28	71	28
Made to include husband	48	58	19	46
Qualified answer	7	14	10	24

"When a father makes a will do you think he should be entirely free to distribute his possessions as he wishes, or should he be made, by law, to include all his sons and daughters in the will?"

					Divorced or separated	
When a father	Husbands %	Wives %	Widowers %	Widows %	Men %	Women %
Entirely free	69	65	65	51	75	61
Made to include child	21	26	27	38	15	34
Qualified answer	10	9	8	11	10	5
When a mother						
Entirely free	73	67	68	54	80	60
Made to include child	20	26	25	38	15	34
Qualified answer	7	7	7	8	5	6

Notes 1. Sources, paras 8.1,8.2,11.4, Todd and Jones, *Matrimonial Property*.
2. The sample cannot be a sample of the complete population, as persons who have never been married are excluded.
3. The question relating to children does not specify the age of the children or whether the spouse has a competing claim.

Chapter 2

THE POLICY OF FAMILY PROVISION

The first step in any critical analysis of family provision as it exists in England and Wales and certain parts of the Commonwealth is to examine the arguments for and against testamentary freedom. The second step is to compare the conclusions on the desirable amount of testamentary freedom with the system of family provision as it actually exists.

The Arguments for Testamentary Freedom

Probably the most substantial argument for testamentary freedom is that it is a logical extension of an owner's freedom to deal with his property during his lifetime. The same reasons which allow a man freedom of disposition during his lifetime should also allow him freedom of disposition after his death. This was the reasoning used by Grotius to justify testamentary freedom,[1] and Mill characterised testamentary freedom as the ultimate extension of private property.[2] A variant upon this argument is that people obtain pleasure by knowing that their wishes as to the destination of their property after their death will be respected.[3]

Whatever the logic of this position, people are generally less concerned with the dispositions of their property after their death than when they are alive and are more interested in and affected by lifetime dispositions than by those after death. While lifetime dispositions are substantially responsible for their efficacy upon the owner, those after death require by their nature greater involvement of other persons and legal institutions to be effective.[4] Capital taxation affords an example of the lesser importance people attach to dispositions of property after their death. One of the rationales of Estate Duty and the higher rates of Inheritance Tax levied on transfers on death is that taxing transfers on death causes least

1. Grotius, *Jurisprudence of Holland*, s 2.14.2.
2. Mill, *Principles of Political Economy* (6th edn), Book II, Ch II, s 4.
3. Sedgwick, *The Elements of Politics* (3rd edn), p 103.
4. Blackstone, Commentaries 10–12 (St George Tucker, ed 1803); Bentham, *Principles of the Civil Code* in *Theory of Legislation* Pt 1, Ch 12 at 122 (Ogden, ed 1931); Morton, 'The Theory of Inheritance' (1894–95) 8 Harv L Rev 161, 162.

resentment among taxpayers. The experience of Estate Duty and Inheritance Tax after the Finance Act 1986 afford an illustration of the amount of people's concern about the disposition of their property after their death – although both taxes could easily be avoided by inter vivos dispositions, it was still paid on many estates where the deceased obviously did not consider that the preservation of his wealth for his successors outweighed the costs of making inter vivos dispositions. That a dead person's wishes are entitled to less respect than a live person's is evidenced in English Law by such provisions as the rule against perpetuities, the rule against accumulations and the mandatory provisions of the Settled Land Act 1925.[5] It follows from this that it might be proper to impose greater restrictions upon dispositions on death than upon dispositions inter vivos.[6]

A second argument in favour of testamentary freedom, or perhaps a variant of the first argument, is that, because restrictions on testation can be avoided by inter vivos dispositions, any regime restricting disposition of property on death will inevitably lead to restrictions on inter vivos dispositions which are undesirable.[7] The experience of post-classical Roman Law and certain civil law systems is that *legitim* soon leads to restrictions on inter vivos dispositions.[8]

A third argument for testamentary freedom is that it enables a living person to extract advantages from others in return for the hope of a favourable mention in the deceased's will. The removal of testamentary freedom would prevent a person from bargaining while alive with the ownership of his property after his death and remove a certain element of its value to the testator. This ability to use the power of testation to extract obedience, respect and attention has been noted by many disparate authors.[9]

Fourthly, it has been argued that testamentary freedom is an incentive to industry and the accumulation of wealth, there being less incentive to accumulate wealth to hand over on death when choice of the persons to whom the wealth is to be given is denied.[10]

5. But note the repeal of the Settled Land Act 1925 by the Trusts of Land and Appointment of Trustees Act 1996 and that Northern Ireland has never had any restrictions on accummulation of income.
6. *Rational Basis of Legal Institutions*, p 448; Morton, op cit .
7. Grotius, *Jurisprudence of Holland*, s 2.14.2.
8. Dawson, *Gifts and Promises*; see also MacDonald, *Fraud on the Widow's Share.*
9. Locke, *Two Treatises on Government* Book II, para 72; *Rational Basis of Legal Institutions*, p 421; *Banks v Goodfellow* (1870) LR 5 QB 549 at 564 *per* Cockburn C J quoting Kent C in *Van Alst v Hunter* 5 Johns Cas (NY) 159; Sedgwick, *The Elements of Politics* (3rd edn), 103; Mill, *Principles of Political Economy* (6th edn), Book II, Ch II, s 4.
10. Bentham, *Supply without Burthen, or Escheat vice Taxation* Essay Two (24/1795); Sedgwick, *The Elements of Politics* (3rd edn), pp 100, 104–105; Wedgewood, *The Economics of Inheritance*, 200–201.

However, while *some* incentive effects of testamentary freedom must exist, the size of such effects upon the national economy must be very small.[11]

A much stronger argument in favour of testamentary freedom is that guaranteed inheritances cause heirs to cease to work and so reduces the total wealth of the country.[12] It is generally thought to be undesirable for society that anybody, particularly a young person, should be so well provided for that he has no need to work.

Finally, an argument in favour of testamentary freedom is that the circumstances of people are so varied that no solution uniformly enforced is likely to do justice to the myriad of different human relations.[13] This was the principal reason for the rejection of Miss Rathbone's Bill in 1931 by the Joint Select Committee.[14] Individualised decisions can also be given by the institutions of the State – this is one of the rationales of family provision – but the cost of making such decisions is likely to be very great and in most cases the deceased will know more about and be far better able to evaluate the claims made upon him than any institutions of the State.[15]

The Arguments Against Freedom of Testation

One of the most compelling arguments for forced share regimes is that they are a recognition that in reality and justice the deceased was not the sole owner of his property, but was a co-owner of it with his family whose efforts helped to produce it.[16] This is the principal rationale for the enlarged standard of provision awarded to spouses under the 1975 Act.[17] However, its relevance to situations other than between spouses in modern England and Wales must be small or

11. See Boswell, *The Rise and Decline of Small Firms* 90–95, 179–198.
12. Morton, 'The Theory of Inheritance' (1894–95) 8 Harv L Rev 161, at 165; Wedgewood, *The Economics of Inheritance* 194; Dalton, *The Inequality of Incomes* 301; Laski, *A Grammar of Politics* (5th edn), 528 and see remarks of Roxburgh J in *Re Pearson-Gregory* (1957) Times, 11 October and of Foster J in *Re Ferguson* (6 June 1980, unreported).
13. *Rational Basis of Legal Institutions* 419.
14. See pp 14–15, *ante*.
15. See the remarks of Lord Wilberforce in 358 HL Parl Deb, col 933 (set out at p 29, *ante*); and see also Spring, *Law, Land & Family* on the uses of testamentary freedom.
16. Mill, *Principles of Political Economy* (6th edn), Book II, Ch II, s 3; Miraglia, *Comparative Legal Philosophy* 745; Unger, 'The Inheritance Act and the Family' (1943) 6 Mod L Rev 215, 225; Ontario Law Reform Commission, *Study Prepared by the Family Law Project* Vol III, Property Subjects, 477.
17. See pp 25–27, *ante* and pp 169–186, *post*; and Gray, *Re-allocation of Property on Divorce*.

non-existent, since units of production centred upon parent and child are the exception and families tend to be small.[18] While it may readily be admitted that it is a sufficient reason for restricting inheritance to protect spouses, and it may be admitted that it has some relevance for rural societies such as New Zealand and nineteenth century France where children work or worked upon their parents' farms for less than economic wages, it has no application for relations other than between spouses in twentieth century urban England and Wales.

Probably the most telling argument against freedom of testation is that a person while alive is not totally free to dispose of his property as he pleases and that therefore, these restrictions should continue after his death. While alive a person can be made to support various members of his family at the instance of those members of the family[19] or at the instance of the State, which wishes to be relieved of the burden of supporting members of the family.[20] Although, since the Dower Act 1833 and the espousal of separate property by the Married Women's Property Act 1882, English Law has lacked any kind of matrimonial property regime, the development in the twentieth century of obligations of support and the wide powers of the courts upon divorce to vary the parties' property rights has led to a de facto matrimonial property regime during the spouse's lifetime. It is clearly anomalous and the cause of hardship to spouses and children and expense to the State that these obligations should cease at death and that the right of a spouse in the quasi-matrimonial property regime should not be enforceable after death. Indeed the position prior to the 1938 Act was somewhat remarkable in that the legally enforceable obligations of support owed by a person to his family ceased on death. While death should not prima facie affect the existence of legal obligations to support, it may properly affect the remedies available for such obligations and the amount awarded under such remedies. The maintenance awarded to a widow after the death of her husband might be legitimately less than that actually provided before death, because the widow is relieved from performing wifely services and is free to remarry, or might be legitimately more because of the economies of scale of two persons, as opposed to one person, living in the same household. In certain circumstances it might be appropriate for maintenance which was

18. Unger, 'The Inheritance Act and the Family' (1943) 6 Mod L Rev 215, 225.
19. Matrimonial Causes Act 1973, s 23(1)(a) (divorce and judicial separation), s 27 (wilful default to maintain during marriage); Domestic Proceedings and Magistrates' Courts Act 1978, s 1; Children Act 1989, Sch I (children).
20. Social Security Administration Act 1992, s 78(6)-(9), s 105(3); Child Support Act 1991.

provided as income during the deceased's lifetime to be awarded as capital to encourage a dependant to make a fresh start after the death of the deceased.[1]

It has been further argued that restrictions upon testamentary freedom will lead to a more equal distribution of wealth by preventing the concentration of wealth through primogeniture. This argument has been examined with some care by Wedgewood who concluded that a system of fixed shares would have only a very marginal effect on the distribution of wealth, which would be essentially to equalise the distribution within the higher social classes rather than between social classes.[2] Any limitation upon testamentary freedom will prevent rich people from leaving their property to charitable and public purposes. The conclusion which must be drawn is that restrictions on testamentary freedom will not significantly affect the distribution of wealth in society, the marginal increase in equality of distribution within classes being offset by the decrease caused by the obstacles placed in the way of giving property for charitable purposes. If it is desired to reduce the inequality of wealth in our society caused by inheritance, this can be best achieved by taxation rather than restricting freedom of testation.

It has been objected that freedom of testation can be abused by being used 'maliciously' and hence should not be permitted. This view, although not articulated in these precise terms, has been put forward by a distinguished Professor of English Law[3] and by a solicitor MP during the Parliamentary Debates on the 1975 Act.[4] It must be observed that, apart from the obligations and property rights owed to infant children and spouses discussed above a person is free to deal with his property as he pleases during his lifetime. As a general principle of English Law merely acting maliciously does not generally make an act lawful in itself unlawful.[5] While it may be a proper rule of the common law that the civil law should not be an instrument of punishment between private parties,[6] it can hardly

1. Compare s 25A of the Matrimonial Causes Act 1973, inserted by Matrimonial and Family Proceedings Act 1984.
2. Wedgewood, *The Economics of Inheritance*, 75–76; see also Dalton, *The Inequality of Incomes*, 301–302; Stephens, *The Law Relating to Family Protection in New Zealand* (2nd edn), 35–39.
3. Guest, 'Family Provision and the Legitima Portio' (1957) 73 LQR 74, 83; see also the remarks of Lord Denning MR in *Re Brocklehurst's Estate* [1978] Ch 14, at 32E–H, [1978] 1 All ER 767, at 776h-777b.
4. Mr Bruce Douglas-Mann MP at 898 HC Parl Deb, cols 191–192.
5. *Bradford Corpn v Pickles* [1895] AC 587, HL; *Allen v Flood* [1898] AC 1, HL; *Lonrho Ltd v Shell Petroleum Co Ltd (No 2)* [1982] AC 173, [1981] 2 All ER 456, HL; Gutteridge, 'Abuse of Rights' (1935) 5 Camb L Jo 22.
6. Compare the common law's refusal to enforce penalties.

be regarded as punishment if a person is denied an inheritance – property to which he had no prior right.

A further reason against free testation is that it discourages disputes after the death of the deceased. This argument certainly found some support among the survey of public opinion carried out for the Law Commission.[7]

Conclusion on Testamentary Freedom

The conclusion which appears from an examination of the arguments in favour of and against testamentary freedom is that it is generally desirable, but that it should be subject to the same or similar restrictions as dispositions of property made inter vivos. This conclusion follows not so much from the strength of the arguments in favour of testamentary freedom, but from the weakness of the arguments against it.

Almost all of the 1938 Act and much of the 1975 Act can be justified on the basis that they extend after a person's death the obligation owed to support before death and the quasi-matrimonial property regime derived from the powers of the Divorce Court. The manner of enforcement is slightly different to take account of the differences created by a person's death. It is curious to note that the State cannot apply, even indirectly, as it can when a person is alive, for provision to be made out of a person's estate for a dependant receiving support from the State. A further curiosity is that at the time of the passing of the 1938 Act a person while alive was legally responsible, at least in theory, for the maintenance of a much wider range of persons than could apply under the Act, including children of any age, parents and grandparents,[8] whereas at the time of the passing of the 1975 Act the legal responsibility to maintain had been reduced to the maintenance of his spouse and children under 16[9] but the class of applicants for family provision had been widened considerably.

Many people might argue that family provision should only apply to applicants who were owed a duty of support by the deceased when alive. This was the conclusion of the Albertan Study on Family

7. Todd and Jones, *Matrimonial Property*: of the spouses questioned who preferred fixed inheritance rights for children, 15% of husbands and 21% of wives gave as *a* reason for their belief that it would prevent disputes and arguments.
8. Poor Law Act 1930, s 14, replacing essentially Poor Law Act 1927, s 41 and the Poor Relief Act 1601, s 7.
9. Social Security Administration Act 1992, s 78(6)-(9), s 105(3).

Provision, which is probably the most sophisticated analysis of family provision by a law reform body in recent years;[10] it concluded that limiting applicants to those to whom a duty of support was owed during the lifetime of the deceased gave 'a clear and rational foundation' for support after death.[11] However, because a person's interest in his property is so much the less when he is dead than when he is alive, it may be justifiable to have a larger class of applicants than those to whom a duty of support is owed during the deceased's lifetime. If sufficiently valid arguments can be advanced it may be justifiable to increase the class of applicants beyond spouses and infant children.

The Claims of Adult Children

The case of claims by adult children has been put forward strongly by various writers, but they have not particularised the grounds on which they base their claims. Professor Guest writing in 1957 is an example:

> But family obligations do not function only when a wife or child is in need, nor do they necessarily cease when a child grows up or marries. The ties of family duty are not so easily severed.[12]

A similar refusal to particularise the reasoning behind the proposition is evident in the speeches of Lord Simon of Glaisdale, who justified the right of *all* adult children to apply under the 1975 Act by reference to certain special cases and the general place of the family among society's institutions.[13]

One of the clearest discussions of the obligations owed to a child by his parent is by Mill. He concluded:

> The duties of parents to their children are those which are attached to the fact of causing the existence of a human being. The parent owes to society to endeavour to make the child a good and valuable member of it and owes to the children to provide, for far as depends on him, such education, and such appliances and means, as will

10. Institute of Law Research and Reform, University of Alberta, Report No 29 *Family Relief* (1978), pp 23–26.
11. *Ibid*, 26.
12. 'Family Provision and Legitima Portio' (1957) 73 LQR 74, 83.
13. 358 HL Parl Deb, cols 925–928, 359 HL Parl Deb, cols 1067–1071. See also the defence of the 'reserve' in the civil law – 'It is not true that the centre of modern society is the individual' Miraglia, *Comparative Legal Philosophy* 760.

> enable them to start with a fair chance of achieving by their own exertions a successful life. To this every child has a claim; and I cannot admit that as a child he has a claim to more.[14]

Few people would disagree with Mill that the obligations arising from the very act of procreation should cease upon adulthood, unless, perhaps, the child is handicapped so as to be incapable of supporting himself. Indeed few children would claim rights, solely by the fact of the relationship of parent and child, after they have reached adulthood. As set out previously it has been thought to be undesirable for people to be guaranteed inheritances as this would be a disincentive to work.[15] Mill summed it up thus, 'it is really no grievance to any man, that for the means of marrying and supporting a family he has to depend upon his exertions'.[16]

The advocates of forced share provisions for adult children stress the importance of the family in society. However there is no evidence that forced inheritance rights will improve the relationship between parents and adult children – indeed an argument can be made to the contrary.[17]

Moreover, the very idea of inheriting property from parents is one which is condemned by a large body of opinion as being unjust and the cause of unnecessary inequality in society.[18] One of the rationales of Inheritance Tax, with its exceptions for gifts for charitable and public purposes, is to restrict the amount of wealth inherited – a system of forced shares for children would run counter to much of the policy behind the present system of capital taxation. Accordingly any device which strengthens the rights of adult children to inherit from their parents might be disapproved of because of its inegalitarian consequences. It is therefore suggested that as there is no consensus in society as to the role of inheritance from parents the private law should not attempt to restrict testators in the exercise of their powers one way or the other.

14. *Principles of Political Economy* (6th edn), Book II, Ch II, s 3; See also Institute of Law Research and Reform, University of Alberta, Report No 29, *Family Relief* (1978) 8–9.
15. See p 37, *ante*.
16. *Principles of Political Economy* (6th edn), Book II, Ch II, s 3.
17. See p 36, *ante*.Compare the facts of *Re Goodchild*, where giving the deceased total freedom of testation might have acted as an incentive for the son to get on better with the deceased's second wife.
18. Morton, 'The Theory of Inheritance', (1894–95) 8 Harv L Rev 161; Wedgewood, *The Economics of Inheritance*; Dalton, *The Inequality of Incomes*; Gold, Note, (1938) 1 Mod L Rev 296; Chester, *Inheritance, Wealth and Society*.

It would seem that public opinion does not support guaranteed inheritance rights for adult children.[19] It is therefore suggested that the case for restricting freedom of testation in favour of adult children, purely because of the relationship of parent and child, has not been made out, except perhaps in the exceptional case of a person unable through handicap to support himself.

A further argument justifying restrictions on disinheriting children and those who have been supported by the deceased prior to his death is that it is wrong to disappoint the expectations of children and those being maintained by the deceased that they will inherit property from the deceased and that their maintenance will continue. The author of a book on the New Zealand Law of family provision stated that, 'it is unethical for a testator to defeat the just expectations of those dependent upon him'.[20] Against this Sedgwick thought that the disappointment of expectations held by children, no matter how painful, was insufficient to justify any state intervention with the power of testation.[1] It is a general proposition in the law of obligations that, in the absence of the most compelling reasons of policy, expectations should only be protected to the extent that a person has suffered a detriment in reliance upon them.[2] The amount of detriment caused by reliance upon an expectation of an inheritance is likely to be small because the time of death is always uncertain, there is no guarantee that a person's estate will remain constant, events such as the remarriage of the person may legitimately destroy all prospects of inheritance and people realise that testators have freedom to disinherit. If it is desired to protect the expectations of prospective heirs the remedy should be to give the same form of action in estoppel where the remedy will reflect the detriment suffered rather than to limit testamentary freedom.[3]

19. See the results of the Survey, Ch 1, p 34A, *ante*; the public opinion surevey in Appendix C Law Commission Report – Family Law: Distribution on Intestacy (No 187, 1989); and the result of representations made to the Institute of Law Research and Reform, University of Alberta, Report No 29, *Family Relief*, p 31.
20. Stephens, *The Law Relating to Family Protection in New Zealand* (2nd edn), 34. One suspects that the keyword in the quotation is 'just' rather than 'expectations'.
1. *The Elements of Politics* (3rd edn), p 101.
2. See Fuller and Perdue, 'The Reliance Interest in Contract Damages' (1936) 46 Yale L Jo 52, 373; Beale, *Remedies for Breach of Contract*, 164–166; Oughton, 'Proprietory Estoppel' (1979) 129 NLJ 449; Atiyah, *Promises, Morals and the Law*.
3. See *Re Basham* [1987] 1 All ER 405, [1986] 1 WLR 1498; *Wayling v Jones* (1993) 69 P & CR 170, [1995] 2 FLR 1029, CA; Lawson, 'The things we do for love:detrimental reliance in the family home'(1996) 16 Legal Studies 218.

Another argument in favour of restricting testamentary freedom is that where a person is being maintained by the deceased, it may be right that such maintenance should not cease on death. To a certain extent this argument encompasses the previous argument about not disappointing expectations. It is examined more fully in Chapter 4 on the discussion of section 1(1)(e) of the 1975 Act – other dependants of the deceased who can apply for provision[4] – and found substantially, but not totally, wanting.

Accordingly it can be concluded, except perhaps in the case of handicapped adult children, that the case for imposing greater restraints on testamentary dispositions other than inter vivos dispositions has not been made out.

The 1975 Act

Applying our conclusions to the 1975 Act, it is found that the Act generally limits testamentary freedom at about the correct point. The Act deviates from the conclusion on the proper limits of testamentary freedom in allowing adult children and any person actually dependent on the deceased to apply. These classes of applicant were the least thought out by the Law Commission and have given the most difficulty to the courts and commentators. They were passed mainly to deal with particular problems of children who sacrificed a great deal to care for aged and infirm parents and the problem of cohabitation outside marriage. But it is questionable whether either the definitions adopted or the choice of family provision are well adapted to deal with these problems effectively. The defects in section 1(1)(e) were recognised by the extension of the class of applicants to cohabitants by the Law Reform (Succession) Act 1995, cohabitation being increasingly recognised by English law as a relationship while not equivalent to marriage having signicant legal consequences.[5] The failure to take the opportunity to repeal section 1(1)(e) is to be regretted.

4. See pp 100–103 and pp 280–282, *post*.
5. Cohabitation is recognised in social security law, eg s 132 of the Social Security Contributions and Benefit Act 1992, in the occupation of dwellinghouses, eg s 38 of the Family Law Act 1996, in succession to residential tenancies, eg s 17(4) of the Housing Act 1988, in relation to damages for loss of dependency, see s 1(3)(b) of the Fatal Accidents Act 1976 as amended. However, it is significant, that save by way of the 'liable relative' procedure, cohabitees can not be obliged to maintain each other before death.

The Basis of Family Provision

It is, therefore, submitted that family provision should be regarded as a means of extending a person's obligations of support owed while alive (and in the cases of spouses the quasi-matrimonial property regime) to the period after a person's death and in a very limited number of situations extending those duties. Parliament in passing family provision legislation and the courts in administering it have not evinced a single coherent basis for family provision, but it is suggested that the idea of continuing a deceased's lifetime obligations is probably the most important basis used by both Parliament and the courts. While the essential factor justifying interference with the operation of a deceased's will or intestacy is the existence of lifetime obligations, these lifetime obligations should not *necessarily* govern the remedies used to enforce those obligations after death. As has been noted previously, death is an important factor to be taken into account, in some cases freeing the applicant from rendering obligations and services to the deceased, in other cases releasing property used for the deceased's support for the use of the applicant or for the first time informing the applicant of the true wealth of the deceased.[6]

The discretionary nature of family provision can be partially justified because rights of support and the quasi-matrimonial property regime during a person's lifetime are discretionary. The discretionary nature of family provision allows an individualised form of justice,[7] and interferes with testamentary freedom only when necessary. The statistics of applications made to the courts do not show that the volume of litigation under the legislation has become unmanageable.[8]

Family provision is essentially a matter concerned with private rights – the State's interest in relieving the public purse is a reason justifying the existence of the jurisdiction but is not the guiding principle governing the exercise of the jurisdiction. Thus it may be possible to answer Sir Claud Schuster's question inquiring whether family provision, 'means that the excluded relations have a right to be protected against destitution or a right to the kind of maintenance

6. Compare *Re Whittle* (5 March 1973, unreported), CA; *Re Borthwick* [1949] Ch 395, [1949] 1 All ER 472.
7. For the individualised system of justice see Atiyah, *From Principles to Pragmatism: Changes in the Function of the Judicial Process*, criticised by Stone, 'From Principles to Principles' (1981) 97 LQR 224.
8. See Appendix A.

to which they have been accustomed'[9] more in the second sense than in the first sense. This means that family provision may be ordered in favour of an applicant who is not destitute or dependent upon the State for support in any way even at the expense of an applicant who is therefore thrown upon the State for support and that provision may be refused to an applicant who while destitute and supported by the State is not otherwise deserving of maintenance from the deceased's estate. It is generally the policy of the modern law that private rights are only enforced when just rather than that the State be relieved of the burden of supporting the destitute to the maximum extent.[10]

What Family Provision Should Not Be

It is the thesis of this book that family provision should be regarded as a method of extending the obligations owed by a person before his death to after death and perhaps in a few limited cases extending them. What family provision should not be is a general jurisdiction to vary the dispositions of a person's will or intestacy as the judge considers just in favour of a limited class of people or a general power to dispense with the requirements for making wills and the rules for their operation.[11] Three cases demonstrate the dangers of this approach.

9. Letter, Schuster to Sir Maurice Gwyer, 19 February 1934, PRO LCO 2/1188, also set out at p 16, *ante*.
10. A husband's duty to maintain his wife under the predecessor of the Social Security Administration Act 1992, ss 105(1), 106(1) was not by itself destroyed by the commission of a matrimonial offence, but this was an important factor in deciding the amount, if any, of any order: *National Assistance Board v Wilkinson* [1952] 2 QB 648, [1952] 2 All ER 255; *National Assistance Board v Parkes* [1955] 2 QB 506, [1955] 3 All ER 1, CA. The House of Lords in *Minton v Minton* [1979] AC 593, [1979] 1 All ER 79 in rejecting the principle of *Hyman v Hyman* [1929] AC 601, HL that the court's jurisdiction to order maintenance for a spouse cannot be ousted by agreement clearly preferred a divorce law which was just between the parties at the expense of a possible extra burden upon the State. It is submitted that the Child Support Act 1991 is not inconsistent with this analysis. See generally Prime, 'Ex-Wife Ex-Family?' (1982) 12 Fam Law 53, 55–56 which approves the argument put forward in the text.
11. For the argument that the court should have wider powers to do justice after the death of a deceased person, see Law Commission Working Paper No 108, para 5.13; Cretney, 'Reform of Intestacy:The Best we can do?'(1995) 111 LQR 77, at 95–99. The title of Dr Cretney's article inevitably invites the retort of 'is this the best that academics and the Law Commission can do?' – more discretion, less guidance upon how this discretion should be exercised, more uncertainty and more litigation. For a valuable critque of 'selective compassion' and incremental changes in the law without any overall view of where the law is going, see Atiyah, *The Damages Lottery*.

In *Re Christie*,[12] a decision of Mr Vivian Price QC, sitting as a Deputy High Court Judge, the deceased originally owned two properties. It was her original intention, expressed in her will, to give one property to her adult daughter and one property to her adult son. Before she died she made a gift of one of the properties to the daughter. She sold the property devised to her son and used the proceeds of sale to purchase another property. Consequently, the gift of the property to the son was adeemed and the replacement property fell into the residue which was divided equally between the son and the daughter. There was some evidence that the deceased wished to alter her will so as to ensure that the replacement property went to the son solely. The disappointed son applied for additional provision out of his mother's estate so that he could be awarded the whole of the value of the replacement property and Mr Vivian Price QC acceded to this application. His Lordship supported his decision by reference to the intention of the deceased to change her will so as to ensure that the replacement property went to the son alone[13] and the desire to preserve equality between the children.[14]

It is suggested that the decision is very wrong both as a means of interpreting the Act in accordance with its legislative history and as a matter of general policy. The Judge expressly found that the 'deceased did not have any special obligations towards the son as opposed to his sister'.[15] What happened in *Re Christie* was an alteration of the deceased's testamentary disposition according to the Judge's discretion, which paid no attention to whether the children were in need of maintenance or ought to receive maintenance for any special reason other than the testator's intention and the desire to preserve equality between the children. In *Re Christie* the Court in effect allowed the deceased to make a new will, her intentions being proved orally by evidence from the person in whose favour the alteration was made and his wife,[16] a result contrary to unrepealed sections of the Wills Act 1833,[17] which sections the Law Reform Committee has recently concluded should remain in force.[18] It is in this context that Lord Wilberforce's remarks about

12. [1979] Ch 168, [1979] 1 All ER 546 – a decision subsequently not followed by other cases.
13. [1979] Ch 176B–C, [1979] 1 All ER 551g-h. Compare *Re Pugh* [1943] Ch 387, [1943] 2 All ER 361.
14. [1979] Ch 176E–F, [1979] 1 All ER 552a.
15. [1979] Ch 175H, [1979] 1 All ER 551e-f.
16. See [1979] Ch 175B, 176B–D, [1979] 1 All ER 550h-551b, 551g-h.
17. Wills Act 1833, s 9 – wills to be in writing and witnessed by two persons; s 15 – gifts to witnesses and their spouses are void.
18. Law Reform Committee: 22nd Report – *The Making and Revocation of Wills* (1980 Cmnd 7902), para 2.20 – approval of existing requirement of writing; para 2.15 – approval of existing law on gifts to witnesses.

the quality of evidence in family provision proceedings are particularly relevant.[19] It is not to be thought that without any discussion of what they were about Parliament in passing the 1975 Act intended to repeal many of the provisions of the Wills Act 1833. If *Re Christie* is correct it means that the court now has a discretion to admit oral wills upon the evidence of beneficiaries and to prevent the ademption of gifts, but only in favour of a limited class of beneficiaries and then only if they are not rich, since whatever meaning 'maintenance' may have rich people must be barred from claiming under the Act.[20] The result is totally absurd.

A not dissimilar misuse of family provision is found in the case of *CA v CC*,[1] a decision of Baker P. The deceased by his will left all his property to his legitimate infant son. After the execution of the will he began associating with a mistress by whom he had an illegitimate child. There was some evidence that prior to his death he wished to alter his will so as to make provision for his mistress and illegitimate son. The illegitimate son and the mistress applied for provision out of the estate and both were successful. Baker P awarded the illegitimate son a share in the estate equal to that of the legitimate son and stated, 'The younger boy *had to* be put on equality with the older boy'.[2] It is submitted that there is no legal compulsion upon a testator to leave equal amounts to his children or not discriminate between his legal and illegitimate children[3] and that Parliament has not by a sidewind caused it to be impossible to discriminate between children. If Parliament had intended to enact a pretermitted child statute[4] it would have done so in express terms. The actual decision in *CA v CC* is unexceptional, since where an estate is insufficient to support all the claims for maintenance made upon it, similarly placed applicants and beneficiaries should be treated alike.

19. See p 29, *ante*.
20. For the argument that relative poverty should not be a pre-requisite for enforcing 'moral claims' on death, see Chatterton, 'Inheritance Act claims by adult children' [1994] Fam Law 330.
1. (1978) Times, 17 November, sub nom *Re C* 123 Sol Jo 35, sub nom *In the Estate McC* 9 Fam Law 26.
2. Emphasis added. The quotation is only found in (1978) 123 Sol Jo 35. The report in (1978) 9 Fam Law 26 includes a reference by Baker P to 'equity is equality'.
3. Compare Family Law Reform Act 1969, s 14(5), which prevented illegitimates taking under entails and the rules which prevent illegitimates succeeding to peerages.
4. For pretermitted child statutes see Page, *Wills* (Bowe-Parker, ed), s 21, pp 105–112 and an example is Uniform Probate Code s 2-302. The only change of circumstances revoking a will is marriage, Wills Act 1833, ss 18 and 19.

In *Re Goodchild*[5] a married couple agreed to make wills in each other's favour and for the survivor to leave his estate to the son of the marriage. The wife died and her estate passed to the husband, who later remarried. The son and the second wife did not get on with each other and the husband made a will leaving his entire estate to his second wife. Upon his death the son, a businessman whose business had fallen on hard times and who had accumulated substantial debts, made two claims, firstly alleging a mutual wills trust and secondly claiming under the 1975 Act. Carnwath J rejected the claim for a mutual wills trust because the deceased and his first wife did not have the requisite intention to make a legally binding agreement, but acceded to the second claim in effect awarding the applicant provision equivalent to the provision had the mutual wills trust been enforced.[6] Both these decisions were subsequently upheld by the Court of Appeal.[7] The same factor which limits the application of a mutual wills trust, namely the reluctance to impose inter vivos restrictions on an apparently absolute gift[8] applies equally to a family provision claim.[9] Moreover the moral claim of an intended beneficary under a mutual will understanding is exactly the same if the beneficiary is rich or poor or child or some other person, but under the approach of *Re Goodchild* a poor, or relatively

5. [1996] 1 WLR 694, [1996] 1 All ER 670; affirmed [1997] 3 All ER 63. Another controversial decision in this area is *Re Leach*[1986] Ch 226, [1985] 2 All ER 754, which is critcised in (1986) 83 LS Gaz 93 and discussed at pp 215–218, *ante* .
6. [1996] 1 WLR 694, [1996] 1 All ER 670.
7. [1997] 3 All ER 63. In the Court of Appeal only Leggatt LJ gave a reasoned judgment on the claim under the 1975 Act and this was less than satisfactory. Leggatt LJ did not refer to *Re Jennings* [1994] Ch 286, [1994] 3 All ER 27, the leading case on claims by adult children (as to which see pp 219–221, *post*), which had been cited and was extensively discussed by Carnwath J at first instance, and *Re Coventry* [1980] Ch 461, [1979] 2 All ER 408 (as to which see pp 211–215, *post* was only referred to on the question of appeals, see [1997] 3 All ER 74j.The reference to *Bosch v Perpetual Trustee Co Ltd* [1938] AC 463, [1938] 2 All ER 14 at [1997] 3 All ER 73g fails to note that the children in *Bosch* were young and that Australasian courts have taken a completely different approach to claims by adult children to English Courts (see pp 121–123 and p 229, *post*) and sits very uneasily with the judgment of the Court of Appeal in *Re Jennings* (but note the approval by Leggatt LJ at [1997] 3 All ER 74a of Carnwath J's holding that the deceased's disposition of that part of his estate which was not derived from his first wife could not be challenged under the 1975 Act). The statement that the estate was of 'modest size' and that therefore appeals should be discouraged ([1997] 3 All ER 74j) seems absurd when the estate was worth between £380,000 and £500,000 before Inheritance Tax and can not stand with *Cameron v Treasury Solicitor* [1996] 2 FLR 716.
8. See per Morritt LJ at [1997] 3 All ER 76b-d.
9. S 10 of the 1975 Act has essentially the same effect as the floating trust set out in *Birmingham v Renfrew* (1936) 57 CLR 666.

poor, child is allowed to succeed under a lower standard of proof, but only in so far as there is no competing beneficiary.[10] The courts have striven to give the anomalous doctrine of mutual wills trust[11] a precise ambit and they seem satisfied with their conclusion,[12] but the decision in *Re Goodchild* creates a two tier test, namely ordinary beneficiaries who must prove a legally binding agreement and applicants under the 1975 Act who must prove merely a morally binding understanding.[13]

10. *Re Goodchild* did not decide the order of priority between a maintenance claim of a surviving spouse and an adult child claiming under 'moral' mutual wills, as the second wife could not and did not claim that her rights under the 1975 Act extended to more than half the deceased's estate,
11. So described by Morritt LJ at [1997] 3 All ER 76b-c.
12. It is a matter of regret that Morritt LJ who delivered extremely lucid, learned and elegant judgments on mutual wills in *Re Dale* [1994] Ch 31; [1993] 4 All ER 129 and in *Re Goodchild* at [1997] 3 All ER 75c-76d did not address the merits of the family provision claim.
13. For the view that relative poverty does not deprive a claim of moral weight, see Chatterton 'Inheritance Act claims by Adult Children' [1994] Fam Law 330.

Chapter 3

CONFLICT OF LAWS

Deceased Died Domiciled in England and Wales

It is a condition precedent to the exercise of the Court's jurisdiction under the Act that the deceased died domiciled in England and Wales.[1] The Act does not extend to Scotland and Northern Ireland.[2] Reference should be made to the text books on the Conflict of Laws for the law relating to domicile.[3] Very briefly, a person dies domiciled in England and Wales:

(1) if his domicile of origin was England and Wales and (a) he has never acquired a domicile of choice in another country, or (b) having acquired a domicile of choice in another country he subsequently abandoned it and had not acquired another domicile of choice;
(2) if, where his domicile of origin was not in England and Wales, he had acquired a domicile of choice in England and Wales and had not abandoned it at the time of his death.

A domicile of origin is determined by the domicile, at the time of the child's birth, of the person upon whom he is legally dependent.

Accordingly a domicile of origin in England and Wales is acquired at birth by:

(1) a legitimate child born to a living father domiciled in England and Wales;
(2) a legitimate child born, after the death of the father, to a mother domiciled in England and Wales;
(3) an illegitimate child born of a mother domiciled in England and Wales.

1. Inheritance (Provision for Family and Dependants) Act 1975, s 1(1). England and Wales are defined in Interpretation Act 1978, Sch 1.
2. S 27(2). There is no analogous legislation for Scotland. But there the surviving spouse is entitled to *terce* and *jus relictae* (or in the case of intestacy the housing right, the statutory legacy and the *jus relictae*) and the children *legitim*, see generally Meston, *The Succession (Scotland) Act 1964* (4th edn); MacDonald, *An Introduction to the Scots Law of Succession*. For Northern Ireland, see Inheritance (Provision for Family and Dependants) (Northern Ireland) Order 1979, SI 1979/924 and Chapter 11 generally.
3. See eg Dicey and Morris, *Conflict of Laws* (12th edn); Cheshire and North's *Private International Law* (12th edn).

A domicile of choice is acquired by the fact of residing in a country other than that of the domicile of origin with the intention of continuing to reside there indefinitely:

(1) in the case of a person not under a disability, by residence in England and Wales with the intention of remaining in England and Wales indefinitely. Although formerly regarded as dependent persons, married women are now free to acquire a domicile of choice on the same terms as other adults.[4] A child is capable of acquiring a domicile of choice independent of its parent upon attaining the age of sixteen or marrying under that age;[5]
(2) in the case of a legitimate infant, on the acquisition of a domicile in England and Wales by the father, unless the father and the mother are living apart and the infant has or has had its home with the mother to the exclusion of the father,[6] in which case the infant will acquire a domicile in England and Wales when the mother does so. If the father is dead, on the acquisition of a domicile in England and Wales by the mother;
(3) in the case of a legitimated infant, on the legitimation if the father is then domiciled in England or Wales, or otherwise in the same way as a legitimate child;
(4) in the case of an illegitimate infant, on the acquisition by the mother of a domicile in England and Wales.

Burden of Proof

The applicant carries the burden of proof that the deceased died domiciled in England and Wales. In *Mastaka v Midland Bank Executor and Trustee Co Ltd*,[7] the deceased testatrix had married a Russian who was in England at the time of the marriage but whose whereabouts at the time of the deceased's death were unknown. There was no direct evidence that either the deceased's husband was dead or had acquired an English domicile. Accordingly there was no evidence that the testatrix's domicile was not the Russian domicile acquired on marriage under the then law by which a wife acquired her husband's domicile on marriage and the application was dismissed.

4. Domicile and Matrimonial Proceedings Act 1973, s 1(1).
5. Domicile and Matrimonial Proceedings Act 1973, s 3(1).
6. Domicile and Matrimonial Proceedings Act 1973, s 4(1) and (2).
7. [1941] Ch 192; *ad idem Re Harmsworth* [1982] CLY 3388.

In most cases no question of domicile will arise for the parties will have lived in England and Wales all their lives. But if the circumstances suggest any doubt as to the domicile of the deceased, for example, if the deceased had emigrated to Australia but had returned to England and Wales and died here, the matter should be expressly dealt with in the evidence stating the grounds for supposing that the Court has jurisdiction.[8]

Effect of the Choice of Law Clause

Under the present requirement the Court can make an order if the deceased was domiciled in England and Wales in respect of all of the deceased's property, except foreign immovables which under the general rules of the conflict of laws are governed by the *lex situs*.[9] There is no reason to think that in administering the jurisdiction the Court is in any way less reluctant to make orders in respect of foreign movables comprised in the estate than other assets of the estate, provided the courts of the country where the movables are situate recognise the Court's order.[10] While foreign immovables are not subject to the jurisdiction of the Court, the devolution of such property is taken into account in deciding whether the provision for an applicant is reasonable.[11] It has been held in New Zealand[12] and Australia[13] that because the sole purpose of family provision legislation is not the relief of the public purse through maintenance

8. For the form of evidence, see pp 353–354, *post*.
9. *Dicey and Morris*, Rules 135, 136 and 140. There is a substantial body of Australasian authority to the effect that there is no jurisdiction to make an order affecting foreign immovable property: *Re Donnelly* (1927) 28 SRNSW 34; *Re Osborne* [1928] QSR 129; *Re Paulin* [1950] VLR 462 at 465; *Re Bailey* [1985] 2 NZLR 656; *Heuston v Barber* (1990) 19 NSWLR 354; *Dicey and Morris* 1037-8; DICKEY, 207-8. In New South Wales this rule has been reversed by legislation – Family Provision (Foreign Land) Amendment Act 1989; but doubt has been expressed about the validity of the legislation: see *Baljan v Nikitin* (1994) 35 NSWLR 51 per Windeyer J; (1994) 68 ALJ 612. Meston, *The Succession (Scotland) Act 1964* (4th edn), 118 states that an English court has no jurisdiction to make an order under the 1975 Act affecting Scottish immovables. For possible jurisdiction to make orders affecting foreign land under *renvoi*, in particular where the lex situs provides that succession to land is governed by the law of the nationality of the deceased (eg Spain), see *Re Bailey* [1985] 2 NZLR 656 and Breslauer (1938) 1 Mod LR 306
10. Kelly, 'Testators' Family Maintenance and the Conflict of Laws' (1967) 41 Aust LJ 382, 384; contra, Morris, 'The Choice of Law Clause in Statutes' (1946) 62 LQR 170, 178.
11. *Re Butchart* [1932] NZLR 125; Compare *Re Carter* (1968) 112 Sol Jo 136.
12. *Re Roper* [1927] NZLR 731
13. *Re Found* [1924] SASR 236, at 239–240; *Re Roper* [1927] NZLR 731 at 743; *Re Donelly* (1927) 28 SRNSW 34 at 35; *Re Perkins* (1958) 58 SRNSW 1 at 7, 9–10. And see *Re Preston* [1969] 1 WLR 317, [1969] 2 All ER 961.

of persons within the jurisdiction applicants who have no connection with the jurisdiction may successfully apply under the legislation.

An English Court normally has jurisdiction over matters of succession to immovables situate in England and Wales, whether or not the deceased was domiciled in England and Wales. As the Court's jurisdiction under the 1975 Act is limited to cases where the deceased was domiciled in England and Wales, this can lead to an anomalous situation, where, for instance, the deceased dies domiciled in Northern Ireland leaving land in England and Wales. In such a case the Northern Irish Court has no jurisdiction over the English land because the devolution of such land is governed by English law, and the English Court has no jurisdiction because the deceased was not domiciled in England and Wales. Thus the two countries having the closest connection with the deceased and the land both have identical family provision legislation, yet neither has jurisdiction to apply family provision legislation to the land. This situation has been strongly criticised by academics,[14] who have argued the adoption of the Australasian rule that the Court has jurisdiction under the family provision legislation whenever the Court has jurisdiction over matters of succession.[15] The removal of the limitation to domicile was pressed upon the Law Commission,

14. Breslauer (1938) 1 Mod LR 306; Laskin, 'Dependants' Relief Legislation' (1939) 17 Can Bar R 181, 181–182; Falconbridge (1941) 19 Can Bar R 539; Morris, 'The Choice of Law Clause in Statutes' (1964) 62 LQR 170, 178–179; Kelly, 'Testators' Family Maintenance and the Conflict of Laws' (1967) 41 Aust LJ 382; *Dicey and Morris*, 1037–1038; Miller (1990) 39 I & CLQ 261. The problem has been substantially solved in Australia by the Jurisdiction of Courts (Cross-Vesting) Act 1987 which confers on each State and Territory the jurisdiction of the other States and Territories. See DICKEY, 203–204. Such legislation could usefully be introduced for England and Wales and Northern Ireland. For discussion of the possible application of *renvoi* where a British national dies domiciled in a country where succession is governed by the law of the nationality of the deceased, see Breslauer.

15. England, Northern Ireland and the Yukon Territory (Dependants' Relief Ordinance 1975, s 3(1)) are the only jurisdictions which have express choice of law clauses limiting jurisdiction to the domicile of the deceased. The Canadian Uniform Dependants' Relief Act enacted in the North West Territories, Ontario and Prince Edward Island expressly provides for jurisdiction if the deceased died domiciled within the jurisdiction or if the deceased died possessed of land within the jurisdiction.

In other jurisdictions where there is no express limitation on jurisdiction the courts exercise jurisdiction if the deceased died domiciled within the jurisdiction and, when he died, possessed of immovables within the jurisdiction (*Re Butchart* [1932] NZLR 731; *Re Perkins* (1958) 58 SRNSW 105), but not when the deceased merely died possessed of immovables within the jurisdiction (*Pain v Holt* (1919) 19 SRNSW 105; *Re Elliot* (1941) 2 DLR 71 (BCSC)).

The Institute of Law Research and Reform, University of Alberta, Report No 29, *Family Relief* (1978) (pp138–139) proposed that Albertan courts should

but the Law Commission rejected this proposal for a change in the law.[16] The Law Commission gave two reasons for its views. Firstly they argued that having a multiplicity of jurisdictions would create problems of co-ordinating applications in more than one jurisdiction, to the detriment of other beneficiaries of the estate. It is submitted that such problems already exist, for instance, where a deceased domiciled in England and Wales leaves land in New Zealand, and that it is not beyond the wit of the courts to make relief granted to applicants conditional upon making co-ordinated applications in other jurisdictions.[17] Secondly, the Law Commission argued that any change in the law should wait for international reform of the basis of jurisdiction for family and succession law.

Power to Vary Maintenance Agreements and Orders

The jurisdiction to vary after death secured periodical payment orders under section 31(6) of the Matrimonial Causes Act 1973,[18]

---

have jurisdiction, if the deceased died domiciled in Alberta, if the deceased died possessed of movables situate in Alberta *and* the applicant is ordinarily resident in Alberta. It was further proposed that where jurisdiction was based only on the deceased dying possessed of immovables within the jurisdiction the Albertan courts should have power to adjourn proceedings until proceedings in the domicile of the deceased had been determined.

The New South Wales Family Provision Act 1982, s 11(1)(c) provided that the court can make an order affecting property situate within or outside New South Wales whether or not the deceased was domiciled in New South Wales. The Family Provision (Foreign Land) Amendment Act 1989 extended this power to foreign land.

The South Australian Inheritance (Family Provision) Act 1972, s 7(1)(a) gives the court jurisdiction if the deceased died domiciled in South Australia or owned land or personal property in South Australia.

16. LAW COM, paras 258–262.
17. In *Re Paulin* [1950] VLR 462, 468 Scholl J stated that it was desirable to co-ordinate applications, but refused to make relief conditional on pursuing applications in other jurisdictions. The South Australian Inheritance (Family Provision) Act, s 7(5) gives the court power to refuse an order or adjourn proceedings if it is of the opinion that proceedings would be more appropriately commenced in another jurisdiction.

    It is submitted that in an *extreme case*, such as the deceased dying domiciled in England and Wales, but possessed of substantial movable assets in New South Wales and negligble assets in England and Wales, with the applicant and beneficiaries resident in Australia, the English courts will stay an application under the 1975 Act in favour of an application in New South Wales on the ground of forum non conveniens. See further *S v S (matrimonial proceedings: appropriate forum)* [1997] 1 WLR 1200 – discussion of forum non conveniens in context of pre-nuptial agreement, covering inter alia death where one party claimed to be domiciled in England and Wales.
18. See pp 416–417, *post*.

and paragraph 7 of the First Schedule to the Children Act 1989[19] is not subject to a requirement that the deceased died domiciled in England and Wales. Jurisdiction under section 31(6) of the Matrimonial Causes Act 1973 is governed by the rules on jurisdiction of the English courts:

(a) (in cases before the Family Law Act 1996 came into effect) to grant decrees of divorce, nullity and judicial separation[20] which operate by reference to the circumstances of *either* party to the marriage as at the date of the commencement of the proceedings;
(b) (in cases after the Family Law Act 1996 came into effect) to grant divorce and separation orders[1] which likewise operate by reference to the circumstances of *either* party to the marriage as at the 'statement date';
(c) under Part III of the Matrimonial and Family Proceedings Act 1984 which enables a court to grant relief after a foreign divorce;
(d) by the rules enabling the English courts to make orders for secured periodical payments in cases of neglect to maintain.[2]

The jurisdiction to make an order for secured periodical payments is relatively wide, subject only to the rules as to service out of the jurisdiction and to the Civil Jurisdiction and Judgments Act 1982.[3] If an application to vary a secured periodical payments order after the death of the payer is made under section 31(6) of the Matrimonial Causes Act 1973, the court has power under section 17 of the 1975 Act to direct that the application shall be deemed to have been accompanied by an application for provision under section 2 of the 1975 Act.[4] Thus in these limited circumstances the court can make orders under the 1975 Act in a case where the

19. See p 420, *post*. The dichotomy between the jurisdictional provisions of the 1975 Act and of the First Schedule to the Children Act 1989 is well illustrated by the case of *A v A (a minor: financial provision)* [1994] 1 FLR 657. This case involved a claim by an illegitimate infant child for periodical payments and/or a lump sum against her father who was domiciled outside England and Wales. Because the child would have no claim under the 1975 Act should the father die, the court ordered the that the periodical payments be secured ([1994] 1 FLR 667H-668A). See also *C v C (financial provision: personal damages)* [1995] 2 FLR 171, at 188E-189F.
20. S 5 of the Domicile and Matrimonial Proceedings Act 1973.
1. S 19 of the Family Law Act 1996.
2. The requirements are to be found in s 27(2) of the Matrimonial Causes Act 1973 as amended by s 6(1) of the Domicile and Matrimonial Proceedings Act 1973.
3. See *Dicey and Morris* Rule 97, pp 841–844.
4. See pp 417–419, *post*.

deceased was not domiciled in England and Wales. Section 17 does not apply to application to vary orders after the death of the payer under paragraph 7 of the First Schedule to the Children Act 1989.

The powers to vary maintenance agreements after the death of the payer under section 36 of the Matrimonial Causes Act 1973 and paragraph 19 of the First Schedule to the Children Act 1989 both require that the payer was domiciled in England and Wales at the date of his death.[5]

Service out of the Jurisdiction

Neither the Brussels Convention nor the Lugano Convention apply to questions of succession.[6] Accordingly service out of the jurisdiction is governed by the provisions of Order 11 of the Rules of the Supreme Court 1965.[7] Curiously, there is no provision in Order 11, rule 1 of the Rules of the Supreme Court 1965 specifically enabling service out of the jurisdiction of proceedings under the 1975 Act.[8] In almost all cases however there will be one party who has been duly served within the jurisdiction and hence service out of the jurisdiction can be justified under Order 11, rule 1(1)(c).[9] It is difficult to visualise a court exercising its discretion not to allow service out of the jurisdiction against a beneficiary when there are personal representatives and other beneficiaries who have been validly served.[10] Difficulties in serving out of the jurisdiction can in some cases be overcome by obtaining representation orders.[11]

It is submitted that where the defendant out of the jurisdiction in respect of whom leave to serve is being sought is only interested in the net estate through being entitled to foreign property which

5. S 36(1) of the Matrimonial Causes Act 1973; para 11(1) of the First Schedule to the Children Act 1989.
6. Art 1(1) of the Convention on Jurisdiction and Enforcement of Judgments in Civil and Commercial Matters; Kaye, *Civil Jurisdiction and Enforcement of Judgments*, 117-29.
7. In the County Court, CCR Ord 8.
8. It is submitted that RSC Ord 11, r 1(1)(k) [CCR Ord 8, r 2(1)(j)] 'a claim for the administration of the estate of a person who died domiciled within the jurisdiction or for any relief or remedy which might be obtained in any such action' is inapt to cover an application under the 1975 Act. It is submitted that the reference to 'any relief or remedy which might be obtained in such action' is a reference to RSC Ord 85, r 2.
9. CCR Ord 8, r 2(1)(c).
10. For an example of an appropriate case for refusing leave to serve out of the jurisdiction , see *Re Dennis* [1981] 2 All ER 140.
11. RSC Ord 15, r 4; CCR Ord 5, r 6. See generally p 350, *post*.

does not vest in the personal representatives, such as being the surviving holder of a joint bank account, the court is likely to adopt a fairly high test of a 'good arguable case' in deciding whether to allow service out of the jurisdiction.[12]

Foreign Property Forming Part of the Net Estate of the Deceased Not Disposable by Will

Whereas the 1938 Act only applied to property disposable by will, the 1975 Act extended the Court's jurisdiction to enable it to order provision out of certain classes of property which do not normally form part of the deceased's estate.[13] Neither the Act nor the Reports of the Law Commission contain any guidance as to the exercise of the Court's powers where such property is situated outside England and Wales or is closely connected with a jurisdiction other than England and Wales. Accordingly the matter must be governed by general principles of the Conflict of Laws.

In considering this two separate questions arise. Firstly, whether the English court has jurisdiction to make orders under sections 8–11 affecting property situate outside England and Wales. Secondly, if the English court has jurisdiction whether, if necessary, the court would order service of proceedings outside the jurisdiction. The question of service outside the jurisdiction has already been discussed.[14]

On general principles the law governing statutory nominations will be the law of the enactment creating the right to nominate. Thus a person who acquires title to property by a nomination under the provisions of a foreign enactment will have such title respected by English law and such nominated property will not form part of the 'net estate' of the deceased.[15]

12. Compare *Re Jogia* [1988] 1 WLR 484, [1988] 2 All ER 328; *Re Paramount Airways Ltd* [1993] Ch 233, at 240H-241G, [1992] 3 All ER 1, at 12j-13f.
13. S 8(1) (statutory nominations), s 8(2) (*donatio mortis causa*), s 9 (property held on a joint tenancy), s 10 (dispositions intended to defeat a family provision application), s 11 (contracts to make wills). For full discussion see Chapter 7.
14. See pp 57–58, *ante*.
15. It is submitted that an English court would not construe the 1975 Act as altering the effect of foreign statutory provisions affecting property abroad. Accordingly the title of a nominee under a foreign statutory nomination will be respected by an English court – *Galbraith v Grimshaw* [1910] AC 508, *Winkworth v Christie Manson and Woods* [1980] Ch 496, [1980] 1 All ER 1121; *Macmillan Inc v Bishopsgate Investment Trust plc (No 3)* [1995] 1 WLR 978, [1995] 3 All ER 747; aff'd [1996] 1 WLR 387, [1996] 1 All ER 585.

Likewise because a *donatio mortis causa* is characterised for the purposes of the Conflict of Laws as an inter vivos transaction rather than as a matter of succession,[16] title to property the subject of a donatio mortis causa effected outside England and Wales will be governed solely by the *lex situs*[17] and such property even if subsequently brought into England and Wales will not form part of the 'net estate'. For example, if a deceased domiciled in England and Wales effects a *donatio mortis causa* of jewellery in Northern Ireland in favour of a friend, and even if the friend later brings the jewellery into England and Wales, the jewellery will not form part of the 'net estate' of the deceased and no order for family provision can be made against the friend in respect of the jewellery.

Similarly the effect of the title acquired by a survivor of a joint tenancy of foreign immovables will be governed solely by the *lex situs* of the immovable because the *lex situs* governs all questions of title to immovables.[18] The effect of the title acquired by a survivor of joint contractual rights, such as a joint bank account, will be governed by the proper law of the contract or the law of the place where the debtor is ordinarily resident.[19] The position of a survivor of a joint tenancy of movables situate outside England and Wales is uncertain. If the operation of survivorship in a joint tenancy is characterised as an inter vivos transaction,[20] then the effect of the title of the survivor will be governed by the *lex situs* of the property,[17] but if it is characterised as part of the law of succession, then the effect of the title of the survivor will be governed by the law of the deceased's domicile.[1] Thus if a deceased domiciled in England and Wales immediately before his death is a joint tenant of land in Northern Ireland, has a joint bank account with a Northern Irish bank and is a joint owner of a motor car situate in Northern Ireland, the English court has no power under section 9 to make an order that the deceased's severable share in the joint tenancy of land and

16. *Re Korvine's Trusts* [1921] 1 Ch 343; *Emery v Clough* 63 NH 552, 4 A 796 (1885). Compare *Re Craven's Estate* [1937] Ch 423.
17. *Dicey and Morris*, Rule 118, *Galbraith v Grimshaw* [1910] AC 508; *Winkworth v Christie, Manson and Woods* [1980] Ch 496, [1980] 1 All ER 1121; *Macmillan Inc v Bishopsgate Investment Trust plc (No 3)* [1995] 1 WLR 978, [1995] 3 All ER 747.
18. *Dicey and Morris*, Rule 117.
19. *Dicey and Morris*, Rule 120; Ehrenzweig, *Treatise on the Conflict of Laws*, s 204; *Kindler v Kindler* 169 Neb 15, 98 NW 2d 88 (1959). However in *Re Patton* [1986] NI 45 a Northern Irish court made an order under s 9 in respect of a severable share in a jointly held bank account in the Isle of Man, but the question of jurisdiction was not argued.
20. Compare *Re Korvine's Trusts*, *supra*.
1. *Dicey and Morris*, Rules 134 and 139.

in the bank account form part of the 'net estate' of the deceased, but it is uncertain whether an order can be made in respect of the deceased's severable share in the jointly owned motor car.

Section 10 which deals with dispositions intended to defeat applications for family provision operates not by upsetting any person's title to property, but by requiring the person benefiting by the impugned disposition to pay money or to transfer property for the purposes of a family provision order.[2] Accordingly the court's powers under section 10 are better characterised for the purpose of the Conflict of Laws as powers to order restitution than as powers to affect the title to property. It is therefore tentatively suggested that in accordance with the Conflict of Laws rules on questions of *legitim*[3] and matrimonial property regimes[4] and with the approach tentatively adopted by English courts with similar statutory powers in bankruptcy[5] and matrimonial proceedings,[6] an English court could make an order under section 10 where the disposition took place outside England and Wales and order that property situate outside England and Wales at the time of the order be transferred, on the general basis that the powers under section 10 are ancillary to matters ordinarily within the jurisdiction of the English court. However, because of the general rule that all matters affecting directly the title to immovables are governed by the lex situs,[7] the Court has no power under section 10 to make an order where the disposition was a disposition of foreign land or to order the donee to transfer foreign land.

Problems relating to contracts to make wills where the proper law of the contract is not that of the domicile of the deceased or that of the site of the land are unlikely to arise in practice.

2. For the operation of s 10 see pp 303–310, *post*.
3. *Dicey and Morris*, Rule 102 – the essential validity (which includes *legitim*) of a will of movables is governed by the law of the domicile of the deceased.
4. *Dicey and Morris*, Rule 139 – the law governing a matrimonial property regime is the law of the marriage.
5. On the court's jurisdiction under the Insolvency Act 1986, see *Trustee of Rousou v Rousou* [1955] 1 WLR 545, [1955] 2 All ER 169, application to set aside dismissed [1955] 3 All ER 468; *Re Paramount Airways Ltd* [1993] Ch 223, [1992] 3 All ER 1; *Dicey and Morris*, p 1170.
6. In *Wyler v Lyons* [1963] P 274, 279, [1963] 1 All ER 821 at 824I Simon P refused to decide whether the powers of the court to set aside dispositions under Matrimonial Causes (Property and Maintenance) Act 1958, s 2 (now Matrimonial Causes Act 1973, s 37) were exercisable over a disposition of property abroad. In *Hamlin v Hamlin* [1986] Fam 11, [1985] 2 All ER 1037 the Court of Appeal held that an order under s 37 of the Matrimonial Causes Act 1973 could affect foreign land.
7. *Dicey and Morris*, Rule 117.

Grant of Probate or Letters of Administration

For an order to be made under the Act there must be a grant of representation to personal representatives. Although normally the Court will not make a grant when the deceased domiciled within the jurisdiction leaves no assets within the jurisdiction, the Court has power to do so if good reason to do so is shown.[8] It is submitted that the existence of foreign movables is a good reason to make a grant when an application under the Act is made.

8. Administration of Justice Act 1932, s 2(1), technically repealed by Supreme Court Act 1981; *In the Estate of Wayland* [1951] 2 All ER 1041; *Tristram and Coote's Probate Practice* (28th edn), para 12.35; *Dicey and Morris*, pp 1002–1004. Normally the personal representative's oath must contain the reason why the grant is sought, *Probate Registrar's Direction* (30 November 1932, unreported).

Chapter 4

APPLICANTS

The 1975 Act considerably enlarged the classes of persons entitled to make an application under it; such persons are described as 'applicants' in the Act. These persons are:

(a) the wife or husband of the deceased;
(b) a former wife or former husband of the deceased, who has not remarried;
(c) a child of the deceased;
(d) any person (not being a child of the deceased) who, in the case of any marriage to which the deceased was at any time a party, was treated by the deceased as a child of the family in relation to that marriage;
(e) any person (not being a person included in the foregoing classes) who immediately before the death of the deceased was being maintained, either wholly or partly, by the deceased.[1]

In respect of individuals dying after 1 January 1996, section 2 of the Law Reform (Succession) Act 1995 adds a further class of applicant, namely:

> (ba) any person (not being included in paragraph (a) or (b) above) to whom subsection (1A) applies.

Subsection (1A) provides:

> This subsection applies to a person if ... during the whole of the period of two years ending immediately before the date when the deceased died, the person was living-
> (a) in the same household as the deceased, and
> (b) as the husband or wife of the deceased.[2]

The burden of proving that the applicant comes within the statutory classes is upon the applicant.[3]

1. S 1(1).
2. Inserted by s 2(3) of the Law Reform (Succession) Act 1995.
3. Eg *Re Peete* [1952] 2 All ER 599; *Re Wilkinson* [1978] Fam 22, at 23E, [1978] 1 All ER 221, at 222j; *Williams v Roberts* [1986] 1 FLR 349, at 354C.

Spouses

Spouses as befits their places at the head of the classes of applicants are the most numerous class of applicants who apply, and provision for spouses is more generous than for other applicants.[4] The burden of proof is on the applicant to show that he was the spouse of the deceased.[5] Generally this burden will be discharged by the evidence including the marriage certificate. Prima facie a marriage certificate is evidence of the validity of the marriage of the parties mentioned therein, but that presumption may be displaced if there is some evidence which causes the Court to doubt its validity.[6] In *Re Peete* the applicant was described in the certificate of marriage to the deceased as a widow. She was unable to produce the death certificate of her previous husband and her evidence of his death was based on hearsay and uncorroborated. It was held that she had not proved that she was the widow of the testator and her application was dismissed. But an applicant may be able to set up a case that her former spouse had disappeared over a long period, in which circumstances she would be entitled to presume that he was dead at the time of the marriage.

In *Re Watkins*[7] the applicant last saw her previous husband in 1922. She remained in touch with his relatives but they never mentioned him. In 1948, being under the impression that her previous husband had died in 1942, she married the deceased and was described in the marriage certificate as a widow. It was held that although the applicant had made no enquiries to trace her previous husband, having regard to the fact that those persons most likely to hear of him had had no word of him since 1922, the applicant was entitled in 1948 to assume that he was dead, and, therefore she was free to marry the deceased whose widow she must be presumed to be.

Where the applicant has been previously married the evidence should, therefore, include the death certificate of the previous spouse or if the applicant had been divorced or granted a decree of nullity of marriage reference to the short title and record of the proceedings.[8] It may be noted that where proceedings for divorce have been instituted a spouse remains such until the decree is made absolute.[9]

4. S 1(2)(a).
5. *Re Peete*, supra; *Re Watkins* [1953] 1 WLR 1323, [1953] 2 All ER 1113.
6. *Re Peete*, supra.
7. *Re Watkins* [1953] 1 WLR 1323, [1953] 2 All ER 1113; see also *Datzoff v Miller & Datzoff* (1963) 37 DLR (2d) 110.
8. For evidence generally, see pp 353–355, *post*.
9. Eg *Re Seaford* [1968] P 53, [1968] 1 All ER 482 and see *Re Hancock* Times 21/1/70, 27/2/70.

An applicant who cannot prove that he is the spouse of the deceased may be able to be treated as a spouse being a bona fide survivor of a void marriage or be able to claim as a person being maintained by the deceased or as a cohabitee.[10]

The surviving spouse's right to claim is not lost by remarriage,[11] but it is unlikely that in such circumstances anything more than a sum to represent maintenance during the period between the death and the remarriage would be awarded.[12]

Foreign Marriages

The status of a spouse of the deceased can be acquired by a marriage outside England and Wales recognised by English courts[13] and can be lost by any divorce outside England and Wales recognised by English courts.[14]

In *Re Sehota*[15] Foster J held that 'wife' in section 1(1)(a) included not only any wife by a monogamous marriage recognised by English law but also any wife by a polygamous marriage recognised by English law. His Lordship refused to follow *Hyde v Hyde and Woodmansee*[16] which held that the divorce legislation only applied to monogamous marriages, because polygamous marriages are generally treated as valid marriages in English law,[17] the rule in *Hyde*

10. For bona fide survivors of a void marriage, see pp 67–69, *post*, for persons being maintained by the deceased, see pp 78–103, *post*, and for cohabitees, see pp 104–108, *post*.
11. See LAW COM, paras 37–43. Compare Matrimonial Causes Act 1973 s 28(3); *Jackson v Jackson* [1973] Fam 99, [1973] 2 All ER 395. Decisions in Australasia on this point are conflicting, see DICKEY, 22–23; DE GROOT AND NICKEL, paras 304-304.1. In *Re Collins* [1990] Fam 56, [1990] 2 All ER 47 Hollings J held that an adoption order made after the death of the deceased prevented a child from bringing a claim against the estate of his natural parent. It is submitted that the remarks of Hollings J that an applicant must be qualified both at the date of death and the date of application ([1990] Fam 60D-E, [1990] 2 All ER 50h) are not necessarily applicable to all classes of applicant. Under s 2(1)(a) of the Family Law Act 1996 the two stage process of decree nisi and decree absolute is abolished.
12. See further pp 128–131, *post*.
13. On the recognition of foreign marriages by English courts, see Dicey and Morris, *The Conflict of Laws* (12th edn), Rules 69–76; Cheshire and North's *Private International Law* (12th edn), 569–626.
14. On the recognition of foreign divorces by English courts, see Part II of the Family Law Act 1986; Dicey and Morris, *The Conflict of Laws* (12th edn), Rules 80–85; Cheshire and North's *Private International Law* (12th edn), 655–690.
15. [1978] 1 WLR 1506, [1978] 3 All ER 385; compare *Re Lazurus* Times 16/11/82.
16. (1866) LR 1 P & D 130.
17. See Dicey and Morris, *The Conflict of Laws* (12th edn), Rule 76.

v Hyde and Woodmansee never applied to matters of succession[18] and in matrimonial proceedings the rule in *Hyde v Hyde and Woodmansee* has been reversed by statute.[19] The effect of *Re Sehota* is reinforced by section 5 of the Private International Law (Miscellaneous Provisions) Act 1995 which provides a potentially polygamous marriage effected outside England and Wales will be recognised by an English court even though one of the parties is domiciled in England and Wales.[20]

Judicially Separated Spouses

A judicially separated spouse comes within the definition of 'wife or husband' who can apply under the Act. However, consistently with section 18(2) of the Matrimonial Causes Act 1973, which treats a decree of judicial separation as a decree of divorce for the purposes of intestacy, a judicially separated spouse (*but not a party to a marriage where a non-cohabitation order has been made by a magistrates' court*[1]) does not have the benefit of the higher standard of reasonable provision awarded to spouses.[2] A judicially separated spouse is denied the higher standard of reasonable provision only if 'at the date of death the decree was in force and the separation was continuing'.[3] 'Separation' probably has the same meaning as 'living apart' as defined for the purposes of the two and five years' separation facts evidencing irretrievable breakdown of marriage for divorce.[4]

Under the Family Law Act 1996 decrees of judicial separation are replaced by 'separation orders'.[5] A spouse whose marriage has been the subject of a separation order is treated in the same way as a judicially separated spouse for the purposes of the 1975 Act, in that such an individual is within the definition of 'wife or husband'

18. *Sinha Peerage Claim* (1939) 171 Lords Journals 350; *Bamgbose v Daniel* [1955] A C 107, [1954] 3 All ER 263; Dicey and Morris, *The Conflict of Laws* (12th edn) 705–708.
19. Matrimonial Proceedings (Polygamous Marriages) Act 1972, now Matrimonial Causes Act 1973, s 47, as amended by the Private International Law (Miscellaneous Provisions) Act 1995.
20. This Act came into force on 8 January 1996 (s 16(2)).
1. Non-cohabitation orders were made under the Matrimonial Proceedings (Matrimonial Courts) Act 1960, s 2(1)(a), but the power to do so was abolished by the Domestic Proceedings and Magistrates' Courts Act 1978.
2. S 1(2)(a).
3. S 1(2)(a), following Matrimonial Causes Act 1973, s 18(2).
4. Matrimonial Causes Act 1973, s 1(2)(d), (e), s 2(6); RAYDEN, para 13.52-3.
5. S 2(1)(b).

and such an individual is denied the higher standard of reasonable provision while the separation order is 'in force'.[6]

Bona Fide Survivors of Void Marriages

The survivor of a void, as opposed to a voidable, marriage is clearly not a spouse, cannot claim any interest on intestacy as a spouse and, but for the statutory provision referred to hereafter, make an application under the Act as a spouse. Before 1971 where a married man, representing himself as unmarried or a widower, married a woman who did not become aware that she was not legally married until after the man's death, the woman could obtain some relief by an action for breach of promise to marry and breach of warranty that the man is free to marry against the man's personal representatives. In *Shaw v Shaw*[7] in 1937 a married man married in such circumstances. His legal wife died in 1950 and he himself died in 1952 intestate. The woman sued the man's personal representatives for breach of promise and breach of warranty and was awarded damages approximately equal to the share on intestacy that she would have received had she been lawfully married to the deceased. When the Law Commission recommended that actions for breach of promise and breach of warranty that a person is free to marry should be abolished, it recognised that for the facts of *Shaw v Shaw* the actions did provide a useful remedy and it proposed that a bona fide survivor of a void marriage could apply to the court under the Inheritance (Family Provision) Act 1938.[8] This recommendation was carried into effect by section 6 of the Law Reform (Miscellaneous Provisions) Act 1970.

In its report on Family Provision the Law Commission approved of section 6 of the Law Reform (Miscellaneous Provisions) Act 1970[9] and with slight alterations section 6 was incorporated into the 1975 Act. Section 25(4) provides that any reference to a spouse includes:

6. Family Law Act 1996, Sch 8, para 27(2). A separation order remains 'in force' while the marriage continues or 'until cancelled by the court on the joint application of the parties' – s 2(3). Under the amendments to the 1975 Act there is no comparable provision covering situations where the 'separation is continuing'. This can be contrasted with s 21(b) of the Family Law Act 1996 which provides that a separation order is only treated as a decree of divorce for the purposes of intestacy if, inter alia, 'the parties to the marriage remain separated'.
7. [1954] 2 QB 429; [1954] 2 All ER 638, compare *Re Lazurus* Times, 16/11/82; *Re P*, Halsbury's Laws of England Monthly Review, para 96/369.
8. Law Commission Report No 26.
9. LAW COM, paras 25, n 27, 42–43.

... a person who in good faith entered into a void marriage with the deceased unless either–

(a) the marriage of the deceased and that person was dissolved during the lifetime of the deceased and the dissolution or annulment is recognised by the law of England and Wales, or

(b) that person *during the lifetime of the deceased*[10] entered into a later marriage.

This definition is wide and covers all survivors of a void marriage provided they entered into the marriage in good faith. It is wider than the factual situation in *Shaw v Shaw* in two ways. First a person who enters into a marriage in good faith can include a person who is not himself free to marry, who thinks that he is free to marry. For instance, the applicant in *Re Peete*[11] who married when in good faith she thought that her first husband was dead is within the definition. Similarly, a divorcing person who mistakenly thinks that a divorce is effective from the date of the decree *nisi* and who remarries before the decree is made absolute is within the definition. The only requirement is good faith and there is no further requirement of reasonableness to be shown. Secondly, the sub-section applies to all void marriages and so includes marriages void by affinity, one of the parties being under age, non-compliance with the procedural requirements or the parties being of the same sex, as well as marriages where one party is not free to marry.

These provisions which treat bona fide survivors of void marriages as spouses complement the provisions which treat parties to void and voidable marriages which have been annulled as former spouse.[12] However there is an incongruity, reflecting the separate derivation of the provisions relating to bona-fide survivors of a void marriage and former spouses, in that a party to a void marriage, who was not in good faith, is not treated as a spouse if the marriage has not been annulled, but is treated as a former spouse if the marriage has been annulled. Such a person in the absence of a decree of nullity can only make an application as a person being maintained by the deceased or as a co-habitee.This incongruity has been removed by the decision of the Court of Appeal in *Whiston v Whiston*[13] which held that a bigamist was barred by public policy from applying for ancillary relief after a decree of nullity.

10. Emphasis added.
11. [1952] 2 All ER 599, *supra.*
12. S 25 (1).
13. [1995] Fam 198; see also *J v S-T (formerly J) (transsexual: ancillary relief)* [1997] 1 FLR 402.

A bona fide survivor of a void marriage is treated as a spouse for all purposes of the Act including the higher standard of provision available to spouses.

Former Spouses

An application can be made by a person whose marriage to the deceased has been dissolved by a decree or order of divorce or annulled by a decree of nullity[14] and who has not remarried.

As originally enacted only a person whose marriage had been dissolved or annulled by a decree of an English Court could apply.[15] The Law Commission considered this problem in 1974, but exercising uncharacteristic caution decided that any reform of the definition of former spouse should await consideration of the issue whether English courts should be able to grant ancillary relief in respect of foreign divorces.[16] In *Quazi v Quazi*[17] both Viscount Dilhorne[18] and Lord Scarman[19] expressed the desire that the question of whether English courts should be able to grant ancillary relief after a foreign divorce should be considered by the Law Commission. In response the Law Commission produced a Working Paper in November 1980[20] and a Report in December 1981.[1] Both recommended that English courts should have power to grant ancillary relief after a foreign divorce subject to there being a substantial connection with England and Wales and provided for a 'filter' process before an application could be made. The Working Paper and the Report also recommended that the definition of former spouse in the 1975 Act should be extended to cover a party to a marriage whose dissolution or annulment is recognised by an English Court.[2] The Law Commission considered that the requirement under the 1975 Act that the deceased died domiciled in England and Wales[3] prevented any problems of 'forum shopping'.[4] Neither the Working Paper nor the Report discussed

14. S 1(2)(b), s 25(1), as amended by Family Law Act 1996, Sch 8, para 27(8).
15. The definition of 'former spouse' in s 25(1) as originally enacted.
16. LAW COM, para 46-50.
17. [1980] AC 744, [1979] 3 All ER 897.
18. [1980] AC 810C–D, [1979] 3 All ER 904f.
19. [1980] AC 819B–G, [1979] 3 All ER 912f-j.
20. Working Paper No 77.
1. Report No 117 'Family Law: Financial Relief after Foreign Divorce'.
2. Working Paper, para 63; Report, paras 2.18–2.19.
3. As to which, see pp 51–52, *ante*.
4. Report, para 2.18.

how a court under the 1975 Act should approach an order made by a foreign court, for instance, where the foreign divorce court limited maintenance on a 'clean break' or 'rehabilitation only' principle when an English divorce court would not have so limited maintenance.[5] The recommendations of the Law Commission were enacted by the Matrimonial and Family Proceedings Act 1984.

Former spouse under the 1975 Act is now defined as:

> 'Former wife' or 'former husband' means a person whose marriage with the deceased was during the lifetime of the deceased either-
> (a) dissolved or annulled by an order or decree of divorce or a decree of nullity of marriage granted under the law of any part of the British Islands, or
> (b) dissolved or annulled in any country or territory outside the British Islands by a divorce or annulment which is entitled to be recognized as valid by the law of England and Wales.[6]

A former spouse is not entitled to the more generous standard of provision available to spouses.

Only former spouses who have not remarried can apply. This limitation is similar to the prohibition on the granting of ancillary relief on divorce after remarriage.[7] The Law Commission considered whether this limitation should be abolished, but decided that it served a useful purpose.[8] It was argued that remarriage may be regarded as a renunciation of claims against the first spouse[9] and in effect as a 'clean break'. It was thought that it would be anomalous if remarriage barred maintenance against a person when alive, but not against his estate after death.[10]

Whether or not an applicant has remarried is determined at the date of death.[11] Where a former spouse remarries between the date of death of the deceased and the hearing it is submitted that provision should be limited to at the most maintenance from the date of death to the date of remarriage.

In order to protect a divorcing spouse where one party dies between the date of the decree absolute and the hearing of the

5. Compare *Holmes v Holmes* [1989] Fam 47, [1989] 3 All ER 786; *M v M (financial provision after foreign divorce)* [1994] 1 FLR 399.
6. S 25(1) of the 1975 Act, inserted by s 25(2) of the Matrimonial and Family Proceedings Act 1984 and amended by the Family Law Act 1996, Sch 8, para 27(8).
7. Matrimonial Causes Act 1973, s 28(3).
8. LAW COM, paras 55–58.
9. LAW COM, para 56.
10. LAW COM, para 57.
11. The Act refers to being 'survived' by an applicant, and see *Bailey v Public Trustee* [1960] NZLR 741; but see *Re Collins* [1990] Fam 56, [1990] 2 All ER 47 and fn 11, p 65, *ante*.

application for ancillary relief, special provisions have been enacted in section 14. This originally provided that where a party to a marriage dies within twelve months of the decree absolute or the granting of an order of judicial separation and either no application for ancillary relief under section 23 and section 24 of the Matrimonial Causes Act 1973 has been made by the other party or such an application has been made but 'the proceedings thereon have not been determined' at the date of death of the deceased the court has power to treat the former spouse as a spouse and so be entitled to the higher standard of provision available to spouses. As a result of the Family Law Act 1996 the wording was altered to refer to death within twelve months of divorce order or separation order having been made under the Family Law Act 1996 in relation to a marriage or a decree of nullity having been made absolute and the reference to an application for ancillary relief was extended to include sections 22A or 23 and section 23A or 24.[12] It is important to note that section 14 only gives the court a *discretionary* power to act '*if it thinks it just to do so*', and does not lay down an automatic rule.[13] For instance, it would not be just to so order when proceedings had not been brought because there was little chance of success or where there was an agreement as to maintenance and property or where the applicant unreasonably delayed the commencement of proceedings.[14] Section 14 applies to orders of judicial separation while such orders are in force and the separation is continuing.[15]

In *Whiston v Whiston*[16] the Court of Appeal held that a person who went through a ceremony of marriage knowing that she was already married could not apply for ancillary relief after a decree of nullity as public policy prevented her from making such a claim. This decision would appear to be applicable to claims under the 1975 Act.[17] It is unclear whether the decision is applicable to a case where both parties know of the inability of one party to enter into the marriage.

12. As amended by Family Law Act 1996, Sch 8, para 27(4).
13. For a case in which an order was made under s 14, see *Eeles v Evans* Court of Appeal, 6 July 1989.
14. Example given by Professor Miller in the commentary to *Current Law Statutes*.
15. S 14(2).
16. [1995] Fam 198. Leave to appeal was refused by the House of Lords – [1995] Fam 208E-F. See further *J v S-T (formerly J) (transsexual: ancillary relief)* [1997] 1 FLR 402, a nullity case of a woman who went through a ceremony of marriage as a man and where there were allegations of approbation by the wife.
17. It is significant that Ward LJ (at [1995] Fam 206D-207B) relied strongly on the family provision case of *Re Royse* [1985] Ch 22, [1984] 3 All ER 339. Interesting issues arise if a bigamous judicially separated spouse can qualify within classes (ba) or (f), but for the express exclusion from these sub-sections of persons coming within other classes.

Children of the Deceased

Under the 1938 Act the only children of the deceased who could apply were:

(i) 'a daughter who has not been married, or who is, by reason of some mental or physical disability, incapable of maintaining herself';
(ii) 'a son who has not attained the age of twenty-one years';[18]
(iii) 'a son who is, by reason of some mental or physical disability, incapable of maintaining himself'.[19]

This definition restricted the categories of adult children who could apply to categories of adult children who would be likely to be actually dependent upon the deceased or particularly deserving. The Law Commission discussed whether the classes of dependants should be extended to include all children.[20] Several cases could be imagined of actual dependence by adult children or other particularly deserving applicants which did not fall within the categories set out in the 1938 Act. For instance the 1938 Act did not cover the case of a married daughter or a son who made considerable sacrifices to care for a parent or a married daughter with infant children who was widowed or divorced and penniless. On the other hand it may be noticed that a parent's duty to maintain his children under the social security legislation ceases at either age 16 or 19,[1] parental contributions for students' grants (which are not legally enforceable) cease to be relevant at the age of 25,[2] liability under the Child Support Act 1991 can not extend beyond age 18,[3] and in divorce proceedings maintenance for a child normally ceases at age 18 or the later completion of a course of full-time education.[4] The Law Commission also paid considerable attention to the absence of any age limit in Irish and Australasian statutes,[5] but it

18. The wording, but not the meaning, of this subsection was altered by the Family Law Reform Act 1969, s 5(1).
19. Inheritance (Family Provision) Act 1938, s l.
20. LAW COM, paras 71–79.
1. S 78(6)(a),(b),(d), s 105(3) of the Social Security Administration Act 1992.
2. Education (Mandatory Awards) Regulations 1994, SI 1994/3044.
3. See the definition of 'child' in s 55.
4. Matrimonial Causes Act 1973, s 29(1), (3) as amended .This provision must be contrasted with the Children Act 1989, Sch I, para 2(1)(a), (b) which allow orders to be made in favour of children over the age of 18 years who are undergoing education or full time training or where there are 'special circumstances'. On this provision, see *T v S (financial provision for children)* [1994] 2 FLR 883; *C v C (financial provision: personal damages)* [1995] 2 FLR 171.
5. LAW COM, para 73.

does not appear that the Law Commission considered how in practice adult children were treated in such jurisdictions. While the Law Commission regarded the categories under the 1938 Act as too restrictive, they did not support any idea of *legitim* and were clearly anxious to restrict claims by adult children to a relatively few deserving cases. Restricting claims by adult children to situations where the child was actually dependent upon the deceased at the date of his death was considered by the Law Commission.[6] This test was rejected by the Law Commission however, as it would not cover cases where a deceased wrongfully refused to maintain an applicant before the death of the deceased (but query whether in the absence of a legal duty to support such failure to support can be *wrongful*) and where the applicant became incapable of supporting himself after the death of the deceased.[7] More importantly experience with a test of actual dependence with applicants under section 1(1)(e) has not been happy and a test of actual dependence would not necessarily cover a child who sacrificed a great deal to care for a parent since such a child is not necessarily dependent upon the parent. The Law Commission eventually recommended that any adult child should be able to apply, but contemplated that only particularly deserving adult children in situations broadly analogous to the categories under the 1938 Act would actually be awarded provision. However, the Law Commission both in its report and its draft Bill, other than by the use of the expression 'reasonable provision', gave no indication as to the exact cases in which provision would be ordered. The Parliamentary debates did not reveal any coherent approach on this matter.

Although adult children have proved to be the most controversial class of applicant under the 1975 Act,[8] the Law Commission when it considered family provision as part of its review of the law of intestacy gave the position of adult children only the most cursory consideration and did not recommend any restriction in the classes of applicant entitled to apply.[9]

Under the 1975 Act any 'child' of the deceased may be an applicant.[10]

The burden of proof of parenthood is upon the applicant,[11] but an applicant may be able to rely upon the presumption of legitimacy if his alleged parents were married at the time of his birth. A child

6. LAW COM, para 75.
7. Compare *Millward v Shenton* [1972] 1 WLR 711, [1972] 2 All ER 1025.
8. See Chapter 6, Part 3.
9. Law Commission Working Paper No 108, para 5.13 (1988); Report, Family Law:The Effect of Divorce on Wills (Law Com 217), paras 58–61 (1989).
10. S 1(1)(c).
11. Eg *Re Peete* [1952] 2 All ER 599.

who fails to prove that he is a child of the deceased may be able to apply as a 'child of the family' or as a person actually maintained by the deceased.

Until 1970 'child' only referred to a legitimate child. As one aspect of the partial assimilation of the rights of illegitimate and legitimate children contained in the Family Law Reform Act 1969 the definition of child in the 1938 Act was extended to cover an illegitimate child.[12] The 1975 Act specifically defines a child as including an illegitimate child.[13] This definition represents a change of emphasis in the legislation; whereas originally the 1938 Act was partly promoted to prefer legitimate issue to illegitimate issue, the effect of the modern legislation is often to enable illegitimate children to obtain provision, often at the expense of legitimate issue.

'Child' includes an adopted child,[14] that is a child adopted in England and Wales and in any foreign country where the adoption is recognised in England and Wales.[15] An adopted child can not make a claim against the estate of his natural parent and a child adopted after the death of his natural parent can not make a claim against the estate of his natural parent.[16]

'Child' includes a child *en ventre sa mère*.[17]

Child of the Family

In line with the matrimonial jurisdiction of the courts the 1975 Act enables a child treated by the deceased as a child of the deceased's family to apply to the court.

Section 1(1)(d) provides that an application may be made by 'any person (not being a child of the deceased) who, in the case of any marriage to which the deceased was at any time a party, was

12. Family Law Reform Act 1969, s 18.
13. S 25(1); see also s 1(1) of the Family Law Reform Act 1987. For children born as a result of artificial insemination, see s 27 of the Family Law Reform Act 1987; Human Fertilisation and Embryology Act 1990; *Re B (parentage)* [1996] 2 FLR 15; *Re M (Child Support Act: parentage)* [1997] 2 FLR 90; *V v W (A-G intervening)* [1997] 3 WLR 739.
14. Adoption Act 1976, s 36(1), (5)(a).
15. Adoption Act 1976, s 38(c), (d), (e). For the recognition of foreign adoptions, see Dicey and Morris, *The Conflict of Laws* (12th edn), Rule 106.
16. *Collins v Collins* [1990] Fam 56, [1990] 2 All ER 47.This case is to be contrasted with *Watson v Willmott* [1991] 1 QB 140, [1991] 1 All ER 473 where an adoption order did not deprive the adopted child of his right to claim as a child of his natural parent under the Fatal Accidents Acts.
17. S 25(1). For an example of an application by a posthumous child, see *Re Trott* [1958] 1 WLR 604, [1958] 2 All ER 296.

treated by the deceased as a child of the family in relation to that marriage'.[18]

This definition of 'child of the family' is taken with one alteration from the definition in the divorce legislation.[19] It must be noted that the provision only applies to cases of marriage and thus a child of a mistress by another man cannot be regarded as a child of the family of the mistress's deceased lover. Significantly, this is unaltered by the Law Reform (Succession) Act 1995 which introduced the new class (ba). However the Act refers to *any* marriage and not merely one subsisting at the deceased's death. There is no upper age limit on when a child is treated as a child of the family and in two reported cases the courts have held that persons came within the statutory definition where the marriage of the deceased took place when the applicants were adults.[20] The courts have specifically rejected arguments that the conduct of the deceased in treating the applicant as a child of the family must be as a 'dependent' or 'unfledged' child.[1] Unlike the definition in the Matrimonial Causes Act 1973 it is not necessary to show that the child was treated as a child of the family by *both* parties to the marriage, but only by the deceased. The treatment must be 'in relation to the marriage' and need not be during the subsistence of the marriage, thus conduct after the death of one party to the marriage can be taken into account.[2] Strictly, the applicant need not be a child of either party to the marriage to be treated as a child of the family. It is extremely doubtful whether either the Law Commission or Parliament foresaw that the definition

18. For examples of applications by children of the family, see *Barnsley v Ward* (18 January 1980, unreported), CA; *Adams v Adams* (22 July 1982, unreported), CA; *Re Callaghan* [1985] Fam 1, [1984] 3 All ER 790; *Re Leach* [1986] Ch 226, [1985] 2 All ER 754. For the compromise of a claim by children of the family, see *Re W (a minor) (claim from deceased's estate)* [1995] 2 FCR 689, at 693E-the report at [1995] 2 FLR 24 *sub nom Re C (leave to apply for provision)* does not deal with this aspect of the case.
19. Matrimonial Causes Act 1973, s 52(1), consolidating Matrimonial Proceedings and Property Act 1970, s 27(1), replacing earlier legislation worded slightly differently.
20. *Re Callaghan* [1985] Fam 1, [1984] 3 All ER 790; *Re Leach* [1986] Ch 226, [1985] 2 All ER 754, affirming [1984] FLR 590.
1. *Re Callaghan* at [1985] Fam 5E-6E, [1984] 3 All ER 793f-794c; *Re Leach* at [1984] FLR 597F-599H, [1986] Ch 235F-237E, [1985] 2 All ER 760j-762c. See further the remarks of Megarry V-C in *Re Beaumont* [1980] Ch 444, at 454D–455B, [1980] 1 All ER 266, at 273e–274a contrasting s 3(3) which merely requires the court to 'have regard whether' the deceased had assumed a responsibility for the applicant's maintenance with s 3(4) which requires the court to have regard to 'the extent to which and the basis upon which the deceased had assumed a responsibility for the applicant's maintenance'.
2. *Re Leach* at [1986] Ch 233H-235A, [1985] 2 All ER 759g-760e.

under the 1975 Act was very considerably wider than the definition under the matrimonial legislation.

The case law on the definition of child of the family in the Matrimonial Causes Act 1973 reveals the following propositions. In order to prove that a child is a child of the family, it must be proved that there was some sort of a family to which the child could belong.[3] Thus if the parties to the marriage at all material times lived separate lives, there cannot be a 'family'.[4] The question of whether the deceased treated the child as a child of the family is to be answered as an ordinary citizen would answer it.[5] To treat a child as a child of the family requires something more than a representation to the outside world that the child is the deceased's. Representations to the Inland Revenue or occasional acts of affection given in the manner of an uncle rather than a father are not, by themselves, sufficient for the child to be treated as a child of the family.[6] With adult children the mere display of affection, kindness or hospitality by a step-parent to a step-child is clearly insufficient.[7] To satisfy the definition it is conduct towards the child, rather than conduct towards the other spouse or third parties, that is required.[8]

One cannot treat a child as a child of the family until he is born.[9] The deceased's knowledge of the true paternity of the child is not relevant in deciding whether the deceased treated him as a child of the family.[10] A child can be the child of two or more families and it is no absolute impediment that a child has a natural parent living who takes an interest in the child,[11] but the existence of a natural parent and the attitude of the deceased towards a natural parent may be evidence that the child was not in fact treated as a child of the family of the deceased.

In deciding whether to award reasonable provision to a child of the family the court is specifically required to consider whether in fact the deceased had assumed any responsibility for the child's maintenance, and if so, the extent to which and the basis upon which the deceased assumed that responsibility, the length of time for

3. *M v M (child of the family)* (1981) 2 FLR 39.
4. *M v M (child of the family)*, *supra*.
5. *M v M (child of the family)*, *supra*.
6. *M v M (child of the family)*, *supra*; *D v D (child of the family)* (1980) 2 FLR 93.
7. *Re Leach* [1986] Ch 226, at 235D-E, [1985] 2 All ER 760g-h.
8. *A v A (family: unborn child)* [1974] Fam 6, at 15D, [1974] 1 All ER 755, at 763b-c .
9. *A v A (family: unborn child)* [1974] Fam 6, [1974] 1 All ER 755.
10. *W (R J) v W (S J)* [1972] Fam 152, [1971] 3 All ER 303.
11. *Newman v Newman* [1971] P 43, [1970] 3 All ER 529.

which the deceased discharged the responsibility,[12] the knowledge of the deceased that the child was not his own child when he assumed and discharged the responsibility to maintain[13] and the liability of any other person to maintain the child.[14]

It is thought that where the deceased treated the child as a child of the family because of some misapprehension as to the child's paternity or where the deceased's actions were only barely sufficient to support a finding that he treated the child as a child of the family, maintenance will not be awarded out of the estate. This follows from the express provisions of section 3(3)(a) and from general principles.[15] It should be noted that the definition of 'child of the family' in the 1975 Act is taken from the Matrimonial Causes Act 1973 where the purpose of the concept 'child of the family' is as much to enable the spouse who is not the parent to claim access to and custody of the child and to define the limits of the court's duty to approve arrangements for the upbringing of the children[16] as to enable maintenance to be obtained from a spouse who is not the parent of the child.

Res Judicata

Whether or not an applicant comes within any of the classes (a), (b), (c), (d) of applicants may be conclusively determined by the operation of the doctrine of *res judicata*.[17] A final judgment (and probably not a default judgment) by a court of competent jurisdiction obtained without fraud and collusion concerning the status of an applicant in litigation between the applicant and the deceased is binding upon the deceased's personal representatives and persons interested in his estate as the deceased's privies.[18]

12. S3(3)(a), taken from Matrimonial Causes Act 1973, s 25(3)(a). On the operation of s 25(3), see *W v W* unreported Court of Appeal cases [1982] CLY 912. However, it is not a *sine qua non* for making an award under the 1975 Act that the deceased should have assumed any responsibility for the maintenance of the child of the family, see *Re Callaghan* [1985] Fam 1, at 6C-D, [1984] 3 All ER 790, at 794b-c.
13. S 3(3)(b) taken from Matrimonial Causes Act 1973, s 25(3)(b). On the operation of s 25(3), see *W v W* unreported Court of Appeal cases [1982] CLY.
14. S 3(3)(c), taken from Matrimonial Causes Act 1973, s 25(3)(c). On the operation of s 25(3), see *W v W* unreported Court of Appeal cases [1982] CLY.
15. Compare *W v W (Child of the Family)* [1984] FLR 796; *Teeling v Teeling* [1984] FLR 808.
16. Matrimonial Causes Act 1973, s 41, as substantially amended.
17. See generally Spencer Bower and Turner, *Res Judicata* (2nd edn); *Halsbury's Laws of England* (4th edn: Reissue) Vol 16, paras 974–996.

However, it is clear that *res judicata* will not prevent evidence being given that a marriage is in fact void,[19] although usually an applicant in this situation will be able to claim as a bona fide survivor of a void marriage.

Declarations as to the legitimacy of a child[20] to which the child is normally a party will bind the deceased's personal representatives and persons interested in his estate. Likewise findings that a child is a child of the family in matrimonial proceedings will bind the deceased's estate, but only if *the child is a party* to such decision. A finding adverse to the child in affiliation and matrimonial proceedings to which the child is not a party creates no *res judicata*,[1] but a finding in favour of the child may create an issue estoppel against the estate.[2]

Other Persons Being Maintained by the Deceased[3]

The 1975 Act extended the classes of applicants for family provision by allowing persons who were actually maintained by the deceased prior to his death whatever their relationship with the deceased. This extension was probably the most controversial change in the law introduced by the 1975 Act and section 1(1)(e) which effected the extension was the most hotly discussed in the House of Commons.

18. Eg *Ampthill Peerage Case* [1977] AC 547. For the definition of 'privies' see *Halsbury's Laws of England* (4th edn: Reissue) Vol 16, paras 990–992.
19. *Hayward v Hayward* [1961] P 152, [1961] 1 All ER 236 where earlier conflicting authorities were considered. *Hayward v Hayward* was approved by the Court of Appeal in *Rowe v Rowe* [1980] Fam 47, at 58C, [1979] 2 All ER 1123, at 1126b. In *Hayward v Hayward* Phillimore J specifically refused to rest his judgment on the Divorce Court's statutory inquisitorial duty, see at [1961] P 159–160, [1961] 1 All ER 243C–D.
20. On declarations generally see Family Law Act 1996, s 55-60 as amended. On declarations as to paternity generally, see *Aldrich v A-G* [1968] P 281, [1968] 1 All ER 345.
1. *Rowe v Rowe* [1980] Fam 47, at 53G, 58E, [1979] 2 All ER 1123, at 1127d,1131d-e.
2. *Rowe v Rowe* [1980] Fam 47, at 58E, [1979] 2 All ER 1123, at 1131d-e. On issue estoppel generally, see *Halsbury's Laws of England* (4th edn: Reissue) Vol 16, para 977.
3. On s 1(1)(e) generally, see Miller, 'Provision for Dependants and Agreements for Testamentary Provision' (1980) 128 NLJ 449; Cadwallader, 'A Mistress's Charter?' [1980] Conv 46; Naresh, 'Dependants' Applications under the Inheritance (Provision for Family and Dependants) Act 1975' (1980) 96 LQR 534; Hand, 'Family Provision: Are the Right People Receiving It?' (1980) 10 Fam Law 140.

The interpretation of section 1(1)(e) has given rise to considerable judicial and academic disagreement. Section 1(1)(e) is widely regarded as an unsatisfactory piece of legislation, creating a class which is over-inclusive in that it permits *any* person actually receiving a net benefit from the deceased to apply and under-inclusive in that it excludes persons who cared for the deceased without reward and persons who contributed indirectly to the deceased's estate but not so as to create any interest by way of a resulting trust, such as mistresses and lovers.[4] The preference of the Act for 'spongers' as against those who contributed to the welfare of the deceased without reward[5] is widely regarded as morally unsatisfactory. The present design of section 1(1)(e) is due to the Law Commission failing to apply the same degree of thought that it applied to technical questions of the orders which a court could make and the definition of the deceased's net estate to the more fundamental questions of the basis of family provision legislation and its functions in society. The survival of the Law Commission's draft section 1(1)(e) into the enacted statute is due to excessive subservience paid by the Bill's promoters in Parliament to the Law Commission.

The defects of section 1(1)(e) were belatedly recognised by the Law Commission when in 1988 it published a Working Paper on the reform of the law of intestacy[6] and in 1989 a full Report on the law of intestacy[7] which led to the enactment of the Law Reform (Succession) Act 1995 creating a new section 1(1)(ba).[8] What is remarkable, and so regretted, is that neither the Law Commission nor Parliament gave any consideration to the abolition of section 1(1)(e) in its present form or its substantial recasting.[9]

The Law Commission's Report

In its Working Paper the Law Commission discussed the question of applications by persons other than a spouse and a child in 38

4. For example, see the difficult remarks of Butler-Sloss LJ in *Bishop v Plumley* [1991] 1 WLR 582 at 587H-588A, [1991] 1 All ER 236 at 242e-f, set out at p 90, *post*. See also the remarkable dictum of Lord Denning MR in *Stott v Ratcliffe* (1982) 126 Sol Jo 310, CA that *Jelley v Iliffe* was wrongly decided. Donaldson LJ specifically reserved his position on this matter.
5. See pp 100–103, *post*.
6. Working Paper No 108.
7. Report, No 187.
8. See pp 104–106, *post*.
9. For example the Law Commission gave no consideration to the classes of applicant proposed by Mr Awdry when the 1975 Act was being considered in committee, as to which see pp 81–82, *post*.

lines.[10] The Working Paper tentatively suggested that the classes of applicants could in appropriate cases be extended and referred to suggestions put forward by the Ontario Law Reform Commission in 1968[11] and by a Working Paper of the Law Reform Committee of Western Australia also in 1968,[12] which allowed any person actually dependent upon the deceased to apply. The Ontario Law Reform Commission emphasised that its aim in extending the class of applicants was to protect persons whose support was suddenly removed from them by the death of the deceased.[13] This approach based on actual dependence rather than any particular relationship with the deceased was tentatively approved by the Law Commission in its Working Paper.[14]

The consensus of the comments on the Working Paper received by the Law Commission favoured an extension of the class of applicants by permitting all persons actually dependent upon the deceased at his death to apply,[15] and this scheme was recommended by the Law Commission's Report.[16]

It is noteworthy that neither the Law Commission's Working Paper nor its Report considered in any depth any alternative criterion for extending the class of applicants. The Law Commission failed to note that the eventual legislation adopted in both Ontario and Western Australia only permitted applications by persons who satisfied a cumulative test of a particular relationship and actual dependence upon the deceased in some cases for a minimum period.[17]

10. WORKING PAPER, para 3.47.
11. Ontario Law Reform Commission, Family Law Project, Vol III 478 and 536–537.
12. Law Reform Committee of Western Australia, Working Paper 'Testators' Family Maintenance'.
13. *Op cit*, 536–537. The excerpt quoted in the WORKING PAPER does not fully convey the reasoning of the Law Reform Commission. Compare *Jelley v Iliffe* [1981] Fam 128, [1981] 2 All ER 29.
14. WORKING PAPER, para 3.47.
15. LAW COM, para 88.
16. LAW COM, paras 89–95.
17. Proposals for extending the class of applicants were considered at the 55th and 56th (1973 and 1974) Conference of Commissioners on Uniformity of Legislation in Canada.

    The draft Uniform Act adopted permits applications by, inter alia:

    (iv) a grandparent, parent or descendant of the deceased who, for a period of at least three years immediately prior to the date of death of the deceased, was dependent upon him for maintenance and support;

    (vi) a person of the opposite sex to the deceased not legally married to the deceased who, for a period of at least three years immediately prior to the date of death of the deceased, lived and cohabited with the deceased as the spouse of the deceased and was dependent upon the deceased for maintenance and support.

The idea that the dependence should have existed for a minimum period was specifically rejected by the Law Commission.[18] The Law Commission's Report clearly shows that whilst it contemplated that some mistresses may fall within the new class (e), the class was not specifically designed for such people.[19]

Class (e) in Parliament

The debates upon section 1(1)(e) in the House of Commons are instructive in that they show that the disadvantages in section 1(1)(e) in its over- and under-inclusive nature were appreciated far more by MPs than by the Law Commission and certain academic commentators. During the Second Reading Debate two speakers commented on clause 1(1)(e) – Mr Awdry welcomed the extension of the classes of potential applicants represented by class (e),[20] and Mr Fletcher-Cooke QC, a rare modern opponent of family provision legislation, thought that it was wrong that clause 1(1)(e) should have no requirement that the applicant have a common residence with the deceased or that the applicant had been openly acknowledged by the deceased as dependent upon him, and observed that clause 1(1)(e) gave people who had 'no obvious connection with the family a power of blackmail'.[1]

During the Committee Stage of the Bill three amendments were proposed adding classes of applicants.[2] The proposed additional classes were,

> (f) any person ... who immediately before the death of the deceased had been living with the deceased and treated by the deceased as a

In Ontario this was enacted as the Succession Reform Act 1977. The Western Australian proposals were reconsidered by a Report of the Law Reform Committee of Western Australia, 'The Protection to be Given to the Family and Dependants of a Deceased Person', (1970). Eventually enacted in Western Australia was the Inheritance (Family and Dependants Provision) Act 1972 which permitted applications by, inter alia:

s 7(d) a grandchild of the deceased who at the time of the death of the deceased was being wholly or partly maintained by the deceased ...

(e) a *de facto* widow of the deceased who at the time of the death of the deceased was being wholly or partly maintained by the deceased, who was ordinarily a member of the household of the deceased, and for whom the deceased, in the opinion of the court had some special moral responsibility to make provision (emphasis supplied; widow includes widower).

18. LAW COM, para 93.
19. LAW COM, para 92.
20. HC Parl Deb, cols 1689–1690 (16 July 1975).
1. HC Parl Deb, cols 1691–1692.

member of the family for an uninterrupted period of not less than 5 years (Mr Awdry)

alternative (f) any person ... who for a period of 5 years before the death of the deceased was maintaining, either wholly or partly, the deceased or lived with and nursed or otherwise cared for the deceased other than as an employee of the deceased ... (Mr Awdry)

(g) any person (... not being a tenant or licensee for value of the deceased) who shared with the deceased for a period of 5 years before the death of the deceased the occupation of a dwelling-house of which the deceased at his ... death owned either the freehold or lease having at least 21 years to run and who contributed substantially with the deceased to the upkeep and maintenance of the dwelling-house. (Mr Penhaligan)

The proposed alternative classes (f), although not free from difficulties of interpretation, were certainly worthy of serious consideration. Persons who satisfied alternative (f) were far more likely to have a moral claim upon the deceased than a person who merely came within class (e) because at the moment of death he received the deceased's largesse.[3] The proposed classes (f) would permit applications by mistresses and persons who cared for aged relations – the five-year time limit would only allow really meritorious claims and would avoid applications arising out of transient relationships. The proposed class (g) is misconceived, since mere physical proximity should not be the basis of an obligation to provide for another on death.

Despite considerable support from MPs the amendments were not pressed by their movers because of opposition from the Solicitor-General, who was in charge of the Bill from the Government side. The Solicitor-General gave as his reasons for opposition that the amendments extended the Bill beyond the scope of its long title,[4] that the matter should be further considered by the Law Commission before such a change was made,[5] and that the proposed amendments further restricted freedom of testation.[6] The Solicitor-General regarded it as unhealthy for persons to help others expecting some reward,[7] but he by his support for class (e) apparently thought that it was acceptable for a recipient of charity to demand and be given further gifts. Equally dubiously the Solicitor-General stated that to extend the classes of applicants to

2. (1974–75) 4 HC Standing Committees, col 3 (29 July 1975).
3. (1974–75) 4 HC Standing Committees, col 5 (Mr D Awdry).
4. (1974–75) 4 HC Standing Committees, col 8.
5. (1974–75) 4 HC Standing Committees, cols 9–10, 13.
6. (1974–75) 4 HC Standing Committees, col 9.
7. (1974–75) 4 HC Standing Committees, cols 8, 15–16 (Mr S Newens).

people who were not in some way dependent upon the deceased would be radically to alter the family provision legislation.[8] It is a great pity that the Solicitor-General threw the Government's weight against the proposed amendments. The result of the Solicitor-General's actions was bad legislation by inadequately considered recommendations of the Law Commission as opposed to far better proposals which had been far more adequately considered by the elected representatives of the people. Few people would now willingly choose class (e) if they had the choice of either or both Mr Awdry MP's classes (f).

Of considerable interest was an example of a person whom Mr Awdry thought would not come within clause 1(1)(e), but would come within either of his proposed additional classes of applicant. He referred to a niece who had lived with an elderly aunt in the aunt's house, perhaps looking after the aunt or paying the majority of the household bills.[9] The Solicitor-General stated that such a lady might well on the facts of any particular case come within clause 1(1)(e).[10] Some of his remarks on this potential applicant are of some interest:

> It is a little difficult to try to pre-empt what the courts will make of the expression 'For full valuable consideration'.
>
> I doubt whether they will assume there was a calculated bargain between the parties and that every time the niece washed up, took the aunt out for the evening, or even made a contribution to the food bill, her actions should be set against the benefit of her having a roof over her head. I would hope that there would be a liberal interpretation of these matters. I think it will be necessary to consider the facts of each case. A number of situations that have been put forward could arguably – I think, fairly strongly arguably – be brought within paragraph (e). However, there might be some situations of a similar kind which fell outside the paragraph. [11]
>
> The court would probably look at the value of living rent free and any other perquisites which accrued in the course of it to the claimant. If these exceeded the contribution made by the deceased, there might be a fairly strong argument for saying that it fell within paragraph (e). If they were substantially less than any contribution

8. (1974–75) 4 HC Standing Committees, col 9.
9. (1974–75) 4 HC Standing Committees, cols 4–5.
10. (1974–75) 4 HC Standing Committees, cols 10, 11, 12.
11. (1974–75) 4 HC Standing Committees, col 12. Note however the Solicitor-General specifically stated that two 'Liver Birds' sharing a flat for reasons of mutual convenience should not be able to claim against the estate of the other (col 13). Further note that Mr Ivan Lawrence took a different view of the construction of s 1(3) (cols 16–17).

> made by the claimant to the deceased, it might be more difficult to argue that they fell within that paragraph.[12]

During the Report Stage and Third Reading of the Bill in the House of Commons there were criticisms from the Conservative benches of the design of clause 1(1)(e) and the possibility of applications by survivors of relationships outside marriage.[13]

After the Bill had been passed the Attorney-General announced in a written answer that the Law Commission had no plans to follow up the suggestions for extending the classes of applicants made during the Committee Stage[14] and legislative change had to wait 20 years until the Law Reform (Succession) Act 1995.

Section 1(1)(e)

Section 1(1)(e) permits an application by:

> ... any person[15] (not being a person included in the foregoing paragraphs of this subsection) who immediately before the death of the deceased was being maintained, either wholly or partly, by the deceased.

This is further explained by section 1(3):

> For the purposes of subsection (1)(e), a person shall be treated as being maintained by the deceased, either wholly or partly, as the case may be, if the deceased, otherwise than for full valuable consideration, was making a substantial contribution in money or money's worth towards the reasonable needs of that person.

All the case law and all but one of the commentators[16] have proceeded on the basis that section 1(3) narrows or qualifies or explains section 1(1)(e). The inter-relationship of section 1(3) and section 1(1)(e) was fully discussed by Megarry V-C in *Re*

12. (1974–75) 4 HC Standing Committees, col 17.
13. 898 HC Parl Deb, cols 171–174 (Mr I Stanbrook), cols 186–190 (Mr I Lawrence) (29 October 1975).
14. 901 HC Parl Deb, col 336 (28 November 1975).
15. 'Person' despite the Interpretation Act 1978, Sch I must be limited to human persons; compare *Re Dodwell & Co Ltd's Trust* [1979] Ch 301, [1978] 3 All ER 738.
16. The exception is Naresh, 'Dependants' Applications under the Inheritance (Provision for Family and Dependants) Act 1975' (1980) 96 LQR 534, 537–539.

Beaumont,[17] whose approach on this matter was approved by the Court of Appeal in *Jelley v Iliffe*.[18] Although section 1(3) begins with the words, 'For the purposes of subsection (1)(e) a person *shall be treated* ...' which suggests that section 1(3) was designed to extend the meaning of section 1(1)(e) – in effect a 'deeming' provision, since section 1(3) is narrower in scope than section 1(1)(e) it is clear that section 1(3) is designed to narrow and explain section 1(1)(e). In effect section 1(3) should be read as if it stated, 'For the purposes of subsection 1(1)(e) a person *shall not be treated as* ... *unless* the deceased ...'[19]

To come within the subsection the deceased must have been making a 'substantial contribution in money or money's worth towards the reasonable needs of the applicant'. There is little authority on the meaning of 'substantial'.[20] In *Re Viner*[1] the payment of a weekly sum of £5 in 1975 to an old age pensioner who appears to have had only her old age pension to live on was regarded as 'substantial'. In *Re Dymott*[2] Purchas J held that the payment of £10

17. [1980] Ch 444, 450D–451D, [1980] 1 All ER 266, 270e–271c. The Naresh article, *supra*, is an excellent, but critical, commentary on *Re Beaumont*. In the Law Commission's Explanatory Notes to their Draft Bill, s 1(3) is described as 'further explaining the meaning of "maintained" ' (LAW COM, p 85). The interchange between the Solicitor-General and Mr Ivan Lawrence MP during the Committee Stage of the 1975 Act suggests that s 1(3) was regarded as qualifying s1(1)(e) ((1974–75) 4 HC Standing Committees, cols 11, 12, 16–17). Coldham, Note, (1982) 45 MLR 100, 101 states that while the interpretation adopted by *Re Beaumont* and *Jelley v Iliffe* 'indicates a rather robust approach to statutory interpretation, it clearly implements the intentions of the Law Commission'.
18. [1981] Fam 128, 136D, [1981] 2 All ER 29, 34h-j (per Stephenson LJ), [1981] Fam 141B, [1981] 2 All ER 38d-e (per Griffiths LJ); see to the same effect *Bishop v Plumley* [1991] 1 WLR 582, 586F, [1991] 1 All ER 236, 241c.
19. Per Megarry V-C at [1980] Ch. 451B–C, [1980] 1 All ER 271a.
20. In *Jelley v Iliffe* [1981] Fam 128, 141D–E, [1981] 2 All ER 38f-h Stephenson LJ stated: 'Only if the balance comes down heavily in favour of the applicant will it be shown that the deceased was "making a substantial contribution in money or money's worth towards the reasonable needs" of the applicant.' It is submitted that this approach is erroneous; the deceased has to be making a substantial contribution to the maintenance first of all and only after the applicant has passed that test are the parties' relative contributions balanced; see *infra*.The difficulties of this statement are exposed in the judgment of Butler-Sloss LJ in *Bishop v Plumley* – compare [1991] 1 WLR 586G-H, [1991] 1 All ER 241d with [1991] 1 WLR 587 B, [1991] 1 All ER 241b. See further *Re Kirby* (1981) 11 Fam Law 210 and *Williams v Roberts* [1986] 1 FLR 349, 354C–D.
1. [1978] CLY 3091. In *Re Green* Daily Mirror, 25/11/81, Daily Telegraph, 25/11/81 a mistress who was given between £25 and £50 per week by her deceased lover was held to have been receiving substantial maintenance.
2. Court of Appeal, 15 December 1980; the report in the Daily Mirror, 26/7/80 does not deal with this aspect of the case.

per week in 1978 to a person in quite modest circumstances was 'substantial' and this was not challenged on appeal.

Section 1(3) is worded so as to require the deceased's contribution to the applicant's maintenance to be *substantial*, but if the deceased did make a substantial contribution and the applicant gave consideration for such contribution, an applicant is only debarred from applying if the consideration is '*full* consideration'; accordingly an applicant does not have to prove a substantial difference between the value of the contribution made by the deceased and the value of the consideration in return. This is a possible explanation of the decision in *Re Wilkinson*.[3] The reference to the 'reasonable needs' of the applicant must imply that the contributions from the deceased should not be solely mere luxuries unrelated to the ordinary standard of living of the applicant. For instance the provision of expensive jewellery and many holidays abroad by a man to his mistress could not be regarded as a contribution to the reasonable needs of the mistress.[4]

The phrase 'otherwise than for full valuable consideration' in section 1(3) is not limited to consideration provided under a contract. This has been held by Arnold J in *Re Wilkinson*,[5] Megarry V-C in *Re Beaumont*,[6] and by the Court of Appeal in *Jelley v Iliffe*.[7] In the case of *CA v CC*[8] either it was not argued that 'valuable

3. [1978] Fam 22, [1978] 1 All ER 221.
4. In *Harrington v Gill* (1983) 4 FLR 265, at 271A-B Dunn LJ equated 'reasonable needs' in s 1(3) with 'needs' in s 3(1)(c) and s 25(2)(b) of the Matrimonial Causes Act 1973. This has been intrepreted to mean 'reasonable requirements'(*Preston v Preston* [1982] Fam 17, at 25B-C, [1982] 1 All ER 41, at 47f-g), being more than needs 'narrowly' defined (*O'D v O'D* [1976] Fam 83, at 91D-E, [1975] 2 All ER 993, at 997f-g), but less than a person's 'wishes'(*Dart v Dart* [1996] 2 FLR 286, at 297A-H).

   In *Rhodes v Dean* (28 March 1996, unreported), CA Micklem J sitting as a judge of the Chancery Division did not pay any regard to the deceased having paid for expensive holidays at home and abroad for his mistress. It is unclear whether the judgment was on the basis that such holidays were not a contribution to the 'reasonable needs' of the applicant or that in the circumstances the court should not exercise its discretion to award the applicant a sufficient sum to enable her to continue having such holidays.
5. [1978] Fam 22, 25F–G, [1978] 1 All ER 221, 224f-g.
6. [1980] Ch 444, 453A–454B, [1980]1 All ER 266, 272e–273b.
7. [1981] Fam 128, 136F–G, [1981] 2 All ER 29, 35a–b (per Stephenson LJ), at [1981] Fam 141D, [1981] 2 All ER 38f–g (per Griffiths LJ); and see also *H v G and D* (1980) 10 Fam Law 98 (Reeve J).
8. (1978) Times, 17 November, *sub nom Re C* 123 Sol Jo 35, *sub nom In the Estate of McC* 9 Fam Law 26. All three reports should be consulted for the full details of this case. The defendant argued that the applicant lived with the deceased under a contractual arrangement to act as the deceased's housekeeper and to provide sexual services. Baker P rejected this because while the applicant originally went to live with the deceased under a contract, by the time of his

consideration' extended beyond consideration provided under a contract or Baker P actually held that the valuable consideration must be provided under a contract. This construction of section 1(3) has been criticised by academic commentators,[9] who have argued that the purpose of the phrase 'otherwise than for full valuable consideration' was merely to exclude applications against the estates of people such as the proprietors of old people's homes who provide accommodation and maintenance contractually and that the construction first adopted in *Re Wilkinson* is likely to exclude applications by deserving mistresses and persons who look after elderly relatives. Three points can be made against these criticisms. Firstly, if the Act intended to limit 'valuable consideration' to that provided under a contract, it would have done so expressly.[10] Secondly, the clear policy and legislative history of section 1(1)(e) was to protect *dependants* and any benefits to mistresses and persons who cared for elderly relatives is only incidental. Accordingly a construction that does not favour mistresses and persons who care for elderly relatives is not *ipso facto* contrary to the intent of the Act. Thirdly, a person who provides consideration equal to or greater than the value of any maintenance received from the deceased can hardly be said to be a 'dependant' of the deceased or to be maintained by him.[11] For instance if two people live together, one providing the accommodation for both of them worth £10 per week and the other providing the food for both of them worth £10 per week, the first person cannot be said to be 'maintained' by the second or vice versa. It would clearly be unsatisfactory if an application could be made by either person in the above example,

---

death the applicant was living with the deceased as a member of his family and a prospective wife and was maintained by him as a result of affection.

9. PVB, (1978) 94 LQR 175; Clark, (1978) 41 MLR 35; Naresh, 'Dependants' Applications under the Inheritance (Provision for Family and Dependants) Act 1975', (1980) 96 LQR 534, 542–546; Hand, 'Family Provision: Are the Right People Receiving It?' (1980) 10 Fam Law 140; Coldham, (1982) 45 MLR 100, 105; Dewar, 'Cohabitees: Contributions and Considerations' (1982) 12 Fam Law 159.
10. Compare s 11(2)(a).
11. *Re Beaumont* [1980] Ch 444, 453C–G, [1980] 1 All ER 266, 272g-j ; see also *Jelley v Iliffe* [1981] Fam 128, [1981] 2 All ER 29. Dewar, 'Cohabitees: Contributions and Considerations' (1982) 12 Fam Law 159, 160 criticises this analysis as failing to distinguish two different situations – firstly, where the consideration provided for the deceased by the applicant would otherwise be available for the applicant's maintenance, and secondly, where the consideration provided for the deceased by the applicant was not easily convertible into providing for the applicant's maintenance. The fallacy with this argument is that where consideration is not easily convertible into matters which can be used for the applicant's maintenance, it will have only a low market value.

but no application could be made if each paid £5 for the accommodation and for the food. That Parliament found it necessary to enact the Law Reform (Succession) Act 1995 suggests that it accepted the construction put upon this question by the courts.[12]

'Valuable consideration' does not include marriage or a promise of marriage.[13]

The Court's function is to value the contributions made by the deceased and any valuable consideration given in return, and to ascertain whether the former exceeds the latter.[14] This is by no means an easy task since most of the relevant contributions are likely to be in kind, such as the provision of accommodation, housekeeping services and companionship, for which there is not necessarily a well organised market.[15] *Re Wilkinson*[16] is a good example of the difficulties which may be experienced. In 1969 the deceased, an elderly arthritic widow, persuaded the applicant, her sister then aged 61 to leave her employment as a housekeeper to provide companionship and to help look after the household. The applicant was told by the deceased that if she did not decide to live with her sister she would be unlikely to receive anything under the sister's will. In 1973 the applicant became less able to do heavy housework and to afford the deceased all the assistance she required, so further help was obtained from a home help and a sister-in-law. At the date of the deceased's death in 1976 the deceased paid for all the outgoings of the house and all the household expenses including

12. See p 104, *post*.
13. S 25(1).
14. See the remarks of Butler-Sloss LJ in *Bishop v Plumley* [1991] 1 WLR 582, 587A, [1981] 1 All ER 236, 241f-g, 'If the flow of benefits from the one to the other is broadly commensurate, full valuable consideration will be demonstrated; if there is an obvious imbalance in favour of the applicant, he or she will have have surmounted the first hurdle'. These remarks were applied by Micklem J in *Rhodes v Dean* (28 March 1996, unreported), CA.
15. In both *Jelley v Iliffe* [1981] Fam 128, 141D-F, [1981] 2 All ER 29,38g-j and *Bishop v Plumley* [1991] 1 WLR 582, 587F, [1991] 2 All ER 242b there are statements about valuing benefits in a 'common sense' way. It is unclear what is meant by these remarks, other than that expert evidence as to the value of services is not required. A 'common sense' finding that a person was or was not dependent upon the deceased can not be made in the face of detailed evidence which is to the contrary. A decision which is probably wrong is the finding in *Re Campbell* [1983] NI 10 that the grandson of the deceased who worked full time for the deceased was within s 1(1)(e).
16. [1978] Fam 22, [1978] 1 All ER 221; further facts are contained in Cadwallader, 'A Mistress's Charter?' [1980] Conv 46. For a case involving extremely complicated figures, see *Williams v Roberts* [1986] 1 FLR 349 and involving slightly less complicated facts, see *Clark v Jones* (2 December 1985, unreported), CA.

food. In return for this the applicant did *light* housework, the cooking and provided companionship for the deceased. Arnold J held, after admitting the difficulty of the decision which he had to make, that the applicant's services as a housekeeper and a companion bearing in mind her own disability did not quite equal the value of the free board and lodging provided by the deceased.[17]

Domestic services such as nursing and housekeeping services are valued on a ' common sense' basis and not necessarily according to the cost of employing a person to provide those services.[18]

It appears from the remarks of Stephenson LJ in *Jelley v Iliffe*[19] that companionship can be regarded as a contribution made by the deceased to the applicant's maintenance and as valuable consideration given in return. In most situations, particularly of man and mistress, companionship is likely to be of equal value to each party and any inequality is only likely to exist when the companionship was the subject of a bargain as in *Malone v Harrison*[20] or where a bargain might have been contemplated as in *Re Wilkinson.*[1]

In *Bishop v Plumley*[2] the applicant and the deceased were an elderly couple who lived together in a house owned free of mortgage by the deceased. The couple pooled their income which consisted of joint payments of Income Support and the deceased's modest part-time earnings. The applicant was the housekeeper in the relationship and as the deceased's health deteriorated she cared for the deceased. The trial judge held that the applicant did not come within section 1(1)(e) because the free accommodation which she was receiving was offset by the housekeeping and care which she gave the deceased. The Court of Appeal reversed that decision. Giving the only reasoned judgment Butler-Sloss LJ relied upon remarks made by Griffiths LJ in *Jelley v Iliffe* as follows:

17. The deceased's will gave the applicant a legacy of £5,000 and furniture (Cadwallader, *op cit*).
18. *Jelley v Iliffe* [1981] Fam 128, 141F, [1981] 2 All ER 29, 38h–j (per Griffiths LJ).
19. [1981] Fam 128, 139D, [1981] 2 All ER 29, 37b. In *Rhodes v Dean* (28 March 1996, unreported), CA Micklem J at first instance specifically held that on the facts of the case mutual companionship between a man and his mistress was of equal value to each.
20. [1979] 1 WLR 1353.
1. [1978] Fam 22, 25B, [1978] 1 All ER 221, 224b–c. Similarly where sexual intercourse is the subject of a bargain, as in the initial situation in *CA v CC* (1978) Times, 17 November, *sub nom Re C* (1979) 123 Sol Jo 35, *sub nom In the Estate of McC* (1979) 9 Fam Law 26 and perhaps in *Malone v Harrison* and *Layton v Martin* [1986] 2 FLR 227. Such sexual intercourse can count as valuable consideration given to the deceased, although this raises interesting questions of illegality.
2. [1991] 1 WLR 582, [1991] 1 All ER 236.

> In striking this balance the court must use common sense and remember that the object of Parliament in creating this extra class of persons who may benefit from an estate was to provide relief for persons of whom it could truly be said that they were wholly or partially dependent on the deceased. It can not be an exact exercise of evaluating services in pounds and pence. By way of example if a man was living with a woman as his wife providing the house and all the money for their living expenses she would clearly be dependent upon him, and it would not be right to deprive her of her claim by arguing that she was in fact performing the services that a housekeeper would perform and it would cost more to employ a housekeeper than was spent on her and indeed perhaps more than the deceased had available to spend upon her. Each case will have to be looked at carefully on its own facts to see whether common sense leads to the conclusion that that the applicant can fairly be regarded as dependent.[3]

Butler-Sloss LJ explained such remarks (uncontroversially) as follows:

> I do not read the judgment as saying more than that, in determining whether or nor the deceased was making a substantial contribution, one must look at the problem in the round; apply a common sense approach, avoiding fine balancing computations involving the value of *normal exchanges of support in the domestic sense.*[4]

However Butler-Sloss LJ went on to say:

> The case for the applicant is that her contribution to the deceased was that of a woman acting as in all ways as a wife. [Her Counsel] argues that her contribution by way of love and support in such a relationship ought to be disregarded in calculating the benefits flowing from her. [Counsel for the beneficiaries] argues that on her own evidence the applicant gave services which were out of the ordinary, and by this exceptional care she was giving him full valuable consideration. I do not consider that the evidence that she did everything for him over a period of years can be assessed in isolation from the mutuality of the relationship. If a man or woman living as man and wife with a partner gives the other extra devoted care and attention, particularly when a partner is in poor health, is he or she to be in a less advantageous position on an application under the Act than one who may be less loving and gives less attention to the partner? I do not accept that this could have been the intention of Parliament in passing this legislation.[5]

3. [1981] Fam 128, 141D-F, [1981] 1 All ER 38g–j.
4. [1991] 1 WLR 587F, [1991] 1 All ER 242b emphasis added.
5. [1991] 1 WLR 587G-588A, [1991] 1 All ER 242c-f.

The judgment goes significantly beyond previous authority which presumed marital companionship to be mutually beneficial[6] and did not value housekeepng services as the cost of employing a professional housekeeper. Butler-Sloss LJ confused the motive for the services (quasi-marital affection) with the quality and value of the services actually provided. Her Ladyship did further elaborate upon the precise extent of the matters which can be ignored because of the motive for their provision and the motives which allow matters to be ignored.[7] It is respectfully submitted that the reasoning of Butler-Sloss LJ is wrong and in due course should be reconsidered by an appropriate court. The answer to the rhetorical question posed by Butler-Sloss LJ is that such unfairness is implicit in section 1(1)(e) and has been belatedly recognised by the Law Commission and Parliament in the enactment of the Law Reform(Succession) Act 1995.

Immediately Before the Death of the Deceased

The applicant must have been maintained by the deceased 'immediately before the death of the deceased'. The same test has been adopted for the new class (ba) of cohibitants.This requirement of dependency at or close to the date of death is surprisingly shared by most Commonwealth jurisdictions who allow claims by de facto spouses or by mistresses if there has been a fixed period of cohabitation unrelated.[8]

6. See p 89, *ante*.
7. Butler-Sloss LJ did not refer to those parts of the judgments in *Jelley v Iliffe* where the court clearly indicated that regard was to be had to the performance of housekeeping tasks between a man and his mistress, see [1981] Fam 140D,142H-143A, [1981] 2 All ER 37j,39h-j. In *Wayling v Jones* (1993) 69 P & C R 170, [1995] 2 FLR 1029 in argument before the Court of Appeal there was some discussion as to the exact ratio of *Bishop v Plumley* during which some Lord Justices expressed difficulty in understanding the precise ratio. The case was ultimately decided upon another point and the judgment did not deal with the claim under the 1975 Act.
8. South Australia, Family Relations Act 1975, s 11; Inheritance (Family Provision) Act Amendment Act 1975 (five years' cohabitation or common parentage of a child).

   The New South Wales Law Reform Commission's Report on the Testators' Family Maintenance and Guardianship of Infants Act 1916, No 28 of 1977, recommended a three-fold test – sometime dependency, membership of the deceased's family (neither linked to the time of the deceased's death) and a reasonable expectation at the time of the deceased's death to his bounty. As eventually enacted the New South Wales Family Provision Act 1982 permitted applications by a person 'who at the time of [his or her] death, was living with the deceased person as [his wife or her husband] on a bona fide domestic basis'

The meaning of 'immediately before the death of the deceased' was discussed at some length by Megarry V-C in *Re Beaumont*.[9] Megarry V-C considered that dependence should not be measured solely on the day or week of death, but that a wider approach should be adopted. Measurement literally 'immediately' before the death of the deceased would exclude many meritorious cases, where the deceased who had maintained the applicant for a long period of time was unable to do so for the weeks before his death because of a terminal illness or the like, and perhaps permit unmeritorious applications where maintenance had been provided merely in the last week before death. Megarry V-C decided that 'immediately' should be approached in a broad sense and that a 'settled basis or arrangement between the parties as regards maintenance'[10] existing at the date of death would suffice for section 1(1)(e), even though maintenance was not actually being provided on the very day or during the very week of death. According to Megarry V-C the

---

and also by grandchildren who were wholly or partially dependent upon the deceased and were living in the same household, see s 6(1) definition of 'eligible person'.

The Northern Territory Family Provision Act 1970 allows an application to be made by 'a de facto partner of a deceased person' (s 7(1)(g)), but only if he 'was maintained by the deceased person immediately before his death' (s 7(2)), a concept which is restrictively defined (s 7(7)).

The Queensland Succession Act 1981 allows an application to be made by a person who was being maintained by the deceased immediately before death *and* who has 'lived in a connubial relationship with' the deceased either for five continuous years terminating on the death of the death or for an aggregate of five years out of a total of six years with the 'connubial relationship' subsisting at the date of death (s 40(d)) or by a person who is the parent of a child of the deceased under the age of 18 years (s 40(b)).

For the tentative conclusions of the Tasmania Law Reform Commission, see Working Paper on Obligations arising from De Facto Relationships (1974).This contains the following remarkable example of paternalism (p 4): 'Above all, it is still necessary to protect women from the exploitation of some men who use them for their sexual gratification and to provide household services but who just as readily abandon them when it suits'. To date Tasmania has not enacted any legislation allowing cohabitants to claim.

The Western Australia Inheritance (Family and Dependants Provision) Act 1972 allows an application by 'a *de facto* widow or widower of the deceased who at the time of the death of the deceased was being wholly or partly maintained by the deceased, who was ordinarily a member of the household of the deceased, and for who the deceased, in the opinion of the Court, had some special moral responsibility to make provision' (emphasis supplied) (s 7(1)(f)).

For discussion of this legislation, see DICKEY, 29–32, DE GROOT AND NICKEL, paras 309–309.7.

Most of the drafting of the Australian leglislation compares favourably with the drafting of s 1(1)(e).

9. [1980] Ch 444, at 451D–453A, [1980] 1 All ER 266, at 271c–272d .
10. [1980] Ch 452F, [1980] 1 All ER 272b.

function of the 'immediately' requirement is to prevent applications where the 'settled basis or arrangement' has terminated before death,[11] for instance where a man and his mistress have separated or where a prolonged illness rules out any prospect of maintenance being restored. This approach of Megarry V-C, while a considerable gloss on the words of the statute, constitutes a most sensible and just solution to a problem of infelicitous drafting. It was approved by the Court of Appeal in *Jelley v Iliffe*,[12] where Stephenson LJ stated what was required was maintenance on a 'settled basis or [the] general arrangement between the parties as regards maintenance during the lifetime of the deceased' and that 'the actual, perhaps fluctuating, variation of [maintenance] which exists immediately before his or her death' should be ignored.

It appears from the approach of Megarry V-C and the Court of Appeal in *Jelley v Iliffe* and in particular the adoption of the requirements of an assumption of responsibility that the 'settled basis' test is a *necessary* rather than merely a *sufficient* test. Thus a person who was actually maintained by the deceased during the last few weeks of his life not under any settled basis is not able to apply. Bearing in mind that the Law Commission rejected any minimum period of dependence,[13] and the specific word 'immediately' used in the Act, it is suggested that the 'settled basis' test is a sufficient test only and that persons actually maintained during the last weeks or days of the deceased's life should satisfy the immediacy requirements,[14] but that their claims should fail on the basis of a lack of assumption of responsibility or their lack of merits.

It is uncertain whether any length of interruption of the settled basis of maintenance because of the deceased's illness prevents an applicant from being regarded as maintained by the deceased *immediately* before his death.

A helpful decision is *Re Dymott*,[15] decided after the full report in *Re Beaumont* became available. In about 1975 the applicant and the deceased began to associate with one another. They retained their separate homes and each supported themselves. From March to August 1978 the deceased supported the applicant by paying her £10 per week. In August 1978 the deceased had a heart attack and

11. [1982] Ch 452G, [1980] 1 All ER 272c–d.
12. [1981] Fam 128, at 136E, [1981] 2 All ER 29, at 34j–35a.
13. LAW COM, para 93.
14. Naresh, 'Dependants' Applications under the Inheritance (Provision for Family and Dependants) Act 1975', (1980) 96 LQR 534, 547–8; Coldham, Note, (1982) 45 MLR 100, 102. In *Re Kirby* (1981) 11 Fam Law 210 Purchas J appeared to treat the 'settled basis' test as a necessary requirement rather than merely a sufficient one.
15. Purchas J [1980] CA Transcript 942.

thereafter until his death in July 1979 the applicant to some extent contributed to his maintenance. Purchas J[16] held that the applicant was not maintained by the deceased *immediately* before his death. An application for leave to appeal out of time was dismissed by the Court of Appeal, Ormrod LJ implicitly stressing the short time that the deceased actually maintained the applicant. He said:

> The view I have come to is that it is not arguable in this case, looking at the evidence, that *the norm of this relationship*[17] was one of dependence on the part of the plaintiff. The whole relationship from 1975 onwards was on the basis of two people with means living together and sharing their lives in whatever way they chose to do. It would seem to me, that the period March to August should be regarded as an exceptional period in their lives, whereas the continuing of mutual independence is the way in which these people chose to live.

It seems implicit in these remarks that a more lengthy and settled basis of dependence prior to the deceased's terminal illness might have enabled the applicant to be regarded as being maintained immediately before the death of the deceased.

Further guidance on the meaning of 'immediately' is contained in the case of *Kourkgy v Lusher.*[18] Between 1969 and July 1979 the deceased and the applicant lived together as man and mistress, before separating on what was likely to be a permanent basis. The deceased died only a matter of days after the permanent separation. Wood J expressly found that the deceased abandoned any assumption of responsibility for maintenance upon the separation and so the applicant was not being maintained 'immediately before the death of the deceased'.

Assumption of Responsibility

A further requirement for an applicant to satisfy to come within class (e) was introduced, without being mentioned in previous cases, by Megarry V-C in *Re Beaumont* and partially approved by the Court

16. Daily Mirror, 26 July 1980.
17. Emphasis added. Megarry V-C's views are to some extent supported by the subsequent case law on children of the family where it has been held that to qualify the deceased need not have assumed a responsibility for the maintenance of the applicant, see p 77, *ante*.
18. (1981) 4 FLR 65. For an example of where a claim by a mistress failed because the relationship ended several years before death, see *Layton v Martin* [1986] 2 FLR 227.

of Appeal in *Jelley v Iliffe*. The requirement is that the deceased should have assumed a responsibility for the maintenance of the applicant in addition to actually maintaining the applicant. An assumption of responsibility for maintenance had not been mentioned in any prior reported cases nor discussed by any commentator. Megarry V-C felt compelled to infer such a requirement from a comparison of sub-sections (3) and (4) of section 3. Section 1 deals with the qualifications of the various classes of applicants and section 3 deals with the matters to which the court is to have regard in the exercise of its powers. Section 3(3) deals with matters especially to be considered in applications by a 'child of the family' and provides that:

> ... the court shall also have regard (a) *to whether* the deceased had assumed any responsibility for the applicant's maintenance and, *if so*, to the extent to which and the basis upon which the deceased assumed that responsibility ...[19]

Section 3(4) deals with applicants within section 1(1)(e) and provides that:

> ... the court shall ... have regard to the extent to which and the basis upon which the deceased assumed responsibility for the maintenance of the applicant and to the length of time for which the deceased discharged the responsibility.

Megarry V-C thought that the absence of the word 'whether' in section 3(4), in direct contrast to section 3(3), must imply that while an assumption of responsibility by the deceased was not technically a requirement for an applicant to come within class (e), any applicant lacking such an assumption of responsibility was *bound* to fail on the merits.[20] The idea of a requirement of an assumption of responsibility ties in nicely with Megarry V-C's views on a settled basis or arrangement for maintenance satisfying the immediacy requirement.[1] Megarry V-C also thought that to come within class (e) an applicant had to show a similar degree of permanence or importance as was revealed with the other classes of applicants.[2] Megarry V-C's views on the need for some kind of an assumption of responsibility for maintenance were in general terms accepted by the Court of Appeal in *Jelley v Iliffe*.[3]

19. Emphasis added.
20. [1980] Ch 454B–456G, [1980] 1 All ER 273c–275d.
1. [1980] Ch 456E–G, [1980] 1 All ER 275a–d.
2. [1980] Ch 452H–453A, [1980] 1 All ER 272d.
3. [1981] Fam 128, at 136H–137B, [1981] 2 All ER 29, at 35c–d (per Stephenson LJ).

It is clear that this assumption of responsibility to maintain is an assumption to maintain during the deceased's life, not necessarily an assumption of responsibility to maintain after his death.[4]

It is doubtful whether this extra requirement of an assumption of responsibility introduced by *Re Beaumont* is a legitimate piece of statutory interpretation.[5] This requirement coupled with the 'settled basis or arrangement' introduces a very substantial gloss upon the words of the statute. The Law Commission's Report nowhere states that an assumption of responsibility was a sine qua non of a successful application.[6] The House of Commons when it discussed section 1(1)(e) was fully aware of the implications of making actual dependence at death the sole criterion for making an application.[7]

The burden of proving an assumption of responsibility is upon the applicant.[8] In *Re Beaumont* the applicant and the deceased lived together as man and mistress from 1940 until the deceased's death in 1976. The parties lived in the deceased's house, which was always regarded as belonging to the deceased alone. The applicant always gave the deceased a weekly sum in respect of his accommodation and contributed to the weekly shopping bill. While originally these contributions were full consideration for the accommodation and board provided by the deceased, towards the end of the deceased's life with the decline in the value of money caused by inflation and because of the declining income of the applicant such contributions did not fully equal the maintenance provided by the deceased. The applicant did work on the deceased's house for which he was paid by the deceased. The parties nursed each other in times of sickness. The applicant admitted in cross-examination that the deceased never expressly agreed to be responsible for the applicant's maintenance.[9] On these facts Megarry V-C held that as the deceased in effect intended that the applicant should pay his way she assumed no responsibility for his maintenance. Megarry V-C specifically

4. *Jelley v Iliffe* [1981] Fam 128, at 137F–138B, [1981] 2 All ER 29, at 35h–36b (per Stephenson LJ).
5. See criticism of *Re Beaumont* in Naresh, 'Dependants' Applications under the Inheritance (Provision for Family and Dependants) Act 1975', (1980) 96 LQR 534, 548–554; see also Coldham, Note, (1982) 45 MLR 100, 102–103.
6. Megarry V-C at [1980] Ch 455F–456A, [1980] 1 All ER 274d–g drew support from LAW COM, para 91. Naresh, *op cit*, 550–551 draws support for his contrary argument from LAW COM, paras 91, 93. Bearing in mind that a Law Commission Report is not a statute, the only safe conclusion that can be drawn from the Report is that the Law Commission did not specifically mention an assumption of responsibility as a necessary requirement.
7. See pp 81–83, *ante*.
8. *Re Beaumont* [1980] Ch 444, at 457E–F, [1980] 1 All ER 266, at 275h–276a and p 63, *ante*.
9. [1980] Ch 458A–B, [1980] 1 All ER 276d.

rejected the argument that the actual provision of maintenance implies an assumption of responsibility for its provision.[10] However, in *Jelley v Iliffe* this statement of Megarry V-C's was overruled. Stephenson LJ stated that the very provision of maintenance 'generally' gives rise to a presumption of an assumption of responsibility to maintain, although this presumption can be rebutted.[11] In *Jelley v Iliffe* the Court of Appeal regarded the mere fact of maintenance provided by a mistress to her lover after a period of cohabitation of perhaps eight years implied that the mistress assumed a responsibility for her lover's maintenance.[12] In *Re Dymott*,[13] a decision of the Court of Appeal given a day before *Jelley v Iliffe*, Ormrod LJ held overruling Purchas J at first instance that the provision of £10 per week by a lover to his mistress for six months in a relationship which lasted for four years where both parties retained a considerable degree of independence was not evidence of an assumption of responsibility. It is suggested that after *Jelley v Iliffe* Ormrod LJ's decision, while it could not be given on an application to strike out a claim, is still good law.

Further guidance as to the meaning of an assumption of responsibility for maintenance is contained in the case of *Kourkgy v Lusher*.[14] The case involved a claim by a mistress against the estate of her deceased lover. Wood J examined the relationship of the applicant and the deceased meticulously. He found that during the period of cohabitation by reason of the deceased's general contribution to the applicant's maintenance he assumed a responsibility for her maintenance. The deceased had refused to accede to the applicant's request to purchase a larger house necessitating a larger mortgage. Wood J regarded this as a divestment by the deceased of a financial responsibility of a capital nature.[15] On the evidence Wood J found that during a temporary separation and during the final separation when the deceased returned to his wife the deceased 'abandoned' his responsibility.[16]

10. [1980] Ch 458B–D, [1980] 1 All ER 276d–f.
11. [1981] Fam 128, at 137B–C, [1981] 2 All ER 29, at 35d-e (per Stephenson LJ), at 142E, 39e–f (per Griffiths LJ).
12. [1981] Fam 128, at 142G–143B, [1981] 2 All ER 29, at 39g–j (per Griffiths LJ). *Jelley v Iliffe* was applied to very similar facts in *Harrington v Gill* (1983) 4 FLR 265.
13. [1980] CA Transcript 942. For a case in which the court had regard both to the statements of the deceased and the fact of maintenance in determining the extent of an assumption of responsibility, in which neither was regarded as conclusive, see *Rhodes v Dean* (28 March 1996, unreported), CA.
14. (1981) 4 FLR 65.
15. (1981) 4 FLR 71B, 75C–E.
16. (1981) 4 FLR 75B–C. Compare the different finding in this type of situation in *Re P* Halsbury's Laws of England Monthly Digest, para 96/369.

An express disclaimer of responsibility for the maintenance of the applicant during the deceased's lifetime is probably effective to prevent an applicant from coming within section 1(1)(e).[17]

It is clear from the wording of section 3(4) which directs attention 'to the *extent* and the *basis* upon which the deceased assumed responsibility' that an assumption of responsibility for another's maintenance need not be total and can take many forms or be at different levels.[18] All that section 3(4) requires is *some* assumption of responsibility by the deceased; the quality of such assumption should only be relevant when the court is deciding whether to exercise its discretion to award provision. For instance, it is submitted that the deceased in *Re Viner*[19] had assumed *some* responsibility for the maintenance of the applicant, so as to satisfy the test put forward in *Re Beaumont*, even though such assumption was made under 'moral duress'. In *Rhodes v Dean*[20] Judge Micklem sitting as a Judge of the Chancery Division found that the deceased had assumed a responsibility for the accommodation of the applicant, but not for any other aspect of her maintenance and used this finding to justify not awarding provision. The Court of Appeal refused to interfere with this finding.

It is probably a fair inference that cohabitation between a man and his mistress over a period of time coupled with actual maintenance implies some sort of an assumption of responsibility to maintain.[1] But this inference may be misplaced if the couple intended to lead separate lives and considered that they have no long term ties to one another[2] or where the cohabitation is merely for

17. *Re Beaumont* [1980] Ch 444, at 458G, [1980] 1 All ER 266, at 276h-j (per Megarry V-C); *Jelley v Iliffe* [1981] Fam 128, at 137F, [1981] 2 All ER 29, at 35h (per Stephenson LJ).
18. It is not apparent that Megarry V-C fully appreciated this point from the report of *Re Beaumont*.
19. [1978] CLY 3091; further facts of *Re Viner* can be found in Davies, 'Inheritance (Provision for Family and Dependants) Act 1975 – Subjective or Objective Test' (1978) 75 LS Gaz 75.
20. (28 March 1996, unreported), CA.
1. *Jelley v Iliffe* [1981] Fam 128, at 137E, [1981] 2 All ER 29, at 35g-h; *Harrington v Gill* (1983) 4 FLR 265; *Kourkgy v Lusher* (1981) 4 FLR 65. This approach should be contrasted with the decision of Carnwath J in *Wild v Pensions Ombudsman* [1996] 2 FLR 680 where a provision in a private pension scheme worded in a similar manner to s 1(1)(e) was held in effect to require an express assumption of responsibility and to exclude a cohabitee who was financially dependent upon the deceased out of choice, as opposed to out of necessity. On the types of co-habitation which give rise to 'family-like' duties, see Freeman and Lyon, 'Towards a Justification of Rights of Cohabitees' (1980) 130 NLJ 228 and Freeman and Lyon, *Cohabitation Without Marriage*.
2. Compare *Helby v Rafferty* [1979] 1 WLR 13, [1978] 3 All ER 1016; but see *Watson v Lucas* [1980] 1 WLR 1493, [1980] 3 All ER 647 with more marginal

convenience of accommodation or of purely sexual relations.[3] Where one is dealing with situations other than support between man and mistress, or perhaps support for an infant child, Stephenson LJ's statement that actual provision of maintenance generally raises a presumption of an assumption of responsibility to maintain is not necessarily true. Where two or more people, not sexually attracted to each other, share accommodation for reasons of economy, such as Megarry V-C's example of the rich and the poor student[4] or the two 'Liver Birds' as discussed in the House of Commons,[5] any imbalance of contributions between them surely infers no assumption of responsibility. Likewise Megarry V-C is probably correct in requiring in an application by a distant relative or former employee to whom no special duty is owed who actually receives maintenance from the deceased there should be an express assumption of responsibility by the deceased.[6]

According to the Court of Appeal in *Jelley v Iliffe* it will be relatively rare that the evidence on affidavit before a trial will be so clear that the applicant was not maintained by the deceased or that the deceased had not assumed a responsibility for the applicant's maintenance that an application can be struck out before trial.[7]

In the light of the decision of the Court of Appeal in *Jelley v Iliffe* that the actual provision of maintenance raises a presumption

---

facts; and see *Re Dymott* [1980] CA Transcript 942, particularly the remarks of Ormrod LJ set out at p 97, *ante*. The failure of the Court of Appeal in *Harrington v Gill* (1983) 4 FLR 265 to consider adequately the significance of the applicant's continued holding of a tenancy of her own flat during the relationship was regrettable. See further Freeman and Lyon, *Cohabitation Without Marriage*, 189–193.

3. Compare *Richards v Dove* [1974] 1 All ER 888, at 894G–H. In *H v G and D* (1980) 10 Fam Law 98 Reeve J did not regard two years' cohabitation as indicative of any assumption of responsibility because the deceased had recently at least two similar relationships and because the applicant and the deceased did not contemplate marriage. In *H v G and D*, a decision prior to *Jelley v Iliffe*, Reeve J indicated that an intention to marry might be evidence of an assumption of responsibility of maintenance. In *Re Green* Daily Mirror, 25/11/81, Daily Telegraph, 25/11/81 Foster J found a sufficient degree of an assumption of responsibility where the deceased and his mistress cohabited for nine months and the deceased provided the mistress with between £25 and £50 per week to supplement her small earnings. The couple clearly intended to marry, but the difference in ages between the parties (the deceased was aged 22, the mistress 29) the difference in occupation (the deceased was a panel beater, the mistress was a model) and the fact that the mistress's first marriage had ended in divorce might indicate that the prospects for marriage were not great.
4. [1980] Ch 452C, [1980] 1 All ER 271j.
5. (1974–75) 4 Standing Committees, col 13 (29 July 1975).
6. [1980] Ch 458D–G, [1980] 1 All ER 276f-j.
7. On striking out applications generally, see pp 358–359, *post*.

of an assumption of responsibility to maintain and bearing in mind that assumptions of responsibility take many different forms there will be very few cases in which some sort of an assumption of responsibility does not exist. While the introduction of the requirement of an assumption of responsibility to maintain in *Re Beaumont* and its refinement in *Jelley v Iliffe* raise interesting theoretical points about the definition of s 1(1)(e), it is most doubtful whether the requirement greatly affects the law in practice, since if an applicant cannot show some sort of an assumption of responsibility he is unlikely to succeed on the merits anyway, and the approach of *Jelley v Iliffe* prevents many cases being struck out before a full hearing.[8]

Conclusion on Class (e)

Few people would claim that class (e) has resulted in a morally satisfactory class of applicants. The test of dependence, and dependence alone, permits successful claims by a 'kept woman'[9] but bars claims by a person who has enriched and cared for a mistress or lover over many years.[10] It permits substantial provision to be ordered to a relative of the deceased who has coerced or tricked the deceased into making some provision for him during the deceased's lifetime,[11] while barring the claim of a relative who cared greatly for the deceased when aged or infirm.[12] The test of dependency emphasises the amount of maintenance that followed from the deceased rather than the amount of maintenance which the applicant gave to the deceased. No account is taken of any detriment which the applicant may have suffered as a result of the conduct of the

8. *Ad idem* Coldham, Note, (1982) 45 MLR 100, 103. After *Jelley v Iliffe* virtually none of the reported case law deals with an assumption of responsibility in the context of coming within s 1(1)(e).
9. Compare *Malone v Harrison* [1979] 1 WLR 1353.
10. *Re Dymott*; *Re Beaumont*. Practitioners are aware of many similar cases where the applicant has been advised not to commence proceedings because he or she has no case. See also for the case of an unmeritorious applicant *Re Kozdrach*, Ewbank J, [1981] Conv 224 – the facts of which can be found in the interlocutory Court of Appeal hearing 9 November 1979, *sub nom Sobesto v Farren* [1981] Conv 224.
11. *Re Viner* [1978] CLY 3091.
12. *Re Wilkinson* [1978] Fam 22, [1978] 1 All ER 221. The author is aware of several cases of relatives who have cared for the deceased at considerable expense and hardship and have been unable to make a claim under the Act because no remuneration had been sought from the deceased.

deceased.[13] The test of dependence penalises generosity by the deceased during his lifetime and acts as an incentive to meanness.

The outcome of the case law on section 1(1)(e) is not the result of malevolent or misconceived construction of the statute by the judiciary as some commentators have argued,[14] but a necessary working out of a concept adopted with inadequate research and thought by the Law Commission and passed reluctantly by a more thoughtful and sceptical Parliament.[15]

The mere fact that one person maintains another during his lifetime *by itself* raises no implication that the maintenance will continue after the deceased's death, is indicative of no moral obligation binding upon the donor (but is perhaps indicative of an obligation binding upon the donee) nor indicative of any social or moral duty. (Matters might be different if the donee has had to incur a detriment to receive the maintenance.[16]) The over-inclusive nature of a test of dependence alone has been recognised by law reform bodies in New South Wales[17] and Alberta.[18]

13. Surely the most meritorious thing about the applicant in *Malone v Harrison* was that her relationship with the deceased prevented her acquiring any training and severely reduced her prospects of employment. Similarly in *Re Wilkinson* it was not unimportant that the applicant gave up employment to nurse the deceased and in *CA v CC* that the applicant gave up her child at the request of the deceased. Such detriment cannot really be regarded as 'valuable consideration' for the purposes of s 1(3) and is accordingly irrelevant in deciding whether the applicant comes within s 1(1)(e). See also *Graham v Murphy* [1997] 1 FLR 860.
14. See articles cited in fn 9, p 87, *ante*. It is uncertain whether Hand is objecting to the judicial interpretation of the Act or to the design of the Act. Compare the very much more restrictive construction placed upon a similarly worded definition in a private pension scheme by Carnwath J in *Wild v Pensions Ombudsman* [1996] 2 FLR 680, where no case law under the 1975 Act was cited.
15. See the remarks of Lord Meston QC in the debates on the Law Reform (Succession) Act 1995 in HL Parl Deb, Vol 561, col 507, set out at p 105, *post*.
16. See fn 13, *ante*.
17. Law Reform Commission of New South Wales, Working Paper on Testators' Family Maintenance and Guardianship of Infants Act 1916, para 6.66 – 'Our present thoughts are that dependency alone is too broad a base from which to invoke the operation of the Act. The circumstances which can give rise to situations of dependency are endless... We do not believe that the principle of testamentary freedom should be encroached to the extent that would be possible if all dependants became eligible applicants under the Act. And we do not believe that opportunities for speculative actions should be enlarged to the extent that they would be enlarged if any person claiming to be a dependant of the deceased could commence proceedings under the Act.'

    See now Family Provision Act 1982 referred to in fn 8, p 92, *ante*.
18. Institute of Law Research and Reform, University of Alberta, Report No 29 Family Relief (1978) 59. The same conclusion was reached by the Manitoba Law Reform Commission Report 'The Testator's Family Maintenance Act' (1985) 50 (generally this is a remarkably lucid and intelligent discussion of the basic issues in family provision legislation).

If dependence is used as a criterion for establishing a claim under the Act (and dependence may be an appropriate test when dealing with claims by siblings, parents, stepchildren not being 'children of the family'), then a dependence plus other factors test should be adopted. Such an approach has been adopted by several Commonwealth jurisdictions[19] and proposed in others.[20] If such an approach is thought suitable for adoption in England and Wales, the legislation should require a minimum period of dependency to prevent applications by persons who have been maintained for only a brief period before the deceased's death.

Belatedly the Law Commission and Parliament have recognised through the enactment of the Law Reform (Succcession) Act 1995 that a test of dependence is an unsuitable device to enable cohabitants to claim. However, in neither of the Law Commission's Reports which led to the 1995 Act[1] nor in the Parliamentary Debates[2] was there any suggestion that section 1(1)(e) should be abolished.Thus a person who can not come within section 1(1)(ba) because the cohabitation has not lasted for two years,[3] because they

19. See fn 8, pp 91–92, *ante*. In addition to Ontario, the Uniform Dependants' Relief Act has been enacted in the North West Territories and Prince Edward Island.
20. Alberta, Institute of Law Research and Reform, University of Alberta, Report No 29, Family Relief (1978) – grandparents, parents and grandchildren if actually maintained for three years prior to death.

 The Australian Capital Territory Family Provision Act 1969 allows applications to be made by stepchildren, grandchildren and parents (s 7(1)(d), (e), (f)), but grandchildren can only claim in very restricted circumstances (s 7(3)) and parents can only claim if they were being actually maintained by the deceased before death (s 7(4)).

 For New South Wales legislation, see fn 8, pp 91–92, *ante*.

 The Northern Territory Family Provision Act 1970 as regards claims by stepchildren, grandchildren and parents is almost identical to the legislation of the Australian Capital Territory.

 The Queensland Succession Act 1981 allows claims by persons financially dependent upon the deceased immediately before death provided they are a parent, a parent with the deceased of an infant child, 'a person under the age of 18 years' or had lived in a 'connubial relationship' for a specified number of years (s 40(a), (b), (c), (d)).

 The South Australia (Family Provision) Act 1972 allows claims by stepchildren who were being maintained by the deceased (s 6(g)) and by grandchildren upon whom no test of dependence is required (s 6(h)).

 The Western Australia Inheritance (Family Provision) Act 1972 allows claims by grandchildren who were being maintained by the deceased (s 7(1)(d)) and by parents upon whom no test of dependence is required (s 7(1)(e)).

 See further fn 8, pp 91–92, *ante* and fn 9, p 103, *post*.

1. Working Paper No 108, Report No 187.
2. For the Parliamentary Debates on the 1995 Act, see fn 2, pp 104–106, *post*.
3. Eg *Re Green* Daily Mirror, 25/11/81, Daily Telegraph, 25/11/81 discussed in fn 3, p 99, *ante*.

were not living in the same household as the deceased[4] or because they are of the same sex[5] may still be able to claim under section 1(1)(e). Having an alternative set of tests for the same broad factual situation is difficult to justify.

The test of dependency is clearly unsuitable to deal with claims by persons who have cared for aged and ill relatives or non-relatives, since many really deserving applicants would be maintaining the deceased. It is doubtful whether family provision legislation is the right vehicle for dealing with claims by such people,[6] since in family provision proceedings a person who looked after the deceased would be postponed to the creditors of the deceased, his claim must be balanced against the claims of other applicants, and any award reflects the applicant's financial circumstances rather than the amount of care provided by the applicant to the deceased and applications can be made only on death. It is suggested that the better way of dealing with claims by such people is by developing principles of contract, implied contracts[7] or proprietory estoppel[8] to cover the situation or by enacting a variant of the New Zealand Testamentary Promises legislation.[9]

4. Eg *Malone v Harrison* [1979] 1 WLR 1353 – the moral claim of a 'kept woman' who has not given birth to the deceased's child must be very weak.
5. Eg *Wayling v Jones* (1993) 69 P & CR 170, [1995] 2 FLR 1029.
6. *Ad idem*, Law Reform Commission of New South Wales, Working Paper on Testators' Family Maintenance and Guardianship of Infants Act 1916, para 6.5.
7. See *Deglman v Guaranty Trust Co of Canada and Consantineau* (1954) 3 DLR 785 (Sup Ct Can applying Ontario law); *Hink v Lhenen* (1974) 52 DLR 3d 301 (Alta Sup Ct App Div); Miller, 'Provision for Dependants and Agreements for Testamentary Provision', (1978) 128 NLJ 449.
8. Naresh, 'Dependants' Applications under the Inheritance (Provision for Family and Dependants) Act 1975', (1980) 96 LQR 534, 538–542 relying upon *Griffiths v Williams* (1977) 248 Estates Gazette 947; see further *Re Basham* [1986] 1 WLR 1498, [1987] 1 All ER 405.
9. For discussion of the New Zealand Testamentary Promises legislation, see Robson, 'The Law Reform (Testamentary Promises) Act 1949, (NZ)', (1950) 13 MLR 353; Coote, 'Testamentary Promises Jurisdiction in New Zealand' *The A.G. Davies Essays in Law* 1–25. Surely the better remedy in *Re Goodchild* [1996] 1 WLR 694, [1996] 1 All ER 670 would have been under a form of testamentary promise legislation rather than straining the definition of 'maintenance' to bring the claim under the 1975 Act.

   The South Australian Inheritance (Family Provision) Act 1972 as amended allows applications by either a parent or sibling of the deceased 'who satisfies the court that he cared for , or contributed to the maintenance of, the deceased person during his lifetime' (s 6(i), (j)). This caring or contribution towards the maintenance need not be immediately before the death of the deceased and in the case of parents would presumably enable virtually every parent to claim.

Cohabitants

In 1988 the Law Commission produced a Working Paper on the law of intestacy.[10] In an insightful discussion of the aims and objectives of the rules of intestacy, the Law Commission raised the questions as to whether cohabitants should be entitled under the rules of intestacy or be allowed to claim under the 1975 Act.[11] After consultation and carrying out a detailed survey of public opinion, the Law Commission produced in December 1989 a Report 'Family Law: Distribution on Intestacy'.[12] The principal recommendation was that if a deceased was survived by a spouse, the spouse should in all circumstances be solely entitled to the estate of the deceased under the rules of intestacy to the exclusion of the issue.This recommendation was unacceptable to the Government and to many commentators.[13] A majority of the persons questioned in the survey of public opinion favoured giving cohabitants automatic rights under the rules of intestacy,[14] but this proposal was rejected by the Law Commission, principally on the ground of the enormous practical problems if a deceased died intestate survived by both a spouse and a cohabitant.[15] Instead the Law Commission proposed that cohabitants should be allowed to claim under the 1975 Act as an additional class of applicants and the Law Commission proposed that the definition of cohabitants under the Fatal Accidents Act 1976 should be adopted.[16]

The Law Reform (Succession) Act 1995 in Parliament

The Law Commission's recommendation that cohabitants should be entitled to apply under the 1975 Act was eventually the centre

10. Working Paper No 108.
11. Paras 3.19, 5.30(iii). While the Working Paper's discussion of the rules of intestacy was thoughtful and lucid, the discussion of family provision generally can only be described as desultory.
12. Report No 187.
13. See the important article Cretney, 'Reform of Intestacy:the best we can do?'(1995) 111 LQR 77.
14. Appendix C, para 2.22-3, para 2.25(v).
15. Para 58. See further Deech, 'The Case Against Legal Recognition of Cohabiatation' in Eekelaar and Katz, 'Marriage and Cohabitation in Contemporary Societies' at 305–306. For a view that it is possible in a system of intestacy to accommodate potentially competing claims of a surviving spouse and cohabitant, see Alberta Law Reform Institute 'Reform of the Intestate Succession Act', Report for Discussion No 16, pp 92–97 (January 1996).
16. Para 59. The definition was introduced by s 3(1) of the Administration of Justice Act 1982.

piece of the Government sponsored Law Reform (Succession) Bill 1995. This was introduced in the House of Lords and was passed without a division or an amendment.[17] During the Second Reading Debate there were speeches by the Lord Chancellor, Lords Irvine of Lairg QC and Mischcon on behalf of the Labour Party and Lord Meston QC on behalf of the Liberal Democrats.[18] Parts of the speech of Lord Meston QC, who through a distinguished practice at the Divorce Bar is one of the few modern legislators familiar with the practical operation of family provision legislation, are worth setting out in full:

> One objective must be to try to minimize the need for recourse to the discretionary family provision legislation.
>
> Litigation under the 1975 Act is costly to estates, which are seldom able to sustain the luxury of legal expenses. It is litigation which is often divisive and distressing to the competing relatives, each of who may have his own idea of what the deceased would or would not have wanted had he got round to making a will. The 1975 Act has a number of distinct limitations and it is also an area of discretionary law in which practioners do not find it particularly easy to advise with certainty, if the case has to go to court.
>
> Therefore, I support the view that, before the safety net of the intestacy rules is altered, the underlying further safety net of family provision should also be checked for holes, strength and positioning. That review is almost certainly too wide anyway to involve this Bill in the special committee procedure of the House.
>
> The existing law requires proof of dependency. Mere financial or other sacrifice for the sake of the deceased does not qualify for a claim under the 1975 Act. That is particularly the result of insufficient thought being given to that problem during the Parliamentary passage of the 1975 Act.[19]

In stark contrast to the political storms which overtook the Family Homes and Domestic Violence Bill 1995 and the Family Law Act 1996,[20] the passage of the 1995 Act through the House of Commons

17. HL Parl Deb, Vol 561, col 502, 1309; Vol 562, col 1409; Vol 265, col 199.
18. HL Parl Deb, Vol 561, cols 502–5411 (13 February 1995).
19. HL Parl Deb, Vol 561, col 507. Lord Meston's father had piloted the Matrimonial Causes (Property and Maintenance) Act 1958 through the House of Lords.
20. The Family Homes and Domestic Violence Bill 1995 had to be abandoned because of opposition from Government backbenchers. The Family Law Act 1996 was probably the most politically contentious piece of legislation in the 1995–96 Parliamentary Session, was heavily amended in both Houses, being eventually passed only by the votes of Opposition MPs and its possible failure was thought likely to precipitate the resignation of the Lord Chancellor. For the view that law reform is most likely to succeed if it is presented as entirely 'technical', see Cretney, 'The Forfeiture Act 1982:the Private Members' Bill as an Instrument of Law Reform', (1990) 10 Ox J Leg Studies 289.

was noted by the complete absence of any opposition, reasoned discussion or amendment.[1]

The Definition of Cohabitants

The 1995 Act adds a new class of applicants to those enumerated in section 1(1) in the following terms:

> (ba) any person (not being a person included in paragraph (a) or (b) above) to whom subsection (1A) below applies.

Subsection (1A) provides:

> This subsection applies to a person if the deceased died on or after 1st January 1996 and, during the whole of the period of two years ending immediately before the date when the deceased died, the person was living...
> *(a)* in the same household as the deceased, and
> *(b)* as the husband or wife of the deceased.

This somewhat convoluted drafting has the effect that if an applicant comes within both section 1(1)(ba) and section 1(1)(e), the applicant's status within section 1(1)(ba) has priority – this has important consequences as the statutory matters to which the Court has regard under section 3 are very significantly different for the two classes of applicant.[2]

Section 1(1)(ba) only applies where the deceased dies on or after 1 January 1996.

Section 1(1)(ba) is derived from the comparably worded class of dependant under the Fatal Accidents Act 1976 as amended.[3]

The Act imposes a strict requirement of cohabitation for a continous period of two years ending immediately before the date of death of the deceased. Thus there can be no claim where

1. HC Parl Deb, Vol 261, col 811; Vol 265, col 199.
2. For s 1(1)(ba), see s 3(2A); for s 1(1)(e), see s 3(4).
3. On the origins of s 1(1)(ba), see Law Commission Report No 187, para 59; HL Parl Deb, Vol 561, col 502-11 (13 February 1995). S 1(3)(b) of the Fatal Accidents Act 1976 was inserted by s 3(1) of the Administration of Justice Act 1982. While there have been a number of reported awards under s 1(3)(b), there has been a paucity of reported case law upon the interpretation of s 1(3)(b). A further comparable statutory provision which may be of some use in interpreting s 1(1)(ba) is s 113(1)(a) of the Housing Act 1985 which refers to 'he and that person living together as husband and wife', a definition adopted by s 62(1) of the Family Law Act 1996.

cohabitation had ceased before death, no matter how shortly before death or how long the previous period of cohabitation.[4] In a case under the Fatal Accidents Act it has been held that 'brief absences' do not interrupt the period of two years.[5] It is submitted that in determining whether cohabitation existed for the whole of the requisite period, the approach of Megarry V-C in *Re Beaumont* which directs attention to the 'settled basis or arrangement between the parties'[6] should be adopted. Thus separation by reason of a terminal illness should be ignored.

The parties must be 'living in the same household'. This definition excludes the traditional mistress who is set up by the deceased in her own house.[7] A person can be simultaneously living in two different households.[8] Particular difficulties may be experienced where two people live physically in the same dwellinghouse, but lead 'separate lives' or live in separate households.[9]

The parties must be 'living ... as the husband or wife of the deceased'. This excludes homosexual relationships.[10] It is noteworthy that the legislation uses the phrase 'as the husband or wife of the deceased' rather than 'as *if he or she were* the husband

4. Compare *Kourkgy v Lusher* (1981) 4 FLR 65; *Layton v Martin* [1986] 2 FLR 227; *Hill v Hill* [1997] 1 FLR 730. For one view of the plight of the discarded mistress, see the Working Paper of the Tasmanian Law Reform Commission, fn 8, p 92, *ante*.
5. In *Pounder v London Underground Ltd* [1995] PIQR P 217 it was held that brief separations between would not break the continuity of cohabitation. For three to four months during the requisite period of two years, the applicant was living in a women's refuge. However during this period the applicant suffered stress as a result of giving birth to a child who subsequently died, which might be treated in the same manner as a spell in hospital, and there was some evidence that the applicant returned to the home of the deceased during this period. The precise ratio of this case is obscure.
6. [1980] Ch 444, at 451D–453A, [1980] 1 All ER 266, at 271c–272d. See generally pp 92–93, *ante*.
7. Eg *Malone v Harrison* [1979] 1 WLR 1353.
8. Compare *Pounder v London Underground Ltd* [1995] PIQR P 217; *Jessop v Jessop* [1992] 1 FLR 591.
9. Compare *Adeoso v Adeoso* [1980] 1 WLR 1535, [1981] 1 All ER 107; *Hollens v Hollens* (1971) 115 Sol Jo 327; s 2(6) of the Matrimonial Causes Act 1973 on the definition of 'living apart' and the situation of persons while living in the same dwellinghouse living in separate households and hence being able to obtain divorces under s 1(2)(d), (e) of the Matrimonial Causes Act 1973 – *Santos v Santos* [1972] Fam 247, [1972] 2 All ER 246.
10. *Harrogate Borough Council v Simpson* (1984) 17 HLR 205; *Fitzpatrick v Sterling Housing Association Ltd* (1997) Times, 31 July; see further the answer of the Lord Chancellor to the question of Lord Meston QC – HL Parl Deb, Vol 561, col 511. Homosexuals may claim under s 1(1)(e), eg *Wayling v Jones* (1993) 69 P & CR 170, [1995] 2 FLR 1029.

and wife of the deceased' [11] and hence it may be arguable that cohabitation where the parties deliberately reject the attributes of marriage and seek to retain their status as unmarried people[12] is excluded. It has to be said that this is not the construction that has been adopted for the similarly worded Domestic Violence and Matrimonial Proceedings Act 1976[13] and the point has never been taken under any reported case under the Fatal Accidents Act 1976, where the courts merely look for cohabitation and do not require the parties to adopt the attributes of marriage.

Bankrupt Applicants

The right to make an application under the 1975 Act, like the right to apply for ancillary relief on divorce, does not vest in a trustee in bankruptcy[14] and accordingly the trustee in bankruptcy can not apply. The applicant can apply,[15] but any award (including an order for periodical payments[16]) may be claimed by the trustee as after-acquired property.[17] This factor makes it extremely unlikely that a court will exercise its discretion in favour of a bankrupt applicant.[18]

11. But see *Adeoso v Adeoso* [1980] 1 WLR 1535, at 1538H, [1981] 1 All ER 107, at 110d–e where Ormrod LJ said that s 1(2) of the Domestic Violence and Matrimonial Proceedings Act 1976 should be read '*as if* they were husband and wife'.
12. Compare *Helby v Rafferty* [1979] 1 WLR 13, [1978] 3 All ER 1016; *Rhodes v Dean* (28 March 1996, unreported), CA where Micklem J at first instance characterised the relationship of a man and mistress who while cohabiting retained several attributes as single people as 'far from the familiar situation of man and wife'; Freeman and Lyon, *Cohabitation Without Marriage*, 189–193, 198–200.
13. S 1(2).
14. See *Williams and Muir Hunter on Bankruptcy* (19th edn), pp 291–294.
15. See *Coffey v Bennett* [1961] VR 264.
16. Because an order under the 1975 Act takes effect as a variation of the will (as to which see Chapter 10, Part 1), an order for periodical payments takes effect as an annuity which is 'property' within s 307 of the Insolvency Act 1986 as opposed to 'income' within s 310 of the Insolvency Act 1986.
17. Under s 307 of the Insolvency Act 1986.
18. See *Davy-Chiesman v Davy-Chiesman* [1984] Fam 48, at 64D-F, 69B-C, [1984] 1 All ER 321, at 332g-h, 336c-d. These matters were discussed at some length at first instance in *Wayling v Jones* (1993) 69 P & CR 170, [1995] 2 FLR 1029, including a discussion as to whether the judge should adjourn the trial so as to await the discharge of the applicant from his bankruptcy (on this latter point, see *Re Crowley* [1949] QSR 189, which it is submitted would not be followed in England). On appeal the Court of Appeal did not find it necessary to determine the claim under the 1975 Act. For the position in Australasia, see DE GROOT AND NICKEL, paras 709, 204.13.

In *Re Abram*[19] the applicant while not bankrupt, was the subject of an Individual Voluntary Arrangement under the terms of which he undertook to apply the proceeds of his application towards his creditors. Judge Roger Cooke sitting as a judge of the Chancery Division held that it was not 'maintenance' to award a lump sum which would pay off the applicant's creditors, but instead settled a substantial sum of money upon protective trusts for the applicant.

Personal Representatives of an Applicant

Where the applicant predeceases the deceased no claim can be made.[20] The courts have held that by analogy with claims for ancillary relief, that claims under the 1975 Act do not survive the death of the applicant.[1] In so holding the courts have rejected an argument that because a spouse's claim under the 1975 Act is partially to correct an unjust matrimonial property regime, the spouse's claim is in the nature of a property right and hence should survive.[2]
Commonwealth jurisdictions differ as to whether a claim for family provision survives the death of the applicant,[3] but in those jurisdictions in which it has been held that it does survive provision has been generally limited to maintenance of the applicant before death.[4]

19. [1996] 2 FLR 379, at 396C–397C.
20. Compare *Re Cummins* [1972] Ch 62, [1971] 3 All ER 782.
1. *Whytte v Ticehurst* [1986] Fam 64, [1986] 2 All ER 158; *R v O* (1985) 16 Fam Law 58; *Re Bramwell* [1988] 2 FLR 263; *O'Reilly v Mallon*, Campbell J (10 March 1995, unreported).
2. *Whytte v Ticehurst* [1986] Fam 64, at 66D–70E, [1986] 2 All ER 158, at 160g-163e; *Re Bramwell* [1988] 2 FLR 263. But compare *Smith v Smith (Smith intervening)* [1992] Fam 69, [1991] 2 All ER 306 where in a *Barder v Caluori* situation the court allowed the deceased wife's estate to retain an award representing her 'property' entitlement, but removed from the deceased wife's estate her 'maintenance' entitlement.
3. A family provision claim has been held not to pass to the personal representatives in Alberta, *Re McMaster* (1957) 10 DLR (2d) 436; Ontario, *Re Kerley* [1949] OWN 187 (Co Ct), but compare *Re McCafferty* (1931) 4 DLR 930 (SC App Div); Saskatchewan, *Re Smith, Wetzel v National Trust Co Ltd* (1956) 4 DLR (2d) 171, CA; New South Wales, *McEvoy v Public Trustee* (1989) 16 NSWLR 92 at 100. A family provision claim has been held to pass to the personal representatives in British Columbia, *Barker v Westminster Trust* (1941) 4 DLR 514, CA; New Zealand, *Re Hawke* [1957] NZLR 152; *Re Shrimpton* [1962] NZLR 1000; South Australia, *In the Estate of Wardle* (1979) 22 SASR 139. See for an excellent discussion of this whole issue DE GROOT AND NICKEL, para 204.12.
4. See generally DE GROOT AND NICKEL, para 204.12 and their particularly useful Table 2.1.

It is submitted that the principles of *Barder v Caluori*[5] apply to appeals in family provision cases where one party dies after the original order.

Homicidal Applicants

A rule of public policy, which has come to be known as 'the forfeiture rule' prevents any person who unlawfully kills another from taking a benefit from his victim's estate.[6] It has been held by the Court of Appeal that this rule applies to family provision and hence a person who unlawfully kills the deceased can not apply under the 1975 Act.[7]

The operation of the forfeiture rule was limited by the Forfeiture Act 1982,[8] a piece of legislation described by a supporter of its aims as legislation 'which its sponsors never expected to see enacted, and which was undeniably technically defective in many ways'.[9] This Act, which is retrospective,[10] abolishes the forfeiture rule for claims

5. [1988] AC 20, [1987] 2 All ER 440. In *O'Reilly v Mallon*, Campbell J (10 March 1995, unreported) it was held that where an applicant died after an interim order had been made in her favour payments due before death but unpaid at the date of death were payable to the applicant's personal representatives.
6. On the general principle that prohibits a person who unlawfully kills another from benefiting by such killing, see Youdan, 'Acquisition of Property by Killing', (1973) 89 LQR 235. On the extent of the forfeiture rule, see *Re Giles* [1972] Ch 544, [1971] 3 All ER 1141; *Re Royse* [1985] Ch 22, [1984] 3 All ER 339; *Re K* [1985] Ch 85, [1985] 1 All ER 403; *Re H* [1990] 1 FLR 441; *Jones v Roberts* [1995] 2 FLR 422, not following *Re H*. For the operation of the forfeiture rule in relation to endowment policies on the joint lives of the deceased and the killer, see *Davitt v Titcumb* [1990] Ch 110, [1989] 3 All ER 417.
7. *Re Royse* [1985] Ch 22, [1984] 3 All ER 339.
8. On the Act generally, see Cretney, 'The Forfeiture Act 1982:the Private Member's Bill as an Instrument of Law Reform', (1990) 10 Ox J Leg Studies 289. For cases under the Forfeiture Act 1982, see *Re K* [1985] Ch 85, [1985] 1 All ER 403; affd [1986] Ch 180, [1985] 2 All ER 833; *Social Security Decision No R(P) 1/88*; *Re H* [1990] 1 FLR 441; *Re S (forfeiture rule)* [1996] 1 FLR 910; *Re Dunbar* Times, 24/7/97. See also the divorce case of *M v M* (1981) 11 Fam Law 118.
9. Cretney, *op cit*, at 290.
10. S 7(3); *Re K* [1985] Ch 85, [1985] 1 All ER 403, affd[1986] Ch 180, [1985] 2 All ER 833.

under the 1975 Act[11] except where the applicant '*stands convicted* of murder'.[12]

11. S 3. The members of the Court of Appeal in *Re Royse* gave two reasons why the application was bound to fail, firstly public policy ([1985] Ch 27H–28C, 29H-30E; [1984] 3 All ER 342b–e, 343g–344b) and secondly that s 2(1) only applied where the dispositions of the deceased's estate effected by his will or the rules of intestacy failed to make reasonable provision for the applicant and that the section could not be read as 'the dispositions of the deceased's estate effected by the rule of public policy'([1985] Ch 27D–H, 30G–31B; [1984] 3 All ER 341g–342b, 344d-g). In *Re Royse* the applicant was the sole beneficiary under the will of the deceased and solely entitled under the rules of intestacy. Both Ackner LJ ([1985] Ch 29C, [1984] 3 All ER 343b–c) and Slade LJ ([1985] Ch 31E-F, [1984] 3 All ER 344j-345a) were of the opinion that s 3 of the Forfeiture Act 1982 did not alter this second reason. (This was accepted by Vinelott J in *Re K* [1985] Ch 85, at 101E-F, [1985] 1 All ER 403, at 415f-g.) This has the effect that a person who was solely entitled under the deceased's will or the rules of intestacy, but who loses his interest under the rules of intestacy, must firstly apply under s 2 of the Forfeiture Act 1982, which has a strict limitation period of three months from the date of conviction (s 2(3)), and then if necessary under the 1975 Act, which has a discretionary time limit of six months from the grant of representation. Thus a homicidal applicant who has no or very little benefit under the will or intestacy of the deceased is placed in a more favourable position than one who has a substantial benefit under the will or intestacy of the deceased. However, in *Re K* [1985] Ch 85, at 101G, [1985] 1 All ER 403, at 415g-h Vinelott J stated that an applicant under s 2 of the Forfeiture Act 1982 would be placed in no worse a position than if she had applied under the 1975 Act. When the case went to the Court of Appeal, Ackner LJ stated that the discretion under s 2 of the Forfeiture Act 1982 was more generous to an applicant than the discretion under the 1975 Act, since the former was not limited by questions of 'need' or in the case of a spouse by a comparison of the provision which would be made on divorce ([1986] Ch 180, at 194F–195B, [1985] 2 All ER 833, at 842f–843a).
12. S 5.

Chapter 5

REASONABLE PROVISION

The 1975 Act is a Continuation of the Legislation it Replaced

The Inheritance (Provision for Family and Dependants) Act 1975 is to be construed in the same manner as the Inheritance (Family Provision) Act 1938 and section 26 of the Matrimonial Causes Act 1965 which it repealed, except where an express change in the statutory provisions has been made, but having due regard to changes in society and other legislation. Consequentially much of the case law on and many of the concepts used in the repealed legislation can be used to interpret the 1975 Act.

In some of the first cases to come to court after the enactment of the 1975 Act it was argued that the previous case law was irrelevant and that the provisions of the 1975 Act had to be considered afresh. This argument was based principally upon the wording of the long title of the statute, which refers to 'An Act to make *fresh* provision for empowering the court ...'[1] It appears to have been accepted by Mr Vivian Price QC sitting as a deputy judge of the High Court in *Re Christie*[2] that the 1975 Act was a totally different piece of legislation from the 1938 Act.

However, this argument was rejected by Oliver J, himself an editor of a book on the 1938 Act,[3] in *Re Coventry*. He stated, that while:

> ... one of the purposes ... was to make 'fresh provision' in the sense that [the 1975 Act] broadened the class of those who could make application for an order and widened the ambit of applications by spouses, ... it was nevertheless in continuation of the previous legislation which it repealed and, except to the extent which, in terms, it goes beyond such previous legislation, it may be construed and applied in the same way.[4]

1. Emphasis added.
2. [1979] Ch 168, [1979] 1 All ER 546, in particular the argument of Mr Gerrey at [1979] Ch 170B. For further discussion of *Re Christie* see pp 47–48, *ante*.
3. Oliver J was the editor of the second edition of Tillard, *Family Inheritance* (1950).
4. [1980] Ch 461, at 472D–E, [1979] 2 All ER 408, at 416a-c. For dicta to the same effect see *Re Leach* [1984] FLR 590, at 600B-D; *Moody v Stevenson* [1992] Ch 486, at 492D-E, 502F, [1992] 2 All ER 524, at 528e-g, 537b; *Re Abram* [1996] 2 FLR 379, at 387D-388H; *Re Krubert* [1997] Ch 97, at 104G–H.

On appeal in *Re Coventry* the point was argued again,[5] and the Court of Appeal expressly affirmed Oliver J's views.[6] This position is supported by the Working Paper and Report of the Law Commission which both regarded the existing law as a structure on which to build – indeed the Working Paper described the then existing system of family provision as a 'known and tried procedure'.[7]

While the case law on the 1938 Act and section 26 of the Matrimonial Causes Act 1973 is highly relevant to the interpretation of the 1975 Act, some caution must be adopted with some of the older authorities. The changes in social attitudes towards and in the law governing marriage since 1938 make some of the older authorities on claims by spouses suspect. The growing equality of the sexes since 1938 means that widowers will now be more favourably treated than in the past and adult unmarried daughters less favourably. Most of the decisions on the quantum of provision prior to 1966 are of strictly limited value, since until the Family Provision Act 1966 the question of the quantum of provision was dominated by the statutory restrictions on the amount of provision. The matter was summed up by Waite J in *Moody v Stevenson*:

> While it may be technically correct, as suggested in *Re Coventry*, that cases decided under the 1938 Act represent a continuing body of case law capable of affording guidance to the exercise of the court's powers under the Act of 1975, the earlier authorities should be approached with caution because of the substantial changes which have occurred in the legislation itself. That is particularly true of claims where a surviving spouse is involved, because of the radical changes introduced in that context by the Act of 1975. Certainly *Re Styler*[8] should now be treated in our judgment as a decision which, though doubtless correct on its facts under the law as it then stood, gives rise to no principle of law relevant to the jurisdiction under the Act of 1975.[9]

Jurisdiction of the Court

If it is satisfied that the dispositions of the deceased's estate effected by his will[10] or the law relating to intestacy or the combination of his will and that law is not such as to make reasonable provision for

5. [1980] Ch 480G–H.
6. [1980] Ch 487B–E, [1979] 3 All ER 821e-g (per Goff LJ).
7. Para 3.7.
8. *Re Styler* [1942] Ch 387, [1942] 2 All ER 201 was an application by a widower.
9. [1992] Ch 486, at 502F-H, [1992] 2 All ER 524, at 537b-d.
10. 'Will' includes codicil, s 25(1).

the applicant, the court may make a variety of orders for financial provision to be made out of the net estate of the deceased in favour of the applicant.[11] To guide the court in the exercise of its powers the Act provides that it is to have regard to the following matters:

(a) the financial resources and financial needs which the applicant has or is likely to have in the foreseeable future;
(b) the financial resources and financial needs which any other applicant for an order under section 2 of this Act has or is likely to have in the foreseeable future;
(c) the financial resources and financial needs which any beneficiary of the estate of the deceased has or is likely to have in the foreseeable future;
(d) any obligations and responsibilities which the deceased had toward any applicant for an order under the said section 2 or towards any beneficiary of the estate of the deceased;
(e) the size and nature of the net estate of the deceased;
(f) any physical or mental disability of any applicant for an order under section 2 or any beneficiary of the estate of the deceased;
(g) any other matter, including the conduct of the applicant or any person, which in the circumstances of the case the court may consider relevant.[12]

Additional guidelines are provided for applications by spouses,[13] children,[14] children of the family,[15] persons being maintained by the deceased prior to death[16] and cohabitees[17] respectively. These guidelines are based upon the guidelines prescribed in section 25 of the Matrimonial Causes Act 1973 to guide the exercise of the court's powers as to maintenance and property rights upon divorce.[18] Like the guidelines in section 25 of the Matrimonial Causes Act 1973, they are of only limited use in assessing whether an applicant is entitled to an order for financial provision.[19] It is greatly to be regretted that the Law Commission did not set out expressly the

11. S 2(1).
12. S 3(1).
13. S 3(2).
14. S 3(3).
15. S 3(3)(a), (b), (c). For discussion of these guidelines see pp 76–77, *ante*.
16. S 3(4). For discussion of s 3(4) see pp 94–100, *ante* and pp 275–280, *post*.
17. S 3(2A) inserted by s 2(3) of the Law Reform (Succession) Act 1995. For discussion of s 3(2A) see pp 290–291, *post*.
18. WORKING PAPER, paras 3.16–3.21; LAW COM, paras 32–34.
19. See *Wachtel v Wachtel* [1973] Fam 72, [1973] 1 All ER 829, where the Court of Appeal found that the guidelines in the Matrimonial Causes Act 1973, s 25(1), were substantially irrelevant to the major principles upon which the Court was to exercise its powers.

principles to be applied by the courts in administering the Act rather than merely setting out a list of guidelines with no priorities mentioned.

The Nature of the Discretion

The jurisdiction under the Act is one which is not easy to administer.[20] Lord Wilberforce's extra-judicial remarks in the House of Lords on the difficulties of administering the jurisdiction have already been cited.[1] Further discussion of the difficulties of the court's discretion is contained in the remarks of Uthwatt J in *Re Catmull*, where he said:

> The court, of course, has a discretion in this class of case, and a judicial discretion. In exercising any judicial discretion the court is bound so far as possible to get rid of its personal views, and to give effect to an informed impersonal outlook on the problem presented to it by the Act and the facts of the case. That is the ideal which one seeks to achieve but, unfortunately, no person can see any problem except through his own spectacles and it is difficult – and to my mind impossible – for a judge in exercising his discretion to get rid of his personal views in these matters, and perhaps equally difficult to state the way in which the varying considerations have influenced his discretion.[2]

In *Re Coventry* Buckley LJ described the judge's role as 'a qualitative decision or what is sometimes called a "value judgment" '.[3]

The jurisdiction is only a limited jurisdiction and is to be exercised carefully,[4] but as the principles upon which the courts act have become clearer and Parliament has endorsed the principle of family provision by enlarging the jurisdiction, it has been exercised in a slightly less cautious manner than previously.[5]

20. *Re Joslin* [1941] Ch 200, at 203, [1941] 1 All ER 302, at 305A (per Farwell J); *Re Goodwin* [1969] 1 Ch 283, at 291, [1968] 3 All ER 12, at 16H (per Megarry J).
1. 358 HL Parl Deb, col 933, set out at p 29, *ante*.
2. [1943] Ch 262 at 268, [1943] 2 All ER 115, at 119B–C.
3. [1980] Ch 461, at 495H, [1979] 3 All ER 815, at 828e.
4. *Re Inns* [1947] Ch 576, at 586, [1947] 2 All ER 308, at 311C (per Wynn-Parry J); *Re Andrews* [1955] 1 WLR 1105, at 1106, [1955] 3 All ER 248, at 249 (per Wynn-Parry J); *Re Brown* (1955) 105 L Jo 169, 219 LT Jo 129 (per Wynn-Parry J); *Re E* [1966] 1 WLR 709, at 716, [1966] 2 All ER 44, at 48 (per Stamp J); *Re Gregory* [1970] 1 WLR 1455, at 1458F, [1971] 1 All ER 497, at 499B–C (per Harman LJ).
5. *Re Brown* (1995) 105 L Jo 169, 219 LT Jo 129 (per Wynn-Parry J); *Re Gregory* [1970] 1 WLR 1455, at 1458F, [1971] 1 All ER 497, at 499B–C (per Harman J).

The jurisdiction is essentially a power of review. The court can only interfere with the dispositions of the deceased's will or intestacy if they fail to make 'reasonable provision' for the applicant and any alteration will be for that end only. The court does not have a licence to rewrite the dispositions of the deceased's estate as it thinks fit.[6] A Judge cannot make an order merely because he thinks that he would have been inclined, if he had been in the position of the deceased, to make provision for the applicant.[7]

No Duty to Make Provision

In *Dillon v Public Trustee of New Zealand*[8] Viscount Simon L C stated that:

> The statute[9] does not impose any duty to frame a will in any particular way, and the testator did not fail to observe any statutory obligation by making his will as he did. What the statute does is to confer on the court a discretionary jurisdiction to override what would otherwise be the operation of a will by ordering that additional provision should be made for certain relatives out of the testator's estate, notwithstanding the provisions which the will actually contains.[10]

This statement has two meanings. Firstly, it is a technical, but unhelpful, description of the operation of family provision legislation. Secondly, it emphasises that an applicant has no prima facie right to provision and that there is no presumption that an

6. *Re Coventry* [1980] Ch 461, at 474G–475C, [1979] 2 All ER 408, at 417j-418c (per Oliver J); at [1980] Ch 486F, [1979] 3 All ER 815, at 821a-b (per Goff LJ); *Brill v Proud* [1984] Fam Law 59, at 60 (per Arnold P); *Re Leach* [1984] FLR 590, at 601A-G (per Mr Michael Wheeler QC); *Jessop v Jessop* [1992] 1 FLR 591, at 598H-599A; *Davis v Davis* [1993] 1 FLR 54, at 59H (per Brown P); *Cameron v Treasury Solicitor* [1996] 2 FLR 716, at 720D-G; *Re Krubert* [1997] Ch 97, at 104G-105C (per Nourse LJ) .
7. *Re Styler* [1942] Ch 387, at 389, [1942] 2 All ER 201, at 204C-D (per Morton J); *Re Pugh* [1943] Ch 387, at 395, [1943] 2 All ER 361, at 365C-D (per Morton J); *Re Inns* [1947] Ch 576, at 586, [1947] 2 All ER 308, at 311C (per Wynn-Parry J); *Re E* [1966] 1 WLR 709, at 714E–F, [1966] 2 All ER 44, at 47G–H (per Stamp J); *Re Ducksbury* [1966] 1 WLR 1226, at 1233G, [1966] 2 All ER 374, at 380D (per Buckley J); *Re Coventry* [1980] Ch 461, at 475A, [1979] 2 All ER 408, at 420f (per Oliver J).
8. [1941] AC 294, at 301, [1941] 2 All ER 284, at 287C-D.
9. The statute referred to is the Family Protection Act 1908 of New Zealand, but it is submitted that Viscount Simon LC's remarks are of general application.
10. *Ad idem Re Brownbridge* (1942) 193 LT Jo 185 (per Bennett J).

applicant who has been omitted from sharing in the deceased's estate under his will or intestacy is entitled to relief.

The Burden of Proof

It is uncertain whether there is any technical burden of proof upon an applicant, but there is a clear onus upon any applicant to show that the operation of the deceased's will or intestacy has given him inadequate provision. In *Re Ducksbury*,[11] a case on the 1938 Act, Buckley J said:

> Mr Sparrow, appearing on behalf of the Plaintiff, has submitted that ... the various classes of dependants ... [have] a prima facie right to be maintained or to be provided for under the will of a deceased person, and that the burden is thrown upon the defendant to show that in fact it was reasonable for the deceased to make no more provision for the plaintiff than in fact he has made. I do not feel at all able to accept that view. It seems to me that the section does not put the burden of proof one way or another. It is for the court to decide upon such evidence as it has before it, whether or not the testator has made reasonable provision for the maintenance of the applicant, and I do not think that the court should start with a leaning one way or another in favour of the view or against the view that the testator owed some sort of moral duty to provide for any particular applicant.

Although in two cases[12] under section 26 of the Matrimonial Causes Act 1965 which used the expression 'if the court is satisfied'[13] rather than the expression 'if the court is of opinion' which is used in the 1938 Act[14] it was held that the burden of proof is upon the applicant, and although the 1975 Act adopts the wording 'if it is satisfied'[15] and although Australasian authority puts the burden of proof on the applicant,[16] Oliver J in *Re Coventry*[17] expressly approved the

11. [1966] 1 WLR 1226, at 1230E–H, [1966] 2 All ER 374, at 378C–D.
12. *Re Talbot* [1962] 1 WLR 1113, at 1118, [1966] 2 All ER 174, at 177G (per Baker J); *Re Harker-Thomas* [1969] P 28, at 30E–F (per Latey J).
13. S 26(2).
14. S 1(1).
15. S 2(1).
16. *Re Green* [1951] NZLR 135, at 141 (per Gresson J); DICKEY, 81.
17. [1980] Ch 461, at 474E–F, [1979] 2 All ER 408, at 417h. In *Tabbenor v Shaw*, Court of Appeal, Thorpe LJ stated that applications under the 1975 Act were inquisitorial rather than adversarial and relied upon their supposed origin in divorce jurisdiction.This fails to take into account that applications under the 1975 Act are governed by RSC Ord 99 and CCR Ord 48 and not by the Family

statement of Buckley J in relation to the 1975 Act. Whether or not there is a burden of proof upon an applicant, it is however clear that there is an evidential burden upon the applicant to show that the provision awarded to him is unreasonable[18] and that there is no presumption in favour of provision being awarded to any particular applicant.

Must be Unreasonable not to Make Provision

The court only has jurisdiction to make an order for financial provision out of the deceased's net estate if the court is satisfied that the disposition of the deceased's estate effected by his will or the law relating to intestacy is not such as to make reasonable financial provision for the applicant.[19] In each case it is not sufficient for the applicant to show that he is in need of maintenance and that there are available assets in the estate, it must be further shown that it is reasonable for the applicant to have a share of those assets. In *Re Coventry* Oliver J stated:

> It cannot be enough to say 'here is a son of the deceased; he is in necessitous circumstances; there is property of the deceased which could be made available to assist him, but which is not available if the deceased's dispositions stand; therefore those dispositions do not make reasonable provision for the applicant.' There must, as it seems to me, be established some sort of moral claim by the applicant to be maintained by the deceased or at the expense of his estate beyond the mere fact of a blood relationship, some reason it can be said that, in the circumstances, it is unreasonable that no or no greater provision was made.[20]

Proceedings Rules. The decision in *Tabbenor v Shaw* was undoubtedly correct on the facts, since the refusal to allow the late exchange of Witness Statements was extremely unjust and the decision in *Beachley Property Ltd v Edgar* (1996) Times, 18 July is to be narrowly construed.

18. While *Re Coventry* is the only authority under the 1975 Act expressly to address the question of the burden of proof, several judges have used language which at the very least puts an evidential burden upon an applicant, see *Re Crawford* (1982) 4 FLR 273, at 278D ('must establish') (per Eastham J); *Williams v Roberts* [1986] 1 FLR 349, at 354C-D ('must satisfy me, the burden being upon her')(per Wood J); *Davis v Davis* [1993] 1 FLR 54, at 61E ('cross the threshold')(Thorpe J); *Re Abram* [1996] 2 FLR 379, at 390D ('must therefore establish')(per Roger Cooke J); *Cameron v Treasury Solicitor* [1996] 2 FLR 716, at 721G ('must satisfy')(per Peter Gibson LJ).
19. S 2(1).
20. [1980] Ch 461, at 475C–E; [1979] 2 All ER 408, at 418e-f. See also *Re Abram* [1996] 2 FLR 379, at 390C, 391C (per Roger Cooke J).

In *Cameron v Treasury Solicitor*[1] the Court of Appeal stressed that the mere fact that the competing beneficiary had no possible moral or legal claim upon the deceased did not of itself make it unreasonable that the applicant received no benefit under the will or intestacy of the deceased.

The Meaning of Reasonableness

Reasonableness in English law means a wide ranging principled discretion which takes into account all the circumstances of the case. However, as a guide to how the courts behave the mere test of 'reasonableness' is of little value unless the principles which guide the discretion are known.[2] A useful insight into the nature of reasonableness is contained in some remarks of Buckley and Goff LJJ in *Re Coventry*[3] who described the type of decision which the court has to make as 'a qualitative decision, or what is sometimes called a "value judgment"'. This was elaborated upon by Hoffmann LJ in *Re Grayan Ltd* where it was stated that such a judgment was not a matter of pure discretion but involved the ranking of various matters[4] and emphasised the wide extent of the matters to be taken into consideration.[5]

Likewise Ormrod LJ in *Re Fullard*[6] said:

> It is impossible to answer the question, 'Is the provision reasonable or alternatively is it reasonable to make no provision?' without considering what 'ought' to have been done for the applicant. Once one introduces the word 'ought,' one inevitably introduces in some way or other some moral question.

1. [1996] 2 FLR 716, at 720F–G.
2. Compare the remarks of Roxburgh J in *Re Pearson-Gregory* (1957) Times, 10 October that 'reasonableness as a standard was never regarded as being void for uncertainty, it was a standard for which all material facts had to be regarded'. See further the remarks of Lord Wilberforce cited at p 29, *ante*.
3. [1980] Ch 461, at 487A–B, [1979] 3 All ER 815, at 821d (per Goff LJ), at [1980] Ch 495H, [1979] 3 All ER 828d-e (per Buckley LJ). These remarks have been cited with approval in many authorities, see per Brandon LJ in *Re Portt* (25 March 1980, unreported), CA; *Williams v Johns* [1988] 2 FLR 488H-489B; *Moody v Stevenson* [1992] Ch 486, at 498B, [1992] 2 All ER 524, at 533e; *Davis v Davis* [1993] 1 FLR 54, at 60D-F; *Re Abram* [1996] 2 FLR 379, at 390D.
4. [1995] Ch 241, at 254G-255F, particularly at 255A-B citing with approval the speech of Lord Bridge of Harwich in *George Mitchell (Chesterhall) Ltd v Finney Lock Seeds Ltd* [1983] 2 AC 803, at 815H, [1983]2 All ER 737, at 743e. See also *Davis v Davis* [1993] 1 FLR 54, at 61C-D.
5. [1995] Ch 241, at 254G-255F, particularly at 255E-F.
6. [1982] Fam 42, at 47D–E, [1981] 2 All ER 796, at 800c. The punctuation in the report has been altered.

The case law on the earlier legislation demonstrates that reasonableness is essentially concerned with justice between private persons, with what is ethically, morally or legally *just* between the deceased and the applicant, rather than relieving the State of the burden of supporting applicants.[7]

The Moral Duty Test

As has been previously noted[8] Australasian courts have adopted the 'moral duty' test as the guiding test for the exercise of the court's discretion. The classic statement of the principle is contained in the judgment of Salmond J in *Allen v Manchester*:[9]

> The Act is on the contrary [not to extend the provisions of the Destitute Persons Act[10] after death, but is] designed to enforce the moral obligation of a testator to use his testamentary powers for the purpose of making *proper and adequate* provision after his death for the support of his wife and children having regard to his means, to the means and deserts of the several claimants and to the relative urgency of the various moral claims upon his bounty. The provision which the court may properly make in default of testamentary provision is that which a just and *wise* father would have thought it his moral duty to make in the interests of his widow and children had he been fully aware of all the relevant circumstances.[11]

A more restrictive analysis had been adopted by Edwards J concurring in the New Zealand Court of Appeal in *Re Allardice*[12] who stated that the court could only intervene when:

> … the testator has been guilty of a manifest breach of that moral duty which a just, *but not a loving*,[13] husband or father owes towards his wife or towards his children.

7. Eg see *Re Andrews* [1955] 1 WLR 1105, [1955] 3 All ER 248 where an application by a person in receipt of National Assistance was dismissed and *Re Canderton* (1970) 114 Sol Jo 208 where the order was deliberately drawn so as not to reduce the applicant's social security. For the court's attitude to state benefits generally, see pp 144–146, *post*.
8. See pp 8–9, *ante*.
9. *Re Allen, Allen v Manchester* (1922) 41 NZLR 218, at 220 approved by Lord Romer in *Bosch v Perpetual Trustee Co Ltd* [1938] AC 463, at 479, [1938] 2 All ER 14, at 21A-E.
10. For the Destitute Persons Act, see p 7, *ante*.
11. Emphasis added.
12. (1910) 29 NZLR 959, at 973. For the current status of the 'moral duty' test in Australasian law, see DICKEY, 73-83.
13. Emphasis added.

The moral duty test has been approved by the Privy Council twice,[14] but has never been expressly adopted in England and Wales as the main test to govern the court's discretion. However, the test of moral duty has been mentioned by the courts throughout the history of the 1938 Act, section 26 of the Matrimonial Causes Act 1965 and the 1975 Act[15] although without the reference to a 'wise' testator and without the contrast to lifetime duties of support as set out in the judgment of Salmond J in *Allen v Manchester*.

In *Re Coventry*[16] it was argued before the Court of Appeal that the test of 'moral obligation' used by Oliver J at first instance[17] to reject the applicant's claim was an erroneous gloss upon the statute. Goff LJ rejected this criticism, saying:

> Oliver J nowhere said that a moral obligation was a prerequisite of an application under s 1(1)(c); nor did he mean any such thing. It is true that he said a moral obligation was required, but in my view that was on the facts of this particular case, because he found nothing else sufficient to produce unreasonableness.[18]

It is suggested that this approach of regarding moral duty as in some cases a component of reasonableness (rather than a gloss upon or substitute for) is both correct in policy terms and as a piece of statutory interpretation.[19] Section 3(1)(d) enjoins the court to take into account 'any obligations and responsibilities which the deceased

14. *Allardice v Allardice* [1911] AC 730, 734 approving the general approach of the New Zealand Court of Appeal; *Bosch v Perpetual Trustee Co Ltd* [1938] AC 463, [1938] 2 All ER 14, where Lord Romer said at [1938] AC 478–479; [1938] 2 All ER 21G–H – 'Their Lordships agree that in every case the court must place itself in the position of the testator and consider what he ought to have done in all the circumstances of the case, treating the testator for that purpose as a wise and just, rather than a fond and foolish, husband or father.'
15. Eg *Re Andrews* [1955] 1 WLR 1105, at 1107, [1955] 2 All ER 248, at 49I–250A (per Wynn-Parry J); *Re Ducksbury* [1966] 1 WLR 1226, at 1230H, [1966] 2 All ER 374, at 378D–E (per Buckley LJ); *Re Coventry* [1980] Ch 461, at 475D–E, [1979] 2 All ER 408, at 418e-f (per Oliver J); *Re Fullard* [1982] Fam 42, at 47E, [1981] 2 All ER 796, at 802g (per Ormrod LJ) and see Megarry, Note, (1955) 72 LQR 18; Guest, 'Family Provision and the Legitima Portio' (1957) 73 LQR 74, 85–87.
16. [1980] Ch 479H, at 480F–G.
17. [1980] Ch 475D–G, [1979] 2 All ER 418e-h.
18. [1980] Ch 487G–H, [1979] 3 All ER 821j-h, approved by Buckley LJ at [1980] Ch 495G, [1979] 3 All ER 828d , by Ormrod LJ in *Re Fullard* [1982] Fam 42, at 47E, [1981] 2 All ER 796, at 800a-b and by Butler-Sloss and Peter Gibson LJJ in *Cameron v Treasury Solicitor* [1996] 2 FLR 716, at 720A-B, 721H-722C.
19. Ie a different approach from the traditional Australasian analysis, as set out in the extracts from *Re Allardice* and *Allen v Manchester*, see further DICKEY, 73-83. The statement of Carswell J in *Re Creeney* [1984] NI 397, at 405A–B that 'moral claim' was a 'convenient shorthand' for reasonableness is wrong.

had towards any applicant ... or towards any beneficiary of the estate ...' and it is clear that the subsection refers to moral as well as legal duties.[20] It has been specifically held that a 'moral duty' or 'moral claim' cannot exist without a 'moral obligation' under section 3(1)(d).[1] To be relevant any 'moral obligation' must be subsisting at the death of the deceased.[2]

English law now treats a 'moral claim' or 'moral obligation' as merely being one of the matters to be considered within section 3(1)(d) and 'moral duty' (with or without the prosaic descriptions of the testamentary duties of a Victorian paterfamilias set out above) no longer forms part of the reasoning process of a court in administering the 1975 Act. Further discussion of 'moral obligation' is generally limited to cases of adult children[3] and weak claims by former spouses[4] and is not found when dealing with other classes of applicant, where the courts employ other aids. Even in these cases the 'moral obligation' test is not particularly helpful since there is no necessary agreement on what constitutes a 'moral obligation'.[5] Indeed the term in claims by adult children is being replaced by 'special circumstances'.[6]

Two Stage Approach

The 1975 Act requires the court to approach an application in two stages.

20. Eg *Re Fullard* [1982] Fam 42, at 50E–F, [1981] 2 All ER 796, at 802 (per Ormrod LJ) .
1. *Cameron v Treasury Solicitor* [1996] 2 FLR 716, at 719E–720B, 722D.
2. *Re Jennings* [1994] Ch 286, at 296B-E, 300E-G, 302C-G, [1994] 3 All ER 27, at 34d-h, 38g-39a, 40d-j.
3. Eg *Re Coventry*; *Re Jennings*.
4. Eg *Re Fullard*; *Cameron v Treasury Solicitor*.
5. The Australasian courts (eg *Re Allardice*; *Hughes v National Trustee* (1979) 143 CLR 134) and some Canadian courts use the 'moral duty' test as justifying provision for adult children, whereas the English courts use the test as a reason for not awarding provision. When English (and Northern Irish) judges have found a 'moral claim', generally their decisions have been highly controversial, see *Re McGarrell* [1983]8 NIJB (Hutton J); *Re Debenham* [1986] 1 FLR 404, at 409E (Ewbank J); *Goodchild v Goodchild* [1996] 1 WLR 694, at 714D-F, [1996] 1 All ER 670, at 689e-g (Carnwath J); affd [1997] 3 All ER 63, at 73f-g (Leggatt LJ- a remarkably wide and, it is submitted, wrong statement); *Re Abram* [1996] 2 FLR 379, at 390D-E (Roger Cooke J).
6. *Re Abram* [1996] 2 FLR 379, at 390D-E. The phrase would appear to be derived from *Re Coventry* and from the legislation which allows adult children to be maintained by their parents during their lifetime, see s 29(3) of the Matrimonial Causes Act 1973, para 3(2)(b), Sch 1 of the Children Act 1989.

Firstly, the court has to be satisfied that the dispositions of the deceased's estate fail to make reasonable provision for the applicant.[7] Secondly, if that question is answered in the affirmative, the court has to decide whether and to what extent it should exercise its powers to order financial provision.[8] The matters set out in section 3 to which the court is to have regard are relevant at both stages.[9] The two-stage approach has been adopted by the courts.[10] In *Re Coventry* Goff LJ distinguished the two questions thus:

> The second part of that composite problem is clearly a question of discretion, but I think the first is not. It is a question of fact but it is a value judgment, or a qualitative decision, which I think ought not to be interfered with by us unless we are satisfied that it is plainly wrong.[11]

While the two-stage approach is enjoined upon the courts by the wording of the Act, it is doubtful whether it serves any useful purpose. The same factors, such as competing claims upon the testator, are taken into account at both stages.[12] Apart from matters peculiarly affecting the quantum and form of financial provision, it is difficult to visualise matters which might affect the court in considering one question but not the other. Furthermore it is difficult to contemplate a court answering the first question in the affirmative but not awarding any provision, except perhaps in cases of conduct unrelated to the deceased occurring after the death of the deceased, such as the applicant physically assaulting a beneficiary of the estate[13] or the applicant committing perjury at the hearing.[14]

7. S 2(1).
8. S 3(1).
9. S 3(1).
10. *Sivyer v Sivyer* [1967] 1 WLR 1482, at 1486–1487, [1967] 3 All ER 429, at 432D–G (per Pennycuick J); *Re Coventry* [1980] Ch 461, at 469G–H, [1979] 2 All ER 408, at 413j (per Oliver J), at [1980] Ch 486G–487B, [1979] 3 All ER 815, at 821b-d (per Goff LJ), at [1980] Ch 492D–E, [1979] 3 All ER 825f-g (per Geoffrey Lane LJ). Reference to the two-stage approach is now *de rigeur* in judgments and citation of authorities setting out the two-stage approach is otiose.
11. [1980] Ch 487A–B, [1979] 3 All ER 821d.
12. By way of example the competing claims upon the testator were taken into account in answering the first question in *Re Joslin* [1941] Ch 200, at 202, [1941] 1 All ER 302, at 304A–H; *Re Talbot* [1962] 1 WLR 1113, at 1118, [1962] 3 All ER 174, at 1771–178B; *Re Bellman* [1963] P 239, at 244–245, [1963] 1 All ER 513, at 517B-518A; *Re E* [1966] 1 WLR 709, at 714E–F, [1966] 2 All ER 44, at 47G–H; *Re Coventry* [1980] Ch 461, at 477E–G, [1979] 2 All ER 408, at 419j-420e.
13. Compare *Jones v Jones* [1976] Fam 8, [1975] 2 All ER 12.
14. Compare *Yelland v Taylor* [1957] 1 WLR 459, [1957] 1 All ER 627. The current practice on ancillary relief is that misrepresentation of assets will not affect the substantive order for provision, but will be reflected in the order for costs, see

It has been suggested by two writers[15] that before the court has jurisdiction to order provision it must be satisfied that the existing provision for the applicant is *unreasonable*, but once it is so satisfied it can award *reasonable* provision, which may exceed the threshold of reasonableness. Accordingly, an applicant who has been treated very badly by the deceased's dispositions will be awarded provision which may exceed the provision given to a similarly placed beneficiary who has been badly treated by the deceased's dispositions, but not so badly treated that the dispositions can be regarded as unreasonable. While this anomaly theoretically exists, it is doubtful whether the courts will administer the jurisdiction so as to produce such striking anomalies which might be regarded as unjust.[16]

Objective or Subjective Test of Reasonableness?[17]

Until 1972 there was a conflict under both the 1938 Act and Matrimonial Causes Act 1965 as to whether the test of reasonableness was subjective, ie if an award is to be made the court has to find that the testator acted unreasonably, or objective, ie an award will be made however the testator acted if in the event the provision is unreasonable in all the circumstances. An objective test was expounded by Megarry J in *Re Goodwin*[18] in the following way:

P v P (financial relief: non-disclosure) [1994] 2 FLR 381; *T v T (interception of documents)* [1994] 2 FLR 1083, both not following *B v B* [1988] 2 FLR 490. In *Re Haig*, Browne-Wilkinson J [1979] LS Gaz R 476; *Re McGarrell* [1983] 8 NIJB and *McGuigan v McGuigan*, Kerr J (25 March 1996, unreported) the applicants were found to have been less than frank in giving evidence, but this did not affect the substantive award. And see *Jelley v Iliffe* [1981] Fam 128, at 140D–E, [1981] 2 All ER 29, at 37j-38a (per Stephenson LJ) on the relevance of post death vacillation by the applicant.

15. ALBERY, 8–10; Guest, 'Family Provision and the Legitima Portio', (1957) 73 LQR 74, 83–84; see also first edition, p 49.
16. It is noteworthy that neither author is able to cite any authority *directly* supporting their proposition. Furthermore every applicant for family provision who commences proceedings may be at risk in terms of costs. Such liability may be an effective way of equalising the positions of a person who is likely to be awarded provision and a person whose provision would be regarded as adequate by the courts.
17. The text in the second edition from pp 125–128 was referred to with approval by Waite J in *Moody v Stevenson* [1992] Ch 486, at 494A, [1992] 2 All ER 524, at 530f.
18. [1969] 1 Ch 283, at 287F–288C, [1968] 3 All ER 12, at 15A-C.

> The statutory language [in section 1(1) of the 1938 Act[19]] is thus wholly impersonal. The question is simply whether the will or the disposition has made reasonable provision, and not whether it was unreasonable on the part of the deceased to have made no provision or no larger provision for the dependant. A testator may have acted entirely reasonably; he may have taken skilled advice on the drafting of his will, intending to make fully reasonable provision, and yet through some blunder of the draftsman (perhaps as to the incidence of estate duty) or by some change in circumstances unknown to the testator in his lifetime, the provision may have been wholly unreasonable. Conversely the testator may have acted wholly unreasonably in deciding what provision to insert in his will, but by some happy accident such as the lapse of a share of residue which then passed to the widow on intestacy, the provision may in fact be entirely reasonable. In my judgment the question is not subjective but objective. It is not whether the deceased stands convicted of unreasonableness, but whether the provision in fact made is unreasonable.

Re Franks[20] is another example of the objective test. In that case where the applicant was born only two days before his mother's death so that she had no chance to change her will and make provision for the applicant Wynn-Parry J pointed out that the relevant words of the Act were 'if the court is of opinion that the will does not make reasonable provision' not 'that the testator has acted unreasonably'.[1]

However, certain other decisions suggested[2] that the test is subjective and a subjective test was expressed in *Re Howell*, a decision of the Court of Appeal, where Sir Raymond Evershed MR[3] approved the statement of Morton J in *Re Styler* who said:

> I think that the court has to find that it was unreasonable on the part of the testator to make no provision for the person in question or that it was unreasonable not to make a larger provision.[4]

Evershed MR accepted this view as follows:

19. S 2(1) of the 1975 Act.
20. [1948] Ch 62, [1947] 2 All ER 638.
1. [1948] Ch 65, [1947] 2 All ER 640A-B; see also *Re Blanch* [1967] 1 WLR 987, at 991 E, [1967] 2 All ER 468, at 471B (per Buckley J).
2. See eg *Re Pugh* [1943] Ch 387, [1943] 2 All ER 361; *Re Inns* [1947] Ch 576, [1947] 2 All ER 308; *Re Clayton* [1966] 1 WLR 969, [1966] 2 All ER 370; and see *Dun v Dun* [1959] AC 272, [1959] 2 All ER 134.
3. [1953] 1 WLR 1034 at 1038, [1953] 2 All ER 604, at 606H–607C.
4. [1942] Ch 387, at 389, [1942] 2 All ER 201, at 204C-D.

> That view of the intention of the Act has so far as I know been consistently acted upon since and should in my judgment be followed now. The question is in making his will did the testator make unreasonable provision for these children? The matter could equally well be put; was the series of dispositions unwarranted in the circumstances as they presented, or should have presented, themselves to the testator at the moment of death? For I think, prima facie, at any rate, that it must be right to judge this matter, whether the testator was unreasonable in the light of the circumstances which did present, or should have presented themselves to him up to the moment of death. No doubt the circumstances must include eventualities reasonably to be foreseen, but the testator ought not to be judged exclusively in the light of circumstances happening after his death, which might very much have altered the situation.

Re Goodwin unfortunately did not settle the conflict, since *Re Howell* does not appear to have been cited there. The matter was subsequently settled for the 1938 Act by the Court of Appeal in the cases of *Re Gregory*[5] and *Millward v Shenton*[6] where the dicta of Evershed MR in *Re Howell* were expressly disapproved and the approach of Megarry J in *Re Goodwin* was specifically endorsed. The objective approach of *Re Goodwin* was similarly approved by Lord Simon of Glaisdale in *Re Shanahan*[7] for cases under section 26 of the Matrimonial Causes Act 1965.

The Law Commission preferred the objective test,[8] as did almost all commentators[9] and, after one false start,[10] the objective

5. [1970] 1 WLR 1455, at 1460H–1461H, [1971] 1 All ER 497, at 502B–H (per Winn LJ).
6. [1972] 1 WLR 711, at 715A–D, [1972] 2 All ER 1025J–1028C (per Lord Denning MR); but compare Stamp LJ *dubitante* at [1972] 1 WLR 716B–C; [1972] 2 All ER 1028J–1029A, but by 1977 Stamp LJ had adopted the objective approach, *Bayliss v Lloyd's Bank Ltd* (9 December 1977, unreported), CA.
7. [1973] Fam 1, at 4E–F, 6A–9A, [1971] 3 All ER 873, at 876e-g, 877f-880d.
8. WORKING PAPER, para 3.15; LAW COM, paras 100–101.
9. Megarry, Note (1948) 64 LQR 19; ALBERY, pp 22–23; Borkowski, 'Reasonable Provision – The Time Factor', (1968) 118 NLJ 1105; Hopkins, 'Family Provision on Death', (1971) 35 Conv (NS) 72; ROSS MARTYN, p 15; but compare Cretney, Note (1969) 85 LQR 331; GILCHRIST SMITH, 106.
10. See the argument of Mr Gerrey in *Re Christie* [1979] Ch 168, at 170B apparently accepted by the Judge at [1979] Ch 174E. It is submitted that the suggestion of Davies, 'Inheritance (Provision for Family and Dependants) Act 1975 – Subjective or Objective Test', (1978) 75 LS Gaz 1005, that *Re Viner* [1978] CLY 3091 imports a subjective test is misplaced. In *Re Viner* the Master limited the amount of provision to a maximum of that provided by the deceased during his lifetime. It is suggested that this is a correct approach for all applicants under s 1(1)(e) and does not import any subjectivity as to whether provision should be ordered.

test has been adopted by the courts in interpreting the 1975 Act.[11] The Court of Appeal in *Moody v Stevenson* specifically confirmed the objective test and depreciated citation of the remarks of Morton J in *Re Styler*.[12] The objective test is clearly the better approach in terms of the actual language of the Act – a matter confirmed by the court's duty to have regard to the facts at the date of the hearing as opposed to the date of death[13] – and of the policy of the legislation.

Time at which Reasonableness is Determined

It has been a matter of some difficulty throughout the history of family provision legislation in the Commonwealth in deciding as to the time at which the court should assess whether an applicant has been left with inadequate provision. The two alternatives times are the date of the deceased's death and the date of the hearing. Because the relevant facts such as the value of the net estate and the means and outgoings of the applicant and beneficiaries of the estate may be different at the two dates, the time at which the court makes its judgment as to the adequacy of the provision given to the applicant and the amount of any provision ordered can be of considerable importance. The facts of two cases afford examples of the importance of the date on which reasonableness is determined. In *Re Howell*[14] the deceased divorced his wife and was granted custody of the two children of the marriage. Subsequently the first wife was denied access to the children. The deceased by his will left his entire estate to his second wife and appointed her testamentary guardian of the children. Shortly after the deceased's death, his second wife became seriously ill and unable to look after the children, who went to live with the first wife. An application for provision was made on behalf of the infant children. If the situation were judged at the date of the deceased's death, then the application was bound to fail because at the date of death it was reasonably anticipated that the deceased's second wife would care for and support the children. If

11. Eg *Re Coventry* [1980] Ch 461, at 474H, [1979] 2 All ER 408, at 418b (per Oliver J); at [1980] Ch 489A, [1979] 3 All ER 815, at 823b (per Goff LJ); *Moody v Stevenson* [1992] Ch 486, at 494E-F, [1992] 2 All ER 524, at 530e-f (per Waite J); *Jessop v Jessop* [1992] 1 FLR 591, at 596G (per Nourse LJ); *Re Jennings* [1994] Ch 286, at 297A; [1994] 3 All ER 27, at 35b (per Wall J).
12. [1992] Ch 486, at 494A-E, 502G-H, [1992] 2 All ER 524, at 529j-530e, 537b-d.
13. S 3(5); *Re Shanahan* [1973] Fam 1, at 8F–H, [1971]3 All ER 873, at 880a-c (per Lord Simon of Glaisdale).
14. [1953] 1 WLR 1034, [1953] 2 All ER 604.

the matter were judged at the date of the hearing of the application would have more chance of success since it was clear that provision for the deceased's second wife would not indirectly benefit the children. In *Dun v Dun*[15] the deceased who died in 1942 bequeathed to his widow various legacies equal to £2,000 and an annuity of £800, his net estate being valued at £22,216. By 1956 the net estate had appreciated in value to £82,000. In 1956 the widow applied out of time for provision to be made out of the estate of her deceased husband. If regard were had to the value of the estate at the date of death the application would fail.[16] However, if regard were had to the enhanced value of the estate at the date of the hearing the application had considerably more merit.

In *Re Howell*, the first English decision directly on point, the Court of Appeal held that regard was to be had to the facts at the date of death and to those reasonably foreseen at the date of death[17] and so rejected the application of the children.[18] The Canadian courts disagreed about which time to assess reasonableness.[19] The Australian courts disagreed about the correct time until the decision of the High Court of Australia in *Coates v National Trustees Co Ltd*[20] decided that the time for judging whether the will or intestacy provided reasonable provision was the date of death taking into account matters which could reasonably be foreseen, but that in deciding the quantum of provision to be awarded regard could be had to matters arising after the death of the deceased. Thus a significant improvement in the circumstances of the applicant between the date of death and the date of the hearing of the application might result in a diminution of the provision ordered. A significant worsening in the circumstances of the applicant between the date of death and the date of the hearing of the application would only be taken into account if it could be shown that the provision in the deceased's will or under his intestacy at *the date of death* was unreasonable. *Coates v National Trustees Co Ltd* was approved and followed by the Privy Council in *Dun v Dun*.[1]

15. [1959] AC 272, [1959] 2 All ER 134.
16. [1959] AC 283, [1959] 2 All ER 137H–I (per Lord Cohen).
17. [1953] 1 WLR 1034, at 1037, 1038, [1953] 2 All ER 604, at 606D–E, 607B–D (per Evershed MR).
18. The application also failed because the court applied a subjective test of reasonableness ([1953] 1 WLR 1037, [1953] 2 All ER 606D–E) and because any provision while being only a modest amount would severely harm the second wife ([1953] 1 WLR 1037, [1953] 2 All ER 606A–B).
19. *Re Hull* [1944] 1 DLR 14 (Ont CA) date of death; *Re Willan Estate* (1951) 4 WWRNS 114(Alta Sup Ct) date of hearing; *Re Urquhart* (1956) 5 DLR (2d) 235 (BC Sup Ct) date of hearing.
20. (1956) 95 CLR 494.
1. [1959] AC 272, [1959] 2 All ER 134.

Lord Cohen justified this conclusion by looking at the words of the statute and by applying the subjective test of reasonableness in that it would be wrong to judge a testator on events which he could not foresee.[2]

He rejected the contrary arguments that the date of the hearing was better because it accorded more with the aims of the legislation, was more realistic and avoided the difficult question as to what the deceased should have reasonably foreseen.[3]

After *Dun v Dun* English courts specifically held that the time for assessing whether reasonable provision had been made was the date of the deceased's death,[4] although regard was had to subsequent events if they qualified uncertainties existing at the date of death[5] and in assessing the quantum of provision which the court should order – in particular changes in the value of the estate between the date of death and the date of hearing were considered.[6] However, in *Re Clark*[7] Plowman J ignored *Dun v Dun* and took into account the death of the principal beneficiary under the deceased's will – a matter which radically improved the merits of the plaintiff's application. In *Re Shanahan*,[8] a case in which *Dun v Dun* was not cited, Lord Simon of Glaisdale stated that the value of the estate was to be assessed at the date of the hearing and thus by implication held that the reasonableness of any provision made by the deceased was to be assessed at such time also.

The Law Commission after a cursory examination of the relevant case law – *Dun v Dun* was not referred to – recommended that the court should consider the facts at the date of the hearing rather than the date of death.[9] This recommendation was carried into effect by section 3(5) of the Act which reads:

2. [1959] AC 290, [1959] 2 All ER 141I.
3. Ibid.
4. *Re Harker-Thomas* [1969] P 28, at 30G–31B, [1968] 3 All ER 17, at 20C-E (per Latey J); *Re Goodwin* [1969] 1 Ch 283, at 298B, [1968] 3 All ER 12, at 15G (per Megarry J); *Millward v Shenton* [1972] 1 WLR 711, at 714H, [1972] 2 All ER 1025, at 1027H (per Lord Denning MR) (*Dun v Dun* not cited); *Lusternik v Lusternik* [1972] Fam 125, at 133H–134A, [1972] 1 All ER 592, at 597f-j (per Cairns LJ).
5. *Re Goodwin* [1969] 1 Ch 283, at 289B–290B, [1968] 3 All ER 17, at 15G-16E (per Megarry J).
6. *Re Goodwin* [1969] 1 Ch 283, at 289B–290B, [1968] 3 All ER 17, at 15G-16E (per Megarry J); *Lusternik v Lusternik* [1972] Fam 125, at 133H–134B, [1972] 1 All ER 592, at 597f-j (per Cairns LJ); *Re Shanahan* [1973] Fam 1, at 8F–9A, [1971] 3 All ER 873, at 880d-e (per Lord Simon of Glaisdale).
7. [1968] 1 WLR 415, at 421F–G; [1968] 1 All ER 451, at 455I–456A. See also *Re Lewis* (13 March 1980, unreported), CA, a case on the 1938 Act, where the Court of Appeal took into account inflation after the death of the deceased.
8. [1973] Fam 1, at 8F–9A. [1971] 3 All ER 873, at 880d-e.
9. WORKING PAPER, para 3.15; LAW COM, paras 102–104.

> In considering the matters to which the court is to have regard under this section, the court shall take into account the facts as known to the court at the date of hearing.

The reference to section 3(1) clearly reverses *Dun v Dun* by holding that both the question whether the provision actually made was reasonable and the determination of the amount of any provision ordered is to be decided on the facts at the date of the hearing.[10] Accordingly, an adult child who becomes disabled after the death of the deceased will have the disability taken into account[11] and the death of a beneficiary after the death of the deceased will similarly be taken into account.[12] The problem, highlighted by *Dun v Dun*, of an application made many years after the death of the deceased and the correct approach of the court in extending time for such applications[13] was not considered by the Law Commission.

It is the practice of the court to consider the value of the net estate and the financial circumstances of the parties as at the date of hearing. Where a substantial time has elapsed between the date of the application and the date of the hearing it is usual for the parties' original evidence as to their financial circumstances and the value of the net estate to be updated.[14]

Provision Limited to Maintenance

Whereas spouses, other than those judicially separated, are entitled to 'reasonable provision' unrelated to their needs for maintenance;[15]

10. This is confirmed by LAW COM, paras 103–104:
    '103. In the light of our proposal that the test of reasonable provision should be an objective one, it seems to us that it is drawing an unnecessarily rigid distinction to ask the court to look at one date in deciding whether the provision made was in fact reasonable and at another date in determining the amount of provision.
    104. We *recommend* that it be made clear in future family provision legislation that the relevant circumstances for the court to consider are those existing at the date of the hearing and not those existing at the date of death."
11. *Re Urquhart* (1956) 5 DLR (2d) 235 (BC Sup Ct); compare *Millward v Shenton* [1972] 1 WLR 711, [1972] 2 All ER 1025 and *Re Testator's Family Maintenance Act* (1916) 12 Tas LR 11. For a child losing the right to apply through being adopted after the death of the deceased, see *Re Collins* [1990] Fam 56, [1990] 2 All ER 47.
12. Eg *Re Clarke* [1968] 1 WLR 415, [1968] 1 All ER 451; *Re Wood* (1982) LS Gaz R 774; Mervyn Davies J, 2 April 1982.
13. See *Stock v Brown* [1994] 1 FLR 840, discussed at p 342, *post*.
14. For evidence generally as to the parties' financial circumstances and the value of the net estate, see pp 353–355, *post*.
15. S 1(2)(a).

all other applicants are only entitled to 'reasonable provision' for the applicants' maintenance. The Act provides that in the case of applications by such applicants 'reasonable provision' means:

> ... such financial provision as would be reasonable in all the circumstances of the case for the applicant to receive for his maintenance.[16]

Although 'maintenance' was used in the 1938 Act, because the amount of provision which could be ordered was limited and because the jurisdiction was exercised carefully the need to define the concept of maintenance did not frequently arise. Few problems arose with the concept of 'maintenance' in the Matrimonial Causes (Property and Maintenance) Act 1958 because of the legislation's links with the divorce jurisdiction. The limits of maintenance were only explored in cases involving extremely large estates and after the Family Provision Act 1966 removed the restrictions on the quantum of provision. The Law Commission in its reports went to considerable lengths to stress that provision for applicants other than spouses should be limited to 'reasonable maintenance', as opposed to 'an equitable share', but the Law Commission did not offer any further guide as to what reasonable maintenance is.[17]

The best analogy for considering the limits of 'maintenance' is that of the dichotomy between maintenance and property rights which characterised matrimonial property law prior to the enactment of the Matrimonial Proceedings and Property Act 1970 and which is still of considerable importance. Section 3(1)(a) of the 1975 Act is derived from section 25(2)(b) of the Matrimonial Causes Act 1973 and refers to 'financial needs'. This concept has been consistently interpreted to mean 'reasonable requirements',[18] being more than needs 'narrowly' defined,[19] but less than a person's 'wishes'.[20]

In *Re Coventry* Oliver J deduced from the reference in section 1(2)(a) to 'provision *required* for his or her maintenance' that the court was concerned with what was *required* for the applicant's

16. S 1(2)(b).
17. WORKING PAPER, paras 3. 6–3.11; LAW COM, paras 12–15, 19–24. The Law Commission used the term 'support rights' virtually interchangeably with maintenance, WORKING PAPER, General Introduction, *passim*.
18. *Preston v Preston* [1982] Fam 17, at 25B-C, [1982] 1 All ER 41, at 47f-g; *Dart v Dart* [1996] 2 FLR 286, at 296D-H. In *Harrington v Gill* (1981) 3 FLR 265, at 271B Dunn LJ said specifically that 'needs' in s 3(1)(a) means 'reasonable requirements'.
19. *O'D v O'D* [1976] Fam 83, at 91D-E, [1975] 2 All ER 993, at 997f-g.
20. *Preston v Preston* [1982] Fam 17, at 25C, [1982] 1 All ER 41, at 47g; *Dart v Dart* [1996] 2 FLR 286, at 297A–H.

maintenance.[1] This was specifically approved by Nourse LJ in *Re Jennings*.[2] The concept of being *required* for the maintenance of the applicant imports a normative element to maintenance, confirming that the test is objective and possibly sugggests that maintenance is to meet some form of *deficiency* of resources.

'Maintenance' is limited to provision of an income nature and excludes provision of a capital nature. In *Re Dennis*[3] Browne-Wilkinson J regarded an application by an adult son for provision in the form of a lump sum to pay Capital Transfer Tax on an inter vivos gift as unarguable, because such payment could not be regarded as 'maintenance'. He said:

> The court has, up until now, declined to define the exact meaning of the word 'maintenance' and I am certainly not going to depart from that approach. But in my judgment the word 'maintenance' connotes only payments which, directly or indirectly, enable the applicant in the future to discharge the cost of his daily living at whatever standard of living is appropriate to him. The provision that is to be made is to meet recurring expenses, being expenses of living of an income nature. This does not mean that provision need be by way of income payments. The provision can be by way of a lump sum, for example, to buy a house in which the applicant can be housed, thereby relieving him pro tanto of income expenditure. Nor am I suggesting that there may not be cases in which payment of existing debts may not be appropriate as maintenance payment for example, to pay the debts of an applicant in order to enable him to continue to carry on a profit-making business or profession may well be for his maintenance.[4]

Further guidance on the limits of maintenance can be obtained from the cases of *Re Christie*[5] and *Re Coventry*.[6] In *Re Christie* Mr Vivian Price QC sitting as a deputy judge of the Chancery Division stated:

1. [1980] Ch 461, at 472F-G, [1979] 2 All ER 408, at 416b-c.
2. [1994] Ch 286, at 295D-E, [1994] 3 All ER 27, at 33h.
3. [1981] 2 All ER 140.
4. [1981] 2 All ER 145H–146A.This passage was cited with approval by Nourse LJ in *Re Jennings* [1994] Ch 286, at 297H-298A, [1994] 3 All ER 27, at 37j-36a. It is a question of fact in each case whether the payment of debts can be regarded as 'maintenance'. It was held not to be maintenance in *Re Dennis* and in *Re Abram* [1996] 2 FLR 379, at 396C-E, but was held to be so in *Re Goodchild* [1996] 1 WLR 694, at 713G-714A, [1996] 1 All ER 670, at 688j-689a. See also *Burridge v Burridge* [1983] Fam 9, [1982] 3 All ER 80.
5. [1979] Ch 168, [1979] 1 All ER 546. For the facts of *Re Christie* see pp 47–48, *ante*.
6. [1980] Ch 461, [1979] 2 All ER 408, [1979] 3 All ER 815.

> In my judgment, the word 'maintenance' refers to no more and no less than the applicant's way of life and well-being, health, financial security and allied matters such as the well-being, health, financial security and allied matters of his immediate family for whom he is responsible.[7]

The width of this definition is illustrated by Mr Vivian Price QC's use of it to justify awarding the applicant who was able to support himself and his family in reasonable comfort approximately £12,800 out of the deceased's net estate instead of approximately £6,800 which the deceased by her will gave the applicant. This wider approach was rejected by Oliver J in *Re Coventry* because it failed to have regard to the case law on the pre-1975 Act[8] and because Parliament by awarding spouses a more generous standard of provision clearly considered 'maintenance' to be more limited than anything reasonably desirable for the applicant's 'financial well-being'.[9] Oliver J's approach was affirmed by the Court of Appeal. Goff LJ said:

> What is proper maintenance must in all cases depend upon all the facts and circumstances of the particular case being considered at the time, but I think that it is clear on the one hand that one must not put a too limited a meaning on it; it does not mean just enough to enable a person to get by; on the other hand, it does not mean anything which may be regarded as reasonably desirable for his general benefit or welfare.[10]

Probably the best statement on the standard of maintenance in family provision legislation was given by Salmond J in *Allen v Manchester*,[11] who stated:

> ... the proper maintenance, which a testator owes to his widow in cases where there are no competing moral claims of other dependants

7. [1979] Ch 174F, [1979] 1 All ER 550f-g. Mr Vivian Price QC's definition of 'maintenance' was apparently accepted by Baker P in *CA v CC* (1978) Times, 17 November, *sub nom Re C* (1979) 9 Fam Law 26.
8. [1980] Ch 472D–F, [1979] 2 All ER 413b-c.
9. [1980] Ch 472F, [1979] 2 All ER 413c.
10. [1980] Ch 485C–D, [1979] 3 All ER 819j-820a. Buckley LJ paraphrased s 1(2)(b) as 'In the case of any other application made by virtue of sub-s (1) above, "reasonable financial provision" means such financial provision as would be reasonable in all the circumstances of the case to enable the applicant to maintain himself in a manner suitable to those circumstances' ([1980] Ch 494F, [1979] 3 All ER 827d-e). Most subsequent cases cite either the judgment of Goff LJ (eg *Re Jennings* [1994] Ch 286, at 297G-H, [1994] 3 All ER 27, at 35j) or *Re Duranceau* [1952] 3 DLR 714 as defining maintenance.
11. [1922] NZLR 218, at 222.

> is such maintenance as will enable her, taken in conjunction with her own means, to live with comfort and without pecuniary anxiety in such state of life as she was accustomed to in her husband's lifetime, or would have been so accustomed to if her husband had then done his duty to her.

Soon after the 1938 Act came into effect the courts rejected any notion that reasonable maintenance meant mere subsistence and was related to any particular level prescribed by social security legislation[12] and this approach has been consistently followed subsequently.[13] An Ontario court stated that reasonable maintenance should be:

> ... sufficient to enable the dependant to live neither luxuriously nor miserably, but decently and comfortably according to his or her station in life.[14]

Ewbank J has more recently defined maintenance as:

> ... sufficient to enable the applicant to live decently and comfortably according to the station in life to which she has been called. It does not mean merely enough to bring her to subsistence.On the other hand, it does not mean sufficient to give her a life of luxury.[15]

Maintenance can include the provision of small luxuries for a mentally or physically disabled person whose wants as regards normal living expenses are already fully provided for.[16] In *Re*

12. In *Re Catmull* [1943] Ch 262, at 268–269, [1943] 2 All ER 115, at 119C–D Uthwatt J stated that the state pension for a widow was adequate maintenance.
13. *Re Borthwick* [1949] Ch 395, at 401, [1949] 1 All ER 472, at 475F-476A (per Harman J); *Re Pringle* (1956) Times, 2 February (per Vaisey J); *Re Parry* (1956) Times, 19 April (per Vaisey J); *Re E* [1966] 1 WLR 709, 715F, [1966] 2 All ER 44, at 48F (per Stamp J); *Thornley v Palmer* [1969] 1 WLR 1037, at 1041E, [1969] 3 All ER 31, at 34E–F (per Harman LJ); *Millward v Shenton* [1972] 1 WLR 711, at 715G–H, [1972] 2 All ER 1025, at 1028E–G (per Lord Denning MR); *Re Christie* [1979] Ch 168, at 174E, [1979] 1 All ER 550e-f (per Mr Vivian Price QC); *Re Coventry* [1980] Ch 461, at 471A–B, [1979] 2 All ER 408, at 414j (per Oliver J), at [1980] Ch 485A–C, 490F, [1979] 3 All ER 815, at 819g-j (per Goff LJ), at [1980] Ch 494C–E; [1979] 3 All ER 827c-d (per Buckley LJ). See also *Bosch v Perpetual Trustee Co* [1938] AC 463, at 476, [1938] 2 All ER 14, at 20A-H (per Lord Romer).
14. *Re Duranceau* [1952] 3 DLR 714, at 720 approved in *Re Coventry* [1980] Ch 461, at 485C, [1979] 3 All ER 815, at 819h-j (per Goff LJ) and in *Harrington v Gill* [1981] 4 FLR 265, at 270G-H (per Dunn LJ).
15. *Re Debenham* [1986] 1 FLR 404, at 408E-F.
16. *Re Pringle* (1956) Times, 2 February (per Vaisey J); *Re Parry* (1956) Times, 19 April (per Vaisey J); *Millward v Shenton* [1972] 1 WLR 711, at 715H, [1972] 2 All ER 1025, at 1028F–G (per Lord Denning MR).

Wood[17] Mervyn Davies J after hearing detailed evidence on the point held that maintenance could include twice-weekly hydrotherapy sessions plus weekly trips out and holidays for a severely subnormal woman aged 30 accommodated in a mental hospital, there being evidence that such activities would bring the applicant pleasure and help in her treatment. Maintenance may even include provision to enable the applicant to save *small* amounts to give to others where such saving can be regarded as a hobby of the applicant.[18] Provision for maintenance may take account of future contingencies such as the retirement of the applicant or his loss of employment.[19]

As the judgments of Salmond J in *Allen v Manchester*[20] and of the Ontario court[1] previously cited indicate, what is reasonable maintenance varies with the status and wealth of the deceased and of the applicant. Thus what would be adequate provision by way of *maintenance* for the widow of a poor man would be inadequate provision for the widow of a wealthy man. Harman J in *Re Borthwick*,[2] stated the position to be as follows:

> It is said that maintenance is the only thing you can look at. What does that mean? It does not mean that you can only give the dependant just enough to put a little jam on his bread and butter. It has already been held that what is reasonable for one may not be reasonable for another. It must depend on the circumstances of the widow, but I think it may also depend on the circumstances of the testator, that is to say, whether he died a rich man or not, because a rich man may be supposed to have made better provision for his wife's maintenance than a poor one. Maintenance does not only mean the food she puts in her mouth. It means the clothes on her back, the house in which she lives, and the money which she has to have in her pocket, all of which vary according to the means of the man who leaves a wife behind him. I think that must be so. Maintenance cannot mean only a mere subsistence.

17. [1982] LS Gaz R 774; 2 April 1982.
18. *Re Parry* (1956) Times, 19 April. The applicant was blind and lived in an old people's home – the court awarded him an annuity of 10s per week, it being likely that he would save 2s 6d per week to give to his children. For the general approach of the courts to provision to enable people to save to give to others see p 148, *post*.
19. *Re Clayton* [1966] 1 WLR 969, at 973H–974H, [1966] 2 All ER 370, at 373D–374A (per Ungoed-Thomas J); future retirement, *Re Bunning* [1984] Ch 480, at 490H-491H, [1984] 3 All ER 1, at 6a-c; and pp 134–141, *post*. See also *Bosch v Perpetual Trustee Co* [1938] AC 463, at 483, [1938] 2 All ER 14, at 24H (per Lord Romer).
20. P 134, *ante*.
1. P 135, *ante*.

As a rule of thumb it can be said that where it is unreasonable not to make provision for an applicant, reasonable maintenance means the maintenance received from the deceased prior to death adjusted for the change in conditions brought about by death. While the court will generally be guided by the actual maintenance provided by the deceased while alive, the test of what is reasonable maintenance remains an objective test for the court. In particular with a very large estate the court will not *necessarily* regard it as reasonable maintenance to continue the applicant's luxurious standard of living at the same level after the deceased's death.[3] Moreover, where the deceased *wrongfully* failed to maintain the applicant at all or adequately prior to death, the amount of provision provided by the deceased while alive is no guide as to what is reasonable maintenance. In *Re Borthwick* Harman J rejected an argument that reasonable maintenance was limited to the inadequate allowance that the deceased gave to his estranged wife prior to his death, when the deceased should have provided a much larger allowance, thus,

> In other words it is said the worse a man treats his wife in his lifetime the less he need leave when he is dead. I cannot accept such a cynical conclusion.[4]

The concept of maintenance in relation to applications by spouses, infant children, adult children and other dependents is discussed in the appropriate sections of Chapter 6, *post*.[5]

2. [1949] Ch 395, at 401, [1949]1All ER 472, at 475G-476A .
3. In *Re Inns* [1947] Ch 576, 581, [1947] 2 All ER 308, at 311E-F Wynn-Parry J said: 'Still less [before the enactment of the 1938 Act] could he be compelled to make provision that his wife, for instance, should be enabled to live in circumstances similar to those in which during his life, he and she lived together. The Act is not designed to bring about any such compulsion.' Compare *Re Besterman* (1982) 3 FLR 255, at 263H, a case of an application by a spouse under the 1975 Act, but which appears to have been principally argued on the basis of maintenance where Judge Mervyn Davies QC awarded the widow £259,250 to enable her to 'maintain herself on a scale of living having some semblance to the scale that was adopted during the marriage'. For a contrary approach, see *Rhodes v Dean* (28 March 1996, unreported), CA.
4. [1949] Ch 395, at 400, [1949] 1 All ER 472, at 475G, followed by *Re Sanderson* (1963) Times, 2 November; *Re Milliken* [1966] NI 68, at 72; *Re Whittle* (5 March 1973, unreported), CA; *Re W* (1975) 119 Sol Jo 439, (1975) Times, 21 April.
5. For discussion of maintenance in relation to applications by spouses, see pp 172–174, *post*, by infant children, see pp 200–203, *post*, by adult children, see pp 222–229, *post*, and by other dependants, see pp 285–289, *post*.

Matters to be Considered by the Court

(i) The Financial Resources and Financial Needs of the Applicant

Section 3(1)(a) of the 1975 Act requires the court to have regard to:

> ... the financial resources and financial needs which the applicant has or is likely to have in the foreseeable future.

This subsection is derived from section 25(1)(a) of the Matrimonial Causes Act 1973.

Normally the applicant is required to adduce evidence of his income, capital and expenditure, both at the present and in the foreseeable future. The failure to do so results in the court drawing extremely adverse inferences. All sources of income, whether earned or unearned, are relevant.[6] Matters such as the right to occupy a house may have to be brought into account.[7] The court will take a broad view of a person's financial position – the ability of the applicant to borrow money or live off capital gains may be considered to be the equivalent of a regular income in an appropriate case.[8]

Section 3(6) specifically enjoins the court to have regard to the 'earning capacity' of the applicant. Accordingly evidence of the applicant's earning capacity should be adduced. The evidence should mention whether the applicant has or has had a job, any qualification he possesses, whether he could resume work if not working at present or whether he is too old or too ill to work.

6. Eg *Re Catmull* [1943] Ch 262, [1943] 2 All ER 115 (state widow's pension); *Re Charman* [1951] 2 TLR 1095 (voluntary pension from testator's employers); *Re E* [1966] 1 WLR 709, [1966] 2 All ER 44 (state retirement pension and income from lodgers); *Re Morris* (1967) Times, 14 April (pension from testator's employers).
7. Eg *Re Blanch* [1967] 1 WLR 987, at 992H–993A, [1967] 2 All ER 468, at 472C–D.
8. In *J-PC v J-AF* [1955] P 215, [1955] 2 All ER 85 a husband had a taxable income of £70, but derived substantial benefit from his business as a property developer by making capital gains and by borrowing against the security of his property. It was held proper in divorce proceedings to have regard to this ability to make capital gains and to raise money in assessing the husband's liability for maintenance. See also *Hardy v Hardy* (1981) 2 FLR 321, at 328H-329B and the remarks of Ormrod LJ in *Preston v Preston* [1982] Fam 17, at 26H, [1982] 1 All ER 41, at 48j. It is implicit in both multiplier calculations, eg *Malone v Harrison* [1979] 1 WLR 1353, at 1365F, and *Duxbury* calculations that an applicant will partly live off the capital of any sum awarded to him.

The court is entitled to consider whether the applicant's unemployment is voluntary or involuntary and may proceed on the basis that the applicant could have a larger income than at present if he wished.[9] A determination by the Benefits Agency that the applicant is involuntarily unemployed is entitled to considerable respect in a court,[10] but is not conclusive of the matter.[11]

(ii) Future and Contingent Financial Resources

The Act requires the court to have regard to the financial needs of the applicant which he 'is *likely to* have in *the foreseeable future*'.[12] Thus the court may have regard to changes in the applicant's financial resources which will only occur sometime in the future or which are merely contingent. For instance the court can have regard to such future property as reversionary interests belonging to the applicant,[13] the loss of income consequent upon retirement, future pensions from employment and gratuities given after service in the armed forces ceases.[14]

Similarly the court can have regard to contingent possibilities such as the possibility of inheriting property from third parties,[15] of appointments being made under discretionary trusts[16] and of provision being made by the trustees of a discretionary pension fund.[17]

The case law on the meaning of 'the foreseeable future' in section 25(1)(a) of the Matrimonial Causes Act 1973 is

9. Eg *Re Pearson-Gregory* (1957) Times, 10 October; *Re Coventry* [1980] Ch 461, at 466F, [1979] 2 All ER 408, at 411e; *Re Bunning* [1984] Ch 480, at 490G-H, [1984] 3 All ER 1, at 5j-6a; similar principles apply upon divorce, *McEwan v McEwan* [1972] 1 WLR 1217, [1972] 2 All ER 708; *Trippas v Trippas* [1973] Fam 134, at 142G–H, [1973] 2 All ER 1, at 6e-f.
10. *Williams (LA) v Williams (EM)* [1974] Fam 55, at 62E–F, [1974] 3 All ER 377, at 382h-383a (per Finer J).
11. *Bromilow v Bromilow* (1976) 7 Fam Law 16; *Burridge v Burridge* [1983] Fam 9, [1982] 3 All ER 80.
12. S 3(1)(a). Emphasis added.
13. Reversionary interests were taken into account upon divorce in *Warren v Warren* (1890) 63 LT 264 (per Hannen P); *Shearn v Shearn* [1931] P 1, at 6 (per Hill J), *Crews-Orchard v Crews-Orchard* (1970) 114 Sol Jo 150; *Calder v Calder* (1976) Fam Law 242.
14. *Priest v Priest* (1978) 1 FLR 189
15. *Morgan v Morgan* [1977] Fam 122, [1977] 2 All ER 515; *Hardy v Hardy* (1981) FLR 321.
16. *Clinton v Clinton* (1866) LR 1 P & D 215; *Martin v Martin* [1919] P 283; *Howard v Howard* [1945] P 1, at 5, [1945] 1 All ER 91, at 95B–C (per Lord Greene MR); *Browne v Browne* [1989] 1 FLR 291; *Mills v New Zealand Insurance Co Ltd* [1958] NZLR 356; compare *Re Berry Estate* (1966) 58 WWR 187 (Sask): and see *Re Wilson* [1973] 2 NZLR 359.
17. Compare *Re Clayton* [1966] 1 WLR 969, at 974B–C, [1966] 2 All ER 370, at 373D–E (per Ungoed-Thomas J).

unsatisfactory, some cases fixing a specific number of years as the maximum of foreseeability[18] whereas other techniques look to the entire life-expectancy of the parties.[19]It is submitted that the corect approach to the term 'foreseeable future' is to examine the probability of an event occurring as opposed to merely counting the number of years before the event is likely to occur.[20]

Under the Inheritance Act there appear to be no limits on the future events to which the courts may have regard. In *Re Clayton* Ungoed-Thomas J considered the situation where the applicant who was aged 56 at the date of the hearing would retire from work presumably at age 65[1] or his possibility of losing his present employment prior to the normal retiring age.[2] In *Re Bunning* Vinelott J took into account the income during retirement and 'a lengthy widowhood' of an applicant aged 55 years.[3] In *Malone v Harrison* the court using the 'multiplier' approach took into account the financial needs until death of an applicant aged 37 years.[4]

Although in one case the Court of Appeal appeared to construe 'likely to' as meaning on a balance of probabilities,[5] it is suggested that lesser probabilities can be considered and evaluated.[6] But clearly fanciful possibilities or remote contingencies must be ignored. Similarly the possibility of benefiting under a discretionary trust should be ignored when it is apparent that there is no real possibility of an appointment being made in favour of the applicant.[7]

It is suggested that when dealing with contingent or future rights the court should adopt the following procedure. When dealing with

18. *Priest v Priest* (1978) 1 FLR 189, at 192-3 (up to 15 years foreseeable); *Ranson v Ranson* [1988] 1 FLR 292 (13 years not foreseeable).
19. Eg *Duxbury* calculations (as to which see pp 388–389, *post*) are related to maintenance up to the date of death. *Duxbury v Duxbury (1985)* [1992] Fam 62n, [1990] 2 All ER 77 involved a life expectancy of 35 years! Compare s 25B, C, D of the Matrimonial Causes Act 1973 introduced by the Pensions Act 1995 which specifically reject any test of foreseeability.
20. *Michael v Michael* [1986] 2 FLR 389, at 396H-397G per Nourse LJ.
1. [1966] 1 WLR 969, at 974B–D, [1966] 2 All ER 370, at 373E–G.
2. [1966] 1 WLR 969 at 973H–974E, [1966] 2 All ER 370, at 373D–E,G.
3. [1984] Ch 480, at 490H-491A, 499A–B, [1984] 3 All ER 1, at 6b, 11j-12a. See to like effect, *Re Crawford* (1982) 4 FLR 273, at 283C–D.
4. [1979] 1 WLR 1353. The annuity approach employed by Judge Mervyn Davies QC (1981) 3 FLR 255 also assumes maintenance to the date of death.
5. *Priest v Priest* (1978) 1 FLR 189 (per Cumming-Bruce LJ), see also *Calder v Calder* (1975) 6 Fam Law 242.
6. Compare the possibility of valuing reversionary interests, JACKSON AND DAVIES, para 7.12, and see *Wells v Wells* [1997] 1 WLR 652, at 681G–H, [1997] 1 All ER 673, at 700h and the type of possibilities considered by Ungoed-Thomas J in *Re Clayton, supra*.
7. *Howard v Howard* [1945] P 1, at 4, [1945] 1 All ER 91, at 95C-D; *Re Berry Estate* (1966) 58 WWR 187 (Sask); *Re Wilson* [1973] 2 NZLR 359.

matters such as the exercise of trustees' powers under discretionary pension funds, the appointment of capital under discretionary trusts, applications for family provision in other jurisdictions[8] and all other matters which are likely to be resolved relatively shortly after the death of the deceased the court should adjourn any proceedings so that it makes any award with full knowledge of the applicant's financial provision.[9] Where the uncertainty will not be removed in the immediate future and the provision is likely to be of a capital nature or it is desired finally to determine the parties' rights the court should act on its best assessment of the applicant's position in the future, fully taking into account the uncertainty of contingencies.[10] Where the uncertainty will not be removed in the immediate future and and in the limited number of situations where provision of an income nature is sought or where a subsequent variation of an award is possible, it is suggested that the court should ignore the future or contingent property, but make any award subject to the condition that the applicant keeps the court informed as to his financial position so that if the applicant obtains the future or contingent property the amount of any award may be varied accordingly.[11]

(iii) All Property and Income of the Applicant to be Considered

In deciding the reasonableness of the provision made by the deceased for the applicant the court has regard to all the property which passed from the deceased to the applicant or other people whether or not such property passed on death and whether or not it forms part of the deceased's net estate.[12] Thus, for example,

8. See p 55, *ante*.
9. Compare the approach of the divorce court in adjourning applications for a substantial period of time, eg *Morris v Morris* (1977) 7 Fam Law 244; *MT v MT (financial provision: lump sum)* [1992] 1 FLR 362. It is submitted that the practice on divorce of adjourning applications for *years*, is not necessarily applicable under the 1975 Act (but see *Re Bateman* (1941) 85 Sol Jo 454 indefinite adjournment and *Re Franks* [1948] Ch 62, [1947] 2 All ER 638 adjournment for two years and three months) and that only adjournments of much shorter duration will be allowed.
10. See the discussion of the two ways of proceeding in *Warren v Warren* (1890) 63 LT 264. Note the increasing sophistication of the calculation of chances with techniques such as *Duxbury* calculations, see *Wells v Wells* [1997] 1 WLR 652, at 681G–H, 685B–D, [1997] 1 All ER 673, at 700g–h, 701–704c–e.
11. See first edition, p 56.
12. Eg *Re Pearson-Gregory* (1957) Times, 10 October (trust fund for applicant); *Re Dyer* (1964) Times, 13 March (lease and goodwill of shop for applicant); *Re E* [1966] 1 WLR 709, [1966] 2 All ER 44 (house for applicant); *Re Morris* (1967) Times, 14 April (pension from employment); *Re Fullard* [1982] Fam 42, [1981] 2 All ER 796 (lump sum payable on divorce).

appointments made under special powers or under discretionary pension schemes are taken into account as well as inter vivos dispositions made more than six years before death whether or not intended to defeat an application for family provision. Three cases afford examples of this.

In *Re Charman*[13] the deceased bequeathed his estate to his mistress and sister, making no provision for his estranged wife, who did however receive a pension as the deceased's widow from his employers. Harman J, taking into account the pension, dismissed the widow's application but added that the position would have been different if there was no pension.

In *Re Carter*[14] the deceased gave £3,000 to a friend four months before his death. In his will the deceased made no provision for his estranged wife and bequeathed all his estate of £4,700 to two friends, one being the recipient of the gift of £3,000. Upon an application by the widow for family provision Buckley J stated that in this case it would not normally be proper to award the widow the whole estate, but because the large gift to a beneficiary under the will had to be taken into account it was proper to award the widow the entire estate.

In *Jessop v Jessop*[15] the deceased left a wife and a mistress. The net estate was very small, but the severable share in the beneficial joint tenancy of the dwellinghouse occupied by the mistress passed to the mistress by survivorship. The deceased's employers appointed a lump sum of £40,000 to the mistress under the terms of the deceased's pension scheme. The Court of Appeal made an order under section 9 making the deceased's severable share part of the net estate and awarded the applicant a lump sum of £10,000. Clearly the Court of Appeal had no wish to imperil the occupation of her dwellinghouse by the mistress and the clear purpose of the order under section 9 was to enable the widow to have access to the lump sum payable under the pension scheme.

If the one-third rule applies to applications by spouses,[16] it must be remembered that the calculation is one-third of the *combined* incomes of the spouse and the deceased and one-third of the *combined* capital of the spouse and the deceased. If an applicant has been provided with capital by the deceased, but has dissipated it prior to the hearing the court will not require the deceased's estate to make up the dissipated assets.[17]

13. [1951] WN 599.
14. (1968) 112 Sol Jo 136. For a very similar case, see *Re F* (1965) 109 Sol Jo 212.
15. [1992] 1 FLR 591. For a not dissimilar case, see *Re Crawford* (1982) 4 FLR 273.
16. For discussion of the one-third rule see pp 194–196, *post*.
17. *Re Pearson-Gregory* (1957) Times, 10 October; *Re Haig* [1979] LS Gaz R 476, Browne-Wilkinson J, 22 February 1979; *Re Dennis* [1981] 2 All ER 140; *Re*

(iv) Reasonable Provision is Secure Provision

The courts have interpreted reasonable provision for the maintenance of the applicant to mean provision which is as secure and free from conditions as is reasonably possible. Thus if an applicant's income from the deceased's estate is precarious because it is derived from a particular source and it can easily be made more secure then the court will make an order for family provision so as to render the income more secure.[18]

In *Rajabally v Rajabally*[19] the deceased left the matrimonial home to his widow and three sons in equal shares. At first instance the widow's application was dismissed on the basis that the sons gave non-legally binding assurances that she could reside in the property. The Court of Appeal reversed Nicholls J and held that the Act was concerned with the parties' legal entitlements and the widow's lack of security made the provision under the will unreasonable.

Where reasonable provision for maintenance includes the provision of a house a gift of a licence for life or a mere right to occupy a particular property will not be regarded as reasonable. For example, in *Re Mason*[20] Plowman V-C made an order varying the deceased's will so as to provide the widow applicant with a full life interest under the machinery of the Settled Land Act 1925, in place of a licence to reside in a particular dwellinghouse, which the widow found to be too large and expensive to maintain. To avoid applications under the Act testators should be advised to give the applicant a full life-interest with the trustees' powers only being exercisable with the consent of the tenant for life rather than make

---

Farrow [1987] 1 FLR 205; *Rhodes v Dean* (28 March 1996, unreported), CA. But see *Re Ducksbury* [1966] 1 WLR 1226, [1966] 2 All ER 374 where the court did not reduce the provision ordered for the applicant where the applicant's mother had fraudulently converted trust money provided by the deceased for the applicant. See also the remarks of Oliver J in *Re Coventry* [1980] Ch 461 at 466F, [1979] 2 All ER 408, at 411e.

18. In *Re Doring* [1955] 1 WLR 1217, [1955] 3 All ER 289, the applicant widow's income under the will of her husband was heavily dependent upon the business being profitable. The court made an award permitting the widow to resort to the income of other parts of the estate should the income from the business be insufficient to meet the widow's annuity. See also *Re Goodwin* [1969] 1 Ch 283, [1968] 3 All ER 12 .
19. [1987] 2 FLR 390.
20. (1975) 5 Fam Law 124; *ad idem*, *Re Lewis* (13 March 1980, unreported), CA; see also *Re Parkinson* (1957) Times, 4 October; but compare *Harrington v Gill* (1983) 4 FLR 265 where a house was settled on a trust for sale rather than on a Settled Land Act 1925 settlement and *Moody v Stevenson* [1992] Ch 486, [1992] 2 All ER 524 where only a right to reside was awarded, but the applicant had been guilty of misconduct.

any attempt at preserving a particular dwellinghouse intact for the remainderman.[1]

If the applicant's provision for his maintenance provided by the deceased in his will is subject to some condition, such as one as to religion, which is likely to make the gift fail,[2] then the court *may* make the provision more secure by exercising its powers to delete the condition.[3] But it must be remembered that the court only has jurisdiction when it is satisfied that the dispositions of the deceased's will do not give reasonable provision for the applicant and the removal of conditions in gifts is only an incidental matter to the awarding of reasonable provision. Furthermore, a deliberate breach of such a condition is a factor to be taken into account in deciding whether to order provision for the applicant.[4]

(v) The Relevance of State Benefits

The history of the treatment of state benefits in family provision applications has not been happy. Originally certain of the Judges of the Chancery Division appeared to regard it as more desirable that an applicant should rely upon (what was then) the Poor Law and National Assistance than that the testator's intentions manifest in his will be interfered with.[5] Moreover no distinction was made between contributory benefits and those available as of right on the one hand and means-tested benefits on the other hand.[6] It is suggested that authorities on matrimonial obligations of support and the general principles of law are a better guide to the law today than some earlier authorities. Three different situations exist.

1. Consideration should be given to making the exercise of the trustees' powers of management subject to the consent of the life tenant under s 8(2) of the Trusts of Land and Appointment of Trustees Act 1996 or delegating powers of management to the life tenant under s 9.
2. In *Re Sylvester* [1941] Ch 87, [1940] 4 All ER 269 the deceased bequeathed the applicant an annuity which was subject to forfeiture on alienation. The court increased the amount of the annuity, but did not remove the forfeiture, to which, it appears, no objection was taken.
3. In *Re Gunn* (1912) 32 NZLR 153 the court removed a condition as to religion, which was likely to cause a forfeiture. But see *Mills v New Zealand Insurance Co Ltd* [1958] NZLR 356 where the court refused to convert a widow's interest in a discretionary trust into a life-interest there being no evidence that the trustees exercised their powers in a manner adverse to the widow; but see further the contrary approach of *Re Lawther* [1947] 2 DLR 510, at 524; *Re WTN* (1959) 33 ALJ 240.
4. See first edition, pp 66–67.
5. *Re Catmull* [1943] Ch 262, [1943] 2 All ER 115 (per Uthwatt J); see also *Re Vrint* [1940] Ch 920, [1940] 3 All ER 470.
6. See the argument in *Re E* [1966] 1 WLR 709, at 714G–715H, [1966] 2 All ER 44, at 47I–48H where it was sought to apply *Re Watkins* [1949] 1 All ER 695 to national assistance.

Firstly, it is clear the *contributory* benefits such as unemployment benefit, widow's pensions, old age pensions and industrial injury benefits are regarded as part of the applicant's means. It is not in any way wrongful for the deceased to require an applicant to claim insurance benefits, private or public, to which he has contributed. The distinction between contributory benefits and non-contributory benefits was illustrated by the decision of Ewbank J in *Re Debenham*[7] who awarded the applicant periodic payments of £6,000 per annum which thereby removed her entitlement to Income Support, but ordered that when the applicant attained the age of 60 years the periodic payments should be reduced by the amount of the old age pension. Similarly universal state services such as state education and the National Health Service can be taken into account. In *Re Wood*[8] Mervyn Davies J took into account a state invalidity pension and a mobility allowance in assessing the means of the applicant – in this case the estate was quite large in relation to the claims made upon it. In *Re Watkins*[9] Roxburgh J considered that a testator was not being unreasonable in allowing his mentally ill adult daughter to be maintained at the state's expense in a National Health Service mental hospital. However, while it is correct to take into consideration such state provision, it is not necessarily a guide to what is reasonable maintenance.[10] In such cases reasonable maintenance may include a small allowance for extra comforts for an applicant accommodated in a local authority old persons' home[11] or a National Health Service mental hospital[12] or even private education and health care.[13]

Secondly, where the deceased's estate is sufficiently large to satisfy all the claims made upon it, whether made by persons qualified as applicants or otherwise, it is wrong for the deceased to attempt to satisfy his duty to make reasonable provision by requiring the applicant to apply for a means-tested non-contributory benefit

7. [1986] 1 FLR 404, at 410G-411B.
8. [1982] LS Gaz R 774, 2 April 1982.
9. [1949] 1 All ER 695, at 699H–700B.
10. Eg see the emphatic rejection of *Re Catmull* by Danckwerts J in *Re Elliot* (1956) Times, 18 May; *Re E* [1966] 1 WLR 709, at 715E-G, [1966] 2 All ER 44, at 48E-G.
11. *Re Parry* (1956) Times, 19 April.
12. *Re Blight* (1946) 96 LJ 233; *Re Pringle* (1956) Times, 2 February; *Re Wood* [1982] LS Gaz R 774; Mervyn Davies J, 2 April 1982.
13. Eg *Bosch v Perpetual Trustee Co Ltd* [1938] AC 463, [1938] 2 All ER 14; *Re Sanderson* (1963) Times, 2 November; *Re Bellman* [1963] P 239, [1963] 1 All ER 513.

such as income support.[14] In such a case any assessment of the applicant's means should exclude any social security benefits.

However, thirdly, where a deceased's estate is insufficient to satisfy all the claims upon it, whether by applicants, potential applicants or otherwise, means-tested and other like non-contributory benefits may be taken into account. In such a case the court may take into account social security benefits.[15] Moreover, the court will be extremely reluctant to make an award which merely has the effect of redistributing social security benefits among the parties.[16]In some cases the court has chosen to award provision in the form of a lump sum so as to prevent the applicant's income support being reduced.[17]

(vi) Inflation

Inflation between the date of the will and the date of death and between the date of death and the date of hearing is taken into account.[18]

In *Bosch v Perpetual Trustee Co Ltd*, a decision extremely favourable to plaintiffs, the Privy Council took future inflation into account.[19] In *Re Besterman* both Judge Mervyn Davies QC at first instance and Oliver LJ in the Chancery Division increased the amount of the lump sum to take account of prospective inflation.[20] In *Re Bunning* Vinelott J took into account the cost of annuities

14. *Re E* [1966] 1 WLR 709, at 715F–G, [1966] 2 All ER 44, at 48F-G; *Millward v Shenton* [1972] 1 WLR 711, at 715G–H, [1972] 2 All ER 1025, at 1028F (per Lord Denning MR); *Re Debenham* [1986] 1 FLR 404; *Re Collins* [1990] Fam 56, at 61G-62D, [1990] 2 All ER 47, at 51h-52c; see also *Askew v Askew* [1961] 1 WLR 725, at 726–727, [1961] 2 All ER 60, at 61I–62B.
15. *Re E* [1966] 1 WLR 709, at 715E–H, [1966] 2 All ER 44, at 48D–H (per Stamp J) . See also per Ungoed-Thomas J in *Re Clayton* [1966] 1 WLR 969, at 971F–G, [1966] 2 All ER 370, at 371H–I.
16. *Re Howell* [1953] 1 WLR 1034, at 1037, [1953] 2 All ER 604, at 606A–G (per Evershed MR). And see *Moody v Stevenson* [1992] Ch 486, at 500A-B, [1992] 2 All ER 524.
17. *Millward v Shenton* [1972] 1 WLR 711, at 715H, [1972] 2 All ER 1025, at 1028F–G (per Lord Denning MR); *Re Canderton* (1970) 114 Sol Jo 208 (per Ungoed-Thomas J); *Wallace v Thorburn* (9 October 1987, unreported), CA. Compare the different approaches to backdating periodic payments taken in *Re Goodwin* [1969] 1 Ch 283, at 292C–E, [1968] 3 All ER 12, at 17B–D and in *Re Debenham* [1986] 1 FLR 404, at 410G.
18. As to taking into account inflation between the date of the will and the date of hearing, see Inheritance (Provisions for Family and Dependants) Act 1974, s 3(5) and *Re Lewis* (13 March 1980, unreported), CA. On falling interest rates between the date of death and the hearing, see *Stock v Brown* [1994] 1 FLR 840.
19. [1938] AC 463, at 483, [1938] 2 All ER 14, at 24H (per Lord Romer).
20. (1982) 3 FLR 255, at 266D–E (per Judge Mervyn Davies QC); varied [1984] Ch 458, at 478F, [1984] 2 All ER 656, at 670g (per Oliver LJ).

which gave a limited protection against inflation.[1] There has been virtually no discussion of inflation in reported cases under the 1975 Act after the early 1980s.

One of the reasons why orders for periodic payments has ceased to be made is that they offer very limited protection against inflation, the power of variation being limited and inevitably expensive to operate.[2]

The reference in section 3(1)(a) to 'the financial needs which any beneficiary ... is likely to have in the foreseeable future' *entitles* the court to have regard to future inflation. The question arises as to *whether* and *how* the court should have regard to prospective inflation. In the calculation of damages in personal injury litigation prospective inflation is ignored, because it is difficult to assess[3] and because the investment component[4] of the multiplier-multiplicand calculations does take into account prospective inflation in a reasonably adequate manner.[5] On divorce *Duxbury* calculations take into account anticipated inflation.[6] In *Wells v Wells*[7] the Court of Appeal assimilated the approach of the courts in assessing personal injury damages and lump sums on divorce and Thorpe LJ held the same approach was applicable to claims under the 1975 Act.[8] Accordingly it is submitted that under the 1975 Act prospective inflation should be taken into account through the selection of investment models and not through the award of an additional lump sum as some form of *Besterman* cushion.[9]

(vii) Financial Obligations and Responsibilities

The phrase 'financial needs' in section 3(1)(a) is further explained by section 3(6) which provides that:

1. [1984] Ch 480, at 499G-H, [1984] 3 All ER 1, at 12f. In *Malone v Harrison* [1979] 1 WLR 1353 Hollings J using a multiplier-multiplicand approach took no account of prospective inflation.
2. The power of variation is contained in s 6, but this is limited to property appropriated to meet the periodical payments, see s 6(6) and this is turn is limited in amount, see s 2(2), (3). See generally pp 402–408, *post*.
3. *Lim Poh Choo v Camden and Islington Area Health Authority* [1980] AC 174, at 193F-G, [1979] 2 All ER 910, at 923c-d.
4. *Wells v Wells* was a dispute about the relative merits of investment in equities and index linked gilt edged securities as a hedge against inflation.
5. *Cookson v Knowles* [1979] AC 556, at 571H-572A, [1978] 2 All ER 604, at 611d.
6. *Wells v Wells* [1997] 1 WLR 652, at 681F-G, [1997] 1 All ER 673, at 700g.
7. [1997] 1 WLR 652, [1997] 1 All ER 673.
8. [1997] 1 WLR 652, at 686D-E, [1997] 1 All ER 673, at 705c-d.
9. On the '*Besterman* cushion' see pp 176, 178–179, *post*. On the demise of the '*Besterman* cushion', see *Dart v Dart* [1996] 2 FLR 286, at 298F-G; *H v H* [1993] 2 FLR 335, at 349F-350A.

> ... in considering the financial needs of any person for the purposes of this section the court shall take into account his financial obligations and responsibilities.

It is difficult to understand the exact effect of this qualifying subsection. Clearly an applicant's obligations, legal or moral, to a third party such as an infant child, mistress or aged relative should be taken into account, but provision can only be ordered to support the applicant and not some third party.[10] Except perhaps where a spouse is awarded a 'just share', provision should not be ordered to enable an applicant to leave property on his death to a third party.[11] If the court suspects that the real motive behind an application is to obtain capital which will be inherited by a third party, any provision ordered should be in the form of periodic payments or a life-interest rather than a lump sum.

(viii) Obligations Owed to Persons other than the Applicant

Section 3(1) further provides that the court shall have regard to the following matters:

> (a) the financial resources and financial needs which any other applicant for an order under section 2 of this Act has or is likely to have in the foreseeable future;

10. In *Talbot v Talbot* [1962] 1 WLR 1113, [1962] 3 All ER 174 Baker J refused to take into account the obligations of a former spouse to support her illegitimate child born after a decree of nullity was pronounced between the deceased and her. He said at [1962] 1 WLR 1117, [1962] 3 All ER 177C, 'Despite the wide terms of s 3(4)(d) of the Matrimonial Causes (Property and Maintenance) Act 1958, I do not consider that I should take into account that she has to provide for her boy now aged fourteen'. But see *Re Goard* (1962) 106 Sol Jo 721 where Cross J awarded an estranged widow provision out of the estate of her deceased husband solely because she was maintaining the deceased's illegitimate child – the application was brought at a time when adulterine bastards could not be legitimated by subsequent marriage and when illegitimate children could not apply under the 1938 Act. Further in *Re Lewis* (13 March 1980, unreported), CA Buckley LJ in considering a claim by a widow under the 1938 Act had regard to the widow's obligation to support her infant child by a prior marriage. See further pp 149–150, *post*.
11. *Page v Page* [1981] 2 FLR 198, at 203E (per Dunn LJ), at 205D (per Wood J); *Preston v Preston* [1982] Fam 17, at 25C, [1982] 1 All ER 41, at 47g (per Ormrod LJ), [1982] Fam 36D, [1982] 1 All ER 56g-h (per Brandon LJ); *S v S*, Court of Appeal, 16 July 1980, cited in *Preston v Preston* [1982] Fam 24E, [1982] 1 All ER 47g. See also *Malone v Harrison* [1979] 1 WLR 1353, at 1365F, 1368B–C (per Hollings J). At first instance in *Re Besterman* Judge Mervyn Davies QC stated that provision would not be ordered to enable the applicant to leave property to a third party on death, [1982] 3 FLR 255, at 265E, 266F, but the Court of Appeal significantly made no similar remarks.

(b) the financial resources and financial needs which any beneficiary of the estate of the deceased has or is likely to have in the foreseeable future;
(c) any obligations and responsibilities which the deceased had towards any applicant for an order under section 2 or towards any beneficiary of the estate of the deceased;

'Beneficiary' is defined to include a person benefiting under a statutory nomination and a *donatio mortis causa*.[12] Although not technically defined as beneficiaries survivors of joint tenancies, persons benefiting under dispositions intended to defeat family provision applications and contracts to make wills are entitled to similar consideration.[13]

In deciding whether the dispositions of the deceased's estate made reasonable provision for the applicant the court considers the competing interests of other applicants and beneficiaries in the estate. Provision for an applicant may be totally unreasonable when viewed in isolation, but not unreasonable when account is taken of the other claims upon the deceased's bounty. In exercising its jurisdiction the court frequently has to balance the financial needs and resources and moral claims of the various parties.[14]

Unless the financial circumstances of beneficiaries are irrelevant, they should adduce evidence of their fiancial situation.[15]

The mere fact that a beneficiary does not fall within the class of applicants set out in the Act does not mean that his claims are valued as any the less by the court. *Re Joslin*[16] is a good example of this. The deceased left an estate of £370 to his mistress for life, remainder to his illegitimate children by his mistress and made no provision for his widow. After his death the mistress was destitute but the widow had a small income of her own. An application by the widow for provision out of the estate was refused, because of the strong claims of the mistress and the illegitimate children who were not at that time permitted to make applications. Merely because the widow was an applicant and the mistress and illegitimate children could not be applicants did not give the widow any preference.

It is suggested that the court should also be able to consider the claims of persons who are are not technically beneficiaries under

12. S 25(1).
13. S 9(1), s10(6), s11(4).
14. Eg *Re E* [1966] 1 WLR 709, [1966] 2 All ER 44.
15. In many cases it will be sufficient for the beneficiaries to state that they are 'comfortably off' and not in need of immediate financial assistance.
16. [1941] Ch 200, [1941] 1 All ER 302; see also *Re E* [1966] 1 WLR 709, [1966] 2 All ER 44.

the obligation to consider 'any other matter'.[17] For instance in assessing the reasonableness of provision made by a man for his cohabitee who comes within section 1(1)(ba) regard might be had to the needs of the cohabitee's child by another man which the deceased had treated as his own, but which could not be 'a child of the family' because the deceased and the mistress did not marry.[18] Similarly where a gift in a will was made to a beneficiary under a moral, but not a legal, duty to give to a person who cared for the deceased during his lifetime, the claims of the person who cared for the deceased should be considered.

(ix) Dilemma Cases

In some cases of relatively small estates where the deceased is unable to satisfy all the conflicting claims made upon him, the deceased often elects to prefer one person with claims upon him to another. In such cases the courts have sometimes refused to upset the testamentary dispositions holding that the deceased has not acted unreasonably in attempting to prefer one claimant to another.[19] The advantage of this approach is that it prevents any of the net estate being swallowed up in legal costs and so allows all of the estate to be applied for the maintenance of those who have claims upon the deceased. However, other judges have felt it more appropriate that the 'misery should be spread around' and have required that the deceased make some provision for the applicant even though the provision made by the deceased or by the rules of intestacy was inadequate for the beneficiaries of the deceased's estate. This approach may help to ensure a rough equality between parties with similar moral claims, but it does invite litigation which causes bitterness and dissipates the estate in costs.

(x) The Obligations and Responsibilities of the Deceased

Detailed discussion of the obligations and responsibilities of the deceased towards each class of applicant is contained in the next chapter.

17. S 3(1)(g).
18. For the definition of 'child of the family' see s 1(1)(d). In *Re Lewis* (13 March 1980, unreported), CA Buckley LJ considered it correct (under the 1938 Act) to have regard to a widow's responsibility to maintain a child by a former marriage. See further fn 10, p 48, *ante*.
19. *Re Joslin* [1941] Ch 200, at 202, [1941] 1 All ER 302, at 304E-H (per Farwell J); *Talbot v Talbot* [1962] 1 WLR 1113, at 1118, [1962] 3 All ER 174, at 1771 (per Baker J). It is noteworthy that in both cases the court thought that the testator had resolved the dilemma correctly. See also *Re Bateman* (1941) 85 Sol Jo 454; *Re E* [1966] 1 WLR 709, [1966] 2 All ER 44.

In *Re Jennings* the Court of Appeal held that section 3(1)(d) only referred to 'obligations and responsibilities' which the deceased had immediately before death.[20] Nourse LJ qualified his remarks by saying , 'at all events as a general rule'.[1] Henry LJ and Sir John May stated the proposition without qualification.[2] Of course events before death can create an obligation which is not discharged at the date of death.[3] An obligation which is not current at the date of death can not be relied upon within section 3(1)(g) as 'any other matter…'.[4]

It is suggested that just as an applicant must prove more than that he is in need and comes within the class of applicants,[5] a beneficiary to have his claims considered must prove more than that he is named in the will or takes on the intestacy and that he is in need.[6] The obligations and responsibilities of the deceased towards any beneficiary which may influence the court would appear to be similar to those which would influence the court in favour of an applicant. It is suggested that some matters favourable to an applicant which are not by themselves sufficient for the court to consider provision for an applicant unreasonable may be sufficient when found in a beneficiary to deny an otherwise successful applicant provision. For instance, the fact that a sizeable portion of the deceased's estate came from a particular source is normally not *in itself* sufficient reason to make an order for provision,[7] but it can be in itself sufficient to refuse provision.[8] That an adult child helped

20. [1994] Ch 286, [1994] 3 All ER 27. *Ad idem, Re Abram* [1996] 2 FLR 379, at 390F. For discussion of this principle in relation to claims by adult children, see pp 234–236, *post*.
1. [1994] Ch 296D-E, [1994] 3 All ER34g.
2. [1994] Ch 300E-G, [1994] 3 All ER 38h-39a (per Henry LJ); [1994] Ch 302F-G, [1994] 3 All ER 40h-J (per Sir John May).
3. [1994] Ch 300F-G, [1994] 3 All ER 38j (per Henry LJ). For a possible example, see *Re Goodchild* [1996] 1 WLR 694, [1996] 1 All ER 670; affd [1997] 3 All ER 63.
4. [1994] Ch 296E, [1996] 1 All ER 34g-h (per Nourse LJ).
5. *Re Coventry* [1980] Ch 461, at 475C–E, [1979] 2 All ER 408, at 418e-g (per Oliver J).
6. Compare *Re Harker-Thomas* [1969] P 28, [1968] 3 All ER 17 where Latey J appears to treat the mere poverty of the beneficiaries as a sufficient reason for refusing the applicant provision.
7. But compare *Sivyer v Sivyer* [1967] 1 WLR 1482, [1967] 3 All ER 429 where provision for an applicant was increased because the bulk of the estate originally came from the applicant's mother. See also *Re Callaghan* [1985] Fam 1, [1984] 3 All ER 790; *Re Leach* [1986] Ch 226, [1985] 2 All ER 754; *Re Goodchild* [1996] 1 WLR 694, [1996] 1 All ER 670; affd [1997] 3 All ER 63.
8. *Re Styler* [1942] Ch 387, at 390, [1942] 2 All ER 201, at 205A-B (per Morton J); *Re Brownbridge* (1942) 193 LT Jo 185; *Re Pugh* [1943] Ch 387, [1943] 2 All ER 361; *Re Canderton* (1970) 114 Sol Jo 208, *Re Iliffe, Jelley v Iliffe* [1981] Fam 128, at 140D-E, [1981] 2 All ER 29, at 37j (per Stephenson LJ); *Rhodes v Dean* (28 March 1996, unreported), CA.

the deceased in his business may be insufficient reason for awarding provision,[9] but may be a sufficient reason for refusing provision to an otherwise entitled applicant.[10] An example of this is the case of *Stephens v Stephens*.[11] In this case the deceased gave his second wife only a life-interest in his estate with remainder to his son by his first marriage. The wife applied under the 1975 Act for provision and the trial judge, reasoning that because the son could not bring a claim himself following *Re Coventry*, awarded the applicant the entire estate. The Court of Appeal reversed the decision on the basis that the trial judge had overstated the widow's claims and that the trial judge had given insufficient attention to the claims of the son.

In *Re Harker-Thomas*[12] Latey J held that the ties of blood of remote relatives taking on intestacy who had little or no contact with the deceased prior to his death were in themselves a 'moral claim' and entitled to consideration. The Law Commission disapproved of this decision and in its Working Paper stated that:

> In our view, the emphasis should be on the deceased's obligations to [the beneficiaries] rather than on preserving their interests in the estate.[13]

It is submitted that this approach is correct, and that Latey J's views, which have not been followed in subsequent cases, should not be regarded as an accurate statement of the law.

(xi) The Size and Nature of the Estate

Section 3(1) further provides that the court shall have regard to:

> (e) the size and nature of the net estate of the deceased.

(xii) Large Estates

If an estate is large it will be able to satisfy all the claims made against it and there will be less need to balance the rights of the various

9. See pp 237–239, *post*.
10. *Re Brownbridge* (1942) 193 LT Jo 185; compare *Re Rowlands* [1984] FLR 813.
11. (1 July 1985, unreported).
12. [1969] P 28, at 31G, [1968] 3 All ER 17, at 21A-B. See also the remarks of Lord Denning MR in *Sobesto v Farren* [1979] Conv 224, CA that the Defendant as 'the only known relative of the deceased ... would have a very considerable claim in respect of any property of his'. The decision of Burgess V-C in *Re Preston* [1969] 1 WLR 317, [1969] 3 All ER 961 to prefer some relatives over others (none of whom had any claim upon the deceased) in determining the incidence of an award seems indefensible.
13. WORKING PAPER, para 3.18; see also LAW COM, para 34, n 46.

applicants and beneficiaries.[14] However, the mere fact that an applicant is in need and that the estate is large enough to afford him provision is not sufficient to justify an award – in every case it must be reasonable for the court to order provision.[15]

(xiii) Small Estates

Throughout the history of family provision legislation the courts have stated that applications in small estates should be discouraged.[16] However, the actual decisions in cases where the estate was small have shown considerable variation – in many, applications have been dismissed,[17] often with costs against the applicant,[18] but in several cases provision has been ordered,[19] indeed in one case somewhat larger provision than usual was ordered because of the impact of costs in a small estate[20] and in another case a 'derisory order' was made to discourage applications in cases of small estates.[1]

The courts' objections to applications in small estates are based upon the problem of costs. In a small estate unless the applicant is awarded the entire estate and costs against the respondents, which is quite rare,[2] the assets available for both the applicant and the

14. *Malone v Harrison* [1979] 1 WLR 1353, at 1364D–E (per Hollings J).
15. *Re Coventry* [1980] Ch 461, at 475D–E; [1979] 2 All ER 408, at 418e-f (per Oliver J); see also *Re Pearson-Gregory* (1957) Times, 10 October; *Re Dennis* [1981] 2 All ER 140; *Cameron v Treasury Solicitor* [1996] 2 FLR 716.
16. *Re Vrint* [1940] Ch 920, at 926, [1940] 3 All ER 470, at 475F-H (per Bennet J); *Re Joslin* [1941] Ch 200, [1941] 1 All ER 302; *Re Catmull* [1943] Ch 262, [1943] 2 All ER 115; *Re Howell* [1953] 1 WLR 1034, [1953] 2 All ER 604; *Re Trowell* (1957) Times, 29 November; *Re E* [1966] 1 WLR 709, at 716A, [1966] 2 All ER 44, at 481 (per Stamp J); *Re Parkinson* (1975) Times, 4 October (per Lord Denning MR, per James LJ, per Bridge LJ); *Re Coventry* [1980] Ch 461, at 486F, [1979] 3 All ER 815, at 820h-821a (per Goff LJ); *Re Fullard* [1982] Fam 42, at 46B, [1981] 2 All ER 796, at 799b-c (per Ormrod LJ); *Brill v Proud* [1984] Fam Law 59 (per Latey J).
17. *Re Vrint* [1940] Ch 920, [1940] 3 All ER 470; *Re Joslin* [1941] Ch 200, [1941] 1 All ER 302; *Re Catmull* [1943] Ch 262, [1943] 2 All ER 115; *Re Howell* [1953] 1 WLR 1034, [1953] 2 All ER 604; *Re E* [1966] 1 WLR 709, [1966] 2 All ER 44.
18. *Re Vrint* [1940] Ch 920, [1940] 3 All ER 470; *Re Joslin* [1941] Ch 200, [1941] 1 All ER 302; *Brill v Proud* [1984] Fam Law 59; an order for costs against the legal aid fund was made in *Re Fullard* [1982] Fam 42, [1981] 2 All ER 796; and see also the remarks of Stamp J in *Re E* [1966] 1 WLR 709, at 716A–D, [1966] 2 All ER 44, at 48I–49B and Cross J in *Re Nesbitt* (1963) Times, 23 November.
19. *Re Parry* (1956) Times, 19 April; *Re Browne* (1957) Times, 14 December; *Re Clayton* [1966] 1 WLR 969, [1966] 2 All ER 969.
20. *Re Parkinson* (1975) Times, 4 October.
1. *Re Trowell* (1957) Times, 29 November.
2. But see the orders for costs made in the Court of Appeal in *Millward v Shenton* [1972] 1 WLR 711, [1972] 2 All ER 1025; *Bayliss v Lloyd's Bank* (9 December 1977, unreported), CA.

beneficiary are likely to be substantially diminished by the costs of any proceedings. The result is that the net value of the estate available to the applicant and the beneficiary who are both likely to be poor is to be substantially reduced. The effect of allowing claims in small estates is to make one party better off, but collectively the persons who have claims upon the deceased, who are likely to be poor, worse off.

It is submitted that the correct approach to claims against small estates was set out by Ungoed-Thomas J in *Re Clayton*:

> The [1938] Act places no bottom limit on the value of the estate in respect of which an application can be made. Dependants of a dead person, including the husband, have the right to make a claim against that person's estate however small it may be. Small sums matter to very many people, and an order under the Act for payment of £1 per week or less might, in certain circumstances, make all the difference to a claimant. However small the estate, all the relevant circumstances have to be considered before the court's decision is made. *The smallness of the estate neither excludes jurisdiction nor full consideration.*[3] Smallness of the estate, however, is significant in relation to (1) the availability of state aid for the claimant; (2) the extent to which the estate can effectively contribute to the claimant's maintenance; and (3) the costs which are necessarily involved in the application.[4]

As has been discussed where the deceased's estate is so small as to be unable to make provision for all persons having claims upon the deceased's estate, then it is proper to take into account means-tested non-contributory state benefits.[5]

Where the claims upon a small estate exceed its value, it may not be appropriate to seek to review the decision which the deceased made as to which persons having a claim upon his estate should benefit.[6] Certainly weak claims will not be acceded to in cases where the estate is small, and attempts at 'fine-tuning' or appeals in small estates will not be encouraged,[7] although an appeal will be

3. Emphasis added.
4. [1966] 1 WLR 971D–F, [1966] 2 All ER 371E–G: *ad idem Re Coventry* [1980] Ch 461, at 486F, [1979] 3 All ER 815, at 820h-821a (per Goff LJ).
5. See pp 145–146, *ante*.
6. See p 150, *ante*.
7. *Re Howell* [1953] 1 WLR 1034, at 1039, [1953] 2 All ER 604, at 607G (per Romer LJ); *Re Gregory* [1970] 1 WLR 1455, at 1460C, [1971] 1 All ER 497, at 501e-f (per Winn LJ), at [1970] 1 WLR 1462E, [1971] 1 All ER 503e (per Fenton Atkinson LJ); *Re Coventry* [1980] Ch 461, at 492G, [1979] 3 All ER 815, at 825g (per Geoffrey Lane LJ), at [1980] Ch 496B–C, [1979] 3 All ER 828f-g (per Buckley LJ); *Re Portt* (25 March 1980, unreported), CA (per Roskill LJ); *Brill v Proud* [1984] Fam Law 59, at 61 (per Latey J).

considered and allowed if there is an important point of principle involved as opposed to the exercise of a discretion.[8] In some cases the estate may be so small that any provision may be comparatively negligible as to not afford any real improvement in the applicant's maintenance.[9]

In some cases the estate is just so small that the cost of commencing proceedings, never mind litigating to judgment, consumes most of the estate. In *Re Clayton* Ungoed-Thomas J said:

> ... claims in cases where the costs of establishing claims leave virtually nothing significant for the claimant deprive the claim of substance and are to be discouraged. There will always be such cases, despite any reduction in costs that may be effected.[10]

Re Vrint[11] is an example of such a case. In 1940 the deceased left a net estate of £138-14s-10d and Bennet J dismissed an application for provision because the necessary costs of any hearing payable out of the estate were likely to exhaust the estate. It is suggested that in assessing this lower limit the costs of commencing proceedings and negotiating a settlement rather than the costs of prosecuting a claim to trial should be considered.[12]

(xiv) The Nature of the Estate

Both the 1938 Act and section 26 of the Matrimonial Causes Act 1965 contained the following restriction upon the court's power:

> ... the court ... shall not order any such provision to be made as would necessitate a realisation that would be improvident having a regard to the interests of the [deceased's] dependants and of the person who, apart from the order, would be entitled to that property.[13]

Although no such provision is found in the 1975 Act, the matter is dealt with under the court's duty to have regard to the interests of other beneficiaries and applicants and to the 'nature of the estate'.

8. *Cameron v Treasury Solicitor* [1996] 2 FLR 716, at 718B–C, 721F-G.
9. *Re Clayton* [1966] 1 WLR 969, at 971H–972A, [1966] 2 All ER 370, at 371I (per Ungoed-Thomas J).
10. [1966] 1 WLR 972A–B, [1966] 2 All ER 371I–372A.
11. [1940] Ch 920, [1940] 3 All ER 470, and see Rem Note (1940) 56 LQR 442.
12. The real value of £138-14s-10d in 1947 at 1997 prices is approximately £2,921 and there was approximately 50% inflation between 1940 and 1947. *Brill v Proud* [1984] Fam Law 59 concerned an estate worth £12,000 in 1980. *Cameron v Treasury Solicitor* [1996] 2 FLR 716 concerned an estate worth £8,000 in 1990. The author would not normally recommend commencing proceedings where the estate is less than £8,000.
13. S 1(5) of the 1938 Act; s 26(5) of the Matrimonial Causes Act 1965.

It is quite clear that the court will have regard to the real cost to the beneficiaries of making an order for provision, where such an order necessitates a premature or infelicitous realisation of a part of the estate. Similarly the court will be slow to order provision which will result in a beneficiary losing his home[14] or being deprived of his income from a business.[15] However, it must be stressed that what is considered are the interests of the beneficiaries and other applicants and that there is no presumption that the assets of the estate such as houses and businesses should remain in specie.[16] The court should consider both the loss to the beneficiary if provision is ordered and the extent of his claims upon the deceased. Thus it may well be proper to make an order for provision which will deprive a beneficiary of his home, if the applicant's claim upon the deceased is strong.[17] The claim of an adult son to inherit his father's business is entitled to far more consideration if he has himself contributed to the success of the business than if his connection with the business only began upon the deceased's death.[18]

If the nature of the estate and the claims upon it do not enable an immediate provision to be made, it is possible for the court to adjourn the summons until circumstances change or until some specified date in the future.[19]In recent years family provision courts have developed fairly subtle techniques to enable the claims of applicants to be met without disturbing the occupation by a

14. Eg *Re E* [1966] 1 WLR 709, [1966] 2 All ER 44; *Re Fergusson*, Foster J (16 June 1980, unreported).
15. Eg *Re Brownbridge* (1942) 193 LT Jo 185; *Re Rowlands* [1984] FLR 813, at 818H (per Anthony Lincoln J), at 824F-H (per Cumming-Bruce LJ).
16. See per Edmund Davies LJ in *Thornley v Palmer* [1969] 1 WLR 1037, at 1043G–1044A, [1969] 3 All ER 31, at 36G–I. In *Re Rowlands* [1984] FLR 813, at 824F-G Cumming-Bruce LJ referred to both the cost to the beneficiaries of realising farming assets and the deceased's wish to preserve the farm intact for successive generations.The remarks of Cumming-Bruce LJ in relation to the dynastic intentions of the deceased were, rightly, given short shrift by Campbell J in *Morrow v Morrow* (5 April 1995, unreported) and Kerr J in *McGuigan v McGuigan* (25 March 1996, unreported).
17. Eg *Re Nesbitt* (1963) Times, 22 November; and note also that the mere loss of accommodation does not give an adult child a claim under the Act, *Re Coventry* [1980] Ch 461, [1979] 2 All ER 408; affd [1979] 3 All ER 815; *Re Fergusson*, Foster J (16 June 1980, unreported). Both Campbell J in *Morrow v Morrow* (5 April 1995, unreported) and Kerr J in *Mcguigan v McGuigan* (25 March 1996, unreported) made orders in favour of surviving wives which to some extent interefered with farming businesses carried on by children.
18. Compare *Re Brownbridge* (1942) 193 LT Jo 185 with the remark of Edmund Davies LJ in *Thornley v Palmer* [1969] 1 WLR 1037, at 1043G–1044A, [1969] 3 All ER 31, at 36G–I.
19. *Re Bateman* (1941) 85 Sol Jo 454; *Re Franks* [1948] Ch 62, [1947] 2 All ER 638; but see fn 9, p 141, *ante*.

beneficiary of a dwellinghouse [20] or the running of a business by a beneficiary.[1] Payment by instalments[2] or some form of deferred charge [3] are ways in which competing claims can be accommodated.

(xv) Source of the Estate

Normally the source of the deceased's estate is of no relevance in deciding whether the deceased has made reasonable provision for the applicant. Just as the source of a person's wealth and income is generally irrelevant in assessing his liability to maintain another when alive,[4] so it is irrelevant when assessing his liability after death.[5] However, the source of the deceased's estate may be relevant in three situations.

In some circumstances property may have been given to the deceased under a moral obligation to leave it by will to a third person. Such an obligation is certainly a matter to be taken into consideration by the court and may have the effect of excluding part of the estate from being available to satisfy an order for family provision.[6] A good example of this is *Re Canderton*.[7] In this case a

20. *Re H (a minor)* (1975) 6 Fam Law 172 concerned an application by an infant child, where the estate devolved upon a second wife and where the only substantial asset in the estate was a house occupied by the widow. Lane J awarded a lump sump of £2,000 but stated that the order was not to be enforced immediately. In *Jessop v Jessop* [1992] 1 FLR 591 the Court of Appeal made an order under s 9 in respect of the deceased's severable share of the dwellinghouse occupied by the deceased's mistress, but the mistress through a lump sum pension payment was able to buy out the applicant. In *Rajabally v Rajabally* [1987] 2 FLR 390 the applicant wife acquired a dwellinghouse absolutely subject to a charge in favour of a child of the deceased, the court having ascertained that the applicant could raise a mortgage with which to discharge the charge. Similar orders were made in *Moody v Haselgrove* (16 November 1987, unreported), CA and *Dixit v Dixit* (23 June 1988, unreported), CA.
1. In both *Re Rowlands* [1984] FLR 813, at 818H,824G-H and *Re Farrow* [1987] 1 FLR 205, at 210C-D there was discussion of how a farm could be mortgaged to realise lump sums with which to meet the applicant's claim.
2. Eg *Re Rowlands* [1984] Fam Law 280.
3. Eg *Rajabally v Rajabally* [1987] 2 FLR 390.
4. Eg *Pearce v Pearce* (1979) 10 Fam Law 209.
5. But see *Sivyer v Sivyer* [1967] 1 WLR 1482, at 1488E–1489, [1967] 3 All ER 429, at 433G–434C where Pennycuick J specifically increased the applicant's award because of the derivation of the estate. Similar remarks were made in similar circumstances by Mervyn Davies J in *Re Wood* [1982] LS Gaz R 774, 2 April 1982 but it is doubtful whether the result of the case was affected.
6. *Re Styler* [1942] Ch 387, at 390, [1941] 2 All ER 201, at 205A-B (per Morton J); *Re Canderton* (1970) 114 Sol Jo 208; *Jelley v Iliffe* [1981] Fam 128, at 140D–E, [1981] 2 All ER 29, at 38a (per Stephenson LJ); *Cumming Burns v Burns* (4 July 1985, unreported), Ca. But see *Dillon v Public Trustee* [1941] AC 294, [1941] 2 All ER 284 and *Re Brown* (1955) 105 L Jo 169, 219 LT 129 where it was held not only that property the subject of a contract to make a will was available to satisfy an order for family provision, *but also that it was proper in the court's discretion* to order such provision.
7. (1970) 114 Sol Jo 208.

substantial portion of the deceased's estate was derived from his mistress who predeceased him. The mistress by the provisions of her will indicated that if her estate did not go to the deceased it was to go to a niece and a friend of the mistress. The deceased in his own will made substantial provision for the niece and the friend. In an application for family provision by the deceased's estranged wife, Ungoed-Thomas J took into account the circumstances in which the deceased came into a large part of the estate and made an award of provision which probably did not substantially reduce the benefits to the niece and the friend which came from the mistress's will. A similar case is *Cumming Burns v Burns*.[8] Here the principal asset in the estate was a property which had been given to the deceased by his second wife. The deceased left his estate to his second wife and the first wife applied for provision. The application was dismissed on the basis that the deceased held the property on a 'moral resulting trust' for his second wife.

Where the deceased received a substantial portion of his estate from his first spouse upon the express understanding that he would leave such property to the children of the marriage and even though the situation did not create a binding mutual wills trust, following *Re Goodchild*,[9] such property is probably immune from a claim by the second wife. There is unfortunately no modern decision on the court's approach to the more common situation where the deceased received a substantial portion of his estate from his first spouse where there was no express understanding with the first spouse that he should leave such property to their children and where the second spouse makes a claim.[10]

Secondly, if the applicant or a beneficiary has contributed to the deceased's estate this may be a factor in deciding whether or

8. (4 July 1985, unreported), CA.
9. [1996] 1 WLR 694, [1996] 1 All ER 670; affd [1997] 3 All ER 63. Note that the second wife did not put forward any affirmative case of her own for provision to be made for her. But would such an agreement be avoided by s 11?
10. The 'moral resulting trust' cases of *Re Styler* [1942] Ch 387, at 390, [1941] 2 All ER 201, at 205A-B; *Re Canderton* (1970) 114 Sol Jo 208 and *Cumming Burns v Burns* (4 July 1985, unreported), CA strongly suggest that provision would not be ordered for a second spouse. However, in *Jelley v Iliffe* [1981] Fam 128, at 140D-E, [1981] 2 All ER 29, at 38a Stephenson LJ appeared to indicate that while it was unlikely that a life-interest would be awarded to the deceased's lover in a property derived entirely from the deceased's first husband and their children, it was not *impossible* for the court to do so. A life-interest to the surviving spouse satisfies the requirement for maintenance, but also preserves the property for the children of the first marriage.

not to order provision.[11] Clearly under the 1975 Act the conduct of a spouse in directly or indirectly contributing to the estate of the deceased is a matter to be considered.[12] Thus it might be proper in dealing with an application by a second wife against the estate of her husband where the second wife did not contribute directly or indirectly to the deceased's estate to award the applicant maintenance from the estate, but not a 'just share'.[13] It may be relevant that a beneficiary under the will of the deceased assisted the testator in his business which made up the bulk of the estate whereas the applicant contributed nothing to the success of the business.[14] In comparing the relative claims of a wife and mistress or between a former wife and wife to maintenance from the deceased's estate regard is had to the relative contribution of each to the deceased's business.[15]

Thirdly, there is a controversial line of cases where adult children have been able to make a claim under the legislation *solely* upon the basis of the deceased's estate coming from a particular side of the family.[16]

(xvi) Any Physical or Mental Disability of an Applicant or a Beneficiary

Section 3(1) further provides that the court shall have regard to:

> (f) any physical or mental disability of any applicant for an order under the said section 2 or any beneficiary of the estate of the deceased.[17]

11. *Re Brownbridge* (1942) 193 LT Jo 185; *Re Pugh* [1943] Ch 387, at 395, [1943] 2 All ER 361, at 365F (per Morton J); *Re Langley* (1964) Times, 27 June; *Re Clayton* [1966] 1 WLR 969, at 973C, [1966] 2 All ER 370, at 372H–I (per Ungoed-Thomas J); *Jelley v Iliffe* [1981] Fam 128, at 140D, [1981] 2 All ER 29, at 38e (per Stephenson LJ).
12. For the position generally of applications by spouses, see Ch 6, Pt 1.
13. Eg *Moody v Stevenson* [1992] Ch 486, [1992] 2 All ER 524. And see the significant case of *Churchill v Churchill* (1980) 11 Fam Law 179 where in divorce proceedings after a short marriage the applicant wife was refused a lump sum award out of a substantial inheritance which the husband obtained after the parties' separation where otherwise the wife was not entitled to maintenance or a lump sum.
14. *Re Brownbridge* (1942) 193 LT Jo 185.
15. *Thornley v Palmer* [1969] 1 WLR 1037, [1969] 3 All ER 31.
16. *Re Callaghan* [1985] Fam 1, [1984] 3 All ER 790; *Re Leach* [1986] Ch 226, [1985] 2 All ER 754; *Re Goodchild* [1996] 1 WLR 694, [1996] 1 All ER 670; affd [1997] 3 All ER 63, discussed in pp 49–50, *ante* and pp 240–242, *post.*
17. Derived from Matrimonial Causes Act 1973, s 25(1)(e).

The relevance of any physical or mental incapacity of any applicant or beneficiary will be discussed in the next chapter where claims by adult children are examined.[18]

(xvii) Any Other Relevant Circumstances of the Case

The final matter with which the court is to have regard to is:

> (g) any other matter, including the conduct of the applicant or any other person, which in the circumstances of the case the court may consider relevant.

In *Re Fullard* Ormrod LJ described section 3(1)(g) as giving the court:

> ... the widest possible powers to take into account any matter which is relevant.[19]

However, Nourse LJ stated in *Re Jennings* that if a matter were held not to come within any of the other specific subsections of section 3, it could not 'be prayed in aid under a general provision such as section 3(1)(g)'.[20]

In *Malone v Harrison* Hollings J drew attention to this reference to conduct being 'in much wider or more general terms than the terms used in the Matrimonial Causes Act 1973'.[1]

As it is difficult to generalise about the relevance of the conduct of an applicant for all classes of applicant, conduct will be discussed in the next chapter where the different types of applicant are discussed separately.

(xviii) Intestacy

When the 1938 Act was extended to cases of total intestacy by the Intestates' Estates Act 1952,[2] the following subsection was added to the Act:

> The court in considering ... whether the dispositions of the deceased's estate effected by the law relating to intestacy, or by the combination

18. See pp 242–247, *post*.
19. [1982] Fam 42, at 46H, [1981] 2 All ER 796, at 799h-j.
20. [1994] Ch 286, at 296E-F, [1994] 3 All ER 27, at 34g-h, *sed quaere*.
1. [1979] 1 WLR 1353, at 1364F, *sed quaere* certainly with applications by spouses the test for conduct is exactly the same under the Matrimonial Causes Act 1973 as it is under the 1975 Act, see pp 189–190, *post*.
2. For the background to the extension of the jurisdiction to cases of intestacy see p 21, *ante*.

> of the deceased's will and that law makes reasonable provision for the maintenance of a dependant shall not be bound to assume that the law relating to intestacy makes reasonable provision in all cases.[3]

Although this subsection is not repeated in the 1975 Act, it is quite clear that the same principle applies.[4] In administering the jurisdiction the courts have made no distinction between cases where the deceased died testate and intestate. In *Re Coventry* Goff LJ stated:

> In my judgment the problem must be exactly the same whether one is dealing with a will or an intestacy, or with a combination of both. The question is whether the operative dispositions make or fail to make, reasonable provision in all the circumstances.[5]

The rules for the distribution of a person's estate upon intestacy are designed for the typical case. It is generally thought that in a typical case the court will not award provision in excess of the share available on intestacy. Certainly the Law Commission did not consider that the enhanced standard of provision for applications by spouses would lead to awards greater than the spouse's share on intestacy.[6] However, in two decisions concerning applications by spouses under the 1938 Act the Court of Appeal awarded the applicants more than their intestate share at the date of death but less than their intestate share if measured at the date of the hearing.[7]

3. S 1(8) of the 1938 Act.
4. See s 1(1) of the 1975 Act.
5. [1980] Ch 461, at 488G–H, [1979] 3 All ER 815, at 822g-h. See also *Cameron v Treasury Solicitor* [1996] 2 FLR 716, at 720F-H per Butler-Sloss LJ that the deceased's estate devolved upon the Crown as bona vacantia does not give an applicant a claim which otherwise does not exist and was 'a neutral factor'. But compare *Re Callaghan* [1985] Fam 1, [1984] 3 All ER 790; *Re Leach* [1986] Ch 226, [1985] 2 All ER 754.
6. WORKING PAPER, para 3.9.
7. In *Bayliss v Lloyd's Bank* (9 December 1977, unreported), CA the deceased died on 5 December 1970 survived by a widow and children. His estate was probably worth about £15,000. Under the rules of intestacy for deaths in 1970 the widow was entitled to the personal chattels, a legacy of £8,750 and a life interest in half the residue. The Court of Appeal awarded the applicant widow the entire estate. By the date of the hearing the spouse's statutory legacy had been increased to £25,000.

   In *Re Lewis* (13 March 1980, unreported), CA the deceased died in March 1974, leaving a net estate of at least £68,000 and survived by a widow and children. Under the rules of intestacy for deaths in 1974 the widow was entitled to the personal chattels, a legacy of £15,000 and a life interest in half the residue. The Court of Appeal awarded the applicant widow the use of £18,000 for her widowhood and capital of £28,000, £18,000 of which being the capitalised value of an annuity. By the date of the hearing the spouse's statutory legacy had increased to £25,000.

Where the facts are not typical such as situations where the interests of the spouse and infant children conflict,[8] or where one of several adult children has a strong moral claim[9] or in applications by former spouses or a cohabitee the intestacy rules offer no guidance as to what is reasonable provision.

(xix) The Reasons of the Deceased

The 1938 Act contained a provision which required the court to:

> ... have regard to the deceased's reasons, so far as ascertainable, for making the disposition made by his will if any, or from refraining from disposing by will of his estate or part of his estate, or for not making any provision, or any further provision, as the case may be, for a dependant,

and permitted the court to receive otherwise inadmissible evidence of such reasons.[10] This elevation of the reasons of the deceased into a matter in itself to be considered by the court was criticised as the test applied by the court was an objective one. One distinguished author wrote:

> If the testator's reasons are good reasons founded on truth, then they come in under section [3(1)(g)], and there is no need to add anything thereto except for the purpose of evidence. If on the other hand they are not good reasons but founded on some misapprehension or absence of full knowledge, then it cannot be right to attach any weight to them.[11]

This criticism was accepted by the Law Commission[12] and consequently the 1975 Act contains no provision elevating the reasons of the deceased into a specific matter to be considered by the court, but the Act formerly contained provisions admitting into evidence the statements concerning the deceased's reasons.[13]

Both these awards to widows involved indirect provision for infant children. The author is not aware of any later case where an applicant spouse was awarded more than her entitlement under the rules of intestacy.

8. Eg *Sivyer v Sivyer* [1967] 1 WLR 1482, [1967] 3 All ER 429; *Re Collins* [1990] Fam 56, [1990] 2 All ER 47.
9. Eg *Re Cook* (1956) 106 L Jo 466.
10. S 1(7) as amended. S 26 of the Matrimonial Causes Act 1965 contained no comparable provision.
11. ALBERY, 23.
12. WORKING PAPER, paras 3.22–3.24; LAW COM, paras 105–108.
13. S 21, repealed by the Civil Evidence Act 1995. Similar Australian provisions have been interpreted to mean that such statements are evidence of the deceased's reasons, but not evidence of the truth of those reasons, DICKEY, 125-8; DE GROOT AND NICKEL, para 606.3; *Hughes v National Trustee* (1979) 143 CLR 134 (High Ct).

Accordingly the reasons of the deceased are not a matter to be considered merely because they are his reasons but on their merits.[14] The mere absence of reasons for the deceased making any particular disposition does not make such a disposition unreasonable.[15] A deceased should not be punished in family provision proceedings merely because his reasons for excluding the applicant are false and dishonourable.[16]

The deceased's intention to benefit the applicant is generally irrelevant.[17] In *Re Coventry* Goff LJ said:

> Indeed I think any view expressed by a deceased person that he wishes a particular person to benefit will generally be of little significance, because the question is not subjective but objective. An express reason for rejecting the applicant is a different matter and may be very relevant to the problem.[18]

Contracting Out of the Act

Although there was no decision on the point,[19] it was always assumed that parties could not contract out of the provisions of the 1938 Act.[20] This was because of the principle of public policy against contracting out of legislation partially designed to relieve the state

14. The stress by Balcombe LJ on the reasons of the deceased in *Stephens v Stephens* (1 July 1985, unreported), CA is erroneous, but the decision is unexceptional.
15. Eg *Re Coventry* [1980] Ch 461, [1979] 2 All ER 408; affd [1979] 3 All ER 815; *Cameron v Treasury Solicitor* [1996] 2 FLR 716.
16. *Re Borthwick* [1949] Ch 395, at 300, 302, [1949] 1 All ER 472, at 475H, 476D (per Harman J).
17. *Re Coventry* [1980] Ch 461, at 488H–489A, [1979] 3 All ER 815, at 822h (per Goff LJ), doubting *Re Christie* [1979] Ch 168, [1979] 1 All ER 546 and *Bosch v Perpetual Trustee Co* [1938] AC 463, at 481, [1938] 2 All ER 14, at 23G (per Lord Romer). See further *Re Brindle* (1941) 192 LT Jo 75; *Re Collins* [1990] Fam 56, at 62H, [1990] 2 All ER 47, at 52g and pp 47–48, *ante*. But compare *Malone v Harrison* [1979] 1 WLR 1353, at 1359E–F, 1365D and see p 167, *post*. In *Re Collins* [1990] Fam 56, at 62H-63A, [1990] 2 All ER 47, at 52g-h lack of intention by the deceased to benefit the beneficiary, confirms reasonableness to make provision for the applicant.
18. [1980] Ch 488H–489A, [1979] 3 All ER 822h. The second sentence of the quotation is a little dubious in the light of the repeal of s 1(6).
19. In *Zamet v Hyman* [1961] 1 WLR 1442, [1961] 3 All ER 933 the plaintiff before her marriage to the deceased executed a deed relinquishing all rights she might have under the 1938 Act against the deceased's estate. It was argued that this provision was void as ousting or tending to oust the jurisdiction of the court, but the court decided the case on another ground.
20. Laskin (1938) 16 Can Bar Rev 669; Note, (1941) 91 L Jo 68, 69. First edition, pp 20–21.

of the burden of supporting needy applicants[1] and by analogy with the similar prohibition on contracting out of the court's powers to order maintenance after divorce.[2] Almost all Commonwealth jurisdictions have prohibited contracting out of the legislation.[3]

It was held in *Re M*[4] that public policy prevented a former spouse from releasing while the deceased was alive her rights to apply to the court under the Matrimonial Causes Act 1965, section 26. Furthermore in *Re S*[5] the court rejected an argument that an agreement not to claim maintenance, while not ousting the jurisdiction of the court, was of such overriding importance that it would be an abuse of the discretion of the court to order provision in proceedings brought under the Matrimonial Causes (Property and Maintenance) Act 1958, section 3.

The Law Commission generally approved of the parties' inability to contract out of the Act, but considered that just as a divorced spouse can validly agree to forego any further claims for maintenance after divorce, so a divorced spouse should be able to forego claims for maintenance out of the estate of the deceased.[6] Accordingly it was recommended that upon a divorce or a decree of nullity or judicial separation *with the consent of the parties* the court could order that either party to the marriage should not be able subsequently to apply for provision under the 1975 Act. This recommendation was carried into effect by section 15 of the 1975 Act. In 1984 the need for the consent of the parties was removed.[7] The Law Commission specifically recommended against giving the courts a power to sanction such agreements debarring an application for family provision before spouses are divorced or judicially separated.[8]

Accordingly it appears that apart from orders made under section 15, which is discussed elsewhere in this book,[9] the parties

1. See *National Assistance Board v Parkes* [1955] 2 QB 506, [1955] 3 All ER 1.
2. *Hyman v Hyman* [1929] AC 601.
3. See generally DE GROOT AND NICKEL, para 209.1; Laskin, (1938) 16 Can Bar Rev 669; Bale, 'Limitation of Testamentary Disposition in Canada', (1964) 42 Can Bar Rev 367, 391–395; New Zealand, *Gardiner v Boag* [1923] NZLR 739; *Parish v Parish* [1923] NZGLR 536; *Dillon v Public Trustee* [1941] AC 294, at 303, [1941] 2 All ER 284, at 289A–B (per Viscount Simon LC); New South Wales, *Lieberman v Morris* (1944) 69 CLR 69; Queensland, *Re Willert* [1937] QWN 35; Victoria, *Re Pearson* [1936] VLR 355.
4. [1968] P 174, [1967] 3 All ER 412; see also *Re S* [1965] P 165, at 170D–G, [1965] 1 All ER 1018, at 1022B–E (per Cairns J).
5. [1965] P 165, at 171B–G, [1965] 1 All ER 1018, at 1022A-E (per Cairns J).
6. WORKING PAPER paras 3.66–3.68; LAW COM, paras 185–188.
7. S 8 of the Matrimonial and Family Proceedings Act 1984.
8. LAW COM, para 186(b).
9. See pp 271–174, *post*.

cannot oust the jurisdiction of the court by agreement. A condition in a will that a gift is forfeited if an application is made under the Act is probably void on the grounds of public policy.[10] Acceptance of a gift in a will which is expressed to be in full satisfaction of all claims by an applicant[11] probably does not bar a subsequent application to the court or create any estoppel against the applicant.[12]

After the Law Commission had reported there were two important developments in the treatment of agreements dealing with maintenance and property matters upon divorce. Firstly, the divorce courts held that while an agreement, arrived at with proper advice[13] and not as a result of unfair pressure[14] or misrepresentation[15] and not substantively grossly unfair to one party did not oust the jurisdiction of the court, it was a matter which greatly affected the exercise of the court's discretionary powers so that the court would normally exercise its powers to give effect to such an agreement.[16] It is submitted that, subject to arguments derived from *Barder v Caluori*,[17] such agreement reached between spouses before death will normally be given effect to if one of the parties dies.

Secondly Parliament in enacting the Matrimonial and Family Proceedings Act 1984 endorsed the concept of a 'clean break' on divorce.[18]

Both these developments have important implications for family provision. It is submitted that while an agreement purporting to deal with the parties' rights to apply to the court under the 1975 Act will not oust the jurisdiction of the court, it is, if not obviously so unfair to a party and fairly negotiated, a matter of such great importance in the exercise of the court's powers that it should normally be given

10. See *Re Gaynor* [1960] VR 640; *Re Chester* (1978) 19 SASR 247; *Re Adams*, Ryan J Queensland (9 September 1987, unreported); *Shah v Perpetual Trustee Co* (1981) 7 Fam LR 97; but compare the rule that enforces conditions against disputing the validity of wills, *Evanturel v Evanturel* (1874) LR 6 PC 1; Theobold, *Wills* (15th edn) 658.
11. Eg *Re Langley* (1964) Times, 27 June.
12. Compare the policy of *Re Ralphs* [1968] 1 WLR 1522, [1968] 3 All ER 285 of distributing prior to the hearing to the applicant in the challenged will.
13. Eg *Backhouse v Backhouse* [1978] 1 WLR 243, [1978] 1 All ER 1158.
14. Eg *Brockwell v Brockwell* (1975) 6 Fam Law 46; *Beetlestone v Beetlestone* (1981) 132 NLJ 297.
15. Eg *Re M* [1968] P 174, [1967] 3 All ER 412.
16. *Dean v Dean* [1978] Fam 161, [1978] 3 All ER 758; *Ladbrook v Ladbrook* (1977) 7 Fam Law 213; *Edgar v Edgar* [1980] 1 WLR 1410, [1980] 3 All ER 887; see also *Smallman v Smallman* [1972] Fam 25, [1971] 3 All ER 717.
17. [1988] AC 20, [1987] 2 All ER 440; *Smith v Smith* [1992] Fam 69, [1991] 2 All ER 306; *Amey v Amey* [1992] 2 FLR 89; *Barber v Barber* [1993] 1 FLR 476.
18. S 25A of the Matrimonial Causes Act 1973, introduced by s 3 of the Matrimonial and Family Proceedings Act 1984.

effect to.[19] In *Re Fullard*[20] the Court of Appeal rejected an argument that merely because an agreement was not contained in an order made under section 15 it was of no relevance to the exercise of the court's powers. Accordingly it is suggested that where an order under section 15 is omitted from the court's order under the Matrimonial Causes Act 1973 by mistake[1] or where such a term could properly be implied into an agreement between spouses on divorce,[2] the court should give effect to such agreement or implied term by dismissing any application. Similarly if the parties had been divorced outside England and Wales,[3] the courts should give effect to orders made in such foreign proceedings which are to the same effect as an order made under section 15. Agreements which the courts should give effect to should include agreements entered into *after the breakdown of the relationship* between separated spouses,[4] parents and adult children.[5] Any compromise of rights under the 1975 Act reached after death is binding.[6]

However, it is doubtful that the courts would wish to exercise their powers so as to enforce ante-nuptial agreements such as are found in many civil law jurisdictions[7] limiting the parties' entitlement to family provision, especially if the marriage were of a long duration.[8]

19. Compare *Dean v Dean* [1978] Fam 161, [1978] 3 All ER 758; *Re Fullard* [1982] Fam 42, [1981] 2 All ER 796.
20. [1982] Fam 42, at 49G–50B, [1981] 2 All ER 796, at 802b-d (per Ormrod LJ), at [1982] Fam 52B, [1981] 2 All ER 803h (per Purchas J); *Re S* [1965] P 165, [1965] 1 All ER 1018 was not cited. *Ad idem*, *Brill v Proud* [1984] Fam Law 59; *Cameron v Treasury Solicitor* [1996] 2 FLR 716.
1. *Cameron v Treasury Solicitor* [1996] 2 FLR 716.
2. Compare *Brill v Proud* [1984] Fam Law 59.
3. Compare *Hewitson v Hewitson* [1995] Fam 100, [1995] 1 All ER 472.
4. Eg in *Edgar v Edgar* [1980] 1 WLR 1410, [1980] 3 All ER 887 the agreement was made prior to divorce.
5. Compare *Re Willert* [1937] QWN 35; and compare *Re Goodchild* [1996] 1 WLR 694, at 714C, [1996] 1 All ER 670, at 686e.
6. *Benson v Benson* [1996] 1 FLR 692. On taking into account post-death vacillation, see *Escritt v Escritt* (1982) 3 FLR 280; *Re Campbell* [1983] NI 10, at 17D-E.
7. See also Uniform Probate Code, s 2-203.
8. See *Zamet v Hyman* [1961] 1 WLR 1442, [1961] 3 All ER 933 and see remarks of the Law Commission against extending the right to apply for an order under s 15 to spouses WORKING PAPER, para 3.67; LAW COM, para 186(b). But see now *S v S (matrimonial proceedings: appropriate forum)* [1997] 1 WLR 1200, at 1203D–1204B, which concerned a pre-nuptial agreement governing both divorce and death; and Harcus 'Pre-Nuptial Agreements' [1997] Fam Law 669. The approach of *Cumming Burns v Burns* (4 July 1985, unreported), CA ('a moral resulting trust') and of *Re Goodchild* [1996] 1 WLR 694, [1996] 1 All ER 670; affd [1997] 3 All ER 63 ('a moral mutual wills trust') does suggest that the parties can in effect remove property from an application under the Act. *Sed quaere* whether such cases have fully taken into account the operation of s 10 and the general prohibition on contracting out. In both cases the property was provided by a third party.

Just as the parties cannot contract out of the jurisdiction of the court under the 1975 Act, so jurisdiction under the 1975 Act cannot be conferred on the court by agreement or consent. However, it is suggested that where the court has jurisdiction to order provision the court can, *consistent with the general principles governing the exercise of its discretion*,[9] take into account the agreement or consent of the deceased or the beneficiaries that the Act should apply or that an award should be made. An example of this unusual situation was *Malone v Harrison*[10] where the deceased told the applicant that he had made no provision for her in his will but sent to her a newspaper cutting relating to the passage of the 1975 Act and the enactment of section 1(1)(e). It appears that Hollings J took this into account as *a* factor in awarding provision.

9. See *Malone v Harrison* [1979] 1 WLR 1353, at 1365D (per Hollings J).
10. [1979]1 WLR 1353, at 1359E–F.

Chapter 6

REASONABLE PROVISION FOR DIFFERENT CLASSES OF APPLICANT

PART 1: SPOUSES

Introduction

The protection of the inheritance rights of a spouse has been the most controversial question affecting testamentary freedom in twentieth century England and Wales. The enactment of the 1938 Act was brought about mainly by feminist pressure[1] and the vast majority of applications under both the 1938 and 1975 Acts were and are made by widows. The 1975 Act effected a major change in the jurisdiction by allowing an award to a surviving spouse in excess of his or her need for maintenance; the somewhat curious way in which the Law Commission arrived at its conclusion that spouses should have an enhanced standard of provision has already been noted. [2] The Law Commission advocated giving spouses a larger standard of provision than maintenance because it considered that the system of matrimonial property law was unjust to wives and more specifically because of the possibility that a spouse might be better off applying under the Matrimonial Causes Act 1973 upon divorce than applying for family provision on death.[3] To effect this conclusion section 1(2)(a) provides that in the case of an application by a spouse 'reasonable financial provision' means:

> ... such financial provision as it would be reasonable in all the circumstances of the case for a husband or wife to receive, whether or not that provision is required for his or her maintenance.

Additionally one of the guidelines laid down specifically for applications by spouses provides that:

> ... the court shall also ... *have regard to* the provision which the applicant might reasonably have expected to receive if on the day

1. See pp 9–19, *ante*.
2. See pp 24–27, *ante*.
3. WORKING PAPER, paras 3.6–3.7; LAW COM, paras 13-8, 26-30.

on which the deceased died the marriage, instead of being terminated by death, had been terminated by a decree of divorce.[4]

The Standard of Provision

Probably no part of the 1975 Act has a more theoretical effect, but twenty years after the legislation came into force, the consensus is beginning to emerge that the enhanced standard of provision has only a very limited effect upon the vast majority of applications by spouses. The interpretation of section 1(2)(a) has not been helped by the considerable uncertainty and flux, both statutory[5] and judicial, in the exercise of the court's powers to award ancillary relief after divorce.

The Functions of the Court's Powers on Divorce

Before the relationship of the court's powers under the 1975 Act and the Matrimonial Causes Act 1973 as amended is discussed, it will be helpful to analyse briefly the court's functions when it exercises its powers to grant ancillary relief under the Matrimonial Causes Act 1973 as amended.

Firstly, the court aims at providing maintenance or support for each party. The duty of a spouse to maintain the other after divorce was historically seen as arising from divorce being a breach of contract by one spouse, or by both spouses, and maintenance being compensation for the other party's breach of matrimonial duty.[6] The protection of a party's expectation loss found its expression in the qualified admonition to the court under the Matrimonial Causes Act 1973 as originally enacted to place the parties in the same position which they would be in had the marriage not terminated.[7] Other analysis, while rejecting the 'promise' based justification for maintenance after divorce, justified the award of maintenance on divorce as compensation for detrimental reliance caused by the marriage,[8] such as one spouse giving up a career with, perhaps, the

4. S 3(2); emphasis added.
5. Principally the Matrimonial and Family Proceedings Act 1984.
6. See Law Commission Report No 103, 'The Financial Consequences of Divorce: The Basic Policy. A Discussion Paper', paras 9–13, 20–27.
7. S 25(1).
8. See Law Commission Report No 103, 'The Financial Consequences of Divorce: The Basic Policy. A Discussion Paper', paras 54–55.

prospects of acquiring capital, in order to bear and bring up children or to look after the other spouse or where one spouse has been taught by the other to expect a high standard of living.[9] Under such analysis maintenance ceases to be a general remedy and is only available in certain cases, often on a 'rehabilitative' basis.[10] A disadvantage of this approach, as opposed to the promise-based approach, is that it can lead to a more individualised approach, with greater uncertainty for the parties and consequent litigation costs to the private and public purse.[11] The need for some certainty in the administration of the law, coupled with the facts that marriage more often than not involves a detriment to one of the parties and that marriage is a voluntary obligation which in the minds of ordinary people still imports some assumption of financial responsibility for the other party, might lead to a rule that the very fact of marriage prima facie imports *some sort* of maintenance obligation.[12]

Secondly, the court recognised the contribution of one spouse to the acquisition of family wealth which might as a matter of strict law be held by the other spouse.[13] This is to correct an unjust matrimonial property regime – unjust because it does not necessarily recognise the contribution a wife makes to the acquisition of the husband's wealth through the division of labour within the marriage[14] and because it does not necessarily compensate a wife who gives up the opportunity of a career. It is suggested that in awarding any sum in recognition of a spouse's contribution to the marriage, a spouse should prove that he has *earned* such a sum and that, in contrast to maintenance, the fact of marriage alone should not raise any presumption that he is entitled to a 'just sum'.

While as a matter of principle, and not merely as a matter of history, the functions of awarding maintenance and a 'just share' should be kept distinct, in many cases the same factors justifying a

9. See p 43, *ante* and compare *Malone v Harrison* [1979] 1 WLR 1353; *Re Besterman* [1984] Ch 458, [1984] 2 All ER 656, (1982) 3 FLR 255.
10. See Law Commission Report No 112, 'The Financial Consequences of Divorce', para 26–27.
11. For criticism of an over-individualised approach, see *Wachtel v Wachtel* [1973] Fam 72, at 87D, 89H-90A, [1973] 1 All ER 829, at 833f-g, 835g-h (per Lord Denning MR); *Dart v Dart* [1996] 2 FLR 286, at 301F-G per Thorpe LJ, 395D-E per Butler-Sloss LJ; Law Commission Report No 112, 'The Financial Consequences of Divorce', paras 12–23; Deech, 'Financial Relief. The Retreat from Precedent and Principle', (1982) 98 LQR 621.
12. Compare Chapter 2 'Contracts, Promises and the Law of Obligations' in Atiyah, Essays on Contract.
13. *Wachtel v Wachtel* [1973] Fam 72, at 90B-C, 92C-94A, [1973] 1 All ER 829, at 835h-j, 837e-839a (in particular references to extra-judicial remarks of Lord Simon of Glaisdale) (per Lord Denning MR).
14. See fn 9, p 28, *ante* and Gray, *Reallocation of Property on Divorce.*

duty to maintain will also justify the award of a 'just share', the same remedies often satisfy each claim[15] and the two claims are infinitely fungible with each other.

The criticsm of the duty in section 25 of the Matrimonial Causes Act 1973 as originally enacted to place the parties so far as practicable and just in the position in which they would have been had the marriage not broken down lead to its repeal by the Matrimonial and Family Proceedings Act 1984.[16] The legislation now has no general statutory aim, the court merely being obliged to give 'first consideration' to the welfare of any minor child of the family[17] and to 'have regard' to various enumerated matters.[18] The duty to give 'first consideration' to the welfare of any child of the family is as much a pious statement of general Parliamentary intent,[19] which can be of no application in very many cases, and the courts have resisted the temptation to make orders totally lop-sided in their effect dependent upon in whose favour a residence order is made.[20] Further, the Matrimonial and Family Proceedings Act 1984 introduced a new section 25A of the Matrimonial Causes Act 1973 directing the court to consider the appropriateness of terminating the financial obligations of the parties to each other after the decree of divorce,[1] a clear admonition to consider the appropriateness of a 'clean break' order and 'rehabilitation only' maintenance.

To date there has been no reported case under the Inheritance Act 1984 which has discussed either of these changes introduced by the Matrimonial and Family Proceedings Act 1984, a matter partially explained by the high average age of applicants.

The Operation of Section 1(2)(a) – *Re Besterman*

It is suggested that the change effected by section 1(2)(a) is more academic than practical and that in all but a limited number of cases the applicant's claim for maintenance will be the decisive factor. In most cases the claim of an applicant spouse for maintenance will be more relevant and advantageous to the spouse than any claim based on the applicant's contribution to the deceased's property.

15. Compare *Van den Boogaard v Laumen* [1997] 3 WLR 284, at 302D-304C.
16. S 3.
17. The new s 25(1) of the Matrimonial Causes Act 1973.
18. The new s 25(2) of the Matrimonial Causes Act 1973.
19. Compare s 25(2)(e) of the Matrimonial Causes Act 1973 and s 3(1)(f) of the 1975 Act on physical or mental incapacity.
20. Eg *Suter v Suter and Jones* [1987] Fam 111, [1987] 2 All ER 336.
1. Introduced by s 3 of the Matrimonial and Family Proceedings Act 1984.

Maintenance for a spouse when capitalised can be a most substantial claim. The claim of an applicant spouse has always been regarded as one of great strength. In the Court of Appeal case of *Re Bayliss*,[2] a decision under the 1938 Act in 1977, the entire estate of not insignificant size was awarded to the applicant wife, whose marriage to the deceased was successful and happy.

An example of how generous an award based on maintenance alone can be is the decision of Judge Mervyn Davies QC sitting as a deputy judge of the High Court in *Re Besterman*.[3] In this case the deceased died in 1976 leaving an estate of £1,370,000 at the date of the trial. The applicant was the deceased's widow who married the deceased in 1958 when she was aged 42 and the deceased was aged 54. It was the deceased's third marriage and the applicant's second marriage. There were no children of the marriage. The deceased bequeathed to the applicant his personal chattels and a life interest in £100,000 nominal value 3.5% War Loan, the residue being devised to the University of Oxford upon charitable trusts relating to the study of the works of Voltaire, which had been the deceased's major interest in life. The applicant had capital assets consisting of jewellery worth £13,000 and her only income, other than from the estate, was the state widow's pension. It was found as a fact that the applicant had no earning capacity. The marriage had been 'not altogether happy',[4] but the couple stayed together and conduct was not an issue. The deceased had introduced the applicant to a very high standard of living, including at the date of death the occupation of a house worth £350,000 with servants.

It was conceded by the University of Oxford that the deceased's will did not make reasonable provision for the applicant and the only issue was that of quantum. Both parties agreed that provision should be in the form of a lump sum. While the claims of the University of Oxford were not to be ignored, the case was not in any real sense a case of competing claims upon the deceased's bounty. Judge Mervyn Davies QC found that:

> ... the applicant [cannot be regarded] as having made any special contribution 'to the welfare of the family of the deceased'.[5] At the same time I fully accept that Mrs Besterman played her part in contributing to the deceased's domestic arrangements and in making his home life happy.[6]

2. 9 December 1977.
3. (1982) 3 FLR 255. Compare the divorce case of *Dart v Dart* [1996] 2 FLR 286.
4. (1982) 3 FLR 258D.
5. A reference to s 3(2)(b).
6. (1982) 3 FLR 264B-C.

His Lordship was referred to two then recently reported divorce cases, *Preston v Preston*[7] and *Page v Page*[8] each involving large amounts of money and large awards to wives. He discussed the contribution that each wife had made to the husband's business and to the marriage generally. Mrs Besterman had already received an interim order under section 5 of £75,000, of which £68,000 had been used to purchase a house outright and other payments of £31,000. Mrs Besterman's annual expenses were estimated by her at £15,325. Judge Mervyn Davies QC rejected the arguments of the applicant's counsel that she should be given a large capital sum because that would enable her to leave property upon her death to a third party.[9] Judge Mervyn Davies QC decided that the applicant should be confirmed in her house, should have some free capital by enlarging her life-interest in the War Loan to an absolute interest and that she should have a further £125,000 absolutely, being a sum a little in excess of what would be required to purchase an annuity of £18,246 gross. The total sum received from the estate was £259,000.

It may be noted that in making his calculations Judge Mervyn Davies QC made no allowance for the possibility of remarriage, which in the circumstances, while not very likely, should not have been treated as miniscule. Furthermore the money advanced to the applicant to purchase a house was given absolutely. The judge's order gave the applicant some free capital and allowed room for error in favour of Mrs Besterman.

The applicant appealed from the judgment of Judge Mervyn Davies QC to the Court of Appeal.[10] The court was a relatively strong one comprising Oliver, Fox and Robert Goff LJJ[11] and the leading judgment, with which the other Lord Justices agreed, was given by Oliver LJ, who in his youth had edited a book on family provision[12] and who had decided the leading case of *Re Coventry*.[13] The judgment was delivered in October 1982, by which time the value of the estate had risen to £1,436,280. Throughout his judgment Oliver LJ greatly stressed the enhanced standard of provision provided for spouses by section 1(2)(a) and the admonition to have regard to the provision which would have been

7. [1982] Fam 17, [1982] 1 All ER 41.
8. (1981) 2 FLR 198.
9. (1981) 2 FLR 265E, 266F.
10. [1984] Ch 458, [1984] 2 All ER 656.
11. But note the comment of Thorpe LJ in *Dart v Dart* [1996] 2 FLR 286, at 298G drawing attention to the fact that none of the Lord Justices had any experience of ancillary relief cases at first instance.
12. Tillard, *Family Provision* (2nd edn, 1950).
13. [1980] Ch 461, [1979] 2 All ER 408.

available on divorce. His Lordship refused to find that Judge Mervyn Davies QC reached a conclusion as to quantum at which no reasonable judge could have arrived.[14] He did however find that Judge Mervyn Davies QC failed fully to have regard to the applicant's requirements and failed fully to have regard to the provision which the applicant would have been awarded on divorce.[15] Consequently he felt that the Court of Appeal could interfere and increased the award to £378,000. Oliver LJ stressed that it was a 'pure' case, where the court was untramelled by the size of the estate and where there were no competing claims.[16] The Court of Appeal refused leave to appeal to the House of Lords and it is understood that a petition for leave to appeal was not made directly to the House of Lords.

On a technical level the judgment of Oliver LJ can be subject to a great deal of criticism.[17] On a general level the judgments of the Court of Appeal in *Re Besterman* made two fundamental mistakes. The first was that whereas it may be proper to regard the fact of marriage as importing a prima facie duty to maintain,[18] it is not proper to regard the fact of marriage as importing a prima facie

14. [1984] Ch 471F-472C, [1984] 2 All ER 665e-j. On the general approach to appeals, see pp 369–370, *post*.
15. [1984] Ch 472C-476B, [1984] 2 All ER 665j-668h.
16. [1984] Ch 479E-480C, [1984] 2 All ER 671d-h.
17. In contrast to *Wachtel v Wachtel* [1973] Fam 72, [1973] 1 All ER 829, the leading case on s 25 of the Matrimonial Causes Act 1973 (before amendment), the court in *Re Besterman* did not fully set out its reasons for arriving at its decision and did not state the policy background to the legislative change. The criticism made by Oliver LJ that Judge Mervyn Davies QC failed to take into account the position on divorce is almost specious and disingenuous. The matter was fully argued before the trial judge and it is clear that he distinguished the two divorce cases cited to him because Mrs Besterman's 'contribution' to the deceased's capital was not great. The criticism that Judge Mervyn Davies QC failed to consider various contingencies which might adversely affect the applicant's position seems misplaced ([1984] Ch 476C-F, [1984] 2 All ER 668j-669c). The trial judge left a considerable margin of error in the applicant's favour and if contingencies increasing the applicant's need for maintenance were ignored, so were contingencies such as remarriage decreasing her need for maintenance. The example of ill health used by Oliver LJ might as easily decrease the applicant's need for maintenance as increase it. Oliver LJ criticises Judge Mervyn Davies QC for not taking into account the possibility of inflation and that by opting for a lump sum rather than periodical payments, the applicant is losing the advantage of applying to the court for an increase in such payments([1984] Ch 476C-D, 476H, [1984] 2 All ER 668h-j, 669d). This assumes a highly disputable point whether it is proper to take prospective inflation into account (see pp 146–147, *ante*) and fails to note that the power to increase provision on a variation of an order for periodical payments is limited (see pp 403–406, *post*).
18. See p 171, *ante*.

right to a 'just share'. The difference between the Court of Appeal and Judge Mervyn Davies QC is illustrated by the following passage from the judgment of Oliver LJ:

> He should I think have looked at the decision as a whole for the purpose of assessing what reasonable provision would be in all the circumstances for the widow of a millionaire with no obligations to anyone else ... What he did in fact ... was to start from the position in the case of a large estate ... the court should start from the position that the provisions of the will must be upheld except to the extent that they are displaced by the obligation to maintain the widow during her lifetime.[19]

Whereas Judge Mervyn Davies QC regarded the divorce cases of *O'D v O'D*,[20] *Preston v Preston*[1] and *Page v Page*[2] as cases where wives had brought up children or contributed to the acquisition of wealth by the husband,[3] Oliver LJ treated these cases as being simply examples of large awards to wives of wealthy husbands.[4] Subsequent case law both under the 1975 Act and on divorce has held that a spouse must 'earn' a 'just share' and that the same will not be presumed to exist.[5] The second mistake arose from some remarks of Oliver LJ:

> ... and *a cushion* in the form of available capital which will enable her to meet all reasonably forseeable contingencies. What that sum is is a matter of judgment ...'[6]

This remark gave rise in divorce practice to the '*Besterman* cushion',[7] an argument for increasing awards of capital to wives.

The Retreat from *Re Besterman*

The first reported case to consider *Re Besterman* was the decision of Vinelott J in *Re Bunning*.[8] This case had a superficial resemblance

19. [1984] Ch 477G-H, [1984] 2 All ER 669j-670a. See also the judgment of Peter Gibson LJ in *Dart v Dart* [1996] 2 FLR 286, at 302C-303C.
20. [1976] Fam 83, [1975] 2 All ER 993.
1. [1982] Fam 17, [1982] 1 All ER 41.
2. (1981) 2 FLR 198.
3. (1982) 3 FLR 264F-265A.
4. [1984] Ch 474G-H, [1984] 2 All ER 667h-j.
5. See pp 184–186, *post*
6. [1984] Ch 478H, [1984] 2 All ER 670j.
7. See per Thorpe LJ in *Dart v Dart* [1996] 2 FLR 286, at 298F; *Stead v Stead* [1985] FLR 16, at 26A-D; RAYDEN, para 29. 112. See further p 179, *post.*
8. [1984] Ch 480, [1984] 3 All ER 1.

to *Re Besterman* in that the deceased left the bulk of his estate to the University of Cambridge on charitable trusts. The deceased was survived by his second wife, who was aged 54 years. There were no children of the marriage, but the applicant had given up a pensionable employment to assist the deceased in his business and generally contributed far more to the acquisition of wealth by the deceased than did the applicant in *Re Besterman.* At the trial in 1984 the net estate of the deceased was £220,000 and the applicant had capital of her own totalling £98,000, much of which was derived from the deceased. Vinelott J particularly cited those parts of the judgment of Oliver LJ in *Re Besterman* which referred to the fact that a person in Mrs Besterman's position could justify moving to a more expensive house[9] and concerning a cushion of capital.[10] He specifically stated that he bore in mind that the deceased's assets were 'built up by his own efforts in large measure before he married'.[11] Vinelott J awarded a lump sum of £60,000, which he calculated as being a sum which would equalise the capital of the applicant and the deceased's estate[12] or being generous and secure maintenance for the applicant.[13] In calculating the maintenance, Vinelott J proceeded upon the basis that the applicant would have a capital interest in her dwellinghouse and a reserve or cushion of capital, took no account of the possibility of remarriage but expected the applicant to work part-time. Vinelott J specifically carried out a hypothetical exercise as to what the applicant would have been awarded had the marriage been terminated by divorce rather than by death coming up with a figure of £36,000,[14] but rejected this figure as limiting the provision under the 1975 Act because the deceased was no longer alive and in need of accommodation and maintenance.[15] This reasoning illustrates that except in the very largest estates,[16] the 'maintenance' claim is likely to be larger and

9. [1984] Ch 495, [1984] 3 All ER 9f-g, quoting from [1984] Ch 479A, [1984] 2 All ER 670j.
10. [1984] Ch 495E, 495H-496A, [1984] 3 All ER 9d-e, g-h, quoting from [1984] Ch 478E-F, 479B-C, [1984] 2 All ER 670g, 671b.
11. [1984] Ch 499A-B, [1984] 3 All ER 12a.
12. [1984] Ch 499C, [1984] 3 All ER 12b.
13. [1984] Ch 499D-500A, [1984] 3 All ER 12c-g.
14. [1984] Ch 498A-G, [1984] 3 All ER 11b-h.
15. [1984] Ch 498H, [1984] 3 All ER 11j.
16. Reported cases under the 1975 Act where the 'just share' claim has been held to be greater than the claim for maintenance are rare, but may include *Kusminow v Barclays Bank Trust Co* [1989] Fam Law 66 and *Re Kubert* [1997] Ch 97. See also the Northern Irish decisions of *McGuigan v McGuigan* (25 March 1996, unreported) and *Morrow v Morrow* (5 April 1995, unreported) in which life-interests for widows were converted into absolute interests and can be regarded as cases where the 'just share' was greater than the maintenance claim.

more important than the claim for a 'just share'. While Vinelott J awarded the applicant a substantial sum of money, it is highly significant that he did not adopt the approach of awarding such provision merely because the applicant was the widow of, if not a millionaire, a relatively rich man.[17]

Subsequent reported case law under the 1975 Act paid very little attention to *Re Besterman,* except on the technical question of section 3(2), the case generally being distinguished upon the basis of being concerned with a 'very large estate'[18] or irrelevant to the practical situation.[19]

The effective burial of *Re Besterman* took place not in an application under the 1975 Act, but in a series of applications for ancillary relief culminating in the well publicised decision of the Court of Appeal in 1996 of *Dart v Dart.*[20] The divorce courts had always regarded the cases of *O'D v O'D, Preston v Preston* and *Page v Page* as being concerned with spouses who had brought up children and in particular contributed to the acquisition of wealth by the husband, rather than being of general application.[1] In a series of cases concerning applications for ancillary relief by wives of exceptionally wealthy husbands where the wife had not contributed to the acqisition of assets, the courts limited the award to the wife's 'reasonable needs' and refused to award the wife any particular fraction of the combined assets of the husband.[2] In *Dart v Dart* the husband's wealth of at least £400,000,000[3] was all inherited. The trial judge awarded the wife a house and a lump sum of £9,000,000, being her 'reasonable requirements'. The Court of Appeal affirmed the decision of the trial judge and rejected a challenge to established authorities that a wife of a rich man who had not contributed to the acquisition of wealth was *ipso facto* entitled to a large *just share* in

17. Compare per Oliver LJ in *Re Besterman* at [1984] Ch 477G, [1984] 2 All ER 669h-670a.
18. *Stead v Stead* [1985] FLR 16, at 22D-E,26C per Purchas LJ; *Eeles v Evans* (6 July 1989, unreported), CA per Dillon LJ.
19. *Stead v Stead* [1985] FLR 16, at 26C per Purchas LJ. In both *Stead v Stead* and *Eeles v Evans* the awards at first instance were not generous and the unsuccessful appeals were not totally devoid of merit. In each case the position of the wife compared favourably with that of the applicant in *Re Besterman.*
20. [1996] 2 FLR 286.
1. Divorce courts have generally regarded *Preston v Preston* [1982] Fam 17, [1982] 1 All ER 41 as restrictive of applications by wives.
2. *O'Neill v O'Neill* [1993] 2 FCR 297; *Thyssen-Bornemisza v Thyssen-Bornesmisza (No 2)* [1986] Fam 1, [1985] 1 All ER 328; *F v F (ancillary relief: substantial assets)* [1995] 2 FLR 45.
3. [1996] 2 FLR 291B.

his assets. The Court of Appeal stated that in so far as *Re Besterman* held to the contrary, it was not to be followed.[4]

As regards the '*Besterman* cushion', the Court of Appeal noted that in 1983 the Court of Appeal had in *O'Neill v O'Neill*[5] reversed a trial judge in ancillary relief proceedings who had awarded a wife an additional lump sum of £50,000 purely as 'rainy day' money for the vicissitudes of life. In *Dart v Dart* Thorpe LJ stated that in so far as the decisions conflicted, *O'Neill v O'Neill* was to be preferred,[6] although it is clear that 'reasonable requirements' might include some element of a reserve for capital[7] and such was actually awarded at first instance in *Dart v Dart.*[8]

Comparison with Provision on Divorce

Section 3(2) sets out three specific matters to which a court is to have regard when dealing with an application by a spouse. The most important guideline provides:

> ... the court shall ... have regard to the provision which the applicant might reasonably have expected to receive if on the day on which the deceased died the marriage, instead of being terminated by death, had been terminated by a decree of divorce.

The sub-section was inserted to amplify the proposition that reasonable provision for a spouse's was not limited to 'maintenance' and that a spouse would not be better off on divorce than on death.[9] However the Law Commission did not offer any explanation as to the precise operation of this sub-section.[10]

The mental gymnastics which this requirement dictates have caused judges considerable problems. The situations on death and divorce are often very different. Divorce rarely has such a drastic

4. [1996] 2 FLR 298F-G. This passage is actually directed to the '*Besterman* cushion', but the entire judgment of the Court of Appeal is a complete rejection of the approach of Oliver LJ in *Re Besterman.*
5. [1993] 2 FCR 297.
6. [1996] 2 FLR 298F-G. See to like effect *H v H (financial provision: capital allowance)* [1993] 2 FLR 335, at 349F-350B, per Thorpe J.
7. [1996] 2 FLR 298G-H; see further p 183, *post.*
8. [1996] 2 FLR 300C-D,302G.
9. LAW COM, para 16–18, 33–34.
10. LAW COM, para 34. This guideline was not mentioned in WORKING PAPER.

effect on the family's finances as does death, which will frequently deprive the family of the deceased's income from employment, but will also frequently remove the need for the deceased to be maintained and may result in new assets in the form of monies under life insurance policies and pension schemes.[11] The process of altering the dispositions of a will or the rules of intestacy under the 1975 Act can be very different from the exercise of the court's powers under the Matrimonial Causes Act 1973.

The guideline in section 3(2) has given rise to two problems. The first concerns the particular facts which are to be assumed in the hypothetical divorce. Specifically the issue has been raised as to whether the hypothetical divorce should assume that one of the parties is about to die and hence not require assets in the estate for his maintenance or whether it should be assumed that both of the parties to the divorce are likely to require maintenance for the foreseeable future.[12]

All the reported cases have proceeded upon the basis that both parties continued to need maintenance to the same extent as before death.[13]

The second concerns the weight to be given to the guideline in section 3(2). It is submitted that while section 1(2)(a) lays down the *test* for reasonable provision, section 3(2) is merely one of several *guidelines*. Bush J in *Re Dawkins* said:

> That is a matter that I have to take into account as one of the items; it is not the test itself.[14]

Oliver LJ in *Re Besterman* said:

> In an application under [the 1975 Act], however, the figure resulting from the section 25 exercise is merely *one* of the factors to which the court is to 'have regard' and the overriding consideration is what is 'reasonable' in all the circumstances. It is, however, obviously a very

11. Eg see per Cazalet J in *Re Krubert* [1997] Ch 97, at 106C-E.
12. For a graphic example of the difference between the two approaches, see *Smith v Smith (Smith intervening)* [1992] Fam 69, [1991] 2 All ER 306.
13. In *Re Besterman* [1984] Ch 458, [1984] 2 All ER 656 Oliver LJ cited reported divorce decisions; *Re Bunning* [1984] Ch 480, at 498E,H, [1984] 3 All ER 1, at 11f-g,j; *Moody v Stevenson* [1992] Ch 486, at 499F-G, [1992] 2 All ER 524, at 534g-h; *Re Krubert* [1997] Ch 97, at 104D-F. In *Winfield v Billington* (30 July 1990, unreported), CA the Court of Appeal was pressed as to the effect upon a hypothetical divorce of a change in care and control of the children of the marriage effected by death, but the Court of Appeal refused to be drawn upon this point.
14. [1986] 2 FLR 360, at 365H.

important consideration and one which the statute goes out of its way to bring to the court's attention.[15]

Re Besterman is a useful example of the importance of section 3(5) in that while Oliver LJ stressed that the sub-section was merely one of several factors to consider, the failure of the trial judge to deal fully with section 3(5) was one of the reasons why the Court of Appeal felt able to interefere. In *Re Bunning* Vinelott J, having assessed what the applicant would have received under the hypothetical divorce, went on to hold that such a figure did not limit the award and that he could take into account other factors, including that the deceased no longer required assets for his maintenance.[16]

A different approach was adopted by Waite J giving the judgment of the Court of Appeal in *Moody v Stevenson.*[17] He said:

> The objective is that the acceptable *minimum* posthumous provision for a surviving spouse should correspond as closely as possible to the inchoate rights enjoyed by that spouse in the deceased's lifetime by virtue of his or her prospective entitlement under the matrimonial law.[18]
>
> In other words the Act of 1975, when stripped to its barest terms, amounts to a direction to the judge to ask himself in surviving spouse cases: 'What would a family judge have ordered for this couple if divorce instead of death had divided them [and thereafter the judge should teake into account the other guidelines in section 3].[19]
>
> 'The *starting point* ... will ... be a consideration of the presumed entitlement under a notional divorce.[20]

In *Moody v Stevenson* (which was undoubtedly a correct result on the facts) it so happened that the order made on the notional divorce was undoubtedly the correct order which should be made under the 1975 Act. The matter was taken up again by the Court of Appeal in *Re Krubert* where Nourse LJ noted that *Re Besterman* had not been cited in *Moody v Stevenson* and while describing the two decisions

15. [1984] Ch 469F-G, [1984] 2 All ER663j-664a. This passage was cited with approval by Browne-Wilkinson V-C in *Dixit v Dixit* (23 June 1988, unreported), CA. In *Jevdjovic v Milenko* (12 March 1990, unreported), CA Dillon LJ described the divorce analogy as 'no more than a cross-check on the calculations'.
16. [1984] Ch 480, at 498H, [1984] 3 All ER 1, at 11j.
17. [1992] Ch 486, [1992] 2 All ER 524.
18. [1992] Ch 498F-G, [1992] 2 All ER 533j.
19. [1992] Ch 499D, [1992] 2 All ER 534e.
20. [1992] Ch 503B, [1992] 2 All ER 537e; a passage specifically cited with approval by Kelly LJ in *Re Weir* [1983] 2 NIJB 45.

as involving a conflict of emphasis, stated that the approach of Oliver LJ in *Re Besterman* should be followed.[1] Cazalet J concurring, stated that a strict analogy with divorce would work an injustice in applications by spouses in small estates.[2]

It is noteworthy that a provision which was inserted into the 1975 Act to confirm the enhanced standard of provision for spouses came to be seen as limiting the potential award to a spouse.

Probably section 3(2) has more application where the parties had separated prior to death, than in cases where the marriage was continuing at the date of death. The argument that neither party should be any better or worse off as a result of death has more force where the parties are actually in the process of a divorce than where divorce is only a theoretical possibility.[3]

While the courts have rejected the hypothetical order on divorce as the starting point for an award under the 1975 Act, it is clearly established that the court has regard to the *general* policy and principles of the exercise of the court's powers on divorce.[4] A particular problem which makes the exact assimilation of the exercise of the courts' powers on divorce and on death impossible are the differences between the factual situation and jurisdictions in relation to pensions.[5]

The Meaning of Maintenance[6]

Maintenance or 'needs' (which is the expression used in section 3(1)(a) and in section 25(2)(b) of the Matrimonial Causes Act 1973) means 'reasonable requirements'.[7] In divorce cases it has been held

1. [1997] Ch 97, at 102G-104F. The difference between *Re Besterman* and *Moody v Stevenson* had been noted previously in *Jessop v Jessop* [1992] 1 FLR 591, at 597F-G.
2. [1997] Ch 106C-F.
3. But compare *Re Bunning* [1984] Ch 480, [1984] 3 All ER 1 where the parties had separated prior to death and where Vinelott J expressly awarded the applicant substantially more than she would have obtained on divorce. For an example of where the analogy with divorce specifically limited provision for the widow, see *Stephens v Stephens* (1 July 1985, unreported), CA. It may be significant that in *Winfield v Billington* (30 April 1990, unreported), CA; *Moody v Stevenson* [1992] Ch 486, [1992] 2 All ER 524 and *Re Weir* [1983] 2 NIJB 45 where s 3(2) figured prominently the parties had separated prior to death.
4. See eg the judgment of Oliver LJ in *Re Besterman.*
5. For discussion of the position as regards pensions, see pp 321–323, *post.*
6. For discussion of 'maintenance' generally, see pp 131–137, *ante.*
7. *Preston v Preston* [1982] Fam 17, at 25B-C, [1982] 1 All ER 41, at 47fg; *Dart v Dart* [1996] 2 FLR 286, at 296D-H.

that this means more than needs 'narrowly' defined,[8] but less than wishes[9] and ultimately the concept is an objective one. 'Reasonable requirements' can be a very generous concept; in *Dart v Dart*[10] an award based on 'reasonable requirements' came to £9,000,000 plus a house. The concept of maintenance or reasonable requirements has proved relatively easy to apply to applications by spouses under the 1975 Act. Although ultimately the concept is objective and hence an award based on maintenance under the 1975 Act can be at a significantly greater level than maintenance before death, particularly if the deceased was *wrongly* failing adequately to maintain the applicant before death,[11] in practice the level of maintenance before death is generally taken to be the appropriate level of maintenance after death.[12]

Just as maintenance upon divorce has been held to entail an element of capital to act as a reserve for minor emergencies and to enable small capital purchases to be made,[13] so under the 1975 Act courts generally regard it as appropriate that a surviving spouse should have access to a limited amount of capital as part of his entitlement to maintenance.[14] Such a sum is not to be awarded as of right, but has to be justified on the facts of each case as being reasonably required.[15] Invariably courts award surviving spouses absolute interests in the personal chattels.[16]

8. *O'D v O'D* [1976] Fam 83, at 91D-E, [1975] 2 All ER 993, at 997f-g.
9. *Preston v Preston* at [1982] Fam 25C, [1982] 1 All ER 47g; *Dart v Dart* [1996] 2 FLR 297A-H.
10. [1996] 2 FLR 286.
11. *Re Borthwick* [1949] Ch 395, [1949] 1 All ER 472.
12. See now specifically s 25(2)(c) of the Matrimonial Causes Act 1973, introduced by s 3 of the Matrimonial and Family Proceedings Act 1984.
13. RAYDEN, para 29.49, fn 6; *Davis v Davis* [1967] P 185, at 193G-194A, [1967] 1 All ER 123, at 127G-H.
14. *Re Lewis* (13 March 1980, unreported), CA; *Re Besterman* [1984] Ch 458, at 478E-F, [1984] 2 All ER 656, at 670g; *Harrington v Gill* (1983) 4 FLR 265 (a lump sum of £5,000); *Stead v Stead* [1985] FLR 16 (£5,000); *Re Dawkins* [1986] 2 FLR 360, at 364F-G ('a capital sum which would allow her to make more comfortable provision for herself by way of furniture and matters of that kind and also by way of capital luxuries of life'); *Eeles v Evans* (6 July 1989, unreported), CA (£5,000 for 'holidays and spending'); *Re Clarke* [1991] Fam Law 364, at 365 ('something to fall back upon to deal with contingencies in the future'); *Jessop v Jessop* [1992] 1 FLR 591, at 599D-F ('a capital reserve for future contingencies').
15. *Dart v Dart* [1996] 2 FLR 286, at 298E-299A, not following *Re Besterman* [1984] Ch 458, [1984] 2 All ER 656 and prefering *O'Neill v O'Neill* [1993] 2 FCR 297.
16. Eg *Harrington v Gill* (1983) 4 FLR 265, at 272A.

The Contribution to the Welfare of the Family of the Deceased

Section 3(2)(b) requires a court to have regard to:

> ... the contribution made by the applicant to the welfare of the family of the deceased, including any contribution made by looking after the home or caring for the children.[17]

This provision was designed to give a spouse a property interest in his partner's property even though he made no direct or indirect *financial* contribution to its acquisition. A spouse's contribution is relevant not only to the acquisition of a 'just share', but also in justifying the award of maintenance in the face of conflicting claims by beneficiaries and in negativing the effect of misconduct by the applicant spouse.[18] A spouse's contribution was always taken into account by courts administering the 1938 Act.[19]

As previously set out in the discussion of *Re Besterman*,[20] and in line with the position on divorce,[1] a spouse is only entitled to the enhanced standard of provision under section 1(2)(a) if he has *earned* such an interest under section 3(2)(b).[2]

It does appear that the courts do attach considerably more importance to a contribution to a spouse's business or career than a contribution by bringing up a family,[3] but the care of and bringing up of a family are still matters of the highest importance.[4] Caring for the family home will not be so highly regarded as the bringing up of children and the precise effect of a wife merely looking after the home is uncertain. Although not strictly within section 3(2)(a),

17. Derived from Matrimonial Causes Act 1973, s 25(1)(f).
18. For examples of 'contributions' being balanced against 'conduct', see *Re Snoek* (1983) 13 Fam Law 18; *Morrow v Morrow* (5 April 1995, unreported).
19. *Re Sylvester* [1941] Ch 87, [1940] 4 All ER 269; *Re Brownbridge* (1942) 193 LT Jo 185; *Re Pugh* [1943] Ch 387, [1943] 2 All ER 361 (absence of contribution by applicant); *Re Blanch* [1967] 1 WLR 987, [1967] 2 All ER 468; *Thornley v Palmer* [1969] 1 WLR 1037, [1969] 3 All ER 31.
20. See pp 175–179, *ante*.
1. RAYDEN, para 29.59; *Page v Page* (1981)2 FLR 198, at 201G; *Preston v Preston* [1982] Fam 17, at 25D-F, [1982] 1 All ER 41, at 47g-j; *Dart v Dart* [1996] 2 FLR 286.
2. [1993] 1 FLR 54.
3. Compare the differing orders made in *Page v Page* (1981) 2 FLR 198 and *Preston v Preston* [1982] Fam 17, [1982] 1 All ER 41; and see *Re Dainesi* Times, 16/11/82; Telegraph, 16/11/82.
4. *Wachtel v Wachtel* [1973] Fam 72, at 93B-94A, [1973] 1 All ER 829, at 838c-839a.

the courts also take into account any detriment suffered by the applicant as a result of the marriage.[5]

While the reported case law under the 1975 Act is replete with dicta to the effect that a spouse's contribution to the welfare of the family and the acquisition of the deceased's wealth is to be taken into account[6] and conversely the lack of any such contribution militates against a generous award,[7] the case law reveals a lack of consistency in the weight which is given to such contribution.

This lack of consistency can be illustrated by four cases. In *Stead v Stead*[8] the marriage was a second marriage for both parties and lasted 24 years. There was fairly cogent evidence that the applicant wife worked hard on the deceased's farm, subsequently took in paying guests and generally lived a frugal life. The deceased died in 1982 leaving an estate of £66,000 and bequeathed the matrimonial home and £6,000 to the applicant for life with the residue to his children by his first marriage. The applicant was aged 82 years at the trial and had only limited requirements for maintenance. At first instance Arnold P increased the applicant's income, but refused to award her any interest in capital. The Court of Appeal dismissed an appeal by the applicant. In *Eeles v Evans*[9] the parties were married for 45 years, although they separated shortly before death. There was one child of the marriage. The applicant wife did not work during the marriage. The deceased died in 1982 leaving an estate at the date of trial of £420,000 net. The deceased bequeathed all his estate to the child of the marriage. The applicant, aged 74 years at the date of the trial, was accommodated in an old people's home. The trial judge awarded the applicant a lump sum of £5,000 together with the income from £85,000 and the trustees had power to advance capital. The Court of Appeal dismissed an appeal by the applicant for additional provision.

5. *Re Sylvester* [1941] Ch 87, [1940] 4 All ER 269 (but compare *Re Styler* [1942] Ch 387, [1942] 2 All ER 201); *Re Hancock* Times 21/1/70, 27/2/70; *Stephens v Stephens* (1 July 1985, unreported), CA (wife giving up house on marriage); *Davis v Davis* [1993] 1 FLR 54, at 57E-G.
6. *Re Snoek* (1983) 13 Fam Law 18; *Re Rowlands* [1984] FLR 813 (a harsh decision); *Stead v Stead* [1985] FLR 16, at 18D-G; *Stephens v Stephens* (1 July 1985, unreported), CA (wife giving up house on marriage); *Dawkins v Dawkins* [1986] 2 FLR 360, at 363C-F; *Rajabally v Rajabally* [1987] 2 FLR 390 at 394F; *Kusminow v Barclays Bank Trust Co* [1989] Fam Law 66; *Davis v Davis* [1993] 1 FLR 54, at 57E-G, 61B-C; *McGuigan v MacGuigan* (25 March 1996, unreported).
7. *Re Bunning* [1984] Ch 480, at 499A-B, [1984] 3 All ER 1, at 11c-d (wealth acquired before marriage); *Re Clarke* [1991] Fam Law 364, at 365; *Moody v Stevenson* [1992] Ch 486, at 499H, [1992]2 All ER 524, at 534h-j.
8. [1985] FLR 16.
9. (6 July 1989, unreported).

A different approach was adopted by Kerr J in the Northern Irish case of *McGuigan v McGuigan*.[10] In this case the marriage of the deceased, who was a farmer, and the applicant lasted 63 years and there were three children. The applicant wife worked on the farm and materially contibuted to the acquisition of the deceased's farming assets. Kerr J awarded the applicant a life-interest in the entire estate and an absolute interest in £5,000 specifically to reflect her contribution to the family and the farm. In *Re Krubert*[11] the applicant and the deceased were married for 44 years. There were no children. The deceased died in 1994 leaving a house worth £59,000 and investments of about £20,000. The applicant wife was aged 89 years. The case was argued essentially on maintenance grounds rather than on the basis of a 'just share'. The Court of Appeal in 1996 reversing a more generous award at first instance awarded the applicant an absolute interest in the investments and a life-interest in the house.

It is submitted that the approach of *McGuigan v McGuigan* and *Re Krubert* is to be preferred and that *Stead v Stead* and *Eeles v Evans* failed to pay sufficient regard to sections1(2)(a) and 3(2)(b). An argument can be made that in cases such as *Stead v Stead* the 'just share' is represented by the actuarial value of the life-interest. It is submitted that this argument can not stand with section 1(2)(a) which must imply that a 'just share' should be greater than the claim for maintenance and sits uneasily with the admonition to have regard to the position on divorce. A problem is that such cases tend to be argued upon the basis of simply a choice between an absolute interest in the entire estate or merely a life-interest, when it is submitted that the correct solution is an absolute interest in part and an absolute interest in part. Particularly useful guidance upon the amount of the absolute interest can be gained from the *Barder v Barder* cases of *Smith v Smith*[12] and *Barber v Barber*[13] where it was held that the maintenance element of an ancillary relief order should be set aside after the death of one party, but not the 'just share' element.

The Age of the Applicant

In the case of an application by a spouse or a former spouse the court is directed to have regard to 'the age of the applicant'.[14] The typical

10. (25 March 1996, unreported).
11. [1997] Ch 97. A decision recognising a spouse's contribution is *Kusminow v Barclays Bank Trust Co* [1989] Fam Law 66.
12. [1992] Fam 69, [1991] 2 All ER 306. See also *Amey v Amey* [1992] 2 FLR 89.
13. [1993] 1 FLR 476.
14. S 3(2)(a).

spouse who applies under the 1975 Act is elderly. Elderly persons often have only limited requirements for maintenance and their limited life expectancy draws attention to the destination of their own estates. Because elderly persons have a low life expectancy and, compared to younger people, a more uncertain life expectancy, gifts upon trust are more suitable for elderly surviving spouses than for younger surviving spouses.[15] There are numerous dicta drawing attention to the age of applicants as a reason for restricting the amount of provision.[16] The courts have been particularly astute in restricting provision so as to prevent applicants benefiting those entitled in their estates at the expense of those entitled under the estate of the deceased. Indeed as the discussion of *Stead v Stead* and *Eeles v Evans* suggests at times their anxiety to prevent persons potentially interested in the estate of the applicant benefiting from an order has unjustly deprived the applicant of an entitlement to a 'just share'.[17]

The Duration of the Marriage between the Applicant and the Deceased

Section 3(2)(a) requires the court to have regard to 'the duration of the marriage between the applicant and the deceased'. In considering the length of marriage the court generally considers only the period when the parties lived together.[18] The court may take into account pre-marital cohabitation,[19] although such cohabitation is never to be fully equated with years of marriage.[20]

15. See text p 385, *post*.
16. *Re Rowlands* [1984] FLR 813, at 824B-D; *Stephens v Stephens* (1 July 1985, unreported), CA; *Eeles v Evans* (6 July 1989, unreported), CA; *Re Clarke* [1991] Fam Law 364; *Moody v Stevenson* [1992] Ch 486, at 499F-G, [1992] 2 All ER 524, at 534g-h; but see *Re Bunning* [1984] Ch 480, at 499A, [1984] 3 All ER 1, at 11j-12a (lengthy widowhood reason for generous provision).
17. See pp 185–186, *ante*. The position under the Matrimonial Causes Act 1973 as amended (not always well articulated) is that a desire to leave property on death is not a 'reasonable requirement', see *Preston v Preston* [1982] Fam 17, at 25C, [1982] 1 All ER 41, at 47g, but once a spouse has 'earned' a just share, it is irrelevant to what use he puts such a sum, see *Duxbury v Duxbury* [1992] Fam 62n, at 67G-H, [1990] 2 All ER 77, at 82j (a not particularly satisfactory decision).
18. Eg *Re Rowlands* [1984] FLR 813 where the parties lived apart for the last 43 years of the 62 years of marriage.
19. *Kokosinki v Kokosinki* [1980] Fam 72, [1980] 1 All ER 1106; *Foley v Foley* [1981] Fam 160, [1981] 2 All ER 857.
20. *Foley v Foley* [1981] Fam 160, [1981] 2 All ER 857; *Hayes v Hayes* (1981) 11 Fam Law 208.

In *itself* the duration of the marriage between the applicant and the deceased, like the duration of dependency of an applicant under section 1(1)(e),[1] is not a matter which should affect a spouse's claim. However, the length of a marriage may be some *evidence* of the amount of detrimental reliance caused by the marriage and the amount that one party has contributed to the acquisition of matrimonial property and to the welfare of the parties. The modern approach on divorce is to pay less attention to the duration of the marriage and to examine closely the effect which the marriage has had on the applicant's position.[2] The difference between the effect of a short marriage between a young couple where there are children of the marriage is obvious, as is the difference between a marriage of an older couple where the applicant gives up pension rights or accommodation as a result of the marriage and one where the applicant suffers no such detriment. Bearing in mind in particular the provisions of the Matrimonial and Family Proceedings Act 1984,[3] it is submitted that a short childless marriage of young people which has not caused any significant detriment to the applicant should not result in substantial provision under the 1975 Act.

Before the 1975 Act the courts' attitude to family provision claims by survivors of short marriages was rather uncertain.[4] A particular problem in family provision concerns the case of a short marriage of elderly parties where the survivor has little income and capital. On divorce a court might well award such an applicant only very limited provision because he has not earned any 'just sum' and his needs must be balanced against the needs of the other party to the marriage. On death while the applicant will not be entitled to a 'just share', his needs can be met by an award from the deceased's estate, whether or not the marriage was only of a limited duration. A good example of this is *Moody v Stevenson*.[5] Here the parties married in 1971 and lived in a house owned by the deceased. The deceased went into a nursing home in 1984 and died in 1988. The applicant did not visit the deceased and generally made only a

1. Compare pp 279–280, *post*.
2. RAYDEN, para 29.56; *S v S* [1977] Fam 127, at 134C-F, [1977] 1 All ER 56, at 60j-61c. In *Re Dawkins* [1986] 2 FLR 360, at 365D-E Bush J refers to the shortness of the marriage and to the fact that during the marriage the applicant lost virtually her entire capital of £10,000.
3. In particular s 25A of the Matrimonial Causes Act 1973 inserted by s 3 of the Matrimonial and Family Proceedings Act 1984.
4. See the very generous provision ordered for the very short marriages in *Re Milliken* [1966] NI 68; *Re Clarke* [1968] 1 WLR 415, [1968] 1 All ER 451; but compare these orders with the remarks on short marriages in *Re Watkins* [1953] 1 WLR 1323, at 1331; *Re W* (1972) 116 Sol Jo 218.
5. [1992] Ch 486, [1992] 2 All ER 524.

limited contribution to the finances of the marriage. Had the parties divorced in a situation where the deceased could adduce any reason for returning to or selling the matrimonial home, the claims of the deceased would clearly have been preferred to those of the applicant. However, under the 1975 Act the Court of Appeal granted the applicant a life interest in the deceased's house.

Conduct of the Parties

Under the 1938 Act the conduct of the deceased and the applicant spouse were matters of considerable importance.[6] Although the court paid great attention to the parties' commission of matrimonial offences, the matter was always considered as a whole and a guilty spouse could be awarded provision[7] and an innocent spouse refused provision.[8] Under the 1975 Act because of the duty to have regard to provision which would be awarded after divorce, conduct will only be relevant if it would be relevant on divorce.[9]

The change in the statutory regime effected by the Matrimonial and Family Proceedings Act 1984 has had surprisingly little effect upon how the divorce courts approach questions of conduct.[10] In very general terms conduct is only taken into account when it is 'obvious and gross',[11] or where it has an economic effect upon the other party.[12]

Although reported cases do not explicitly support the proposition,[13] it is arguable that conduct should have more influence where an obligation to maintain is concerned than where a 'just share' is claimed. While it would be generally wrong to deprive a spouse of her 'property' because of the commission of a matrimonial offence,[14] it is not necessarily wrong to deprive a spouse of her right

6. See first edition, pp 59–64.
7. Eg *Re Goard* (1962) 106 Sol Jo 721.
8. Eg *Re E* [1966] 1 WLR 709, [1966] 2 All ER 44.
9. S3(2); see also LAW COM, paras 35–36; per Wood J in *Re Snoek* (1983) 13 Fam Law 18.
10. S 25(1)(g) of the Matrimonial Causes Act 1973 introduced by s 3 of the Matrimonial and Family Proceedings Act 1984.
11. RAYDEN, paras 29.60–29.66; JACKSON AND DAVIES, paras 3.20–3.22; CRETNEY, 448–453.
12. RAYDEN, para 29.64; JACKSON AND DAVIES, para 3.21; Gray, *Reallocation of Property on Divorce*, 243–265.
13. But compare *Robinson v Robinson* [1983] Fam 42, [1983] 1 All ER 391, a case concerned with a maintenance obligation, with *Backhouse v Backhouse* [1978] I WLR 243, at 252D-254G, [1978] 1 All ER 1158, at 1166H-1168H, a case of a 'just share'.
14. See *Wachtel v Wachtel* [1973] Fam 72, at 90B-E, [1973] 1 All ER 829, at 835j-836b; *Backhouse v Backhouse* [1978] 1 WLR 243, [1978] 1 All ER 1158.

of maintenance which may have some sort of a contractual basis[15] if the other party has repudiated the marriage contract.

While 'conduct' will have only a limited relevance under the 1975 Act, a party's 'contribution' to the marriage is very important[16] and the two matters cannot always be conveniently separated. On divorce it appears that conduct is never totally ignored.[17] It is therefore suggested that in proceedings under the 1975 Act the court will always to some extent consider the *general* conduct of the parties, although it will be reluctant to adjudicate on individual incidents and matrimonial offences, unless they are 'obvious and gross' or have a major economic effect on the parties. In *Re Chatterton,*[18] an application under the 1975 Act, Reeve J certainly took into account the conduct of the applicant spouse, which might well have been described as 'obvious and gross', and the shortness of the period of cohabitation in awarding the applicant only a very small amount of provision. Similarly in *Re Snoek*[19] Wood J awarded a wife who had been married to the deceased for 20 years and had borne him four children *only* £5,000 out of an estate of £40,000 because of her 'atrocious and vicious behaviour'.

Where the parties are living together at the date of death, the courts are most reluctant to consider the conduct of the applicant, as opposed to his contribution to the marriage, except in very extreme circumstances such as *Re Snoek.*[20] Attempts to raise the conduct of the applicant where the parties were living together at the date of death have almost uniformly had very little effect upon the court.[1]

15. See pp 170–171, *ante*. The argument that maintenance has a contractual nature is less easy to advance after the Matrimonial and Family Proceedings Act 1984.
16. S 3(2)(b); see pp 184–186, *ante*
17. Barrington Baker, Eekelaar, Gibson and Raikes, *The Matrimonial Jurisdiction of Registrars*; Law Commission Report No 112, 'The Financial Consequences of Divorce', para 38.
18. (11 July 1978, unreported). The wife did not appeal to the Court of Appeal, 1 November 1978. The applicant's conduct was expressly taken into consideration in *Dixit v Dixit* (23 June 1988, unreported), CA; *Winfield v Billington* (30 July 1990, unreported), CA and *Moody v Stevenson* [1992] Ch 486, [1992] 2 All ER 524, where to a greater or lesser extent conduct reduced, but did not extinguish the applicant's claim.
19. (1983) 13 Fam Law 18. In *Morrow v Morrow* (5 April 1995, unreported) the marriage lasted 52 years and there were three children. The applicant wife made a substantial contribution to the marriage. Campbell J sitting in the Northern Irish High Court held that it would be wrong to allow the last year or so of the marriage when the applicant behaved badly towards the deceased in any way to counterbalance her contribution through 50 years of marriage.
20. (1983) 13 Fam Law 18.
1. *Re Watkins* [1953] 1 WLR 1323; *Re Langley* (1964) Times, 27 June; *Re Blanch* [1967] 1 WLR 987, [1967] 2 All ER 487; *Re Wilson*, Judge Holt (23 September 1980, unreported); *Re Besterman* (1982) 3 FLR 255; varied [1984] Ch 458, [1984] 2 All ER 656; *Stephens v Stephens* (1 July 1985, unreported), CA.

Is a Life-interest Sufficient?

A question of great practical importance, particularly in the context of second marriages, is whether reasonable provision for a surviving spouse can be limited to a life-interest or whether a surviving spouse is entitled to some form of absolute interest. This question has arisen in a number of reported cases where it has been held that *in certain circumstances* a life-interest can be adequate provision.

The case of *Stead v Stead*[2] has already been discussed.[3] There the Court of Appeal in 1984 refused to interfere with a decision of Arnold P awarding the applicant widow essentially only a life-interest. Likewise the Court of Appeal refused to interfere in the case of *Eeles v Evans.*[4] In *Stephens v Stephens*[5] the marriage was a second marriage for both parties and lasted 20 years. The widow was aged 80 at the date of the hearing. The deceased effectively left an estate of £27,500 to the widow for life. At first instance the judge awarded the widow the entire estate absolutely, but this decision was reversed by the Court of Appeal who instead awarded the applicant an absolute interest in 60% of the estate. In *Re Clarke*[6] the marriage was a second marriage for both parties and lasted 12 years. The net estate of the deceased came to £180,000 and the deceased bequeathed to the applicant wife a life-interest in his house and £25,000. The applicant had her own capital of £32,000. In 1990 Scott Baker J dismissed the widow's application. *Davis v Davis*[7] concerned a marriage of seven years, which was a second marriage for the deceased and where there were no children. Shortly before he died the deceased gave £15,000 to the applicant. The deceased bequeathed the applicant a life-interest in his estate, which was worth about £177,000. In addition the estate had an interest in remainder in the estate of the deceased's father which was likely to fall in in the near future and was worth £90,000. The executors purchased a house worth £70,000 for the occupation of the applicant. The applicant applied for an absolute interest in the house. Manifestly this was not a case where she had made a large contribution to the welfare of the deceased or the acquisition of his wealth. Her claim was dismissed by Thorpe J whose decision was affirmed by the Court of Appeal in 1991. In *Re Krubert*[8] the marriage

2. [1985] FLR 16.
3. See p 185, *ante.*
4. 6 April 1989, discussed at p 185, *ante.*
5. 1 July 1985.
6. [1991] Fam Law 364. Compare *Re Mason* (1975) 5 Fam Law 124.
7. [1993] 1 FLR 54.
8. [1997] Ch 97.

lasted 42 years, but was childless. The applicant was aged 87 years at the date of the hearing. The estate consisted of a dwellinghouse worth £59,000 in which the applicant probably had an interest by way of a resulting trust and £25,000 in cash. The deceased bequeathed a legacy of £10,000 to the applicant absolutely together with a life interest in the residuary estate with remainder to the deceased's siblings who were elderly and had no particular claim on the deceased. At first instance the county court judge awarded the applicant the entire estate absolutely but with immediate legacies totalling £7,000. In 1996 the Court of Appeal reversed the trial judge and, after specifically citing *Davis v Davis*,[9] awarded the applicant an absolute interest in the cash, but only a life-interest in the deceased's dwellinghouse.

In deciding whether a life-interest is sufficient reasonable provision for a surviving spouse, certain matters must be borne in mind. Firstly, in the reported cases, the courts have endeavoured to ensure that the surviving spouse will have relatively generous maintenance, including access to significant sums of capital. Under the rules of intestacy, a surviving spouse is entitled to a substantial absolute legacy before a life-interest becomes relevant. In *Davis v Davis* the applicant had been given £15,000 immediately before the death of the deceased. In *Re Krubert*[10] Nourse LJ specifically said that an absolute legacy of £10,000 was insufficient. This can be illustrated by the case of *Jevdjovic v Milenko*,[11] the facts of which were complicated and somewhat uncertain. The applicant who had a claim to a 'just share' was bequeathed a life-interest in a property worth up to £112,000. At first instance the applicant was awarded an absolute interest in this property. The Court of Appeal substituted a lump sum of £50,000 together with a life interest in the balance of the proceeds of sale of the property. It is only in a case such as *Moody v Stevenson*,[12] where there are competing beneficiaries or the applicant has been guilty of misconduct, that a bare life-interest will be sufficient.

Secondly, in all these cases (with the exception of *Stead v Stead*[13]) the surviving spouse has had no or only a limited entitlement to a 'just share'.[14] Further it is significant that in *Jevdjovic v Milenko*[15] and *Re Krubert*[16] where the applicants had some entitlement to a

9. [1997] Ch 104H-106A.
10. [1997] Ch 105G-106A.
11. (12 March 1990, unreported), CA.
12. [1992] Ch 486, [1992] 2 All ER 524.
13. [1985] FLR 16; see also p 185, *ante*.
14. On a 'just share', see pp 184–186, *ante*.
15. (12 March 1990, unreported), CA.
16. [1997] Ch 97.

'just share' and in *Stephens v Stephens*[17] where the applicant had incurred a detriment, the Court of Appeal did award some form of absolute interest. A bare life-interest is rarely likely to be sufficient where an applicant has a claim to a 'just share', a position illustrated by *McGuigan v McGuigan*[18] and *Smith v Smith.*[19]

Thirdly, the older the applicant is, the more suitable is a life-interest.[20] *Re Bayliss*[1] is a classic example of where a younger widow was awarded an absolute interest. The younger the applicant the less pressing a problem is that an award to a surviving spouse will merely substitute as ultimate beneficiaries those entitled under the applicant's estate for those entitled under the deceased's estate.

Fourthly, the courts have been assiduous in protecting the rights of adult children by earlier marriages. This can be illustrated by the case of *Stephens v Stephens*[2] where Micklem J at first instance reasoned that because adult children themselves would not normally be entitled to the court awarding them provision,[3] they had no interests to consider and accordingly the entire estate should be awarded to the second wife. The Court of Appeal reversed this decision. With charities and more distant relatives, the courts have been less protective of the interests of beneficiaries.[4]

Fifthly, the courts have never fully considered the practice of divorce courts in endeavouring to award parties absolute interests in houses. In *Re Besterman* [5] and *Re Bunning* [6] the applicants were awarded absolute interests in houses as a matter of course and without any discussion.

While it is clear law that in deciding upon an investment strategy, trustees are obliged to balance the interests of beneficiaries entitled to income and capital, there is no accepted approach as to how this is acheived. A surviving spouse may have legitimate concerns about a life interest where the trustees are friendly to the remaindermen. In this situation thought should be given to

17. (1 July 1985, unreported), CA.
18. Kerr J (25 March 1996, unreported), discussed p 186, *ante*. See also *Morrow v Morrow*, Campbell J, (5 April 1995, unreported).
19. [1992] Fam 69, [1991] 2 All ER 306.
20. See p 385.
1. (9 December 1977, unreported), CA.
2. (1 July 1985, unreported), CA.
3. See p 191, *ante*.
4. Eg *Re Besterman* [1984] Ch 458, [1984] 2 All ER 656; *Re Bunning* [1984] Ch 480, [1984] 3 All ER 1.
5. [1984] Ch 458, [1984] 2 All ER 656.
6. [1984] Ch 480, [1984] 3 All ER 1. The decisions of *Re Parkinson* (1975) Times, 4 October and *Re Bayliss* (9 December 1978, unreported), CA turned on the problem of costs and debts of the applicant and can not be considered to be decisive of the issue.

appointing *independent* professional trustees[7] or a trustee specifically to represent the interests of the beneficiaries entitled to income or including in a will a direction as to the minimum proportion of the fund to be invested to produce an income. A direction that the trustess are not bound to balance the interests of various types of beneficiary in choosing investments[8] may invite an application under the 1975 Act and is best avoided.

Under the rules of intestacy a surviving spouse may 'redeem' his life-interest in one half of the residue.[9] It is unresolved whether a surviving spouse who has been left a life interest can bring an application under the 1975 Act *solely* to obtain the actuarial value of the life-interest.

The 'One-Third Rule'

In considering the applicability of the 'one-third rule' to claims under the 1975 Act by surviving spouses, the first point to be made is that, as set out above, the duty to have regard to provision which would be awarded on divorce is merely one of several guidelines and is not the overriding criterion.[10] Further, it is important to bear in mind the justification of the rule on divorce and its current status in divorce law.

The modern rebirth of the rule in *Wachtel v Wachtel*[11] that a wife should be awarded sufficient capital and income so that she has one-third of the *joint* capital and income of herself and her husband was justified by Lord Denning MR in two ways. Firstly, a wife should only have an income equal to one-third of the joint income because the husband would have to pay a housekeeper to look after him.[12] Secondly, the wife should only be awarded one-third of the joint capital because her husband would in all probability be paying additionally periodical payments to the wife and children.[13] While this reasoning can easily be criticised,[14] the general approach of the 'one-third rule', both in that it is a rule and that it is set at about the correct level, has generally been liked by practitioners. It might be that a figure of one-third of joint incomes

7. *Davis v Davis* [1993] 1 FLR 54, at 59G-H.
8. Eg Kessler, *Drafting Trusts and Will Trusts: A Modern Approach*, 2nd edn, para 14-030.
9. S 47A of the Administration of Estates Act 1925.
10. See pp 179–182, *ante*.
11. [1973] Fam 72, [1973] 1 All ER 829.
12. [1973] Fam 94D-F, [1973] 1 All ER 839d-f.
13. [1973] Fam 95B-E, [1973] 1 All ER 839f-840d.
14. Stone, *Family Law*, pp 175–177.

is an amount which does not impose too great a burden on husbands.[15] Moreover, a figure of one-third might accurately quantify a wife's 'just share' by contribution to the family in her husband's property, bearing in mind that the modern tendency to place the legal title of the matrimonial home in joint names[16] might suggest that the number of cases where the principles of law and equity do not give a 'just' answer are declining.[17] It may be noted that the one-third rule is very rarely employed to take property away from a wife with the legal title.

On divorce, the 'one-third rule' has been severely affected by the changes to taxation of maintenance orders effected by the Finance Act 1988 as regards periodical payments.[18] As regards capital payments, it has been decisively rejected as regards 'very big cases'[19] and 'very small cases', but remains 'a flexible starting point in an appropriate case'.[20] It is important for courts in exercising their jurisdiction under the 1975 Act to be aware of the *current* status of the 'one-third rule' on divorce and not to overstate its importance.

Because the basis of the 'one-third rule' as regards maintenance, namely balancing the needs of a husband and wife, disappears with claims under the 1975 Act as the deceased no longer requires maintenance for himself, it is submitted that the 'one-third rule' has no application for the very many cases which are decided purely on the applicant's need for maintenance. Thus with many small estates it may be proper to give the applicant the entire estate.[1] In cases of competing claims or where the parties had separated before death,[2] it may be that the 'one-third rule' has *some* limited relevance. In cases where the matter turns upon the spouse's claim for a 'just share', which will tend to be the meduim sized estates,[3] it is submitted that the 'one-third rule' will be of considerable relevance. It must be

15. Lord Denning MR in *Wachtel v Wachtel* [1973] Fam 72, at 94F, [1973] 1 All ER 839e states, 'In any case, where there are two households, the greater expense, will, in most cases, fall on the husband than the wife'; and see Law Commission Report No 113, 'The Financial Consequences of Divorce: The Basic Policy. A Discussion Paper', para 25.
16. See generally Todd and Jones, *Matrimonial Property*.
17. Compare generally Zuckerman, 'Ownership of the Matrimonial Home – Common Sense and Reformist Nonsense', (1978) 94 LQR 26.
18. See RAYDEN, para 29.84; *Furniss v Furniss* (1982) 3 FLR 46.
19. Eg *Dart v Dart* [1996] 2 FLR 286.
20. *Slater v Slater* (1982) 3 FLR 364; JACKSON AND DAVIES, para 3.18.
1. *Re Parkinson* (1975) Times, 4 October; *Re Bayliss* (9 December 1977, unreported), CA.
2. See p 182, *ante*.
3. See pp 178–179, 184–186, *ante*.

remembered that the rule has a decreasing application the larger the sums which are involved.[4] In *Re Besterman*[5] Oliver LJ stated:

> In arriving at this figure [the total provision ordered] I have not taken as a starting point the *Wachtel* proportion, but it has been suggested that this is a useful cross-check. Adding back the value of the house to the present value of the estate this provision constitutes approximately a quarter of the available total and confirms one in the belief that it is not excessive.

Applying the 'one-third rule' under the 1975 Act involves having regard to the combined assets of the deceased's estate and of the applicant.[6] It also involves the often difficult task of calculating the relative value of capital and an income stream, such as a pension or wages from employment of the applicant.

The Effect of Remarriage and Cohabitation

In theory the effect of remarriage upon an application under the 1975 Act should be relatively straightforward. Firstly, because a spouse's 'just share' is in the nature of a property right which has been earned, it should not be reduced by the applicant's remarriage.[7] Secondly, a claim for maintenance should terminate on remarriage.

However, several factors operate to make the law in practice much less straightforward. Periodical payments do not automatically terminate upon remarriage. This was a change introduced by the 1975 Act and contrasts with the position under the Matrimonial Causes Act 1973[8] and with applications by former spouses under the 1975 Act.[9] The Law Commission justified the change by

4. For the ultimate authority on this point, see *Dart v Dart* [1996] 2 FLR 286.
5. [1984] Ch 458, at 479E, [1984] 2 All ER 656, at 671c-d. For an example of a 'cross-check', see *Re Bunning* [1984] Ch 480, at 499B-D, [1984] 3 All ER 1, at 12b-c. Brown P applied the 'one-third rule'in *Kusminow v Barclays Bank Trust Co* [1989] Fam Law 66 – a medium sized estate where the applicant was entitled to a' just share'. Dillon LJ rejected the 'one-third' approach in *Eeles v Evans* (6 July 1989, unreported), CA – a medium to large estate where the applicant had a limited claim to a 'just share', discussed p 185, *ante* (a somewhat harsh decision).
6. *Re Bunning* [1984] Ch 480, at 499B-D, [1984] 3 All ER 1, at 12b-c; *Kusminow v Barclays Bank Trust Co* [1989] Fam Law 66.
7. *Wachtel v Wachtel* [1973] Fam 72, at 96G-H, [1973] 3 All ER 829, at 841d–e (per Lord Denning MR). See also *Smith v Smith* [1992] Fam 69, [1991] 2 All ER 306.
8. S 28(1).
9. S 19(2).

comparison with the position on intestacy and modern trends in will-making and because the remarriage of an elderly widow will not always bring her any financial advantage.[10] At no time did the Law Commission consider the *policy* of extending a deceased's obligations beyond remarriage;[11] it merely considered the *needs* of the applicant. A further factor to consider is that it is not always easy to separate an award of a 'just share' and an award made for maintenance – the two generally overlap and a maintenance obligation will often be satisfied by an award of a lump sum. Moreover, it is often forensically difficult and invidious to assess a person's chances of remarriage.[12]

Since the 1975 Act has been in force the courts have not adopted any consistent approach as to whether the obligations of a deceased cease upon the remarriage of his surviving spouse.[13]

The absence of a provision in the 1975 Act terminating periodical payments upon remarriage for an applicant spouse leaves the court with a choice whether it should limit the maintenance obligation to the applicant's widowhood. It is tentatively suggested that as a matter of principle, in line with the position after divorce, maintenance should generally cease upon remarriage and possibly be suspended on cohabitation. However, no limits should be placed upon the *form* of the orders used and the whole question should be approached in a practical manner, having due regard to the invidiousness of some attempts to ascertain the likelihood of a widow or a widower remarrying. It is suggested that where remarriage has already taken place, is imminent or very likely to take place an award of maintenance as opposed to a 'just share' should be limited to the time of remarriage.[14] If periodical payments are ordered or property settled for a limited period, the interest of the applicant should cease

10. WORKING PAPER, para 3.23; LAW COM, paras 37–43.
11. See generally Hayes, 'Cohabitation Clauses' in Financial Provision and Property Adjustment Orders – Law, Policy and Justice', (1994) 110 LQR 124.
12. *Wachtel v Wachtel* [1973] Fam 72, at 96H-97A, [1973] 3 All ER 829, at 841d-e (per Lord Denning MR). But see Atiyah, *Accidents, Compensation and the Law*, (5th edn) pp 115–116.
13. In virtually every reported case under the 1975 Act the possibility of remarriage has been ignored. With particularly aged applicants this is not surprising. But future marriage and cohabitation was taken into account in the s 1(1)(e) cases of *Malone v Harrison* [1979] 1 WLR 1353, at 1365D; *Re Haig*, Browne-Wilkinson J [1979] LS Gaz R 476.
14. In *Winfield v Billington* (30 July 1990, unreported), CA the court took account of the applicant husband's remarriage. The limited award at first instance can be justified not on the basis of a 'just share' or maintenance before marriage, but as a contribution to the 'welfare' of the children (the amended s 25(1) of the Matrimonial Causes Act 1973). Even so any award seems very difficult to justify.

on remarriage or cohabitation,[15] but it might be beneficial to pay a capital sum ('a dowry') upon the event of remarriage in order to encourage remarriage and compensate him or her for the loss of the payments.[16] Where a lump sum is calculated on the basis of capitalised periodical payments, the possibility of remarriage should be considered,[17] but the courts should approach the matter of remarriage with due regard to the applicant's dignity.

Applications by Husbands

When the 1938 Act came into effect there was considerable diversity of approach in dealing with applications by widowers.[18] However, by the 1960s it was recognised that a widower could make a successful claim and should in principle be treated in exactly the same way as a widow.[19] The modern approach was expounded by Ungoed-Thomas J in *Re Clayton* as follows:

> I certainly do not see in the Act of 1938 a greater onus of proof on the surviving husband than on the surviving wife. It is simply a question in each case, be the claimant husband or wife, whether in all the circumstances as established in evidence the deceased's failure to make any, or enough, provision for the surviving spouse is unreasonable; and I for my part, find no material assistance nowadays from contemplating the sex of the claimant, or considering it a circumstance on its own when all material circumstances have to be considered.[20]

Equality between the sexes is also the rule under the Matrimonial Causes Act 1973.[1]

15. See *Wachtel v Wachtel* [1973] Fam 72, at 97B, [1973] 1 All ER 829, at 841b-c; *Chadwick v Chadwick* [1985] FLR 606; *Clutton v Clutton* [1991] 1 WLR 359, [1991] 1 All ER 340; Hayes, "Cohabitation Clauses' in Financial Provision and Property Adjustment Orders – Law, Policy and Justice', (1994) 110 LQR 124.
16. For discussion of a 'dowry' in this context see Royal Commission on Civil Liability and Compensation for Personal Injury (Cmnd 7054 – 1978) Vol 1, paras 409–417.
17. As in *Malone v Harrison* [1979] 1 WLR 1353, at 1365D. See Law Commission Consultation Paper No 148 'Claims for wrongful death', paras 3.65–3.66.
18. *Re Sylvester* [1941] Ch 87, [1940] 4 All ER 269 (provision ordered); *Re Pointer* [1941] Ch 60, [1940] 4 All ER 372 (provision ordered), but Morton J doubted the correctness of his decision in *Re Styler* [1942] Ch 387, [1942] 2 All ER 201 (application dismissed); *Re Lawes* (1946) 62 TLR 231 (provision ordered).
19. *Re Parry* (1956) Times, 19 April; *Re Bonham* (1962) 112 L Jo 634; *Re Beale* (1964) Times, 4 June; *Re Clayton* [1966] 1 WLR 969, [1966] 2 All ER 370.
20. [1966] 1 WLR 969, at 972F-G, [1966] 2 All ER 370, at 372E-F.
1. *Calderbank v Calderbank* [1976] Fam 93, [1975] 3 All ER 333.

In practice there may well be some differences in approach between applications by husbands and wives. In so far as the 'one-third rule' applies under the 1975 Act,[2] in the case of an application by a husband he will only be entitled to one-third of the joint assets.[3] Whereas the very fact of marriage in the case of a wife may be treated as indicating an assumption of an obligation to maintain and indicating financial dependence upon the deceased, in the case of an application by a husband, the court is likely to attach less importance to the fact of marriage and more to the underlying reasons for making an award.[4]

PART 2: INFANT CHILDREN

Infant children have probably the strongest moral claim upon the deceased's estate. Few moral claims are as strong as the claim of one who has been brought into existence by the act of another and who is incapable of supporting himself.[5] This strong moral claim is reflected in family provision proceedings. In all the reported cases concerning applications by infant children, there is only one case[6] where the applicant was refused provision, whether direct or indirect, present or future, and that decision would probably not be followed today.[7] In *Re Bateman*[8] Uthwatt J stated that 'the testator's infant child had first claim on the estate'. More recently Wilson J in *Re C* stated that the 'substantial award' for an illegitimate

2. See pp 170–171, *ante.*
3. See *Calderbank v Calderbank* [1976] Fam 93, at 103E-G, [1975] 3 All ER 333, at 340e-g (per Cairns LJ); *P v P (financial provision: lump sum)* [1978] 1 WLR 483, [1978] 3 All ER 70.
4. See the instructive remarks of Ungoed-Thomas J in *Re Clayton* [1966] 1 WLR 969, at 972E-F, [1966] 2 All ER 370, at 372D; and note the particularly strong facts of *Re Sylvester* [1941] Ch 87, [1940] 4 All ER 269 and *Re Lawes* (1946) 62 TLR 231. For applications by husbands under the 1975 Act, see *Winfield v Billington* (30 July 1990, unreported), CA; *Moody v Stevenson* [1992] Ch 486, [1992] 2 All ER 524.
5. This passage in the second edition was cited with approval by Carswell J in *Re Patton* [1986] NI 45, at 51B-C. See also s 25(1) of the Matrimonial Causes Act 1973 inserted by s 3 of the Matrimonial and Family Proceedings Act 1984 which requires that 'first consideration be ... given to the welfare of a minor child of the family who has not attained the age of eighteen years' when exercising the powers of the court to grant ancillary relief.
6. *Re Howell* [1953] 1 WLR 1034, [1953] 2 All ER 604.
7. *Re Howell* adopted a subjective approach and regard was had only to matters at the date of death. Nowadays an objective approach is taken, see pp 125–128, *ante*, and regard is had to facts at the date of hearing, s 3(5). Compare *Re H (A Minor)* (1976) 6 Fam Law 172.
8. (1941) 85 Sol Jo 454.

child of the deceased aged eight years where the estate of the deceased after Inheritance Tax was £500,000 and where the deceased's will made no provision for the applicant was 'inevitable'.[9] Further, the state's interest in parents maintaining their infant children has been reasserted in recent years through the Child Support legislation.[10] While an infant child may have first claim on the deceased's estate this need not be satisfied by an award in his favour, but may be satisfied by an award in favour of his parent or guardian who will maintain him.

The Standard of Provision

Reasonable provision for infants is:

> ... such financial provision as it would be reasonable in all the circumstances of the case for the applicant to receive for his maintenance.[11]

In deciding whether reasonable provision has been made and how to exercise its powers to order reasonable provision the court is required to:

> ... have regard to the manner in which the applicant was being or in which he might expect to be educated or trained.[12]

It is quite clear that provision can be ordered, where appropriate, to enable the applicant to receive private education.[13] The wording of section 3(3) clearly indicates that the amount of the deceased's estate available for the applicant's maintenance is not the sole criterion as to whether such things as private education are appropriate for the applicant. For instance it would not necessarily be proper to order maintenance to include private education where the applicant had no prospect of receiving such while the deceased was alive and the deceased's estate was greatly enlarged on death by death benefits under pension schemes and insurance policies,

9. [1995] 2 FLR 24, at 29F-G.
10. See Child Support Acts 1991, 1995.
11. S 1(2)(b).
12. S 3(3), derived from s 25(2) of the Matrimonial Causes Act 1973.
13. Eg *Bosch v Perpetual Trustee Co* [1938] AC 463, [1938] 2 All ER 14; *Re Franks* [1948] Ch 62, [1947] 2 All ER 638; *Talbot v Talbot* [1962] 1 WLR 1113, [1962] 3 All ER 174; *Re Bellman* [1963] P 239, [1963] 1 All ER 513; *Re Cohen*, John Mills QC (23 February 1979, unreported).

or where a rich man has maintained his illegitimate child but at the level appropriate to the child's poorer mother and has not had contact with the child.[14]

In line with recent legislation removing disabilities from illegitimate children illegitimacy *per se* is not a factor which will affect the standard of provision, although the court will have regard to the manner in which each child was being and should be brought up.[15]

Three recent cases demonstrate the amount of provision which may be ordered where there are no competing claims and the estate is reasonably large.

Re Cohen[16] concerned an application by an illegitimate child against the estate of his deceased father under the 1938 Act. The deceased, who lived with his wife, had a longstanding relationship with his mistress. A child was born of this relationship in 1966. The deceased maintained his mistress and child lavishly, purchasing an expensive house for the mistress in 1971, sending the applicant to a private school at age five and giving the mistress up to £100 per week for the maintenance of herself and the child. The deceased died in 1974, leaving a will which bequeathed his entire estate to his widow. The net estate at the date of the hearing was stated to be about £70,000, but it was strongly suspected that it was considerably larger. The widow had in the circumstances a strong claim of her own, but had a substantial estate of her own. In 1979 Mr John Mills QC sitting as a deputy judge of the Chancery Division awarded the applicant £3,000 per year until age 20.

In *Re Chatterton*[17] the husband and wife cohabited for only four months before separating. The applicant was born after the separation. The deceased husband did not know the child's name and took no interest in her, but he did voluntarily maintain her at £5

14. Compare *Re C (leave to apply for provision)* [1995] 2 FLR 24, at 29F-G where Wilson J refused to commit himself upon whether the eight year old illegitimate daughter of a peer of the realm who had not been maintained by the deceased while alive and who lived with her mother in local authority accommodation dependent upon state benefits should be entitled to be privately educated-for a fuller report of this case see [1995] 2 FCR 689 *sub nomen Re W (a minor) (claim from deceased's estate)*; and compare also the facts of *Re Chatterton* (1 November 1978, unreported), CA.
15. See the perceptive judgment of Carswell J in *Re Patton* [1986] NI 45, at 51D-52D discussing the remarks of Baker P in *In the Estate of of McC* (1979) 9 Fam Law 26, discussed at p 48, *ante*. See also the reluctance of Wilson J to commit himself on the question of private education in *Re C (leave to apply for provision)*, discussed in the preceeding footnote.
16. Mr John Mills QC (23 February 1979, unreported). Mr Stephen Weeks of Counsel kindly supplied me with a note of the evidence and of the judgment.
17. (1 November 1978, unreported), CA. A similar order was made with capital to the children at age 25 in *C A v C C* (1978) Times, 17 November, this aspect of the case being reported only in (1979) 123 Sol Jo 35 *sub nom In the Estate of McC*.

per week. A magistrates' court refused to order the deceased to maintain his wife. The deceased died in 1977, leaving a net estate of £18,000 and a will providing for a quarter share to the applicant at age 18 with full powers of maintenance and advancement and three quarters to various animal charities. In 1978, Reeve J in an unreasoned judgment awarded the widow £1,000 and increased the applicant's provision to half the residue (£8,500) to be held upon the same trusts as before. An appeal by the applicant requesting further provision and for the provision to be made absolute was refused by the Court of Appeal. While on the facts of the case where there were no competing claims the award was clearly unexceptionable, the judgment of Brandon LJ which emphasised that the applicant would probably receive maintenance of £14 per week, being the interest on £8,500, *and a capital sum of £8,500 at age 18* evinces an erroneous approach. Lump sum awards are made to infants as commuted annual maintenance payments, to make provision against inflation,[18] not to provide legacies when children become adults.[19] If the sum of £14 per week is adequate maintenance, the applicant should have been awarded a lesser capital sum sufficient to purchase an annuity of £14 per week up to age 18.

In *Re Patton*[20] the deceased was the father of twin illegitimate boys who were born in 1973. The deceased did not live with the mother of the children and at the date of death was obliged by court order to pay £4. 25 per week for the maintenance of each of the children. The deceased died in 1984 leaving an estate of £47,000 together with a severable share in a joint bank account worth £5,000. The deceased made no provision for his children and the beneficiaries under the will of the deceased had no particular claim upon the estate. Each child did however receive a pension from the deceased's employer of £407 per annum and some provision was also made for their mother. In 1986 Carswell J awarded each child a lump sum of £10,000.

Because provision is limited to maintenance, and in line with the divorce court's refusal to order capital provision for infant children beyond their needs for maintenance,[1] it is suggested that

18. For inflation generally see pp 146–147, *ante*.
19. 'Maintenance' is of an income not a capital nature, *Re Dennis* [1981] 2 All ER 140. The criticism of the remarks of Brandon LJ in the second edition were accepted as valid by Carswell J in *Re Patton* [1986] NI 45, at 53B-C.
20. [1986] NI 45.
1. *Harnett v Harnett* [1973] Fam 156, at 161D, [1973] 2 All ER 593, at 598f-g; *Chamberlain v Chamberlain* [1973] 1 WLR 1557, [1974] 1 All ER 33; *Lord Lilford v Glynn* [1979] 1 WLR 78, [1979] 1 All ER 441; *Kiely v Kiely* [1988] 1 FLR 248. See for the similar position under the Children Act, Sch 1, *A v A (a minor: financial provision)* [1994] 1 FLR 657; *T v S (financial provision for children)* [1994] 2 FLR 883; *J v C* [1997] Fam Law 512.

rovision should not be ordered so as to enable the applicant to have capital sum when he attains his majority. The Act refers to maintenance' not 'advancement'.[2] Of course a legitimate omponent in maintenance can be a small sum of capital to meet ninor emergencies and to pay for out of the ordinary expenditure 'rainy day money'. If lump sums are ordered, the trustees will ormally be given the widest powers of advancement and naintenance (including a power to resort to capital for naintenance).[3]

ompeting Claims upon the Deceased

he maintenance of an infant child, both before and after death, hould be the responsibility of both parents.[4] Neither the deceased or the surviving partner can put the entire burden of supporting n infant child upon the other.

Whereas the courts have on occasions allowed the deceased to hoose which partners he should benefit on death, where his estate is nadequate to satisfy all the claims made upon him[5] with infant children he courts do not permit the deceased to choose which ones to benefit. n example of this is *Re Lecoche*.[6] The deceased died in 1965 leaving n estate of about £5,000, mostly a dwellinghouse in which he lived vith his mistress and survived by a mistress, an estranged wife, three egitimate children and an illegitimate child. The deceased by his will eft his entire estate to his illegitimate infant son. Plowman J remarked hat the deceased had 'so many to provide for and so little with which o do it'. An application by the widow, who received a benefit from the leceased's pension, failed, but the court ordered that provision should e made for the two legitimate infant children.

ompeting Claims between Infant Children and arents

Vhere a parent is maintaining a child their interest in family rovision proceedings are essentially similar. It matters little to an

2. This passage in the second edition was approved by Carswell J in *Re Patton* [1986] NI 45, at 53A-C.
3. Eg per Browne-Wilkinson V-C in *Dixit v Dixit* (23 June 1988, unreported), CA.
4. S 1(1) of the Child Support Act 1991. Compare the remarks of Brandon LJ in *Preston v Preston* [1982] Fam 17, at 36H-37A, [1982] 1 All ER 41, at 57a.
5. For 'dilemma' cases, see p 150, *ante*.
6. (1967) 111 Sol Jo 136.

infant whether money paid to his parent for his maintenance i nominally his or his parent's.

The advantages of provision being provided for the infant chil directly are that there is some assurance that the money will actuall be used for the infant's benefit and that there is a reduced risk o the funds being dissipated before the child attains his majority. A advantage of provision being made to a parent is that there is greate flexibility in managing the provision, for instance, the purchase o a house for the mother of a child is a very good form of provisio for the child, but is difficult to achieve when property is held in trus for an infant. A lump sum awarded to a surviving spouse is probabl more tax efficient for the purposes of Income Tax and Inheritanc Tax than periodical payments to an infant ceasing at age 18.

Whereas an infant's claim is of an income nature and only last until adulthood is attained, a surviving spouse's claim is under th 1975 Act also a claim to capital and is generally of a longer duratio The courts have recognised the longer duration of the spouse's clai by awarding a spouse who has been left with inadequate provisio by the deceased provision out of gifts of capital given to infan children. In both *Re Lidington*[7] and *Re Hills*[8] provision was ordere out of gifts of capital given to the deceased's infant children in favou of the deceased's widow who was maintaining the children. In *R Bateman*[9] Uthwatt J refused to order provision in similar circum stances, but adjourned the widow's application until the chil attained the age of 21. Thus, with the exception of the case wher the deceased left his infant child an interest in the income of th estate terminating on adulthood,[10] where a surviving spouse is le with inadequate provision and the deceased gave gifts to his infan children who are being maintained by the applicant, it may be prope to order provision out of the infant children's interests for th surviving spouse.[11]

Where provision is ordered at the expense of an infant child i favour of his parent, the court has to be satisfied that the parent wi actually maintain the child. Usually reading the evidence i sufficient,[12] but an undertaking to the court to maintain has bee

7. [1940] Ch 927, [1940] 3 All ER 600.
8. [1941] WN 123.
9. (1941) 85 Sol Jo 454; see also *Re Franks* [1948] Ch 62, [1947] 2 All ER 63
10. *Re Bateman* (1941) 85 Sol Jo 454.
11. An example is *Re Weir* [1993] 2 NIJB 45 where the deceased left a moderate substantial estate to his daughter, aged 15 years at the date of trial, and n provision for his estranged wife, who was caring for the child. Provision wa ordered for the wife at the expense of the daughter.
12. Eg *Re Hills* [1941] WN 123; *Re Bayliss* (9 December 1977, unreported), CA *Re Lewis* (13 March 1980, unreported), CA; *Dixit v Dixit* (23 June 198 unreported), CA.

required in one case[13] and in some cases it may be appropriate to obtain a report from the court welfare officer.

It is clear that where a parent and a child being maintained by that parent both make applications, the court will frequently make an award in favour of the parent and no award in favour of the child, the indirect provision being considered adequate.[14] But where there is a real doubt about the parent's ability or intention to maintain the child it is inappropriate to combine their interests and regard provision for one as indirect provision for the other.

Where an award is made to a surviving spouse on the basis that he will maintain an infant child, thought should be given to the child's position if the surviving parent dies before the child becomes an adult.[15] If a periodical payments order is made in favour of the applicant parent, the infant child can apply for the original order to be varied in its favour.[16] If an order in the form of capital provision is made, consideration should be given to using the court's power to settle property[17] so that provision is assured for the infant child in the case of the surviving parent's death or to requiring the spouse to undertake to make provision for the infant child in his estate – this may obviate the need for the child subsequently to apply out of time for provision out of his parent's estate or apply for provision out of the surviving parent's estate.

Furthermore, in some cases it would be inappropriate or unjust to order more than a small sum for the parent because of his behaviour[18] or where provision for a parent would be limited anyway[19] separate provision should be ordered for both parent and child. Similarly in some cases, to a limited extent, it may be desirable to obtain symmetry between the parties and this may make it

13. *Re Lidington* [1940] Ch 927, [1940] 3 All ER 600.
14. *Re Bayliss* (9 December 1977, unreported), CA; *Re Lewis* (13 March 1980, unreported), CA; see also *Preston v Preston* [1982] Fam 17, [1982] 1 All ER 41 and the remarks of Lord Donaldson MR in *Re J (a minor)* (9 December 1991, unreported), CA. But compare the remarks of Lord Romer in *Bosch v Perpetual Trustee Co* [1938] AC 463, at 482, [1938] 2 All ER 14, at 24A-D and Harman J in *Re Borthwick* [1949] Ch 395, at 402–403, [1949] 1 All ER 472, at 476F-G.
15. ALBERY, 40.
16. S 6. See pp 401–408, *post*.
17. S 2(1)(d); ALBERY, 40.
18. Eg *Re Chatterton* (1 November 1978, unreported), CA; *Dixit v Dixit* (23 June 1988, unreported), CA; *Re Snoek* (1983) 13 Fam Law 18; but compare *Re Goard* (1962) 106 Sol Jo 721.
19. It is arguable that the amount of provision which can be ordered to an applicant under s 1(1)(e) is limited to the amount of his dependency, see further pp 282–285, *post*, but provision for a cohabitant within s 1(1)(ba) is not so limited. Note that in many cases a spouse's claim will be limited to maintenance and will not extend to a 'just share', eg *Winfield v Billington* (30 July 1990, unreported), CA.

appropriate to obtain separate provision for both parent and child.[2]
An example of these principles is the case of *Winfield v Billington.*
In this case a young married couple had two infant children. Th
husband left the wife, committing adultery. Subsequently the wif
died and the husband and his second wife acquired care and contro
of the two children. The deceased's estate consisted of her half shar
in the matrimonial home and £9,000 in investments and had bee
bequeathed to the children of the marriage contingent upo
attaining the age of 18 years. By agreement the deceased's share o
the matrimonial home had been applied in the purchase of a nev
house. The husband applied for provision under the 1975 Act. Judg
Stuart-White in the county court reduced the children's interest i
the matrimonial home by a third and converted it into a charge
realisable when each child attained the age of 21 years, but otherwis
dismissed the husband's application. The Court of Appeal dismisse
an appeal by the husband. The order made protected th
maintenance claims of the children of the marriage and the husband
but also gave effect to the legitimate desire of the deceased that he
capital should go to her children as opposed to her husband an
his second wife.

Competing Claims between Infant Children and Second Spouses

Although the possibility of conflict between the interests of infan
children and survivors of the parent's subsequent marriages was th
reason for the extension of family provision legislation to cases o
intestacy in 1952,[2] there are remarkably few reported cases on suc
situations. It does seem clear that both the infant child and th
deceased's partner have strong claims and in a typical case the cour
will divide the estate to give each a share. The method of divisio
depends upon a variety of factors affecting the surviving spouse'
claim, but it is thought that particular regard should be paid to th
ability of the other parent to support the child. In *Re H (a minor)*
the deceased was survived by a 10 year old child of his first marriag
and his second wife. The sole asset in the deceased's estate was hi

20. See *Re Lecoche* (1967) 111 Sol Jo 136; *C A v C C* (1978) Times, 17 Novembe *sub nom Re C* (1979) 123 Sol Jo 35, *sub nom In the Estate of McC* (1979) 9 Fa Law 29 – on this aspect of the case see p 48, *ante.*
1. (30 July 1990, unreported), CA.
2. See p 21, *ante.*
3. (1976) 6 Fam Law 172.

half share in his matrimonial home occupied by his second wife worth £3,500. In 1975 Lane J awarded the daughter a lump sum of £2,000 charged on the property, enforcement of which was stayed pending an investigation of the means of the widow raising the sum of £2,000. In *Re J (a minor)*[4] the deceased was survived by a daughter of his first marriage aged 14 years at the date of death and aged 16 years at the date of trial, his second wife and a daughter of the second marriage aged five years. His severable share in the matrimonial home passed to his second wife by survivorship and she was solely entitled to his estate of £30,000. The county court judge awarded the daughter of the second marriage a lump sum of £7,500, which the Court of Appeal reduced to £5,000, Lord Donaldson MR stating that but for the existence of the five year old daughter of the second marriage who was being maintained by the second wife, £7,500 would have been the appropriate award. An equal division of the estate[5] is only justifiable when the estate is insufficient to satisfy all the claims made against it and there are no other factors to aid the court in its determination.

When is an Infant Child Treated as an Adult Child for the Purposes of Family Provision?

Whereas it will be a rare case where an infant child will be left without some form of provision, direct or indirect, it will be an almost equally rare case in which family provision will be ordered on the application of an adult child.[6] It is therefore important to ascertain when an infant child ceases to be treated as such for the purposes of family provision. When a child reaches such an age he will only be entitled to provision if he satisfies the higher standards required for adult children.

A wide variety of ages for determining when a parent ceases to be financially responsible for a child is found in legislation. For social security purposes a parent ceases to be under a duty of support at between ages 16 and 19.[7] Under the Matrimonial Causes Act 1973 and the First Schedule to the Children Act 1989 an order for periodical payments for a child cease at age 18 or at the end of his

4. (9 December 1991, unreported), CA.
5. As suggested as appropriate in *Sivyer v Sivyer* [1967] 1 WLR 1482, at 1488D-E, [1967] 3 All ER 429, at 433G-H (per Pennycuick J).
6. Eg Compare *Re H (a minor)* (1976) 6 Fam Law 172 with *Re Coventry* [1980] Ch 461, [1979] 2 All ER 408; affd [1979] 3 All ER 815.
7. S 78(6)(a), (b), (d), s 105(3) of the Social Security Administration Act 1992.

education or training unless 'special circumstances' exist.[8] Liability under the Child Support Act 1991 can not extend beyond age 18.[9] Parental income ceases to be relevant for the purposes of calculating a student's grant at age 25.[10] When the Family Law Reform Act 1969 reduced the age of majority from 21 to 18, it specifically preserved the right of a son who had not reached the age of 21 to apply for provision under the 1938 Act.[11]

The Albertan study in 1978 which recommended against allowing adult children to apply for provision recommended that a child should cease to be able to apply at age 23 if he were in full-time education.[12] The pre-1970 cases under the 1938 Act tend to order provision up to age 21 for sons.[13] In *Re Cohen*[14] a post-1969 case under the 1938 Act Mr John Mills QC sitting as a deputy judge of the High Court after some discussion of the point held that for a daughter being privately educated periodic payments should end at age 20.

It is suggested that the test applied by the Matrimonial Causes Act 1973 of ceasing payments at age 18 or the cessation of full-time education or training is the correct test to be applied in family provision proceedings. This jurisdiction is used considerably and is closely analogous to family provision proceedings.[15] In the House of Lords debates on the 1975 Act there were several references to this power of the divorce court to order maintenance to children above the age of 18.[16] The

8. S 29(1), (2), (3) of the Matrimonial Causes Act 1973 as amended; para 2(1), Sch 1 of the Children Act 1989; *ad idem* s 5(1), (3) of the Domestic Proceedings and Magistrates' Courts Act 1978.
9. See the definition of 'child' in s 55.
10. Education (Mandatory Awards) Regulations 1994, SI 3044/1944.
11. Family Law Reform Act 1969, s 5(1).
12. Institute of Law Research and Reform, University of Alberta, Report No 29, Family Relief (1978), p 33. Exactly the same conclusion was reached by the Manitoba Law Reform Commission Report 'The Testators' Family Maintenance Act'(1985) 70. In his note of reservation to Law Reform Commission of British Columbia 'Report on Statutory Succession Rights'(LRC 70) (December 1983) Arthur L Close proposed an age limit of 19 years unless physically or mentally disabled.
13. *Re Lidington* [1940] Ch 927, at 938, [1940] 3 All ER 600, at 607D; *Re Bateman* (1941) 85 Sol Jo 454; *Re Westby* [1946] WN 141; but see *Re Lecoche* (1967) 111 Sol Jo 136 where payments were to end at age 16.
14. (23 February 1979, unreported). In *Re Bayliss* (9 December 1977, unreported), CA Deputy Judge Ellison, at first instance awarded an infant applicant income until she ceased full-time education. In *Re Snoek* (1983) 13 Fam Law 18 the court varied the entitlement of beneficiaries so that property was to be held upon trust for a child until he attained the age of 21 years with a view to providing for his education.
15. See also WORKING PAPER, paras 3.39, 3.43; LAW COM, paras 76–77.
16. See pp 28–30, *ante*.

reference to 'educated or *trained*'[17] in section 3(3) is a partial confirmation of the correctness of this approach. Where a child is being educated or trained maintenance should cease when the child ceases full time education or training, with perhaps a maximum of age 25.[18]

In recent years as a result of decreasing opportunities for employment for children under 21 years, coupled with less social security provision for such persons and increased opportunities for further education, there has grown up a class of children in an economic 'no man's land' between childhood and adulthood. The courts have in reported awards awarded provision to such children. In *Re Collins*[19] the applicant was aged ten at the date of death of her mother and aged 19 at the date of the hearing. At the time of the hearing the applicant was unemployed, having recently completed a Youth Training Scheme and dependent upon Income Support. In 1989 Hollings J awarded her a lump sum of £5,000. In *Re J (a minor)*[20] the applicant was aged 14 years at the date of death of her father and 16 years at the date of the hearing. She worked part-time in a fish and chip shop and hoped to go into further education. In 1991 the Court of Appeal awarded her a lump sum of £5,000. Both these cases can be partly explained upon the basis of awarding maintence for the period between the date of death and the date of hearing.

It is suggested that a child's claim to maintenance above age 16 while undergoing full-time education and training is less strong than that of a child under 16. Accordingly if there are competing claims upon the deceased, for instance those of a second spouse, the child's claims are entitled to more consideration when he is under 16 than when he is over 16.[1]

17. Emphasis added. See the remarks of Oliver J in *Re Coventry* [1980] Ch 461, at 467E-F, [1979] 2 All ER 408, at 419e-f, discussed by Goff LJ at [1980] Ch 492B-C, [1979] 3 All ER 815, at 825d-e.
18. At age 25 parental income ceases to be relevant for student grants, Education (Mandatory Awards) Regulations 1994, SI 1994/3044.
19. [1990] Fam 56, [1990] 2 All ER 47.
20. (9 December 1991, unreported), CA. In *Re Tomlinson* (3 July 1996, unreported) Judge Moseley QC sitting as a judge of the Chancery Division awarded a similarly placed daughter maintenance up to age 23. The estate was large (£250,000), the beneficiaries had no competing claim and the deceased during his lifetime had not maintained the applicant through concealment of assets. See also the remarks of Carswell J in *Re Patton* [1986] NI 45, at 53 D: 'The needs of the applicants will not cease when they become 16 or 18 years of age, and I consider that if the deceased had been making reasonable provision for them he would have provided a sum which would give them an income not only during their teens, but extending into the future.'
1. Compare *Re Lecoche* (1967) 111 Sol Jo 136.

Conduct of the Infant

The conduct of the deceased towards the infant is only of a very limited relevance. The mention of 'the manner … in which he might *expect* to be educated or trained' in section 3(3) suggests that while the standard of provision is objective, the way in which the deceased actually maintained the applicant while alive is a relevant factor in determining the amount of reasonable provision.[2]

The conduct of a young child towards the deceased is clearly irrelevant. In particular it is irrelevant that the applicant sides with one parent against another in a divorce.[3]

It is uncertain how far an older infant child may forfeit his right to maintenance by his conduct toward his parents. Two contrasting cases are *Re Mastaka*[4] and *Downing v Downing.*[5] In the former case the 20 year old daughter of the deceased had had no contact with the deceased since shortly after birth and had rejected the deceased as her mother. Farwell J held, *obiter,* that it would not be right to order provision.[6] *Downing v Downing* was a divorce case. A daughter of the divorced parents, aged 20, had effectively rejected both her father and mother and applied, herself, for maintenance to support her at university. Payne J did not decide the merits of the matter, but his judgment did imply that the applicant's conduct was not necessarily a total bar to relief.[7]

Child Support Act 1991

The Child Support Act has no application where the 'absent parent' is dead. Because the calculations under the Child Support Act 1991 take no account of capital,[8] it is unlikely that such calculations will be of any practical utility in determining the amount of reasonable provision for an infant child.

2. See *Re Patton* [1986] NI 45, at 51D-52D; and the discussion of private education at pp 200–201, *ante.*
3. For an extreme example, see *Re Ducksbury* [1966] 1 WLR 1226, at 1229A-B, 1231G-1232D, [1966] 2 All ER 374, at 377C-D, 378–399E.
4. [1941] Ch192, [1941] 1 All ER 236.
5. [1976] Fam 288, [1976] 3 All ER 474. See further *MacDonald v Macdonald* Times, 22/10/97.
6. [1941] Ch 194–195, [1941] 2 All ER 237H–238C.
7. [1976] Fam 294E, [1976] 3 All ER 479c-d.
8. See *Phillips v Peace* [1996] 2 FLR 230. Of more practical use are National Foster Care Association recommended allowances, set out in *At A Glance.*

PART 3: ADULT CHILDREN

The law on claims by adult children can not be understood without a chronological examination of the leading cases on claims by adult children. The 1975 Act permitted any adult child to apply to the court for reasonable provision out of the estate of their deceased parent. The Law Commission in their reports stressed that they considered that few claims by adult children would succeed and implied that claims would only be successful in situations broadly analogous to situations where claims could be brought under the 1938 Act.[9] However, the Law Commission did not offer any further elucidation as to the types of cases where adult children should succeed in their applications.

With so little guidance it is not surprising that initially the courts exhibited considerable diversity of approach in their treatment of applications by adult children. In the first case to be reported, *Re Christie,*[10] Mr Vivian Price QC sitting as a deputy judge of the Chancery Division made an order for provision for a married able-bodied son who appeared to be in good financial circumstances and who had no particularly strong claim upon the deceased's bounty.

A considerable change in direction came with the decision in *Re Coventry.*[11] In *Re Coventry* the deceased died aged 77 in 1976 intestate, his estate consisting mainly of a two-thirds interest in a dwellinghouse of a total value of about £12,000. The applicant was the deceased's only son aged 46 at the date of the hearing. The applicant had lived with the deceased from 1957 until the date of his death, rent free but contributing to the household expenses. The applicant was self-employed, had only a modest income and was required to pay maintenance to his divorced wife and children.

By the operation of the rules of intestacy, the deceased's estate devolved upon his estranged wife. The widow had virtually been forced to leave the matrimonial home by the combined pressure of the deceased and the applicant in 1957. The widow after this separation had not been supported at all by the deceased, was now

9. WORKING PAPER, paras 3.39–3.43; LAW COM, paras 71–79.
10. [1979] Ch 168, [1979] 1 All ER 546. For the facts of *Re Christie* see pp 47–48, *ante.* The earlier decision of Judge Toyn sitting as a deputy judge of the Family Division in *Re Homer, Rann v Jackson* appears to be unreported.
11. [1980] Ch 461, [1979] 2 All ER 408. Some further information on the activities of the defendant's legal advisers is contained in *In Re Solicitors; In Re Taxation of Costs* [1982] 1 WLR 745, [1982] 2 All ER 683.

aged 74 and lived in straitened circumstances. It was agreed that the widow by reason of her contribution to the purchase of the house was entitled to a third interest in the house. The applicant applied for family provision and was awarded £2,000 by Master Gowers. Being dissatisfied with this award the applicant had the summons adjourned to Oliver J.

After a very careful review of the evidence Oliver J characterised the applicant's son's claim as resting substantially on two limbs only, namely:

> (a) that he is a son of the deceased with whom it might be thought that there would be a bond of natural affection and (b) that although he is in employment and capable of maintaining himself his circumstances leave him little or no margin for expenditure on anything other than the necessaries of life.[12]

These two limbs were an insufficient basis on which to enable the court to order any provision for the applicant and Oliver J dismissed the summons, discharging the Master's award of £2,000. Parts of his judgment deserve setting out in full, in particular:

> It cannot be enough to say 'here is a son the deceased; he is in necessitous circumstances; there is property of the deceased which could be made available to assist him but which is not available if the deceased's dispositions stand; therefore those dispositions do not make reasonable provision for the applicant'. There must, as it seems to me be established some sort of moral claim by the applicant to be maintained by the deceased or at the expense of his estate beyond the mere fact of the blood relationship, some reason why it can be said that, in the circumstances, it is unreasonable that no or no greater provision was in fact made.[13]

In his judgment Oliver J, differing from the approach of Mr Vivian Price QC in *Re Christie*,[14] stressed that the 1975 Act was a continuation of the 1938 Act.[15] The case law on the 1938 Act was still relevant to the 1975 Act.[16] In particular Oliver J referred to the approach of the court to applications by able-bodied widowers and quoted[17] Morton

12. [1980] Ch 478B-C, [1979] 2 All ER 420h-j.
13. [1980] Ch 475C-E, [1979] 2 All ER 418e-f.
14. [1979] Ch 168, [1979] 2 All ER 408.
15. [1980] Ch 472D-E, 473H-474D, [1979] 2 All ER 416a-c, 417b-f; see pp 113–114, *ante*. Oliver J had been the editor of a book on the 1938 Act, Tillard, *Family Provision* (2nd edn, 1950).
16. [1980] Ch 472G–473E, 474A-C, [1979] 2 All ER 416d-h, 417e-f.
17. [1980] Ch 472H-473D, [1979] 2 All ER 416d-h.

J in *Re Styler*[18] to the effect that such applications should only succeed in 'exceptional' circumstances. Oliver J, after explaining the limited function of the court when dealing with applications under the 1975 Act, stated in effect that only if certain matters existed would the dispositions of the deceased's estate be unreasonable[19] – in the Court of Appeal Buckley LJ put it that 'some special circumstance is required'.[20] In many cases this 'special circumstance' takes the form of a 'moral duty',[1] – in the present case Oliver J found that there was no moral duty.[2] In his judgment Oliver J indicated 'special circumstances' which would enable an adult child to be awarded provision *might* be if the applicant had substantially looked after the deceased at a cost to himself,[3] if the applicant was actually dependent upon the deceased,[4] if the applicant because of a physical or mental disability was incapable of earning a living[5] or if the applicant was still being trained for a vocation.[6]

The ratio of *Re Coventry* at first instance is that the mere existence of a blood relationship and the comparative poverty of an adult child are insufficient reasons to entitle a court to interfere with the disposition of the deceased's estate. Although the outcome of the case can be justified as turning upon the greater claim of the widow, Oliver J clearly preferred not to decide the matter upon the priority of conflicting claims, but upon the failure of the applicant to satisfy the court that he had any claim to be considered under the Act at all.[7]

18. [1942] Ch 387, at 388–389, [1942] 2 All ER 201, at 204B-F; these dicta with regard to applications by widowers do not necessarily represent the law today, see pp 198–199, *ante*.
19. [1980] Ch 475C-G, [1979] 2 All ER 418e-f.
20. [1980] Ch 495A-B, [1979] 3 All ER 827g-h. The provision enabling the divorce court to order maintenance for a child over the age of 18 years if 'special circumstances' exist was first enacted in s 8(3)(b) of the Matrimonial Proceedings and Property Act 1970.
1. [1980] Ch 475D, [1979] 2 All ER 418e-f. On the test of moral duty, see the instructive remarks of Goff LJ at [1980] Ch 487G-H, [1979] 3 All ER 821j-822a and pp 121–123, *ante*.
2. [1980] Ch 476F-477D, [1979] 2 All ER 419f-420b.
3. [1980] Ch 477C-D, [1979] 2 All ER 419j-420a and see pp 233–237, *post*.
4. [1980] Ch 465F, 471A, 471D, [1979] 2 All ER 410g, 414h-j, 415b-c, and see generally pp 231–232, *post*.
5. Oliver J speaks of 'able-bodied' applicants at [1980] Ch 465G, 472A, 472G, 473F, 474B, 474D-E, [1979] 2 All ER 410h, 415g, 416d, 417a-b, 417d-e, 417g. See generally pp 242–247, *post*.
6. [1980] Ch 476E-F, [1979] 2 All ER 419e-g. S 3(3) requires the court in dealing with applications by children and by children of the family to have regard to 'the manner in which the applicant was being or in which he might expect to be educated or trained. ' See generally pp 207–209, *ante*.
7. See the remarks of Oliver J at [1980] Ch 476D-477D, 478D, [1979] 2 All ER 419d-420b, 420j-421a.

Thus the decision would have been the same had the deceased left his entire estate by will to a charity.

Although Oliver J at first appeared to think that the court should treat applications by adult children with a special scepticism and reservation,[8] he eventually stated that the test was the same as with other classes of applicants. He said:

> I think ... that I ought not to approach this application with any preconceived notion that there is some especially heavy burden on a male applicant of full age beyond that which must, as a practical matter, necessarily exist when a person who applies to be maintained by somebody else is already capable of adequately maintaining himself.[9]

It is submitted that this approach is correct. While there is no special test for adult children, it is clear that different classes of applicants will be able to satisfy the court of the *unreasonableness* of the dispositions of the deceased's estate with different degrees of ease. This approach has been affirmed by the Court of Appeal in *Re Fullard*,[10] where Ormrod LJ stated that few applications by former spouses would succeed because of the difficulty of proving that the dispositions of the deceased's estate were unreasonable.[11]

The applicant's son appealed against the judgment of Oliver J but his appeal was unanimously dismissed by a strong Court of Appeal.[12] Whereas the ratio of Oliver J's judgment is obvious and clearly stated, the judgments of the Court of Appeal are less clearly stated and are more difficult to understand. All three judgments are written within the framework of the limited degree of appellate review permitted in family provision proceedings[13] and take the form of approval or criticism of Oliver J's judgment rather than an original statement of the law. Although *Re Christie*[14] was not formally overruled[15] and although some criticism of Oliver J's judgment was ventilated,[16] it is clear that both Goff and Buckley LJJ approved much of the reasoning of Oliver J, but without completely authoritive

8. [1980] Ch 465F-H, [1979] 2 All ER 410g-j.
9. [1980] Ch 474D-E, [1979] 2 All ER 417f-g.
10. [1982] Fam 42, [1981] 2 All ER 796. For the facts of this case see pp 254–256, *post*.
11. [1982] Fam 42, at 49E-F, [1981] 2 All ER 796, at 801j-802a.
12. [1980] Ch 748, [1979] 3 All ER 815. The court consisted of Buckley, Goff and Geoffrey Lane LJJ.
13. For the general approach to appeals see pp 369–370, *post*.
14. [1979] Ch 168, [1979] 1 All ER 546.
15. See the remarks of Goff LJ at [1980] Ch 490F-G, [1979] 3 All ER 824c.
16. Per Goff LJ at [1980] Ch 490H-491B, [1979] 3 All ER 824d-824f, per Geoffrey Lane LJ at [1980] Ch 493A, [1979] 3 All ER 826b.

statements of principle in what was argued as very much a 'test case'.[17] Although Geoffrey Lane LJ stated that he would have come to the same conclusion as Oliver J,[18] his judgment does not contain a complete endorsement of the ratio of Oliver J.

Independently Toyn J sitting as a deputy judge of the Family Division in *Re Homer, Rann v Jackson*[19] regarded it as monstrous that a father should be under any obligation to provide for a daughter aged 54 who was married and had children. Oliver J's approach was further confirmed by the judgment of Ormrod LJ in *Re Fullard*[20] which emphasised the considerable regard which is had to the deceased's duties to maintain during his lifetime and that within a class of applicants only a small number would be successful. In *Rann v Jackson*[1] and *Re Portt*[2] the Court of Appeal dismissed appeals by adult children whose applications had failed at first instance. In each case the applicant had no real merit and in neither case did the Court of Appeal lay down any authorititive statement of principle. Until *Re Leach* the approach of Oliver J was consistently followed at first instance.[3]

The law was thrown into a degree of uncertainty by the case of *Re Leach.*[4] In this case the applicant was an able-bodied unmarried

17. See the remarks of Goff LJ at [1980] Ch 492A, [1979] 3 All ER 825c-d (set out at pp 224–225, *post*) and of Buckley LJ at [1980] Ch 494G, [1979] 3 All ER 827e-f. That Goff and Buckley LJJ differred from Oliver J on the meaning of 'maintenance' and did not stress the countervailing claims of the widow, indicates their endorsement of the general approach of Oliver J. (A particular problem with the judgment of Buckley LJ is his failure to comment upon his own decision at first instance in *Re Ducksbury* [1966] 1 WLR 1226, [1966] 2 All ER 374 where he awarded an able-bodied adult daughter substantial provision.) In *In Re Solicitors; In Re Taxation of Costs* [1982] 1 WLR 745, at 749E, [1982] 2 All ER 683, at 687c it was stated that the appeal in *Re Coventry* was expected to 'provid[e] a definitive judgment'.
18. [1980] Ch 493G, [1979] 3 All ER 826g. Geoffrey Lane LJ's judgment is open to the interpretation that if somebody other than the widow was entitled to the deceased's estate, the applicant would have succeeded.
19. See the extract from Toyn J's judgment in the Court of Appeal, 6 November 1978.
20. [1982] Fam 42, [1981] 2 All ER 796.
1. (6 November 1978, unreported).
2. (25 March 1980, unreported).
3. *Re Embelton* Telegraph, 3/3/79 Purchas J; *Re Fergusson* (16 June 1980, unreported) Foster J; *Re Dennis* [1981] 2 All ER 140, Browne-Wilkinson J; *Re Lazurus* Times, 16/11/82 Toyn J; *Re Rowlands* [1984] FLR 813, Anthony Lincoln J. The Northern Ireland judges were more benevolent to adult children, see *Re McGarrell* [1983] 8 NIJB; *Re Creeney* [1984] NI 397.
4. [1986] Ch 226, [1985] 2 All ER 754, affirming [1984] FLR 590. While the case of *Re Callaghan* [1985] Fam 1, [1984] 3 All ER 790 raises difficult issues as to the concept of 'maintenance' and the quantum of an award, the decision to award provision in a case where the applicant and his wife gave up work for a time to look after the deceased is unremarkable.

lady aged 55 years who was in secure employment. The applicant's mother had died in 1959 and her father remarried the deceased in 1960. The Plaintiff was on very affectionate terms with her step-mother, although apart from holidays and visits and several months spent nursing her parents in 1959, she had not lived with either her parents or the deceased since she was aged 21 years. In 1974 the applicant's father died and the majority of his estate passed to the deceased. The deceased died intestate in 1981 and her estate devolved upon her sibling, who had no moral or other claim upon the deceased. At the trial the estate was stated to be of the order of £45,000 and was mainly derived from the applicant's father's estate and a house purchased in the name of the deceased with funds probably provided by the applicant's father. There was some evidence that the deceased had stated that she would leave the applicant half her estate and the applicant had taken this into account when deciding to purchase another a house.

In 1983 Mr Michael Wheeler QC sitting as a judge of the Chancery Division held that the applicant, despite being 32 years of age at the date of the marriage between her father and the deceased, was in relation to that marriage 'a child of the family' within section 1(1)(d).[5] He further held that the rules of intestacy did not make reasonable provision for the applicant and that she was in need of maintenance and awarded a lump sum of £19,000. In his judgment Mr Michael Wheeler QC quoted extensively from the judgments of both Oliver J and the Court of Appeal in *Re Coventry*. Expressly differing from Goff LJ in *Re Coventry*,[6] he regarded the intention of the deceased to leave property to the applicant,[7] together with the applicant's purchase of a house in reliance upon statements from the deceased to this effect (which was conceded not to have created any kind of estoppel)[8] created a moral obligation entitling the applicant to reasonable provision. The applicant's take home pay was £6,250 per annum, she owned a half share in a house subject to a mortgage of £14,000, had savings of £1,200 and other debts of £8,000, payment of which was not being immediately sought. On these figures the trial judge held that the applicant was in need of maintenance and awarded £19,000, being calculated either as half the estate less costs or sufficient to enable

5. [1984] FLR 590, at 596H-599H. On this issue, see pp 75–76, *ante*.
6. [1980] Ch 488F-H, [1979] 3 All ER 822f-j.
7. [1984] FLR 602A-E, 605D-606D.
8. [1984] FLR 606D-E.

to pay off her debts and leave her with some money for her current needs and when she retired.[9]

The beneficiaries appealed to the Court of Appeal (O'Connor, Slade and Robert Goff LJJ) who save as to quantum dismissed the appeal.[10] A single reserved judgment was given by Slade LJ. Although the trial judge had in his judgment cited extensively from *Re Coventry,* endeavouring to set out in the respects in which he was following or not following the decision and although extensive arguments based upon *Re Coventry* were put by Counsel for the beneficiaries,[11] the judgment of Slade LJ on the question of whether reasonable provision had been made for the applicant contains only one reference to *Re Coventry* or any other authority and then only to a passage in the judgment of Goff LJ on the limited nature of appellate review.[12] It is not particularly easy to ascertain the precise matters which Slade LJ regarded as creating a 'moral obligation'. He certainly regarded the applicant's commitment to purchasing a house in reliance upon the statement that she would inherit half the deceased's estate as creating a moral obligation (even if it did not create any form of estoppel).[13] Likewise that the estate of the deceased was derived from the applicant's father created a moral obligation,[14] although Slade LJ said that he would have found for the applicant even if this were not the case.[15] Slade LJ specifically stated that if he had been the trial judge, he would have reached the same conclusion.[16] At the hearing before the Court of Appeal, it emerged that the value of the estate had been overstated and was only £34,000. As a consequence the Court of Appeal reduced the lump sum to £14,000.[17] This reduction is difficult to justify – if the

9. [1984] FLR 606607A-G. Some evidence as to how the lump sum was calculated can be found in the judgment in the Court of Appeal at [1986] Ch 245G-246A, [1985] 2 All ER 768b-c. ROSS MARTYN, 42 sums up the position of the applicants in *Re Callaghan* and *Re Leach* as being 'not in special need'. Neither the trial judge nor the Court of Appeal made any attempt to compare the financial position of the applicants in *Re Coventry* and *Re Leach*, a comparison which is highly instructive – see Oughton (1986) 83 LS Gaz 93, at 94.
10. [1986] Ch 226, [1985] 2 All ER 754.
11. I am indebted to Mr Bernard Weatherill of Counsel for informing of the course of the argument in the Court of Appeal.
12. [1980] Ch 487A-B, [1979] 3 All ER 821d, cited at [1986] Ch 244C-D, [1985] 2 All ER 767a-b. The judgment on the question of reasonable provision has to be contrasted with the judgment of whether the applicant was a child of the family which is approximately 2½ pages in length and in which five cases were cited.
13. [1986] Ch 243G-244A, [1985] 2 All ER 766g-j.
14. [1986] Ch 244A-B, [1985] 2 All ER 766j.
15. [1986] Ch 244C, [1985] 2 All ER 767a.
16. [1986] Ch 244D-E, [1985] 2 All ER 767b.
17. [1986] Ch 245G-246A, [1985] 2 All ER 768b-c.

applicant has a case for provision and the beneficiaries have no countervailing claim, then the size of the estate should be irrelevant – the inference is that the Court of Appeal was enforcing the oral will of the deceased whereby she was to leave half her estate to the applicant.

For those timorous souls who were reluctant to advance an argument that *Re Leach*, being a reserved judgment of a three judge Court of Appeal was *per incuriam,*[18] *Re Leach* was regarded as merely *extending* the number of 'special circumstances' in which adult children could successfully claim. After *Re Leach* there was a dearth of reported authorities on claims by adult children. While first instance judges in *Re Debenham*[19] and *Williams v Johns*[20] adopted diametrically opposite approaches to claims by adult children, in neither case was *Re Leach* cited.

The next case of significance is the unreported decision of *Riggs v Lloyds Bank plc*[1] in 1992. The deceased died in 1989 survived by an adult son and daughter. The estate of the deceased was worth at least £130,000, possibly much more as certain land had considerable development potential. The deceased left all his estate by will to his son. The deceased's daughter applied for provision under the 1975 Act and a declaration that by virtue of proprietory estoppel she had become the owner of a small garden worth approximately £5,000. The applicant was aged 42 years, married with two infant children. The deceased had given the applicant the land upon which her house was built. The applicant and her husband owned a house worth £80,000 subject to a mortgage of £8,000. The applicant's husband was employed as a hospital technician. Dillon LJ described the applicant and her husband as 'living comfortably'. The applicant's case was that living close to the deceased, she had cared for him and assisted in the deceased's business cleaning out chalets which he let out. The judgment in the Court of Appeal does not particularise the extent of caring and assistance given, but implicitly it appears not to have been particularly substantial. At first instance Judge Weeks QC sitting as a judge of the Chancery Division held that even taking into account the inter vivos gift of the land upon which the applicant's house was built and the garden acquired by way of proprietory estoppel, reasonable provision had not been made for the applicant and awarded her a lump sum of £20,000. The claim for proprietory estoppel was also successful. The son appealed to

18. Compare (1986) 83 LS Gaz 93.
19. [1986] 1 FLR 404, per Ewbank J, an approach critical of *Re Coventry*.
20. [1988] 2 FLR 475, per Micklem J an approach strongly following *Re Coventry*.
1. (27 November 1992, unreported), CA.

the Court of Appeal (Dillon, Butler-Sloss and Simon Brown LJJ), who allowed the appeal against the award under the 1975 Act, but dismissed the appeal against the finding of proprietory estoppel. The case is significant in that the Court of Appeal was prepared to overrule a decision of a first instance judge. Dillon LJ gave a judgment with which his judicial siblings concurred, referring at some length to the remarks of both Oliver J and the Court of Appeal in *Re Coventry* on the meaing of maintenance. Dillon LJ stated that the applicant and her husband were 'living comfortably' and had adduced no *evidence* of any need for maintenance and accordingly held that the application should be dismissed. The judgment did not deal with the issue of whether if the applicant had been in need of maintenance, it would been appropriate to award the applicant any provision. Dillon LJ did not refer to *Re Leach* and it is unclear whether it was cited to the Court of Appeal.

The uncertainties in the law were substantially removed by the decision of the Court Of Appeal in *Re Jennings*.[2] In this case the applicant was aged 50 at the date of the hearing in the Court of Appeal. When he was aged two, his parents separated and he was brought up by his mother. The applicant's mother requested the deceased to contribute towards the maintenance of the applicant, but he did not do so and the deceased had no contact with the applicant while he was an infant. Significantly the applicant's mother did not take any proceeedings to compel the deceased to maintain the applicant.[3] The deceased died in 1990 leaving a net estate of £300,000, bequeathing his residuary estate to charities. The applicant was married with two adult daughters. Through his own efforts he had become a successful businessman. He and his wife owned a four bedroomed house with an outside swimming pool and three and a half acres of grazing land. The house was worth £400,000 subject to a mortgage of £43,000. The capital value of the deceased's companies was not before the court, but there was evidence from which it might be inferred that they had a value in excess of £500,000.[4] The only suggested financial need of the applicant was that the value of his pension policy was only £23,000.

2. [1994] Ch 286, [1994] 3 All ER 27. (There is no explanation why an appeal from a judge of the Family Division is reported in the Chancery Division Reports!). I am grateful to Mr Ian Leeming QC for kindly supplying me with copies of the Skeleton Arguments in the Court of Appeal which incidentally contain extracts from the judgment at first instance of Wall J.
3. This is made clear from the evidence set out in the Skeleton Argument of the beneficiaries. It is also clear that the applicant's step-father not ungenerously supported the applicant while an infant.
4. [1994] Ch 292B-E, [1994] 3 All ER 30f-j.

Wall J relying upon the failure of the deceased to maintain the applicant while he was an infant or to take any interest in the applicant as an infant awarded the applicant a lump sum of £40,000.[5] The beneficiaries appealed to the Court of Appeal (Nourse and Henry LJJ and Sir John May) who allowed the appeal and set aside the award of Wall J.[6] All three judges gave judgments and specifically rejected the claim on two bases, firstly that the applicant was not in need of maintenance and, secondly, that there was nothing to show it was unreasonable for the deceased not to have made provision for the applicant. All three judgments approached the matter as one of principle. The decision is highly significant since unlike previous authorities, it involved the Court of Appeal reversing a judge at first instance, it did not involve any balancing of competing claims since the residuary beneficiaries had no competing claim and all the judges made it clear that their decision was not solely based upon the concept of 'maintenance'.

The reasoning of Nourse LJ is encapsulated in the following passage:

> It was established by the decisions of Oliver J and this court in *Re Coventry* that, on an application by an adult son of the deceased who is able to earn, and earns his own living there must be some special circumstance, typically a moral obligation of the deceased toward him, before the question can be determined in his favour ... In that case Oliver J was of the opinion that financial provision was reasonably required for the applicant's maintenance.[7] But his application failed because the deceased owed him no moral or other obligation and no other special circumstance was shown. The decision was affirmed by this court.[8]

Nourse LJ then rejected the trial judge's reliance upon the failure to maintain while an infant as constituting a 'moral obligation' and concluded:

> No other legal or moral obligation or special circumstance having been suggested, the judge was wrong to decide the first question in favour of the plaintiff. His error being one of law or principle, it matters not which, this court can and must interfere.[9]

5. There is some suggestion in the judgment at first instance that the mere relationship of parent and child created a lifetime obligation to maintain.
6. [1994] Ch 286, [1994] 3 All ER 27.
7. With respect Oliver J found that the applicant was not in need of maintenance, but the Court of Appeal in *Re Coventry* did not accept this part of the judgment.
8. [1994] Ch 295E-G, [1994] 3 All ER 33j-34a.
9. [1994] Ch 296H, [1994] 3 All ER 34j-35a.

Henry LJ specifically agreed with Nourse LJ[10] and specifically approved the remarks of Oliver J that the purpose of the 1975 Act was not to 'provide legacies or rewards for meritorious conduct'.[11]

Sir John May said:

> [Counsel] for the plaintiff, accepted both before the judge and in this court that in the case of an adult child the mere fact of the relationship of father and son is not of itself sufficient to require the deceased father to make financial provision from his estate for his (the child's) benefit if the latter is able-bodied and capable of earning a living.[12]

The effect of *Re Jennings* is to give the authority of the Court of Appeal to the judgment of Oliver J at first instance in *Re Coventry* and to remove any doubts arising from the less emphatic judgments of the Court of Appeal in that case. *Re Jennings* lays down a clear rule that an adult child will not succeed under the 1975 Act unless he can show a 'moral obligation or special circumstance'.[13] While it is implicit in *Re Jennings* that such 'moral obligations or special circumstances' will be comparatively rare, and *Re Jennings* specifically rejected certain matters as constituting 'moral obligations or special circumstances', the Court of Appeal did not attempt to define authoritively what constituted 'moral obligations or special circumstances'.[14]

Wall J cited from *Re Leach* in his judgment at first instance.[15] In the Court of Appeal counsel for the beneficiaries did not in any way criticise *Re Leach* and indeed relied upon the case as an example of a more meritorious applicant than the applicant in the present case.[16] Counsel for the applicant while referring to *Re Leach*, did

10. [1994] Ch 299G, [1994] 3 All ER 37h.
11. [1994] Ch 301A-C, [1994] 3 All ER 39c-e, quoting from [1980] Ch 474F-475A, [1979] 2 All ER 417h-418418c.
12. [1994] Ch 302B-C, [1994] 3 All ER 40c-d. *Query* whether such a concession should have been made, and whether it might not have been appropriate to argue that Parliament in the 1975 Act had given the court an unfettered discretion in dealing with claims by adult children. There is some suggestion that Wall J at first instance stated that the relationship of parent and child created a lifetime obligation to maintain.
13. It is significant that counsel for the beneficiaries cited the divorce cases of *Lord Lilford v Glynn* [1979] 1 WLR 78, [1979] 1 All ER 441 and *Griffiths v Griffiths* [1984] Fam 70, [1984] 2 All ER 626 on the reluctance of the divorce court to award provision for adult children, see [1994] Ch 289D-E.
14. A matter exploited fully in the subsequent case of *Re Goodchild* [1996] 1 WLR 694, [1996] 1 All ER 670; affd [1997] 3 All ER 63.
15. Skeleton Argument on behalf of the applicant.
16. [1994] Ch 289F.

not place it in the forefront of his argument.[17] The judgments in the Court of Appeal did not refer to *Re Leach,* but significantly did not expressly criticise the decision. Because the precise reasoning of Slade LJ in *Re Leach* is obscure and because the judgment of Slade LJ does not explain how the reasoning sits with *Re Coventry,*[18] it is submitted that after *Re Jennings, Re Leach* can not be regarded as laying down any wide proposition upon the claims of adult children, but in terms of precedent (if not necessarily in terms of principle) the decision remains authoritative on its own facts.

In *Re Goodchild,*[19] a decision after *Re Jennings,* Carnwath J had no hesitation in holding that an adult son in a precarious financial position had no claim under the 1975 Act on the part of his father's estate which he had not inherited from his first wife.

Maintenance for Adult Children

Provision for adult children is limited to 'maintenance'.[20] Whereas with other categories of applicant there are either existing jurisdictions for the payment of maintenance while the payer is alive or the actual provision of maintenance before death which can guide the courts as to the concept of 'maintenance', with adult children there is no such guidance and the courts have been left to develop a test of 'maintenance' without assistance from existing legal regimes. It is therefore not surprising that the courts have found the concept of 'maintenance' for adult children difficult to apply in practice, but the lack of consistency shown by the courts is not a good advertisement for the case law system.

In *Re Coventry*[1] the applicant in 1978 had take-home pay of £52 per week, out of which he had to pay maintenance of £12 per week towards the maintenance of his children. He accepted that the house which he had shared with the deceased should be sold. He sought a lump sum of £7,000 with which to use as a down payment on a small house or flat.[2] There was evidence of dubious worth that the rent for a small furnished flat would be between £20 and £28 per week.[3] The

17. [1994] Ch 290B, and Skeleton Argument on behalf of the applicant.
18. See pp 217–218, *ante.*
19. [1996] 1 WLR 694, at 714C-D, [1996] 1 All ER 670, at 689d-e. See also *Re Abram* [1996] 2 FLR 379, at 390C-D. For full discussion of *Re Goodchild* see pp 240–242, *post.*
20. S 1(2)(b). On 'maintenance' generally, see pp 131–137, *ante.*
1. [1980] Ch 461, [1979] 2 All ER 408; affd [1979] 3 All ER 815.
2. [1980] Ch 468B-C, [1979] 2 All ER 412f-g.
3. [1980] Ch 468B, [1979] 2 All ER 4412f.

judgment of Oliver J is noticeable for two statements of law. Firstly, Oliver J deducing from the reference in section 1(2)(a) to 'provision *required* for his or her maintenance' concluded that in dealing with an applicant other than a spouse the court was directed to consider what was *required* for maintenance.[4] The concept of provision being 'required' for maintenance adds a normative element to maintenance and confirms that it is an objective test. Secondly, Oliver J rejected the approach of Mr Vivian Price QC in *Re Christie*[5] that 'maintenance' is to be equated with 'well being' or 'benefit'.[6] However, Oliver J in his judgment does not expressly make any finding as to whether the provision was required for the applicant's maintenance. He characterised the applicant as 'earning an adequate living, [but] clearly not well-to-do',[7] but stated that:

> If, therefore, *financial need* were the sole criterion, then I think that undoubtedly exists although its stringency may have been to some extent the plaintiff's own responsibility. But the mere fact that the plaintiff finds himself in *necessitous circumstances* can not, in my judgment, by itself render it unreasonable that no provision has, in the events which have happened, been made for his maintenance out of the deceased's estate.[8]

One possible reading of the judgment of Oliver J is that if a person is able to cover his weekly outgoings, provision is not required for his maintenance.

In the Court of Appeal Goff LJ dealing with the question of 'maintenance' quoted with approval the Canadian case of *Re Duranceau*:[9]

> Is the provision sufficient to enable the dependant to live neither luxuriously nor miserably, but decently and comfortably according to his or her station in life?

and added:

> What is proper maintenance must in all the circumstances depend upon all the circumstances of the particular case being considered at the time, but I think it is clear on the one hand that one must not put too limited a meaning on it; it does not mean just enough to

4. [1980] Ch 472F-G, [1979] 2 All ER 416b-c.
5. [1979] Ch 168, [1979] 1 All ER 546.
6. [1980] Ch 471C-H, [1979] 1 All ER 415a-f.
7. [1980] Ch 477C-D, [1979] 1 All ER 420a-b.
8. [1980] Ch 476D-E, [1979] 1 All ER 419d-e.
9. [1952] 3 DLR 714, at 720.

> enable a person to get by; on the other hand, it does not mean anything which may be regarded as reasonably desirable for his general benefit or welfare.[10]

Goff LJ treated Oliver J as having found as a fact that the applicant was in need of maintenance, but that the application failed because there was nothing unreasonable in the deceased not making provision for the applicant.[11] It is a fair conclusion from the judgments in the Court of Appeal that while emphatically rejecting the wider approach of *Re Christie* to maintenance, the Court of Appeal would have unhesitatingly found that the applicant in *Re Coventry* was in need of maintenance.

In *Re Dennis*[12] an adult son sought provision in the form of a lump sum to enable him to pay Capital Transfer Tax upon an inter vivos gift made by the deceased to him. Siginificantly he did not claim that he had any other requirement for maintenance.[13] The applicant claimed that if he was not awarded provision, the Capital Taxes Office would make him bankrupt. The applicant did not lead evidence that bankruptcy would make him homeless, or evidence of any conviction that bankruptcy would prevent him earning a living.[14] Browne-Wilkinson J refused his application to bring an application notwithstanding that more than six months had elapsed since representation had first been taken out to the estate of the deceased. In giving probably the most incisive discussion of the concept of 'maintenance', he said:

> To my mind the applicant is not really applying for 'maintenance'; he is asking for a capital sum to pay his creditors ... In [*Re Coventry*] both Oliver J at first instance and Goff LJ in the Court of Appeal disapproved of the decision in *Re Christie,* in which the judge had treated maintenance as being equivalent to providing for the well-being or benefit of the applicant. The word 'maintenance' is not as wide as that ... But in my judgment the word 'maintenance' connotes only payments which, directly or indirectly, enable the applicant in the future to discharge the cost of his daily living at whatever standard of living is appropriate to him. The provision that is to be made is to meet recurring expenses, being expenses of living of an income nature. This does not mean that the provision need be by way of income payments. The provision can be by way of a lump sum, for example, to buy a house in which the applicant can be housed, thereby relieving him pro tanto of income expenditure. Nor am I

10. [1980] Ch 485C-D, [1979] 2 All ER 819h-820a.
11. [1980] Ch 488E-F,490F-H, [1979] 2 All ER 822e-f, 824b-d.
12. [1981] 2 All ER 140.
13. [1981] 2 All ER 143d-e.
14. [1981] 2 All ER 142g-h,146b.

> suggesting that there may not be cases in which payment of existing debts may not be appropriate as a maintenance payment; for example, to pay the debts of an applicant in order to enable him to continue to carry on a profit-making business or profession may well be for his maintenance. But no such case is made here. It is not suggested that the payment of capital transfer tax will do anything to help the applicant's future maintenance. It may save him from bankruptcy, but there is no evidence that being made bankrupt is going to prevent the applicant from earning his living ...[15]

In *Re Callaghan*[16] the applicant in 1984 was earning £7,850 per annum gross and his wife was earning £3,900 per annum from part-time employment. The applicant and his wife had no appreciable capital and were intending to purchase their own house under the Right-to-Buy legislation for £13,250. There was no evidence that the applicant was unable to pay his outgoings and indeed had decided to purchase his house whether or not his claim under the 1975 Act succeeded. In a judgment in which there was no reference to any previous authority on the issue of maintenance nor any substantial discussion of maintenance, Booth J awarded the applicant a lump sum of £15,000 'to enable him to purchase his present home'.[17]

The facts of *Re Leach* have already been discussed at some length.[18] At first instance, both Counsel agreed that the test was accurately set out in the remarks of Goff LJ in *Re Coventry.*[19] There was no evidence that the applicant was unable to pay her outgoings.[20] The applicant had liabilities under a mortgage and a loan to purchase a car,[1] but there was no evidence that the loans had not been granted other than by applying normal lending criteria or that the applicant was unable to make the payments as and when they arose. In awarding a lump sum of £19,000, the judge did refer to the possible need to make provision for the applicant's retirement and in case the friendship between the applicant and the lady with whom she jointly owned her house broke down.[2] On appeal Slade LJ did not discuss the concept of the 'maintenance'. His remarks that:

15. [1981] 2 All ER 145g-146b.
16. [1985] Fam 1, [1984] 3 All ER 790.
17. [1985] Fam 7G, [1984] 3 All ER 795c. See the similar approach taken in *Graham v Murphy* [1997] 1 FLR 860.
18. [1984] FLR 590; affd [1986] Ch 226, [1985] 2 All ER 754, discussed in pp 215–218, *ante*.
19. [1984] FLR 600C-H.
20. [1984] FLR 607C-D.
1. [1984] FLR 607B-C.
2. [1984] FLR 606G, 607H-608A.

> ... as part of the reasonable provision for her maintenance, she requires financial assistance in discharging her share of the heavy running expenses (including mortgage repayments) of the house which she shares ...[3]

ignore the evidence that the applicant was able to pay such expenses as and when they arose and a mortgage debt equal to one's annual income after income tax can not be described as onerous.[4]

In *Re Debenham*[5] the applicant and her husband were aged respectively 58 and 63 years. Both were unemployed and in receipt of Income Support. They owned a small bungalow and the husband was in receipt of an occupational pension of £500 per annum. In 1984 Ewbank J awarded the applicant a lump sum of £3,000 together with periodical payments of £4,500 per annum, which would be the amount of the applicant's old age pension when it became payable in two years' time. Ewbank J stated that he aimed to give the applicant an income of £6,000 per annum.[6]

In *Riggs v Lloyds Bank plc*, the facts of which have already been given,[7] the Court of Appeal reversed the trial judge on the question of maintenance. Dillon LJ in giving the judgment of the Court of Appeal quoted extensively from both Oliver J and Goff LJ in *Re Coventry*, but the judgment did not refer to any other authority on the question of 'maintenance'.

In *Re Jennings*[8] the applicant was in effect a millionaire. The only possible evidence that he was in need of maintenance was that his house was subject to a mortgage of £50,000 and that he had only one pension policy worth £23,000. All three judges of the Court of Appeal specifically overruled Wall J on the question of maintenance and held that reasonable provision was not needed for the applicant's maintenance. *Re Dennis*, *Re Leach*, *Re Callaghan* and *Riggs v Lloyds Bank plc* were all cited to the Court of Appeal. Both

3. [1986] Ch 226, at 245E-F; [1985] 2 All ER 754, at767j.
4. The remarks of Carswell J in *Re Creeney* [1984] NI 397, at 403H-404A that 'So long as one does not depart from the concept of maintenance [presumably meaning an income concept] as the necessary foundation for an applicant's claim, his own financial need is not the touchstone or sole criterion. The financial provision made under a will or intestacy ... may not be reasonable even if the applicant is not suffering significant financial hardship if comparisons with other beneficiaries or applicants and such moral factors as the conduct of the persons concerned are imported into the determination' can stand neither as a matter of principle nor in the light of the authorities. On the facts of the case in 1984 the applicant was earning £6,000 per annum gross and his wife was earning £7,000 gross, and Carswell J held that the applicant was in need of maintenance.
5. [1986] 1 FLR 404.
6. [1986] 1 FLR 410G-411A.
7. (27 November 1992, unreported), CA, discussed at pp 218–219, *ante*.
8. [1994] Ch 286, [1994] 3 All ER 27.

Nourse LJ and Henry LJ specifically approved the conclusion of Oliver J that under section 1(2)(b) maintenance must be reasonably 'required' for an applicant.[9] Nourse LJ specifically approved the remarks of Goff LJ on what constituted 'maintenance'[10] and the judgment of Browne-Wilkinson J that 'maintenance' connoted only payments which will directly or indirectly enable the applicant in the future to discharge the cost of his daily living at whatever standard of living is appropriate to him.[11] Nourse LJ stated that the applicant was not in need of a sum with which to discharge his mortgage, because he was able to pay the instalments due under his mortgage out of his income.[12] Nourse LJ stated that the evidence did not disclose a single need which required provision for the applicant's maintenance, as opposed to an award for what might be 'reasonably desirable for his benefit or welfare', adding 'but an award on that basis is impermissible'.[13] Nourse LJ distinguished the decision of Booth J in *Re Callaghan* on the facts in that:

> ... [the Applicant in *Re Callaghan*] had a need [to buy his rented home] which enabled him to say that the provision was reasonably required for his maintenance. Here, I repeat, no *real need* has been demonstrated.[14]

Henry LJ said:

> In my judgment on the figures in this case there was no requirement for maintenance for the applicant made out. The judge's findings that the applicant was 'not merely self-sufficient but in reasonably comfortable financial circumstances' and that his companies 'provide the plaintiff and his family with a comfortable standard of living' and that 'there is no evidence that the plaintiff is likely to encounter financial difficulties provided he maintains his health and his capacity to work' should in my judgment have compelled him to conclude that no requirement for maintenance has been made out.[15]

While it is clear that Nourse LJ approved of the decision of *Re Callaghan* on the issue of maintenance, no member of the Court of Appeal addressed the decision of *Re Leach* on the issue of maintenance. It is significant from the refusal of the Court of Appeal in *Riggs v Lloyds Bank plc* to take account of possible future costs of

9. [1994] Ch 295D-E, 301E-F, [1994] 3 All ER 33h, 39g-h.
10. [1994] Ch 297G-H, [1994] 3 All ER 35j.
11. [1994] Ch 297H-298A, [1994] 3 All ER 35j-36a.
12. [1994] Ch 298D-E, [1994] 3 All ER 36e.
13. [1994] Ch 298F-G, [1994] 3 All ER 36 g.
14. [1994] Ch 299E, [1994] 3 All ER 37e; emphasis added.
15. [1994] Ch 301G-H, [1994] 3 All ER 39j-40a.

educating the applicant's children and in *Re Jennings* to take account of the limited provision which the applicant had made for his pension[16] that any need for maintenance must have a substantial basis in fact and must be evaluated against the general financial position of the applicant.

Re Goodchild[17] was a decision of Carnwath J in 1995. In this case the applicant had an annual salary of £13,000. His wife was dependent upon Invalidity Benefit. He had substantial assets, but very substantial debts. There was evidence that if the applicant sold his home to pay his debts, he would be homeless, and if he sold some business premises, he would lose his employment.[18] Distinguishing *Re Dennis* as being a case where the payment of debts would not assist the applicant to earn a living, Carnwath J held that the applicant required maintenance and in principle awarded him provision.[19]

In *Re Abram*[20] the applicant was aged 52 years, unemployed and his wife had an income of about £150 per week. His business had failed and he was subject to an Individual Voluntary Arrangement. The applicant's evidence about his likely future finances and his current and future financial needs was meagre. Despite this and a full citation of authorities, in 1996 Roger Cooke J sitting as a judge of the Chancery Division awarded the applicant a protected life interest in £200,000. The only guide to why the judge chose this sum was a statement that this sum when invested would produce a gross annual income of £8,000 to £10,000.[1] However, the lengthy discussion in the judgment of the deceased's testamentary intentions[2] may give rise to the suggestion that the judge, like the Court of Appeal in *Re Leach,* was to some extent making an oral will for the deceased.

This body of case law leaves the line between those situations where maintenance is required and those where it is not as a relatively fine line running between the facts of *Re Leach* and of *Riggs v Lloyds Bank plc*. The difference between there being 'not much at the end of the month'[3] and 'living comfortably',[4] appears to be as

16. [1994] Ch 298E, [1994] 3 All ER 36f.
17. [1996] 1 WLR 694, [1996] 1 All ER 670.
18. [1996] 1 WLR 713H, [1996] 1 All ER 688j-689a.
19. [1996] 1 WLR 715D-F, [1996] 1 All ER690d-f.
20. [1996] 2 FLR 379.
1. [1996] 2 FLR 397B-C.
2. [1996] 2 FLR 382B-D, 382G-383C, 384B-385A, 390H-391H.
3. The words of the applicant quoted by Mr Michael Wheeler QC in *Re Leach* at [1984] FLR 607C-D. In 1983 the applicant had an after tax income of £6,250 and was liable to pay a half share of a mortgage equal to £7,000.
4. The words of Dillon LJ in *Riggs v Lloyds Bank plc*. In 1992 the applicant's husband had an income of £13,000 per annum and the applicant and her husband's house was subject to a mortgage of £8,000. Between 1983 and 1992 inflation was approximately 64%.

much based upon a subjective view of the merits of an applicant as any objective consideration of the financial circumstances.

The Mere Existence of a Parent and Child Relationship

After *Re Coventry* and the judgments of the Court of Appeal in *Re Jennings*[5] set out previously the mere fact that an applicant is an adult child of the deceased does not entitle him to an order for provision.

In coming to this conclusion the English courts have not had to consider the Australasian line of cases,[6] commencing with the Privy Council case of *Allardice v Allardice,*[7] which awarded adult children substantial provision in the absence of special factors such as physical incapacity or the applicant having sacrificed much in order to care for the applicant. In *Re Homer, Rann v Jackson*[8] the appellant applicant pressed the Court of Appeal with *Allardice v Allardice,* but Sir David Cairns erroneously regarded the case as only an authority on the level of maintenance and the appeal was dismissed without hearing the respondents. It is submitted that the line of authorities emanating from *Allardice v Allardice* conflicts totally with modern English law and policy and must be rejected.[9]

The effect of *Re Jennings* is to overrule certain cases under the 1938 Act where the court had awarded substantial provision to adult unmarried daughters and such cases can not be relied upon today as indicating the approach of the courts to such claims.[10]

5. See pp 220–221, *ante.*
6. See generally WRIGHT, 117–126; DE GROOT AND NICKEL, paras 314–318; DICKEY, 88–91.
7. [1911] AC 730. The facts of *Allardice v Allardice* are set out at p 8, *ante.* For criticism of the manner in which the decision in *Allardice v Allardice* was arrived at see fn 8, p 8, *ante.*
8. (6 November 1978, unreported).
9. Any attempt at unifying family provision law in the Commonwealth is likely to fail since Australian courts have recently turned away from *Allardice v Allardice* with its emphasis on 'moral duty'. In *Hughes v National Trustee* (1979) 23 ALR 321 (Aust HC on appeal from Victoria) Murphy J stated that all an adult child had to prove to obtain provision was that he was in need of provision and that the estate had available assets – the legal, moral or ethical claims of the applicant are irrelevant. In *Hughes' Case* the applicant had unlawfully evicted his mother from her farm shortly before her death. Although *Hughes' Case* is extreme, it is not out of line with Australasian authority generally, see DE GROOT AND NICKEL, paras 316, 318.
10. For discussion of these cases see pp 230–231, *post.* For detailed discussion of *Re Ducksbury* [1966] 1 WLR 1226, [1966] 2 All ER 374, see second edition 164-165. Modern cases which have to be reconsidered in the light of the decision of the Court of Appeal in *Re Jennings* include *Re McGarrell* [1983] 8 NIJB; *Re Creeney* [1984] NI 397; *Re Debenham* [1986] 1 FLR 404.

Unmarried Daughters

Under the 1938 Act[11] an adult unmarried daughter could apply for provision without proving any mental or physical incapacity. In several cases in the first 15 years of the Act the courts appeared to award adult unmarried daughters provision fairly freely where no special circumstances existed such as the daughters being disabled or having sacrificed much to care for the parent.[12] Subsequently, although the facts of the reported cases were slightly different, the courts became much less sympathetic to such applications.[13] No doubt heavily influenced by the changed social conditions since the Second World War the courts thought it more appropriate that unmarried adult daughters support themselves.[14] In *Re Pearson-Gregory*[15] Roxburgh J specifically referred to the change of attidudes towards the support of unmarried women since Victorian times and recommended that the applicant should work for a living.

Bearing in mind the Law Commission's preference for equality between the sexes,[16] and the change in social attitudes to parental obligations to unmarried daughters, it is suggested that there should be no difference in approach between applications by male and female adult children. The matter was put beyond doubt by Nourse LJ in *Re Jennings* who, referring to the *Re Coventry* line of cases, said:

> Although these decisions were in terms confined to the case of a son, the principle of them is applicable no less to the case of a daughter and, with developments in the structure of society, instances of its application in such cases may become more common.[17]

11. S 1(1)(b).
12. *Re Pointer* [1941] Ch 60, [1940] 4 All ER 372; *Re Blight* (1946) 96 LJ 233; *Re Borthwick* [1949] Ch 395, [1949] 1 All ER 472; *Re Black* (1953) Times, 24 March; *Re Ducksbury* [1966] 1 WLR 1226, [1966] 2 All ER 374; but see *Re Watkins* [1949] 1 All ER 695.
13. *Re Andrews* [1955] 1 WLR 1105, [1955] 3 All ER 248; *Re Pearson-Gregory* (1957) Times, 11 October. Compare similar developments in Australasian law, see DE GROOT AND NICKEL, para 314; DICKEY, 89.
14. *Re Ducksbury* might be regarded as an anachronism even in 1966.
15. (1956) Times, 18 May.
16. WORKING PAPER, para 3.40; LAW COM, para 72.
17. [1994] Ch 286, at 295F, [1994] 3 All ER 27, at 33j; Henry LJ specifically agreed with the judgment of Nourse LJ and referred to 'child' as opposed to 'son' ([1994] Ch 299G-GH, [1994] 3 All ER 37h-j). See to the same effect the judgment of Micklem J in *Williams v Johns* [1988] 2 FLR 475, at 488E-F.

Reported cases under the 1975 Act show no distinction between claims by adult children of either sex and show many claims by adult daughters failing.[18]

Actual Dependence upon the Deceased

It is probably the law that the actual dependence of an adult child upon the deceased for maintenance is a sufficient reason for an award of provision. This appears to have been the basis of *Re Black*[19] and to have been implicitly accepted by the Law Commission.[20] The matter is put beyond doubt by the enactment of section 1(1)(e) which is premised on the basis that a person actually receiving such provision should have such provision continued after death.[1]

As has been pointed out the provision of maintenance inter vivos simpliciter does not import any obligation upon the estate of the person providing the maintenance and the protection of a person's expectations of future maintenance is an insufficient basis for interference with a deceased's testamentary dispositions.[2] It must further be noted that provision for applicants under section 1(1)(e) is by no means automatic[3] and frequently successful applicants have incurred considerable detriment in order to benefit the deceased.[4] Accordingly even if an adult child proves dependence he should not necessarily be awarded provision. In *Re Fergusson*[5] an application

18. Claims by adult daughters failed in the following cases, *Rann v Jackson* (6 November 1978, unreported), CA (married applicant); *Re Embelton* Telegraph, 3/7/79 (married applicant); *Re Fergusson* Foster J (16 June 1980, unreported) (single applicant); *Re Portt* (25 March 1980, unreported), CA (widowed applicant); *Re Rowlands* [1984] FLR 813 (one applicant married, the other applicant divorced); *Williams v Johns* [1988] 2 FLR 475 (divorced applicant).
19. (1953) Times, 24 March.
20. WORKING PAPER, para 3.41; LAW COM, para 73.
1. See pp 100–103, *ante*.
2. See pp 43–44, *ante*.
3. Eg *Kourkgy v Lusher* (1983) 4 FLR 65; *Rhodes v Dean* (28 March 1996, unreported), CA.
4. Eg *Re Wilkinson* [1978] Fam 22, [1978] 1 All ER 221 applicant gives up paid employment to nurse deceased; *Malone v Harrison* [1979] 1 WLR 1353 applicant cannot train for any vocation because of relationship with the deceased; *CA v CC* (1978) Times, 17 November, *sub nom Re C* 123 Sol Jo 35; *sub nom In The Estate of McC* 9 Fam Law 26: applicant gives up child at request of deceased.
5. Foster J (16 June 1980, unreported). In *Williams v Johns* [1988] 2 FLR 475 the deceased had periodically made gifts to the applicant, although not on a regular basis and not immediately before her death. This was held not to entitle the applicant to provision.

under the 1975 Act failed where the adult child could show a small degree of dependence through the provision of accommodation. This case can be contrasted with *Re Campbell*[6] where an adult son aged 53 years who had lived on his father's farm since birth and who had worked on the farm all his adult life was awarded a non-assignable licence for life to occupy the farmhouse and an increased share in the residuary estate.

Being Brought Up With the Idea that One Need Not Work for a Living

There is mention in the cases of adult children being entitled to provision solely on the basis their parents had brought them up with the idea that they need not work for their support.[7] *Re Black*[8] was a decision of Vaisey J in 1953 concerning an application by an unmarried daughter born in 1889 against the estate of her deceased father. He had been a rich man and had settled on the applicant investments providing an income of about £1,000 per annum. He left a net estate of £123,000, and his will made no substantial provision for the applicant, who had never been trained for any kind of occupation and was in poor health. Vaisey J awarded the applicant £1,500 per annum from the estate. The application was not substantially opposed and Vaisey J expressly stated 'that this was an unusual case, so unusual ... it could [not] be a guide to ... any other case'.

A not dissimilar application was decisively rejected by Roxburgh J in *Re Pearson-Gregory*[9] three years later. On the facts Roxburgh J found that the applicant who was born in 1915 had not been brought up with the idea that she need not work. Even if the applicant had been brought up with such ideas, they were 'outmoded' and it was not a father's duty to maintain an adult daughter in idleness. Roxburgh J emphasised that attitudes to people working for a living had changed greatly since the reign of Queen Victoria.[10]

Despite this emphatic rejection of being brought up with the idea that one need not work was sufficient basis to order provision,

6. [1983] NI 10.
7. *Re Black* (1953) Times, 24 March; *Re Ducksbury* [1966] 1 WLR 1226, at 1231A-B, [1966] 2 All ER 374, at 378-F.
8. (1953) Times, 24 March.
9. (1957) Times, 11 October, separately reported at [1957] CLY 3741.
10. One wonders whether the reference in the report at (1957) Times, 11 October to 1899 is a misprint for 1889, the date of birth of the applicant in *Re Black*.

Buckley J in *Re Ducksbury*[11] in 1966 stated that the expectation of *some* financial support was a reason for awarding the applicant provision.

It is unlikely, as Roxburgh J stated in *Re Pearson-Gregory*,[12] that many people these days are brought up with the idea that they need not work for a living. Even with the very large estate in *Re Dennis*[13] such a claim appeared to be unarguable on the facts. In the few cases where such expectations can be proved to exist there should not be a sufficient reason for the court to intervene and order provision,[14] unless the applicant has incurred a significant detriment in reliance upon such expectation[15] and even then sparingly since it cannot be good policy for the law to discourage people from wanting to work.

Children Caring for Parents

It seems generally accepted that if an adult child expends great effort in caring for an aged or infirm parent then it may be unreasonable for such a child to be denied provision from the parent's estate. The debates in both Houses of Parliament on the 1975 Act demonstrated the concern of MPs and peers for children, particularly daughters, who sacrifice much to care for aged or infirm relatives.[16] While it seems well established that it may be unreasonable for such children to be denied maintenance, there are only a few reported cases of such circumstances.[17] While the justice of awarding provision to such children cannot be criticised, the appropriateness of family provision which is limited to maintenance and partially dependent upon the applicant's financial circumstances as a vehicle for aiding such

11. [1966] 1 WLR 1226, at 1231A-B, [1966] 2 All ER 374, at 378E-F.
12. (1957) Times, 11 October.
13. [1981] 2 All ER 140.
14. See pp 43–44, *ante*. It must be very doubtful whether being brought up with the idea that one need not work for a living can constitute a 'special circumstance' within *Re Jennings*.
15. See pp 43–44, *ante*. Compare *Re Leach* [1986] Ch 226, [1985] 2 All ER 754.
16. See pp 29–30, *ante*. The case of children caring for aged or infirm parents is virtually ignored by the Law Commission in its two reports; this omission must cast some doubt on the Commission's understanding of the realities of family provision litigation.
17. *Re Cook* (1956) 106 L Jo 466; *Re Fletcher* Telegraph, 8/6/56 ; *Re McGarrell* [1983] 8 NIJB ; *Re Callaghan* [1985] Fam 1, [1984] 3 All ER 790; *Re Abram* [1996] 2 FLR 379, at 383G-H; see also *Re Gonin* [1979] Ch 16, [1977] 2 All ER 16 and the remarks of Roxburgh J in *Re Pearson-Gregory* (1957) Times, 11 October, Oliver J in *Re Coventry* [1980] Ch 461, at 477C-D, [1979] 2 All ER 408, at 420b and Micklem J in *Williams v Johns* [1988] 2 FLR 475, at 488G.

people can be criticised.[18] Probably the courts take into account care provided for the deceased's spouse[19] and care provided by the applicant's spouse.[20]

It does not appear to have been decided whether provision is ordered essentially to compensate the applicant for a detriment incurred in order to help the aged and infirm parent or simply because of the help actually given to the aged and infirm parent whether or not this has been at the financial expense of the applicant. In some cases the courts have emphasised the detriment incurred, such as the giving up of the prospect of marriage[1] or a career.[2] In *Re Coventry* Oliver J states in a passage not expressly connected with adult children who have cared for aged and infirm parents:

> It is not the purpose of the [1975] Act to provide legacies or rewards for meritorious conduct.[3]

The example given by Oliver J[4] and approved by the Court of Appeal[5] of an adult child to whom a moral duty is owed by his deceased parent is one *who gives up employment* to care for the parent. In *Re Jennings* Henry LJ specifically approved this remark of Oliver J[6] and gave the following example of a moral obligation binding upon a parent:

> ... a child of the deceased might have given up a university place to nurse the deceased through his last long illness and now wish to take up that place. The moral obligation there would be both current and clear.[7]

Such remarks and the emphasis in the judgment of Henry LJ that only conduct which affected the applicant's financial position at the date of death,[8] tend to suggest that caring which does not cause financial detriment will not enable an adult child to claim.

18. See p 103, *ante.*
19. Compare *Re Leach* [1984] FLR 590, at 595F.
20. *Re Callaghan* [1985] Fam 1, at 4B-C, [1984] 3 All ER 790, at 792f-g; *Re Creeney* [1984] NI 397, at 398D; *Re Abram* [1996] 2 FLR 379, at 383G-H.
1. Eg *Re Homer, Rann v Jackson* (6 November 1978, unreported), CA.
2. Eg *Re Coventry* [1980] Ch 461, at 477C-D, [1979] 2 All ER 408, at 420b; compare *Re Gonin* [1979] Ch 16, [1977] 2 All ER 16.
3. [1980] Ch 474G, [1979] 2 All ER 418a.
4. [1980] Ch 477C-D, [1979] 2 All ER 420b; see to the same effect the remarks of Micklem J in *Williams v Johns* [1988] 2 FLR 475, at 488G.
5. [1980] Ch 490A, [1979] 3 All ER 823f (per Goff LJ), [1980] Ch 495G, [1979] 3 All ER 828d (per Buckley LJ).
6. [1994] Ch 286, at 301B, [1994] 3 All ER 27, at 39g.
7. [1994] Ch 300F-G, [1994] 3 All ER 38j.
8. [1994] Ch 300H, [1994] 3 All ER 39b-c; Sir John May's judgment was to the same effect, see [1994] Ch 303A, [1994] 3 All ER 41b. Nourse LJ did not deal with the question of a child caring for the deceased in his judgment.

Despite these remarks it is submitted that in principle there is o reason why caring for the deceased *in itself* should not in an ppropriate case be a special circumstance entitling an adult child) claim. While the claim of a person who has been impoverished 1 order to aid the deceased is clearly much greater than that of a erson who has merely aided the deceased, it does not follow that ie latter's claim does not exist. Public opinion as evidenced by the ebates in the Houses of Parliament and the reaction to the working ut of section 1(1)(e)[9] might suggest that merely caring for an aged r infirm parent should entitle the applicant to provision. In *Re 'allaghan*[10] the applicant who gave up work temporarily to care for ie deceased was awarded substantially more than his lost wages.

In *Re Jennings* the Court of Appeal held that 'the obligations nd responsibilities which the deceased had towards an applicant' ithin section 3(2)(d) referred to obligations and responsibilities 'hich the deceased had immediately before his death.[11] Henry LJ 1 the passage set out previously refers to a moral obligation arising om caring from the deceased being *current*.[12] While this covers a

9. See pp 85–88, *ante* ; and in particular the remarks of Butler-Sloss LJ in *Bishop v Plumley* [1991] 1 WLR 582, at 587G-588A, [1991] 1 All ER 236, at 242c-f set out at p 90, *ante*.

10. [1985] Fam 1, [1984] 3 All ER 790. In this case the applicant took four months off work (for which he was paid approximately £7,850 per annum gross) in order to look after the deceased. His wife left her job, but at the time of the hearing had found other employment. The award could further be justified upon the basis that the deceased's estate was substantially derived from the applicant's mother, see pp 240–242, *post*. *Re McGarrell* [1983] 8 NIJB is a case where the applicant cared for the deceased without incurring any financial detriment and was awarded provision, but it is very doubtful if the case is in any event correctly decided and can stand with *Re Coventry* or *Re Jennings*.

11. [1994] Ch 286, at 296D-G, 300E-G, 302C-G, [1994] 3 All ER 27, at 34f-j,38g-39a,40d-j. Nourse LJ did qualify his judgment as referring to such obligations existing at the date of death as being 'a general rule'([1994] Ch 296E, [1994] 3 All ER 34g) and did leave open the possibility of conduct in relation to an infant child still having some effect upon the applicant when he was an adult ([1994] Ch 296F-G, [1994] 3 All ER34j; see also [1994] Ch 302F-G, [1994] 3 All ER 40h). *Re Abram* [1996] 2 FLR 379 was a decision subsequent to *Re Jennings*, in which *Re Jennings* was cited. However the judge did not address the remarks of Henry LJ. The judge did make findings that the conduct of the deceased had a substantial detrimental effect upon the applicant, see [1996] 2 FLR 393C, but he did not (and possibly on the facts could not) find that the conduct of the deceased had any adverse effect upon him immediately prior to death. Compare the case of *Re Creeney* [1984] NI 397 where the applicant's decision not to go to university in 1944 was held to have affected his earning potential in 1982; but note *Re Rowlands* [1984] FLR 813, at 815H-816C, 819F-820A where an adult daughter acted as 'woman of the house' in varying degrees after the deceased's wife left between 1938 and 1954. The deceased died in 1981 and Anthony Lincoln J dismissed her claim.

12. See p 234, *ante*.

moral obligation to make good a loss subsisting at the date of deat caused by caring for the deceased, it is unclear what the effect the judgment is upon situations where the applicant has cared fc the deceased, but is suffering from no financial loss at the date death. It can not be the law that only caring for the decease immediately before his death entitles the applicant to provision.

If caring for a parent which does not cause an applicant financi loss entitles him to provision, the courts require any caring for a aged or infirm parent to be something considerably more than th usual acts of affection and caring expected of an adult child towarc his parent.[13] In *Re Pearson-Gregory*[14] Roxburgh J distinguishe between 'filial' and rendering 'special services'. In *Re Christie*[15] M Vivian Price QC as a deputy judge of the Chancery Division saic

> In the evidence before me there was some attention paid to such matters as how frequently the son, on the one hand, visited Mrs Christie [the deceased] as compared with his sister, and also whether he did more maintenance and odd jobs around the house for his mother than did the daughter or her family. I am bound to say that I attach no importance to such matters since, it seems to me, that visiting and helping a widowed mother is no more or less than an expression of natural affection as between a son and his mother, on the one hand, and a daughter and her mother, on the other hand. I do not think it is useful or desirable for a court when considering an application such as the present one, to attempt to strike a balance-sheet between the expressions of natural affection of one child of the deceased as against another.

Merely living in the same house as the deceased does not by itse imply any special degree of care for the parent by the child. A pointed out in the discussion of section 1(1)(e) mere physic propinquity implies no moral obligation.[16] In *Re Coventry*[17] Oliver found that the sharing of accommodation by the applicant with th

13. It is questionable whether the degree of care reported in *Re Cook* (1956) 106 466 satisfied this test(the report of the facts is very brief) and see also *Re McGarr* [1983] 8 NIJB. In *Re Andrews* [1955] 1 WLR 1105, [1955] 3 All ER 248 a degr of caring by the applicant for the deceased did not enable the applicant to obta provision. In *Riggs v Lloyds Bank plc* (27 November 1992, unreported), CA t applicant generally 'helped' her father in his domestic chores and to a limit extent with his business. The Court of Appeal decided the case upon the basis 'maintenance' and hence did not have to address whether the applicant's ac entitled her to provision. It is submitted that they did not.
14. (1957) Times, 11 October.
15. [1979] Ch 168, at 175F-H, [1979] 1 All ER 546, at 551d-e.
16. See p 82, *ante*.
17. [1980] Ch 461, at 466H-467D, 476F-G, [1979] 2 All ER408, at 411g-412 419f-g.

eceased was merely a matter of mutual convenience. In *Re Christie*[18] Ir Vivian Price QC sitting as a deputy judge of the Chancery Division attached no significance to the defendant daughter having ccommodated the deceased for a period of five years.

Any Detriment Incurred by an Adult Child at the Request of the Deceased Parent

: is a logical extrapolation from the principle that if an adult child incurs detriment at the request of the deceased in order to care for the eceased he may be owed a moral duty by the deceased, to a principle hat if an adult child incurs any significant detriment at the request of he deceased in order to benefit the deceased he may be owed a moral uty by the deceased. Such a principle appears to have been implicitly ccepted by both Oliver J and the Court of Appeal in *Re Coventry*.[19]

The applicant in *Re Coventry* argued that he was owed a moral uty because he gave up the opportunity of re-enlistment in the oyal Navy with considerable prospects of advancement in order o live with his father and by reason of sharing his father's house he ost the opportunity of buying a house on what inflation has shown o be favourable terms. Oliver J rejected these claims as they were ot made out on the facts and the degree of detriment anyway was isignificant.[20] But his reasoning did imply that a moral duty could xist if the applicant had made out his case on the facts and had icurred a significant detriment.

A possible example of this wider principle is the incompletely eported case of *Re Murphy*.[1] In this case the applicant had married t the age of 18 'at the wish of her father' and was subsequently ivorced from her husband, with whom she had never lived, also at er father's request. She successfully applied for maintenance out f her deceased father's estate.

This principle *may* enable an adult child to be awarded provision here he has helped to build up the deceased's business.[2] In at least

8. [1979] Ch 168, at 175E-F, [1979] 1 All ER 546, at 547f.
9. [1980] Ch 461, [1979] 2 All ER 408, [1979] 3 All ER 815.
0. [1980] Ch 461, at 476H-477D, [1979] 2 All ER 408, at 419g-420b, approved at [1980] Ch 489D-490A, [1979] 3 All ER 823c-g (per Goff LJ), at [1980] Ch 492H, [1979] 3 All ER 826a (per Geoffrey Lane LJ), at [1980] Ch 496D, [1979] 3 All ER 828h (per Buckley LJ).
1. Evening Standard 17/12/42. See also *Re Abram* [1996] 2 FLR 379, at 382A-B, 393C.
2. Certainly this is a reason for not awarding provision at the expense of a child who has helped to build up the deceased's business eg *Re Brownbridge* (1942) 193 LT Jo 185; and see pp 151–152, *ante*.

three cases the court has ordered provision on the basis that an adul child helped in the deceased's business. In *Re Fletcher*[3] the applicant' daughter was employed by the deceased in his business and as hi housekeeper for 40 years without any wages. By consent Danckwert J awarded her substantial provision out of the deceased's estate. I *Re Creeney*[4] the applicant when he left school in 1944 instead o proceeding to university went to work for the deceased in the famil shop. The applicant received low wages and his wife worked in th business for no wages. The deceased promised him the business an in 1964 gave the applicant the business. The business did no prosper and the applicant ceased trading in 1972. Thereafter th applicant and the deceased quarrelled. In 1984 Carswell J awarde the applicant £18,000.

While it is submitted that if a detriment is incurred at the reques of the parent in order to benefit the parent it is right that such child may be entitled to be awarded family provision, this principl should only apply where the detriment is real and substantial an where the court considers it just. In *Re Abram*[5] the applicant worke in the deceased's business from 1960 to 1978. The applicant wa paid very low wages, a matter proved by specific figures.[6] He cease working for the deceased because he could not support himself o the wages he was paid, although subsequently there was a degre of assistance given by the applicant to the deceased's business.[7] I 1996 Roger Cooke J sitting as a judge of the Chancery Division gav these matters as a reason for awarding the applicant very substanti provision.[8]

Family provision should not be a means whereby an adult chil is compensated upon his parent's death for every erroneou suggestion made by the parent to the child. Oliver J was correct t reject the argument of the applicant in *Re Coventry*[9] that the loss o an opportunity to buy a house created a moral obligation upon th deceased – family provision should not be used to compensate th applicant for every loss of an investment opportunity. Where a clai is made on the basis that the applicant had contributed to th deceased's business, something more than the applicant being pai rather less than the market rate should be shown, such as the tota absence of remuneration in *Re Fletcher*[10] or the proven very low rat

3. Telegraph, 8/6/56.
4. [1984] NI 397.
5. [1996] 2 FLR 379.
6. [1996] 2 FLR 381F-H.
7. [1996] 2 FLR 383H-384A.
8. [1996] 2 FLR 392D-E.
9. [1980] Ch 461, [1979] 2 All ER 408.
10. Telegraph, 8/6/56.

of remuneration in *Re Abram*.[11] It is doubtful whether an arrangement reached at arm's length or with independent legal and accountancy advice would give a child any claim.[12] With matters such as choices of career and even the choice of spouses, bearing in mind the vicissitudes of life it may be difficult to know whether a particular choice would have worked out for the better. In *Re Coventry* it is doubtful whether the applicant would have been better off re-enlisting in the Royal Navy to become a Chief Petty Officer rather than leaving the Navy when he did to acquire the skilled trade of a toolmaker. Consideration should be given to the benefits of any choice made. In *Re Coventry* the applicant had the benefit of free accommodation for 20 years. An applicant who works for a parent may have a greater security of employment and other benefits to compensate for a reduced level of remuneration. In *Re Creeney*[13] the deceased provided the applicant with comfortable free accommodation for 14 years and was given by the deceased the benefit of his business – this might be thought to have been sufficient to compensate the applicant for any detriment incurred.

All the above cases concern situations where the detriment by the child *benefited* the parent. A case where the detriment did not benefit the deceased was *Re Leach*.[14] In this case the deceased told the applicant that she would receive half of her dwellinghouse upon death and in reliance upon this the applicant purchased a house or a more expensive house than would otherwise have been the case. It was conceded that this did not found an estoppel because the deceased did not request the applicant to purchase a house.[15] Both Mr Michael Wheeler QC at first instance[16] and Slade LJ in the Court of Appeal[17] regarded this as creating some form of 'moral obligation' and as *a* matter justifying an award of provision. It may be questioned whether this is a correct approach. The doctrine of estoppel is applied to give relief for representations as to testamentary intentions in a generous and highly non-technical manner[18] and it is difficult to justify adult children in need of 'maintenance' having to satisfy a less onerous test than other persons

1. [1996] 2 FLR 379, at 381F-H.
2. *Re Goodchild* [1996] 1 WLR 694, at 714C, [1996] 1 All ER 670, at 689d.
3. [1984] NI 397, at 398E. See also the examination and ultimate rejection of a possible estoppel in *Re Abram* [1996] 2 FLR 379, at 391D-392C.
4. [1984] FLR 590; affd [1986] Ch 226, [1985] 2 All ER 754.
5. But query whether in the light of *Taylors Fashions Ltd v Liverpool Trustees Co* [1982] QB 133n, [1981] 1 All ER 897 this concession was correctly made.
6. [1984] FLR 606D-E.
7. [1986] Ch 243G-244A, [1985] 2 All ER 766g-j.
8. See *Re Basham* [1986] 1 WLR 1498, [1987] 1 All ER 405; *Wayling v Jones* (1993) 69 P & CR 170, [1995] 2 FLR 1029.

who may have relied upon testamentary promises. The genuinel[y] meritorious cases will satisfy the requirements of a claim for estoppe[l] and bearing in mind the number of situations in which parents mak[e] vague statements as to their testamentary intentions it seem[s] inappropriate to have a 'half way house' where such statements ar[e] enforceable by a limited class of beneficiaries.

This body of case law must be re-examined in the light of th[e] remarks of the Court of Appeal in *Re Jennings* that 'the obligation[s] and responsibilities which the deceased had towards the applicant should be subsisting at the date of death.[19]

Detriment Incurred by a Third Party

In *Re Callaghan*[20] the estate of the deceased, who was the applicant'[s] step-father, was substantially derived from the estate of th[e] deceased's mother and ultimately from the applicant's late father[.] There was no evidence that the applicant's mother had expresse[d] any wish that her estate should ultimately devolve upon th[e] applicant. Booth J stated that the *origin* of the estate was *a* reaso[n] for awarding the applicant provision.[1] Booth J did not state ho[w] important this factor was in awarding provision and the award coul[d] in any way be justified by the care which the applicant and his wif[e] gave to the deceased. In *Re Leach*[2] the facts were essentially the sam[e] as in *Re Callaghan*. Again there was no evidence that the applicant'[s] parent had expressed any wish that his estate should ultimatel[y] devolve upon the applicant. Both Mr Michael Wheeler QC an[d] Slade LJ in the Court of Appeal indicated that this was *a* facto[r] justifying an award in favour of the applicant, although neithe[r] judgment articulated the precise reasoning for this conclusion. Although it may be a proper reason for refusing or limiting provisio[n] in favour of an applicant,[4] it is submitted that the mere fact that th[e] estate of the deceased was derived from one side of the family i[s] not a sufficient reason to award an adult child provision. If the origi[n] of the estate of the deceased is a sufficient reason in itself fo[r] awarding an adult child provision, then it is a factor that can easil[y] be outweighed by other matters. It is significant that in both *R*[e]

19. See pp 49–50, *ante*.
20. [1985] Fam 1, [1984] 3 All ER 790.
1. [1985] Fam 7D, [1984] 3 All ER 794j.
2. [1984] FLR 590; affd [1986] Ch 226, [1985] 2 All ER 754.
3. [1986] Ch 244B, [1985] 2 All ER 766j.
4. See pp 151–152, *ante* on matters which while in themselves do not justify claim can act as a defence to a claim.

Callaghan and *Re Leach* the beneficiaries were relatively distant relations who took on intestacy and had no competing cliam upon the deceased whatsoever.

Of more sigificance is the case of *Re Goodchild.*[5] In this case the deceased and his first wife made wills in each other's favour but with their son taking if the spouse did not survive the testator. The deceased's wife died and her estate passed to the deceased. The deceased then remarried and by his will bequeathed his estate to his second wife. The deceased's son commenced proceedings to assert a mutual wills trust binding upon the deceased and in the alternative applied for provision under the 1975 Act. Carnwath J after an extremely detailed investigation of the law and the facts held that while there was 'some loose understanding or sense of moral obligation'[6] between the deceased and his first wife, there was insufficient evidence of a legally enforceable agreement between the parties and accordingly he dismissed the mutual wills claim. He did however hold that the deceased as a result of the mutual discussions he had with his first wife was under 'a moral obligation' to leave that part of his estate he had derived from his first wife to his son and that under the 1975 Act this was a sufficient reason for awarding an adult child provision out of that part of the estate.[7] Carnwath J specifically stated that the applicant had no claim under the 1975 Act over the part of the deceased's estate which he had not inherited from his first wife. The estate was sufficient to meet the claims of the deceased's second wife and accordingly there was no need to balance the claims of the son.

Re Goodchild is a stronger decision than both of *Re Callaghan* and *Re Leach* in that there was clear evidence that the deceased parent intended her estate to pass to her son and arguably *detriment* by her in that had the deceased not evinced a similar intention, she would have made different testamentary dispositions. *Re Goodchild* however remains a difficult one. The same reasons which cause the courts to require a reasonably high standard of proof before enforcing mutual wills trusts, namely uncertainty as to whether the parties really intended to bind each other legally, uncertainty as to the terms of the agreement between the parties which makes enforcement difficult and reluctance to assume that the parties fully intended to be subject to the floating trust which enforcement of a

5. [1996] 1 WLR 694, [1996] 1 All ER 670; affd [1997] 3 All ER 63.
6. [1996] 1 WLR 706D-E, 714D-E, [1996] 1 All ER 681h, 689e-f.
7. [1996] 1 WLR 714D-F, [1996] 1 All ER 689e-g; this reasoning was specifically approved by Legatt LJ who gave the only reasoned judgment on this point in the Court of Appeal at [1997] 3 All ER 73c-75a.

mutual trust entails[8] are also applicable under the Inheritance Act 1984. The distinction between being satisfied on a balance of probabilities that the parties intended a legally enforceable obligation and that they only intended a 'morally enforceable' obligation is likely to be small and satisfied in only a very small number of cases. A court hearing a claim under the 1975 Act has no greater ability to ascertain the scope and extent of an agreement than a court being asked to enforce a mutual wills trust. Section 10 of the 1975 Act has much the same effect as equity's floating trust. It is difficult to justify a poor adult child being able to enforce an otherwise unenforceable mutual wills trust whereas a better off adult child or a person other than a child is unable to do so. In general terms it is highly questionable whether the Inheritance Act should be used to give effect to detriments incuured by third parties in their dealings with the deceased. What *Re Goodchild* did not have to address is the balancing of claims by an adult child under a 'morally binding' mutual wills trust and a surviving spouse.

Misbehaviour by a Parent

In *Re Jennings*[9] the deceased following the separation of himself and his wife took no interest in the applicant when he was an infant and did not maintain the applicant at all. Henry LJ graphically dismissed this as a reason for awarding the applicant provision thus:

> ... it is in my judgment simply irrelevant that this father behaved as he did – however much this behaviour may be deplored. It is not the purpose of the Act of 1975 to punish or redress past bad or unfeeling parental behaviour where that behaviour does still not impinge on the applicant's present financial situation.[10]

Any Physical or Mental Disability of an Adult Child

The importance Parliament attached to any physical or mental disability of an adult child was evidenced by sons over 21 years of

8. *Birmingham v Renfrew* (1936) 57 CLR 666.
9. [1994] Ch 286, [1994] 3 All ER 27.
10. [1994] Ch 301D-E, [1994] 3 All ER 39f-g. In the light of these remarks the decision in *Re Ducksbury* [1966] 1 WLR 1226, [1966] 2 All ER 374 and that part of the reasoning in *Re Debenham* [1986] 1 FLR 404, at 409F-H as refers to the misconduct of the deceased should be taken to be overruled. In *Re Abram* [1996] 2 FLR 379 the judge conspicuously failed to address these remarks.

age and married daughters who 'by reason of some mental or physical disability, were incapable of maintaining' themselves being able to apply under the 1938 Act.[11] The 1975 Act requires the court to have regard to:

> ... any physical or mental disability of any applicant for an order under ... Section 2 or any beneficiary of the estate of the deceased.[12]

While it seems generally accepted that adult children who are physically or mentally disabled should be awarded family provision, the reasoning for such a rule has never been fully set out. If an adult child is disabled from supporting himself, an award of provision to him cannot act as a disincentive to work.[13] The main justification of a parent's obligation to support an infant child, that of the intentional creation of a new being who is incapable of supporting himself,[14] can be used to justify a parent's obligation to support an adult disabled child, but only where the disability existed at birth, or perhaps where it arose during childhood.[15] While alive a parent owes no duty to support his adult disabled child and there is no public pressure to change the law. Even while an infant it is not always thought to be wrong for a parent to refuse to maintain or care for a severely disabled child.[16] Discussing the matter the Albertan Institute of Law Research and Reform[17] was in two minds whether to recommend that adult disabled children should be able

11. S 1(1)(b), (d).
12. S 3(1)(f), derived from s 25(1)(e) of the Matrimonial Causes Act 1973. CRETNEY, 447 states that the original comparable provision in the Matrimonial Proceedings and Property Act 1970 was not a suggestion of the Law Commission but was introduced because of Parliamentary pressure.
13. See p 37, *ante*.
14. See the remarks of J S Mill quoted at pp 41–42, *ante* and also pp 199–200, *ante*.
15. See the remarks of Sir John May in *Re Jennings* [1994] Ch 286, at 302E-F, [1994] 3 All ER 27, at 40h.
16. Eg see the costs order made *in favour of* the parents who reject their severely handicapped child and wished it to die in *Re B (a minor) (wardship: medical treatment)* [1981] I WLR 1421. Neither s 29 of the Matrimonial Causes Act 1973, para 2(1), Sch 1 of the Children Act 1989 nor s 5(1), (3) of the Domestic Proceedings and Magistrates' Courts Act 1978 specifically enable orders for maintenance to be in favour of mentally or physically disabled adult children. There is only one reported case where it has been held that the physical or mental disability of an adult child constituted a 'special circumstance' within the meaning of these statutory provisions, see *C v C (financial provision: personal damages)* [1995] 2 FLR 171, at 188E-189F.
17. Institute of Law Research and Reform, University of Alberta Report, No 29 Family Relief (1978) 40–44. The Report of the Manitoba Law Reform Commission 'The Testator's Family Maintenance Act' (1985) 77–80 was equally unsure of the correct approach, noting in particular the anomalous situation of a duty to maintain after death, but no duty to maintain before death.

to apply for family provision. The Institute stressed that a parent while alive is not obliged by law to maintain a disabled adult child, but noted that after death the deceased's parent's estate is not required for the maintenance of the parent.[18] Ultimately the Institute decided that adult disabled children should be permitted to apply for family provision.[19] While sentiment in favour of ordering provision for adult disabled children is fairly strong, the rationale for doing so, where the incapacity arose after childhood, is rather hard to find.

This uncertain rationale is well illustrated by two contrasting cases. In *Re Andrews*[20] the applicant daughter in 1911 then aged 25 left the deceased's home to live as the mistress of a man separated from his wife by whom she had six children. When the applicant left the deceased's house they became estranged, but they were subsequently reconciled and the applicant saw the deceased and looked after him on occasions before his death. The deceased died in 1953 and his will made no provision for the applicant. She was at the time of the hearing before Wynn-Parry J in 1955 aged 69, in ill-health and consequently unable to support herself. Her lover was similarly unable to support himself and the only source of income for both was National Assistance. The applicant applied for provision out of the deceased's estate under the 1938 Act on the basis that she was an unmarried daughter and that she was a daughter incapable of supporting herself. Wynn-Parry J dismissed the applicant's summons. He argued that as soon as she set up permanent home with her lover the responsibility for her maintenance was that of her lover and that the deceased was under no moral duty to make provision for her in his will as an unmarried daughter. *Likewise* upon the applicant leaving the deceased's home and setting up a permanent home with her lover, the deceased ceased to be under any moral duty to make provision for her in his will on the basis that she was by reason of a disability incapable of supporting herself.[1]

A completely different approach was taken by the Court of Appeal in *Millward v Shenton.*[2] In this case the deceased widow died in 1970 leaving an estate of £3,144 and six adult children, one daughter who predeceased the deceased having died of cancer. The deceased left her entire estate to a charity for cancer research, making

18. Page 41.
19. Page 42. The same ultimate conclusion was reached by the Manitoba Law Reform Commission.
20. [1955] 1 WLR 1105, [1955] 3 All ER 248.
1. [1955] 1 WLR 1107, [1955] 3 All ER 249I–250A.
2. [1972] 1 WLR 711, [1972] 2 All ER 1025.

no provision for any of her children because she feared that they would quarrel after her death about the division of the estate and in the belief that they were all self-supporting. However one of her adult sons had been severely disabled since 1966 and was incapable of supporting himself. He was aged 52 in 1970, his wife was also severely handicapped with arthritis and his only source of income was social security benefits. His application for provision under the 1938 Act was refused by the county court judge, but succeeded in the Court of Appeal, where he was awarded 11/12ths of the estate with the costs of the appeal to be paid by the charity.[3] On the evidence it was clear that the deceased was ignorant of the applicant's disability.[4] Although the Court of Appeal debated whether the test to be applied by the court was subjective or objective and the relevance of state benefits, no substantial reasons were advanced by the court to justify its emphatic conclusion that the applicant was entitled to provision. Although *Re Andrews* was cited in argument, it and the argument that a parent's moral duty to provide for a disabled child ceases upon marriage were not discussed in the judgments.

A comparison of the facts of *Re Andrews* and *Millward v Shenton* reveals that the applicants were similarly placed in most respects, save that the applicant daughter in *Re Andrews* had over a period of 34 years on occasions nursed the deceased,[5] whereas the applicant son in *Millward v Shenton* could not claim to have rendered 'special services' to the deceased.[6] One of the most remarkable features of *Millward v Shenton* was that although the applicant claimed to have been a dutiful son and to have had a good relationship with his mother,[7] news of the applicant's severe disability did not reach the deceased for the four years between the onset of the disability and the making of the will. On the facts of *Millward v Shenton* it is doubtful whether the relief of suffering was better served by giving money to the applicant disabled son or for cancer research.

In *Re Wood*[8] Mervyn Davies J in 1982 followed the approach of *Millward v Shenton* and awarded the applicant substantial

3. The unusual nature of this fraction and the extremely succinct judgments of Megaw and Stamp LJJ might suggest that the actual order was a result of a compromise among members of the court.
4. [1972] 1 WLR 714D-G, [1972] 2 All ER 1027C-G.
5. [1955] 3 All ER 248G-H.
6. [1972] 1 WLR 714G, [1972] 2 All ER 1027F-G.
7. [1972] 1 WLR 614G, [1972] 2 All ER 1027F-G.
8. [1982] LS Gaz R 774, 2 April 1982. The author knows of a large number of similar cases which have been compromised in a similar manner to *Re Wood*. See also *C v C (financial provision: personal damages)* [1995] 2 FLR 171, at 188E-189F.

provision. However the case for a substantial award was conceded and the matter was argued solely on the question of quantum. The facts of the case were much stronger than in either of *Re Andrews* and *Millward v Shenton* in that the applicant had been severely mentally subnormal since birth, had been visited extensively by the deceased while in a mental hospital – some of the provision ordered was to be used to pay for trips out formerly provided by the deceased during her lifetime – and was unmarried. In *Re Debenham* [9] the applicant was aged 58 years, suffered from severe epilepsy and was awarded provision.

Although the reasoning for doing so can be criticised as resting essentially upon sentiment, it is probably the law that the physical or mental disability constitutes special circumstances entitling an adult child to provision out of his deceased's parent's estate. This conclusion can be partly justified by the mention of physical or mental disability in both the 1938 and 1975 Acts. [10] There are a substantial number of obiter dicta suggesting that adult children who are unable to support themselves are entitled to provision out of the estate,[11] although most recently Sir John May in *Re Jennings*[12] appeared to restrict provision to disabled adult children where the disability was 'continuing' from childhood. *Millward v Shenton*,[13] being a decision of the Court of Appeal, must be taken to have overruled *Re Andrews*,[14] however unsatisfactory the treatment of the latter case was.

It is likely that the court will pay particular regard to the possibility of an adult child incapable of maintaining himself by reason of a physical or mental disability being maintained by other people such as a spouse.[15] It is implicit in *Millward v Shenton*[16] that little other than the incapacity of the applicant needs to be proved

9. [1986] 1 FLR 404.
10. 1938 Act, s 1(1) (b), (d); 1975 Act, s 3(1) (f).
11. *Re Watkins* [1949] 1 All ER 695, at 700A-G (per Roxburgh J), who held that the applicant was adequately maintained in a National Health Service mental hospital, but who stated that had such accommodation not been available he would have awarded the applicant provision; *Re Black* (1953) Times, 24 March (per Vaisey J); *Re Pearson-Gregory* (1957) Times, 11 October (per Roxburgh J); *Re Coventry* [1980] Ch 461, at 474D-E, [1979] 2 All ER 408, at 417g (per Oliver J); *Re Jennings* [1994] Ch 286, at 295E-F, [1994] 3 All ER 27, at 33j (per Nourse LJ),[1994] Ch 302F-G, [1994] 3 All ER 40h (per Sir John May).
12. [1994] Ch 286, at 302E-F, [1994] 3 All ER 27, at 40h.
13. [1972] 1 WLR 711, [1972] 2 All ER 1025.
14. [1955] 1 WLR 1105, [1955] 3 All ER 248.
15. In *Re Wood* [1982] LS Gaz R 774, 2 April 1982, Mervyn Davies J gave as *a* reason for awarding the quite large provision which he did to the applicant the inability of the applicant's father, who was divorced from the deceased, to make any contribution to the applicant's well-being and maintenance.
16. [1972] 1 WLR 711, [1972] 2 All ER 1025.

for the court to be satisfied that special circumstances which entitle the adult child to provision, although it is clear that incapacity does not override all other relevant considerations. Certainly in considering the analogous provision on divorce the courts have not allowed disbilities of the most severe kinds to preclude consideration of other factors.[17]

Although the 1975 Act is differently worded to the 1938 Act, requiring the court to have regard to ' *any* physical or mental disability'[18] of an applicant or a beneficiary as opposed to only permitting an application if an adult child was '*incapable of maintaining himself*'[19] by reason of some disability, it is suggested that the difference in language is not significant and that the court will only pay attention to a disability where it affects the applicant's ability to support himself.

Before the discussion of physical or mental disabilities is concluded, three situations which might be regarded as essentially similar to physical or mental disabilities will be discussed.

Is Old Age a 'Physical or Mental Incapacity'?

It is uncertain whether old age by itself comes within the statutory definition of 'any physical or mental disability'. While advancing years frequently lead to physical or mental incapacity, it is doubtful whether old age as such can be regarded as coming within the definition – certainly the most natural method of drafting would have included old age expressly within the definition had it been intended to include it.

In *Re Rowlands*[20] an adult daughter aged at least 60 years at the date of trial and described as 'elderly' who looked after a disabled adult son and the deceased's widow was refused provision by Anthony Lincoln J, who did not regard old age and straitened circumstances as a reason for awarding provision. This case is to

17. Eg *Wagstaff v Wagstaff* [1992] 1 WLR 320, [1992] 1 All ER 275.
18. S 3(1)(f) (emphasis added).
19. S 1(1)(b), (c) (emphasis added).
20. [1984] FLR 813, at 819F-820A. In *Re Black* (1953) Times, 24 March, Vaisey J ordered provision for the applicant's old age; In *Re Andrews* [1955] 1 WLR 1105, [1955] 3 All ER 248 provision was refused to an applicant aged 69. In *Re Pearson-Gregory* (1957) Times, 11 October Roxburgh J found that provision for the applicant's old age was in any event adequate and also otherwise rejected her application completely on its merits. In *Re Portt* (25 March 1980, unreported), CA an application by a widow aged 70 failed because, inter alia, her means were already adequate and because of her conduct.

be contrasted with *Re Debenham*[1] where Ewbank J specifically awarded periodic payments to a daughter who suffered from severe epilepsy to extend beyond the applicant's 60th birthday. Much of Ewbank J's judgment can not stand with *Re Jennings* and the extent to which the effects of epilepsy would go beyond the effects of age when she reached retirement age was not discussed. In *Cameron v Treasury Solicitor*[2] the Court of Appeal rejected the claim of a former spouse whose age was not stated, but must have been, at least 56 years and who was in 'ill-health'. The significance of the case is that two Lord Justices regarded Oliver J's judgment in *Re Coventry*[3] as applicable and as determining the case against the applicant.

Other 'Disabilities'

A comment by the late John Hall[4] on the case of *Re Rodwell*[5] had considerable influence upon the Law Commission's decision to permit all adult children to apply for family provision. Hall thought it highly anomalous that a daughter whose voidable marriage had been annulled could apply by reason of the existing law[6] under the 1938 Act as 'a daughter who has not been married',[7] but that a widowed daughter left penniless with young children to support could not. The Law Commission paid particular attention to this criticism of the 1938 Act and recommended that all adult children should be able to apply for provision.[8] This argument is equally applicable to situations where a married daughter has been deserted by her husband with young children to support and daughters who are unmarried mothers, but in many of these situations it could be argued that the applicant to a considerable extent is the author of her own misfortune.

1. [1986] 1 FLR 404, at 407D-E, 410H. In *Re Abram* [1996] 2 FLR 379 Roger Cooke J sitting as a judge of the Chancery Division awarded the applicant, aged 52 at the date of the hearing a protected life interest in a substantial sum of capital. The judge made no enquiry as to the pension entitlement of the applicant.
2. [1996] 2 FLR 716.
3. Butler-Sloss and Peter Gibson LJJ at [1996] 2 FLR 719E-720F, 721H-723B. Thorpe LJ referred to *Re Fullard* at [1996] 2 FLR 723F-G.
4. Hall, Casenote, [1970] Camb L Jo 313; see also first edition, p 20.
5. [1970] Ch 726, [1969] 3 All ER 1363.
6. The law was subsequently altered by s 5 of the Nullity of Marriage Act 1971.
7. S 1(1)(b).
8. WORKING PAPER, para 3.42; LAW COM, para 78.

On a technical level this argument has lost its force by reason of the assimilation by the courts of the position of adult sons and daughters.[9]

Such case law as has considered the position of adult children who are in a difficult family circumstance has rejected the claims of such children. In *Re Rowlands*[10] Anthony Lincoln J rejected an application by an elderly married adult daughter who lived in straitened circumstances and who cared for her 90 year old mother and an adult handicapped son.

Unemployed Adult Children

In *Re Coventry*[11] the applicant was in work, albeit his income was modest. There is a considerable tension in the judgment of Oliver J who refers to the applicant as being 'in, or capable of, gainful employment',[12] but also enunciates the proposition that it is insufficient to assert that merely being in necessitous circumstances is sufficient to enable an adult child to succeed in his application.[13] This tension was repeated in *Re Jennings* where Nourse LJ and Sir John May both referred to 'an adult son of the deceased who is able to earn, and earns, his own living',[14] whereas the rest of the judgments emphasise that the deceased must have owed the applicant some moral or legal duty at the date of death.[15]

These tensions are resolved by the judgment of Goff LJ in *Re Coventry* who stated:

> ... his [Oliver J's] conclusion was not that the plaintiff was not in need of maintenance, but that on the facts of the case he was not in a position to show that the intestate's disposition failed to make reasonable provision for his maintenance.[16]

9. See pp 230–231, *ante*.
10. [1984] FLR 813.
11. [1980] Ch 461, [1979] 2 All ER 408; affd [1979] 3 All ER 815.
12. [1980] Ch 465E-F, G, [1979] 2 All ER 410f-g, h.
13. [1980] Ch 475C-E, [1979] 2 All ER 418e-f.
14. [1994] Ch 286, at 295E-F,302C, [1994] 3 All ER 27, at 33j, 40d.
15. [1994] Ch 295G-296H, 300D-301D, 302C-303D, [1994] 3 All ER 34b-35a, 38g-39e, 40d-41d.
16. [1980] Ch 492A, [1979] 3 All ER 825c. Buckley LJ adopted the same reasoning, see [1980] Ch 494G, [1979] 3 All ER 827e-f, but did refer to a person 'in adult male employment' at [1980] Ch 495A-B, [1979] 3 All ER 827g. See also the emphatic holding of Carnwath J in *Re Goodchild* [1996] 1 WLR 694, at 714C-D, [1996] 1 All ER 670, at 689d-e rejecting the claim of an adult child in employment, but otherwise in a perilous financial situation, to the half of the deceased's estate not derived from his first wife.

With one exception,[17] courts have rejected applications by adult children who have relied upon partial[18] or total unemployment.[19] In *Cameron v Treasury Solicitor*[20] the Court of Appeal rejected the claim of a former spouse who was accepted by the Court of Appeal to be 'in straitened circumstances'. The significance of the case is that two Lord Justices regarded Oliver J's judgment in *Re Coventry*[1] as applicable and determining the case against the applicant.

Conclusion on 'Disabilities'

All three situations – old age, being a single parent with young children to support and being unemployed – are essentially the same financial hardship caused by factors external to the applicant, although in the latter two situations in many cases it is likely that the applicant may be to varying extents the cause of his own financial hardship. To order provision in these cases would be to deny Oliver J's central proposition of law, affirmed by the Court of Appeal in *Re Jennings*[2] and reasserted emphatically in *Re Fullard*,[3] that:

> It cannot be enough to say 'here is a son of the deceased; he is in necessitous circumstances; there is property of the deceased which could be made available to assist him but which is not available if the deceased's dispositions stand; therefore those dispositions do not make reasonable provision for the applicant'. There must, as it seems to me, be established some sort of moral claim by the applicant to be maintained by the deceased or at the expense of his estate beyond the mere fact of a blood relationship, some reason why it can be said that, in the circumstances, it is unreasonable that no or no greater provision was in fact made.[4]

In almost all the 'special circumstances' where family provision is awarded to adult children, the obligation to do so arises from some

17. *Re Debenham* [1986] 1 FLR 404.
18. *Re Fergusson* Foster J (16 June 1980, unreported).
19. *Re Pearson-Gregory* (1957) Times, 11 October; *Re Dennis* [1981] 2 All ER 140; *Williams v Johns* [1988] 2 FLR 475. In all these cases unemployment was to some extent voluntary. There is no reported case on unemployment existing at a time or within a social class that can not to some extent be described as voluntary.
20. [1996] 2 FLR 716.
1. Butler-Sloss and Peter Gibson LJJ at [1996] 2 FLR 720C-D. At 723B, Thorpe LJ relied upon *Re Fullard.*
2. [1994] Ch 286, [1994] 3 All ER 27.
3. [1982] Fam 42, [1981] 2 All ER 796.
4. [1980] Ch 475C-D, [1979] 2 All ER 418e-f.

act of, or conduct towards,[5] the deceased parent. In the other situations under discussion all that the applicant can rely upon is the financial hardship caused in certain ways. To award family provision in such circumstances would be to increase very substantially the number of family provision applications, going a considerable way to introducing *legitim* for certain classes of adult child applicant – an erroneous policy choice and one opposed by public opinion[6] which will inevitably involve the courts in exceptionally difficult questions of conduct.[7] It is suggested that the present law's hesitant refusal to award provision in such circumstances is correct.

The case of a physically or mentally disabled adult child is essentially the same as the three other situations – financial hardship caused by the act of a third party or by nature (unless subsisting since childhood[8]) and it is submitted that it should be treated in the same way. It is therefore suggested that such adult children relying upon their disability alone should not be awarded provision, that the Court of Appeal decision in *Millward v Shenton* [9] is to be rejected and that the inclusion of section 3(1)(e) in the 1975 Act was erroneous.

Married Adult Children

The Law Commission in recommending that adult children who had been married should be able to apply for family provision stressed that the court should pay particular regard to the ability, if it existed, of the child's spouse to maintain him or her in deciding whether to award provision and should normally accept that the principal liability to maintain a wife should be that of her husband not her father.[10] This approach of paying particular regard to the ability and responsibility of a spouse to maintain an adult child, but not completely barring such applications is sensible but may be

5. The case of an adult child caring for an aged or infirm child. This might also justify the decisions of *Re Leach, Re Callaghan* and *Re Goodchild.*
6. See table of public opinion at p 34A, *ante* and also the public opinion survey on intestacy, in Law Commission Report No 187, Family Law: Distribution on Intestacy.
7. Compare *Re Andrews* [1955] 1 WLR 1105, [1955] 3 All ER 248; *Re Embleton* Telegraph, 3/3/79: *Re Portt* (25 March 1980, unreported), CA; *Re McGarrell* [1983]8 NIJB ; *Re Creeney* [1984] NI 397.
8. Note the possibly significant remarks of Sir John May in *Re Jennings* at [1994] Ch 302F-G, [1994] 3 All ER 40h-j referring to 'continuing disability'.
9. [1972] 1 WLR 711, [1972] 2 All ER 1025.
10. WORKING PAPER, para 3.42; LAW COM, para 78.

inappropriate where a married child is entitled to provision because of her caring for the parent or otherwise having incurred a detriment to benefit the parent.[11] The reported case law suggests that in considering the means of an adult child, his means are aggregated with those of his spouse.[12]

Conduct of the Adult Child

Where an adult child relies upon the fact that he has cared for the deceased or incurred a detriment to benefit the deceased, his conduct is the very basis of her right to family provision.

It is clear from the discussion of the facts of *Millward v Shenton*[13] that where an applicant suffers from a physical or mental disability the applicant's conduct is of very limited importance. However, conduct in such a case is not entirely irrelevant because Lord Denning MR did state that:

> There was no personal reason for cutting him out of the will. The judge found that the relationship between this son and his mother had been a normal affectionate one.[14]

If family provision is ordered in favour of adult children for reasons other than mental or physical handicap, the courts become involved with questions of conduct: it is unthinkable that English courts would follow the approach of Murphy J in *Hughes v National Trustee*[15] in ignoring conduct and only looking at need. In reported cases where adult children have had their claims rejected the judges have often fortified their conclusions by references to the misconduct of the applicants[16] and while 'meritorious conduct' by an adult child

11. Examples of sucessful applications by married adult children include *Re Callagan* [1985] Fam 1, [1984] 3 All ER 790; *Re McGarrell* [1983] 8 NIJB; *Re Creeney* [1984] NI 397; *Re Debenham* [1986] 1 FLR 404; *Re Goodchild* [1996] 1 WLR 694, [1996] 1 All ER 670. These cases are to be contrasted with *Re Rowlands* [1984] FLR 813, at 819F, 820B where Anthony Lincoln J followed *Re Andrews* and held that marriage effectively barred an adult daughter's claim.
12. A very clear example of this is *Riggs v Lloyds Bank plc* (27 November 1992, unreported), CA which turned almost exclusively upon the means of the applicant's husband.
13. [1972] 1 WLR 711, [1972] 2 All ER 1025.
14. [1972] 1 WLR 714G, [1972] 2 All ER 1027F-G.
15. (1979) 23 ALR 321 (Aust HC on appeal from Victoria). See further fn 9, p 229, *ante*.
16. *Re Coventry* [1980] Ch 461, [1979] 2 All ER 408 (son's conduct helped to cause widow to leave matrimonial home); *Re Embleton* Telegraph, 3/3/79 (estrangement of daughter from father and refusal to visit deceased); *Re Portt*

will not in itself justify an award of provision, misconduct is capable of preventing an otherwise justified claim from succeeding.

PART 4: FORMER SPOUSES

The right of former spouses to apply for family provision out of the estate of the deceased was governed by different legislation and was administered by different courts to that of the 1938 Act.[17] There were differences of approach between the Chancery Division and the Probate, Divorce and Admiralty Division in the interpretation and operation of the respective legislation.[18] The 1975 Act by creating a uniform code abolished these differences and it is submitted that the same approach will be adopted whichever Division of the High Court now exercises jurisdiction.

Of more importance than the formal changes to the legislation enabling former spouses to apply have been the changes to the powers and attitudes of the courts in financial matters after divorce. When in 1958 former spouses were first given the right to apply for family provision, the courts had only limited powers to vary the parties' property rights and relief was generally limited to periodic payments orders. Since then the courts have acquired and liberally exercise extensive powers to vary the parties' property rights. In more recent years considerable scepticism has arisen as to the appropriateness of life-long duties of support and the courts have in some cases enthusiastically adopted the principle of the 'clean break' on divorce.[19] With the increase of 'clean break' orders on

(25 March 1980, unreported), CA (quarrels with deceased and excessively litigious nature of applicant); *Re Fergusson*, Foster J (16 June 1980, unreported) (quarrels with step-father, refusal to grow up and excessive interest in dogs); *Re Dennis* [1981] 2 All ER 140 (reckless spending of assets); *Williams v Johns* [1988] 2 FLR 475 (quarrels with the deceased, commission of criminal offences and generally feckless lifestyle – a particularly strong case); but compare *Re Ducksbury* [1966] 1 WLR 1226, [1966] 2 All ER 374 (estrangement of daughter from father and unpleasant conduct by daughter towards father held not to disbar daughter from being awarded provision); *Re Goodchild* [1996] 1 WLR 694, [1996] 1 All ER 670 (unhappiness between the applicant and the deceased following the deceased's remarriage held to be irrelevant).

17. See pp 21–23, *ante*.
18. See first edition, pp 103–105.
19. See generally *Minton v Minton* [1979] AC 593, [1979] 1 All ER 79; *De Lasala v De Lasala* [1980] AC 546, [1979] 2 All ER 1146; Law Commission Report No 112; The Financial Consequences of Divorce (1981), paras 28–30; s 25A of the Matrimonial Causes Act 1973, inserted by s 3 of the Matrimonial and Family Proceedings Act 1984.

divorce and in particular orders under section 15,[20] the number of applications by former spouses under the 1975 Act has very substantially decreased.

Many of the principles governing applications by former spouses can be found in the parts of this Chapter dealing with applications by spouses and in books on divorce law and only matters which are peculiar to applications by former spouses will be stressed in this part.

The law on applications by former spouses was revolutionised by the decision of the Court of Appeal in *Re Fullard*[1] in 1981. The applicant and the deceased married in 1938 and had two children both of whom had left the matrimonial home. In 1976 the parties separated and were divorced. The parties, each being advised by solicitors, agreed that the applicant would pay the deceased £4,500 for his half share in the matrimonial home and that neither party would make any maintenance payments to the other. This agreement was not embodied in an order of the court. The husband left the matrimonial home and took lodgings with the respondent, an elderly lady. The deceased died in 1978 leaving his estate of £7,100, much of which consisted of the money paid by the applicant for the deceased's share of the matrimonial home, by will to the respondent. The applicant who was aged over 60 was working but still had to pay off a mortgage taken out in order to buy out the deceased. The applicant's application for provision was dismissed by Bush J and her appeal was rejected by a Court of Appeal consisting of Ormrod LJ and Purchas J.

Certain parts of Ormrod LJ's judgment dealing with the general approach of the court to applications by former spouses are of such importance that they deserve to be set out in full. Ormrod LJ said:

> In approaching these applications by a party who has been divorced, I think it is important to bear in mind ... the history of the legislation ...
>
> To go to the history briefly, the Act of 1975 is a composite of the former Inheritance (Family Provision) Act 1938 and what was originally section 3 of the Matrimonial Causes (Property and Maintenance) Act 1958 ...
>
> It is very important to remember that, at the time that section first came into existence, the court had no power to deal with capital adjustments between spouses. At that period the Court's powers were

20. On s 15 orders, see pp 271–274, *post*. See the remarks of Ormrod LJ in *Re Fullard* at [1982] Fam 49E-F, [1981] 2 All ER 801j.
1. [1982] Fam 42, [1981] 2 All ER 796. Prime, 'Ex-Wife Ex-Family?' (1982) 12 Fam Law 53 is an excellent case-note on *Re Fullard*.

> greatly restricted in relation to ancillary relief because they could not deal adequately with the situation when (usually) a husband came into a substantial capital sum, either because he earned it or for some other reason, after the ancillary relief order had been made. So there were many cases in and around that time where ex-wives were in receipt of periodic payments which ceased on the death of their former husbands and were placed in a position of extreme difficulty. There is no doubt that that section was passed originally to give the court power to deal with that sort of situation when it arose. With the coming into effect of the Matrimonial Proceedings and Property Act 1970 with the new powers to make property adjustment orders and very much freer power to order lump sums, the court now has power to make appropriate capital adjustments as between spouses after divorce and those powers, although they are not necessarily comprehensive ... nonetheless the number of cases in which it would be possible for an applicant to bring himself (or herself) within the terms of section 2 of the Inheritance (Provision for Family and Dependants) Act 1975 in my judgment, would be comparatively small. Where the estate – like this one – is small, in my view the onus on an applicant of satisfying the conditions of section 2 is very heavy indeed ...[2]

Ormrod LJ approved emphatically the decision in *Re Coventry*,[3] and accepted that an applicant had to do more than show that he comes within one of the classes of applicant and that he is in necessitous circumstances to be awarded provision. Ormrod LJ stated that a deceased's 'obligations and responsibilities' within the meaning of section 3(1)(d) towards a former spouse were limited.[4] He said:

> ... [the trial judge] said quite rightly that the deceased had no legal obligations or responsibilities for the beneficiary. To my mind he had no moral obligations or responsibility either, in the circumstances of the case, to the plaintiff. The judge referred to his having towards the plaintiff: '... the responsibility and obligations of a former husband for the maintenance of his former wife'. I am not quite clear what he had in mind because the responsibility and obligations of a former husband for the maintenance of a former wife are to comply with such orders as the court has made or that the parties may have agreed between themselves. There are certainly no other legal

2. [1982] Fam 45B-46B, [1981] 2 All ER 798e-799c, see also [1982] Fam 49D-E, [1981] 2 All ER 801j. Purchas J agreed with the judgment of Ormrod LJ at [1982] Fam 50G-H, [1981] 2 All ER 802j.
3. [1980] Ch 461, [1979] 2 All ER 408, approved at [1982] Fam 47B-H, 50H, [1981] 2 All ER 799j-800h.
4. See generally pp 150–152, *ante*.

> obligations. In these days it might be quite difficult to say that he had a moral obligation – though there may be cases where it could be argued that he had.[5]

On the facts of *Re Fullard* the court found that the parties' obligations towards each other ceased on divorce. The parties had made a settlement of their rights and obligations which was intended to be permanent and was intended to effect a 'clean break'. It was irrelevant that this agreement, being fairly negotiated, was not included in a court order and that no order under section 15 barring an application for provision had been made.[6] In the present case no periodic payments ceased on death[7] and there had been no significant change of circumstances between the date of the divorce and the date of death,[8] – if either of these matters existed the applicant might well have been awarded provision. In *Re Fullard* the applicant was trying to obtain maintenance by way of periodic payments from the deceased's estate which she could not obtain while he was alive[9] and was trying to recover £4,500 which she had paid the deceased for his share of the matrimonial home[10] – claims which the court regarded as clearly unreasonable.

It appears from *Re Fullard* that former spouses will be likely to be awarded provision from the estate of the deceased in essentially three situations: firstly when there has not been a proper settlement of financial matters on divorce; secondly when there has been a really significant change of circumstances between the date of the divorce and the date of death; and thirdly where there has been a continuing financial obligation or actual provision for the applicant which terminated on death. Although this analysis flows from *Re Fullard,* it is submitted that most of the previous reported cases are congruent with this analysis. These three situations are probably the only matters which would justify a finding that the dispositions of the deceased's estate were unreasonable in not providing for a former spouse and it is extemely unlikely that an applicant who cannot bring himself within these three situations will be awarded provision.[11] The Court of Appeal has twice rejected submissions to limit the full vigour of *Re Fullard.*[12] In *C v C (financial provision: personal*

5. [1982] Fam 50D-F, [1981] 2 All ER 802e-g.
6. [1982] Fam 49G-50B, 51F-52C, [1981] 2 All ER 802a-d, 803h-8-4b. To the same effect is *Cameron v Treasury Solicitor* [1996] 2 FLR 716.
7. [1982] Fam 49E-F, 52E-F, [1981] 2 All ER 801j, 804b-c.
8. [1982] Fam 49F-G, 52F-G, [1981] 2 All ER 801j-802a, 804c-d.
9. [1982] Fam 51G, [1981] 2 All ER 803g.
10. [1982] Fam 49C-E, [1981] 2 All ER 801g-h.
11. *Cameron v Treasury Solicitor* [1996] 2 FLR 716.
12. *Brill v Proud* [1984] Fam Law 59; *Cameron v Treasury Solicitor* [1996] 2 FLR 716.

damages)[13] Singer J regarded it as axiomatic that if periodical payments were not ordered on divorce, a claim under the 1975 Act would fail and that accordingly a section 15 order should be made.

It is clear that *Re Fullard* with its emphasis upon the deceased's obligations towards the applicant *during his lifetime*[14] and the need to show a really significant change of circumstances between the date of divorce and the date of death,[15] has overruled previous authorities which had adopted the 'two bites at the cherry' approach. In both *Re S*[16] and *Re M*[17] it was held that the absence of a duty to maintain a former spouse while alive was neither an absolute bar to an order for provision nor a matter controlling the exercise of the court's discretion to bar an application for provision. Although neither *Re S* nor *Re M* was cited to the Court of Appeal in *Re Fullard,* the clear ratio of *Re Fullard* must be taken as having implicitly overruled them.

No Proper Settlement of Financial Matters on Divorce

It is submitted that if there has not been a proper settlement of financial matters on divorce, the absence of any continuing financial obligation upon the deceased or of any really significant change of circumstances will not prevent an applicant from being awarded provision. While *Re Fullard* rejected the 'two bites at the cherry' approach, it did not in any way reject the proposition that the 'one bite' should be a proper one.

It is implicit in the judgment of Ormrod LJ emphasising the enlargement over time of the divorce court's powers in ancillary matters,[18] that a settlement of financial matters made prior to the coming into force of the Matrimonial Proceedings and Property Act 1970 might not be regarded as a final settlement of the obligations stemming from the marriage. It must however be pointed out that the deficiency in the court's powers prior to 1970 was in regard to its inability to transfer property and a former spouse's claim for family provision is limited to maintenance.

13. [1995] 2 FLR 171, at 187E-188E.
14. See the remarks of Ormrod LJ at [1982] Fam 50D-F, [1981] 2 All ER 802e-g set out at pp 265–266, *ante.*
15. [1982] Fam 49F-G, [1981] 2 All ER 801j-802a (per Ormrod LJ); [1982] Fam 52F, [1981] 2 All ER 804c-d (per Purchas J).
16. [1965] P 165, at 170A-171F, [1965] 1 All ER 1018, at 1021E-1022I (per Cairns J).
17. [1968] P 174, at 179G-180A, [1967] 3 All ER 412, at 416E-H (per Stirling J).
18. [1982] Fam 45C-46B, [1981] 2 All ER 798f-799b set out at pp 254–255, *ante.*

The absence of an application for ancillary relief on divorce *may* be a sufficient reason for making an award of provision. But it must be remembered that just as the court's decision to treat a former spouse as a spouse under section 14 is by no means automatic,[19] so the failure of a spouse to pursue a claim for ancillary relief does not necessarily indicate that it is unreasonable for the deceased not to have made provision for the applicant.[20] In *Re Fullard*[1] although there was no actual determination by the court of the application for ancillary relief, this was because the applicant was properly advised that the agreement reached was the best obtainable in the circumstances. *Re W*[2] a decision of Rees J in 1975 under section 26 of the Matrimonial Causes Act 1965, is an example of where the court rightly took into account the failure to apply for ancillary relief on divorce. The deceased and the applicant married in 1934 and were divorced in 1946. On divorce the applicant wife did not apply for maintenance because she was advised that no maintenance would be awarded as she was earning more than the deceased. In fact the deceased was very careful not to reveal to the applicant the full extent of his wealth. He did at one stage agree to pay the applicant £12 per month, but he only made two or three payments. He died in 1972, leaving an estate of at least £28,000 and making in his will no provision for the applicant. Rees J awarded the applicant £11,000 from the estate and stressed that the deceased had never revealed his true means to the applicant and that he had been able to build up his estate partly because he had not been obliged to maintain the applicant.[3]

The principle of a 'clean break' does not apply to cases where the agreement is manifestly unfair to one party or where it has been obtained as a result of fraud or unfair bargaining procedures.[4] A

19. See p 71, *ante*.
20. An example is the case of *Re Legat* (2 May 1980, unreported) where although there had been no settlement of matters of divorce, Dillon J held that in the circumstances and paying particular regard to the means of the applicant it was not reasonable to award a former wife provision.
1. [1982] Fam 42, at 49B-C, 51F-H, [1981] 2 All ER 796, at 801f, 803f-g.
2. (1975) Times, 21 April, 116 Sol Jo 218; see also *Re M* [1968] P 174, [1967] 3 All ER 412; *Lusternik v Lusternik* [1972] Fam 125, at 133C, [1972] 1 All ER 592, at 597a-b.
3. Compare *Re Sanderson* (1963) Times, 2 November; *Re Milliken* [1966] NI 68.
4. Viscount Dilhorne in *Minton v Minton* [1979] AC 593, at 601E-F, [1979] 1 All ER 79, at 81c-d referred to the court being 'satisfied that adequate or generous provision has been consented to'. See also the courts' attitude to approving agreements negotiated between the parties, *Dean v Dean* [1978] Fam 161, [1978] 3 All ER 758; *Backhouse v Backhouse* [1978] 1 WLR 243, [1978] 1 All ER 1158; *Ladbrook v Ladbrook* (1977) 7 Fam Law 213; *Edgar v Edgar* [1980] 1 WLR 1410, [1980] 3 All ER 887.

consent order can be challenged and set aside if obtained by misrepresentation or non-disclosure.[5] Where a final settlement of financial matters after divorce can be so challenged, the court may award provision in favour of a former spouse. Any misrepresentation or non-disclosure must have been material and have affected the terms of the consent order – moreover the court must be satisfied that at the date of the hearing under the 1975 Act application it remains reasonable for the applicant to be awarded provision. In *Brill v Proud*[6] it was alleged that the deceased had failed to disclose in an application for ancillary relief the existence of an insurance policy upon the life of the deceased maintained by his employers and that this enabled his former wife to be awarded provision. The Court of Appeal rejected this argument holding that the value of the policy at the date of the ancillary relief hearing would have been small and would not have affected the order made which was already generous to the former wife and that in any event it was doubtful whether the former wife had a sufficient claim to provision bearing in mind her means and the claims of the beneficiary under the estate.

But in such cases it must be remembered that family provision proceedings are not appeals from hearings of applications for ancillary relief on divorce. Family provision for former spouses is limited to reasonable provision *for their maintenance*[7] assessed on the facts known at the date of the hearing.[8] Except perhaps in fixing an upper limit[9] the *source* of an obligation is no guide to the *quantum* of an award of maintenance. In *Re W*[10] and certain cases under the 1938 Act of applications by spouses[11] the courts appear to have awarded applicants provision in excess of what is needed for their maintenance in order to compensate them for the deceased's wrongful failure to maintain them while alive. In *Re W* the applicant aged 75 was awarded £11,000 in 1975. While such practice is justified with applications by spouses under the 1975 Act when provision can be awarded in excess of maintenance, it is submitted that in other cases such an approach is incorrect as it mistakes the source of the obligation with the measure of relief.

5. *Re M* [1968] P 174, [1967] 3 All ER 412. On the jurisdiction generally to set aside consent orders see *Thwaite v Thwaite* [1982] Fam 1, [1981] 2 All ER 789; *Livesey v Jenkins* [1985] AC 424, [1985] 1 All ER 106.
6. [1984] Fam Law 59.
7. S 1(2)(b).
8. S 3(5).
9. See pp 282–285, *post*.
10. (1975) Times, 21 August, 116 Sol Jo 218.
11. *Re Sanderson* (1963) Times, 2 November; *Re Milliken* [1966] NI 68.

Contact Between the Former Spouse and the Deceased after Divorce

In certain cases considerable regard has been paid to acts of affection and other contact between the parties after divorce.[12] These can be criticised in that the Act only permits former spouses to apply and does not permit friends or girlfriends to apply.[13] Regard must be had to the totality of the deceased's obligations and while pre-marital cohabitation *may* be taken into account in assessing the mutual obligations of the parties to a marriage,[14] on divorce it has been held that post-marital relations may not be taken into account.[15] Just as pre-marital cohabitation takes many forms and does not involve the same degree of commitment as marriage,[16] so post-marital relations do not involve the same degree of obligation as marriage and, if post-marital relations are taken into account, they should not be equated with marriage.

It may be that the court may pay regard to the parties' relations after marriage. Such cases may be some of the limited number of cases in which Ormrod LJ considered that a former husband had a moral obligation to provide for a former wife.[17] But such post-marital relations should only be taken into account if they significantly affect the applicant, such as the incurring of a substantial detriment by giving up a job or employment opportunities.[18] The activities should be referable to the marriage, such as a reconciliation[19] or caring for the children of the marriage[20]

12. *Re Bellman* [1963] P 239, [1963] 1 All ER 513; *Lusternik v Lusternik* [1972] Fam 125, [1972] 1 All ER 592 and see also the facts of *Escritt v Escritt* (1981) 3 FLR 280.
13. Compare *Hewitson v Hewitson* [1995] Fam 100, at 106C-D, 108A-B, [1995] 1 All ER 472, at 477b-c, 478h-j.
14. *Kokosinski v Kokosinski* [1980] Fam 72, [1980] 1 All ER 1106; *Foley v Foley* [1981] Fam 160, [1981] 2 All ER 857.
15. In *Hewitson v Hewitson* [1995] Fam 100, at 108A-B, [1995] 1 All ER 472, at 478h Balcombe LJ stated, 'cohabitation subsequent to an English divorce is not a basis for the English court to grant *matrimonial* financial relief' (emphasis supplied) and all three Lord Justices specifically doubted *S v S (financial provision: post-divorce cohabitation)* [1994] 2 FLR 228.
16. *Foley v Foley* [1981] Fam 160, at 167F-H, [1981] 2 All ER 857, at 861e-g.
17. *Re Fullard* [1982] Fam 42, at 50D-F, [1981] 2 All ER 796, at 802g set out at pp 255–256, *ante*.
18. *Re Bellman* [1963] P 239, at 244, [1963] 1 All ER 513, at 516H-I; *Escritt v Escritt* (1981) 3 FLR 280.
19. *Re Bellman* [1963] P 239, at 244, [1963] 1 All ER 513, at 516H-I; *Escritt v Escritt* (1981) 3 FLR 280.
20. *Re Bellman* [1963] P 239, [1963] 1 All ER 513.

and no attention should be paid to acts of mere friendship or relations purely of convenience.[1]

This line of cases needs to be re-examined in the light of the decision of the Court of Appeal in *Hewitson v Hewitson*[2] which was a decision under Part III of the Matrimonial and Family Proceedings Act 1984 as to whether to allow an application for ancillary relief in England following a foreign divorce. A married couple were divorced in California and by consent a 'clean break' order was made in California. Subsequently the parties moved to England where they cohabited. In emphatic terms the Court of Appeal held that the wife would not be granted leave under Part III of the Matrimonial and Family Proceedings Act 1984 and stated that a divorced spouse had no greater rights arising from cohabitation outside marriage than did a person who had never been married.[3] *Hewitson v Hewitson* was applied by Holman J in the case of *Hill v Hill*.[4] In this case the parties divorced in 1969 and there was a comprehensive consent order disposing of all capital claims. However, within six months of the decree absolute, the parties resumed cohabitation and indeed cohabited for 25 years. Upon the parties ceasing to cohabit, the wife attempted to set aside the consent order on the basis of *Barder v Calvori*.[5] Holman J refused the application and following *Hewitson v Hewitson* stated that post-divorce cohabitation was not a ground for setting aside a settlement of claims for ancillary relief.[6] The

1. Compare *Lusternik v Lusternik* [1972] Fam 125, at 133B, [1972] 1 All ER 592, at 597a. In *Re Legat* (2 May 1980, unreported) Dillon J did not regard the applicant providing the deceased with rent-free accommodation for one year well after the divorce as of any siginificance. In *Cameron v Treasury Solicitor* [1996] 2 FLR 716, at 720C-D 'the continuing friendship' of the applicant and the deceased after divorce was held to be irrelevant.
2. [1995] Fam 100, [1995] 1 All ER 472.
3. All members of the court rested their judgments upon the lack of availability of a relief being granted after an English divorce, as opposed to questions of international comity. All members of the Court of Appeal specifically disapproved *S v S (financial provision) (post-divorce cohabitation)* [1994] 2 FLR 228. The House of Lords refused leave to appeal, see [1995] Fam 108C.
4. [1997] 1 FLR 730.
5. [1988] AC 20, [1987] 2 All ER 440.
6. But query whether *Hewitson v Hewitson* and *Hill v Hill* can ever be totally determinative of applications under the 1975 Act. Since both s 1(1)(ba) and s 1(1)(e) are defined to exclude former spouses, and since it can not have been the intention of Parliament that former spouses are to be in a worse position than non-former spouses, it is submitted that where post-divorce events would otherwise bring a former spouse within s 1(1)(ba) or s 1(1)(e) then they should be able to be awarded provision. Note that under s 1(1)(ba) and s 1(1)(e) the cohabitation or financial dependency must exist 'immediately before the death of the deceased'.

decision of Holman J was reversed by the Court of Appeal,[6a] which held that on divorce regard could be had to post-divorce cohabitation and thereby left the authority of *Hewitson v Hewitson* in a state of considerable uncertainty.

A Significant Change of Circumstances between the Date of Divorce and the Date of Death

The Court of Appeal in *Re Fullard*[7] suggested that a significant improvement in the value of the deceased's estate between the date of divorce and the date of death *might* be a reason for awarding a former spouse provision. Ormrod LJ said that provision might be awarded 'where a substantial capital fund was unlocked by the death of the deceased, such as insurance or pension policies'.[8] Purchas J agreed and further developed these views.[9]

It is clear that the mere existence of an increase in the value of the deceased's estate is not a sufficient reason for awarding provision and the court must always be satisfied that it is reasonable in all the circumstances to order provision. Purchas J stated that provision would be ordered:

> ... where the death itself unlocks a substantial capital sum of which the testator should have been aware, and from which, had he made a will at the time immediately before his death, *he ought, within the criteria of the Act, have made some provision.*[10]

It seems likely that the capital must be capital which did not exist at the date of the divorce. The use of the word 'unlock' by both judges[11] and the examples given of insurance and pension policies[12] indicate that the capital should arise on death. Purchas J specifically states that death is generally not a sufficient change of circumstances between the date of the divorce and the date of death to justify an award of provision.[13] Therefore the mere release of capital which had been used to support the deceased during his lifetime, such as

6a. [1997] Fam Law 657.
7. [1982] Fam 42, [1981] 2 All ER 796.
8. [1982] Fam 49F, [1981] 2 All ER 801j-802a.
9. [1982] Fam 52F-G, [1981] 2 All ER 804c-e.
10. [1982] Fam 52F-G, [1981] 2 All ER 804c-d (emphasis added).
11. [1982] Fam 49F-G, 52F-G, [1981] 2 All ER 801j-802a, 804c-d.
12. [1982] Fam 49F-G, [1981] 2 All ER 801j-802a.
13. [1982] Fam 52D, [1981] 2 All ER 804d.

investments which provided the deceased with an income and the house in which he lived, would not justify an award of provision.

It may be doubted whether the remarks of Purchas J represent the last word on this subject. In principle it would appear that where on divorce no lump sum or periodical payments was ordered because of the lack of means of the deceased, the subsequent release of funds on death *should be* be a reason for awarding a spouse provision and it is difficult in this situation to justify any distinction between assets in existence at the date of divorce, such as a house occupied by the deceased or investments used to support the deceased, and assets becoming available on death. Of course such cases are likely to be relatively rare, since if a former spouse has a *strong enough* case for a periodical payments order or a property adjustment order a court on divorce is likely to make such an order even at the cost of disturbing the deceased's occupation of a dwellinghouse or causing him to dispose of income producing investments. There is no guidance in the authorities to the approach of the court to nominal order for periodical payments.[14]

In *Brill v Proud* [15]the Court of Appeal held emphatically that the payment of insurance monies on death did not enable a former wife who had consented to a 'clean break' order to obtain provision.

In *Re Fullard* Purchas J stated that the mere accretion of wealth to the deceased's estate between the date of divorce and the date of death would not justify an award of provision.[16] These dicta must be taken to have overruled the contrary remarks of Lane J in *Eyre v Eyre*[17] at first instance, which were not cited to the Court of Appeal.

14. In *Re Fullard* Purchas J stated that although there had been no technical abandonment of the applicant's claim for periodical payments, the absence of any substantial order for periodical payments made it not unreasonable that the deceased made no provision for the applicant ([1982] Fam 51H-52B, [1981] 2 All ER 803g-j). This may infer that the existence of a nominal order for periodical payments is of no significance. In *Whiting v Whiting* [1988] 2 FLR 189 the Court of Appeal refused to terminate a nominal order for periodical payments in favour of the wife and at the same time refused to make a s 15 order against the wife. This might suggest that a nominal order for periodical payments *may* justify an award under the 1975 Act. In *Walker v Walker* (10 May 1988, unreported), CA an order for substantial periodical payments was made on divorce, but was subsequently suspended. A large part of the estate of the deceased consisted of the proceeds of insurance policies. The former spouse's application under the 1975 Act was dismissed on the basis of the superior claims of the second wife and the considerable means of the applicant and there was no discussion of the significance of the suspended order for periodical payments.
15. [1984] Fam Law 59.
16. [1982] Fam 52F-G, [1981] 2 All ER 804d.
17. [1968] 1 WLR 530, at 543A-C, [1968] 1 All ER 968, at 977I–978A.

Maintenance Payments Made during the Lifetime of the Deceased

Both members of the Court of Appeal in *Re Fullard* stated that if there was a legal obligation upon the deceased to maintain the applicant during his lifetime it might be reasonable to make an order for provision in favour of such spouse.[18] It is likely that most successful applications for provision by former spouses will be made where the former spouse was in receipt of or entitled to receive maintenance payments during the lifetime of the deceased. Most reported cases of applications by former spouses fall into this category.[19] It is clear from some remarks of Purchas J[20] that the form of the order embodying the obligation to maintain is irrelevant. Although the members of the Court of Appeal in *Re Fullard* both spoke of an order for periodic payments or an obligation to maintain,[1] it seems clear by analogy with claims under section 1(1)(e) that the mere provision of maintenance without any obligation to do so may entitle a former spouse to provision.[2]

The general approach of the court to applications by former spouses where they have been or were entitled to receive periodic payments during the lifetime of the deceased is essentially the same as the approach of the court on a variation of an order for periodic payments under the Matrimonial Causes Act 1973.[3] As a general rule the court will, subject to any change of circumstances brought

18. [1982] Fam 49E-F, 50E-G, [1981] 2 All ER 801j, 802f-g per Ormrod LJ, [1982] Fam 52E-F, [1981] 2 All ER 804b-c per Purchas J.
19. *Askew v Askew* [1961] 1 WLR 725, [1961] 2 All ER 60; *Talbot v Talbot* [1962] 1 WLR 1113, [1962] 3 All ER 174; *Re Bellman* [1963] P 239, [1963] 1 All ER 513; *Roberts v Roberts* [1965] 1 WLR 560, [1964] 3 All ER 503; *Re F* (1965) 109 Sol Jo 212; *Eyre v Eyre* [1968] 1 WLR 530, [1968] 1 All ER 968; *Re Harker-Thomas* [1969] P 28, [1968] 3 All ER 17; *Lusternik v Lusternik* [1972] Fam 125, [1972] 1 All ER 592; *Re Shanahan* [1973] Fam 1, [1971] 3 All ER 873; *Re Crawford* (1983) 4 FLR 273; *Cumming Burns v Burns* (4 July 1985, unreported), CA; *Farrow v Farrow* [1987] 1 FLR 205; *Wallace v Thorburn* (9 October 1987, unreported), CA.
20. [1982] Fam 52E-F, [1981] 2 All ER 804c.
1. [1982] Fam 50E-F, [1981] 2 All ER 802f-g (per Ormrod LJ), [1982] Fam 52E-F, [1981] 2 All ER 804c (per Purchas J)..
2. Compare *Re Harker-Thomas* [1969] P 28, [1968] 3 All ER 17 and *Cumming Burns v Burns* (4 July 1985, unreported), CA both of which involved a maintenance obligation in a separation deed. See pp 43–44 and pp 231–232, *ante*.
3. See the reference to variation of a maintenance agreement in *Re Harker-Thomas* [1969] P 28, at 32D, [1968] 3 All ER 17, at 21F per Latey J. The power to vary such orders is contained in s 31 of the Matrimonial Causes Act 1973. On the exercise of the court's powers under this section see JACKSON AND DAVIES, paras 3.66–3.68.

about by the death of the deceased or otherwise, endeavour to provide the former spouse with the same amount of maintenance after death which she was receiving before death. In *Eyre v Eyre* Lane J said:

> As to the former wife receiving as much after as before the death of the husband: assuming that her needs and her means apart from the estate remain as they were before the husband's death, and assuming further that the net estate is sufficient for the purpose, then, to my mind, it is reasonable that she should continue to receive the same provision as that agreed or found to be appropriate during the husband's lifetime.[4]

It is submitted that this approach has been confirmed and strengthened by Ormrod LJ's narrow definition of the deceased's obligations to a former spouse put forward in *Re Fullard*[5] and the general emphasis in *Re Fullard* on the continuity of the deceased's obligations before and after death. It must however be remembered that the words of the Act give the court a very free hand, changes of circumstances taken into account by the court are not limited to those brought about by death and that the jurisdiction to vary an order for periodic payments under the Matrimonial Causes Act 1973 is relatively wide.[6] Thus it is possible for a substantial divergence to exist between orders burdening the deceased while alive and after death.[7]

What is not clear on the authorities is the extent to which an order made during the deceased's lifetime creates an estoppel per rem judicata in proceedings for family provision. It is submitted, especially in the light of the link stressed by the Court of Appeal in *Re Fullard*[8] between duties of support before and after death that on general principles a court will be bound to follow or pay considerable respect to[9] a decision as to maintenance made during

4. [1968] 1 WLR 530, at 541F-G, [1968] 1 All ER 968, at 976H; *Re Farrow* [1987] 1 FLR 205, at 211H-212D, 215G-H. But see Eastham J in *Re Crawford* (1982) 4 FLR 273, at 280H-282F.
5. [1982] Fam 50D-F, [1981] 2 All ER 802f-g set out at pp 255–256, *ante*.
6. *Lewis v Lewis* [1977] 1 WLR 409; [1977] 3 All ER 902; JACKSON AND DAVIES para 3. 67.
7. Eg *Talbot v Talbot* [1962] 1 WLR 1113, [1962] 3 All ER 174; *Re Harker-Thomas* [1969] P 28, [1968] 3 All ER 17; *Re W* (1975) Times, 21 April, 116 Sol Jo 218.
8. [1982] Fam 42, [1981] 2 All ER 796.
9. There is no exact identity between duties of support before and after death: see pp 38–41, *ante*. See also *Re Goard* (1962) 106 Sol Jo 721; *Coates v Thomas* [1947] NZLR 779.

the lifetime of the deceased in family provision proceedings where there has been no change of circumstances after death.[10] Of course where there has been a significant change of circumstances between the date of the order and the date of death the court should not be bound by the order.[11] But where the order was based on a matter such as the conduct of the parties, then after the death of the deceased the court cannot go behind the finding as to conduct[12] and award provision ignoring such finding.[13]

It must be borne in mind that death often effects a dramatic change of circumstances, removing the deceased's income from employment as being able to support the former spouse but freeing the deceased's estate from the costs of supporting the deceased. In many cases these factors cancel each other out, but in some situations these factors may result in very dramatic changes between the positions before and after death. Although both members of the Court of Appeal in *Re Fullard*[14] did not regard death as a significant change of circumstances causing the court to vary the arrangements made on divorce, it has already been suggested that this takes too little account of the radical changes often brought about by death.[15] Although most of the reported cases before 1970 resulted in a reduction of the amount payable to the applicant as against the amount payable while alive,[16] this is probably due to the loss of the deceased's income from employment and the effects of estate duty. With the more recent higher levels of inflation and with the introduction of Inheritance Tax, which is less severe on small estates than estate duty, the number of cases in which the court will award applicants more provision than they were receiving before death of

10. See generally, *R v Nottingham Justices ex p Davies* [1981] QB 38, [1980] 2 All ER 775. It is submitted that *Lewis v Lewis* is not an authority to the contrary. On *res judicata* binding a person's estate, see *Halsbury's Laws of England* (4th edn, Reissue) Vol 16, para 990.
11. In *Re Harker-Thomas* [1969] P 28, at 32D, [1968] 3 All ER 17, at 21F the provisions of the separation deed ceased to govern the rights of the parties because of the applicant's increase in wealth, not because of any different view of the parties' conduct.
12. *Coates v Thomson* [1947] NZLR 779.
13. If and in so far the judgment in *Talbot v Talbot* [1962] 1 WLR 1113, [1962] 3 All ER 174 is based upon Baker J taking a different view as to that taken when maintenance was ordered after the decree of nullity of the applicant's conduct it is submitted that it is wrong.
14. [1982] Fam 49F, [1981] 2 All ER 801j per Ormrod LJ, [1982] Fam 52C-D, 52E-G, [1981] 2 All ER 803j-804b, 804c-d per Purchas J.
15. See generally pp 262–263, *ante*.
16. *Askew v Askew* [1961] 1 WLR 725, [1961] 3 All ER 60; *Talbot v Talbot* [1962] 1 WLR 1113, [1962] 3 All ER 174; *Re Bellman* [1963] P 239, [1963] 1 All ER 513; *Roberts v Roberts* [1965] 1 WLR 560, [1964] 3 All ER 503; *Re F* (1965) 109 Sol Jo 212; *Re Harker-Thomas* [1969] P 28, [1968] 3 All ER 17.

he deceased is likely to increase[17] and there have been several more ecent reported cases where the effect of the order has been broadly ɔ replicate provision before death.[18]

The Matrimonial and Family Proceedings Act 1984 introduced new section 25A and section 31(7) of the Matimonial Causes Act 973 which directed the court to have regard to the desirability of miting a former spouse's financial dependence upon the other party ɔ the marriage to a specific period.[19] In principle these provisions hould be applicable to applications by former spouses under the 975 Act, but to date there have been no reported cases specifically onsidering this legislation.[20]

An award of secured periodical payments on divorce[1] which will emain payable after the death of the payer is not regarded *by itself* s a predetermination and limit of a former spouse's entitlement to amily provision.[2] This is partly because it is the usual practice not ɔ award secured provision for more than about half of a spouse's ntitlement to periodical payments.[3]

)isabled, Poor or Aged Former Spouses

: appears clear from the remarks of Ormrod LJ on the limited nature f a deceased's legal and moral obligations towards a former spouse[4] nd the whole decision of *Re Fullard*[5] that by itself the disability, overty or old age of a former spouse does not entitle that spouse ɔ an award of provision. The matter was considered in the case of

7. Eg *Lusternik v Lusternik* [1972] Fam 125, [1972] 1 All ER 592.
8. *Re Crawford* (1982) 4 FLR 273; *Re Farrow* [1987] 1 FLR 205 (a somewhat generous decision).
9. On the operation of these provisions see generally JACKSON AND DAVIES, para 3.9 and RAYDEN, paras 29.75–29.78.
0. In *Re Crawford* (1982) 4 FLR 273 the applicant had applied before the death of the deceased for a variation of the order for periodical payments with a view to obtaining a lump sum on a clean break basis, but the deceased died before the application could be heard. In his judgment Eastham J did not refer to the jurisdiction to award a lump sum in return for a clean break, but the order actually made is compatible with such a jurisdiction.
1. The power to award secured periodic payments is contained in s 23(1)(b) of the Matrimonial Causes Act 1973.
2. *Eyre v Eyre* [1968] 1 WLR 530, at 536C–537C, [1968] 1 All ER 968, at 972H–973E.
3. *Shorthouse v Shorthouse* (1898) 78 LT 687, 79 LT 366; JACKSON AND DAVIES, para 4.13.
4. *Re Fullard* [1982] Fam 42, at 50D-F, [1981] 2 All ER 796, at 802e-g set out at pp 255–256, *ante*.
5. [1982] Fam 42, [1981] 2 All ER 797.

Cameron v Treasury Solicitor[6] where it was held that in a situatio where there had been a clean break on divorce, but no section 1 order, a former spouse who 'suffered from ill-health and was in ve straitened circumstances' was not entitled to provision. Th authority is a strong one in that the Court of Appeal reversed th trial judge, specifically stated that the matter was one of princip and the beneficiary being the Crown taking by way of bona vacant had no possible countervailing claim.

Specific Guidelines

The only guidelines laid down by the 1975 Act specifically f applications by former spouses are in section 3(2), which provid that the court is to have regard to:

(a) the age of the applicant and the duration of the marriage;
(b) the contribution made by the applicant to the welfare of th family of the deceased, including any contribution made b looking after the home or caring for the children.

These two guidelines also apply to applications by spouses[7] and the appear to have no special implications as regards former spouses

Former Spouses whose Marriages have been Annulled

When granting ancillary relief after a decree of nullity, the cour pay more attention to the circumstances of the decree and th conduct of the parties than after a decree of divorce and becaus these circumstances vary considerably no general rule as to th exercise of the powers to grant ancillary relief can be laid down.[8] is suggested that this approach should be adopted when considerin

6. [1996] 2 FLR 716 at 720C-D, 723B. The court consisted of Peter Gibso Butler-Sloss and Thorpe LJJ.
7. For discussion of these guidelines in the context of applications by spouse see pp 184–189, *ante*.
8. JACKSON AND DAVIES, para 3.25. The cases relied upon all pre-date t Matrimonial Proceedings and Property Act 1970, but it is submitted that, wi modifications, the approach of the court after 1970 is essentially the same. C public policy in relation to bigamous marriages, see *Whiston v Whiston* [199 Fam 198; *J v S-T (formerly J) (transsexual: ancillary relief)* [1997] 1 FLR 402

applications for family provision by former spouses whose marriages have been annulled rather than dissolved. The few reported cases on such applications throw no light upon what weight is given to the fact that the applicant's marriage to the deceased was annulled rather than dissolved.[9]

Balancing the Claims of Former Spouses and Spouses

There is no rule that a former spouse and the spouse at the date of death or even between several former spouses should be treated equally in family provision proceedings.[10] The claims of each applicant and beneficiary must be considered on their merits and there is no rule that a deceased must make equal provision for each. This is particularly pertinent under the 1975 Act where a spouse is entitled to a greater standard of provision than a former spouse while the latter might well have had the benefit of a property adjustment or lump sum order on divorce. The matter was well stated by Lane J in *Eyre v Eyre*:[11]

> In my view, there cannot be any general rule that a first wife applying under section 26 [of the Matrimonial Causes Act 1965] should be accorded financial equality with a widow. Even where there is nothing to choose between them so far as conduct is concerned, there are so many other factors to be considered in each case, such as age, health etc., that such a rule to say the least would be of no practical value. The claim of either a former wife or widow may be paramount and many estates may be insufficient to provide adequate maintenance for both.
>
> See *In Re Talbot*[12] [where the former spouse failed in her application] and *Roberts v Roberts*[13] [where the spouse retained more from the estate than the former spouse].

9. *Talbot v Talbot* [1962] 1 WLR 1113, [1962] 3 All ER 174; *Lamberton v Lamberton* (1966) 110 Sol Jo 288, 116 NLJ 697, [1966] CLY 3917.
10. *Eyre v Eyre* [1968] 1 WLR 530, at 537E-541E, [1968] 1 All ER 968, at 973F–976G. See also *Thornley v Palmer* [1969] 1 WLR 1037, [1969] 3 All ER 31. Recent case law shows each case turning on its own facts, *Re Crawford* (1982) 4 FLR 273 (generous provision for first wife, but substantial sums available to second wife through pension etc); *Cumming Burns v Burns* (4 July 1985, unreported), CA (second wife preferred); *Wallace v Thorburn* (9 October 1987, unreported), CA (former wife preferred to friend of the deceased); *Walker v Walker* (10 May 1988, unreported), CA (second wife preferred, first wife had capital payment on divorce).
11. [1968] 1 WLR 530, at 541B–C, [1968] 1 All ER 968, at 976D–E.
12. [1962] 1 WLR 1113, [1962] 3 All ER 174.
13. [1965] 1 WLR 560, [1965] 3 All ER 503.

It is however clear that similarly placed former spouses and spous with similar claims upon the deceased should be treated alike.[14]

Applications by Male Former Spouses

The same principles of equality that apply to applications by widow and widowers[15] apply to applications by male and female forme spouses. It will be rare however that a male former spouse will b able to satisfy a court that on the facts of the case it was unreasonabl for the deceased not to have made provision for him; this i particularly so because the provision ordered on divorce in favou of a husband is invariably of a capital nature and orders for periodica payments – the principal factor justifying an award of famil provision – are rare. There is no reported case of an application fo family provision being made by a male former spouse.

Duration of Orders for Periodical Payments

An order for periodic payments made in favour of a former spous or a spouse whose marriage to the deceased was the subject of decree of judicial separation which was in force and where th 'separation was continuing'[16] or a spouse whose marriage to th deceased was subject to a separation order under the Family Lav Act 1986 in force[17] at the date of death shall cease to have effec upon the remarriage of the applicant.[18] This automati determination cannot be circumvented by applying for a variatio of the order under section 6 so as to convert the order for periodi payments into an order for a lump sum. For the purpose of the 197 Act a person has remarried if he has entered a void or voidabl marriage.[19]

It is thought that a former spouse should not be able t circumvent this limitation by cohabiting with another person withou

14. *Eyre v Eyre* [1968] 1 WLR 530, at 541D, [1968] 1 All ER 968, at 976F; *R Shanahan* [1973] Fam 1, at 9B–E, [1873] 3 All ER 873, at 880e-f.
15. See pp 198–199, *ante*.
16. For the meaning of this expression, see p 66, *ante*.
17. Reference to orders of judicial separation introduced by para 27(7), Sch 8 o the Family Law Act 1996. For the definition of when a separation order is 'i force' see s 2(2) of the Family Law Act 1996.
18. S 19(2).
19. S 25(6).

marrying that person.[20] When exercising their powers under the Matrimonial Causes Act 1973 the courts have rejected the former approach of including a 'dum casta' limitation in any order,[1] because in line with the lesser emphasis now on conduct in divorce law generally it is thought wrong that an isolated act of unlawful sexual intercourse should terminate the order, but have found it difficult to formulate verbally the type of relationship which should be treated as being equivalent to marriage.[2] It is submitted that an order for periodic payments should not be subject to any condition, but that if the former spouse associates with another person an application for variation of the order should be made.[3] Where an order is made for the settlement of specific property, such as giving the applicant an interest determinable upon death or remarriage in a dwellinghouse, a condition should also be imposed determining the interest upon some form of cohabitation with another person. Until the divorce courts adopt a uniform and satisfactory form of words,[4] it is suggested such a condition might be worded to incorporate a statutory definition of cohabitation so as to achieve certainty.[5]

Orders Under Section 15

In their reports on family provision the Law Commission considered that it was wrong for a former spouse with the sanction of the court validly to contract out of the right to maintenance after divorce and not to be able to do so after death. They recommend that the court should have power upon a decree of a divorce, nullity or judicial separation to make an order with the consent of the parties that either party to the marriage should not be able to apply for family provision out of the estate of the other.[6] This recommendation was

20. See *Re Haig* [1979] LS Gaz R 476 per Browne-Wilkinson J. Compare the statutory provisions which provide that a person cannot receive a widowed mother's allowance or a widow's pension if she and a man 'to whom she is not married are living together as husband and wife', s 37(4)(b), s 38(3)(c) of the Social Security Act 1975.
1. RAYDEN, para 29.91; JACKSON AND DAVIES, para 3.14; Hayes, '"Cohabitation Clauses" in Financial Provision and Property Adjustment Orders-Law, Policy and Justice' (1994) 110 LQR 124.
2. See generally Hayes, op cit; RAYDEN, para 29.70; JACKSON AND DAVIES, paras 3.22–3.23. In *Re Haig* [1979] LS Gaz R 476 Browne-Wilkinson J stated that an interest in a house should be determinable upon the applicant who came within s 1(1)(e) 'being maintained by somebody else'.
3. On the power to vary orders for periodical payments, see pp 401–408, *post*.
4. See Hayes, op cit, at 133–138.
5. Perhaps the definition in s 1(1)(ba) could be adopted.

carried into effect by section 15 of the 1975 Act. In its report on the Financial Consequences of Divorce published in December 1981 the Law Commission recommended that on divorce a court should have the power to make a section 15 order without the consent of the parties[7] and this was carried into effect by section 8(1) of the Matrimonial and Family Proceedings Act 1984.

A court can only make an order under section 15 'if it considers it just to do so'.[8] Guidance upon whether the court can make a section 15 order without the consent of a party was given by Balcombe LJ in *Whiting v Whiting*[9] who said:

> ... before the court can consider it just to make an order depriving a divorced spouse of an opportunity to claim financial provision from the estate of the other spouse, it should be given some indication of what the estate is likely to consist of and some details of the persons whom the applicant considers to have a prior claim in the event of his decease.

Balcombe LJ stressed the need for an applicant for a section 15 order to lay an evidential foundation before the court.[10] These remarks were distinguished by Singer J in *C v C (financial provision: personal damages)*[11] who said that they did not apply in a case where the court had dismissed all the applicant's claims for ancillary relief or imposed a 'clean break' and this accords with practice in the divorce courts.

As originally enacted an order under section 15 can be made on the granting of a decree of divorce, nullity or judicial separation 'or at any time thereafter'.[12] An order can be made before the decree of divorce or nullity is made absolute but is only effective when the decree is made absolute.[13] An order made after a decree of judicial separation is only effective if the 'decree is in force and the separation is continuing'.[14]

Following the coming into force of the Family Law Act 1986

6. WORKING PAPER, para 3.68; LAW COM, paras 185–188.
7. LAW COM, No 112, para 45(6).
8. The wording is the same for the original s 15(1), the s 15(1) inserted by s 8(2) of the Matrimonial and Family Proceedings Act 1984 and the s 15(1) inserted by para 27(5), Sch 8 of the Family Law Act 1986.
9. [1988] 2 FLR 189, at 201B-C.
10. [1988] 2 FLR 201D-E.
11. [1995] 2 FLR 171, at 197E-188E. See also *Whiting v Whiting* [1988] 2 FLR 189, at 201D. In *Cameron v Treasury Solicitor* [1996] 2 FLR 716, at 723E-F Thorpe LJ proceeded as if s 15 were made with great frequency after the Matrimonial and Family Proceedings Act 1984.
12. S 15(1).
13. S 15(2).
14. S 15(3); for the meaning of 'the separation is continuing' see p 66, *ante*.

an order can be made at 'any time when the court has jurisdiction under section 23A or 24 of the Matrimonial Causes Act 1973 to make a property adjustment order in relation to that marriage' or would have jurisdiction had it not already been exercised.[15] The order is only effective after the dissolution of the marriage, the decree of nullity has been made absolute or when a separation order is in force and the separation is continuing.[16]

An order under section 15 can be made at 'any time' after a decree of divorce, nullity or judicial separation and a divorce or separation order[17] and need not be made upon a hearing of an application for ancillary relief consequent upon a decree. For example an order under section 15 can be made prior to one former spouse entering into a second marriage even though there is no order for periodic payments subsisting or any other application for ancillary relief pending. A county court having divorce jurisdiction has jurisdiction to make a section 15 order even if it is not ancillary to a divorce proceeding in that county court.[18] An order under section 15 can affect applications by one or both former spouses,[19] but usually the order prohibits applications by both spouses.

An order under section 15 can be set aside on all the grounds for which a contract can be set aside,[20] and because the order is an order of the court the wider powers of the court to set aside matrimonial orders or to allow appeals out of time are available.[1]

The effect of a section 15 order is to totally deprive a court of jurisdiction to consider an application by a former spouse against whom the order is made.[2] It appears that a section 15 order can not be made to apply conditionally in certain circumstances and can only operate as an absolute bar. A section 15 order prevents an application to vary a secured order for periodical payments or a maintenance agreement from being treated as an application under section 2.[3]

It seems clear that if the parties had made an agreement to the

15. S 15(1) inserted by para 27(5), Sch 8 of the Family Law Act 1996.
16. S 15(2) inserted by para 27(6), Sch 8 of the Family Law Act 1996.
17. S 15(1). The words 'at any time' have been unaffected by the successive amendments of s 15. See *Whiting v Whiting* [1988] 2 FLR 189, at 201E for successive applications.
18. S 15(1) inserted by s 8 of the Matrimonial and Family Proceedings Act 1984. Previously the position on jurisdiction was obscure.
19. S 15(1).
20. *Tommey v Tommey* [1983] Fam 15, [1982] 3 All ER 385.
1. RAYDEN, para 49.71. Note in particular the power to appeal or set aside an order after the death of one of the parties, *Barder v Caluori* [1988] AC 20, [1987] 2 All ER 440.
2. S 15(3).
3. S 18(3).

same effect as an order under section 15 the court will give effect to the agreement by refusing an application for provision.[4]

The absence of an order under section 15 does not raise any presumption that a former spouse is entitled to provision and the absence of such an order is rarely a matter which is relevant to the question of whether it was reasonable for the deceased not to have made provision for the applicant. In *Re Fullard* Ormrod LJ said:

> I regard section 15 as a form of insuring against applications under the 1975 Act which some people may very reasonably wish to do having made financial provision of a capital nature for a former spouse. People obviously have other commitments – second wives (or husbands) and children and so forth. I do not regard section 15 as materially affecting the quesion the court has to answer as the condition precedent to these applications.[5]

These remarks were followed by the Court of Appeal in *Cameron v Treasury Solicitor*.[6] Significantly Thorpe LJ stated that more significance should be given to the absence of a section 15 order in situations after the Matrimonial and Family Proceedings Act 1984 came into force, than in situations before when such orders could be made with consent.

Where the court exercises jurisdiction to grant ancillary relief after a foreign divorce under Part III of the Matrimonial and Family Proceedings Act 1984, the court can make an order having the same effect as a section 15 order.[7]

Variation of Secured Periodical Payment Orders and Maintenance Agreements

The powers of the court to vary an order for secured periodical payments or a maintenance agreement after the death of the payee[8] and their interrelation with applications under section 2[9] are dealt

4. *Re Fullard* [1982] Fam 42, [1981] 2 All ER 796; *Brill v Proud* [1984] Fam Law 59; *Cameron v Treasury Solicitor* [1966] 2 FLR 716. See also in the context of ancillary relief, *Sandford v Sandford* [1986] 1 FLR 412; *Hill v Hill* [1997] 1 FLR 730, at 738F-741C.
5. [1982] Fam 50A-B, [1981] 2 All ER 802c-d.
6. [1966] 2 FLR 716.
7. S 15A inserted by s 25(3) of the Matrimonial and Family Proceedings Act 1984. See [1996] 2 FLR 723D-724B.
8. S 31(6), s 36 of the Matrimonial Causes Act 1973.

with in Chapter 9.[10]

PART 5: OTHER DEPENDANTS

The history of the enactment of section 1(1)(e),[11] its interpretation and operation[12] and the policy implications of it[13] have already been discussed at considerable length – a discussion of disproportionate length compared with the class's practical importance. Provision for applicants within section 1(1)(e) is limited to provision for their maintenance.[14] Because the persons who can come within section 1(1)(e) are very diverse – 'kept women',[15] male and female cohabitees,[16] homosexual lovers,[17] sisters[18] and children of mistresses[19] – it is difficult to draw many general conclusions as to what the courts regard as reasonable provision for an applicant within section 1(1)(e).

The Assumption of Responsibility

The only guidance which the 1975 Act specifically gives to considering applications under section 1(1)(e) is contained in section 3(4) which provides:

> Without prejudice to the generality of paragraph (g) of subsection (1) above, where an application for an order under section 2 of the Act is made by virtue of section 1(1)(e) of this Act, the court shall, in addition to the matters specifically mentioned in paragraphs (a) to (f) of that subsection, have regard to the extent to which and the basis upon which the deceased assumed responsibility for the maintenance of the applicant and to the length of time for which the deceased discharged that responsibility.

The implication from this provision made by *Re Beaumont*[20] and

9. S 16, s 17, s 18.
10. See pp 416–417, *post*.
11. See generally pp 78–84, *ante*.
12. See generally pp 84–100, *ante*.
13. See generally pp 100–103, *ante*.
14. S 1(2)(b).
15. Eg *Malone v Harrison* [1979] 1 WLR 1353.
16. Eg *Re Beaumont* [1980] Ch 444, [1980] 1 All ER 266; *Williams v Roberts* [1986] 1 FLR 349.
17. Eg *Wayling v Jones* (1993) 69 P & CR 170, [1995] 2 FLR 1029.
18. Eg *Re Wilkinson* [1978] Fam 22, [1978] 1 All ER 221.
19. Eg *Barnsley v Ward* (18 January 1980, unreported), CA.

approved by *Jelley v Iliffe*[1] that to qualify within section 1(1)(e) an applicant has to show that the deceased assumed a responsibility for the applicant's maintenance has already been discussed.[2] The practical importance of this requirement is substantially diminished by the need only to prove *some kind* of an assumption[3] rather than a total assumption and the presumption that the actual provision of maintenance usually implies an assumption of responsibility.[4] This treatment of an assumption of responsibility as *a qualifying condition* has been unfortunate, because it has tended to divert attention from the more important question as to how the existence and extent of the assumption of the responsibility for the maintenance of the applicant affects the court's decision as to whether reasonable provision has been made. It is suggested that an assumption of responsibility is not a once and for all barrier to be surmounted and then ignored, but is a matter which assumes its real importance as *a* dominant matter to which regard must be had when the court exercises its discretion in determining whether reasonable provision has been made for the applicant and, if not, the amount of provision which the court would order.

The Basis of the Assumption of Responsibility for the Maintenance of the Applicant

This reference to the basis on which the deceased assumed responsibility for the maintenance of the applicant was designed by the Law Commission, inter alia, as a means of preventing a successful application being made when the deceased expressly disclaimed any intention of maintaining the applicant after his death.[5] In *Jelley v Iliffe* Stephenson LJ stated that in order to qualify as an applicant within section 1(1)(e) an applicant did not have to prove positively that the deceased's assumption of responsibility for maintenance extended to the period after the deceased's death. He said:

> ... there is, in my judgment, a distinction to be drawn between an

20. [1980] Ch 444, [1980] 1 All ER 266.
1. [1981] Fam 128, [1981] 2 All ER 29.
2. See pp 94–100, *ante*.
3. See p 97, *ante*.
4. *Jelley v Iliffe* [1981] Fam 128, at 137B-C, [1981] 2 All ER 29, at 35e (per Stephenson LJ).
5. LAW COM, para 91.

> intention to maintain during the lifetime of the giver ... and an intention to provide continuing support after death ... If it is necessary, or relevant, to prove an intention on the part of the deceased to maintain a dependant, qualified to apply under section 1(1)(e), after the deceased's death, the only case in which there will be the required qualification will be those where the deceased's intention has been defeated by accident, eg by his dying intestate and leaving children or having made an invalid will in the dependant's favour.
>
> I do not read the Act as expressing so limited a legislative intention. Its object is surely to remedy, wherever reasonably possible, the injustice of one who has been put by a deceased person in a position of dependency upon him being deprived of any financial support, either by accident or design of the deceased, after his death. To leave a dependant, to whom no legal or moral obligation is owed, unprovided for after death may not entitle the dependant to much, or indeed any financial provision in all the circumstances, but he is not disentitled from applying for such provision if he can prove that the deceased by his conduct made him dependent for maintenance whether intentionally or not.[6]

It is clear that the absence of any assumption of responsibility for the applicant's maintenance after the deceased's death is *a* relevant matter when the court has to decide whether reasonable provision has been made for the applicant. In his tentative discussion of the merits in *Jelley v Iliffe* Stephenson LJ comments that the deceased's desire in her will that her house should go to her children who had previously surrendered their interest in remainder in the house was an important factor tending to show that the application would fail or only result in a small award.[7]

The regard which the court pays to an assumption of responsibility for the applicant's maintenance after the deceased's death leads to a considerable regard being paid to the deceased's intentions[8] and to a degree of subjectivity[9] in deciding what is reasonable provision for the particular applicant. Thus if a deceased dies intestate or leaves a will made before the applicant became dependent upon him, an application under section 1(1)(e) may be more likely to succeed than if the deceased dies leaving a will made

6. [1981] Fam 128, at 137G–138B, [1981] 2 All ER 29, at 36a-c; see also at [1981] Fam 139E–F, [1981] 2 All ER 37c-d and *Re Haig*, Browne-Wilkinson J [1979] LS Gaz R 476.
7. [1981] Fam 140D–F, [1981] 2 All ER 37j-38b.
8. On the relevance of the deceased's intentions generally see pp 47–48 and pp 162–163, *ante*.
9. See Davies, 'Inheritance (Provision for Family and Dependants) Act 1975 – Subjective or Objective Test', (1978) 75 LS Gaz 1005.

at a time when the claims of the applicant were before him, because such a will is *evidence* that any assumption of responsibility for maintenance ceased on death.[10] The exact weight to be attached to the contrary provisions of a will as evidence of only a limited assumption of responsibility is very uncertain. Stephenson LJ in *Jelley v Iliffe* appeared to consider that on the facts of the case the provisions of the deceased's will as evidence militating against an assumption of responsibility for maintenance after death were strong evidence but not conclusive of the matter.[11] In *Re Haig*[12] on the other hand, a case on not dissimilar facts, Browne-Wilkinson J paid only a limited amount of attention to the provisions of the deceased's will, made at the time the parties began to cohabit, leaving all his estate away from the applicant, but there was also some evidence dehors the will that the deceased wished the applicant to remain in his house for the rest of her life.

Because the factual situations in applications under section 1(1)(e) are so varied and reported cases so few, it is difficult to draw any general conclusions as to the court's classification of the bases on which the deceased assumed responsibility for the applicant's maintenance. However, sufficient reported cases do exist on claims by mistresses to offer some insight into the court's general approach. In *Malone v Harrison*[13] where the deceased insisted that the applicant was to be virtually at his continual beck and call and where he provided her with all she reasonably wanted, the deceased was held to have assumed a total responsibility for her maintenance. The deceased manifested an assumption to maintain the applicant after his death by omitting her from his will, but sending her a newspaper cutting discussing the enactment of the 1975 Act.[14] In *Re Haig*[15] Browne-Wilkinson J considered the nature of the deceased's assumption of responsibility at some length. He said that in the absence of any express agreement as to the basis on which the parties lived together:

> ... the regard [must be had] to the basis on which they actually lived together as indicating the nature of the responsibility which the deceased assumed.

10. Compare *Wayling v Jones* (1995) 69 P & CR 170, [1995] 2 FLR 1029 where the deceased had made a will devising a particular property to the applicant, but which devise had been adeemed.
11. [1981] Fam 128, at 137G–138B, [1981] 2 All ER 29, at 36a-c set out above.
12. [1979] LS Gaz R 476.
13. [1979] 1 WLR 1353.
14. [1979] 1 WLR 1359E-F, 1365D.
15. [1979] LS Gaz R 476.

Browne-Wilkinson J held that although there was no express agreement that the deceased would maintain the applicant after his death, and although the refusal of the deceased to marry the applicant and the provisions of his will implied that the deceased's obligations after his death to the applicant were limited, the circumstances of their cohabitation, which entailed the applicant giving up her own home, and during which the deceased maintained her, implied some sort of an assumption of a responsibility for the deceased's maintenance, particularly the provision of accommodation, after his death.

In *Rhodes v Dean*[16] the deceased and the applicant cohabited. Micklem J sitting as a judge of the Chancery Division found that the deceased had assumed a responsibility for the applicant's accommodation, but not for her general living expenses, and dismissed her application because the proceeds of a joint bank account were sufficient to meet her needs for accommodation. Judge Micklem reached this conclusion partly on the basis of the deceased's express statements, partly on evidence that the parties had chosen not to marry and to retain certain aspects of living as single people,[17] and partly on the basis of the level of provision provided before death. The Court of Appeal refused to interfere.

The Length of Time for which the Deceased Discharged the Responsibility for the Applicant's Maintenance

The court is required to have regard to the length of time for which the deceased discharged any responsibility for the applicant's maintenance. The length of time during which the deceased maintained the applicant can be evidence that the deceased assumed responsibility for the applicant's maintenance to a large extent. For example, in *Malone v Harrison*[18] the provision of maintenance for twelve years was evidence that the deceased's involvement with the applicant was not a passing fancy and that there was a significant assumption of responsibility.

Similarly the Court of Appeal in *Re Dymott*[19] regarded the provision of maintenance for only six months of a relationship

16. Court of Appeal, 28 March 1996. Conversely in *Re P*, Halsbury's Laws Monthly Review, para 96/369 it was held that the deceased had assumed an obligation to provide living expenses, but not accommodation.
17. Compare *H v G and D* (1980) 10 Fam Law 98.
18. [1979] 1 WLR 1353.
19. [1980] CA Transcript 942.

between the applicant and the deceased which subsisted for four years as *a* factor negativing an assumption of responsibility by the deceased.

It is suggested that this specific reference to the length of time that the deceased maintained the applicant, borrowed from divorce law provisions relating to children of the family,[20] (and repeated in the legislation allowing cohabitees to claim)[1] is misconceived. The only relevance of the length of time for which maintenance was provided is as *evidence* of the basis on which the deceased assumed responsibility for the applicant's maintenance. In itself the length of time during which the deceased maintained the applicant is of no significance.[2] Considerable care should be taken by the courts to ensure that too much regard is not had to the mere length of the applicant's dependence. An example of a correct approach to the length of the applicant's dependency is *Graham v Murphy*.[3] Here the judge expressly took into account not only the nine years dependency, but also the nine years previous non-dependent cohabitation and the applicant's caring for the deceased during her final illness.

Provision is Discretionary

An award of provision to any class of applicant by a court is discretionary – in each case a court must be satisfied that the dispositions of the deceased's estate were unreasonable in not making provision for the applicant and this decision will frequently require that the claims of one applicant be balanced against the claims of beneficiaries and other applicants. Bearing in mind that the giving of financial support rarely imposes any obligation upon the donor, one would expect that reported cases would reveal judges frequently exercising their discretion against applicants within section 1(1)(e). However, reported cases evince a judicial reluctance

20. S 25(3)(a) of the Matrimonial Causes Act 1973 as originally enacted, s 25(4)(a) as substituted by the Matrimonial and Family Proceedings Act 1984.
1. S 3(2A)(a) inserted by Law Reform (Succession) Act 1995.
2. See generally the instructive analysis in RAYDEN, para 29.56. Compare the remarkable case of *Re P* Halsburys Laws Monthly Review, para 96/369 where the relationship lasted only 19 months, but the District Judge awarded the applicant a lump sum of £101,500. Quaere if the parties had been married, whether a court would have awarded the applicant as much on divorce – compare *S v S* [1977] Fam 127, [1977] 1 All ER 56 with *Robertson v Robertson* (1982) 4 FLR 387.
3. [1997] 1 FLR 860.

to deprive qualified applicants of an award of provision. In *Re Viner*[4] Master Chamberlain made an award to an applicant to whose support the deceased had unwillingly contributed and to whom it is hard to see that he owed any moral obligation whatsoever. In *Malone v Harrison*[5] Hollings J rejected an argument that the applicant had already received enough money from the deceased and so should not be awarded any further provision, an argument implicitly premised on the basis that a 'kept woman' was not a worthy applicant. In contrast to this in *Kourkgy v Lusher*[6] Wood J indicated *obiter* that if the applicant had come within section 1(1)(e), he would not have made any award, a decision not totally premised on the superior competing claims of the widow, but also premised on the mistress's own resources and on a disapproval of her general conduct towards the deceased. Similarly in *Jelley v Iliffe*[7] Stephenson LJ indicated, again *obiter*, that at any trial the applicant might be awarded nothing in the exercise of the court's discretion and Ormrod LJ made a similar *obiter* remark in *Re Dymott*.[8] In *Rhodes v Dean*[9] Micklem J having held that the applicant came within section 1(1)(e), dismissed her application upon the basis that the deceased had made reasonable provision for the application through a joint bank account.

The repeal of the original section 25(1) of the Matrimonial Causes Act 1973 exhorting the divorce court to place the parties in the position in which they would be if the marriage had continued,[10] the enactment of provisions directing the court to consider 'rehabilitation only' maintenance on divorce[11] and the very modest provision often awarded to spouses after very short marriages[12] should be borne in mind by courts when exercising their discretion in applications made under section 1(1)(e). It would be quite wrong for a mistress claiming on death to obtain more than a wife claiming on divorce.[13] A good illustration of these principles in action is the

4. [1978] CLY 3091.
5. [1979] 1 WLR 1353, at 1365E.
6. (1981) 4 FLR 65, at 82B-C. Compare the cases of *Re Coventry* [1980] Ch 461, [1979] 2 All ER 604, [1979] 3 All ER 815; *Re Fergusson* Foster J (16 June 1980, unreported), CA where the courts dismissed claims by adult children who were financially dependent upon the deceased.
7. [1981] Fam 128, at 140D-F, [1981] 2 All ER 29, at 37h-38b.
8. [1980] CA Transcript 942.
9. (28 March 1996, unreported), CA.
10. Repealed by the Matrimonial and Family Proceedings Act 1984.
11. S 25A(3) of the Matrimonial Causes Act 1973, inserted by s 3 of the Matrimonial and Family Proceedings Act 1984.
12. Eg *Robertson v Robertson* (1982) 4 FLR 387.
13. Compare *Re P*, Halsburys Laws Monthly Review, para 96/369.

case of *Graham v Murphy.*[14] Here the applicant had been dependent upon his deceased mistress for free accommodation and additional benefits for nine years and during this period had a 'high standard of living'. The applicant was employed at a relatively modest wage. Robert Walker J held that the applicant was not entitled to 'a particularly high standard of living for the rest of his life' and awarded him a lump sum of £35,000 to enable him to purchase with the assistance of a small mortgage a 'modest house or a flat in a less expensive area'.

In exercising its discretion, the court must consider in addition to the claims of the applicant, the competing claims of other applicants and beneficiaries in the estate. It is submitted that the claims of an applicant within section 1(1)(e) who relies upon the provision of maintenance and an assumption of responsibility for the applicant's maintenance *simpliciter* are entitled to very little regard when compared with the competing claims of those for whom the deceased had while alive a legal duty of support. A relatively large award was permissible in *Malone v Harrison*[15] because the deceased's estate was sufficiently large to satisfy quite adequately all the competing claims upon the deceased. An award to the mistress applicant in *CA v CC*[16] was justified, although the estate was relatively small and the competing claims of a legitimate and illegitimate child were exceptionally strong, because the applicant had in addition to having been maintained by the deceased, given away her own child at the deceased's request and borne the deceased a child. In *Kourkgy v Lusher*[17] Wood J clearly considered that the claims of the widow were much greater than those of the applicant mistress.

Is Reasonable Provision for a Class (e) Applicant Limited to the Amount of Maintenance Received by the Applicant during the Deceased's Lifetime?

It has not been decided whether reasonable provision for an applicant within section 1(1)(e) is limited to the amount of provision

14. [1997] 1 FLR 860. The estate was £240,000 and the applicant was aged 54 at the date of the trial.
15. [1979] 1 WLR 1353.
16. (1978) Times, 17 November, *sub nom Re C* 123 Sol Jo 35, *sub nom In The Estate of McC* 9 Fam Law 26.
17. (1981) 4 FLR 65.

actually received by the applicant prior to the deceased's death or to the amount of the assumption of responsibility for the maintenance of the applicant. The argument that it is so limited is that an award of provision should reflect the sole reason – actual provision by the deceased when alive – enabling the application to be made. This argument is to some extent strengthened by the emphasis in *Re Fullard*[18] on the relevance of the deceased's duties of support before death to family provision proceedings. The contrary argument is that the Act refers to 'reasonable provision' for the applicant's maintenance generally and there is no statutory indication that an award of provision for an applicant within section 1(1)(e) should be on any different basis to that for any other class of applicant. Section 3(4) provides that a court 'shall have *regard*'[19] to the extent of the actual maintenance provided, which would seem to imply that the court is not totally bound by the amount of actual maintenance.[20]

In *Jelley v Iliffe*[1] Stephenson LJ appeared to have regarded the limited amount of the applicant's net dependency upon the deceased as *a* reason why the applicant would very likely be awarded nothing or very little. There are several reported cases in which provision was ordered on a basis either compatible or incompatible with a limitation of provision to the amount of the maintenance or the assumption of responsibility, but in none is there any clear discussion of the point.[2]

In *Harrington v Gill*[3] Dunn LJ stated that:

18. [1982] Fam 42, [1981] 2 All ER 796.
19. Emphasis added.
20. But compare the interpretation of s 3(4) as imposing *a requirement* that the deceased assumed responsibility for the applicant's maintenance adopted in *Re Beaumont* [1980] Ch 444, [1980] 1 All ER 266 and *Jelley v Iliffe* [1981] Fam 128, [1981] 2 All ER 29.
1. [1981] Fam 128, at 140D-F, [1981] 2 All ER 29, at 37h-38a.
2. In *Re Viner* [1978] CLY 3091 Master Chamberlain expressly stated that the award of provision was limited to the amount of maintenance before death (see further Davies, 'Inheritance (Provision for Family and Dependants) Act 1975 – Subjective or Objective Test', (1978) 75 LS Gaz 1005. Conversely in *Re Dr Kozdrach, Sobesto v Farren* [1981] Conv 224, CA there was an obiter dictum of Lord Denning MR and a subsequent award at trial by Ewbank J of a sum probably well in excess of the amount of lifetime maintenance. The approval by Thorpe LJ in *Wells v Wells* [1997] 1 WLR 652, at 682F, [1997] 1 All ER 673, at 701f-g of *Duxbury* calculations being used in applications under s 1(1)(e) and of the decision of *Nott v Ward* Judge Bromley QC (13 December 1994, uneported) does suggest that the prima facie award for an applicant under s 1(1)(e) is to reflect the amount of maintenance being received before death.
3. (1983) 4 FLR 265, at 271B-C.

> ... the relevance of section 4(3) is that, in considering reasonable requirements or reasonable financial provision under section 1(1) the court will, *amongst other things,* consider the extent to which the deceased has undertaken responsibility for the maintenance of the plaintiff, that is to say, the court will consider as *a* relevant factor the standard of living enjoyed by the plaintiff during the deceased's lifetime and the extent to which the deceased contributed to that standard of living.[4]

These remarks of Dunn LJ cannot be regarded as clear authority for either view. While Dunn LJ was clearly not anxious to fetter the court's discretion, the actual maintenance provided by the deceased was a very important factor to guide the court. The matter was not fully argued, particularly since the applicant partially justified her appeal for more provision on the basis that the trial judge failed to have sufficient regard to the deceased's assumption of responsibility for her maintenance and the actual order made, essentially the same as in *Re Haig*,[5] did not give the applicant on a rough and ready basis any more than she received during the deceased's lifetime.

The issue has been addressed by two inconclusive cases in the Court of Appeal. In *Clark v Jones*[6] the beneficiary appealed against an award in favour of a mistress upon the basis that the award represented an excess of capitalised maintenance during the lifetime of the deceased. In 1985 the Court of Appeal dismissed the appeal. The matter was not fully argued, the facts being rather unclear and the sums involved were very modest. In *Rhodes v Dean*[7] a mistress appealed against the decision of Micklem J sitting as a Judge of the Chancery Division dismissing her application upon the basis that the deceased had assumed only a limited degree of responsibility for her maintenance and that the proceeds of a joint bank account were sufficient to satisfy that claim. The Court of Appeal refused to interfere. Of more significance was Micklem J's holding that he should have regard to the applicant's standard of living *before* she met the deceased, rather than the higher standard of living which she enjoyed when living with the deceased, and that 'reasonable provision' was merely such as would be sufficient to restore her to the position in which she was prior to meeting the deceased.

An alternative approach is to have regard to any detriment incurred by the applicant in order to become dependent upon the deceased. In *Jelley v Iliffe* Stephenson LJ refers to the position of an

4. Emphasis added.
5. Browne-Wilkinson J [1979] LS Gaz R 476.
6. (2 December 1985, unreported).
7. (28 March 1996, unreported).

applicant 'who has been *put* by a deceased person in a position of dependency'.[8] This approach might justify a large award in a case such as *Re Wilkinson*[9] where the amount of net dependency was low, but where the applicant incurred a substantial detriment in order to become dependent upon the deceased. Likewise in *C A v C C*[10] the applicant gave up a child to become dependent upon the deceased and in both *Re Haig*[11] and *Rhodes v Dean*[12] the applicants gave up houses to live with the deceased. Just as adult children to whom the deceased owed no duty of support while alive might be awarded provision if they incurred a significant detriment at the deceased's request,[13] it might be proper to award applicants within section 1(1)(e) provision in excess of that received prior to the deceased's death. Indeed in many cases protecting the 'reliance' interest is a more morally satisfying approach than protecting the 'expectation' interest.[14]

Limiting the Award

Whether or not the courts should aim to protect the expectation or reliance interest of applicants under section 1(1)(e), it is submitted that the applicant should be under a duty to ' mitigate' his loss. On divorce the courts are now obliged to have regard to the appropriateness of terminating the financial dependency of one party upon the other[15] and it would be grossly inappropriate if an applicant under section 1(1)(e) were in a better position than a wife on divorce

8. [1981] Fam 128, at 137H-138A, [1981] 2 All ER 29, at 36a.
9. [1978] Fam 22, [1978] 1 All ER 221, emphasis added. In *Malone v Harrison* [1979] 1 WLR 1353 it was surely not irrelevant that the deceased 'monopolised the applicant for twelve years' and the association with the deceased damaged the applicant's career prospects.
10. (1978) Times, 17 November; *sub nom Re C* 123 Sol Jo 35; *sub nom In the Estate of McC* 9 Fam Law 26.
11. Browne-Wilkinson J [1979] LS Gaz R 476.
12. (28 March 1996, unreported), CA.
13. See pp 233–240, *ante.*
14. On the interests in contract damages, see Fuller and Perdue, 'The Reliance Interest in Contract Damages', (1936) 46 Yale LJ 52, 372; Atiyah, *Promises, Morals and Law.* The repeal of the original s 25(1) of the Matrimonial Causes Act 1973 can be seen as a move away from protecting the expectation interest on divorce. (Query if *Re Viner* and *Malone v Harrison* are cases protecting the expectation interest and *Rhodes v Dean* is a case limiting recovery to the reliance interest, does *Re Goodchild* represent protection of the restitutionary interest?)
15. S 25A of the Matrimonial Causes Act 1973 introduced by the Matrimonial and Family Proceedings Act 1984.

or claiming under the 1975 Act. In *Rhodes v Dean*[16] Micklem J refused to award the applicant any provision upon the basis that the deceased had through the proceeds of a joint bank account placed the applicant in exactly the same position as if she had not met the deceased – the classic 'rehabilitation only' award of maintenance. In *Re Haig*[17] Browne-Wilkinson J provided that the applicant's interest in her new dwelling was to end when she became dependent upon another. The approach of such limiting an award to such as might enable the applicant to recover as quickly as possible from dependence upon the deceased was urged upon Hollings J in *Malone v Harrison,* but rejected by him.[18] This submission might have met with more favour in *Malone v Harrison* if the deceased's estate were smaller, if the relationship with the deceased had not damaged her earning capacity or if the judge took a more critical moral view of the applicant's relationship with the deceased. Less defensible is the decision in *Re P*[19] where a 19-month relationship was held to entitle the applicant to a sum based upon *lifetime* maintenance, with no allowance for the possibility that had the deceased lived the relationship would have ceased or for the possibility of the applicant remarrying or forming other relationships.

A Typical Award for Applicants under Section 1(1)(e)

In so far it is possible to generalise from the many different circumstances that come within section 1(1)(e), it is possible to say that in the case of a man and woman living together in the house owned by the deceased with 'free accommodation' being the net maintenance, the applicant will typically be awarded some form of life-interest in the deceased's dwellinghouse[20] determinable on cohabitation,[1] together with possibly an absolute interest in the deceased's chattels[2] and a small sum of capital.

16. (28 March 1996, unreported), CA.
17. [1979] LS Gaz R 476. In *Malone v Harrison* [1979] 1 WLR 1353, at 1365D Hollings J stated that he would have regard to the possibility of the applicant marrying.
18. [1979] 1 WLR 1353, at 1365E. See also Bennett, 'Recent Cases on the Inheritance (Provision for Family and Dependants) Act 1975', (1981) 131 NLJ 1151, at 1153.
19. Halsbury's Laws Monthly Review, para 96/1321.
20. *Re Haig*, Browne-Wilkinson J [1979] LS Gaz R 476; *Harrington v Gill* (1983) 4 FLR 265; see also *Moody v Stevenson* [1992] Ch 486, [1992] 2 All ER 524. The author has settled a significant number of cases on this basis.
1. *Re Haig*, Browne-Wilkinson J [1979] LS Gaz R 476. And see pp 196–198, *ante*.
2. *Harrington v Gill* (1983) 4 FLR 265, at 272A.

The Calculation of Reasonable Provision

A controversial method of calculating reasonable provision for an applicant within section 1(1)(e) was adopted by Hollings J in *Malone v Harrison.*[3] In this case Hollings J found that the deceased had assumed a complete responsibility for the applicant's maintenance.[4] He rejected arguments from the defendants that reasonable provision for the applicant should be limited because (implicitly) of the immorality of her relationship with the deceased and because she had already received enough from the deceased or that provision should only be awarded on a rehabilitative basis.[5] It was agreed that the deceased provided the applicant with at least £4,000 per annum during his lifetime, which was the sum which Hollings J assessed as her needs.[6] The applicant's earning capacity was assessed at £2,000 per annum and Hollings J also took account of the possibility of marriage.[7] Hollings J thought that the applicant, now aged 38, was likely to work until age 60 and after that age she would have a life expectancy of a further 16 years. He found that, exclusive of her flat, furs and jewellery, the applicant had free capital of £23,000.[8] Hollings J used the approach of multiplier and multiplicand as used in the calculation of damages for personal injuries[9] and made the following calculations:[10]

Needs	£4,000 per annum
Less earning capacity	£2,000
	£2,000 for 22 years
Apply multiplier of 11: 11 x £2,000	£22,000

Life expectancy 38 years to 76, therefore 16 years after retirement

Apply multiplier of 5: 5 x £4,000	£20,000

3. [1979] 1 WLR 1353.
4. [1979] 1 WLR 1364H.
5. [1979] 1 WLR 1365D–E.
6. [1979] 1 WLR 1365C, H.
7. [1979] 1 WLR 1365H.
8. [1979] 1 WLR 1365G–H.
9. On this method of calculating damages generally see *Royal Commission on Civil Liability and Compensation for Personal Injuries* (1979) Cmnd 7054, paras 646–725; McGregor, *Damages* (15th edn), paras 1453–1480, 1557–1593.
10. I gratefully adopt the tabular form used by Bennett, 'Recent Cases under the Inheritance (Provision for Family and Dependants) Act 1975', (1980) 130 NLJ 566.

	£42,000
Less present capital resources available for maintenance	£23,000
	£19,000

His Lordship consequently made a lump sum award of £19,000. Hollings J considered whether he should make the order conditional upon the applicant granting an interest in remainder in her flat to the beneficiaries of the estate, but decided against doing so because such an order would be of limited use to the beneficiaries who had the greatest claims upon the deceased and because of doubts as to the jurisdiction.[11]

The approach of Hollings J in using multipliers and multiplicands aroused some surprise and considerable criticism.[12] The criticism has been on two levels, technical points as to the details of the calculations and a more general criticism of the whole approach. In making the calculations Hollings J expressly took no account of inflation. However, to some extent inflation was taken into account indirectly in the selection of the multiplier.[13] Hollings J expressly ignored the effects of income tax.[14] This is a more serious deficiency since the applicant's needs were calculated on a basis which ignored income tax and she presumably did not pay income tax on the gifts from the deceased during his lifetime. Although with low rates of Income Tax it is unlikely that the applicant would have any penal problems with income tax on any investment income, this is a serious critique of Hollings J's calculations. The overall effect of the failure to consider income tax is somewhat diminished by the failure to consider the possibility of the applicant receiving a pension at age 60.

11. [1979] 1 WLR 1366B–C.
12. Bryan, Casenote, (1980) 96 LQR 165. In *Re Wood* [1982] LS Gaz 774, 2 April 1982, a case of a disabled adult child, Mervyn Davies J was pressed with calculations based on *Malone v Harrison.* He said that he found the 'suggestion for a mathematical calculation interesting and instructive', but preferred to use a more generalised approach, which however reached almost exactly the same result. In *Williams v Roberts* [1986] 1 FLR 349, at 357D-E Wood J said that he did not find the approach of Hollings J helpful in that particular case where the figures were unclear. To a greater or lesser extent the approach of Hollings J was adopted in *Clark v Jones* (2 December 1985, unreported), CA and in *Re P*, Halsbury's Laws Monthly Review, para 96/369.
13. See *Cookson v Knowles* [1979] AC 556, at 570F–571E, [1978] 2 All ER 604, at 610c-611d (per Lord Diplock); *Wells v Wells* [1997] 1 WLR 652, [1997] 1 All ER 673.
14. [1979] 1 WLR 1365H.

The more general criticism of the use of personal injuries techniques, it is submitted, is misplaced and was rejected by Thorpe LJ in the important case of *Wells v Wells*.[15] He expressly stated that there was no distinction of 'fundamental principle' between providing for 'the future needs' of plaintiffs in personal injury litigation and for applicants for ancillary relief and under the 1975 Act.[16] Thorpe LJ stated that in such cases the 'preferred' approach was to use *Duxbury* calculations.[17] and specifically approved the use of *Duxbury* calculations in the section 1(1)(e) case of *Nott v Ward*.[18]

It is submitted that the general approach of Hollings J in *Malone v Harrison* and of Thorpe LJ in *Wells v Wells* are both permissible correct means of calculating reasonable provision in a case where there is a sufficiently large estate with no competing claims and it is appropriate to award the applicant the full amount of his dependency. They are both welcome approaches, because they stress that provision is limited to maintenance and that provision should not be made so as to enable the applicant to leave property to other persons by will.[19] They can pay full regard to the possibilities of the applicant marrying and working[20] and resorting to her own capital for her maintenance. It is submitted that such matters may not have been taken into account in *Re Dr Kozdrach, Sobesto v Farren*[1] where an unnecessarily large award appears to have been made.

PART 6: COHABITANTS

The history of the enactment of the new class of cohabitants and its definition has already been discussed. [2]

15. *Wells v Wells* [1997] 1 WLR 652, at 680H-686E, [1997] 1 All ER 673, at 699j-705d. The House of Lords has granted leave to appeal, [1997] 1 WLR 870.
16. [1997] 1 WLR 686D, [1997] 1 All ER 705c-d.
17. [1997] 1 WLR 684H, [1997] 1 All ER 703j. On *Duxbury* calculations, see fn 10, p 388.
18. [1997] 1 WLR 682F, [1997] 1 All ER 701f-g. *Nott v Ward* Judge Bromley QC sitting as a Judge of the Chancery Division (13 December 1994, unreported), CA, (no report of this case is available).
19. [1979] 1 WLR 1365F.
20. See *Wells v Wells* at [1997] 1 WLR 685B-E, [1997] 1 All ER 704c-e where it is explained that the basic *Duxbury* program does not allow for varying circumstances such as remarriage, going out to work, but that it does permit variable circumstances to be added to the program.
1. [1981] Conv 224, letter from defendant to the author. See also *Re Green* Daily Mirror, 25/11/81, Daily Telegraph, 25/11/81, discussed in fn 3, p 99, *ante*
2. See pp 104–108, *ante*.

Section 3(2A) sets out the specific matters to which the court has regard when considering applications by cohabitants as follows:

(a) the age of the applicant and the length of the period during which the applicant lived as the husband or wife of the deceased and in the same household as the deceased;
(b) the contribution made by the applicant to the welfare of the deceased, including any contribution made by looking after the home or caring for the family.

These matters are taken from the specific matters to which the court is to have regard when considering an application by a spouse.[3] It would appear therefore that reported cases upon applications by spouses are a good guide to applications by cohabitants, save that the analogy with divorce is inapplicable, a cohabitee is only entitled to maintenance and can not claim a 'just share' and cohabitation is not necessarily to be equated with cohabitation.[4]

That an applicant who is qualified within both section 1(1)(ba) and section 1(1)(e) is to be treated as coming within section 1(1)(ba)[5] suggests that such an applicant will never receive less under section 1(1)(ba) than he or she would have done under section 1(1)(e). In *Jelley v Iliffe*[6] the Court of Appeal indicated *obiter* that on the merits that the applicant would probably fail or be awarded very modest provision because, inter alia, the amount of net maintenance he received was small. Now claiming under section 1(1)(e) the applicant would stand a better chance of being awarded siginificantly greater provision. Accordingly the amount of net maintenance which the applicant was receiving immediately prior to death can never act as an upper limit on the amount of provision,[7] but it may be a factor to be taken into consideration. For instance in the case of a couple where there were no children and the applicant incurred no detriment to enter into or during the relationship, the amount of any net maintenance flowing from the deceased should be an important factor in determining the level of provision.[8] In practice many reported cases under section 1(1)(e), such as *Re Haig*,[9]

3. S 3(2).
4. *Foley v Foley* [1981] Fam 160, at 167F-H, [1981] 2 All ER 857, at 861e-g.
5. See p 106, *ante*.
6. [1981] Fam 128, [1981] 2 All ER 29.
7. See pp 282–285, *ante*.
8. For a contrary view, see Harrap, 'Provision for Cohabitants on Death'[1997] Fam Law 422, at 424.
9. Browne-Wilkinson J [1979] LS Gaz R 476.

Harrington v Gill,[10] *Williams v Roberts*[11] and *Graham v Murphy*,[12] can be treated as good guides to the outcome of applications under section 1(1)(ba).

In a similar manner to applications by spouses[13] and under section 1(1)(e),[14] the courts take into account the possibility of future marriage or cohabitation by an applicant and limit provision accordingly. Likewise the approach of limiting maintenance to sufficient to enable the applicant to rehabilitate himself from the cohabitation may be appropriate.[15]

10. (1983) 4 FLR 265.
11. [1986] 1 FLR 349.
12. [1997]1 FLR 860, a particularly appropriate authority.
13. See pp 146–148, *ante*.
14. See pp 285–286, *ante*.
15. See s 25A of the Matrimonial Causes Act 1973 and pp 285–286, *ante*.

Chapter 7

THE DECEASED'S NET ESTATE

Definition of Net Estate in 1938 Act

The 1938 Act limited the property out of which provision could be ordered to property which the deceased had power to dispose of by will after deducting all liabilities of the estate.[1] The 1938 Act thus made no attempt at all to control lifetime dispositions and it postponed the rights of dependants to those of creditors. This definition was widely criticised as being too restrictive, in that it did not cover several non-testamentary means of passing property on death and that it was exceptionally easy to avoid the Act by inter vivos transactions.[2]

New Definition of Net Estate in 1975 Act

The validity of these criticisms was substantially accepted by the Law Commission and the 1975 legislation considerably extended the categories of property out of which family provision could be ordered. However, the basic scheme of the legislation remains the same in that creditors are not postponed to dependants and inter vivos transactions are only affected in that they have a testamentary aspect. The new definition is contained in section 25(1).

Property Disposable by Will

Firstly, the 'net estate' includes all property of which the deceased had power to dispose of by will less the amount of his funeral, testamentary and administration expenses, debts and liabilities payable out of his estate on his death.[3] Where the deceased is not of full age or capacity, for the purposes of the definition of the 'net estate', he is treated as having power to dispose by will of all property

1. Inheritance (Family Provision) Act 1938, s 5(1).
2. See eg first edition, pp 23–28; Mellows, *The Law of Succession* (2nd edn) Ch 14.
3. S 25(1)(a).

of which he would have had power to dispose by will if he had been of full age and capacity.[4] This is the original definition in the 1938 Act. It includes an unbarred entail vested in the deceased, since this can be barred by will,[5] and property subject to a general testamentary power of appointment, but not property subject to a special power of appointment which is specifically excluded from the definition. The Law Commission did consider whether the definition should be extended to include property subject to a special power of appointment, but finally rejected any change in the law.[6] The Law Commission argued that it would be wrong to interfere with the exercise of a power where the property subject to the power had been given and the limited objects of the power had been selected by a third party.

Scheme of the Enlarged Definition of the Net Estate

The new types of property added by the 1975 Act which may be used to satisfy an order for family provision fall into three classes, property which is automatically part of the 'net estate', property which is part of the 'net estate' if the court thinks it just so to order, and property which is part of the 'net estate' only if it forms part of a disposition intended to defeat an application for family provision and the court in its discretion orders that it form part of the 'net estate'.

Non-Testamentary General Powers of Appointment

Property subject to a non-testamentary general power of appointment is automatically part of the 'net estate',[7] on the basis

4. S 25(2).
5. Law of Property Act 1925, s 176. For a case where the deceased barred an entail by will, see *Re W (a minor) (claim from deceased's estate)* [1995] 2 FCR 689 – the report in [1995] 2 FLR 24 *sub nomen Re C (leave to apply for provision)* does not deal with this aspect of the case. From 1 January 1997 it has not been possible to create new entails, see Trusts of Land and Appointment of Trustees Act 1996, Sch 1, para 5.
6. LAW COM, paras 129–133. It is uncertain whether a hybrid or intermediate power such as a power to appoint to all the world except the donee (eg *Re Manisty* [1974] Ch 17, [1973] 2 All ER 1203) is to be regarded as a general or special power or neither for the purposes of the 1975 Act. The definition in the Perpetuities and Accumulations Act 1964, s 7 only applies for the purposes of the rule against perpetuities. See further Fleming, 'Hybrid Powers', (1948) 13 Conv (NS) 20.
7. S 25(1)(b).

that immediately before death the donee could make himself the absolute owner of the property.

Statutory Nominations

By virtue of certain statutory provisions property such as Savings Bank accounts and money payable to a member by a Friendly Society (usually limited to specific sums) can be disposed of on death by nominations during the lifetime of the deceased. Any property passing on death as a result of a nomination made by the deceased in his lifetime in accordance with the provisions of '*any enactment*' is automatically part of the 'net estate'.[8] The amount of the property or sum of money included in the 'net estate' is limited to the value of the property or the sum of money at *the date of death*, less any Inheritance Tax payable in respect thereof by the nominee.[9]

Donatio Mortis Causa

Property or a sum of money passing by way of donatio mortis causa is automatically part of the 'net estate'.[10] The amount of property or sum of money included in the 'net estate' is limited to the value

8. S 8(1). Some provisions are enumerated in the Administration of Estates (Small Payments) Act 1965, Sch 2. The limit for such nominations from 11 May 1984 is £5,000: Administration of Estates (Small Parties) (Increase of Limit) Order 1984, SI 1984/539.

   Other enactments providing for nominations are the Friendly Society Act 1992, Sch 2 (limit £5,000); Industrial and Provident Societies Act 1965, s 23, s 24 (limit £5,000); Trade Union and Labour Relations Act 1974, Sch 1, para 31; The Trade Union (Nominations) Regulations 1977, SI 1977/789, amended by the Trade Union (Nominations)(Amendment) Regulations 1984, SI 1984/1290 (limit £5,000). The right to make nominations in respect of monies in the Trustee Savings Bank was abolished with effect from 1 May 1979 and in respect of monies in the National Savings Bank and National Savings Certificates with effect from 1 May 1981, although nominations before those dates remain effective.

   On the general law as to statutory nominations, see Samuels, 'Nominations in Favour of a Nominee to Take Effect on Death', (1967) 31 Conv (NS) 85; Chappenden, 'Nominations and Law of Succession', (1982) 56 ALJ 270.

   For a case involving nominations of national savings, see *Stephens v Stephens* (1 July 1985, unreported), CA.

   On non-statutory nominations, which are not part of the 'net estate', see pp 320–321, *post*.
9. S 8(1) and (3).
10. S 8(2). For the requirements of a donatio mortis causa, see Snell's *Equity* (29th edn), pp 380–386; *Halsbury's Laws of England* (4th edn, Reissue) Vol 20, paras 67–100; and see *Woodard v Woodard* [1995] 3 All ER 980.

of the property or the sum of money at *the date of death*, less any Inheritance Tax payable in respect thereof by the donee.[11] This provision is likely to assume more importance now that it has been recognised that a donatio mortis causa of land is possible.[12]

This provision makes it necessary to distinguish between inter vivos gifts and donatio mortis causa even when the gift has been fully completed by delivery according to the rules for inter vivos gifts. If the gift was made in contemplation of death and conditional upon death, then the gift is a donatio mortis causa and automatically part of the 'net estate', whereas if the gift was unconditional the gifted property would only form part of the 'net estate' if the gift was made with an intention to defeat a claim for family provision and if the court so orders.

Liability in Respect of Statutory Nominations and Donatio Mortis Causa

Persons who give effect to statutory nominations[13] or donatio mortis causa[14] by paying over money or by completing the gift are expressly excluded from liability for doing so. Thus a Friendly Society can safely pay a nominee without regard to any proceedings for family provision. By necessary inference from these express exemptions and on general principles a nominee or donee is probably under similar liabilities to a personal representative if he disposes of the nominated or gifted property without regard to any family provision claim.

Thus it would appear that a nominee or a donee who dissipates property nominated to him or the subject of a donatio mortis causa within six months of death is liable in the same manner as a personal representative to a successful applicant if provision is ordered out of the nominated property or the property forming the donatio mortis causa. Accordingly a nominee or donee would be well advised not to dispose of the nominated or gifted property within eight or so months of the death of the deceased. He should furthermore inquire whether a grant of representation to the estate of the deceased has been taken out and if so whether any claim under the Act has been notified to the personal representatives. Because

11. S 8(2) and (3).
12. *Sen v Headley* [1991] Ch 425, [1991] 2 All ER 638, reversing [1990] Ch 728, [1990] 1 All ER 898. Leave to appeal to the House of Lords was granted ([1991] Ch 441D) and it is understood that the action was subsequently compromised.
13. S 8(1).
14. S 8(2).

neither a nominee's title nor a donee's title depends upon a grant of representation being taken out, it is submitted that where a grant of representation is not taken out within the usual period of a few months from the date of the deceased's death and where the court grants an extension of time under section 4 a court should entertain a reluctance to make orders affecting nominated property or donationes mortis causa. In particular the court should recognise the defence of change of position in reliance upon the absence of a family provision claim by the nominee or donee.[15]

It is submitted that a court has jurisdiction to grant interlocutory injunctions to restrain a donee or nominee disposing of the nominated property or the property the subject of the donatio mortis causa either on the basis that the applicant has a claim against the estate and the nominee or donee is subject to some form of fiduciary duty or under the court's general jurisdiction to preserve property during litigation concerning the title to such property.[16]

Because donatio mortis causa and statutory nominations are *automatically* part of the 'net estate' it is submitted that in deciding the incidence of any family provision order, no discrimination should be shown between property passing to personal representatives and statutory nominations and donationes mortis causa and such latter dispositions should be treated as bequests.

Property Held on Joint Tenancies

The deceased's severable share in property held on a joint tenancy is available to satisfy a family provision order 'to such extent as appears to the court to be just in all the circumstances'.[17] 'Property' is specifically defined to include a chose in action,[18] thus the provisions of the Act apply to joint bank accounts and joint insurance policies.[19] The value of the property out of which the court can order family provision is limited to the value of the severable share of the deceased immediately before *the death of the deceased* and after deduction of Inheritance Tax payable in respect thereof by the survivor.[20]

15. See Farren, 'Some Aspects of the Inheritance (Provision for Family and Dependants) Act 1975', [1980] Conv 60.
16. For the jurisdiction to preserve specific property pending litigation, see pp 375–377, *post*.
17. S 9(1).
18. S 9(4).
19. *Powell v Osbourne* [1993] 1 FLR 1001, at 1004G-H.
20. S 9(1) and (2).

The effect of valuing assets 'immediately before the death of the deceased' was discussed by the Court of Appeal in *Powell v Osbourne*.[1] In this case the deceased and his mistress owned a dwellinghouse as beneficial joint tenants. The property had been recently purchased with the assistance of a substantial mortgage and the parties also had taken out an endowment policy on their joint lives which was treated as being held on a benefecial joint tenancy.[2] Immediately before the death of the deceased the policy had no surrender value, but on death it matured and was sufficient to repay the mortgage. The deceased's widow whose application for ancillary relief had not been determined before the death of the deceased applied for an order under section 9. The Court of Appeal rejected an argument that because the deceased's severable share had to be valued 'immediately before his death' it had no value and that the increase in value caused by death should be ignored. Both Dillon and Simon Brown LJJ stated that the reference to 'immediately before his death' was because this was the last time when the joint tenancy could be severed[3] and that if death were certain the value of the policy immediately before death was equal to the proceeds of the policy.[4] Accordingly the Court of Appeal held that they could make an order under section 9 affecting one half of the proceeds of sale of the property unincumbered by the mortgage.[5]

Thus if a long time elapses between the date of death and the date of the order and the formerly jointly owned property appreciates in value, the court is limited to the lower value at the date of death. Conversely if the formerly jointly owned property depreciates in value between the date of death and the date of the hearing, the court can make an order up to the higher value at the date of death, but is unlikely to do so. For the same reason and because the provisions of the section do not render any person liable for anything done before an order under the Act is made,[6] it is submitted that interest

1. [1993] 1 FLR 1001.
2. On implied trusts of endowment policies, see *Smith v Clerical Medical and General Life Assurance Society* [1993] 1 FLR 47.
3. [1993] 1 FLR 1005A (Dillon LJ), 1006G (Simon Brown LJ).
4. [1993] 1 FLR 1006B-C, H. Compare s 171 of the Inheritance Tax Act 1984.
5. In both *Powell v Osbourne* and *Jessop v Jessop* [1992] 1 FLR 591 the deceased died intestate and the applicant widow was solely entitled under the rules of intestacy. Despite the words of s 1(1) giving the court jurisdiction where 'the disposition of the deceased's estate effected by his will or the law relating to intestacy ... is not such as to make reasonable financial provision for the applicant', the Courts considered that they had jurisdiction to make an order under s 9 and thereafter an order under s 2(1). It is submitted that any other construction would emasculate s 9 in a large number of cases. See further *Kourgky v Lusher* (1981) 4 FLR 65, at 79C–81E, discussed below.
6. S 9(3).

on a formerly joint bank account accruing between the date of death and the date of the order belongs to the survivor.[7]

The deceased's severable share cannot be made the subject of an order if an application for family provision is made more than six months from the date on which representation was first taken out.[8] This provision is designed to protect survivors from tardy applications, but it is less effective than it first appears because there is no obligation to take out a grant of representation in good time; indeed where the only asset of any value in the 'net estate' is the severable share in jointly held property, as not infrequently happens where a deceased dies leaving only personal chattels and a jointly held dwellinghouse passes by survivorship, there is rarely any need for a grant of representation to be taken out.[9] It is submitted that where a grant of representation is taken out unusually late, then the court should be reluctant to exercise its powers to make the severable share part of the 'net estate' and in particular should recognise the defence of change of position by a survivor who had relied upon the absence of a family provision application.

A severable share in jointly held property is available if and only to the extent that the court thinks just. The courts have repeatedly stated that section 9 confers a wide jurisdiction.[10]

In *Kourkgy v Lusher*[11] in a judgment which contains the most detailed discussion of the approach of the court to the making of orders under section 9, Wood J stated that the discretion under the section should be exercised *before* the court considers whether reasonable provision has been made for an applicant, so that the court can at that stage take into account the availability of the severable share . In particular Wood J held that the words 'for the purpose of facilitating financial provision for the applicant' did not prevent the court from having regard to the severable share in

7. In *Re Crawford* (1982) 4 FLR 273 it appears to have been accepted that the survivor was entitled to interest accruing after death.
8. S 9(1). In determining the date on which representation was first taken out, see s 23, pp 331–333, *post*.
9. For a graphic illustration of this see *Re McBroom* [1992] 2 FLR 49; Farren, 'Some Aspects of the Inheritance (Provision for Family and Dependants) Act 1975' [1980] Conv 60. In this situation the applicant can cite those with a prior right to take out a grant and failing which the applicant's own nominee could apply for a grant under Supreme Court Act 1981, s 116.
10. *Re Crawford* (1982) 4 FLR 273, 280F–G where Eastham J stated that 's 9 contained everything which is necessary for the purpose of guiding the court' in the exercise of its discretion; *Kourkgy v Lusher* (1981) 4 FLR 65, at 81B; *Jessop v Jessop* [1992] 1 FLR 591, at 596F.
11. (1981) 4 FLR 65, at 79C–81E. This aspect of the judgment was specifically followed in *Re Patton* [1986] NI 45, at 48G–H.

deciding whether reasonable provision had been made.[12] This general approach was specifically approved by Nourse LJ in *Jessop v Jessop*[13] although it is unclear how far all the reasoning of Wood J was adopted.

As the creation of a joint tenancy in property is just as much the making of an alternative will as a donatio mortis causa or a statutory nomination, on principle, jointly held property should be automatically part of the 'net estate'. It is submitted that the reason why the statute provides that jointly held property is only part of the 'net estate' if the court so orders is because jointly held property is frequently used and occupied by the survivor both before and after the death of the deceased and that to make the deceased's severable share in a joint tenancy available to meet a family provision claim may cause grave hardship to the survivor. For example, where a spouse or a mistress is the survivor of a joint tenancy with the deceased of a dwellinghouse, to make the severable share available for family provision might result in a sale of the property. Whereas it is rare for a statutory nominee or a recipient of a donatio mortis causa to have in any way relied upon the nomination or donatio mortis causa, it is not uncommon for the survivor of a joint tenancy to have expended money or given up opportunities in the belief that his occupation of the property is secure for his lifetime. It is submitted that in exercising its discretion to make the severable share part of the 'net estate' a court should not disturb the occupation of formerly jointly held property by the survivor without very good cause. Thus it is submitted that a court should less readily exercise its powers where the jointly held property is actually occupied and used by the survivor, such as a jointly owned dwellinghouse or car than where the jointly held property's utility is purely financial, such as joint bank accounts and jointly owned land subject to tenancies.

Reported case law is broadly congruent with this analysis. Orders under section 9 have been made in respect of severable shares in joint bank accounts with considerable facility.[14] In *Kourkgy v Lusher*[15] Wood J refused to make an order under section 9 which would have adversely affected the occupation by the deceased's widow of the former matrimonial home, but in a hypothetical example he implied that he would have been prepared to make an order under section 9 in respect of a large expensive house which the survivor was proposing to vacate in any event.[16] In *Jessop v*

12. (1981) 4 FLR 81B.
13. [1992] 1 FLR 591, at 596E–F.
14. *Re Crawford* (1981) 4 FLR 65; *Re Patton* [1986] NI 45.
15. (1981) 4 FLR 65, at 81F–H.
16. (1981) 4 FLR 80F–G.

Jessop[17] the Court of Appeal made an order under section 9 in respect of the deceased's severable share of the house occupied by his mistress in the knowledge that the mistress could fund the provision made out of a lump sum payment made under a pension scheme which was not part of the 'net estate'.[18]

This special treatment of joint tenancies, as opposed to other alternatives to wills, such as statutory nominations and donatio mortis causa, is a recognition that even in the late twentieth century, despite criticism by academics,[19] the operation of joint tenancies usually achieves a just result[20] and is known about by the general public and as such appreciated.[1]

Of all the extensions to the definition of the 'net estate' made by the 1975 Act, section 9 is the only provision frequently used in practice and it is difficult to envisage family provision legislation without some form of power to effect a severable share passing by survivorship. However, bearing in mind the enormous value of property which passes by survivorship each year, relatively few orders under section 9 will actually be made in respect of severable shares in dwellinghouses occupied by the survivor.

The Operation of Section 9

It is important to realise that a court can make an order under section 9(1) directing that the severable share of a deceased form part of the 'net estate' at a different and earlier time to the making of an order for actual provision under section 2(1) and can actually make

17. [1992] 1 FLR 591.
18. In *Powell v Osbourne* [1993] 1 FLR 1001 the Court of Appeal did make an order affecting the deceased's severable share in the house which he shared with his mistress. However, the Court of Appeal did not address the merits, but merely chose between two alternative figures put forward by the parties. The report does not state whether any monies were payable under an occupational pension scheme and, if so, which party received such monies.
19. Eg Bandali, 'Injustices and Problems of Beneficial Joint Tenancy', (1977) 41 Conv (NS) 243; LAW COM, para 140; and see the interchange between Professors Thompson and Prichard at [1987] Conv 273, 275. In most American jurisdictions these criticisms have been heeded and it is now difficult or impossible to create joint tenancies of real property – Cunningham, Stoebuck and Whitman, *The Law of Property*, para 5.3
20. See *Joyce v Barker Bros (Builders) Ltd* (1980) 40 P & CR 512, at 514–515 where these matters were discussed.
1. See Todd and Jones, *Matrimonial Property*, pp 10–12. Of married couples who held the matrimonial home jointly, 51% stated that the automatic transfer on death was an important reason for their decision to put the property into joint names.

an order that the severable share form part of the 'net estate' and then subsequently make no order for family provision. This follows from the wording of section 9(1) and (3). Therefore to ensure that a survivor does not dissipate the formerly jointly held property, an applicant may be well advised to seek an order under section 9 at an early stage in the proceedings before the substantive application.

Section 9(3) reads:

> Where an order is made under subsection (1) above, the provisions of this section shall not render any person liable for anything done by him before the order was made.

This subsection was designed to protect institutions such as banks and building societies who pay money to a survivor of a joint account,[2] and it clearly has such effect. However, the subsection is not limited to such institutions, as is section 8(2), and the specific mention of 'any person' must imply that a survivor is under no liability until an order is made under section 9(1).[3] Once an order under section 9(1) has been made, it would appear that the survivor is subject to similar liabilities as a personal representative or at least holds the property on trust to be applied, so far as necessary, towards any award.

The widely worded section 9(3) leaves an applicant in a weak position. He should consider the possibility of applying to the court for an order under section 9(1) before the substantive hearing of the application. The wording of section 9(3), 'any person *liable* for anything *done*', suggests that section 9(3) is only concerned with personal liability for breach of trust, and would not prevent the court from granting an interlocutory injunction to prevent the disposal of the severable share pending the trial or possibly a proprietary claim based on the doctrine of tracing.

Once an order under section 9(1) affecting land has been obtained, it should be registered as an order affecting land.[4] The position whether a *lis pendens* can be registered prior to an actual order under section 9(1) is unclear. It is clear that a claim to have land transferred by order of the court when there is no pre-existing proprietary interest is a 'pending land action' within the statutory definition.[5] It is however not clear whether a claim for an undivided share of the proceeds of sale of land in respect of land beneficially

2. LAW COM, para 142.
3. Professor J G Miller in the commentary to Current Law Statutes argues that 'any person' does not include the survivor.
4. Land Charges Act 1972, s 6(1)(a); Land Registration Act 1925, s 59(1).
5. Land Charges Act 1972, s 5(1)(a), s 17(1); Land Registration Act 1925, s 59(1); *Whittingham v Whittingham* [1979] Fam 9, [1978] 3 All ER 805.

owned by the survivor is a 'pending land action' when 'land' in this context is specifically defined as excluding 'an undivided share in land'.[6] It is tentatively submitted that a claim for an order under section 9(1) would be regarded as falling within the definition of 'pending land action' because of the modern trend to keep broad the definition of 'pending land action',[7] the general trend to view interests behind a trust for sale of land as interests in land[8] and because the claim, although made to create an undivided share in land, is made *against* land which is presently not an undivided share.

Dispositions Intended to Defeat Family Provision Claims[9]

The 1938 Act and the Matrimonial Causes Acts, which enabled divorced spouses to claim, only enabled claims to be made against the deceased's estate and accordingly the effect of the legislation could easily be avoided by inter vivos dispositions.[10] The obvious ease of avoiding the legislation led the Law Commission to consider proposals to attack inter vivos dispositions which made a family provision claim ineffective.[11] The Law Commission had to balance the need to remove very easy methods of avoidance which (at least theoretically) severely damaged the effectiveness of the legislation against the insecurity of title which would result from inter vivos transactions being set aside and the interference with previously untrammelled freedom of disposition. It is noteworthy that a person while alive only owes duties of support to his spouse, his former spouse and infant child, and that the introduction of measures to set aside dispositions which defeat family provision claims would

6. Land Charges Act 1972, s 17(1); *Taylor v Taylor* [1968] 1 WLR 378, [1968] 1 All ER 843. *Taylor v Taylor* is not based upon any general view of the nature of an interest behind a trust for sale of land but upon the specific statutory definition. After the coming into effect of the Trusts of Land and Appointment of Trustees Act 1996 this is much less of a practical issue.
7. *Whittingham v Whittingham* [1979] Fam 9, [1978] 3 All ER 805; *Greenhi Builders Ltd v Allen* [1979] 1 WLR 156, [1978] 3 All ER 1163.
8. *Williams & Glyn's Bank v Boland* [1981] AC 487, [1980] 2 All ER 408.
9. On the general problem of inter vivos transactions defeating succession right, see Macdonald, *Fraud on the Widow's Share*; on the specific provisions of the Act see Sherrin, 'Defeating the Dependants', [1978] Conv 13. For the position prior to 1976, see first edition, pp 24–28.
10. Indeed ALBERY, 67 contained a precedent for a settlement to avoid the 1938 Act.
11. WORKING PAPER, paras 3.69–3.75.

indirectly lead to a regime where a person holds property for the benefit of those to whom he owes no present duty of support.[12]

The Law Commission decided that the best way of dealing with the problem was to enact a variant of section 37 of the Matrimonial Causes Act 1973 which enables the court to set aside dispositions intended to defeat a claim for financial provision on divorce.[13] Section 10 of the 1975 Act gives the court a discretionary power to order a person benefited by a voluntary disposition to deliver property or pay a sum of money for the purposes of making an order for family provision and so form part of the 'net estate' if the disposition took effect less than six years before the death of the deceased and was made with an intention to defeat a family provision application. The provisions of section 10 act personally against the donee rather than against any particular property. Thus a donee can pass good title to any third party and the donee's duty to account is not dependent upon the presence in his hands of any identifiable property.

The court's powers extend to any 'disposition',[14] which is widely defined to include 'any payment of money (including the payment of a premium under a policy of assurance) and any conveyance, assurance, appointment or gift of property of any description, whether made by instrument or otherwise'.[15] This definition probably covers any arrangement whereby property passes; but it probably does not cover arrangements whereby *value* passes out of property but the ownership of the property is left undisturbed[16] and probably an omission to act cannot be regarded as a 'disposition'.[17] Thus the failure to exercise a power of revocation in a settlement is not a 'disposition'. A 'disposition' by a deceased includes a disposition by a trustee for the deceased or by a company controlled by the deceased acting upon his direction.[18] Specifically excluded from the definition are provisions in a will, statutory nominations and donationes mortis causa which form part of the 'net estate' by reason of other sections of the Act.[19] In *Clifford v Tanner*[20] the

12. For discussion of some of the effects of restricting inter vivos gifts in jurisdictions having *legitim*, see Dawson, *Gifts and Promises*.
13. LAW COM, paras 190–221.
14. S 10(2)(a).
15. S 10(7).
16. Compare Taxation of Chargeable Gains Act 1992, ss 29 and 30.
17. Compare Inheritance Tax Act 1984, s 3(3). It is submitted that the word 'disposition' implies some positive action by the disposer. In *Crittenden v Crittenden* [1990] 2 FLR 361 it was held that 'deal with' in s 37 of the Matrimonial Causes Act 1973 did not extend to omissions.
18. *Kemmis v Kemmis*[1988] 1 WLR 1307, at 1327E–G, 1331F–H; but see *Crittenden v Crittenden* [1990] 2 FLR 361.
19. S 10(7)(a).
20. [1987] CLY 3881, CA.

deceased had a personal right under a covenant to occupy a house, which Nicholls LJ stated would be the subject of an order for specific performance. The deceased had released this right gratuitously to the owner of the house, his daughter. Nicholls LJ stated that the release of the right to occupy was 'a gift of property of any description'. An argument that because the right could not be assigned it had no value to the deceased and hence could not be a 'disposition' was rejected, Nicholls LJ stating that the owner of the property would be prepared to pay a substantial sum of money for a release of the right. Testamentary special powers and general powers of appointment, whether exercisable before or upon death, are excluded from the definition because they are specifically dealt with by other sections of the Act.[1] The exercise of a special power of appointment during the deceased's life is not a 'disposition'.[2] This is because of the general view of the Law Commission that the family provision legislation should not impinge on the exercise of special powers.[3] The provisions of the Act do not apply to dispositions made before 1 April 1976, the commencement of the Act.[4]

Only dispositions made less than six years before the date of death are subject to the provisions of section 10.[5] This is an arbitrary limit – there is no time limit on section 37 of the Matrimonial Causes Act 1973 – but it is designed to prevent litigation when witnesses' memories are unlikely to be clear and not to permanently discourage donees from disposing of property given to them.[6] Furthermore it is unlikely that any disposition made many years before death was actually intended to defeat a family provision claim. However, the time limit may permit some avoidance. For example, if a deceased ten years before his death settled property on himself for life, remainder to his mistress and reserved to himself a power of revocation, neither the settlement nor the failure to exercise the power of revocation before death would be a reviewable disposition within section 10.

The disposition to fall within section 10 must not have been made for 'full valuable consideration'.[7] 'Valuable consideration' cannot be marriage or the promise of marriage,[8] but need not be

1. S 10(7)(b).
2. S 10(7)(b).
3. LAW COM, paras 208–210.
4. S 10(8), s 27(3).
5. S 10(2)(a).
6. LAW COM, para 201; New South Wales has selected a period of three years – see s 23(b)(i) of the Family Provision Act 1982. Somewhat surprisingly the other Australasian jurisdictions do not have any legislation comparable to s 10.
7. S 10(2)(b).
8. S 25(1).

provided by the person benefited by the disposition ('the donee').[9] The scheme of section 10 is that the absence of full consideration brings section 10 into effect, but the court in exercising its discretion has regard to the amount of the consideration actually provided.[10] It is unlikely that a court would exercise its powers to order transfer of property or payment of money worth more than the difference between the consideration actually provided and the value of the property or money disposed of.

Furthermore a disposition to be subject to section 10 must be made with the requisite intention to defeat an application for family provision.[11] This is defined as an intention 'in making the disposition or contract ... to prevent an order for financial provision being made under this Act or to reduce the amount of the provision which might otherwise be granted by an order thereunder'.[12] It is provided that this intention need not be the sole intention of the deceased[13] and that the existence of the intention is proved on a balance of probabilities.[14] After one false start,[15] it has been held by the Court of Appeal that section 37 of the Matrimonial Causes Act 1973 requires proof of a subjective intention.[16] In *Kemmis v Kemmis* Lloyd LJ said:

> ... in determining whether a spouse has the requisite state of mind, a court may have regard to the natural consequences of his act. It is true that there is no presumption.....Nor, generally, would the natural consequences of the disposition be enough by itself to support an inference of intention. But the natural consequences of the disposition would certainly be a factor to be taken into account in deciding whether or not to draw the inference of intention in any case.[17]

9. S 10(2)(b).
10. S 10(6).
11. S 10(2)(b).
12. S 12(1).
13. S 12(1).This was applied in both *Re Weir* [1993] 2 NIJB 45 and *Morrow v Morrow*, Campbell J (5 April 1995, unreported)(Northern Ireland).
14. S 12(1).
15. *Jordan v Jordan* (1965) 109 Sol Jo 353.
16. *K v K (avoidance of reviewable dispositions)* (1982) 4 FLR 31; *Kemmis v Kemmis* [1988] 1 WLR 1307, at 1315H–1316B per Purchas LJ, 1326E–F per Lloyd LJ.
17. [1988] 1 WLR 1326G-H. See also Purchas LJ at [1988] 1 WLR 1316A-B. In *Re Dawkins* [1986] 2 FLR 360 Bush J found that the requisite intention under s 10 existed by having regard to the natural effect of the transaction, the surrounding circumstances and an admission by a beneficiary. In both *Re Weir* [1993] 2 NIJB 45 and *Morrow v Morrow* Campbell J (5 April 1995, unreported)(Northern Ireland) the judges relied heavily upon statements which had been made by the deceased.

There are conflicting dicta as to whether a finding that a spouse had the requisite intention under section 37 requires any finding of morally bad behaviour.[18] It has been held that the 'badges of fraud' associated with section 172 of the Law of Property Act 1925 are not a useful tool for determining whether a spouse has an intention within section 37.[19]

By analogy with section 37 of the Matrimonial Causes Act 1973, section 10 requires proof of a subjective intention. This approach gains support from the rejection of a proposal that certain transactions should be rebuttably presumed to have been made with the requisite intention – a proposal rejected upon the ground that such a presumption was unlikley to be true,[20] is supported by most commentators[1] and appears to have been adopted in the limited reported case law on section 10.[2]

Proving the requisite intention within section 10 can involve difficult questions of legal professional privilege.[3]

In *Re Kennedy*[4] it was held that it was not necessary for the deceased to have in mind the provisions of the 1975 Act when he made the transaction, but that an intention to defeat a claim against his estate after his death was a sufficient intention to bring the transaction within section 10.

A disposition can only be made subject to the court's powers under section 10 if it 'would facilitate the making of financial provision'.[5] Thus a donee cannot be made to disgorge if the 'net estate' is otherwise adequate to satisfy any order which the court might make.

Once all the conditions precedent to the court's jurisdiction have been satisfied, the court has a discretion whether to exercise its powers. In exercising this discretion it is provided that the court shall have regard to:

18. In *K v K (avoidance of reviewable dispositions)* (1982) 4 FLR 31, at 36F Ormrod LJ deprecated references to 'fraud' in s 37. In *Kemmis v Kemmis* [1988] 1 WLR 1307, at 1331E Nourse LJ refers to a 'dishonest and fraudulent intention'.
19. *K v K (avoidance of reviewable dispositions)* (1982) 4 FLR 31, at 37C–G, 41A–B per Ormrod LJ.
20. WORKING PAPER, para 3.72; LAW COM, para 200-2.
1. Sherrin, 'Defeating the Dependants' [1978] Conv 13, 16–18; ROSS, 53–55.
2. *Re Kennedy* [1980] CLY 2820 would have been decided in favour of the applicant if the judge had adopted an objective approach. In *Re Dawkins* [1986] 2 FLR 360 Bush J appeared to adopt a subjective approach. In both *Re Weir* [1993] 2 NIJB 45 (a very dubious decision on the facts) and *Morrow v Morrow*, Campbell J (5 April 1995, unreported) (Northern Ireland) the judges expressly adopted a subjective approach.
3. See p 363, *post*.
4. [1980] CLY 2820.
5. S 10(2)(c).

> ... the circumstances in which any disposition was made and any valuable consideration which was given therefor, the relationship, if any, of the donee to the deceased, the conduct and financial circumstances of the donee and all other circumstances.[6]

It is difficult to draw out any general conclusions from such a list of statutory considerations. It is clear that a court would not impugn any transaction where the donee would himself have a strong claim under the Act. The reference to the 'relationship ... of the donee to the deceased' might perhaps suggest that a member of the family of the deceased, even if he is in no financial need at all, would be treated more favourably than a person not a member of the family, such as a charity. It is likely that in exercising its discretion a court will recognise the defence of change of position in the case of a donee who does not know of the deceased's intention to defeat a claim for financial provision. An applicant's consent to a transaction is a defence to an application under section 37 of the Matrimonial Causes Act 1973,[7] and similarly if an applicant approves of a transaction impugnable within section 10, a court would be unlikely to exercise it powers against a donee. Mere knowledge of the transaction would not be enough, since it is unlikely that an applicant has any power to restrain a transaction before the deceased's death.[8]

The Law Commission rejected a suggestion that the court be empowered to approve specific transactions when they were made. The Law Commission thought that such proceedings would turn out to be very complicated and expensive and might well be unnecessary in the light of subsequent events.[9]

Orders Made Under Section 10

The court when it exercises its powers does so by ordering the donee to provide a sum of money or other property as specified in the order.[10] This money or property need not represent in any way the money or property given to the donee and it is not a condition precedent to the court's powers that the donee has any interest in the money or property given by the deceased.[11] The value of any

6. S 10(6).
7. *Jordan v Jordan* (1965) 109 Sol Jo 353.
8. An application made during the lifetime of the deceased failed in *Dower v Public Trustee* (1962) 35 DLR (2d) 29 (Sup Ct Alta).
9. LAW COM, paras 220–221.
10. S 10(2).
11. Ibid.

money or property ordered to be provided by the donee where the disposition consisted of the payment of money is limited to *the amount of the payment* after deducting any Inheritance Tax borne by the donee in respect thereof.[12] Thus if money paid by the deceased is invested any interest or rise in the value of the investment between the date of the disposition and the date of the order belongs to the donee. Where insurance premiums are paid by the deceased under a policy to benefit the donee, the donee cannot be made to pay back more than the maximum amount of the premiums paid by the deceased coming within section 10.[13] Where the disposition consisted of the transfer of property the value of any money or any property ordered to be provided by the donee is limited to the value of the property at *the date of the death of the deceased* or at the date of the earlier disposal of the property by the donee or his personal representatives after deducting any Inheritance Tax borne in respect thereof by the donee.[14] Thus if the deceased gave a donee investments worth £5,000 five years before his death and they are worth £10,000 on his death the donee can be ordered to provide £10,000. 'Value of the property' probably means capital value and so a donee is entitled to interest, rent, dividends and other income of the property accruing between the date of the disposition and the date of death or earlier disposal.[15] If the value of the property falls between the date of death and the date of the order, the court in exercising its discretion is unlikely to make an order exceeding the value of the then current value of the property.

The court has a wide power to give consequential directions for giving effect to an order under section 10.[16] Such directions cannot involve upsetting the title to property of any third party who has acquired property from the donee.[17]

12. S 10(3).
13. LAW COM, paras 203–206.
14. S 10(4), s 12(4)(a). For further discussion of aspects of valuation see Sherrin, 'Defeating the Dependants' [1978] Conv 13, 20–22.
15. It is implicit in *Clifford v Tanner* [1987]CLY 3881, CA that where an asset is not readily saleable, but a person would pay a substantial sum for its release, the 'value of the property' is the amount which that person would pay for its release.
16. S 12(3).
17. Compare Matrimonial Causes Act 1973, s 37(3); *Green v Green* [1981] 1 WLR 391, [1981] 1 All ER 97, not following *National Provincial Bank v Hastings Car Mart (No 2)* [1963] 3 All ER 649, 654C–E, and see Sherrin, 'Defeating the Dependants', [1978] Conv 13, 19.

An order under section 10 can be made in respect of an insolvent estate and in this situation an applicant will be preferred to creditors of the deceased.[18]

Orders Against Personal Representatives

Orders under section 10 can be made against the donee's personal representatives, in the same manner as against the donee personally.[19] However, no order can be made against the personal representatives 'in respect of any property forming part of the estate of the donee' which has been distributed by the personal representatives.[20] 'Any property' in this context probably means the property which the court orders the personal representative to transfer, rather than the property originally given to the donee. The personal representatives are under no liability for distributing the estate without making provision for an application under section 10 unless they have 'notice' of the making of an application under section 10.[1] 'Notice' probably includes constructive notice.[2] The provisions protecting personal representatives probably do not prevent the applicant from following the assets of the deceased into the hands of beneficiaries under the estate of the deceased donee.[3]

Orders Against Trustees

Where a disposition is made to a trustee, the trustee is regarded as a donee. There are different rules limiting the value of property or

18. Eg *Re Dawkins* [1986] 2 FLR 360; *Clifford v Tanner* [1987] CLY 3881, CA. Under para 26, Part II, Sch I of the Administration of Insolvent Estates of Deceased Persons Order 1986, SI 1986/1999 the provisions of s 339 of the Insolvency Act 1986 relating to setting aside transactions at an undervalue are applied to the insolvent estates of deceased persons. Many transactions caught by s 10 will also be caught by s 339. If a court makes orders under both s 10 and pursuant to s 339, it is submitted that the order under the insolvency legislation should have priority upon the basis that the general scheme of the 1975 Act is to prefer creditors to applicants.
19. S 12(4).
20. S 12(4).
1. S 12(4).
2. *Kemmis v Kemmis* [1988] 1 WLR 1307; *B v B (P Ltd intervening) (No 2)* [1995] 1 FLR 374. On the meaning of notice in Trustee Act 1925, s 27(2), see Wolstenholme and Cherry, *Conveyancing Statutes* (13th edn) Vol 4, 37.
3. On the following of assets into the hands of an overpaid beneficiary see *Ministry of Health v Simpson* [1951] AC 251, [1950] 2 All ER 1137. Compare s 20(1) and Trustee Act 1925, s 27(2)(a) which preserve the right to follow with specific words.

money which can be ordered to be provided for ordinary donees and trustee donees. Where the disposition involved the payment of money the trustee can only be ordered to provide money or property not exceeding the value of money originally given and money or property representing or derived from the money originally paid which is in the hands of the trustee at *the date of the order* and after deducting any Inheritance Tax borne by the trustee in respect of the disposition.[4] The aim of this provision is to protect trustees against orders when they have distributed the trust fund. However, the provision is so worded that any rise in the value of property purchased with money originally given to a trustee and any income from the original money or property purchased with the original money between the date of the disposition and the date of the order may be ordered to be provided by a trustee. This may be more favourable to an applicant than an order against an ordinary donee, since in that case the order is limited to the amount of money actually paid. Where the disposition involved the transfer of property the trustee can only be ordered to provide money or property not exceeding the value of the property originally given to the trustee and money or property representing the original property in the hands of the trustee *at the date of the order* and after deducting any Inheritance Tax borne by the trustee in respect of the disposition.[5] Again the aim of this provision is to protect trustees against orders when they have distributed the trust fund, but it can act to the advantage of the applicant in that the property is valued at the date of the order not the date of death or earlier disposal, income from the property is included as is property purchased out of the original property and the income thereof. For example, if a gift of land subject to a lease is given on trust for a beneficiary with a direction to accumulate income an applicant under section 10 has a choice of donees against whom to claim. A claim against the beneficiary in respect of his equitable interest in the trust fund will be limited to the value of the land at the date of death of the deceased excluding the accumulated income after deducting any inheritance tax borne by the beneficiary. A claim against the trustee will be limited to the (probably higher) value of the land or property representing the land at the date of the order including the accumulated income but after deducting any inheritance tax paid in respect of the disposition, provided that the land or other property representing it is still held by the trustee at the date of the order.

A trustee is under no liability for distributing the trust fund without taking into account the *possibility* of an application under

4. S 13(1)(i).
5. S 13(1)(ii).

section 10,[6] but he may be liable if he has actual knowledge of a claim being made.

Donee's Right to Challenge Other Dispositions Within Section 10

When an order is made against a donee or his personal representative, if an order under section 10 could have been made against another donee under another disposition, the donee against whom the order is made can make an application against such other donee and the court has jurisdiction to make such other donee satisfy the original section 10 application – in effect one donee liable under section 10 can claim contribution from another potentially so liable.[7]

Common Law Powers to Set Aside Transactions in Fraud of Family Provision Claims

Aside from the specific provisions of section 10, there is no basis at common law on the ground of *public policy* for challenging any inter vivos transaction which has the effect of defeating an application for family provision.[8] However, the Court of Appeal in *Cadogan v Cadogan*[9] held that an *arguable* case had been made out in a claim by a potential family provision applicant to set aside a conveyance of property which destroyed her application on the ground that she was a 'person thereby prejudiced' by a conveyance which came within section 172 of the Law of Property Act 1925 and on the general jurisdiction as to fraud.[10] In *Cadogan v Cadogan* the deceased died before the 1975 Act had been enacted. It is submitted that since Parliament has repealed section 172 of the Law of Property Act 1925[11] and has enacted a detailed scheme of legislation in section

6. S 13(2).
7. S 10(5), s 12(4)(b).
8. *Cadogan v Cadogan* [1977] 1 WLR 1041, [1977] 1 All ER 200, Slade J. Compare the old law on dispositions in fraud of marital rights.
9. [1977] 1 WLR 1041, [1977] 3 All ER 331. In *Re Thomson* [1933] NZLR 59, 62 Kennedy J specifically held that a family provision applicant could not take advantage of the Statute of Elizabeth (13 Eliz I c 5) as he was not a 'creditor'. *Re Thomson* was followed in *Dower v Public Trustee* (1962) 35 DLR (2d) 29 (Sup Ct Alta). Neither *Re Thomson* nor *Dower v Public Trustee* was cited in *Cadogan v Cadogan*.
10. *Blenkinsopp v Blenkinsopp* (1852) 1 De GM & G 495.
11. Sch 10, Part IV of the Insolvency Act 1986.

10 to undo transactions effected to defeat family provision claims any common law power is no longer applicable. It can not be right that an applicant can circumvent the carefully drawn limits on orders under section 10 by relying upon a general common law power.[12]

Contracts to Make Wills[13]

A testator can validly make a contract as to the contents of his will. A will made in breach of such a contract will be admitted to probate,[14] but a legal remedy in the form of damages or equitable relief in the form of an order for specific performance or the imposition of a constructive trust may be awarded against the estate for the breach of contract. The effect of a contract to make a will on a family provision application has been the subject of considerable controversy. It has been argued that the court's jurisdiction under the family provision legislation cannot be ousted by any contract and that therefore provisions in a will made pursuant to a contract are fully subject to the court's jurisdiction under the family provision legislation. Against this it has been argued that provisions in a will made pursuant to a contract are immune from the court's jurisdiction, since if the testator had not made a will in conformity with the contract, the promisee could obtain damages or equitable relief which would be a liability of the estate and hence preferred to any family provision claim. Furthermore before the death of the testator, the promisee has sometimes been held to have a present interest in the testator's property,[15] and he certainly has a valuable chose in action and to fail to give effect to such a contract is to deprive the promisee of a present property right, rather than a mere *spes*.

The relationship of contracts to make wills and family provision legislation has come before the Privy Council twice. In *Dillon v Public*

12. No argument based upon *Cadogan v Cadogan* appears to have been advanced in any case under the 1975 Act. For instance in *Clifford v Tanner* [1987] CLY 3881, CA a gift of a house was immune from attack under s 10 because it was made more than six years before death and no argument was advanced upon the basis of *Cadogan v Cadogan*; JACKSON AND DAVIES, paras 16.1, 16.9; ROSS MARTYN, 62 and Hanbury & Martin, *Modern Equity* (14th edn) 352 all appear to accept that *Cadogan v Cadogan* is still applicable to claims under the 1975 Act.
13. On contracts to make wills generally see Sparks, *Contracts to Make Wills*; Lee, 'Contracts to Make Wills', (1972) 122 NLJ 576 and see also Miller, 'Provision for Dependants and Agreements for Testamentary Provision', (1978) 128 NLJ 449.
14. Eg *In the Estate of Heys* [1914] P 192.
15. Eg *Birmingham v Renfrew* (1936) 57 CLR 666; Sparks, *Contracts to Make Wills*, Ch 5.

Trustee of New Zealand[16] the Privy Council on appeal from New Zealand held that provisions of a will made in pursuance of a contract are not immune from the court's jurisdiction under the family provision legislation and that a contract to make a will is an attempt to contract out of a statutory jurisdiction and ineffective as such. Viscount Simon LC in giving the advice of the Privy Council stated that any damages for a breach of contract to make a will must be calculated on the basis that a testator's freedom was restricted by family provision legislation and so are reduced by the amount of any order made by the court.[17] *Dillon* was badly received academically[18] – it was noted that an earlier contrary case was not cited to the Board.[19] However, *Dillon* was followed by an English court in 1955.[20] Matters stood still until 1971 when the Privy Council in deciding *Schaefer v Schuhmann*,[1] an appeal from New South Wales, held by a majority that *Dillon v Public Trustee of New Zealand* was wrongly decided. In overruling *Dillon* the Board held that provisions of a will made pursuant to a contract cannot be the subject of an order for family provision and that damages for breach of such a contract are to be calculated without regard to the family provision legislation. Lord Simon of Glaisdale dissented on the basis that family provision legislation was of such importance that it should prevail over lesser contractual rights.[2] While *Schaefer v Schuhmann* is probably the more intellectually satisfying decision and on its facts a most just decision,[3] it did open up a means of deliberately avoiding the legislation and it could cause considerable injustice where the value of the consideration given to the testator in return for his promise or the value of any reliance upon the promise by the promisee is small in relation to the value of the promised provisions in the will.

16. [1941] AC 294, [1941] 2 All ER 284.
17. [1941] AC 294, at 304–305, [1941] 2 All ER 294, at 289F–290A.
18. Gordon (1941) 19 Can Bar Rev 603; contra, Anon, (1941) 19 Can Bar Rev 756; Gordon, (1942) 20 Can Bar Rev 72; first edition, pp 26–27.
19. *Re Richardson's Estate* (1938) 29 Tas LR 949.
20. *Re Brown* (1955) 105 L Jo 169. *Dillon* was doubted *obiter* in *Olin v Perrin* [1946] 2 DLR 461 (CA Ont) and *In Re Willan's Estate* (1951) 4 WWRNS 114. Several Canadian Provinces have reversed *Dillon* by legislation, see Bale, 'Limitations on Testamentary Disposition in Canada', (1964) 42 Can Bar Rev 367, 385–386.

1. [1972] AC 572, [1972] 1 All ER 621.
2. [1972] AC 572, at 593C–600F, [1972] 1 All ER 621, at 633g–639h.
3. The applicants in *Schaefer v Schuhmann* were all adult daughters of the testator, and three of them were married. The promisee was the housekeeper of the testator who had worked for no wages in reliance upon the promise of the testator.

The matter was considered by the Law Commission.[4] The Law Commission accepted the principle of *Schaefer v Schuhmann*, but sought to mitigate some of the worst abuses to which the decision potentially gave rise. The Law Commission had a choice of approaches. Either it could use the power to set aside inter vivos dispositions under section 10 or adopt Canadian legislation specifically on contracts to make wills. Such legislation provides that provisions in wills are exempt from family provision orders if they are made pursuant to 'bona fide' contracts and to the extent of the value of the property passing under the contract to the testator.[5] The Law Commission chose to combine both approaches by giving the court power to review any contract to make a will if it was made with an intention to defeat a family provision application and by enacting that a contract for 'no valuable consideration' is rebuttably presumed to be made with an intention to defeat a family provision application.

The 1975 Act's Provisions on Contracts to Make Wills

By virtue of section 11 the court has jurisdiction to order property bequeathed pursuant to a contract to make a will to be made available to satisfy a claim for family provision. Such contracts include mutual will contracts,[6] but exclude contracts to die intestate, as such can hardly be described as contracts 'to leave by his will a sum of money or other property'. Also specifically included are contractual agreements by a deceased that his personal representatives will pay money or transfer property out of the estate.[7] The contract must have been made after 1 April 1976,[8] but subject to this, unlike the provisions of section 10, there is no time limit on when the contract was made. Section 11 requires a 'contract' and hence would not apply to a situation where the deceased had made a representation to leave property by will, which while not

4. LAW COM, paras 22–42.
5. Canadian Draft Uniform Relief Act, s 16, based upon very similar provincial legislation.
6. *Re Richardson's Estate* (1938) 29 Tas LR 949; and see generally *Re Dale* [1994] Ch 31, [1993] 4 All ER 129 and Burgess, 'A Fresh Look at Mutual Wills', (1970) 34 Conv (NS) 230. For a family provision case where mutual wills were not established, see *Re Goodchild* [1996] 1 WLR 694, [1996] 1 All ER 670; affd [1997] 3 All ER 63.
7. S 11(2)(a).
8. S 11(6), s 27(3).

amounting to a contract, was enforceable against his estate by way of proprietary estoppel.[9] Thus a representee may be obliged to argue that while an estoppel has arisen, no binding contract exists.[10]

The contract must have been made for less than full valuable consideration.[11] Valuable consideration is defined as excluding marriage consideration or a promise of a marriage.[12] In deciding whether full consideration was given, the consideration is valued 'when the contract was made'.[13] Thus if a testator with a life expectancy of one year receives shares worth £1,000 in return for a promise to bequeath a legacy of £1,500, the contract will have been made for less than full consideration, even if at the date of death the shares had risen in value to £2,500. In valuing the consideration regard must be given to factors such as the time between payment of the consideration and the date of the death of the testator and the possibility of the estate being insolvent or otherwise unable to comply with the contract. Thus if a testator with a life expectancy of ten years promises a legacy of £250 in return for an immediate payment of £100, the transaction is for full consideration if regard is had to the expected length of time before the death of the testator (£100 at 10% per annum interest compounded annually for ten years is £259.37) and to the possibility that the testator's estate is insolvent. The Act specifically states that the consideration must pass or be promised at the time the contract was made and can be provided by the promisee (called 'the donee' in the Act) or by a third party[14] – an important point when considering mutual wills.

The contract must have been made with the requisite intention to defeat an application for family provision,[15] which is defined as the same intention required under section 10.[16] Section 12(2) provides that where '*no valuable consideration*' is provided by the

9. Eg *Re Basham* [1986] 1 WLR 1498, [1987] 1 All ER 405; and see *Wayling v Jones*[1995] 2 FLR 1029.Consider also the possibility of a restitutionary claim in this situation – *Deglman v Guaranty Trust Co of Canada and Constantineau* [1954] 3 DLR 785.
10. For example because there has been no compliance with s 40 of the Law of Property Act 1925; s 2(1) of the Law of Property (Miscellaneous Provisions) Act 1989.
11. S 11(2)(c).
12. S 25(1).
13. S 11(2)(c).
14. S 11(2)(c). For discussion of the problems of valuing consideration in contracts to make wills, see Institute of Law Research and Reform, University of Alberta, Report No 29 (1978)138–139; Law Reform Commission of New South Wales, Working Paper on Testator's Family Maintenance and Guardianship Act 1916, para 11.56 and s 22(1)(b), (6) of the Family Provision Act 1982.
15. S 11(2)(b).
16. S 12(1). For detailed discussion of the requisite intention see pp 306–307, *ante*.

promisee or any other person it is rebuttably presumed that the contract was made with the requisite intention to defeat a family provision application. It is not easy to understand what 'no valuable consideration' means, because if there is no consideration present the contract is unenforceable and if the subsection only applied to contracts in consideration of marriage it would have expressly referred to them. One cannot import any idea of inadequacy into the definition of 'consideration', because the context clearly shows that 'consideration' is used in its technical meaning and because the provisions of section 11(2)(c) contemplate that 'valuable consideration' can be less than full consideration. The Report of the Law Commission gives no help as the only example of the operation of the presumption given concerns marriage consideration.[17] It is tentatively submitted that 'no valuable consideration' means contracts where the only consideration is marriage or a promise of marriage,[18] a deed,[19] but not nominal consideration.[20] In the light of the decision of the House of Lords in *Midland Bank v Green* it is unlikely that the court will make any inquiries of the contract to ascertain whether in reality it is of the nature of a gift rather than a contract, if *some* consideration is present.[1]

Deciding when the rebuttable presumption applies is not the only difficulty with it. Its very inclusion in the Act is mistaken because the presumption is a false one – one that is likely to be rebutted in almost every case where evidence is available. The Law Commission rejected the imposition of any presumption as to intention in section 10, because it was felt that such a presumption would be unlikely to be true.[2] The same reasoning should have been applied to the presumption when a contract is made for 'no valuable consideration'. Whenever any contract to make a will is made, the testator's mind is directed to questions of succession, but the lack of 'valuable consideration' is unlikely to be indicative of any intention to defeat a family provision application. Indeed in the

17. LAW COM, paras 229–231.
18. S 25(1).
19. Most textbooks treat the presence of a seal as an alternative to consideration rather than as falling within the definition of consideration *eg* Chitty, *Contracts* (27th edn) Vol 1, para 1-034; Treitel, *The Law of Contract* (9th edn), pp 146–147; Cheshire, Fifoot and Furmston, *Law of Contract* (13th edn), p 29. In equity a deed has never been treated as consideration, Snell's *Equity* (29th edn), p 592; *Jeffreys v Jeffreys* (1841) Cr & P 138.
20. See *Midland Bank Trust Co v Green* [1981] AC 513, at 531G–H, [1981] 1 All ER 153, at 159d-f; *Mountford v Scott* [1975] Ch 258, [1975] 1 All ER 198.
1. [1981] AC 513.
2. LAW COM, paras 201–202.

example cited by the Law Commission – marriage consideration – a testator is more likely than not intending to aid the policy of the family provision legislation by making provision for his wife, the most important potential applicant under the Act. The inclusion of the rebuttable presumption was erroneous and was the result of trying to combine two different and essentially incompatible approaches – the Canadian approach which treats the difference in value between the consideration given and the promised provisions in the will as essentially a gratuitous transfer on death and the approach of subjecting contracts to make wills to the provisions of section 10 – essentially treating them as inter vivos dispositions.

The power of the court to make orders restricting the operation of contracts to make wills is a discretionary one and in exercising the power, the court is to 'have regard to the circumstances in which the contract was made, the relationship, if any, of the donee to the deceased, conduct and financial resources of the donee and all the other circumstances of the case'.[3] This list is similar to the list of matters to which regard is had under section 10 and the same principles which govern the court's discretion under section 10 should govern the exercise of the discretion under section 11.[4]

The Court's Powers Under Section 11

The court has power to make orders which restrict the operation of contracts to make wills 'to facilitate the making of financial provision for an applicant under the Act'.[5] If the personal representatives have performed the contract by transferring money or property to the donee, the court can order the donee to provide money or property specified in the order for the purposes of a family provision order.[6] The wording of the Act would suggest that such an order need not specify the same money or property as had been transferred to the donee. If the personal representatives have not performed the contract in whole or in part by transferring money or property to the donee, the court may order the personal representatives not to transfer such of the money or property as may be specified in the order.[7]

3. S 11(4).
4. See pp 307–308, *ante*.
5. S 11(2)(d).
6. S 11(i).
7. S 11(ii).

An order may be made against a donee's personal representatives,[8] but the same restrictions on liability exist as exist for applications under section 10.[9]

Any order which the court may make is limited to the difference in value between the consideration provided by or on behalf of the donee and the value of the money or property transferred or transferable under the contract.[10] Property transferred or transferable under the contract is valued at the date of the hearing;[11] but, although the Act is not totally clear on this, the consideration is valued when it is provided – such valuation probably includes allowance for the time between the date the consideration passed and the date of death of the testator.[12] For example, if a testator with a life expectancy of two years makes a contract to bequeath shares worth £100 at the date of the contract in return for an immediate payment of £40 and the shares are worth £150 at the date of death and £200 at the date of the hearing, the court can make an order up to the amount of £200 minus £40 plus two years' interest. If, however, the shares drop in value after the date of death to £50 at the date of the hearing the court can effectively make no order. But if the same testator made a contract to bequeath shares worth £100 at the date of the contract in return for an immediate payment of £82 and the shares have risen to £1,000 at the date of the hearing, the court can make no order because the contract at the time it was made for was for full valuable consideration.[13]

Orders against trustees are subject to the same limits as orders against trustees under section 10.[14] It is obscure whether limitations on orders against trustees are alternatives to the ordinary limitations or merely additional, cumulative limitations.[15] As the section specifically defines a 'donee' as including a person 'for *the benefit of whom* the contract was made'[16] where the benefit of a contract is held in trust for a person an order can be made directly against the beneficiary.

8. S 12(4).
9. S 12(4). See pp 308–309, *ante*.
10. S 11(3).
11. S 11(3).
12. See p 316, *ante*.
13. S 11(2)(c).
14. S 13(1)(b).
15. Whether the limitation contained in s 13 is an alternative to the limitations contained in s 10(3) and (4), s 11(3) or additional thereto is a most difficult question. The words of s 13(1), 'shall be subject to the following limitation (in addition, in the case of an application under s 10, to any provision regarding the deduction of Inheritance Tax)' would tend to suggest that the various provisions are truly alternatives.
16. S 11(2)(c).

In exercising its powers the court has a wide general power to give directions.[17]

The Effect of Section 11 on Contractual Remedies

When the court exercises its powers to order personal representatives to transfer money or property to a family provision applicant, prima facie according to *Schaefer v Schuhmann*[18] the estate would be liable for damages for breach of contract. However, section 11(5) provides that the contractual rights of the donee are modified by the court's order and contractual relief is only available to the extent that such relief is not inconsistent with the court's order. Section 11(5) does not appear to be worded to deal with the situation where a testator makes a contract to make a will, fails to die testate in accordance with the contract and the promisee sues for damages or specific performance. In such a situation the promisee's rights are a liability of the estate,[19] and section 11(5) cannot apply, since it requires a court to have made an order under section 11(2) to deal with 'money paid or other property ... transferred ... *in accordance with the contract*'. These words would seem to leave a large and unintended gap in supposedly comprehensive legislation.

Occupational and Other Pension Schemes[20]

Considerable amounts of wealth are held through various occupational and other pension schemes. These frequently provide that on the death of the pensioner, benefits are available to the dependants and family of the deceased. Sometimes these benefits are fixed by the terms of the pension agreement, but frequently there is some discretion in the choice of a person entitled to the benefits after death of the pensioner. In some cases the pensioner has a power of nomination, in others trustees have a discretion but may be influenced by a nomination and in others the trustees have unfettered discretion. The Law Commission, apparently ignoring the possibility that a nomination by the deceased might be effective

17. S 12(3).
18. [1972] AC 572, [1972] 1 All ER 621.
19. *Re Richardson's Estate* (1938) 29 Tas LR 949, approved in *Schaefer v Schuhmann*.
20. Rosettenstein, 'Occupational Pensions and the 1975 Inheritance Act', (1979) 123 Sol Jo 661.

by itself, decided against specifically including benefits payable under occupational pension schemes on the ground that the pension trustees usually exercise the discretion satisfactorily and that it would be wrong to graft different duties on to powers exercisable in a certain way and generally exercised responsibly.[1]

Accordingly occupational pension schemes are governed by the general provisions of the Act. If a pensioner can nominate a person to receive benefits after his death and the pension scheme is contained in an 'enactment' such as a statutory instrument, as happens with some public sector pensions, then the nominated property automatically forms part of the 'net estate' under the provisions relating to statutory nominations.[2] If the pension scheme is not contained in any 'enactment', then the only way in which nominated property can form part of the 'net estate' is under section 10.[3] Such a nomination *probably* comes within the wide definition of 'disposition',[4] but it may be rare to find the requisite intention in making such nomination, except where the effect of not making such nomination is that the nominated benefits go to the deceased's estate. Since a nomination is in reality the making of a will, there would seem to be good reasons for extending the operation of section 8(1) to cover non-statutory nominations. Where the trustees exercise any kind of discretion, the benefits thereby disposed of cannot form part of the 'net estate', but it is clearly prudent for the exercise of the trustees' discretion and the application to the court to be co-ordinated.[5] Further, following the decision in *Brooks v Brooks*,[6] certain pension schemes may constitute an ante-nuptial or post-nuptial settlement and so be capable of being affected by an order under section 2(1)(f).[7]

1. LAW COM, para 213.
2. S 8(1).
3. *Re Cairnes* (1982) 4 FLR 225.
4. 'Disposition' is defined in s 10(7). In *Danish Bacon Co Staff Pension Fund Trusts* [1971] 1 WLR 248, [1971] 1 All ER 486 Megarry J held that a nomination under a pension scheme was not a 'disposition' within the meaning of the Law of Property Act 1925, s 53(1)(c). See further Chappenden, 'Non-Statutory Nominations', [1972] JBL 20 and *Baird v Baird* [1990] 2 AC 548, [1990] 2 All ER 300, which would tend to suggest that such a nomination is purely contractual and hence not a special power of appointment, which is by s 10(7)(b) specifically excluded from the definition of 'disposition'.
5. Compare the problem of applications in several jurisdictions, see p 55, *ante*.
6. [1996] AC 375, [1995] 3 All ER 257.
7. See generally pp 397–399, *post*.

Pensions on Divorce

In the 1990s there has been considerable discussion about extending the power of the divorce courts to make ancillary relief orders affecting pensions. This led to the enactment of legislation in the Pensions Act 1995 and the Family Law Act 1996. Section 166 of the Pensions Act 1995 enacted new sections 25B, 25C, 25D of the Matrimonial Causes Act 1973. These new provisions apply to divorce petitions filed on or after 1 July 1996.[8] The court is enabled to make an order under section 23 of the Matrimonial Causes Act 1973 in respect of income payments made to a spouse under a 'pension scheme'.[9] Such an order is unlikely to fall within section 36(6) of the Matrimonial Causes Act 1973 because normally the pension payments will cease upon the death of the member of the pension scheme.[10] The court can make a lump sum order to affect a lump sum payable upon death, whether the lump sum is payable at the discretion of trustees,[11] at the nomination of a member of the pension scheme[12] or to the member's estate.[13] The court has no power to make an order affecting a widow's pension. 'Pension scheme' for this purpose includes an occupational pension scheme,[14] personal pension scheme,[15] retirement annuity contract[16] and SERPS.[17]

The Family Law Act 1996 conferred upon the court power to split pensions.[18] This legislation has not been brought into force and is unlikely to be brought into force without significant amendement. The Act did not attempt to overrule *Brooks v Brooks*.

Both the Pensions Act 1995 and the Family Law Act 1996 give the divorce courts significantly greater powers than a court exercising the jurisdiction under the 1975 Act. This anomaly was not commented upon in either the Green or the White Papers published to discuss the implementation of the pension splitting provisions of the Family Law Act 1996.[19] The current position is that a spouse

8. Pensions Act 1995 (Commencement) (No 5) Order 1996, SI 1996/1675.
9. S 25B(4).
10. For s 31 of the Matrimonial Causes Act 1973, see pp 416–417, *post*. S 31(6) might be applicable where a secured periodical payments order is made over a pension or annuity which is payable for a guaranteed number of years.
11. S 25C(2)(a).
12. S 25C(2)(b).
13. S 25C(2)(c).
14. S 25D(4); s 1 of the Pension Schemes Act 1993.
15. S 25D(4); s 1 of the Pension Schemes Act 1993.
16. S 25D(3)(a).
17. S 25D(4); s 1 of the Pension Schemes Act 1993.
18. S 16.
19. 'The Treatment of Pension Rights on Divorce', (Cm 3345, 1996); 'Pension Rights on Divorce', (Cm 3564 1997).

can be significantly better off on divorce than on death, thereby defeating the most important aim of the enactment of the 1975 Act. The position is particularly striking if a divorcing spouse dies before the completion of an application for ancillary relief – at the very least some form of 'reverse' section 14[20] should be enacted so that a party is not deprived of a share of a pension by death occurring before the conclusion of an ancillary relief application – and a comparison of the position of a separated spouse and a spouse who has divorced shows the separated spouse in a much weaker position.

Property Subject to Testamentary Options

Where property is made the subject of a contract by the will of the deceased such as by the creation of a testamentary option,[1] such property comes within the definition of the 'net estate' of the deceased, being property of which the deceased had power to dispose by his will. Accordingly the court can make an order which defeats a testamentary option. A claim by an applicant to have provision made out of land subject to a testamentary option should be registered as a pending action,[2] because a person enforcing the option, even within six months of the grant of representation, will take the land as a purchaser for value and will therefore take free of any matter that should have been registered as a pending action unless he has actual notice of it.[3] A person who is given by a will a contractual right is a 'beneficiary' within the meaning of section 25(1), since he is 'beneficially interested' in the estate.[4]

Criticism of the Definition of the 'Net Estate'

The 1975 Act considerably widened the categories of property available to satisfy a family provision order. The extensions were in two directions, extending the operation of the Act to include

20. For s 14, see pp 70–71, *ante*.
1. On testamentary options generally, see Barnsley, *Land Options* (2nd edn), 139–155.
2. Land Charges Act 1972, s 5(2), s 17(1); Land Registration Act 1925, s 59(1); *Whittingham v Whittingham* [1979] Fam 9, [1978] 3 All ER 805
3. Land Charges Act 1972, s 5(7); Land Registration Act 1925, s 59(6); *Whittingham v Whittingham* [1979] Fam 9, [1978] 3 All ER 805
4. At least where the option is granted at an undervalue, *Re Lander* [1951] Ch 546, [1951] 1 All ER 672.

transfers on death which cannot be made the subject of provisions in a will and enacting certain limited anti-avoidance measures. The extensions to include transfers on death which cannot be governed by provisions in a will can wholeheartedly be welcomed. The Act as drafted forms an intellectually consistent code and the precise provisions of the Act are a model of clarity compared with the law on the similar problem whether property passing on death but not forming part of the estate of the deceased is liable for the deceased's debts.[5] The only significant omission in the Act is non-statutory nominations and this omission was due to the Law Commission's mistaken belief that such nominations were never in themselves effective and always depended ultimately on the discretion of trustees.[6]

The Law Commission justified the introduction of anti-avoidance measures because it was thought that 'it is a matter of overriding importance that family provision laws are effective'.[7]

While it may be a matter of 'overriding importance' that family provision laws are effective when the deceased while alive is legally obliged to support the applicant, it can hardly be a matter of such 'overriding importance' when the deceased while alive was under no legal duty to support the applicant and where the deceased could lawfully squander his property and die with no estate. Where the deceased was under no legal duty to support the applicant during the deceased's lifetime, the only justification for family provision legislation is that after death a person's wishes as to the ownership of his property as against society's wishes are entitled to less respect than when he was alive. This justification does not support the upsetting of inter vivos transactions. Having said that, the specific provisions of the Act are sufficiently limited not seriously to disturb the security of title of donees. The detailed provisions of the Act dealing with anti-avoidance are on the whole well drafted, although the Act does contain some errors and obscurities. The usefulness of such detailed provisions, dealing with situations which will only rarely, if ever, occur,

5. The Administration of Estates Act 1925, s 32(1) sets out the property available for the payment of the deceased's debts. Donationes mortis causa are usually thought of as liable for the deceased's debts, but this has been doubted, Warnock-Smith, 'Donatio Mortis Causa and the Payment of Debts' [1978] Conv 130. It is uncertain whether nominated property is liable for the debts of a deceased, see Samuels, 'Nominations in Favour of a Deceased to Take Effect on Death', (1967) 31 Conv (NS) 85; Chappenden, 'Non-Statutory Nominations', [1972] JBL 20. Anomalously a severable share of a joint tenancy is not liable for the deceased's debts, see *Re Palmer* [1994] Ch 316, [1994] 3 All ER 835. This can result in family provision being ordered out of an insolvent estate where orders under s 9 and s 10 are made, eg *Re Dawkins* [1986] 2 FLR 360.
6. LAW COM, para 213; see also ROSS MARTYN, 61.
7. LAW COM, para 191.

can be demonstrated by regard to the unsatisfactory experience of American courts[8] and civil law countries[9] and the rather unhappy decisions of British courts in *Dillon v Public Trustee*,[10] *Schaefer v Schuhmann*[11] and *Cadogan v Cadogan*[12] where the application of open-textured and conflicting general principles of law has caused the law to wallow in intellectual and practical confusion.

The treatment of pensions by the 1975 Act is profoundly unsatisfactory and with judicial decisions and legislation on divorce has become very capricious. Whether lump sums are capable depends upon whether a nomination is made pursuant to a statutory pension scheme,[13] whether a nomination can be challenged under section 10, a difficult question both factually and as a matter of law,[14] or whether the pension scheme can be regarded as an 'ante-nuptial or post-nuptial settlement', which is determined by the wording of the scheme and the date of the marriage in relation to when the deceased joined the scheme or took out the policy.[15] Further legislation has enhanced the powers of the court on divorce, but not under the 1975 Act.[16]

While the enlarged definition of the 'net estate' is to be welcomed intellectually, it is doubtful whether the new provisions will actually be used greatly. Since in any event property passing on death but not disposable by will is taken into account in deciding whether the provision is reasonable,[17] and apart from jointly owned property, the amount of wealth passing by such means is very small, it is most unlikely that many orders will be actually made in reliance upon the new provisions. As has been pointed out the courts are unlikely in practice to upset the accretion of property by survivorship.[18] The provisions on avoidance again are unlikely to be greatly employed, because actual avoidance was and is comparatively rare. While the 1938 Act was exceptionally easy to avoid, in practice very few people actually took steps to avoid it – like estate duty the amazing thing is not the ease of avoidance but the number of people who did not utilise the methods of avoidance.

8. See Macdonald, *Fraud on the Widow's Share*.
9. See Dawson, *Gifts and Promises*.
10. [1941] AC 294, [1941] 2 All ER 284.
11. [1972] AC 572, [1972] 1 All ER 621.
12. [1977] 1 WLR 1041, [1977] 1 All ER 200; revsd [1977] 3 All ER 831.
13. See p 321, *ante*.
14. See p 321, *ante*.
15. See pp 397–399, *post*.
16. See pp 322–323, *ante*.
17. *Re Carter* (1968) 112 Sol Jo 136.
18. See pp 300–301, *ante*.

Chapter 8

PROCEDURE

PART 1: TIME FOR APPLICATION

Limitation Period

In its original form the 1938 Act stated that except as provided by section 4 (variation of orders[1]) an order could only be made on an application made within six months from the date on which representation in regard to the testator's estate for general purposes was first taken out.[2]

Unlike the New Zealand Act, which provided that the application must be made within twelve months from the grant and gave the court jurisdiction to extend the time for application,[3] there was no provision enabling the court to extend the time for making an application.[4]

1. See pp 401–408, *post*.
2. The Inheritance (Family Provision) Act 1938, s 2(1). The date on which representation was first taken out is not included in calculating the six month period from that date, see *Trow v Ind Coope (West Midlands) Ltd* [1967] 2 QB 899, [1967] 1 All ER 19. 'Month' means calendar month, see Interpretation Act 1978, Sch I; *Dodds v Walker* [1980] 1 WLR 1061, [1980] 2 All ER 507; affd [1981] 1 WLR 1027, [1981] 2 All ER 609. The application is made when the originating summons or application is *issued*, not when it is served: *Re Chittenden* [1970] 3 All ER 562.
3. Family Protection Act 1906, s 33(9), now Family Protection Act 1955, s 9. In Australia time limits vary from three months from the date of the grant in Tasmania to two years from the date of the grant in the case of New Zealand, see the table in DE GROOT AND NICKEL, para 402.
4. The period of six months cannot be shortened by means of a notice under the Trustee Act 1925, s 27. However, in exercising its powers to extend time under s 4, the court will have regard to any failure to reply to such a notice (compare *Escritt v Escritt* (1981)3 FLR 280) and any distribution sanctioned by an order of the court within the six-month period, as to which see *Re Ralphs* [1968] 1 WLR 1522, [1968] 3 All ER 285 and pp 356–357, *post*. In New Zealand the courts have, with a view to an immediate distribution, required applicants to lodge their claims under the Act within 30 days or risk a distribution at the expiration of the period; see *Re Barber* [1928] NZLR 113. The New South Wales legislation (now s 17 of the Family Provision Act 1981) expressly provides for the shortening of time by notice to lodge a claim; such a notice protects the personal representatives, but not the beneficiaries.

Extension of Time

The Intestates' Estates Act 1952 gave the court a limited power to extend the period of time in which an application could be made.[5] The Act provided that if it was shown to the satisfaction of the court that the limitation of six months would operate *unfairly*:

(a) in consequence of the discovery of a will or codicil involving a substantial change in the disposition of the deceased's estate (whether or not involving a further grant of representation), or
(b) in consequence of a question whether a person had an interest in the estate, or as to the nature of an interest in the estate, not having been determined at the time when representation was first taken out, or
(c) in consequence of some other circumstances affecting the administration or distribution of the estate,

the court might extend the period.

These grounds for extension were discovered, in the light of experience, to be too restricted. The limitation period was also inconsistent with that under section 3 of the Matrimonial Causes (Property and Maintenance) Act 1958 (subsequently section 26 of the Matrimonial Causes Act 1965) which provided that an application under that section should not be made except:

(a) before the end of the period of six months beginning with the date on which representation in regard to the estate of the deceased is first taken out, or
(b) with the permission of the court, after the end of that period but before the administration and distribution of the estate have been completed.

This inconsistency was undesirable[6] and the 1966 Act changed the limitation provisions governing both applications under the 1938 Act and section 26 of the Matrimonial Causes Act 1965 to give the court a general power to override the six-month limitation period.[7] The case law on the pre-1966 law is of little use in predicting how the court will exercise its general discretion to extend the six-month

5. Intestates' Estates Act 1952, s 7, Sch 3, introducing the Inheritance (Family Provision) Act 1938, s 2(1A).
6. See the comments of Russell LJ in *Re Kay* [1965] 1 WLR 1463, at 1469, [1965] 3 All ER 724, at 727–728.
7. S 5.

period, since it is mostly concerned with the interpretation of the specific conditions introduced by the Intestates' Estates Act 1952 which permitted the court to extend time. The decisions on the pre-1966 law are listed below.[8]

The Law Commission approved of the six-month limitation period as a bar to tardy applications, but with the court's general powers to extend time where appropriate.[9] Accordingly section 4 of the 1975 Act repeated the provisions of the 1966 Act.

Each Applicant Must Apply in Time

An application by one applicant does not enure for the benefit of other applicants and each applicant has to apply personally in time or have the period of time extended under section 4.[10] However, where one application has been made in time, a court is very likely to exercise its powers to extend time for the second application.

Applicants under a Disability

Unlike the position under the Limitation Act 1980[11] and in certain Australasian jurisdictions,[12] the time limit under section 4 applies without modification to applicants under a disability. However, a disability will be a material factor in deciding whether the court should exercise its powers to extend time.[13]

8. Cases where an extension was granted: *Re Bone* [1955] 1 WLR 703, [1955] 2 All ER 555; *Re Trott* [1958] 1 WLR 604, [1958] 2 All ER 296; *Re McNare* [1964] 1 WLR 1255, [1964] 3 All ER 373; *Re John* (1966) 111 Sol Jo 15. Cases where an extension was refused: *Re Greaves* [1954] 1 WLR 760, [1954] 2 All ER 109; *Re Kay* [1965] 1 WLR 1463, [1965] 3 All ER 724; *Re Bluston* [1967] Ch 615, [1966] 3 All ER 220; *Re Hodgkinson* (1956) Times, 26 October, [1956] CLY 9251; affd (1957) [1967] Ch 634n, [1966] 3 All ER 226n; *Re Miller* [1969] 1 WLR 583, [1968] 3 All ER 844.
9. WORKING PAPER, para 3.48; LAW COM, para 144.
10. Eg *Re Trott* [1958] 1 WLR 604, [1958] 2 All ER 296. For the practice in some Australasian jurisdictions, see DICKEY, 15.
11. S 28. The contrast between the 1975 Act and Limitation Act 1980 was noted by Wilson J in *Re C* [1995] 2 FLR 24, at 28G–H.
12. See s 9(2)(a) of the Family Protection Act 1955 (New Zealand); s 41(7) of the Succession Act 1981 (Queensland); s 3(5)of the Testator's Family Maintenance Act 1912 (Tasmania).
13. See per Wilson J in *Re C* [1995] 2 FLR 24, at 28H. For an earlier case involving an infant, see *Re Trott* [1958] 1 WLR 604, [1958] 2 All ER 296

Application before Grant

The issue of whether an application can be made before a grant of representation has been taken out has been the subject of two conflicting reported authorities. In *Re Searle*[14] Roxburgh J arguing that the time limit was directed towards preventing applications from being too late, not too early,[15] held that an application could validly be made before a grant of representation was taken out. No actual order for provision or for interim provision could be made until there was an actual grant of representation. This is the position in Australasia.[16]

Nearly 43 years later Eastham J reached the opposite conclusion in *Re McBroom*.[17] In that case the applicant who was probably entitled to the estate of the deceased under the rules of intestacy, sought orders under section 9 against the deceased's severable share in property passing by survivorship. Eastham J struck out as premature the application because no grant of representation had been taken out.

Neither decision is particularly satisfactory. In *Re Searle* a grant of representation had been obtained prior to the trial and the personal representatives were before the court. The principal reason which Roxburgh J gave was that the objection that the action was premature was only a procedural objection and it was too late to make it at the trial.[18] *Re Searle* was not cited in *Re McBroom*. In *Re McBroom* there had been no attempt to obtain a grant of representation before the hearing and no intimation that one would be obtained before the trial. Eastham J reached his conclusion with regret[19] and relied principally upon arguments relating to the need for personal representatives to be before the court at the time the court made an order.[20]

It is submitted that *Re Searle* is the better decision and should be followed. To follow*Re McBroom* would mean that in a case of a contested probate action an application under the Inheritance Act 1984 could not be begun until after the trial of the probate action,

14. [1949] Ch 73, [1948] 2 All ER 426.
15. [1949] Ch 76-7, [1948] 2 All ER 427B.
16. *Re Purnell* [1961] QWN34; *Leue v Reynolds* [1986] 4 NSWLR 590; DICKEY, 11. The decision in *Re Dawkins* [1986] 2 FLR 360, at 361D–E where a final order was made before any grant of representation was taken out (the court made an order under s 10) must be regarded as *per incuriam*!
17. [1992] 2 FLR 49.
18. [1949] Ch 76-7, [1948] 2 All ER 427F-H.
19. [1992] 2 FLR 52F; Eastham J also granted leave to appeal.
20. [1992] 2 FLR 51C–52F.

thereby preventing the convenient, expeditious and less expensive course of having the trial of the application under the Inheritance Act 1984 immediately after the trial of the probate action.[1] If *Re McBroom* is correct a court may not have jurisdiction to grant interlocutory relief preserving property until a grant of representation has been taken out.[2] The matter is made more unsatisfactory because of doubts whether a grant of representation *ad litem* is sufficient to start time running for the purposes of section 4.[3]

When Representation is First Taken Out[4]

In considering when representation was first taken out, a grant limited to settled land or to trust property shall be left out of account and a grant limited to real estate or personal estate shall be left out of account unless a grant limited to the remainder of the estate has previously been made or is made at the same time.[5]

By analogy with the above statutory exclusion and adopting a purposive construction it is generally thought that the grant of representation must in any event be a general grant, not one limited to particular property (but may be save and except settled land). A grant limited in duration, but giving the personal representatives full powers to distribute the estate, such as a grant *durante minore aetate*, is clearly a grant of representation for the purposes of the limitation period. The position with regard to grants limited for a particular purpose, such as a grant *ad collingenda bona*, or *ad litem*, is not certain. In *Re Johnson*[6] Latey J held that a grant *ad litem* to enable proceedings to be taken for an action for personal injuries did not start time running. Such grants do not usually permit the personal representative to distribute the estate and the personal representative will not necessarily know the nature and extent of the estate or the identity of the persons who are interested therein. On the other hand such grants are not specifically excepted from the statutory definition of a 'grant of representation' and where a grant *ad litem* for the purposes of defending a family provision claim

1. See the factual situation in *Re Freeman* [1984] 1 WLR 1419, [1984] 3 All ER 906.
2. See pp 375–377, *post*.
3. See below.
4. See generally, Andreae, 'Maintenance Claim and Grant of Representation', (1970) 120 NLJ 293.
5. S 23.
6. [1987] CLY 3882.

is made, there are clear policy reasons for regarding the limitation period as running from the making of such a grant.

Successive Grants

Before the Intestates' Estates Act 1952 extended the jurisdiction of the court to cover cases of intestacy, the time limit was expressed to run from 'the date on which representation in regard to the *testator's* estate... is first taken out'.[7] In reliance upon the specific mention of the '*testator's* estate' the Court of Appeal in *Re Bidie*[8] held that where letters of administration were granted and subsequently revoked when a will was discovered, the six-month period only ran from the date of the grant of probate. The majority of the Court of Appeal expressed the view, *obiter*, that where a grant of probate is subsequently revoked on the discovery of a later will, the period of limitation runs from the date of the second grant.[9] Somervell LJ in particular expressed the view that: '"representation" means "the representation ... which the plaintiff is seeking to attack"'.[10] Thus where a subsequent testamentary disposition is subsequently admitted to probate, the limitation period will run from the later grant of representation. Most commentators concluded that the obiter dicta of the Court of Appeal were incorrect,[11] arguing that they stretched the language of the Act too far in the face of the plain use of the word 'first' and drawing comfort from the fact that Parliament when it passed the Intestates' Estates Act 1952 considered it necessary specifically to include as a ground for extending the time limit the discovery of a will or codicil *whether or not involving a further grant of representation.*[12] The uncertainty was resolved by the decision of Thomas J sitting as a judge of the Chancery Division in *Re Freeman.*[13] In this case a grant of probate

7. The Inheritance (Family Provision) Act 1938, s 2(1).
8. [1949] Ch 121, [1948] 2 All ER 995, reversing [1948] Ch 697, [1948] 1 All ER 885. The case was a strong one in that under the then legislation no application could be made in the case of an intestacy and thus it was utterly impossible for the applicant to apply under the original letters of administration.
9. Lord Greene MR at [1949] Ch 133, [1949] 2 All ER 1000H–1001A specifically reserved his opinion; Somervell LJ at [1949] Ch 135, [1948] 2 All ER 1002C; Evershed LJ at [1949] Ch136-7, [1948] 2 All ER1003A–C.
10. [1949] Ch 135, [1948] 2 All ER 1002A.
11. ALBERY, 10-13; Andrae, 'Maintenance Claims and Grants of Representation', (1970) 120 NLJ 243; second edition, p 239.
12. Intestates' Estates Act 1952, s 7, Sch III introducing the Inheritance (Family Provision) Act 1938, s 2(1A)(a).
13. [1984] 1 WLR 1419, [1984] 3 All ER 906.

in favour of a will which benefited the applicant was revoked on the ground of want of due execution and letters of adminstration for an intestacy were granted. Thomas J, following the obiter dicta in *Re Bidie*, held that time only started running from the date of the letters of administration.

It is, however, clear that a grant in solemn form confirming an earlier grant in common form does not affect the running of time,[14] and it is submitted that where an executor to whom power has been reserved subsequently proves, proof by such an executor does not affect the running of time. In most cases of successive grants where the effect of the new grant is different the court is likely to extend the time for an application. It is however important for an applicant to know whether he is entitled as of right to apply or must rely upon the court's power to extend time.

The Court's Discretion to Extend the Time Limit

There has been a surprising amount of reported case law and decisions of the Court of Appeal upon the exercise of the discretion to extend the time limit.[15]

In 1980 Megarry V-C laid down in *Re Salmon*[16] certain principles or guidelines upon the exercise of the court's discretion to extend the time limit. While, except on one point,[17] subsequent judges have not expressly overruled or refused to follow the principles laid down by Megarry V-C, the attitude of subsequent judges to *Re Salmon* has varied enormously, from enthusiastic

14. *Re Miller* [1969] 1 WLR 583, [1968] 3 All ER 844.
15. Since 1966 the following cases have dealt with extensions of time: *Re Stone* (1969) 114 Sol Jo 36; *Re Ruttie* [1970] 1 WLR 89, [1989] 3 All ER 1633; *Re Gonin* [1977] 2 All ER 720, 735 – the report at [1979] Ch 16 does not deal with the application for family provision; *Re Salmon* [1981] Ch 167, [1980] 3 All ER 532; *Re Dennis* [1981] 2 All ER 140; *Re Longley* [1981] CLY 2885; *Adams v Adams* (22 July 1981, unreported), CA; *Escritt v Escritt* (1981) 3 FLR 280; *Re Bowell* Times, 18/11/82; *Re Campbell* [1983] NI 10; *Polackova v Sobolewski* (28 October 1985, unreported), CA; *Clifford v Tanner* [1987] CLY 3881, CA; *Smith v Loosley* (18 June 1986, unreported), CA; *Re Johnson* [1987] CLY 3882; *Perry v Horlock* (18 November 1987, unreported), CA; *Stock v Brown* [1994] 1 FLR 840; *Baker v Fear* (12 November 1993, unreported), CA (a decision under s 20(2) of the Administration of Justice Act 1980); *Re C* [1995] 2 FLR 24; *Re Abram* [1996] 2 FLR 379, at 385A–F. See also *Lilley v Public Trustee* [1981] AC 839 (a decision under the New Zealand Law Reform (Testamentary Promises) Act 1949).
16. [1981] Ch 167, [1980] 3 All ER 532.
17. That relating to the relevance of a claim for negligence against the applicant's legal advisers, see pp 340–341, *post*.

endorsement of the judgment of Megarry V-C[18] to an emphasis upon the broad unfettered nature of the discretion.[19] Since 1980 the general tendency of the courts has been to become increasingly liberal in the grant of leave under section 4. *Re Salmon* remains the only *comprehensive* discussion of how the courts exercise their discretion – the subsequent case law being decisions on particular factual situations – and is an invaluable framework as to how the court should exercise its discretion.

Firstly, Megarry V-C stated that (in contrast to the position to the limited jurisdiction under the Intestates' Estates Act 1952) the jurisdiction is wide and unfettered. The discretion is to be exercised judicially and in accordance with what is 'just and proper'.[20]

Secondly, Megarry V-C said:

> ..... the onus lies on the plaintiff to establish sufficient grounds for taking the case out of the general rule, and depriving those who are protected by it of its benefits. Further, the time limit is a substantive provision laid down in the Act itself,[1] and is not a mere procedural time limit imposed by rules of court which will be treated with the indulgence appropriate to procedural rules. The burden on the applicant is thus, I think, no triviality: the applicant must make out a substantial case for it to be just and proper for the court to exercise its statutory discretion to extend time.[2]

While the logic of Megarry V-C's reasoning is impeccable, the effect of more recent case law has been to significantly reduce the burden upon applicants. Dicta and decisions to the effect that the mere passage of time is a sufficient reason not to extend time are now rare[3]

18. Eg Browne-Wilkinson J in *Re Dennis* [1981] 2 All ER 140; Dillon LJ in *Baker v Fear* (12 November 1993, unreported), CA.
19. In both *Escritt v Escritt* (1981) 3 FLR 280, at 284G–H and *Adams v Adams* (22 July 1981, unreported), CA Ormrod LJ emphasised the unfettered nature of the discretion. See to like effect the judgment of Croom-Johnson LJ in *Smith v Loosley* (18 June 1986, unreported), CA.
20. [1981] Ch 175A–B, [1980] 3 All ER 537a-b, *ad idem* per Dunn LJ in *Adams v Adams* (22 July 1981, unreported), CA and per Sir John Donaldson MR in *Perry v Horlick* (18 November 1987, unreported), CA.
1. This has the consequence that appeals, both from the Master or District Judge to the Judge, and to the Court of Appeal are final and not interlocutory appeals (but see per Wilson J in *Re C* [1995] 2 FLR 24, at 27G–H); and compare *Hughes v Jones* (1996) Times, 18 July. Further the rules on the admissibility of hearsay in interlocutory applications (RSC Ord 41, r 5(2)) do not apply to applications for leave under s 4.
2. [1981] Ch 175B, [1980] 3 All ER 537b–c, cited with approval in *Re C* [1995] 2 FLR 24, at 27G-H. See also per Thorpe J in *Stock v Brown* [1994] 1 FLR 840, at 841F.
3. For dicta that the mere passage of time is sufficient to prevent an extension of time, see *Re Gonin* [1977] 2 All ER 735-6; *Re Longley* [1981] CLY 2885. In

and some judgments proceed upon the basis that prejudice suffered by respondents is almost a *sine qua non* for not granting an extension of time. The more recent case law with its emphasis upon prejudice to respondents,[4] its less rigorous examination of the reasons for delay[5] and its refusal to inquire into the merits save as a purely threshold test[6] has, at least superficially, gone far to treat the time limit as equivalent to a procedural time limit. As a counterbalance to the remarks of Megarry V-C and representing the modern practice of the courts are the remarks of the Court of Appeal in *Re Stone*[7] that in the case of a *short delay* 'leave should have been granted almost as a matter of course' and of Ormrod LJ in *Adams v Adams* stressing the need to 'balance the claims of the plaintiff and the defendants'.[8]

Thirdly, Megarry V-C stated that it is material to consider how promptly and in what circumstances the applicant has sought the permission of the court after the expiry of the time limit. This is not a mere counting of days between the expiration of six months and the date of issue of proceedings, because regard must be had to all the circumstances of the case.[9] It is however correct to say that the greater the delay the greater the burden on the applicant.[10] The reported case law shows that over the years the courts have allowed increasingly longer extensions of time.[11]

Megarry V-C also stated that regard could be had to whether the applicant had warned the respondents that the

Polackova v Sobolewski (28 October 1985, unreported), CA and *Stock v Brown* [1994] 1 FLR 840 arguments based on the passage of time were rejected. In *Clifford v Tanner* the Court of Appeal approved a concession that the delay was insufficient to prevent the court granting an extension of time.

4. Lack of prejudice was stressed in *Adams v Adams* (22 July 1981, unreported), CA and *Perry v Horlick* (18 November 1987, unreported), CA. *Baker v Fear* (12 November 1993, unreported), CA is a rare modern example of where leave was refused despite a lack of prejudice to the beneficiary. In *Re Gonin* at [1977] 2 All ER 736e Walton J referred to the 'prejudice' of a beneficiary being kept out of his money. Apart from a weak echo of this in *Re Salmon* at [1981] Ch 136C, [1980] 3 All ER 538e, such sentiments have not been repeated in subsequent judgments.
5. See pp 336–338, *post*.
6. See p 341, *post*.
7. (1969) 114 Sol Jo 36.
8. (22 July 1981, unreported), CA.
9. [1981] Ch 175C-D; [1980] 3 All ER 537c-d.
10. *Stock v Brown* [1994] 1 FLR 840 at 841H.
11. Leave has been granted in the following cases: *Adams v Adams* (22 July 1981, unreported), CA (19 days); *Re Johnson* [1987] CLY 3882 (3½ years – earlier grant of representation revoked); *Polackova v Soblewski* (28 October 1986, unreported), CA (3½ months?); *Clifford v Tanner* [1987] CLY 3881, CA (8 months); *Smith v Loosley* (18 June 1986, unreported), CA (45 days); *Stock v Brown* [1994] 1 FLR 840 (5½ years); *Re C* [1995] 2 FLR 24 (18 months); *Re Abram* [1996] 2 FLR 379, at 385A-F (6 months). Leave was refused in *Baker v Fear* (12 November 1993, unreported), CA (5¾ years).

application would be made,[12] and how quickly the applicant has acted to apply out of time.[13] Some judges have had regard to the length of time between the date of death and the date upon which representation was taken out, particularly if the applicant could influence the taking out of a grant,[14] to the interval between the issue and service of proceedings and to the general conduct of proceedings.[15]

The adequacy of a reason for the delay can be overstated and it is submitted that the correct approach to giving an explanation for any delay was laid down by Croom-Johnson LJ in *Smith v Loosley*:[16]

> It was submitted to us on behalf of the beneficiaries..... that the reason why the application is being brought is something which has to be *satisfactorily explained* before one proceeds further in order to see whether or not the application should be entertained. It was submitted that, if the explanation is missing or is in some way unsatisfactory, bound up as it may be with the length of the delay, that is something which in effect should *conclude* the matter. But in my view that is not the right approach. The discretion, which is in the court, as to whether it will extend time under section 4 ... is a *whole discretion*.

Smith v Loosley was a strong case. While the applicant, a widow aged 86 years, unversed in legal and financial matters and acting without *independent* legal advice, could legitimately be described as having dithered over her general attitude to the provisions of the deceased's will, the case for an extension of time was otherwise strong. The period of delay was short (45 days) and a warning letter was sent to the executors the day before the time limit expired. Less defensible is the decision of the Court of Appeal in *Polackova v Sobolewski*[17] where (affirming the decision of the trial judge) leave to proceed

12. [1981] Ch 175D, [1980] 3 All ER 537d–e. In *Baker v Fear* (12 November 1993, unreported), CA Waite LJ said, '... there must be a clear public policy interest in encouraging those who have an application under s 20(2) [Administration of Justice Act 1980] in contemplation to be open about it and disclose their intentions at the earliest moment'.
13. [1981] Ch 175D-E, [1980] 3 All ER 537d-e.
14. *Re Gonin* at [1977] 2 All ER 736E-G; *Re C* [1995] 2 FLR 24, at 27H; and see also *Re Longley* [1981] CLY 2885.
15. In *Re Dennis* [1981] 2 All ER 140, at 144b-e regard was had to delays in issuing proceedings after the decision to commence proceedings was made, in the service of the originating summons and in serving the affidavit in support.
16. (18 June 1986, unreported), CA. Emphasis added.
17. (28 October 1985, unreported), CA. A similar benevolent attitude to delays by the applicant's legal advisers was shown by the Court of Appeal in *Perry v Horlick* 18 November 1987 *reversing* the county court judge.

out of time was granted notwithstanding that the only explanation for six months of total inactivity by both solicitors and applicant was that the client did not receive a letter from her solicitors asking for further instructions. In *Re C*[18] the mother of an infant child who knew about the death of the deceased and presumably the prospect of a claim under the Act did not take any steps to make a claim under the Act for nearly three years after the death of the deceased and could give no satisfactory explanation for this. Despite this and other delays Wilson J allowed the infant to bring a claim out of time. It is implicit in the reasoning of Wilson J that had the mother herself been applying she would probably not have been successful.[19] That giving a satisfactory explanation for the delay is still a relevant factor is illustrated by the decision of the Court of Appeal in *Baker v Fear*[20] where (reversing the decision of the trial judge) one of the reasons given for refusing an extension of time under section 20(2) of the Administration of Justice Act 1980 (a provision identical to section 4) was the failure of the plaintiffs' legal advisers to consider over a period of years whether an application should be made under section 20.

Where the applicant does not learn of the death of the deceased or of the dispositions of his estate, or is not born[1] within a few months of the death of the deceased, the court would be likely to extend time for such an applicant, provided that the lack of knowledge was not totally unreasonable. In *Smith v Loosley*[2] and *Stock v Brown*[3] it was held that time should be extended in favour of an applicant who did not learn of the possibility of making a claim under the 1975 Act until some time after the expiry of the time limit. In neither case was it necessary for the court to balance the applicant's lack of knowledge with prejudice suffered by the beneficaries.[4] A similar indulgence is likely to be shown to an application by an individual who was misled, innocently or not, by the defendants or a third party

18. [1995] 2 FLR 24.
19. See at [1995] 2 FLR 28D–29B.
20. (12 November 1993, unreported), CA.
1. Compare *Re Trott* [1958] 1 WLR 604, [1958] 2 All ER 296.
2. (18 June 1986, unreported), CA.
3. [1994] 1 FLR 840. See also *Re Brown* [1949] NZLR 509 where the applicant only learned of family provision legislation 6½ years after the death.
4. In both *Smith v Loosley* and *Stock v Brown* the judges stressed in coming to their decisions the absence of prejudice to the defendants, but it is doubtful whether the judges in either case were laying down a rule that distribution of the estate would bar an extension of time by an applicant who only acquired knowledge of the possibility of making a claim some time after the grant of representation. See further pp 339–340, *post*.

about the merits of a claim[5]or the running of time.[6] If potential defendants wish to rely upon the time limit they should ensure that a potential applicant receives independent legal advice.

Fourthly, Megarry V-C stated that it was material whether negotiations had been commenced within the limit.[7] Such negotiations inform the defendants that a claim is being made and lull the applicant into a false sense of security. Negotiations might also be regarded as a waiver by the defendants of the time limit.[8] Negotiations commenced after the time limit might also aid the applicant, at any rate if the defendants have not taken the point that the time limit has expired.[9] In *Re Ruttie* negotiations were a crucial factor in the court extending the time limit.[10] It is also an important matter if investigations are made which will benefit both parties.[11] Similarly if the defendants make informal promises to allow the applicant more than he is entitled to under the will or the rules of intestacy the court will extend time if the applicant has relied upon such promise.[12] In *Re John*[13] the applicant was informally promised an allowance at the testator's funeral by a majority, but not all, of the beneficiaries under the deceased's will, probate was taken out on 18 November 1960 and the application was made on 2 January 1963. Cross J extended time and awarded provision.

The defendants' knowledge within the time limit that a claim is intended is a factor in favour of the court extending time.[14] While

5. *Re Dennis* [1981] 2 All ER 140, at 144c-e (advice by solicitors of a third party that applicant had no claim). In *Re C* [1995] 2 FLR 24 Wilson J refused to penalise an infant applicant whose mother had for no good reason refused to consult solicitors for nearly 3½ years. See also *Smith v Loosley* (18 June 1986, unreported), CA.
6. In *Perry vHorlick* (18 November 1987, unreported), CA it was a factor in favour of extending time that the personal representatives innocently misled the applicant about whether a grant of representation had been taken out. The court did not refer to the possibility of a Standing Search, as to which see p 345, *post*.
7. [1981] Ch 175F-G, [1980] 3 All ER 537f.
8. Per Megarry V-C in *Re Salmon* [1981] Ch 174D-E, [1980] 3 All ER 536e-h relying upon *Wright v John Bagnall & Sons Ltd* [1900] 2 QB 240; *Lubovsky v Snelling* [1944] KB 44.
9. [1981] Ch 175F-G, [1980] 3 All ER 537f.
10. [1970] 1 WLR 89, [1969] 3 All ER 1633; see also *Re McNare* [1964] 1 WLR 1255, at 1257, [1964] 3 All ER 373, at 376A-G.
11. *Re Ruttie* at [1970] 1 WLR 92E-F, [1969] 3 All ER 1634E-F.
12. In *Adams v Adams* (22 July 1981, unreported), CA the applicant could not rely upon any offer of settlement because the defendants stated that the time limit was to be strictly adhered to.
13. (1966) 111 Sol Jo 15.
14. *Re Stone* (1969) 114 Sol Jo 36; *Adams v Adams* (22 July 1981, unreported), CA; *Re C* [1995] 2 FLR 24, at 27E-F and see the remarks of Megarry V-C in *Re Salmon* at [1981] Ch 174C-D, 175D-E, [1980] 3 All ER 536f-h.

an express statement by the personal representatives that they will strictly insist on the time limit being adhered to is *a factor* militating against allowing an extension of the time limit, it is not an absolute bar to an extension.[15] However, a conscious decision by an applicant not to apply may act as a very substantial impediment to the grant of an extension. In *Escritt v Escritt*[16] the applicant being fully advised as to the merits of an application decided not to make an application. Three years later she changed her mind, there having been a slight change in her circumstances, and she applied for permission to bring an application out of time. Arnold P held that she had advanced insufficient reasons – the small change of circumstances since her decision and the fact that the estate had not been distributed – to go back upon her conscious decision made with full legal advice. The President's decision was unhesitatingly affirmed by the Court of Appeal.

Fifthly, Megarry V-C stated that it was important whether the estate had been distributed or not.[17] If the estate has been distributed, the personal representatives are immune from liability.[18] In considering whether the estate has been distributed the courts are unconcerned with the change in capacity from personal representative to trustee which occurs when administration is complete.[19] While the distribution of the estate is an important factor, being the clearest example of prejudice to defendants, it is not yet completely clear how far the distribution of the estate or any change of position is an absolute bar to an extension of time. Certainly there is no reported case where leave has been granted where the estate has been fully distributed. In *Re Salmon* Megarry V-C attached considerable importance to the mere fact of distribution, but he also stated that the court could go behind the mere fact of distribution to ascertain whether any of the beneficiaries have actually changed their position.[20] In *Re Bowell*[1] Mervyn Davies

15. *Adams v Adams* (22 July 1981, unreported), CA.
16. (1981) 3 FLR 280; *ad idem Re Campbell* [1983] NI 10, at 17C-E. In *Perry v Horlick* (18 November 1987, unreported), CA a decision by the applicant who occupied the major asset in the estate to do nothing and await events was not criticised. In *Re C* [1995] 2 FLR 24, at 28D–E Wilson J refused to apply *Escritt v Escritt* to prevent an application by an infant whose mother had decided to make no claim on his behalf.
17. [1981] Ch 175G-176D, [1980] 3 All ER 537g-538b.
18. S 20(1).
19. *Escritt v Escritt* (1981) 3 FLR 280, at 283 per Arnold P; *Stock v Brown* [1994] 1 FLR 840. The position under New Zealand law is to the contrary – *Lilley v Public Trustee* [1981] AC 839. In Australia see *Easterbrook v Young* (1977) 136 CLR 308; DICKEY, 48–52; DE GROOT AND NICKEL, para 411.
20. [1981] Ch 176C–D, [1980] 3 All ER 538c-b; in *Re Longley* [1981] CLY 2885 Blackett-Ord V-C noted that the estate had been distributed, but was still intact, being invested in a building society and hence still available to satisfy an award.
1. Times, 18/5/82.

J refused leave to apply out of time where the estate had been distributed and had been used by the beneficiary to purchase a house. It is tentatively suggested that the distribution of the estate would normally be a good reason for refusing an extension of time except in cases where the most compelling reasons are advanced when conditional leave should be given so as to protect beneficiaries *to the extent that* they have changed their position. On the other hand in itself the mere fact that the estate has not been distributed does not justify allowing an extension of time, which would otherwise not be justifiable.[2]

A related form of prejudice or lack of it concerns the existence of other litigation affecting the estate. In *Perry v Horlock*[3] the Court of Appeal gave as *a* reason for reversing the decision of the county court judge and allowing an extension of time that the applicant had commenced proceedings claiming a beneficial interest in the principal asset of the estate and thus there would be litigation in any event over the estate of the deceased. *Perry v Horlock* has to be contrasted with the earlier decision of Walton J in *Re Gonin*[4] where on essentially the same facts an application for an extension of time was heard immediately after the trial of the claim for the beneficial interest and refused and with *Baker v Fear*[5] where the Court of Appeal refused to allow an extension of time even though proceedings concerning the same subject matter were on foot.

Sixthly, Megarry V-C, Walton J and Blackett-Ord V-C considered it to be a relevant factor whether the applicant has a claim against a third party, usually his legal advisers.[6] However, the matter was discussed at some length by the Court of Appeal in *Adams v Adams*,[7] where all the case law on the relevance of an action against a plaintiff's legal advisers to striking out claims for want of prosecution and to the limitation periods in personal injury actions were cited and the previous authorities overruled. The Court of Appeal held that while the existence of a possible action for negligence against an applicant's legal advisers was not to be totally

2. *Re Gonin* [1977] 2 All ER 720; *Escritt v Escritt*(1981) 3 FLR 280; *Baker v Fear* (12 November 1993, unreported), CA.
3. (18 November 1987, unreported), CA.
4. [1977] 2 All ER 720.
5. (12 November 1993, unreported), CA.
6. *Re Gonin* at [1977] 2 All ER 736D-E; *Re Salmon* at [1981] Ch 176E-G, [1980] 3 All ER 538b-e; *Re Longley* [1981] CLY 2885. In *Re C* [1995] 2 FLR 24, at 28H-29B Wilson J gave as a reason for extending time that the infant applicant could sue neither his legal advisers nor his mother for the delay in bringing the claim.
7. (22 July 1981, unreported).

ignored,[8] it was not a factor of any great importance and would not counterbalance other important factors favouring the applicant. The Court of Appeal specifically reversed Reeve J who had held that the applicant's right to sue her solicitors for negligence was the decisive factor justifying a refusal to grant leave. The Court of Appeal noted that the right to sue one's solicitors was not precisely the same as the right to apply under the Act, since such litigation necessarily involved a change of solicitors[9] and that the measure of damages where the applicant sought a settlement under section 2(1)(d) and other similar orders would be difficult to calculate.

In deciding whether to allow applications out of time the courts have adopted a threshold test of whether the applicant can show an arguable case or whether there is a triable issue.[10] In particular the courts have rejected arguments that although the case for the applicant is arguable, generally it is weak and that this weakness is a factor which should count against an extension of time.[11] Taking into account the considerable legal costs of any application under the 1975 Act[12] and in particular the ability of a legally aided plaintiff to litigate at no risk to himself and having regard to the 'wide and unfettered' discretion, it is submitted that the courts should have employed applications for leave to proceed out of time as a sieve to exclude weak, but not entirely hopeless, claims.[13]

8. That such a factor is not to be ignored completely is supported by *Donovan v Gwentoys Ltd* [1990] 1 WLR 472, at 479F, [1990] 1 All ER 1018, at 1025a.
9. Following Lord Diplock in *Thompson v Brown Construction* [1981] 1 WLR 744, at 750F-751A, [1981] 2 All ER 296, at 301H-302B.
10. *Re Stone* (1969) 114 Sol Jo 36 per Lord Denning MR; *Re Dennis* at [1981] 2 All ER 144j-145a; *Polackova v Sobolewski* (26 October 1985, unreported), CA; *Clifford v Tanner* [1987] CLY 3881, CA; *Smith v Loosley* (18 June 1986, unreported), CA per Croom-Johnson LJ; *Perry v Horlick* (18 November 1987, unreported), CA; *Stock v Brown* at [1994] 1 FLR 841E-F; *Baker v Fear* (12 November 1993, unreported), CA. In both *Clifford v Tanner* and *Baker v Fear* the Court of Appeal overruled first instance judges solely upon the issue of whether an arguable case had been shown.
11. *Polackova v Sobolewski* (10 June 1986, unreported), CA; *Perry v Horlick* (18 November 1987, unreported), CA. In *Escritt v Escritt*(1981) 3 FLR 280, at 286C the court rejected an argument that the substantive merits of the case justified an extension of time. In *Re C* [1995] 2 FLR 24, at 29F-G where it was rightly conceded that an infant child would to some extent succeed in his substantive application, Wilson J treated the very strong merits as a reason for granting an extension of time.
12. See pp 365–367, *post*.
13. In *Re Salmon* Megarry V-C did not expressly take into account the merits of the applicant's claim as a reason for not extending time, but the judgment does contain a fairly extensive discussion of the merits. The applicant's claim, while not unarguable, was modest and generally not strong and the effect of the judgment was to prevent this relatively weak claim from being brought.

In *Stock v Brown*[14] the deceased died in 1986 leaving a will which gave his widow a life-interest in the matrimonial home and in investments of £75, 000. Probate was granted in 1987. The widow, who had no independent legal advice after the death of the deceased, applied for leave in 1993. Her application was precipitated by a fall in interest rates which led to a dramatic reduction in the income from her life-interest and by increases in the costs of her care. Thorpe J, relying no doubt upon the fact that the estate was intact, granted the applicant leave to proceed out of time. The decision is in effect authority for the proposition that events since the expiry of the time limit, principally a change in investment conditions,[15] can justify an extension of time and hence represents an extreme application of section 3(5) which provides that the court has regard to facts known at the date of the hearing.[16] *Stock v Brown* does result in estates where property is left upon trust[17] as opposed to being given absolutely being far more vulnerable to applications for an extension of time, a questionable policy. *Stock v Brown* also raises the conundrum that had the widow applied in 1987 for provision and been refused, as well she might,[18] she would have been unable to make a second application. Equally had the court awarded her a life-interest in 1987, she would have been unable to come back to court six years later to seek a variation.[19] Likewise had the widow been advised in 1987 that her application would fail, it is unlikely that an application for an extension of time would have succeeded.[20] Thus by not taking independent legal advice the widow in *Stock v Brown* may have been considerably better off.

While the courts frequently extend time where the tardiness of the application is caused by errors and mistakes of the applicant's legal advisers, the cases do not afford any clear guidance as to which errors will be excused and which not. Most reported decisions turn principally upon other factors. While as the judgment of Croom-Johnson LJ in *Smith v Loosley*[1] shows the absence of a completely adequate explanation for the delay can not outweigh an otherwise strong case, it is prudent for an applicant to state in his evidence

14. [1994] 1 FLR 840.
15. See [1994] 1 FLR 842C-D.
16. See pp 128–131, *ante*. There was no discussion in the judgment of s 3(5) or of the Privy Council case of *Dun v Dun* [1959] AC 272, [1959] 2 All ER 134 which had similar facts.
17. As to the advantages and disadvantages of which, see pp 386–387, *post*.
18. Eg *Davis v Davis* [1994] 1 FLR 54.
19. On the power of variation, see pp 401–408, *post*.
20. See *Escritt v Escritt*(1981) 3 FLR 280 where a change of financial circumstances after a conscious decision not to apply under the 1975 Act was held to be insufficient to justify an extension of time.
1. Set out at p 336, *ante*.

the reasons for any delay with *the utmost candour and fullness*.[2] The courts may excuse errors and misjudgments,[3] even total incompetence,[4] but matters should be fully explained to them.

Delays in granting legal aid are a matter which will influence the court in extending the time limit,[5] but delay in granting legal aid does not give an applicant *carte blanche* to ignore the time limit.[6] Where the Legal Aid Board is taking its time in deciding whether to grant legal aid (an all too common occurrence), a solicitor is under a duty to remind the legal aid committee of the urgency of the matter, to inform the personal representatives by letter of the impending action,[7] and to consider whether proceedings should be started using the applicant's own resources[8] or an emergency legal aid certificate.[9]

A solicitor who realises that the time limit has expired should act quickly. He should issue proceedings at once (it is always possible to supplement inadequate evidence by later affidavits), inform the defendants of the commencement of proceedings, and where appropriate register a *lis pendens*[10] and seek an interlocutory injunction to restrain the personal representatives from distributing the estate.

In all cases where litigation in addition to a family provision application is considered, such as a construction summons, an action to revoke a grant of representation or an action seeking a declaration that the applicant has an interest in the deceased's property under a resulting or a constructive trust, it is always the best policy to start

2. See Megarry V-C in *Re Salmon* at [1981] Ch 177F-G, [1980] 3 All ER 539b–c; and compare *Savill v Southend Health Authority* [1995] 1 WLR 1254 on the necessity of putting forward some evidence as to the reason for the delay when seeking leave to appeal out of time. A comparison of the evidence and the judge's remarks on the evidence in cases where applications under s 4 succeeded, eg *Re Ruttie* and in those where applications failed, eg *Re Gonin*, *Re Salmon*, *Re Dennis* and *Baker v Fear* is instructive.
3. Eg *Perry v Horlick* (18 November 1987, unreported), CA.
4. Eg *Polackova v Sobolewski* (28 October 1985, unreported), CA.
5. Eg *Re Trott* [1958] 1 WLR 604, [1958] 2 All ER 296; *Perry v Horlick* (18 November 1987, unreported), CA. In *Re C* [1995] 2 FLR 24, at 27F a delay of five months in obtaining legal aid was effectively excused by the court.
6. *Re Salmon* [1981] Ch 167.
7. [1981] Ch 173B, [1980] 3 All ER 535f-g.
8. [1981] Ch 177F-H, [1980] 3 All ER 539b-c.
9. [1981] Ch 177G-H. The provisions governing emergency legal aid certificates are Reg 21 of the Civil Legal Aid (General) Regulations 1989, SI 1989/339, as amended.
10. An application for an order under s 2(1)(c), (d) is registerable as a *lis pendens*, see Land Charges Act 1972, s 5(1)(a); Land Registration Act 1952, s 59(1); *Whittingham v Whittingham* [1979] Fam 9, [1978] 3 All ER 805. See generally p356, *post*.

family provision proceedings and have such proceedings adjourned, rather than to await the outcome of the other proceedings and then seek an extension.[11] It is unwise to assume that the existence of other proceedings will automatically lead to an extension of time.[12]

Procedure

The application for an extension of time should be made a separate head of relief and the supporting affidavit should set out *in full* the reasons why an extension should be granted.[13] Normally an extension of time is granted at a hearing before any substantive hearing. The almost invariable practice is for such applications to be tried by Masters or District judges in both the High Court and the County Court.[14] The order usually provides for the time to be extended to a particular date – the date of the issue of the summons[15] or the day after that day.[16] Because the order under section 4 is that of the court[17] it is submitted that a court can refuse an application by consent to extend time, although the factual circumstances when a court would refuse such an application are almost inconceivable.[18] Because a personal representative has usually no power to compromise claims under the Inheritance Act 1984,[19] personal representatives should oppose an application under section 4 unless authorised by all beneficiaries potentially adversely affected not to do so or unless all such beneficiaries are already parties to the application.

Where an application under section 4 is contested, costs almost invariably follow the event.[20]

11. *Re Bone* [1955] 1 WLR 703, [1955] 2 All ER 555. As to the possible effect of not applying in time when other proceedings are contemplated, see *Re Miller* [1969] 1 WLR 583, [1968] 3 All ER 844; *Re Gonin* [1977] 2 All ER 735.
12. *Baker v Fear* (12 November 1993, unreported), CA.
13. Para 3, *Practice Note (inheritance: family provision)* [1976] 1 WLR 418, [1976] 2 All ER 447.
14. For the jurisdiction of Masters and District Judges, see p 348, *post*.
15. *Re Trott* [1958] 1 WLR 604, [1958] 2 All ER 296.
16. *Re Bone* [1955] 1 WLR 703, [1955] 2 All ER 555.
17. This follows from the wording of s 4 and see the judgment of Croom-Johnson LJ in *Smith v Loosley* (18 June 1986, unreported), CA.
18. An example might be where the parties were improperly attempting to take advantage of s 146 of the Inheritance Tax Act 1984. See per Morritt LJ in *Re Goodchild* [1997] 3 All ER 63, at 76d-77f and compare the remarks of Ferris J in *Re Carecraft Construction Co Ltd* [1994] 1 WLR 172, at 182A-E, [1993] 4 All ER 499, at 508f-509b.
19. See pp 364–365, *post*.
20. This is the almost invariable result of the cases set out at fn 15, p 333.

Although there is no authority on the point, it is submitted that the court in exercising its power to extend time under section 4 can make a conditional order or an order only upon an applicant's undertaking. For instance, if an estate has been half distributed, the applicant might be required to undertake not to seek provision out of that part of the estate already distributed.

Standing Searches

In order to aid applicants to discover when a grant of representation has been made and to discourage the unnecessary entry of caveats, the Probate Registry in 1975 introduced a 'standing search' procedure whereby an applicant would be informed of any grant to a particular person's estate which was made within a six-month period after the initial search.[1] The current fee for such a search is £2.

PART 2: GENERALLY

The Courts

The High Court has unlimited jurisdiction under the 1975 Act. County Courts were first granted jurisdiction to hear family provision claims by the Family Provision Act 1966 where the value of the deceased's net estate did not exceed £5,000.[2] This limit was increased in 1981 to where the value of the deceased's net estate did not exceed £30,000.[3] However, as a result of the changes introduced by the Courts and Legal Services Act 1990 with effect from 1 July 1991 the County Court has unlimited jurisdiction under the 1975 Act.[4] The position under the 1975 Act is in stark contrast to the probate and general equity jurisdiction of the County Court which is limited to

1. Rule 43 of the Non-Contentious Probate Rules 1987 as amended; Tristram and Coote, *Probate Practice* (28th edn), paras 21.09–21.21. 12, p 1073. Since a caveat is a clearly inappropriate procedure to protect a prospective claim under the 1975 Act, a person who lodges such a caveat solely to protect a claim under the 1975 Act will be liable under the tort of malicious abuse of process.
2. S 7.
3. County Courts Jurisdiction (Inheritance – Provision for Family and Dependants) Order 1981, SI 1981/1636.
4. S 25 of the County Courts Act 1984 as inserted by the High Court and County Courts Jurisdiction Order 1991, SI 1991/724.

estates or funds not exceeding £30,000 and which was unaffected by the reforms of the Courts and Legal Services Act 1990.[5]

The choice of which court should try an application and transfers between the High Court and the County Court is governed by the provisions of the High Court and County Courts Jurisdiction Order 1991,[6] which lays down a presumption that an application where *the value of the action*[7] (not the value of the estate) is less than £25,000 should be tried in the County Court[8] and is £50,000 or over should be tried in the High Court.[9] In practice the provisions of the High Court and County Courts Jurisdiction Order are often applied flexibly in family provision claims, since trial in the High Court by a Master or District Judge[10] may be cheaper and more convenient than by a county court judge and in the Chancery Division in London there is official encouragement to transfer claims in excess of £50,000 to the Central London County Court.[11]

Divisions of the High Court

As part of a political compromise,[12] jurisdiction to hear an application under the 1975 Act is assigned to both the Chancery and Family Divisions.[13] Although the usual procedures for transferring a matter from one Division of the High Court to another are available, the general rule is that the applicant has the choice of forum.[14] Where two applications are made in different Divisions, one application will normally be transferred so that both applications can be heard together.[15] Where an application under the 1975 Act

5. S 23, s 25 of the County Courts Act 1984.
6. SI 1991/724.
7. Defined by Art 9.
8. Art 7(3).
9. Art 7(4).
10. See pp 348–349, *post* and see Chancery Guide, para 11. 2 and Supreme Court Practice 1995, Vol 1, para 99/8/3 (a particularly good commentary).
11. See Chancery Guide, para 11. 2 referring to the Chancery List at the Mayor's and City of London Court. With effect from 1 April 1996 the Chancery List at the Mayor's and City of London Court is replaced by the Chancery List at the Central London County Court, see *Practice Direction (Chancery: Transfer of Business)* [1996] 1 WLR 76, [1996] 1 All ER 265.
12. See pp 30–32, *ante*.
13. RSC Ord 99, r 2.
14. S 64 of the Supreme Court Act 1981; *Midland Bank Ltd v Stamps* [1978] 1 WLR 635, at 638G-H, [1978] 3 All ER 1, at 4A-B (per Donaldson J).
15. The power to transfer between Divisions of the High Court is contained in RSC Ord 4, r 3.

is affected by other proceedings, such as an application for the custody of infant children[16] or the construction of a will or trust[17] the application should be brought or transferred to the Division where the other proceedings are being heard.

Although the Family Division has the reputation of being considerably more favourable to applicants than does the Chancery Division, reported cases do not show any significant difference in the making of awards between the two Divisions.[18]

Procedural Scheme of the High Court

Proceedings under the 1975 Act are begun by originating summons.[19] Order 99 of the Rules of the Supreme Court provides a uniform code for both the Chancery and Family Divisions,[20] so avoiding the pre-1976 position where the procedures of each Division were often quite different. As regards proceedings in Chambers before the matter reaches the judge, the Chancery Division practice will apply to both Divisions.[1] The only procedural distinction between the two Divisions is that in the Family Division, the provisions of the Family Proceedings Rules relating to the drawing up and service of orders apply.[2]

16. Compare *Dennis v MacDonald* [1982] Fam 63.
17. See *Re Besterman* [1984] Ch 458, [1984] 2 All ER 656 which succeeded a construction summons to determine the validity of the residuary bequest in the deceased's will *Re Besterman* (1980) Times, 22 January. It is suggested that *Re Cairnes* (1982) 4 FLR 225, a decision of Comyn J, where the principal issue being the construction of a deed of trust of a pension scheme, might have been more suitable for hearing in the Chancery Division. See also para 4 of the *Practice Note*. Compare also *McCain International Ltd v Country Fair Foods Ltd* [1981] RPC 69, passing off claims are more suitable for the Chancery Division and *Boobyer v Holman (David) & Co* [1992] 2 Lloyd's Rep 436; certain types of Lloyd's litigation should be heard in the Commercial Court as opposed to the Chancery Division. Note the comment of Thorpe LJ in *Dart v Dart* [1996] 2 FLR 286, at 298G that none of the members of the Court of Appeal in *Re Besterman* (a case which ultimately turned very heavily upon divorce principles) had any experience of ancillary relief cases at first instance.
18. The real problem in both Divisions is a diversified judiciary having limited familiarity with family provision claims.
19. RSC Ord 99, r 3(1).
20. There is also a uniform Practice Note, *Practice Note (inheritance: family provision)* [1976] 1 WLR 418, [1976] 2 All ER 447.
1. RSC Ord 99, r 8, applying Ord 32, r 14(1).
2. RSC Ord 99, r 10; the reference is to r 2.43 and r 10.17 of the Family Proceedings Rules 1991, SI 1991/ 1247.

An Originating Summons may be issued out of the Central Office, the Principal Registry of the Family Division or *any* District Registry.[3]

Order 99, rule 8, adopting the technique which gives Chancery Masters their jurisdiction to make final orders, provides: 'Any proceedings under the Act may, if the court so directs, be disposed of in chambers.' No formal direction as to the type of case which Masters, Registrars and District Registrars may hear has been made,[4] but the *Practice Note* states that while they may deal:

> ... with either contested or uncontested applications, it is envisaged that they will exercise their discretion so as to refer to a judge any case which is likely to involve a long or complex issue of fact or law or a question of jurisdiction, unless the amount of the estate is small.[5]

This power is in addition to a Master's jurisdiction to try a matter with the consent of both parties under RSC Ord 36, r 9. While the power in Ord 99, r 8 is quite well used, it does not appear to have been generally used in the face of strong opposition from one of the parties,[6] except perhaps in cases of small estates. The predominant, but not universal, practice is for applications for leave to proceed out of time and for interim payments to be determined in the first instance by Masters and District Judges.

An appeal from a decision of a Master or District Judge lies to a Judge.[7] Because of this possibility of an appeal, it is usual for steps

3. RSC Ord 99, r 3(1); so avoiding the restriction on the issue of Originating Summonses contained in Ord 7, r 5(2). Unlike in the County Court [CCR 1981 Ord 48, r 3(1)] there are no requirements for commencing proceedings in a District Registry that the deceased has any connection with the District; however if proceedings are commenced in a wholly inappropriate District, the matter is likely to be transferred under Ord 4, r 6(4) with a cost penalty for the plaintiff.
4. See the remarks of Megarry V-C in *Re Beaumont* [1980] Ch 444, at 460G-H, [1980] 1 All ER 266, at 278d-f referring to Ord 32, r 14(4).
5. Para 6, *Practice Note (inheritance: family provision)* [1976] 1 WLR 418, [1976] 2 All ER 447. This includes the power to approve compromises *Supreme Court Practice 1995* Vol 1, para 99/8/4.
6. See in particular the remarks of Megarry V-C in *Re Beaumont* [1980] Ch 444, at 459A–461A, [1980] 1 All ER 266, at 277b-h. This is perhaps less true in the 1990s than at the date of the second edition owing to the general increase in jurisdiction and status of Masters and District Judges and the increased pressure on the time of High Court Judges. The statement of Roger Cooke J in *Re Abram* [1996] 2 FLR 379, at 388H-389A that 'the jurisdiction is now comparatively rarely exercised by a judge in open court, but more usually by Masters and District Judges in Chambers' does not accord with the author's experience.
7. Ord 58, r 1.

to be taken to record oral evidence given before the Master or District Judge.[8]

Procedural Scheme in the County Court

Applications in the County Court are made by originating application.[9] Rules provide that the application is to be brought in the court for the district where the deceased resided at the date of his death, or if the deceased did not reside in England and Wales, the district where the respondent or one of the respondents resides or carries on business or in default where the estate or part of the estate is situate or if none of the foregoing matters apply in the district in which the applicant resides or carries on business.[10]

In the County Court the District Judge has power to determine any application under section 1 of the 1975 Act,[11] subject to any contrary direction by the judge.[12] This power appears to be exercised in a similar manner to the similar power in the High Court and is generally exercised only where the parties do not object or where the estate is small. It is a very useful provision where the court's consent to a compromise is required.

Parties

The plaintiff or plaintiffs will be the person or persons applying for provision. Where there are two or more applicants (for example, the deceased's widow and his infant children), whose interests could conflict, all should be made plaintiffs initially. Subsequently either an application should be made for an order reconstituting the action by making those plaintiffs whose interests are adverse to the first named plaintiff defendants or an application should be made under RSC Ord 99, r 6 that the plaintiffs be separately represented.[13] In practice it is often simpler to issue separate proceedings.

8. *Practice Direction (family provision: application)* [1978] 1 WLR 585, [1978] 2 All ER 167. It is submitted that the substance of this direction has survived the substitution of an appeal for an adjournment of a summons.
9. CCR 1981 Ord 48, r 2(1).
10. CCR 1981 Ord 48, r 3(1).
11. CCR 1981 Ord 48, r 7.
12. Under CCR 1981 Ord 50, r 3.
13. There is no comparable provision in the County Court Rules 1981 and Ord 99, r 6 cannot be applicable to the County Court by virtue of s 76 of the County Courts Act 1984 as it is not a 'general principle' of practice.

Where separate applications have been made, they should be dealt with together. If an application is made on behalf of an infant or a mental patient it should be made by his next friend or by the Official Solicitor.[14]

The defendants will be the personal representative or representatives of the deceased or one or those of them who is not an applicant and such of the beneficiaries who may be affected by the order sought.[15] An application is validly made if the only persons initially made defendants are the personal representatives and beneficiaries are added subsequently as defendants. The plaintiff's legal advisers should give full consideration as to which beneficiaries should be joined as defendants, balancing the need to have all beneficiaries potentially affected by an order before the court with the aim of not unnecessarily increasing the costs of the proceedings generally – thus minor pecuniary and other legatees should rarely be joined as parties.[16] An infant or a mental patient will defend proceedings by a guardian ad litem. The court has an extensive power to add persons as parties,[17] and at the first hearing of the originating summons or at the pre-trial review the Master or District Judge is under a duty to ascertain that all proper persons have been joined or been given notice of the proceedings.[18] Where the defendants are numerous a representation order can be made in an appropriate case.[19]

The modern tendency is for defendants, whether they are personal representatives or beneficiaries, to be represented by the same solicitors and counsel, unless their interests conflict by reason of there being a likely argument as to the incidence of any award. Where the personal representatives have no beneficial interest in the estate and are separately represented, after the initial affidavit or answer by them, separate representation of the personal representatives becomes expensive and serves very little use. It is

14. Eg *Re Wood* [1982] LS Gaz R 774 where the applicant, a mental patient, sued the Official Solicitor as her next friend.
15. *Re Lidington* [1940] WN 279; *Re Blight* (1946) 96 LJ 233.
16. In cases of difficulty it may be better to issue against merely the personal representatives and the principal beneficiaries and seek the guidance of the court at the first hearing of the Originating Summons or at the Pre-trial Review as to the joinder of particular beneficiaries. It is to be hoped that in extreme cases of unnecessary joinder of defendants, the court will be prepared to make wasted costs orders (RSC Ord 62, r 11) against plaintiffs' legal advisers who unnecessarily join minor beneficiaries as defendants.
17. RSC Ord 99, r 4(1); CCR 1981 Ord 48, r 4(1).
18. See in particular the notes to CCR 1981 Ord 48, r 3(3) in The County Court Practice 1997.
19. RSC Ord 99, r 4(2); CCR 1981 Ord 48, r 4(2).

suggested that in such a case, the personal representatives seek a direction from the court that either they cease to play an active part in the proceedings or more properly that the beneficiaries' counsel be their counsel at the trial.

While it is generally undesirable for an applicant to be the sole personal representative, there is no reason in principle why an application under the 1975 Act can not be brought by a sole personal representative. In practice an applicant should only renounce probate or his right to apply for letters of administration if there is some other person who is able and willing to take out a grant of representation expeditiously.[20] If the applicant is already the sole personal representative one of the beneficiaries should be joined as the defendant.[1] If no one has taken out a grant of representation, the applicant may apply for his nominee to be appointed administrator under section 116 of the Supreme Court Act 1981.[2]

Issue of Proceedings

In the High Court the originating summons is in the expedited form.[3] Before the summons is issued, the applicant *must* lodge with the court an affidavit which *must* exhibit an official copy of the grant of representation to the deceased's estate and of every testamentary document admitted to proof.[4] It is suggested that where it is necessary to issue proceedings in cases of extreme urgency in order to be within the time limit, the court should be prepared to relax[5] the requirement as to the affidavit and the official copy of the grant of probate.

Although the summons should seek such reasonable provision as the court thinks fit in general terms, it is often advisable to specify

20. See Supreme Court Practice 1995, Vol 1, para 99/4/2. An example is *Re Gonin* [1977] 2 All ER 720. In this respect the first edition 84 does not represent current practice.
1. The appropriate defendant may be a person against whom an order under s 9 (eg *Re McBroom* [1992] 2 FLR 49) or under s 10 (eg *Re Dawkins* [1986] 2 FLR 360) is sought. Any originating summons or originating application should contain all the matters required by RSC Ord 99, r 5 and CCR Ord 44, r 5. It is the author's experience that having an applicant as a sole personal representative rarely creates significant problems and is generally preferable to appointing a nominee under s 116 of the Supreme Court Act 1981.
2. *In the Estate of Simpson; In the Estate of Gunning* [1936] P 40.
3. Ord 99, r 3(2).
4. Ord 99, r 3(3).
5. Under Ord 2, r 1.

in affidavits the precise orders sought.[6] The summons should specifically seek, as separate heads of relief, permission for the application to be brought out of time and for any order under sections 9, 10 and 11. Interim relief need not be asked for specifically in the summons.

In the County Court the originating application will provide for a pre-trial review[7] and is only issued if an official copy of the grant of representation and of every testamentary document admitted to proof is produced.[8] Every originating application *must* state:[9]

(a) the name of the deceased, the date of his death and his country of domicile at that date;
(b) the relationship of the applicant to the deceased or other qualification of the applicant for making the application;
(c) the date on which representation with respect to the deceased's estate was first taken out and the names and addresses of the personal representatives;
(e) whether the disposition of the deceased's estate effected by his will or the law relating to intestacy was such as to make any provision for the applicant and, if it was, the nature of the provision;
(f) to the best of the applicant's knowledge and belief, the persons or classes of persons interested in the deceased's estate and the nature of their interests;
(g) particulars of the applicant's present and foreseeable resources and financial needs and any other information which he desires to place before the court on the matter to which the court is required to have regard under section 3;
(h) where appropriate, a request for the court's permission to make the application notwithstanding that the period of six months has expired from the date on which representation in regard to the estate of the deceased was first taken out, and the grounds of the request;
(i) the nature of the provision applied for.

As with an originating summons, an originating application should contain specific prayers for permission to bring proceedings out of time and for any order under sections 9, 10 and 11.

6. On the usefulness of this see p 356, *post*.
7. Ord 48, r 3(3).
8. Ord 48, r 3(2)(a).
9. Ord 48, r 2(2); there is a non-prescribed County Court Form N423 available for such applications.

Form of Evidence

In the High Court evidence is given by affidavit[10] and at any trial leave may be given for the deponents to be cross-examined on their affidavits.[11] Affidavits, so far as possible, should set out the facts in a narrative form and in chronological order. The plaintiff's affidavit should include all the matters which are required to be included in an originating application. A plaintiff's affidavit should exhibit a birth or marriage certificate or a decree absolute proving that the applicant is qualified to bring an application. The applicant's financial needs, resources and circumstances generally should be stated with considerable particularity. The history of the deceased's relationship with the applicant should be set out. For instance, in the case of an application by a spouse, the history of the marriage between the deceased and the applicant should be set out fully. In the case of a former spouse, the affidavit should refer fully to the divorce proceedings and the orders for ancillary relief made after divorce and to any other arrangements made between the parties. Often it is useful to give some explanation as to the reason why the dispositions of the deceased's estate did not make reasonable provision for the applicant. Evidence in support of an application under sections 9, 10 or 11 should be stated with the utmost particularity.

Similar comments apply to the contents of an originating application. Strictly evidence in support of originating applications is oral and affidavit evidence can not be led as of right.[12] However, witness statements are now normally ordered[13] and these have the same practical effect as affidavits.

If the application gives rise to a substantial conflict of fact, further affidavits by other persons may have to be sworn on behalf of the plaintiff.

Evidence on Behalf of Defendants

An affidavit in answer to the application *must* be served by a defendant who is a personal representative within 21 days after the

10. Ord 99, r 3(3).
11. RSC Ord 38, r 2(3).
12. Save where affidavit evidence is allowed by order of the court (CCR Ord 20, r 6) or upon notice (CCR Ord 20, r 7).
13. See CCR Ord 20, r 12A. For a case on Witness Statements in applications under the 1975 Act, see *Tabbenor v Shaw* [1997] 4 CL 95.

service of the summons on him.[14] Any other defendant *may*, and would usually want to, likewise put in evidence by affidavit, but there is no obligation on him to do so.[15] The affidavit lodged by the personal representative must state to the best of the deponent's ability:

(a) full particulars of the value of the deceased's net estate, as defined by section 25(1);
(b) the person or classes of person beneficially interested in the estate, giving the names and (in the cases of those who are not already parties) the addresses of all living beneficiaries, and the value of their interests so far as ascertained;
(c) if such be the case, that any living beneficiary (naming him) is a minor or a patient...
(d) any facts known to the deponent which might affect the exercise of the Court's powers under the Act.[16]

The duty to make an affidavit containing the specified information, particularly the last general sub-paragraph only applies to matters within the knowledge of the deponent qua personal representative and not qua beneficiary. Thus a personal representative who is also a principal beneficiary of the estate cannot be compelled to disclose by affidavit his own financial circumstances.[17]

While a beneficiary defendant cannot be compelled to depose to his own financial circumstances by affidavit, the failure to do so may be taken into account by the court, as can the failure to adduce by affidavit any other evidence.[18] A beneficiary defendant can be obliged to give evidence as to his means by calling him as a witness, by obtaining discovery against him or by serving a *sub poena duces tecum* on him[19] subject to the court being satisfied as to the relevance of the evidence, as to the cost of producing evidence and having due regard to reasons of privacy.[20]

14. Ord 99, r 5(1).
15. Ord 99, r 5(1); *Re Clark* [1981] CLY 2884.
16. Ord 99, r 5(2).
17. *Re Clark* [1981] CLY 2884, following *Wynne v Wynne* [1981] 1 WLR 69, [1980] 3 All ER 659.
18. *Re Leach* [1984] FLR 590, at 606F; *Sivyer v Sivyer* [1967] 1 WLR 1482, at 1485G-H, [1967] 3 All ER 429, at 431F-G.
19. In *Re Clark* [1981] CLY 2884 Hollings J stated that a claim under the 1975 Act was a claim against the deceased's estate and that therefore for all purposes as to evidence a defendant-beneficiary was not a 'party' to the action. This statement was unnecessary for the decision and entirely wrong, there being nothing in the 1975 Act, decided cases or any general principles to hold that a party to an action is in some sense not a party thereto.
20. See generally *Senior v Holdsworth, ex p Independent Television News Ltd* [1976] QB 23, [1975] 2 All ER 1009; *Morgan v Morgan* [1977] Fam 122, [1977] 2

If the value of the net estate has changed between the date of the first affidavit and the time of the trial, it is usual for the personal representatives to file a subsequent affidavit giving the up to date value of the net estate shortly before the hearing.[1]

Affidavits by defendant beneficiaries should in content mirror those of plaintiffs, setting out with considerable particularity the defendant's financial circumstances, the reasons why the deceased made the dispositions, all other relevant matters and so far as is appropriate and relevant answering the matters set out in the plaintiff's affidavit.

In the County Court a personal representative *must* file an Answer within 21 days of the service on him of the originating application containing the same matters as a personal representative is obliged to depose to in an affidavit in answer to an originating summons in the High Court.[2] Defendant beneficiaries, as in the High Court, are not under any obligation to file an Answer, but it is generally advisable to do so and it will contain the same matters which are found in an affidavit by a defendant beneficiary in the High Court.

Other Proceedings and Proceedings under the 1975 Act

There are no theoretical objections to applications under the 1975 Act and other proceedings being made by the same originating process.[3] While there are considerable dangers in combining in one set of proceedings claims which are normally brought by writ and claims which must be brought by originating summons, it is the usual and acceptable practice to have one originating summons where the plaintiff raises all claims appropriate for an originating summons.[4]

All ER 515. Note that a witness can be ordered to produce documents at a hearing arranged for that purpose before the trial – *Williams v Williams* [1988] QB 161, [1987] 3 All ER 257; *Khanna v Lovell White Durrant* [1995] 1 WLR 121, [1994] 4 All ER 267.

1. See the remarks of Lord Greene MR in *Re Borthwick* [1948] Ch 645, at 651, [1948] 2 All ER 635, at 637G.
2. Ord 48, r 5.
3. RSC Ord 15, r 1; CCR 1981 Ord 5, r 1.
4. Eg *Re Cummins* [1972] Ch 62, [1971] 3 All ER 782 (claim under 1938 Act and s 17 of the Married Women's Property Act 1882); *Wayling v Jones* [1995] 2 FLR 1029, 69 P & CR 170 (claim under 1975 Act and for proprietory estoppel); *Riggs v Lloyds Bank plc* (27 November 1992, unreported), CA (claims under 1975 Act and for proprietory estoppel consolidated).

Pending Actions

Where the applicant seeks an order for a transfer of specific property under section 2(1)(c), the settlement of specific property under section 2(1)(d) or a lump sum order which will affect the entire estate, the application may be registered against land as a 'pending action'.[5] In order to be able to register a pending action an applicant should in the affidavit in support of the originating summons or in the originating application particularise the precise relief entitling him to register the pending action.[6] Even if an applicant validly registers his pending action, if his claim to the relief entitling him to register the pending action is weak, the court under its inherent jurisdiction may vacate the land charge[7] or require the applicant to give an undertaking in damages as a condition of continued registration.[8] An application under section 9[9] or section 10 can be registered as a pending action. It remains uncertain whether a pending action can be registered if the consent of the court is needed to bring the application out of time.[10]

Distribution Pending an Application

Personal representatives should not generally part with any of the estate within the six-month period when there is the possibility of a claim. This is because the incidence of an award is a matter for the

5. Under Land Charges Act 1972, s 5(1)(a); Land Registration Act 1925, s 59(1); *Whittingham v Whittingham* [1979] Fam 9, [1978] 3 All ER 805.
6. *Sowerby v Sowerby* (1982) 44 P & CR 192, at 195–196 (per Megarry V-C); *Calgary and Edmonton Land Co Ltd v Dobinson* [1974] Ch 102, at 107B–H, [1974] 1 All ER 484, at 488h-489f. In *Perez-Adamson v Perez-Rivas* [1987] Fam 89, [1987] 3 All ER 20 the Court of Appeal severely restricted the remarks of Megarry V-C in *Sowerby v Sowerby*.
7. *Sowerby v Sowerby* (1982) 44 P & CR 192, at 197 (per Megarry V-C). On the court's inherent jurisdiction to vacate a land charge, see *Rawlplug Co Ltd v Kamvale Properties Ltd* (1968) 20 P & CR 32; *Clearbrook Property Ltd v Verrier* [1974] 1 WLR 243, at 246B–G, [1973] 3 All ER 614, at 617E–J.
8. *Tiverton Estates v Wearwell* [1975] Ch 146, [1974] 1 All ER 209; *Tucker v Hutchinson* (1987) 54 P & CR 106.
9. See pp 302–303, *ante*.
10. In *Selim Ltd v Bickenhall Ltd* [1981] 1 WLR 1318, [1981] 3 All ER 210 Megarry V-C held that an action under the Leasehold Property (Repairs) Act 1938 for leave to commence proceedings for forfeiture of a lease was registerable as a pending action. On the other hand in *Sowerby v Sowerby* (1982) 44 P & CR 192 Megarry V-C held that an application to set aside a consent order dismissing an application for ancillary relief on divorce was not registerable as a pending action.

court's discretion and there are no presumptions that particular types of gifts, such as legacies as opposed to residue, will suffer the burden of an award.[11] While this general duty not to distribute the estate pending an application exists, it can in some cases result in hardship and some guidelines as to when it may be proper to distribute part of the estate before an application were given by Cross J in *Re Ralphs*.[12] Firstly, it is often proper for a benefit given in a will or on intestacy to an applicant who seeks additional provision to be paid.[13] The only proper reason for withholding a benefit in a simple case – that of retaining a fund from which any costs awarded against the applicant can be paid – will rarely justify withholding the benefit.[14] Secondly, where a legacy is 'trifling in comparison with the size of the residue' or because the legatee has a strong claim on the deceased and is in need, that it is very unlikely that the court would direct the legacy to suffer the burden of an award, then the benefit can be distributed.[15] In any other case the personal representatives are at risk if they distribute. However, rather than adopt a purely negative attitude, the personal representatives with the assistance of their advisers should make up their own minds as to the payments which can be made and seek the consent of those applicants and beneficiaries likely to be affected.[16] If such consent was not forthcoming, the personal representatives should apply to the court for leave to make the payment, when the court may order any party who is withholding his consent unreasonably to pay the costs of the application.[17]

Discovery

Proceedings under the 1975 Act are subject to the usual rules on discovery applicable to proceedings by originating summonses.[18] Discovery is not automatic, but has to be the subject of a specific application[19] and will be ordered if it is relevant and unless there is some good reason why it should not be ordered.[20] Discovery is

11. *Re Simson* [1950] Ch 38, at 42–43, [1949] 2 All ER 826, at 828H-829A (per Vaisey J).
12. [1968] 1 WLR 1522, at 1524C–1525H, [1968] 3 All ER 285, at 287E–288G.
13. [1968] 1 WLR 1525A–B, [1968] 3 All ER 288A–B.
14. [1968] 1 WLR 1525B–C, [1968] 3 All ER 288B–C.
15. [1968] 1 WLR 1525E, [1968] 3 All ER 288D.
16. [1968] 1 WLR 1525F–G, [1968] 3 All ER 288E–F.
17. [1968] 1 WLR 1525F–G, [1968] 3 All ER 288F–G.
18. *Re Borthwick* [1948] Ch 645, at 649, [1948] 2 All ER 635, at 636D-G.
19. RSC Ord 24, r 3.
20. RSC Ord 24, r 8; *Coni v Robertson* [1969] 1 WLR 1007, [1969] 2 All ER 609.

invariably ordered in family provision applications. Courts and the parties' legal advisers should endeavour to ensure that discovery is focused on specific financial and other transactions, rather than becoming an open ended trawl through the affairs of the deceased and the parties to the application.[1] Discovery can be ordered against any party to the action.[2] Similar principles apply in the County Court.[3]

Striking Out Applications Disclosing No Reasonable Cause of Action

It is often the case that applications are made under the 1975 Act by applicants who have only very weak claims in the hope that their 'nuisance value' will lead the defendants to make some offer of compromise, rather than delay the administration of the estate and risk costs being awarded out of the estate of being irrecoverable from the applicant.[4] This prospect has led defendants at an early stage to apply under RSC Ord 18, r 19 and the inherent jurisdiction of the court[5] to strike out applications which do not disclose a reasonable cause of action. The advantage of saving costs all round has been recognised by the courts.[6] It is quite clear that an applicant who is not qualified within section 1 can have his application struck out.[7] Where a person's qualifications depend upon complicated facts and inferences from them, a court will not strike out an application before trial unless failure is certain.[8] In *Jelley v Iliffe*, concerning an

1. Although the actual decision of *Re Borthwick* [1948] Ch 645 was overruled by RSC Ord 24, r 3, 8, the remarks of Lord Greene MR at [1948] Ch 650–651, [1948] 2 All ER 637A-H are still relevant. The various Rules Committees might give consideration to requiring all principal parties to answer a questionnaire on their financial circumstances or a requirement that all principal parties present their financial situation in a particular manner.
2. RSC Ord 24, r 3(1) refers to 'any party' and see RSC Ord 24, r 6(3); and see fn 19, p 354, *ante*.
3. CCR 1981 Ord 14, rr 1, 8.
4. *Re Beaumont* [1980] Ch 444, at 458F–G, [1980] 1 All ER 266, at 276f-h (per Megarry V-C).
5. So as to allow evidence to be admitted.
6. *Jelley v Iliffe* [1981] Fam 128, at 140G–H, [1981] 2 All ER 29, at 38b-c (per Stephenson LJ), [1981] Fam at 143B–C, [1981] 2 All ER 40a (per Griffiths LJ).
7. *Re Dymott* [1980] CA Transcript 942; *Jelley v Iliffe* [1981] Fam 128, at 140A–C, [1981] 2 All ER 29, at 37e (per Stephenson LJ).
8. *Jelley v Iliffe* [1981] Fam 128, at 140B–C, [1981] 2 All ER 29, at 37g-h; *Re Kirby* (1982) 11 Fam Law 210.

application by a lover under section 1(1)(e) against his deceased mistress's estate, Stephenson LJ said:

> There must be few cases indeed where the result of the balancing of contributions of deceased and alleged dependant is so plain before the trial that the court is entitled to strike out an application under section 1(1)(e). In many cases there must be real doubt whether an applicant will be able to prove dependency within section 1(1)(e) ... If there is such doubt the case is not one for the exercise of the court's inherent jurisdiction to stop it without a full hearing because the court cannot say it is bound to fail.[9]

Accordingly an application will only be struck out by the court on the ground that the applicant is unqualified in a very clear case.[10] Secondly, an application can be struck out, even if the applicant is qualified to apply, if the application on the merits is bound to fail.[11] The application must be certain to fail, merely being very likely to fail is not sufficient.[12] Such a procedure will allow applications by wealthy adult children to be struck out[13] or even applications by former spouses who are adequately provided for and who were not in receipt of periodical payments or had some other claim upon the deceased.

Applications to strike out should only be made in very clear cases[14] and should be discouraged when the evidence on such an application would be as full as that on the full application.[15] If the defendants are faced with a very weak application, but one with sufficient possible merit to survive striking out, the better course would be to proceed very quickly to a full hearing[16] or to have the question whether the plaintiff is qualified as an applicant tried as a preliminary issue.[17]

9. [1981] Fam 128, at 140B–C, [1981] 2 All ER 29, at 37g-h.
10. Such a case was *Re Dymott* [1980] CA Transcript 942, a case decided a day before *Jelley v Iliffe*, but not inconsistent with it.
11. See the remarks of Megarry V-C in *Re Beaumont* [1980] Ch 444, at 455D–E, [1980] 1 All ER 266, at 274b-d ; and of Stephenson LJ in *Jelley v Iliffe* [1981] Fam 128, at 140C–F, [1981] 2 All ER 29, at 37h-38c.
12. See the very careful analysis of Stephenson LJ in *Jelley v Iliffe* [1981] Fam 128, at 140C–F, [1981] 2 All ER 29, at 37j-38b.
13. Compare *Re Dennis* [1981] 2 All ER 140.
14. *Jelley v Iliffe* [1981] Fam 128, at 140C–G, 143A–B, [1981] 2 All ER 29, at 37j-38c, 39h-j.
15. *Re Dymott* [1980] CA Transcript 942 (per Ormrod LJ).
16. *Jelley v Iliffe* [1981] Fam 128, at 143C, [1981] 2 All ER 29, at 40h (per Griffiths LJ).
17. Under RSC Ord 33, r 3; CCR 1981 Ord 13, r 2(1); eg *Re S* [1965] P 165, [1965] 1 All ER 1018.

Other Procedural Matters

Interim orders and the court's powers to preserve property during litigation are discussed in Chapter 9.[18]

The Hearing

When the Master or District Judge is satisfied that the evidence is in order and that all interlocutory matters have been dealt with, the summons will be adjourned to the Judge or for hearing by the Master or District Judge. The trial will be according to the usual rules for originating summonses. Evidence will be given by affidavit, unless an order for the deponent to be cross-examined has been made.[19] The hearing before the Judge is in open court.[20]

In the County Court the proper officer of the court will fix a hearing date.[1]

Rules of Evidence

The usual rules of evidence apply to proceedings under the 1975 Act. In particular the rule against hearsay applies and hearsay evidence in affidavit is only admissible in accordance with the machinery of the Civil Evidence Act 1995.[2]

The admissibility of evidence of the deceased's mental capacity was the subject of a *Practice Note*[3] made by Vaisey J after consulting the other judges of the Chancery Division, which was refined by some remarks of Buckley J in *Re Blanch*[4] likewise made after

18. See pp 372–377, *post*. For a case where a claim under the 1975 Act was struck out for want of prosecution, see *Bilton v Bilton* [1996] 5 CLY 760.
19. RSC Ord 38, r 2(3).
20. *Re F* (1985) Times 11 February.
1. CCR 1981 Ord 17, r 9.
2. The Civil Evidence Act 1995 came into force on 31 January 1997, see Civil Evidence Act 1995 (Commencement No1) Order 1996, SI 1996/3217. The relevant rules are now RSC Ord 38, rr 20-24 and CCR 1981 Ord 20, rr 14–17. Hearsay notices do not have to be given for affidavits, see RSC Ord 38, r 21(3)(a) and CCR Ord 20, r 15(3)(a). For the rules under the Civil Evidence Act 1968, see RSC Ord 38, rr 21–25; CCR 1981 Ord 20, rr 15–16; with affidavit evidence, there is no requirement of serving a notice of an intention to rely upon hearsay – RSC Ord 38, r 21(4) and CCR 1981 Ord 20, r 15(4).
3. [1945] WN 210.
4. [1967] 1 WLR 987, [1967] 2 All ER 468.

consulting his fellow judges. Clearly proceedings under the 1975 Act cannot be used as an indirect way of challenging a will for want of testamentary capacity[5] and because the test in proceedings under the 1975 Act is objective, evidence of want of testamentary capacity is unlikely to be relevant.[6] However, where the evidence of mental incapacity is otherwise relevant, such as where the applicant cared for the deceased during a long mental illness, the evidence of mental incapacity is admissible.[7] Mental incapacity is not a reason for the deceased's dispositions which was formerly admissible within section 21,[8] but is available in assessing the weight and credit of such evidence of the deceased's reasons for making the particular dispositions.[9]

The 1938 Act had a specific provision enjoining the court to have regard to the deceased's reasons for making the particular testamentary dispositions and for admitting in evidence any statement by the deceased as to the reason for such dispositions.[10] The specific admonition to the court to consider the reasons of the deceased was not repeated by the 1975 Act as it was considered unnecessary.[11] The Law Commission at first thought it unnecessary to repeat the provision that the deceased's statements of the reasons for his dispositions be admissible, as the matter was already covered by the Civil Evidence Act 1968.[12] Subsequently the Law Commission changed its mind because there remained a doubt whether evidence by the deceased in proceedings in which the deceased could never give evidence while alive was admissible under section 2 of the Civil Evidence Act 1968 and because a specific provision might draw people's attention to the possibility of making such a statement.[13] Accordingly section 21 was enacted, which provides:

5. *Re Blanch* [1967] 1 WLR 987, at 991G–H, [1967] 2 All ER 468, at 471–E (per Buckley J). See to like effect *Williams v Johns* [1988] 2 FLR 475, at 44B-C. Technically a grant of representation is an order of the court and binding on all by virtue of *res judicata*. It is to be hoped that in extreme cases the courts will not hesitate to strike out allegations suggesting that a will was not properly admitted to probate.
6. *Practice Note* [1945] WN 210; *Re Blanch* [1967] 1 WLR 987, at 991D–E, [1967] 2 All ER 468, at 471B–C (per Buckley J).
7. *Re Blanch* [1967] 1 WLR 987, at 991B–F, [1967] 2 All ER 468, at 4701–471C (per Buckley J).
8. *Practice Note* [1945] WN 210; *Re Blanch* [1967] 1 WLR 987, at 991H, [1967] 2 All ER 468, at 471E (per Buckley J). On s 21 generally, see p 362, *post*.
9. *Re Blanch* [1967] 1 WLR 987, at 991D, [1967] 2 All ER 468, at 471A–B (per Buckley J).
10. S 1(7); s 26 of the Matrimonial Causes Act 1965 had no comparable provision.
11. See pp 162–163, *ante*.
12. WORKING PAPER, para 3. 23.
13. LAW COM, paras 105–108.

> In any proceedings under this Act a statement made by the deceased, whether orally or in a document or otherwise, shall be admissible under section 2 of the Civil Evidence Act 1968 as evidence of any fact stated therein in like manner as if the statement were a statement falling within section 2(1) of the Act ...

Unlike section 1(7) of the 1938 Act this is not limited to '*reasons*' of the deceased and covers all statements.

The rules upon the admission of hearsay have been simplified and relaxed by the Civil Evidence Act 1995. Since under the Act hearsay of all kinds is prima facie admissible, there is no need for section 21 and it is repealed by the Civil Evidence Act 1995.[14] This repeal affects only the machinery for the admission of statements by the deceased and does not in any way affect the weight or lack of weight to be given to such statements or the desirability in certain cases of a testator making such a statement.

In many cases it is desirable for a testator to make a statement while alive justifying his dispositions and when a testator is making a will in a situation where he might face a claim under the 1975 Act he should consider making a statement setting out his reasons for making the particular dispositions.[15] Such reasons should not be contained in the will, because the court has a power to omit parts of the will containing offensive allegations from probate[16] and because a will is a public document. Such a statement should set out clearly, without bitterness and exaggeration, the deceased's reasons and refer to any agreements, court hearings and other matters with considerable detail. Because the maker of the statement will not be able to give evidence personally, the facts contained in such a statement may not be able to withstand challenge by witnesses who can give evidence personally to the court.[17] The real value of such a statement is not so much as evidence, but as a pleading, addressing arguments to the court, and as an aid to the defendants in indicating the kind of evidence that might be adduced.

Certain facts, such as proof of a particular relationship[18] or the commission of a matrimonial offence, such as adultery[19] or

14. S 15(2), Sch 2.
15. TBFR, 'Exclusion of the Family from Testamentary Benefits', (1948) 98 L Jo 270, 285; Note, (1960) 230 LT 302.
16. Tristram and Coote, *Probate Practice* (28th edn), paras 3. 264–3.271. But the court may order that a statement which might have an effect on proceedings under the Act should not be struck out; see *In the Estate of C* (1960) Times, 28 July; *In the Estate of Townsend* (1960) Times, 13 October, referred to in Note, (1960) 230 LT 302.
17. See *Re Borthwick* [1949] Ch 395, [1949] 1 All ER 472; *Re Preston* [1969] 1 WLR 317, [1969] 2 All ER 963.
18. See pp 77–78, *ante*.
19. *Coates v Thomas* [1947] NZLR 779.

desertion,[20] which have been adjudicated upon during the deceased's lifetime may create an estoppel per rem judicata in proceedings under the 1975 Act between the applicant and those claiming under the deceased's estate.[1] Such an estoppel is binding only as to the facts of the matter adjudicated upon and do not decide the overall question whether the applicant is entitled to provision.[2]

Earlier wills of the testator are admissible and are not privileged.[3]

There are two issues concerning legal professional privilege and claims under the 1975 Act which arise reasonably frequently in practice, but which have been authoritatively determined by the courts. The first is to the extent that legal professional privilege for communications between the deceased and his legal advisers can be asserted in family provision actions. While legal professional privilege survives the death of the client,[4] it can not be asserted in a dispute between two persons both claiming under the deceased and probate proceedings fall within this category.[5] While claims under the 1975 Act would also appear to be claims between persons both claiming under the deceased, the failure to allow professional privilege to be claimed might have very capricious results. For instance if a spouse should die in the middle of an application for ancillary relief, it would seem grossly inappropriate that the other spouse should be able to see communications passing between the deceased and his lawyers in the matrimonial proceedings in a claim under the 1975 Act which is in reality a continuation of the claim for ancillary relief. The second and to some extent related issue is whether the decision in *Barclays Bank plc v Eustice*[6] that legal professional privilege can not be claimed in transactions intended to defraud others is applicable to applications under section 10. In practice persons defending applications under section 10 often find it appropriate to reveal the full history of a transaction.[7]

20. *Re Goard* (1962) 106 Sol Jo 721.
1. On res judicata generally, see Spencer Bower and Turner, *Res Judicata* (2nd edn); Halsbury's *Laws of England* (4th edn, Reissue) Vol 16, paras 961–996.
2. *Re Goard* (1962) 106 Sol Jo 721.
3. See *Re Moore* [1965] NZLR 895 (a case under the Testamentary Promises legislation).
4. *Bullivant v A-G of Victoria* [1901] AC 196, at 206.
5. *Russell v Jackson* (1851) 9 Hare 387; *Bullivant v A-G of Victoria* [1901] AC 196, at 206; *Halsbury's Laws of England* 4th edn, Vol 17, para 880.
6. [1995] 1 WLR 1238, [1995] 4 All ER 511; compare *Bullivant v A-G of Victoria*.
7. Eg *Clifford v Tanner* [1987] CLY 3881, CA.

Compromise

Most applications are compromised. A compromise where all parties are ascertained and sui juris before the matter reaches court can be contained in a simple agreement varying the dispositions of the deceased's estate, which is usually in the form of a deed of family arrangement. If a court order embodying the terms of the compromise is made, it can either be a straightforward consent order or an order staying further proceedings on agreed terms in the Tomlin form. A Tomlin order is not technically an order under the 1975 Act, but this distinction has few consequences now.[8]

Where an infant or patient is involved, the sanction of the court is needed for the approval of any compromise. Usually an application for a compromise is supported by an affidavit sworn by the infant's or patient's next friend or guardian ad litem.[9]

Where property is to be held on trust by charitable trustees, such trustees have full power to compromise a claim under the 1975 Act,[10] as does a corporate charity where its memorandum or articles permit. In other cases the Charity Commissioners have power to authorise a compromise,[11] as does the Attorney General when he is a party to the proceedings.[12] Alternatively the power of the Charity Commissioners or the Attorney General to authorise charities to make ex gratia payments to the deceased's relatives[13] can be used to compromise a claim under the 1975 Act.

Personal representatives have no power to compromise claims under the 1975 Act,[14] unless the beneficiaries affected confer on them actual authority or unless the court makes some form of representation order.

The court has a limited power to approve a compromise on behalf of unascertained persons, persons who cannot be found or persons who are not before the court, where a party is appointed to represent the absent person and consents to the compromise or

8. See fn 12, p 451, *post* and p 431, *post*.
9. See generally RSC Ord 80, r 11; Supreme Court Practice 1997, Vol 1, para 80/10–11/1–4.
10. S 15 of the Trustee Act 1925; *Re Earl of Strafford* [1980] Ch 28, [1979] 1 All ER 513.
11. S 26(2) of the Charities Act 1993.
12. Tudor, *Charities* (8th edn), 341.
13. S 27 of the Charities Act 1993.
14. The submission made by counsel in *Stock v Brown* [1994] 1 FLR 840, at 841 G–H that the trustees had a power to compromise a claim under the 1975 Act was *per incuriam*.

where a party to the proceedings has the same interest as the absent person and consents to the compromise.[15]

Costs

After the 1938 Act was passed, the courts did not adopt a coherent and uniform approach to costs. In the case of an applicant failing in the application, the cases seem almost equally divided between those where the court ordered the applicant to pay the costs,[16] where there was no order for costs[17] and those where the applicant was awarded costs out of the estate.[18] Albery writing in 1950 was able to detect some trends.[19] If the estate was small, a losing applicant was more likely to have to pay the costs than where the estate was large.[20] If the case involved a difficult point of law, then the applicant was less likely to pay the costs of the application.[1]

In the years 1950–1970 little changed as to the court's attitude to costs. In *Re Ralphs* Cross J said, 'The court would only [require an unsuccessful applicant to pay the costs of the action], however, in a case where the application was totally unmeritorious',[2] but these remarks did not represent a uniform approach of the courts; indeed so little had changed that the first edition of this book could repeat Albery's summary of the law as representing the position in 1970.[3]

After 1970 the courts began to award costs on a more orthodox basis more closely following the event. This change may have been influenced by the possibility after 1966 of an applicant being awarded the entire estate, which resulted in an order that all costs be paid out of the estate might seriously reduce the value of an award

15. RSC Ord 15, r 13(4): CCR 1981 Ord 5, r 6(3). Both these rules are expressly extended to proceedings under the 1975 Act – RSC Ord 99, r 4(2); CCR 1981 Ord 48, r 4(2).
16. Eg *Re Vrint* [1940] Ch 920, [1940] 3 All ER 470; *Re Joslin* [1941] Ch 200, [1941] 1 All ER 302.
17. Eg *Re Pugh* [1943] Ch 387, [1943] 2 All ER 361; *Re Dorgan* [1948] Ch 366, [1948] 1 All ER 723.
18. Eg *Re Catmull* [1943] Ch 262, [1943] 2 All ER 115; *Re Inns* [1947] Ch 576, [1947] 2 All ER 308.
19. ALBERY, 41–42.
20. ALBERY, 41–42; compare *Re Vrint* [1940] Ch 920, at 926, [1940] 3 All ER 470, at 475H (per Bennet J) with *Re Inns* [1947] Ch 576, [1947] 2 All ER 308.
1. ALBERY, 41; *Re Pugh* [1943] Ch 387, [1943] 2 All ER 361; *Re Dorgan* [1948] Ch 366, [1948] 1 All ER 723.
2. [1968] 1 WLR 1522, at 1525C, [1968] 3 All ER 285, at 288B–C.
3. First edition, pp 91–92.

to a successful applicant.[4] The use of legal aid to assist weak applications caused some apprehension among the judiciary.[5] In the related field of matrimonial property law costs generally followed the event[6] and were regarded as a device for discouraging litigation. By 1980 costs tended to follow the event in family provision proceedings. This change had not been brought about by any one leading case, but was the general practice of the courts. When in *Re Fullard*, Ormrod LJ said:

> … for that reason I would be disposed to think that judges should reconsider the practice of ordering costs of both sides in these cases to be paid out of the estate. That is probate practice:[7] this is something quite different. I think judges should look very closely at the merits of each application before ordering that the estate pays the applicant's costs if the applicant is unsuccessful, [8]

he is more setting out what the practice of the courts is than merely advocating a change.

The modern practice as to costs in family provision matters would appear to be as follows. Firstly, a personal representative *in his capacity as such* is always entitled to have his costs paid out of the estate on the indemnity basis.[9] A defendant who opposes the application essentially in his capacity as a beneficiary should not be allowed his costs automatically out of the estate,[10] but costs such as the cost of the obligatory affidavit[11] and Answer[12] by a personal representative should always come out of the estate. Secondly, the almost universal rule is that costs follow the event. If the applicant

4. See the comments of Simon P in *Roberts v Roberts* [1965] 1 WLR 560, at 567C-E, [1964] 3 All ER 503, at 5081–509A and see the order made in *Millward v Shenton* [1972] 1 WLR 711, [1972] 2 All ER 1025.
5. See the remarks of Stamp J in *Re E* [1966] 1 WLR 709, at 716D, [1966] 2 All ER 44, at 49B; and the particularly strong remarks of both members of the Court of Appeal in *Brill v Proud* [1984] Fam Law 59.
6. *Martin v Martin* [1976] Fam 335, [1976] 3 All ER 625; *Gojkovic v Gojkovic (No 2)* [1992] Fam 40, [1992] 1 All ER 267.
7. Surely a mistake for will construction litigation, since in contentious probate matters costs generally follow the event.
8. [1982] Fam 42, at 46C, [1981] 2 All ER 796, at 799c.
9. See *Alsop Wilkinson v Neary* [1995] 1 All ER 431, at 435j; and see generally RSC Ord 62, r 6(2), applied to the County Court by CCR 1981 Ord 38, r 1. Eg *Graham v Murphy* [1997] 1 FLR 860.
10. See further *Alsop Wilkinson v Neary* [1995] 1 All ER 431, at 435j-436b; compare *National Anti-Vivisection Society Ltd v Duddington* (1989) Times, 23 November 1989 and on the two roles of a personal representative-beneficiary – *Re Clark* [1981] CLY 2884.
11. RSC Ord 99, r 5.
12. CCR 1981 Ord 48, r 5.

is successful and is awarded the entire estate, the defendants in their capacity as beneficiaries are ordered to pay the costs.[13] If the applicant is successful and is awarded less than the whole estate, the usual order is that all parties' costs are payable out of the estate.[14] Costs are awarded on the standard basis, save in the case of personal representatives.[15] If the application is unsuccessful, the applicant is ordered to pay the costs of the application[16] and in an appropriate case the Legal Aid Fund may be ordered to pay the costs both at first instance[17] and on appeal.[18] Thirdly, there are still some cases where costs do not strictly follow the event. Most of these cases, but not all, can be explained on the basis that the application and opposition to it was not wholly without merit,[19] there was an interesting point of law involved[20] or the interests of a person under a disability were involved.[1]

The usual rules as to costs in interlocutory proceedings, either that the costs be costs in the cause or follow the event apply.[2] The usual rules as to security for costs on an appeal apply.[3]

A 'without prejudice' offer in the *Calderbank v Calderbank*[4] form applies to proceedings under the 1975 Act. Because costs normally follow the event, to be effective a *Calderbank* offer should include an offer to pay the applicant's costs to date to be taxed on the standard basis.

13. Precise authority is lacking, but see the orders made on appeal in *Millward v Shenton* [1972] 1 WLR 711, [1972] 2 All ER 1025 and *Re Bayliss* (9 December 1977, unreported), CA.
14. Eg *Re Besterman* (1981) 3 FLR 255.
15. *Graham v Murphy* [1997] 1 FLR 860, at 871A-B.
16. E g *Re Fergusson* Foster J (16 June 1980, unreported).
17. *Re Fergusson* Foster J (16 June 1980, unreported).
18. *Re Dymott* [1980] CA Transcript 942; *Re Fullard* [1982] Fam 42, [1981] 2 All ER 796; *Cumming Burns v Burns* (4 July 1985, unreported), CA; *Eeles v Evans* (6 July 1989, unreported), CA; *Winfield v Billington* (30 July 1990, unreported), CA; *Davis v Davis* [1993] 1 FLR 54.
19. Eg *Re Wilson* Judge Holt (23 September 1980, unreported) where the application under the 1975 Act was intimately connected with a construction summons. The applicant's success in the construction summons made her application under the 1975 Act almost otiose.
20. Eg *Re Dorgan* [1948] Ch 366, [1948] 1 All ER 723; *Cameron v Treasury Solicitor* [1996] 2 FLR 716.
1. Eg *Re Watkins* [1949] 1 All ER 695; *Re Chatterton* (1 November 1978, unreported), CA.
2. Eg *Barnsley v Ward* (18 January 1980, unreported), CA; *Sobesto v Farren* [1981] Conv 224, CA.
3. *Midland Bank Trust Co v Nobbs* (1981) 131 NL Jo 342; and see Reg 123 of the Legal Aid (General) Regulations 1989, SI 1989/339.
4. [1976] Fam 93, [1975] 3 All ER 333; *Gojkovic v Gojkovic (No 2)* [1992] Fam 40, [1992] 1 All ER 267; *Graham v Murphy* [1997] 1 FLR 860, at 870A–871A. On the procedure where the defendants are under a disability, see *Abada v Gray* (1997) Times, 9 July.

Legal Aid

Legal Aid is available to prosecute and defend proceedings under the 1975 Act,[5] although it will not normally be granted to a defendant whose *sole* interest in the dispute is in a fiduciary capacity.[6] Where the time limit is about to expire, use should be made of an emergency legal aid certificate.[7]

Where property is recovered or *preserved*,[8] the Legal Aid Board has a charge over such property;[9] but this charge does not apply to any order for interim provision under section 5[10] or the first £2,500 of any order made under section 2 or section 6 or any agreement to like effect.[11] It should be noted that periodical payments under the 1975 Act totalling more than £2,500 are subject to the charge.[12] With an order made under the 1975 Act being either a 'home' or money with which to purchase a home, the enforcement of the statutory charge can be postponed or transferred to another property.[13] The operation of the charge should be borne in mind by all practitioners.

The courts have by making orders for costs against the Legal Aid Board deprecated the grant of legal aid to applicants with weak claims,[14] and this should be borne in mind when applicants apply for legal aid.

5. S 7(1) of the Legal Aid Act 1974. For limited guidance upon the circumstances in which Legal Aid is granted in family provision claims, see Legal Aid Board, Matrimonial and Family Guidance Revision (June 1997), s 9.
6. See Reg 33 of the Civil Legal Aid (General) Regulations 1989, SI 1989/339. See further Legal Aid Board, Matrimonial and Family Guidance Revision (June 1997), para 9.2.
7. See p 343, *ante*.
8. On the meaning of 'preserved' see *Hanlon v Law Society* [1981] AC 124, [1980] 2 All ER 199.
9. S 14 of the Legal Aid Act 1988.
10. Reg 94(b) of the Civil Legal Aid (General) Regulations 1989, SI 1980/339.
11. Reg 94d)(ii) of the Civil Legal Aid (General) Regulations 1989, SI 1989/339.
12. The wording of Reg 96(c) relating to periodical payments of maintenance would seem inappropriate to cover payments made out of a deceased's estate.
13. Regs 96, 97, 98 of the Civil Legal Aid (General) Regulations 1989, SI 1989/339, as amended by SI 1991/2784, SI 1993/1756, SI 1994/229, SI 1994/1822. See further *Practice Direction (legal aid: property recovered: form of order)* [1991] 1 WLR 955, [1991] 3 All ER 896.
14. *Re E* [1966] 1 WLR 709, at 716D, [1966] 2 All ER 44, at 49B (per Stamp J); *Re Fergusson*, Foster J (16 June 1980, unreported); *Re Dymott* [1980] CA Transcript 942; *Re Fullard* [1982] Fam 42, [1981] 2 All ER 796; *Brill v Proud* [1984] Fam Law 59.

Appeals

An appeal in an application under the 1975 Act lies from both the High Court and the County Court to the Court of Appeal. Except in interlocutory matters[15] leave to appeal is not necessary.

Except where there is a clear point of law,[16] the Court of Appeal will be reluctant to interfere with the exercise of the trial judge's discretion in a procedural matter, including applications for an extension of time. Despite these general principles, the Court of Appeal has intervened in a surprising number of applications for an extension of time.[17]

Because the jurisdiction under the 1975 Act is discretionary, the general rules limiting the power of the Court of Appeal to interfere with the discretion of the trial judge apply.[18] Describing the nature of the discretion and the consequent limitations upon the power of the Court of Appeal, Buckley LJ said in *Re Coventry*:

> It is a qualitative decision, or what is sometimes called a 'value judgment'. A decision of that kind is one which is particularly difficult to disturb on appeal, unless the Judge of first instance has clearly proceeded on some error of principle.[19]

This point was taken up by Hoffmann LJ in *Re Grayan Ltd* when referring, inter alia, to appeals under the 1975 Act:

> ... the vaguer the standard and the greater the number of factors which the court has to weigh up in deciding whether or not the standards have been met, the more reluctant an appellate court will be to interefere with the trial judge's decision.[20]

It is certainly the case that the Court of Appeal will not interefere merely because it might have come to a different conclusion.[1]

15. RSC Ord 59, r 1B(1)(f).
16. *Re Borthwick* [1948] Ch 645, [1948] 2 All ER 635; *Re Bidie* [1949] Ch 121, [1949] 2 All ER 995; *Jelley v Iliffe* [1981] Fam 128, [1981] 2 All ER 29.
17. *Re Stone* (1969) 114 Sol Jo 36; *Adams v Adams* (22 July 1981, unreported), CA; *Clifford v Tanner* [1987] CLY 3881, CA; *Perry v Horlock* (18 November 1987, unreported), CA.
18. On the powers of the Court of Appeal in relation to discretionary jurisdiction, see Supreme Court Practice 1997, Vol 1, para 59/1/59.
19. [1980] Ch 461, at 495H–496A, [1979] 3 All ER 815, at 828e.
20. [1995] Ch 241, at 254G–H.
1. *Thornley v Palmer* [1969] 1 WLR 1037, at 1040H, [1969] 3 All ER 31, at 331 (per Harman LJ); *Re Chatterton* (1 November 1978, unreported), CA (per Brandon LJ); *Stead v Stead* [1985] FLR 16, at 24F (per Purchas LJ); *Eeles v Evans* (6 July 1989, unreported), CA.

Reported case law[2] shows that the Court of Appeal will interfere if the trial judge made an error of law,[3] took into account irrelevant matters or omitted to take into account relevant matters,[4] made a material error of fact[5] or simply reached a decision which was 'unjust' or excessive.[6] The Court of Appeal is generally reluctant to interfere with the decsion of the trial judge in a small estate,[7] unless there is a point of principle;[8] but there remain several cases involving small estates where the Court of Appeal has intervened merely on the ground that the quantum has been seriously wrong.[9]

In recent years beneficiaries have been as successful as applicants in persuading the Court of Appeal to reverse decisions of trial judges.[10]

2. The limits on the jurisdiction of the Court of Appeal are conveniently summarised by Nourse LJ in *Jessop v Jessop* [1992] 1 FLR 591, at 597C-D.
3. Eg *Moody v Stevenson* [1992] Ch 486, [1992] 2 All ER 524; *Re Jennings* [1994] Ch 286, [1994] 3 All ER 27; *Cameron v Treasury Solicitor* [1996] 2 FLR 716.
4. Eg *Re Besterman* [1984] Ch 458, [1984] 2 All ER 656; *Jessop v Jessop* [1992] 1 FLR 591, at 598C-D.
5. Eg *Re Leach* [1986] Ch 226, [1985] 2 All ER 754; *Dixit v Dixit* (23 June 1988, unreported), CA.
6. Eg *Re Bayliss* (9 December 1977, unreported), CA; *Re Lewis* (13 March 1980, unreported), CA; *Jevdjovic v Milenko* (12 March 1990, unreported), CA.
7. *Re Howell* [1953] 1 WLR 1034, at 1039, [1953] 2 All ER 604, at 607G (per Romer LJ); *Re Gregory* [1970] 1 WLR 1455, at 1462E, [1971] 1 All ER 497, at 503E (per Fenton Atkinson LJ); *Re Coventry* [1980] Ch 461, at 492G–H, [1979] 3 All ER 815, at 825j (per Geoffrey Lane LJ), at [1980] Ch 496B–C, [1979] 3 All ER 828f-g (per Buckley LJ); *Re Portt* (25 March 1980, unreported), CA (per Ackner and Roskill LJJ); *Brill v Proud* [1984] Fam Law 59, at 60 (per Latey J).
8. *Cameron v Treasury Solicitor* [1996] 2 FLR 716, at 718B–C.
9. *Re Parkinson* (1975) Times, 4 October, but note the judgment of Bridge LJ 65; *Wallace v Thorburn* (9 October 1987, unreported), CA; *Re J* (9 December 1991, unreported), CA.
10. Eg *Re Jennings*; *Cameron v Treasury Solicitor*; *Re Krubert* [1997] Ch 97.

Chapter 9

THE ORDER

Form of Provision

Before the enactment of the 1975 Act the court could only make an award consisting of an order for periodical payments or a lump sum. The 1975 Act considerably increased the type of order which the court could make and assimilated the court's powers to make orders in family provision proceedings with those on divorce.[1]

The court may, if it is satisfied that the disposition of the deceased's estate effected by his will or the law relating to intestacy is not such as to make reasonable financial provision for the applicant, make any one or more of the following orders:

(a) an order for the making to the applicant out of the net estate of the deceased of such periodical payments and for such term as may be specified in the order;
(b) an order for the payment to the applicant out of that estate of a lump sum of such amount as may be so specified;
(c) an order for the transfer to the applicant of such property comprised in that estate as may be so specified;
(d) an order for the settlement for the benefit of the applicant of such property comprised in that estate as may be specified;
(e) an order for the acquisition out of property comprised in that estate of such property as may be so specified and for the transfer of the property so acquired to the applicant or for the settlement thereof for his benefit;
(f) an order varying an ante-nuptial or post-nuptial settlement (including such a settlement made by will) made on the parties to a marriage to which the deceased was one of the parties, the variation being for the benefit of the surviving party to that marriage, or any child of the marriage, or any person who was treated by the deceased as a child of the family in relation to that marriage.[2]

1. The comparable provision in the Matrimonial Causes Act 1973 is s 23(1), s 24. The background to the enlargement of the court's powers is contained in WORKING PAPER paras 3.27–33; LAW COM, paras 109–126.
2. S 2(1).

Interim Orders

The power to make an interim order was introduced by section 6(1) of the Family Provision Act 1966 after the court's limited jurisdiction to protect applicants before an order was made was revealed by *Re Ferrar.*[3] This power was essentially re-enacted in section 5 of the 1975 Act.

To be awarded an interim order for provision an applicant must satisfy three cumulative requirements. Firstly, it must appear to the court:

> ... that the applicant is in immediate need of financial assistance, but that it is not yet possible to determine what order (if any) should be made under [section 2].[4]

The test of 'immediate need of financial assistance' is a fairly strict test and is stricter than the test employed by the court to determine whether reasonable provision has been made for the applicant's maintenance.[5]

Secondly, it must appear to the court:

> ... that property forming part of the net estate of the deceased is or can be made available to meet the need of the applicant.[6]

In *Barnsley v Ward*[7] the Court of Appeal considered that property could be made available if it could easily be sold, even though it was arguable that it might increase in value if retained in the estate.

Thirdly, an applicant must satisfy the court that it is right in the exercise of the court's discretion to order provision.[8] In exercising its discretion, the court shall 'so far as the urgency of the case admits' have regard to the matters specified in section 3 to which the court is required to have regard.[9] As the usual order for interim provision has no requirement that the applicant repay to the estate any award of interim provision made if no order under section 2 is eventually made and in any event it is not unlikely that the applicant will have

3. [1966] P 126, [1966] 3 All ER 78.
4. S 5(1)(a).
5. For an example of the application of being 'in immediate need of financial assistance' to the facts of a particular case, see *Barnsley v Ward* (18 January 1980, unreported), CA.
6. S 5(1)(b).
7. 18 January 1980.
8. S 5(1).
9. S 5(3).

spent the award, it is suggested that the court should in its discretion make an interim order only if the applicant has a strong prima facie case for provision. It may also be a legitimate approach for the court in making an interim order to seek to insure that any undue delay between the date of death and the hearing does not apply unfair pressure on an applicant. In *Barnsley v Ward*[10] Ormrod LJ said, 'The whole purpose of an interim order is to hold the situation as reasonably and fairly as possible pending final determination'.

The court's power to make interim orders is limited to ordering the payment of 'such sum or sums ... as the court thinks reasonable'.[11] This power clearly includes the power to order lump sums to be paid, as well as periodical payments. For example in *Barnsley v Ward*[12] Vinelott J, whose decision was affirmed by the Court of Appeal, made an interim order in favour of an applicant within section 1(1)(e) that she should be paid £50 per week and receive £400 towards the cost of effecting repairs. In *Re Besterman*[13] the Master made in favour of a widow applicant an interim order of a lump sum of £75,000 of which £68,000 was used to purchase a house and periodical payments which totalled £31,000 at the date of the hearing of the substantive application. The expression 'such sum or sums' would suggest that an order is limited to the provision of money and cannot include an award of other property. The power does not include all the jurisdiction of the court under section 2(1) – in particular the court lacks the statutory power to permit an applicant to reside in a particular house pending resolution of the application[14] and the power to authorise personal representatives to purchase property for the applicant's use.[15]

The court has power to determine the length of time for which payments may continue and the intervals at which they are made, but such payments must cease at the substantive hearing of the application.[16] The court has express power under section 5(1) to

10. (18 January 1980, unreported).
11. S 5(1).
12. (18 January 1980, unreported), CA.
13. [1984] Ch 458, at 463A–C, [1984] 2 All ER 656, at 659c-e.
14. This was the issue in *Re Ferrar* [1966] P 126, [1966] 3 All ER 78 and appears to have been the factual situation in many cases eg *Re Parkinson* (1975) Times, 4 October; *Re Haig* Browne-Wilkinson J [1979] LS Gaz R 476; *Sobesto v Farren* [1981] Conv 224, CA and see pp 375–377, *post*.
15. S 5 clearly authorises a lump sum to purchase a house outright – *Re Besterman* [1984] Ch 458, [1984] 2 All ER 656, but it is doubtful whether it authorises the purchase of a house to be held in trust for the applicant as happened in *Re Lewis* (13 March 1980, unreported), CA.
16. S 5(1). In *Re Besterman* the interim order was continued until the final order was carried out. This order appears to have been in excess of the court's jurisdiction, but the order could have been validly made under s 2.

vary an interim order: for instance, provision might be increased if the applicant's financial circumstances deteriorated or reduced if the applicant's financial position improved. In *Barnsley v Ward*[17] the Court of Appeal varied the order of Vinelott J so that the periodical payments ran until judgment in the action or further order, which would appear to be the most common form of the order. The detailed provisions of section 2[18] relating to the form of periodical payments apply to interim orders.[19]

The court has power to make an interim order, 'subject to such conditions and restrictions, if any, as the court may impose'.[20] The Act contains the specific power to impose a condition that any sum paid under an interim order is to be regarded as paid on account of any provision made by an order under section 2.[21] This condition is, and should be, invariably imposed. In *Re Ralphs*[1] where the will gave the applicant a legacy which had not been paid by the executors, Stamp J made an interim order in favour of the applicant on condition that the amount of the order was brought into account against the income of the legacy. In *Barnsley v Ward*[2] Vinelott J required the applicant to give an undertaking to use her best endeavours to obtain employment. A possible condition might be that the applicant repays to the estate all sums paid under the interim order, if the court makes no order in favour of the applicant on the hearing of the application under section 2.

Although section 5 nowhere states it expressly, it is implicit in the Act that money paid under an interim order need not be repaid to the estate if the court makes no order upon the hearing of the application under section 2 or if the applicant dies before the hearing,[3] unless a condition requiring repayment has been imposed. It is submitted that the power of the court to make 'a further order'[4] does not permit the court *retrospectively* to order monies the subject of an interim order to be repaid to the estate.[5] A personal representative who pays out money to an applicant under an interim order is under no liability by reason of the net estate being

17. (18 January 1980, unreported).
18. S 2(2), (3), (4) and see pp 377–378, *post*
19. S 5(2).
20. S 5(1).
21. S 5(4).
1. [1968] 1 WLR 1522, at 1524A–B, [1968] 3 All ER 285, 287C–D.
2. (18 January 1980, unreported), CA.
3. See first edition, p 71. On the effect of the death of tbe applicant see pp 109–110, *ante*.
4. S 5(1).
5. The use of the word 'confirming' an interim order by Judge Mervyn Davies QC in *Re Besterman* (1981) 3 FLR 255, at 265G–H is obscure.

insufficient to make the payment, 'unless at the time of making the payment he has reasonable cause to believe that the estate is not sufficient'.[6]

For the purpose of appeals the question whether the applicant is in immediate need of financial assistance but it is not yet possible to determine the order which should be made, and the question whether there is property forming part of the estate which is or can be made available for the applicant are questions of fact and the trial judge's discretion whether or not to make an interim order will rarely be interfered with on appeal.[7] In the light of this if the beneficiaries are dissatisfied with the interim order made, the better course might be to ensure that the substantive hearing comes on quickly rather than to appeal. If the applicant in whose favour an interim order has been made appears to be delaying the substantive hearing, an application might be made to vary the interim order.

The Court's Jurisdiction to Preserve Property during Litigation

Although it might more properly be discussed in Chapter 8 on Procedure, and although it is technically not an order of the court made under the 1975 Act, it is convenient to discuss the court's jurisdiction to preserve property during litigation[8] in relation to family provision proceedings with interim orders, since they fulfil essentially the same function.

In *Re Ferrar's Application*[9] the applicant former wife attempted to prevent the personal representatives from selling the house in which she and the applicant's infant children were residing. The Court of Appeal held, by a majority, that the court's jurisdiction to preserve property the subject of litigation was not available because the house was not the subject of the litigation – there being no power to award the applicant the house *in specie* as opposed to periodical payments or a lump sum.[10] Under the 1975 Act the court has power

6. S 20(2).
7. *Barnsley v Ward* (18 January 1980, unreported), CA.
8. On the court's jurisdiction to preserve the subject-matter of litigation see RSC Ord 29, r 2; *Leney & Sons Ltd v Callingham* [1908] 1 KB 79, at 84; *Chaplin v Barnett* (1912) 28 TLR 256; *Roche v Roche* (1981) 11 Fam Law 243; *Walker v Walker* (1982) 4 FLR 455; *Shipman v Shipman* [1991] 1 FLR 250; *Barry v Barry* [1992] Fam 140, [1992] 3 All ER 405.
9. [1966] P 126, [1966] 3 All ER 78.
10. [1966] P 126, at 141E–F, [1966] 3 All ER 78 at 82H–I (per Davies LJ), at 143A–C, [1966] 3 All ER 83G–I (per Russell LJ).

to award an applicant specific items of property and accordingly the court has jurisdiction to preserve specific assets during an application for family provision.[11] This power is particularly useful when it is sought to preserve the dwellinghouse in which the applicant is residing pending the resolution of the application. To persuade a court to make an order preserving property in family provision litigation the applicant must satisfy the court that he has at least an arguable case that provision should be made for him *and take the form of an order under section 2(1)(c),(d) in respect of that particular item of property* and that it is proper in the court's discretion to make the order bearing in mind the claims of beneficiaries and of creditors and the personal representatives' duties in administering the estate.[12]

The court in exercising its jurisdiction to preserve property is likely to impose conditions upon an applicant applying for such an order, for example, that the outgoings of a particular property are discharged and may require an undertaking in damages, possibly supported by a charge over other assets of the applicant.

This jurisdiction even extends to ordering the purchase of a dwellinghouse for the occupation of an applicant pending the final hearing.[13]However, such an order will not be allowed to fetter the court's powers on a final hearing.[14]

In *Andrew v Andrew*[15] Judge Fricker QC sitting in Doncaster County Court held that the County Court had no jurisdiction to grant either an 'ouster' or a 'non-molestation' injunction ancillary to an application under the 1975 Act. It is submitted that both the High Court and the County Court[16] have jurisdiction to grant such injunctive relief on the basis of the jurisdiction to preserve property during litigation[17] and to prevent one party from applying improper

11. S 2(1)(c), (d); *Sobesto v Farren* [1981] Conv 224, CA.
12. *Sobesto v Farren* [1981] Conv 224, CA; compare the remarks of Russell LJ in *Re Ferrar's Application* [1966] P 126, at 143C–E, [1966] 3 All ER 78, at 83H–84A on the regard to be had to the personal representative's duties.
13. *Barry v Barry* [1992] Fam140, [1992] 3 All ER 405.
14. *Barry v Barry* at [1992] Fam150A–B, [1992] 3 All ER 413h-j. A similar result was acheived in *Re Besterman* [1984] Ch 458, [1984] 2 All ER 656 by the use of a large lump sum paid by way of an interim order.
15. [1990] 2 FLR 376.
16. Since *Andrew v Andrew* the powers of the County Court to grant injunctions have been assimilated to those of the High Court by the amended s 38 of the County Courts Act 1984 introduced by the Courts and Legal Services Act 1990; see *Burris v Azadani* [1995] 1 WLR 1372.
17. See p 375, *ante*; it is submitted that Judge Fricker QC's remarks at [1990] 2 FLR 377E–F fail to consider this jurisdiction.

pressure to another party during litigation.[18] However, the number of cases in which it is appropriate to grant such injunctive relief and where no other jurisdiction[19] is available must be very small indeed.

Periodical Payments

Orders for periodical payments were, with the exception of small estates,[20] the only orders which could be made until 1966. Until the early 1970s such orders were still the most common order made and it is arguable that most orders in the form of capital provision should be calculated as capitalised periodical payments.

The court has wide powers as to the form of the order for periodical payments. Provisions originally introduced after the decision in *Re Gale*[1] revealed limitations on the original power to order periodical payments enable the court to make an order which may provide for:

> (a) payments of such amount as may be specified in the order;
> (b) payments equal to the whole of the income of the net estate or of such portion thereof as may be so specified;
> (c) payments equal to the whole of the income of such part of the net estate as the court may direct to be set aside or appropriated for the making out of the income thereof payments [under section 2] ... or may provide for the amount of the payments or any of them to be determined in any other way the court thinks fit.[2]

Where an order is made for the payment of a fixed sum, this is paid out of income, with a power to resort to capital if the income is insufficient and any excess income goes to the beneficiaries.[3] The power to make types of orders not specifically set out by the Act

18. *Montgomery v Montgomery* [1965] P 46, at 51C-E, [1964] 2 All ER 22, at 24E-F; *Pinckney v Pinckney* [1966] 1 All ER 121, at 121H-I; *South Carolina Insurance Co v Assurantie NV* [1987] AC 24, at 40D, [1986] 3 All ER 487, at 496 a-b. It is submitted that these authorities justify the jurisdiction of the court to grant injunctions on the application of a party to the litigation and not solely on the application of the Attorney General.
19. Eg the Protection from Harassment Act 1997; the jurisdiction relating to children.
20. S 1(4) of the 1938 Act.
1. [1966] Ch 236, [1966] 1 All ER 945.
2. S 2(2).
3. *Wainwright v Wainwright* (1947) 91 Sol Jo 148; *Re Bonham* (1962) 112 L Jo 634; *Re Gale* [1966] Ch 236, at 242B–C, [1966] 1 All ER 945, at 947 H-I per Harman LJ). There is no objection in the court making an order for periodical payments in excess of the anticipated income of the estate – *Re F* (1965) 109 Sol Jo 212.

might permit orders to be made which vary with the applicant's income or with a price index.[4]

If an order under section 2(2)(a) is made the court *may* direct that part of the estate be set aside or appropriated for the making of the order.[5] If this power is exercised no larger part of the net estate shall be set aside or appropriated than is sufficient, *at the date of the order*, to produce by the income thereof the amount required for the making of these payments.[6] Because this power of appropriation and restriction on the amount of appropriation only applies to orders under section 2(2)(a) which cover fixed amounts, although possibly subject to conditions,[7] it should be relatively easy to calculate the amount of the net estate which should be set aside.[8] This power of appropriation is in addition to any expressly included in the deceased's will, available to the personal representatives under the general law[9] or given to the personal representatives under the court's power to give consequential directions.[10]

Periodical Payments Usually Annual

The amount of the periodical payments can be calculated by reference to any period of time, but the modern tendency is to specify annual sums.

The Commencement of Periodical Payments

The court has a discretion as to the date from which periodical payments should run.[11] The three dates which are usually chosen

4. Compare *Re Doring* [1955] 1 WLR 1217, [1955] 3 All ER 389 and see ROSS MARTYN, 46. In Australia the jurisdiction to relate payments to price indices is well established, see DICKEY, 144–145; *White v Baron* (1980) 144 CLR 431, at 452 (NSW law); *Goodman v Windeyer* (1980) 144 CLR 490, at 503, 503-4, 511-512; *Re Saxon* (1975) 12 SASR 110 at 118, 120.
5. S 2(3).
6. S 2(3).
7. Eg *Re Doring* [1955] 1 WLR 1217, [1955] 3 All ER 389.
8. Some guidance on this operation of this provision is contained in the remarks of Harman LJ in *Re Gale* [1966] Ch 236, at 242B–C, [1966] 1 All ER 945, at 947G-I and of Buckley J in *Re Blanch* [1967] 1 WLR 987, at 992C–F, [1967] 3 All ER 468, at 471H–472B.
9. See Williams, Mortimer and Sunnucks, *Executors, Administrators and Probate* (17th edn) pp 685–687, 1020–1023.
10. S 2(4).
11. *Askew v Askew* [1961] 1 WLR 725, at 726, [1961] 2 All ER 60, at 61G (per Marshall J); *Lusternik v Lusternik* [1972] Fam 125, at 134E–F, [1972] 1 All ER 592, at 598b-d per Cairns LJ.

are the date of death,[12] the date of the application[13] and the date of the order.[14] Factors which influence the court's discretion may include any delay in making the application,[15] any delaying tactics employed by the defendants in the proceedings,[16] the existence of an interim order or benefits under the will for the applicant,[17] but not generally any social security benefits paid to the applicant,[18] and the general administrative convenience of making the payments run from the date of the order.

It was at one time thought that the cases of *Askew v Askew*[19] and *Re Goodwin*[20] laid down a general rule that this discretion should normally be exercised to order that payments should begin from the date of death, which is what would happen in the absence of an order to the contrary, as the order is deemed to have effect from the deceased's death[1] and which would have happened had the reasonable provision been made by the deceased's will or the rules of intestacy.[2] It should be no objection to backdating the order that it results in the making of a small capital award, because the operation of the deceased's will if it had made reasonable provision would have caused the same situation.[3]

However in *Lusternik v Lusternik*,[4] in which *Re Goodwin*[5] was not cited, Cairns LJ denied that the discretion should normally be

12. Eg *Askew v Askew* [1961] 1 WLR 725, [1961] 2 All ER 60; *Re Bellman* [1963] P 239, [1963] 1 All ER 513; *Re Ducksbury* [1966] 1 WLR 1226, [1966] 2 All ER 374; *Re Blanch* [1967] 1 WLR 987, [1967] 2 All ER 468; *Re Goodwin* [1969] 1 Ch 283, [1968] 3 All ER 12; *Stead v Stead* [1985] FLR 16.
13. Eg *Re Eyre* [1968] 1 WLR 530, [1968] 1 All ER 968.
14. Eg *Re Lecoche* (1967) 111 Sol Jo 136.
15. *Lusternik v Lusternik* [1972] Fam 125, at 134F, [1972] 1 All ER 592, at 598c.
16. *Lusternik v Lusternik* [1972] Fam 125, at 134G, [1972] 1 All ER 592, at 598d.
17. *Lusternik v Lusternik* [1972] Fam 125, at 134G–H, [1972] 1 All ER 592, at 598 d-e; *Re Cohen*, John Mills QC (23 February 1979, unreported).
18. *Askew v Askew* [1961] 1 WLR 725, at 726–727, [1961] 2 All ER 60 at 61I–62A; *Re Goodwin* [1969] 1 Ch 283, at 292A–D, [1968] 3 All ER 12, at 16I–17D. In *Re Debenham* [1986] 1 FLR 404, at 410F–G Ewbank J did not backdate periodical payments to the date of death because the applicant had been in receipt of social security benefits and receipt of backdated payments would cause problems.
19. [1961] 1 WLR 725, [1961] 2 All ER 60.
20. [1969] 1 Ch 283, at 292A–E, [1968] 3 All ER 12, at 16I–17D.
1. S 19(2).
2. *Re Goodwin* [1969] 1 Ch 283, at 292B–C, [1968] 3 All ER 12, at 17A–B (per Megarry J).
3. *Re Goodwin* [1969] 1 Ch 283, at 292A–D, [1968] 3 All ER 12, at 16I–17D (per Megarry J). In *Re Debenham* [1986] 1 FLR 404, at 410G–H a lump sum of £3,000 was awarded expressly, inter alia, to obviate the need for backdating the order for periodical payments and a similar order was made in *Re Farrow* [1987] 1 FLR 205, at 216A.
4. [1972] Fam 125, at 134E–135A, [1972] 1 All ER 592, at 598b-e.
5. [1969] 1 Ch 283, [1968] 3 All ER 12.

exercised so that the payments commence from the date of death and deprecated backdating where the order was made several years after the death of the deceased because the applicant could obtain a large capital sum. In *Lusternik v Lusternik* the Court of Appeal affirmed Hollings J in dating the order for periodical payments 15 months before the date of the order, where the deceased died five and a half years before the original hearing, stating that the fact that there had been some provision in the will for the applicant was a reason for not making the order run from an earlier date.[6] While *Re Goodwin* was not cited, the ratio of this case was put in argument.[7]It is respectfully submitted that the approach of Megarry J in *Re Goodwin* is to be preferred to the approach of Cairns LJ.

An interim order will generally provide for payment as from the date of the order or from the first day of the month in which the order is made.

Suspensory Orders

It is sometimes the case that at the date of the hearing while the applicant's claim to some sort of an order is clear it is very uncertain what form the provision should take. Examples of uncertainty include where the needs and income of the applicant and the beneficiaries are uncertain,[8] and where the value or income of the estate is uncertain and an immediate realisation improvident.[9] The solution to this problem would appear to be to declare generally that the applicant is entitled to provision or make a nominal order in favour of the applicant and subsequently fix or increase the amount of the provision. This suggestion conflicts with one of the aims of

6. [1972] Fam 125, at 134G–H, [1972] 1 All ER 592, at 598d-e.
7. See the argument of Counsel for the appellant at [1972] Fam 128A-F. In *Re Cohen*, John Mills QC (23 February 1979, unreported), CA *Re Goodwin*, *Lusternik v Lusternik* and the first edition, p 75 were cited. The payments were ordered to begin shortly before the date of the hearing, but in this case there had been an interim order and some *ex gratia* payments. In *Wells v Wells* [1997] 1 WLR 652, at 680H–686D, [1997] 1 All ER 673, at 699j-705d Thorpe LJ in an important judgment stated that, *ceteris parabus*, awards under the 1975 Act should be calculated in a similar way to damages for loss of income in personal injury actions and orders under the Matrimonial Causes Act 1973 using *Duxbury* principles. As such jurisdictions calculate awards from the date of injury, death or separation, *Wells v Wells* is a powerful endorsement of a prima facie rule that payments should run from the date of death.
8. Eg *Re Bateman* (1941) 85 Sol Jo 454; *Re Franks* [1948] Ch 62, [1947] 2 All ER 638.
9. Eg *Roberts v Roberts* [1965] 1 WLR 560, [1964] 3 All ER 503.

the legislation, made manifest in the time limit,[10] the restrictions on the amount of capital which can be appropriated to provide for periodical payments[11] and the limitation on the power of variation of periodical payments orders to the property appropriated for such orders[12] that the beneficiaries shall not be vexed with multiple applications and should be able to ascertain the burden of any order reasonably quickly. Because of this general policy and the fact that the three enumerated orders all limit themselves to specific amounts of capital in the estate, it would seem that the power to make an order for periodical payments not in any of the three forms set out in section 2(2) is subject to an implied limitation that in general terms only sufficient capital can be appropriated to make the payments due at the time of the order or anticipated in the near future. The existence of index linked gilt edged securities and other investments which purport to keep up with the general level of inflation should enable orders for periodical payments to be made which vary with a price index.[13] Because of this general policy and the duty to appropriate only sufficient capital to service the order for periodical payments at the date of the order,[14] it has been held that there is no power to make a suspensory order directing a part of the estate to be retained and charged with such payment for the maintenance of the applicant as the court may subsequently order having regard to the changed circumstances of the applicant.[15]

Three techniques have been developed or are available to circumvent this prohibition on suspensory orders.

Firstly, it has been held that an application can be stood over for a considerable period of time until a specified date or event in the meantime.[16]

Secondly, the court can make a substantial order, but reduce its effect by the imposition of conditions which might take effect

10. S 4; but see *Stock v Brown* [1994] 1 FLR 840 where leave to bring proceedings five and a half years out of time was granted because of changed investment conditions.
11. S 2(3).
12. S 6(6); WORKING PAPER, para 3.60; LAW COM, paras 172–176.
13. See fn 4, p 378, *ante*.
14. Originally s 3(2) of the 1938 Act.
15. *Re Franks* [1948] Ch 62, at 65–66, [1947] 2 All ER 638 at 640C–E (per Wynn-Parry J); *Welsh v Mulcock* [1924] NZLR 673, at 687 (per Salmond J). For the position in Australasia see DE GROOT & NICKEL, para 702; DICKEY, 159.
16. *Re Bateman* (1941) 85 Sol Jo 454; *Re Franks* [1948] Ch 62, at 66–67, [1947] 2 All ER 638, at 640E–H; *Re Rodwell* [1970] Ch 726, at 730A–B, [1969] 3 All ER 1363, at 1364D and see (1948) 92 Sol Jo 163. It seems doubtful whether the power to adjourn can be exercised for any length of time in the face of opposition from the beneficiaries.

upon subsequent events. In *Re Doring*[17] Wynn-Parry J made a periodical payments order, but such payments were only to be made if the applicant's income from another source fell below a certain limit.

Thirdly, use might be had of the court's power to settle property upon trusts varying with the applicant's situation.[18]

While these powers exist they should only be exercised having regard to the interests of beneficiaries and the statutory policy of fixing the parties' rights at an early stage. It is therefore suggested that orders having a suspensive effect should only be made where there is real uncertainty as to the value of the estate or where such an order will probably be of more immediate benefit to the beneficiary than an immediate order in favour of the applicant.[19]

Termination of Periodical Payment Orders

An order for periodical payments terminates, if it is not ended earlier, upon the death of the applicant.[20] The court has a discretion in fixing the duration of the order.[1] The only limit on duration of an order for periodical payments under the 1975 Act is that an order in favour of a former spouse or a judicially separated spouse must cease upon the remarriage[2] of the applicant.[3] Where a periodical payments order terminates the applicant can apply for a variation of the order to extend the period for which the payments are to be made or to have a lump sum paid out to him;[4] but his power does not cover the termination of payments to a former or judicially separated spouse who remarries.[5]

It is submitted that normally payments should be made to terminate upon the remarriage of a spouse or the attainment of

17. [1955] 1 WLR 1217, at 1218–1219, [1955] 3 All ER 389, at 390–391. See also *Re Blanch* [1967] 1 WLR 987, at 992H–993A, [1967] 2 All ER 468, at 472C–D and *Re Mason* (1975) 5 Fam Law 124. In *Re Debenham*[1986] 1 FLR 404, at 410H–411A an order for periodical payments was to be reduced by the amount of the applicant's old age pension when she became entitled to it in two years' time.
18. S 2(1)(d).
19. Eg*Re Bateman* (1941) 85 Sol Jo 454; *Re Franks* [1948] Ch 62, [1947] 2 All ER 638 .
20. See p 109, *ante*. The doubts as to this point expressed in ROSS MARTYN, p 47 are misplaced.
1. S 2(1)(a).
2. 'Remarriage' includes the entry into a void or voidable marriage, s 25(5).
3. S 19(2).
4. S 6(3).
5. Ibid.

adulthood by an infant child. In these cases while there is no *requirement* that the payments should cease, in the normal case the deceased's obligations will have ceased upon the terminating event. If exceptional reasons for continuing the payments exist, the power of variation is available[6] and it is submitted that the onus of applying for a variation should be upon the applicant alleging some unusual reason for prolonging the payments – this approach results in a lower number of applications for variation than the alternative of putting the onus upon the beneficiaries. In the case of spouses, former spouses, cohabitees and individuals coming within section 1(1)(e) thought should be given to imposing a condition terminating payments upon cohabitation with another.[7]

Orders have in the past been made to terminate, in the case of an order in favour of a widow on the deceased's children coming of age,[8] on the applicant's capital or income reaching a specified amount[9] and in the case of an unmarried daughter applicant upon her mother's death with liberty then to apply for further provision.[10] Such conditions would not necessarily be imposed today.

Lump Sums

The power to award a lump sum was originally limited to small estates,[11] but since 1966 it has been available generally.

When an order is made the court can order that the lump sum be paid in a number of instalments[12] – this power appears to be exercisable only at the time the order was made.[13] An order that the lump sum be paid by instalments once made can subsequently be varied, upon the application of the applicant, the personal representatives and any trustees by whom lump sums are payable.[14] The power of variation enables the means by which the lump sum is payable to be altered, but not the total amount of the lump sum.

6. S 6.
7. *Re Haig*, Browne-Wilkinson J [1979] LS Gaz R 476; but see the remarks of Lord Denning MR in *Wachtel v Wachtel* [1973] Fam 72, at 97A–B, [1973] 1 All ER 829, at 841d-e and see generally pp 196–198, *ante*.
8. *Re Lidington* [1940] Ch 927, [1940] 3 All ER 600.
9. *Re Pointer* [1941] Ch 60, [1940] 4 All ER 372; *Re Hills* [1941] WN 123.
10. *Re Borthwick* [1949] Ch 395, [1949] 1 All ER 472.
11. S 1(4) of the 1938 Act, amended by s 7(c) of the Intestates' Estates Act 1952.
12. S 7(1).
13. S 7(1) refers to 'An order under s 2(1) ... may provide for the payment of that sum by instalments of such amount as may be specified *in the order*'.
14. S 7(2).

A lump sum order has much the same effect as a legacy,[15] and it is submitted that it will bear interest as a legacy, in the absence of any contrary provision in the order. However, as the rules on the dates from which legacies bear interest may be difficult to apply to lump sum orders,[16] as there is uncertainty as to the proper rate of interest payable on legacies[17] and as the consequences of a lump sum order in relation to interest are not always appreciated by the court, it is suggested that the court should give specific directions under its general power to give consequential directions[18] as to the payment of interest, if any, on lump sum orders.

The Appropriateness of Lump Sums

Lump sums are particularly appropriate in certain types of cases. Where a spouse is claiming a 'just share' in the deceased's estate a lump sum is a correct way of recognising his property rights in the estate.[19] A lump sum is also appropriate where it is thought reasonable that the applicant should have provision for a specific purpose, such as to return to her home abroad,[20] to purchase a house[1] or where it is thought that maintenance includes a small element of capital to meet future contingencies.[2] It is also a suitable order where the deceased's estate is insufficient to satisfy all the claims upon it and those claims have to be balanced against each

15. By virtue of s 19(1).
16. See Theobold, *Wills* (15th edn), pp 269–275.
17. Williams, Mortimer & Sunnucks, *Executors, Administrators and Probate* (17th edn), p 1036.
18. S 2(4). In *Re Shanahan* [1973] Fam 1, [1971] 3 All ER 873 Lord Simon of Glaisdale made an order that the lump sum should bear interest at 6% from the date of the application. In *Re Lewis* (13 March 1980, unreported), CA the Court of Appeal made an order as to interest to run from the Court of Appeal judgment. In *Riggs v Lloyds Bank plc* (27 November 1992, unreported), CA the trial judge specifically directed that the lump sums should only bear interest from specific dates and see to like effect *Graham v Murphy* [1997] 1 FLR 860.
19. See *Trippas v Trippas* [1973] Fam 134, at 140D, [1973] 2 All ER 1, at 4d-e per Lord Denning MR.
20. Eg *Re Preston* [1969] 1 WLR 317, at 321D-E, [1969] 2 All ER 961, at 963I
1. Eg *Re Besterman* (1981) 3 FLR 255 Judge Mervyn Davies QC.
2. Eg *Re Sanderson* (1963) Times, 2 November (here periodical payments were ordered); *Re Lewis* (13 March 1980, unreported), CA; *Re Besterman* (1981) 3 FLR 255, Judge Mervyn Davies QC; [1984] Ch 458, at 479C–D; [1984] 2 All ER 656, at 671b-c per Oliver LJ; *Re Bunning* [1984] Ch 480, at 499F, [1984] 3 All ER 1, at 12d per Vinelott J; *Stead v Stead* [1985] FLR 16, at 26H-27B (£2,500); *Jessop v Jessop* [1992] 1 FLR 591, at 599D-F per Nourse LJ. In *Re Debenham* [1986] 1 FLR 404, at 410G-H Ewbank J awarded a lump sum of £3,000 for, inter alia, 'immediate capital needs'.

other.[3] Arguably, lump sums are appropriate where the applicant's claim is limited to compensation for a detriment incurred at the request of the deceased.[4]

There are a limited number of situations where orders for periodical payments are particularly appropriate. One example is where the only asset in the estate is a dwellinghouse occupied by a beneficiary, in which situation an order for periodical payments charged on the dwellinghouse will not disturb the beneficiary's occupation.[5] Another example is where the order for periodical payments is likely to endure for a short, but uncertain, period, such as an order in favour of a male applicant aged 80 years or to a child until he ceases full-time education.[6]

The Decline of Periodical Payments

Orders for periodical payments are rarely made by modern courts. In many cases this is because the estate is insufficiently large to satisfy all claims made upon it. In other cases where the estate is sufficiently large to satisfy all the claims made upon it, almost invariably applicants and beneficiaries request the court to make orders for lump sums rather than for periodical payments. An order for periodical payments operates by way of a trust and trusts of income producing assets frequently involve relatively high administrative costs.[7] Except for relatively large sums of money, trusts are generally

3. Eg *CA v CC* (1978) Times, 17 November , *sub nomen Re C* 125 Sol Jo 35, *sub nomen In the Estate of McC* 9 Fam Law 26.
4. Eg *Re Leach* [1986] Ch 226, [1986] 2 All ER 754.
5. See *Re Nesbitt* (1963) Times, 23 November; *Re H (A Minor)* (1975) 6 Fam Law 172.
6. *Re Debenham* [1986] 1 FLR 404, at 410F-G; see also *Stead v Stead* [1985] FLR 16, at 26G (widow aged 82 years). In practice with an elderly applicant both parties will prefer to proceed by a lump sum with which the applicant can purchase an annuity. Likewise a modern court approaching the situation in the cases in fn 5 is likely to proceed upon the basis that the beneficiary should be able to raise a lump sum by mortgaging the dwellinghouse. In *Re Collins* [1990] Fam 56, at 62F, [1990] 2 All ER 47, at 52e Hollings J gave as *a* reason for awarding a lump sum instead of periodical payments 'the difficulty of assessing an appropriate amount' of any periodical payments. In *Re Farrow* [1987] 1 FLR 205, at 215C–D periodical payments were awarded because the applicant had previously dissipated a lump sum and because the Respondents would find periodical payments easier to fund.
7. It will frequently be necessary to employ professional trustees. Trustees have to submit their own income tax returns which frequently require professionally drawn accounts. See also the remarks of Judge Weeks QC at first instance in *Riggs v Lloyds Bank plc* (27 November 1992, unreported), CA.

less tax efficient than individuals holding investments absolutely.[8] Periodical payments will adversely affect an individual's entitlement to Income Support than will a lump sum.[9] A lump sum order gives the applicant full control over his award and the ability to make his own investment decisions[10] and conversely gives the beneficiaries immediate enjoyment of the balance of the estate rather than having it tied up in a trust for many years. The decline in orders for periodical payments made under the 1975 Act mirrors the virtual disappearance of annuities in modern wills[11] and the general decline in paternalistic control as to how others (particularly women) should deal with their own assets.

In *Re Collins* Hollings J said in 1989 that in the particular case it was not appropriate to award periodical payments having regard to:

(1) the difficulty of assessing an appropriate amount,
(2) the comparatively small amount of the net estate in any event, and
(3) the desirability of acheiving finality.[12]

Similar considerations to those which have made 'clean break' orders on divorce popular have made periodical payment orders less popular under the 1975 Act.[13] Lump sum orders give both parties certainty and finality and remove any necessity for persons who may be hostile to each other from having to deal with each other in the

8. Eg trustees can not invest in PEPs,TESSAs, etc. Trustees have only half the annual exemption for Capital Gains Tax of individuals [Sch 1, para 2(2) of the Taxation of Chargeable Gains Act 1992].
9. All periodical payments are 'Income Resources' within the Income Support (General) Regulations 1987, SI 1987/1967 as amended. Capital is only taken into account in excess of £3,000 and an applicant may be able to expend a lump sum on assets which improve his standard of living without becoming 'Capital Resouces'. Such considerations were taken into account in *Re Canderton* (1970) 114 Sol Jo 208; *Millward v Shenton* [1972] 1 WLR 711, at 715H, [1972] 2 All ER 1025, at 1028F–G; *Re Debenham* [1986] 1 FLR 404, at 410F-G. In *Wallace v Thorburn* (9 October 1987, unreported), CA the applicant who was on Income Support did not seek periodical payments, but sought a lump sum with which to buy a house because of these considerations.
10. Compare a spouse's power to redeem his life-interest under the rules of intestacy – s 47A of the Administration of Estates Act 1925.
11. In their study of a sample of actual wills Finch, Mason, Masson, Wallis and Hayes, *Wills, Inheritance and Families*, p 107 found that a succession of interests was rare for gifts of personal property, but not uncommon with gifts of houses.
12. [1990] Fam 56, at 62F, [1990] 2 All ER 47, at 52E.
13. In *Re Crawford* (1982) 4 FLR 273, at 279E–F Eastham J referred to the advantages of a 'clean break' for beneficiaries. In that case a lump sum was calculated according to the cost of an annuity. See also *Graham v Murphy* [1997] 1 FLR 860, at 869E–F.

future. In this context the power to vary periodical payments[14] is a less than attractive feature. Both parties may consider that issues such as the remarriage and future cohabitation of an applicant are better dealt with by a lump sum calculated to take account of the chances of remarriage and future cohabitation[15] rather than by an order for periodical payments terminating on remarriage of future cohabitation.

The perceived disadvantages of orders for periodical payments do not necessarily apply to orders being made settling dwellinghouses upon applicants for life or lesser periods. Trusts thereby created, so long as there is no investment income, do not give rise to administrative costs , to tax problems[16] nor to Income Support problems.[17] Both applicant and respondent gain some protection against inflation, since in the long term residential housing has more than kept pace with inflation. Such trusts are relatively common in modern wills and modern orders under the 1975 Act.[18]

The Calculation of Lump Sums

The principles governing awards of capital for spouses have been discussed previously.[19]

Where lump sums are awarded for applicants, whose claim is limited to maintenance and the estate is sufficient to satisfy all the claims upon it, it is suggested that the lump sum should be calculated essentially on the basis of capitalised periodical payments.[20] Methods of capitalisation vary – in *Malone v Harrison*[1] Hollings J made use of the principles of multiplier and multiplicand as used in personal injuries litigation. In *Re Besterman*[2] where at first instance Judge

14. S 6; see pp 401–408, *post*.
15. See pp 196–198, *ante*.
16. There is no charge to Capital Gains Tax on a disposal of a private residence occupied by a beneficiary under a trust – s 225 of the Taxation of Chargeable Gains Act 1992.
17. The capital value of a life-interest is disregarded when assessing a person's resources – Sch 10, para 13 of the Income Support (General) Regulations 1987, SI 1987/1967, as amended.
18. Eg *Moody v Stevenson* [1992] Ch 486, [1992] 2 All ER 524; *Re Krubert* [1997] Ch 97; significantly the court awarded a life-interest in the house and an absolute interest in the remainder of the estate.
19. See Chapter 6, Part 1 generally.
20. Compare *Brett v Brett* [1969] 1 WLR 487, at 493B–C, [1969] 1 All ER 1007, at 1012E–F.
1. [1979] 1 WLR 1353; see pp 287–289, *ante*.
2. (1981) 3 FLR 255, at 267D–G.

Mervyn Davies QC regarded reasonable provision for the applicant spouse under the 1975 Act as being limited to maintenance, albeit on a very generous scale, a capital sum was awarded partly on the basis that the applicant could purchase an annuity to satisfy her reasonable needs for maintenance. On appeal [3] the Court of Appeal held that Judge Mervyn Davies QC adopted a too restrictive approach generally and used the capital which would generate sufficient income for the anticipated maintenance of the applicant as *an* approach to the calculation of maintenance.[4] In *Re Bunning* Vinelott J had regard to both the capital which would produce a particular income after deduction of Income Tax with a 'reasonably balanced portfolio of investments' and the cost of an annuity both at the date of the hearing and at a future date when the applicant might reasonably expect to retire.[5] There is no reason why in an appropriate case a lump sum should not be calculated by reference to the amount of additional pension contributions to give a particular level of income in the future.[6] In the personal injury case of *Wells v Wells* Thorpe LJ stated that there was no:

> ... distinction in principle between providing for the future needs of plaintiffs in personal injury litigation and in applicants in proceedings under the Matrimonial Causes Act 1973 or [the 1975 Act].[7]

He specifically deprecated any distinctions based upon differing treatment of Income Tax, inflation or investment strategies between the various jurisdictions.[8] While *Malone v Harrison* was approved,[9] Thorpe LJ stated that the *Duxbury*[10] approach was the most preferable approach. He said:

3. [1984] Ch 458, [1984] 2 All ER 656. For discussion and criticsm of the decision of the Court of Appeal in *Re Besterman* , see pp 172–179, *ante*.
4. [1984] Ch 479B–C, [1984] 2 All ER 656, at 671a-b. This must be wrong since it means that no regard is paid to the life-expectancy of the applicant.
5. [1984] Ch 480, at 499D–H, [1984] 3 All ER 1, at 12c-g. In *Re Crawford* (1982) 4 FLR 273, at 283 F-G a lump sum was calculated as the cost of an annuity for the applicant.
6. Compare the discussion of future inflation linked annuities in *Re Bunning* at [1984] Ch 499G-H, [1984] 3 All ER 12e-g.
7. [1997] 1 WLR 652, at 686D–E, [1997] 1 All ER 673, at 705c-d.The House of Lords has granted leave to appeal, [1997] 1 WLR 870.
8. [1997] 1 WLR 686D, [1997] 1 All ER 705d.
9. [1997] 1 WLR 681E, [1997] 1 All ER 700e.
10. Named after *Duxbury v Duxbury* [1992] Fam 62n, [1990] 2 All ER 77. On *Duxbury* calculations, see JACKSON AND DAVIES, 197-199, the current edition of *At A Glance* and *Wells v Wells* at [1997] 1 WLR 681E-683B, 684G-685G, [1997] 1 All ER 700e-702b, 703h-704h. *Duxbury* calculations take into account inflation and taxation and assume that on the anticipated date of death all capital will have been expended. They do not take into account the possibility of remarriage or future cohabitation.

> Once the utility of the computer program method [ie *Duxbury* calculation] became apparant it was adopted for large claims in the Chancery Division once the dependency was admitted or established. A recent example is *Nott v Ward.*[11]

The judgment is an emphatic endorsement as to the utility of using concepts from personal injury and ancillary relief litigation under the 1975 Act and that the *Duxbury* was the preferred approach.

Maintenance may also include once and for all expenses, such as a journey to another country[12] or repairs to a dwellinghouse.[13] In particular, maintenance for an applicant is often usefully provided by the purchase of a dwellinghouse or furniture for such a house[14] and it is suggested that a lump sum may be calculated on the basis of the sum needed to purchase or help to purchase a dwellinghouse – although as a matter of principle the lump sum should only be sufficient to enable the applicant to acquire a life-interest in the dwellinghouse.[15]

A Transfer of Property Order

The power to order that property comprised in the net estate may be transferred to the applicant[16] was an innovation introduced by the 1975 Act. Like the similar power in the Matrimonial Causes Act 1973[17] it is a power which is likely to be regularly used, particularly in order to give the applicant the deceased's dwellinghouse or where a lump sum order might lead to an improvident realisation of the estate.[18]

In cases where the principal asset in the estate is a dwellinghouse and the court is not minded to award the applicant the whole estate, but is anxious to preserve the occupation by the applicant of the dwellinghouse, the court has transferred the house to the applicant

11. [1997] 1 WLR 682F, [1997] 1 All ER 701f-g. *Nott v Ward* was a decision of Judge Bromley QC (13 December 1994, unreported). No report of the decision is available.
12. Eg *Re Preston* [1969] 1 WLR 317, at 321D–E, [1969] 2 All ER 961, at 963I.
13. Eg *Barnsley v Ward* (18 January 1980, unreported), CA.
14. Eg *Davis v Davis* [1967] P185, at 193E–194A, [1967] 1 All ER 123, at 127B–H; expense of replacing a motor car, see *Re Crawford* (1982) 4 FLR 273, at 283F.
15. *Malone v Harrison* [1979] 1 WLR 1353, at 1366C; *Re Haig*, Browne-Wilkinson J [1979] LS Gaz R 476. In *Graham v Murphy* [1997] 1 FLR 860 a lump sum was awarded to the applicant which together with his ability to borrow by way of a mortgage would enable him to acquire a suitable dwelling.
16. S 2(1)(c).
17. S 24(1)(a).
18. ROSS MARTYN, p 49.

subject to a legacy in favour of a beneficiary.[19] In cases where the claims of the applicant do not justify awarding him an absolute interest in all of a dwellinghouse, the court appears to have power to order the transfer of the house subject to the payment of the outstanding proportion of the value of the house.[20]

'Property' includes a chose in action.[1] It also includes a periodic tenancy from a private or public landlord,[2] but the power to order a transfer of a periodic tenancy will not be exercised where the landlord is unwilling to consent to any assignment when his consent is necessary and where it would interfere with a local authority's statutory duties.[3] However, the machinery for a statutory succession to both private[4] and public[5] residential tenancies means that the power to order a transfer of a periodic tenancy will be rarely exercised.[6]

An order for a transfer of property order cannot be varied.

19. *Rajabally v Rajabally* [1987] 2 FLR 390; *Moody v Haselgrove* (16 November 1987, unreported), CA. It is submitted that before such orders are made the court should consider whether the applicant will be able to discharge the sums charged on the property and that postponement of a problem is rarely synonymous with its solution. Also thought should be given as to the means of enforcing such charges. Rather than leaving the legatee to bring an administration action or an action for sale, it might be appropriate for the court to exercise its powers under s 2(4) (as to which see pp 408–412, *post*) so as to provide a timetable for the raising of the charge with an order for sale in default.
20. *Re Dr Kozdrach* [1981] Conv 224. Note also the power to acquire property under s 2(1)(e) (see pp 393–394, *post*). This power may usefully be employed where the applicant is only entitled to a life-interest and the applicant wishes to acquire the interest in reversion.
1. S 25(1). In *Graham v Murphy* [1997] 1 FLR 860 a transfer of property order was made in respect of a three-quarters interest in a car.
2. *Thompson v Thompson* [1976] Fam 25, [1975] 2 All ER 208; *Hale v Hale* [1975] 1 WLR 931, [1975] 2 All ER 1090; *Hutchings v Hutchings* (1975) 237 Estates Gazette 571; *Regan v Regan* [1977] 1 WLR 84, [1977] 1 All ER 428; *Rodewald v Rodewald* [1977] Fam 192, [1977] 2 All ER 609.
3. *Brent v Brent* [1975] Fam 1, at 8A, [1974] 2 All ER 1211, at 1215b (per Dunn J), *Thompson v Thompson* [1976] Fam 25, [1975] 2 All ER 208; *Hale v Hale* [1975] 1 WLR 931, [1975] 2 All ER 1090; *Hutchings v Hutchings* (1975) 237 Estates Gazette 571; *Regan v Regan* [1977] 1 WLR 84, [1977] 1 All ER 428; *Rodewald v Rodewald* [1977] Fam 192, [1977] 2 All ER 609; *K v K (minors: property transfer)* [1992] 2 FLR 220; *J v J (a minor: property transfer)* [1993] 2 FLR 56.
4. S 2(1)(b), Part 1, Sch 1 of the Rent Act 1977, as amended by s 76 of the Housing Act 1980 (protected and statutory tenants); s 3 of the Rent (Agriculture) Act 1976 as amended by s 76(3) of the Housing Act 1980 (protected agricultural occupier); s 17 of the Housing Act 1988 (assured tenants).
5. Ss 87–90 of the Housing Act 1985 (secure tenants).
6. Possible examples might be business tenancies which included residential accommodation or an assured tenancy where the deceased did not leave a surviving spouse and hence there can not be a statutory succession.

Settlement of Property

A further innovation introduced by the 1975 Act is the power to order property comprised in the net estate to be settled for the *benefit* of the applicant.[7] This power only extends to property 'comprised in' the net estate, but other property can be acquired for settlement by settling cash or the proceeds of sale by the use of the power in section 2(1)(e) for the acquisition of property for settlement.[8] The power to order a settlement of property is a particularly useful one. While obviously being of use where the applicant is an infant or unable to manage his own affairs, it is of great value in dealing with future contingencies, particularly when the applicant's claim is limited to maintenance.[9] A determinable life-interest is a particularly appropriate form of order where an applicant requires maintenance for his life or until remarriage.[10]

The power to settle property is a wide one and settlements created under this power could vary between a simple charge,[11] an unassignable licence for life,[12] protective trusts[13] or an extremely complicated discretionary trust.[14]

It is suggested that 'benefit' should be construed in the same way as 'benefit' has been construed in statutory provisions dealing with variation of ante-nuptial and post-nuptial settlements, rather than in the same way as 'benefit' has been construed in legislation dealing with the law of trusts.[15] This construction allows third parties to have interests in the settlement, but only if it is to the overall financial benefit of the applicant. Non-pecuniary benefits for the applicant can be considered,[16] but the settlement overall must be

7. S 2(1)(c); the section is derived from s 24(1)(b) of the Matrimonial Causes Act 1973.
8. On acquisition of property see pp 393–394, *post.*
9. See generally pp 385–386, *ante.*
10. See pp 385–386, *ante.*
11. *Hector v Hector* [1973] 1 WLR 1122, at 1125A–C, [1973] 3 All ER 1070, at 1073B–D; see also *Re H (a minor)* (1976) 6 Fam Law 172.
12. *Re Campbell*[1983] NI 10.
13. *Re Abram*[1996] 2 FLR 379.
14. In *Stead v Stead* [1985] FLR 16, at 20E trustees were given a discretionary power to pay the income of the proceeds of sale of a property to the applicant; a similar power was conferred at first instance in *Eeles v Evans* (6 July 1989, unreported), CA.
15. Power of maintenance, s 31(1)(i) of the Trustee Act 1925; power of advancement, s 32(1) of the Trustee Act 1925; varying trusts, s l(1) of the Variation of Trusts Act 1958.
16. *Scollick v Scollick* [1927] P 205; *Garforth-Bles v Garforth-Bles* [1951] P 218, [1951] 1 All ER 308; *Best v Best* [1956] P 76, [1955] 2 All ER 839; *Purnell v Purnell* [1961] P 141, [1961] 1 All ER 369.

for the financial benefit of the applicant.[17] While theoretically the court has the power under section 2(1)(d) to make a settlement giving interests to persons other than the applicant and beneficiaries in the estate, it is doubtful whether the court will ever in its discretion consider it proper to give a person who is not either a beneficiary or an applicant any, or any substantial, interest in a settlement.[18]

An order settling property cannot be varied under the 1975 Act but the settlement itself may contain certain powers of appointment and variation which may permit the trusts to be altered in the future and recourse may be had to the general powers of the court to vary trusts.[19]

Considerable care should be taken in the drafting of the substantive and administrative provisions of the settlement. Particular regard should be paid to the trustees' powers of investment and a settlement should contain a power to purchase land for occupation by the applicant or his family.[20] As has already been submitted,[1] where land is settled upon an applicant for life in respect of deaths before 1 January 1997 the machinery of the Settled Land Act 1925 rather than that of a trust for sale should be adopted and in respect of deaths after the life-tenant's consent should be required for the exercise of the trustees' powers of management.[2]

Reported authorities do not reveal any consensus as to what terms, if any, should be imposed upon an applicant where property is ordered to be settled on him for life or some lesser period. In *Moody v Stevenson* the Court of Appeal considered that it had insufficient evidence to come to a decision on this issue.[3] It is submitted that a court should only impose a repairing obligation if

17. *Whitton v Whitton* [1901] P 348; *Scollick v Scollick* [1927] P 205; *Newson v Newson* (1934) 50 TLR 399; *Tagart v Tagart* (1934) 50 TLR 399; *Garforth-Bles v Garforth-Bles* [1951] P 218, [1951] 1 All ER 308; *Best v Best* [1956] P 76, [1955] 2 All ER 839; *Purnell v Purnell* [1961] P 141, [1961] 1 All ER 369.
18. No need has been found to include third parties in orders under s 24(1)(b) of the Matrimonial Causes Act 1973 and indeed the courts have deprecated the practice of giving reversionary interests to children of the marriage – *Chamberlain v Chamberlain* [1973] 1 WLR 1557, [1974] 1 All ER 33; *A v A (a minor: financial provision)* [1994] 1 FLR 657.
19. Eg s 57 of the Trustee Act 1925; Variation of Trusts Act 1958.
20. To circumvent the decision in *Re Power* [1947] Ch 572, [1947] 2 All ER 282. Such a power was added in *In the Estate of McC* (1979) 9 Fam Law 26; this aspect of the case is not dealt with in the reports in (1978) Times, 17 November and (1979) 123 Sol Jo 35.
1. See pp 143–144, *ante; Re Mason* (1975) 5 Fam Law 124; *Re Lewis* (13 March 1980, unreported), CA.
2. Under s 10 of the Trusts of Land and Appointment of Trustees Act 1996 the consent of a tenant for life can be required for the exercise of trustees' powers of management.
3. [1992] Ch 486, at 504D–E, [1992] 2 All ER 524, at 538f-g.

the applicant is likely to have the resources with which to comply with the obligations.[4] Repairing obligations in settlements, like repairing obligations in leases, have a superficial attraction which often hides capricious effects.[5] Accordingly it is submitted that a court should not normally go beyond requiring the applicant to insure and use the property in a tenant-like manner and in particular should not impose an obligation to *put* the property in any better state of repair than it is at the date of death or at the date of the hearing.[6]

Acquisition of Property

The powers to transfer specific items of property and to settle property only extend to property which is already part of the estate. Section 2(1)(e) permits the court to make an order that property be acquired out of property comprised in the net estate and that such acquired property be transferred or settled for the benefit of the applicant. This power is particularly useful where the net estate does not contain a dwellinghouse or where it is desired that the applicant should move to a smaller house.[7]

A good example of the use of the power to acquire property is *Re Haig*.[8] In this case Browne-Wilkinson J held that reasonable

4. See the remarks of Waite J in *Moody v Stevenson* [1992] Ch 486, at 504D-E, [1992] 2 All ER 524, at 538f-g. In *Re Mason* (1975) 5 Fam Law 124, at 125 Plowman V-C said that the deceased's duty 'was not only to provide a home for [the applicant] but to provide the wherewithall to live in the house... It seemed quite useless to provide a roof over the plaintiff's head if she could not afford to live in it'.
5. On the interpretation of such clauses and their effect, see Gover, *Capital and Income* (3rd edn). See the remarks of Cumming-Bruce LJ in *Pascoe v Turner* [1979] 1 WLR 431, at 439B, [1979] 2 All ER 945, at 951g on rights of entry for repair.
6. See *Re Mason* (1975) 5 Fam Law 124 where the court replaced a licence to reside subject to keeping the property in 'reasonable repair' with a tenancy for life under the Settled Land Act 1925 to enable the applicant to sell the property which she could not afford to keep in repair. In *Moody v Stevenson* at [1992] Ch 503H, [1992] 2 All ER 538c Waite J referred to the applicant who had been awarded a life tenancy compensating the remainderman for any 'deterioration' in the property during his occupancy. In *Re Haig* [1979] LS Gaz R 476 Browne-Wilkinson J, using non-technical language imposed an obligation on the applicant to keep the property in repair. In *Stead v Stead* [1985] FLR 16 the will obliged the widow to insure and 'keep' the former matrimonial home in good repair. Arnold P at first instance restricted the widow's obligations to internal repair and placed an *obligation* upon the residuary estate to effect external repairs and to insure.
7. As happened on the facts in *Re Lewis* (13 March 1980, unreported), CA; *Re Besterman* (1981) 3 FLR 255.
8. [1979] LS Gaz R 476.

provision for the applicant would be an award of accommodation for life. Unfortunately the deceased's house, in which the applicant lived, was very close to the house of the beneficiary of the deceased's estate and relations between him and the applicant were extremely bad. Browne-Wilkinson J therefore made an order requiring the estate to purchase a house of comparable value to the present house which was to be settled on the applicant for life or until she became financially dependent on another.

Variation of Nuptial Settlements

As a further innovation the 1975 Act gave the court power to make an order varying an ante-nuptial or post-nuptial settlement.[9] The jurisdiction to vary an ante-nuptial or post-nuptial settlement was for many years the Divorce Court's only power to make orders affecting the parties' capital and as such was a particularly important jurisdiction. The Divorce Court extended the definition of ante-nuptial and post-nuptial settlement beyond the classic marriage settlement to virtually any property relationship in which the parties to the marriage both had an interest and which was in any sense referable to the marriage. In particular, it was extended to include a matrimonial home which was held by the parties as joint tenants or tenants in common.[10] After the coming into effect of the Matrimonial Proceedings and Property Act 1970 this extended definition became largely redundant, and orders affecting the matrimonial home are usually now orders for the transfer of property. While the extended definition of ante-nuptial and post-nuptial settlement is virtually unused by the modern divorce courts and has been called 'almost a legal fiction',[11] the definition has not been judicially overruled.

The Law Commission in its Working Paper considered whether the court should have a power to vary ante-nuptial and post-nuptial settlements in family provision proceedings.[12] It tentatively decided against giving the court such a power, but invited comments. The Law Commission argued that, in accordance with its general policy of not affecting settlements made on the deceased by the third parties,[13] it would be wrong to give the court such a power to do so

9. S 2(1)(f).
10. Eg *Brown v Brown* [1959] P 86, [1959] 2 All ER 266.
11. *Guerrera v Guerrara* [1974] 1 WLR 1542, at 1547C–D (per Ormrod LJ). The report in [1974] 3 All ER 460 does not contain this remark.
12. WORKING PAPER, para 3.30.
13. See LAW COM, paras 129–133 and p 294, *ante*.

in the case of nuptial settlements. The jurisdiction to vary on divorce existed because a divorce was not usually contemplated by the settlor, whereas the death of the deceased was a matter almost always within the contemplation of the settlor and covered by express provisions of the settlement.

Where the deceased was himself the settlor, the jurisdiction to set aside dispositions intended to defeat an application for family provision would be an adequate protection.

After receiving conflicting comments[14] the Law Commission in its Report decided in favour of giving courts in family provision proceedings the power to vary ante-nuptial and post-nuptial settlements, but only to benefit parties to the marriage, children of the marriage and children of the family in relation to that marriage.[15] This conclusion was reached because of the desire to give the courts analogous powers upon divorce and upon death.[16]

The power under section 2(1)(f) to vary a settlement applies to 'any ante-nuptial or post-nuptial settlement'. The settlement can be made by the will of a third party.[17] The phrase 'ante-nuptial or post-nuptial settlement' has become a term of art and no attempt in this book will be made to discuss all the nuances of the definition.[18] The definition has two limbs, firstly it must be a nuptial settlement in relation to the particular marriage of the deceased and secondly it must be a 'settlement'. To be a nuptial settlement, the settlement need not be a classic marriage settlement or anything like such a settlement, nor need it be expressed as a marriage settlement because the court looks to the substance not the form.[19] The settlement must be in some way referable to the parties' capacity as a married couple; Hill J in *Hargreaves v Hargreaves*[20] defined it as:

> ... a settlement made in contemplation of, or because of, marriage and with reference to the interests of married people, or their children.

The settlement need not refer to the husband or wife by name[1] nor it appears must the marriage be the principal motive for making the

14. LAW COM, para 121.
15. LAW COM, paras 121–123.
16. LAW COM, para 122.
17. S 2(1)(f).
18. For a full discussion, see *Halsbury's Laws of England* (4th edn), Vol 13, paras 1136–1144; JACKSON AND DAVIES, Ch 8; RAYDEN, Ch 29, Section XII.
19. *Joss v Joss* [1943] P 18, at 20–21, [1943] 1 All ER 102, at 103H–104D (per Henn Collins J).
20. [1926] P 42, at 45.
1. In *Lort-Williams v Lort-Williams* [1951] P 395, [1951] 2 All ER 241 the insurance policy was to benefit 'the widow or children'. In *Brooks v Brooks* [1995] Fam 70, [1994] 4 All ER 1065 the provision in the pension was to benefit a 'spouse or any other person ... financially dependent upon' the deceased.

settlement.[2] Co-owned residential property[3] or business property[4] has sufficient reference to the marriage to be a nuptial settlement. A settlement can be within the definition if it is made before the marriage in anticipation of the particular marriage, but not if it is made in anticipation of marriage generally.[5]

A settlement which is made in anticipation of a dissolution of the marriage is not a 'post-nuptial settlement'.[6] The settlement must be an ante-nuptial or a post-nuptial settlement in relation to a marriage *of the deceased*.[7]

'Settlement' is not limited to the case where successive interests exist, but includes any arrangement whereby the two spouses have concurrent or successive interests or where there is a continuing legal obligation owed by one of the married partners to the other, such as the obligation to make periodical payments.[8] A provision in an occupational pension scheme whereby an employee can appoint, either as a matter of trust law or contract, pension benefits to, inter alia, a spouse is a 'settlement'.[9] It does not however cover a gift, which has been completed and where all the interest is vested in one party.[10] It can include a jointly owned matrimonial home[11] or a separation deed.[12]

The power of variation can only be exercised to benefit certain applicants. Firstly, it can be exercised to benefit a surviving party[13] to the marriage to which the settlement is referable. It cannot be used to benefit a 'former spouse', but probably a court has power

2. See in particular the remarks of Neill LJ in *Brooks v Brooks* [1995] Fam 70, at 94A–95B, [1994] 4 All ER 1065, at 1087f-g. In *Brooks v Brooks* an ocupational pension scheme which contained, among many very standard terms, a power to appoint a part of the fund as a pension to a spouse or other financial dependent was held to have a sufficient element of nuptiality. There is considerable force in the dissent of Hoffmann LJ on this point ([1995] Fam 88G–89A, [1994] 4 All ER 1081g-j).
3. Eg *Brown v Brown* [1959] P 86, [1959] 2 All ER 266.
4. Eg *Parrington v Parrington* [1951] 2 All ER 916; *Dixit v Dixit* (23 June 1988, unreported), CA.
5. *Hargreaves v Hargreaves* [1926] P 42. It is doubtful whether an ante-nuptial settlement can exist when one of the parties is already married – *Burnett v Burnett* [1936] P 1, at 15–16.
6. *Young v Young* [1962] P 27, [1961] 3 All ER 695.
7. S 2(1)(f).
8. The definition of 'settlement' in s 670 of the Income and Corporation Taxes Act 1988 is a helpful analogy.
9. *Brooks v Brooks* [1996] AC 375, [1995] 3 All ER 257 affirming [1995] Fam 70, [1994] 4 All ER 1065.
10. *Prescott v Fellowes* [1958] P 260, [1958] 3 All ER 55.
11. *Brown v Brown* [1959] P 86, [1959] 2 All ER 266.
12. *Jump v Jump* (1883) 8 PD 159.
13. For discussion of who is a spouse, see pp 64–69, *ante*. It is assumed that this definition applies to the words 'surviving party'.

under section 14[14] to treat a former spouse where the decree of divorce absolute was made within twelve months of the death of the deceased as a spouse. Secondly, the power can be exercised to benefit 'a child of [the] marriage'[15] to which the settlement is referable. This probably includes a legitimated child.[16] Thirdly, the power can be exercised to benefit any 'child of the family'[17] in relation to the marriage to which the settlement is referable.

The word 'benefit' is likely to be construed in the same manner as 'benefit' in the comparable provisions of the Matrimonial Causes Act 1973.[18] In deciding whether a variation is to the benefit of a particular person regard is had to both pecuniary and non-pecuniary benefits, but the variation overall must provide for a net pecuniary benefit for the applicant.[19]

Cases in which the court has used its powers to vary a nuptial settlement in an application under the 1975 Act are exceedingly rare. An example is *Dixit v Dixit*[20] where an investment property was held upon trusts which gave the surviving wife a life interest in half the proceeds of sale with the remaining interests being vested in the deceased's children. On an application by the wife Waite J, using the power in section 2(1)(f), enlarged the wife's interest in the trusts of the investment property to a life-interest in all of the property and 'compensated' certain of the children by awarding them under the power to give consequential directions[1] with interests in remainder in another property which passed under the will of the deceased.

Pension Schemes and the Power to Vary Nuptial Settlements

In *Brooks v Brooks* the House of Lords[2] unanimously affirmed a

14. For discussion of s 14, see pp 70–71, *ante*.
15. For the definition of 'child', see s 25(1) and pp 72–74, *ante*.
16. S 8 of the Legitimacy Act 1976, but is such a child '*a child of the marriage*'?
17. For the definition of 'child of the family', see s 1(1)(d) and pp 74–77, *ante*.
18. S 24(1)(b), (c).
19. *Whitton v Whitton* [1901] P 348; *Scollick v Scollick* [1927] P 205; *Newson v Newson* (1934) 50 TLR 399; *Tagart v Tagart* (1934) 50 TLR 399; *Garforth-Bles v Garforth-Bles* [1951] P 218, [1951] 1 All ER 308; *Best v Best* [1956] P 76, [1955] 2 All ER 839; *Purnell v Purnell* [1961] P 141, [1961] 1 All ER 369.
20. (23 June 1988, unreported), CA. The decision of Waite J was substantially altered on appeal as the Court of Appeal took a different view of the practicality of the order, but there was no criticism of Waite J's willingness to use s 2(1)(f).
1. S 2(4); see generally pp 408–412, *post*.
2. [1996] AC 375, [1995] 3 All ER 1257.
3. [1995] Fam 70, [1994] 4 All ER 1065.

majority decision of the Court of Appeal[3] which itself affirmed a decision of Ewbank J[4] that a divorce court could vary an occupational pension scheme as a post-nuptial settlement. The court had jurisdiction because the pension scheme enabled an employee to allot part of his entitlement to a pension to his 'spouse' or other dependant. The court has no jurisdiction if the pension scheme was set up before marriage[5] and the position is unclear if the deceased joins an existing scheme after his marriage.[6] This decision is applicable to section 2(1)(f) of the 1975 Act and is capable of applying to the common situation of where a lump sum is payable upon death at the discretion of pension fund trustees among a class of persons including a surviving spouse and where the trustees have regard to, but are not bound by, a nomination by the deceased. Whereas tax considerations prevent the court from exercising its powers *on divorce* in virtually all multi-member occupational pension schemes,[7] tax considerations will not normally prevent a court from making an order affecting a lump sum payable upon death or even discretionary pensions payable to dependants.[8] Further, the reasoning of *Brooks v Brooks* would appear to be applicable to lump sums payable upon death under retirement annuity contracts and personal pensions.[9]

The majority of the Court of Appeal rejected an argument that as a matter of policy the court should never exercise its powers to vary nuptial settlements in relation to occupational pension schemes[10] and this decision was implicitly affirmed by the House of Lords. It is entirely unclear how much regard the court will have to the exercise of discretionary powers by entirely disinterested trustees.

The decision in *Brooks v Brooks* makes the law capricious in effect, since a court can have jurisdiction to vary a pension scheme where the deceased joined after marriage, but not where the deceased joined the scheme before marriage and where benefits may be paid to 'a spouse and other dependants', but not where benefits may be paid to 'all dependants'. None of the nine judgments in *Brooks v Brooks* mentions the 1975 Act, yet it may well be that the decision's greatest practical impact will be in relation to family

4. [1993] Fam 322, [1993] 4 All ER 917.
5. Per Neill LJ at [1995] Fam 94H, [1994] 4 All ER 1087e-f.
6. Salter [1994] Fam Law 520, at 523.
7. [1996] AC 396B-D, [1995] 3 All ER 267f-h per Lord Nicholls of Birkenhead.
8. Rearden, *Allied Dunbar Pension Guide* (3rd edn), para 4.14.
9. See in particular the passage in the speech of Lord Nicholls of Birkenhead at [1996] AC 393A–C, [1995] 3 All ER 264g-j; Plumstead and Salter [1995] 25 Fam Law 490, at 492.
10. [1995] Fam 86D–87A, [1994] 4 All ER 1079j-1080a.

provision proceedings. The decision of the House of Lords completely outflanks the carefully thought out statutory scheme defining the 'net estate'.[11] It is to be hoped that, at least in relation to family provision, the decision in *Brooks v Brooks* will be reversed by Parliament.

Conclusion on the Power to Vary Nuptial Settlements

Section 2(1)(f) has the effect of greatly enlarging the 'net estate' of the deceased out of which the court can order provision and it surreptitiously undermines the carefully thought out concept of the 'net estate' in the Act.[12] The 1975 Act's definition of the deceased's 'net estate' is a carefully thought out and coherent concept, extending beyond property disposable by will to other dispositions of property made by the deceased which may be technically inter vivos but have a testamentary aspect, but not covering dispositions by third parties, and the extension to property not disposable by will carefully protects the interests of third parties who have dealt with the property.[13] Section 2(1)(f) allows this elaborate and balanced scheme to be circumvented. In the normal situation a severable share of a joint tenancy of property can only be made part of the net estate in circumstances more limited than it merely being reasonable to make an order for provision[14] and provisions protect third parties dealing with the survivor prior to the court's order.[15] If however the same joint tenancy were held by a deceased and his spouse, the court under section 2(1)(f) could make an order without being tied by any of the restrictions of section 10 and such an order, unless the contrary were stated,[16] could relate back to the date of death[17] possibly to the prejudice of third parties. Moreover, an order under section 2(1)(f) need not be limited to the deceased's severable share but could attach to the whole of the jointly owned property. For example, if a husband and wife purchased property each contributing a half of the purchase price and the husband dies, the court could, theoretically at least, on the application of a disabled

11. See pp 323–325, *ante*.
12. 'Net estate' is defined by s 25(1) and see Ch 7 generally.
13. See Ch 7 generally, particularly at pp 293–294.
14. S 9(1); pp 299–301, *ante*.
15. S 9(3).
16. Eg by virtue of s 2(4).
17. S 19(1).

adult child of the marriage make an order under section 2(1)(f) conveying the whole of the jointly held property to the adult child. In effect section 2(1)(f) can create an inter vivos duty to support where none previously existed or should exist.

The Law Commission decided against making property subject to a special power of appointment of which the deceased was the donee part of the net estate, because the power had usually been given by a third party.[18] However, where the settlement containing the special power has the slightest element of nuptiality this limitation is discarded. Likewise, the Law Commission decided against making most benefits under occupational and other pension schemes part of the net estate because it was reluctant to interfere with a jurisdiction which was usually exercised responsibly.[19] However, if *Brooks v Brooks*[20] remains the law rights in a large number of pension schemes will be capable of being subject to orders under the 1975 Act.[1]

It is submitted that the inclusion of section 2(1)(f) in the 1975 Act was a considerable error of judgment. The power enables the proper limitations on the scope of the net estate to be circumvented at will and enables the court to disregard completely the interests of third parties who created the settlement, have interests in the settlement or who have dealt with interests in the settlement after the death of the deceased but before the court's orders. Where it is proper to vary any nuptial settlement, the court otherwise has the necessary jurisdiction under the definition of the net estate and in particular the power to set aside a settlement made by the deceased under section 10.[2] If any other settlement has to be varied, it should be done under the Variation of Trusts Act 1958, where the variation has to be for the 'benefit' of *all* the beneficiaries and not one applicant.

There is only one reported case of section 2(1)(f) being actually used by a court[3] and it is generally thought that the power is very rarely employed, although *Brooks v Brooks* may mean that it is employed far more frequently. It is hoped that section 2(1)(f) will generally be used as a purely procedural device and that the full width of its substantive jurisdiction will not be employed, so that it will not be used to circumvent any of the restrictions contained in

18. LAW COM, paras 129–133; pp 293–294, *ante*.
19. LAW COM, para 213; and see pp 320–321, *ante*.
20. [1996] AC 375, [1995] 3 All ER 257.
1. See pp 397–398, *ante*.
2. On s 10 see pp 303–312, *ante*.
3. *Dixit v Dixit* (23 June 1988, unreported), CA.
4. See generally Ch 7.

the provisions of the 1975 Act extending the net estate[4] and that full regard will be paid to the interests of third parties, such as the settlor, other beneficiaries in the settlement and persons who have dealt with the property between the date of death and the court's order.

Subsequent Variation of a Nuptial Settlement

Once an order has been made under section 2(1)(f) it cannot be varied under the Act. However, the variation itself may permit some subsequent variation of the settlement by introducing conditional and determinable interests and powers of appointment. Furthermore the general jurisdiction to vary any trust is available.[5]

Variation of Orders

The 1938 Act gave the court a power to vary an order for periodical payments if 'any material fact was not disclosed to the court' or if any 'substantial change of circumstances' has taken place.[6] The variation could increase, decrease or totally extinguish the amount of periodical payments, but it could only affect the income out of which the provision was already being made.[7] The application could be made to benefit any applicant in receipt of periodical payments or any person who was a dependant at the time of death and at the time of the application to vary although not an original party and could also be made by any beneficiary of the estate or a trustee.[8] The same principles applied to variations when former spouses were permitted to apply by the Matrimonial Causes (Property and Maintenance) Act 1958.[9]

After some discussion,[10] the essentials of this scheme – only periodical payments orders may be varied, the variation cannot affect property other than that set aside to meet the periodical payments order and permitting other applicants to have the benefit of the variation – were retained in the 1975 Act. The Law Commission considered whether a power of variation was desirable as a matter

5. See generally Snell, *Principles of Equity* (29th edn), pp 239-44.
6. S 4(1).
7. S 4(1).
8. S 4(1)(b),(2).
9. S 4.
10. WORKING PAPER, paras 3.54–3.65; LAW COM, paras 156–184.

of principle. A will which makes reasonable provision for an applicant will not contain a power of variation and the possibility of an order being varied can cause great uncertainty to the beneficiaries of the estate and can delay the final administration of the estate.

Against these arguments it must be noted that an order for periodical payments is very like an order made in matrimonial proceedings which can be varied and that variation of an order leads to a more just result by adjusting maintenance upwards and downwards to meet more exactly the needs of the applicant.[11] It must be noted that a power of variation more often than not is to the advantage of the beneficiaries rather than of the applicant, because the existence of the power of variation may lead to the amount of orders being less than they would otherwise be[12] and because the power of variation more usually is, and often can only be, used to decrease rather than increase the amount of provision, so compensating the beneficiaries for any loss of certainty and loss of the power to deal with the property. The Law Commission decided, rightly it is submitted, that the power to vary should be retained, but having due regard to the need for certainty and due regard for the interests of the beneficiaries that it should only apply to orders for periodical payments and should only extend to property out of which the periodical payments are made.

Only an Order for Periodical Payments May be Varied

The court can only vary an order for periodical payments made within section 2(1)(a);[13] all the other forms of orders are in their individual ways final. An order varied once, under the power of variation in section 6(1), can be varied subsequently.[14] An order for periodical payments made under the earlier legislation of the 1938 Act and section 26 of the Matrimonial Causes Act 1965, except an interim order, whether made before or after 1 April 1976, may be varied under section 6.[15]

11. WORKING PAPER, paras 3.57–8.65; LAW COM, paras 160–161.
12. See p 387, *ante*.A modern example is *Stead v Stead* [1985] FLR 16.
13. S 6(1); *Fricker v Fricker* (1982) 3 FLR 288. The remarks of Browne-Wilkinson J in *Re Haig* [1979] LS Gaz R 476 that an order settling acquired property under s 2(1)(e) can be varied are *per incuriam*, as were the remarks of Simon P in *Roberts v Roberts* [1965] 1 WLR 560, at 567B, [1964] 3 All ER 503, at 508G–H that an order for periodical payments can be increased generally on a variation.
14. S 6(4).
15. S 26(3), (4); *Fricker v Fricker* (1982) 3 FLR 228.

The Order Which Can Be Made on a Variation

The court when an order for periodical payments is varied can 'vary' the order,[16] which includes the power to increase or decrease the amount of the periodical payments and alter any conditions attached to the periodical payments.

Probably the power to vary an order for periodical payments includes the power to remit previously accrued arrears.[17] The court has express jurisdiction to 'discharge the original order or to suspend any provision of it temporarily or to revive the operation of any provision to suspend',[18] which implies that an order once discharged as opposed to being suspended cannot be revived. Additionally the 1975 Act gave the court two new and wide powers on a variation of an order for periodical payments, so that a court could make a lump sum order out of the property out of which the periodical payments are payable[19] or a transfer of property order in respect of the property out of which the periodical payments are payable.[20] It is expressly provided that on a variation the court has no jurisdiction to make an order for the settlement of property, for the acquisition of property, for the variation of an ante-nuptial or post-nuptial settlement, for making a severable share of a former joint tenancy part of the net estate or for setting aside a disposition intended to defeat an application for financial provision or a contract to make a will.[1] It is hard to see why a court cannot order property to be settled on a variation since such a settlement is much like a lump sum order in its effect.

Upon a variation the power to order a lump sum or a transfer of property enables the amount of provision to be significantly increased. Previously an increase in the amount of provision on a variation of an order for periodical payments would only be obtained if the income of the property out of which the payments were payable had increased or if an order in favour of one applicant had determined. The Law Commission suggested that such a power could be used to enable a deposit to be paid on a new house or to pay the costs of a widow applicant moving house.[2]

The ability to pay capital might be a way of dealing with the vexed question of whether a spouse's periodical payments should

16. S 6(1).
17. Compare *Warden v Warden* [1982] Fam 10, [1981] 3 All ER 193 on s 35 of the Matrimonial Causes Act 1973.
18. S 6(1).
19. S 6(2)(b).
20. S 6(2)(c).
1. S 6(9).
2. LAW COM, para 169(a).

cease on remarriage,[3] and the problems of a widow or widower cohabiting without remarriage,[4] by terminating the periodical payments on remarriage but awarding a capital sum to the applicant as a 'dowry' to help him in his new partnership and to remove any incentive to remain dependent upon the order for periodical payments.[5] The power to vary an order for periodical payments by awarding capital can radically affect the incidence of an award. For instance if a particular beneficiary considered that his fair burden of any award would be to subject his absolute interest to an order for periodical payments, the relative burden of the award would be dramatically altered if the power of variation were used to award a capital sum thereby extinguishing the interest in remainder.

An order for the variation of a periodical payments order can only affect 'relevant property', which is defined as:

> ... property the income of which is at the date of the order applicable wholly or in part for the making of periodical payments to any person who has applied for an order under this Act.[6]

Where an order for periodical payments has ceased to be payable, the 'relevant property' is the property out of which the periodical payments were previously payable.[7] This limitation to property which has been set aside for the purpose of making payments under the periodical payments order represents the old law and was the subject of considerable discussion by the Law Commission.[8] The Law Commission, supported by all persons it consulted, eventually decided that any wider power would result in considerable uncertainty and weaken the important principle of finality.[9]

Where an order for periodical payments terminates on the occurrence of a particular event or the expiration of a specified time an application for a variation of the order can be made at any time up to six months after the termination of the event,[10] unless the

3. See pp 196–197, *ante*.
4. See pp 197–198, *ante*.
5. For discussion of a 'dowry' in this context, see Royal Commission on Civil Liability and Compensation for Personal Injury (Cmnd 7054–1978) Vol 1, paras 409–417. A 'dowry' of one year's payments was paid upon the remarriage of a widow entitled to Widow's Benefit under the Industrial Injuries Scheme – s 67(2)(b) of the Social Security Act 1975. This benefit was abolished by the Social Security Act 1986.
6. S 6(6)(a); property which is set aside for the *occupation* by an applicant is not 'relevant property' – *Fricker v Fricker* (1982) 3 FLR 228.
7. S 6(6)(b).
8. WORKING PAPER, paras 3.60–3.63; LAW COM, paras 172–176.
9. LAW COM, paras 174–176.
10. S 6(3),(10).

terminating event is the remarriage of a former spouse.[11] There is no power to extend the period of six months. On such a variation the court has the same jurisdiction to make an order as if the application for a variation was made during the continuance of the order and any order for periodical payments can be backdated to the date of the termination of the original order.[12] It is to be hoped that this power should be used sparingly, with due regard to the principles of *res judicata*[13] and not as an appeal from the original order.

Who Can Apply for a Variation

An applicant for a variation under section 6 can be made by the applicant in receipt of the varied order for periodical payments[14] or any other successful applicant.[15] A person qualified as an applicant at the date of the deceased's death may also apply and benefit from a variation, even though the applicant did not apply within the time limit or did apply and was refused permission.[16] This represents the law under the 1938 Act.[17] There is no reported case under any legislation of an application to vary being made by one applicant at the expense of another[18] and it is thought that such applications are extremely rare. In such a case it will have to be shown that circumstances have changed so that it is just to reduce the original applicant's provision *and* just to give a new applicant provision *and* just to do so having regard to the interests of the beneficiaries. The Law Commission considered that this power to benefit new applicants would be useful where a person's circumstances deteriorated after the date of the original order.[19] Such a power is particularly useful where provision is made for a parent of an infant child on the basis that the parent will care for the infant child and the parent applicant dies prematurely, so enabling the infant child to 'take over' his parent's order.[20] It is suggested that there should

11. S 6(3),(10).
12. S 6(3).
13. See p 407, *post*.
14. S 6(5)(a).
15. S 6(5)(b), (2).
16. S 6(5)(b), (2).
17. See ALBERY, 38–39; first edition, 35–36.
18. In *Re Dorgan* [1948] Ch 366, [1948] 1 All ER 723 the court rejected an attempt by a new applicant to rely upon the power of variation as there had been no original order.
19. LAW COM, paras 178–179. Compare *Re Urquhart* (1956) 5 DLR (2d) 235 (BC Sup Ct) and see pp 128–131, *ante*.
20. ALBERY, 40 and pp 204–206, *ante*.

be a heavy burden upon any applicant who did not apply originally or whose application was refused to prove a sufficient case to be considered as a person who should benefit from a variation – in particular the power of variation should not be used as a means of circumventing the time limit of six months or of appealing against a refusal of provision at an earlier hearing and full regard should be paid to the principle of *res judicata*.[1]

Applications to vary a periodical payments order can also be made by persons who would benefit by a reduction or termination of the order. An application can be made by a personal representative of the deceased[2] or by the trustees of any 'relevant property'.[3] The 1938 Act merely referred to 'trustees'[4] and this definition might have caused difficulties where the personal representatives had not sufficiently administered the estate to become trustees. An application to vary can be made by a 'beneficiary' of the deceased's estate.[5] 'Beneficiary' presumably includes any person on whom a beneficiary's interest has devolved since the original order and is given an enhanced definition by section 25(1) so as to include statutory nominees and recipients of donatio mortis causa, but curiously it does not include a survivor of a joint tenancy where the deceased's severable share has been made part of the net estate by an order under section 9, or a person interested in a disposition or a contract to make a will set aside under section 10 and section 11.[6] The inability of such persons to apply for a variation is an important lacuna in the 1975 Act.

Consequential Directions on a Variation

On a variation under section 6 the court has full power to give consequential directions.[7]

1. See p 407, *post*.
2. S 6(5)(a).
3. S 6(5)(b); 'relevant property' is defined by s 6(6).
4. S 4(2).
5. S 6(5)(d).
6. Compare pp 149–150, *ante*.
7. S 6(8); for discussion of the power to give consequential directions under s 2(4), see pp 408–412, *post*.

How the Power to Vary is Exercised

Section 6(7), adopting the wording used in section 26 of the Matrimonial Causes Act 1965[8] and by the power to vary inter vivos orders for periodical payments in the Matrimonial Causes Act 1973,[9] provided:

> In exercising the powers conferred by this section the court shall have regard to all the circumstances of the case, including any change of circumstances of the case, including any change in any of the matters to which the court was required to have regard when making the order to which the application relates.

While a very literal reading of section 6(7) would appear to give the court a virtually unfettered discretion, it is suggested that the court's discretion is not without limits. While literally the court's powers to vary are not limited to a change in circumstances, it is suggested that the principles of *res judicata*[10] and the general policy against frequent applications to vary which increase costs and decrease certainty and against allowing applications for variations to be used as a form of appeal against the original order[11] require that the power to vary should only be exercised if there is a change of circumstances since the original order.[12] However, when a court is exercising its powers of variation, its jurisdiction is not limited to a mere mechanical alteration of the order in line with the circumstances which has changed.[13]

Changes of circumstances will generally be a change in the means or needs of an applicant or beneficiary or of the value of the estate, but are not limited to such changes. An order can be varied to make an allowance for inflation.[14] While a change of

8. S 27(4).
9. S 31(7).
10. See generally *R v Nottingham Justices, ex p Davies* [1981] QB 38, [1980] 2 All ER 775.
11. Compare *Hunter v Chief Constable of West Midlands* [1982] AC 529, [1981] 3 All ER 727; *Powys v Powys* [1971] P 340, at 355B–D, [1971] 3 All ER 116, at 127j-128c; but see *Arnold v National Westminster Bank plc* [1991] 2 AC 93, [1991] 3 All ER 41.
12. See pp 405–406, *ante*, doubting the wider implications of *Lewis v Lewis* [1977] 1 WLR 409, [1977] 3 All ER 992.
13. *Lewis v Lewis* [1977] 1 WLR 409, [1977] 3 All ER 992.
14. On inflation generally, see pp 146–147, *ante*; eg the remarks of French J in *Fricker v Fricker* (1982) 3 FLR 228.

circumstances enables a court to exercise its powers of variation, it is not bound to do so. In *Re Gale*[15] Russell LJ differing from Harman LJ[16] held that an accumulation of capital by an applicant was in itself a change of circumstances, but one which need not lead to a variation – 'though ordinarily a dependant will not, so to speak, be penalised for thrift'.[17]

There is only one reported case of a family provision order being varied and generally such variations are rare. Like many parts of the 1975 Act, the complexity of the drafting is in inverse proportion to the practical importance of the provision.

Consequential Directions

The 1938 Act gave the court power to subject any order to 'such conditions or restrictions, if any, as the court may impose'[18] and also the power to give consequential directions for the purpose of giving effect to an order made under the Act.[19]

Comparable provisions are now to be found in section 2(4) which permits an order under section 2 to contain:

> ... such consequential and supplemental provisions as the court thinks necessary or expedient for the purpose of giving effect to the order.

Without prejudice to the generality of the powers under section 2(4), such directions can:

> ... vary the disposition of the deceased's estate effected by the will or the law relating to intestacy ..., in such manner as the court thinks fair and reasonable having regard to the provisions of the order and all the circumstances of the case.[20]

Such conditions can be imposed either to define more exactly the amount of provision ordered or for administrative purposes. Conditions relating to the former purpose can also be imposed under the court's wide jurisdiction as to the variety of periodical payment

15. [1966] Ch 236, [1966] 1 All ER 945.
16. [1966] Ch 244B, [1966] 1 All ER 949A.
17. [1966] Ch 248F, [1966] 1 All ER 951I; Diplock LJ appeared to agree with Russell LJ at [1966] Ch 246G, [1966] 1 All ER 950G-H.
18. S 1(1); s 26(2) of the 1965 Act.
19. S 3(2); s 28(2) of the 1965 Act.
20. S 2(4)(b).

orders it can make[1] and as to settling property.[2] Conditions have been imposed making any order conditional on the applicant not receiving income from another source[3] or requiring the applicant to inform the personal representatives of any capital or income which she receives so that an application to vary can be made[4] and provision has been ordered upon an undertaking by the applicant to maintain a child of the deceased.[5] In one case where the will bequeathed an interest to an applicant subject to a condition against alienation, the judge considered it proper to subject the additional provision ordered to the same condition.[6] The court can order a partition of property settled upon the applicant for life, remainder to others, thereby converting the interest of the remaindermen from an interest in remainder in the whole to an absolute interest in part[7] and can replace an interest in the proceeds of sale of land with a charge on the land securing the same value.[8]

Conditions of an essentially administrative nature have included conditions preventing applicants having the powers of a tenant for life under the Settled Land Act 1925,[9] conditions directing the setting up of a Settled Land Act 1925 settlement,[10] as to the payment of interest[11] and the maintenance of settled property.[12]

Where an applicant has occupied property in the estate, but without any right to do so under the original disposition of the deceased's estate or under the order, it may be appropriate to give a direction under section 2(4) as to whether the applicant should be liable for mesne profits.

Without prejudice to the generality of the powers under section 2(4) the court can:

1. S 2(2).
2. S 2(1)(d), (e).
3. *Re Doring* [1955] 1 WLR 1217, [1955] 3 All ER 389; *Re Mason* (1975) 5 Fam Law 124.
4. *Re Pointer* [1941] Ch 60, [1940] 4 All ER 372; *Re Hills* [1941] WN 123.
5. *Re Lidington* [1940] Ch 927, [1940] 3 All ER 600; *Re Westby* [1946] WN 141.
6. *Re Sylvester* [1941] Ch 87, at 90, [1940] 4 All ER 269, at 272D–E; now the matter would be dealt under s 2(1)(d).
7. *Rajabally v Rajabally* [1987] 2 FLR 390; *Moody v Haselgrove* (16 November 1987, unreported), CA.
8. *Winfield v Billington* (30 July 1990, unreported), CA.
9. *Re Hills* [1941] WN 123.
10. *Re Mason* (1975) 5 Fam Law 124; *Re Lewis* Blackett-Ord V-C (13 March 1980, unreported), CA.
11. *Re Shanahan* [1973] Fam 9, [1971] 3 All ER 873; see p 384, *ante*. In *Riggs v Lloyds Bank plc* (27 November 1992, unreported), CA the judge at first instance made an order for a lump sun to be paid in instalments to prevent an improvident realisation of the estate.
12. *Re Haig*, Browne-Wilkinson J [1979] LS Gaz R 476; *Stead v Stead* [1985] FLR 16 and see pp 392–393, *ante*.

> ... order any person who holds any property which forms part of the *net estate* of the deceased to make such payment or transfer such property as may be specified in the Order.[13]

This enables the court to make an order in respect of property forming part of the net estate, but not under the control of the personal representatives, for example, where property held by a survivor of a joint tenancy[14] or by a statutory nominee[15] or a beneficiary in the estate who has received the property from the personal representatives. The expression 'such payment or transfer' would permit the payment or transfer to someone other than the applicant directly, such as a trustee for the applicant or the personal representatives if the transferred property is going to be administered as part of the estate.[16] This provision is limited to property forming part of the *net estate*; [17] the Law Commission rejected a proposal that any beneficiary could be required to pay money or transfer property directly to the applicant, whether or not it was contained in the net estate, because of the unnecessary complications which would be caused by such a provision.[18]

Without prejudice to the generality of the powers under section 2(4), the court can:

> confer on the trustees of any property which is the subject of an order under [section 2] such powers as appear to the court to be necessary or expedient.[19]

This is a very useful provision and it is often possible to give trustees wider powers as to investment, appropriation, advancement and maintenance than were given by the will or general law. In *CA v CC*[20] Baker P authorised the trustees of an infant's interest to have power to help in the accommodation of the infant's mother with whom he lived. In *Moody v Haselgrove*[1] the executors were given

13. S 2(4)(a); emphasis added.
14. See s 9(1); pp 297–303, *ante*.
15. See s 8(1); pp 295–297, *ante*.
16. See the comments of Professor JG Miller in the commentary to *Current Law Statutes*.
17. Defined by s 25(1), and see Ch 7.
18. WORKING PAPER, para 3.53; LAW COM, para 155.
19. S 2(4)(c).
20. Sub nom *In the Estate of McC* (1979) 9 Fam Law 26 – this aspect of the case is not dealt with in the reports in The Times, 17 November 1978; *sub nom Re C* (1979) 123 Sol Jo 35. For the use of a deferred charge, as in ancillary relief proceedings, acheiving the same result, see *Winfield v Billington* (30 July 1990, unreported), CA.
1. (16 November 1987, unreported), CA, affirming Falconer J.

powers to mortgage a dwellinghouse so as to enable legacies to be paid out while at the same time not disturbing the occupation of the deceased's widow. Frequently the courts give directions as to the maintenance of infants.[2]

Where there is considerable ill-feeling between the parties, it is often useful to include a direction, if the administration of the estate is at an advanced stage, directing that certain assets be transferred to new trustees or new trustees appointed. In *Re Haig*[3] where a great deal of animosity subsisted between applicant and the beneficiary Browne-Wilkinson J appointed the parties' solicitors[4] as trustees. In an intestacy or where a will is being administered by administrators, if the order results in the creation of an interest for a minor or a life interest, it may be appropriate for an application to be made for the appointment of a second administrator,[5] or if the administration is well advanced for a second trustee to be appointed.[6]

It is doubtful whether the power under section 2(4) extends to the actual appointment or replacement of a personal representative, as opposed to a trustee, as there is an extensive statutory code relating to this.[7]

The powers under section 2(4) can be exercised 'as the court thinks necessary *or* expedient'.[8] These are fairly wide words and section 2(4) and its predecessors have been construed widely. Section 2(4) can not be used where an application is dismissed,

2. Compare the remarks of Mervyn Davies J in *Re Wood* [1982] LS Gaz R 774 on the maintenance of an applicant who was a mental patient whose affairs were under the control of the Court of Protection.
3. [1979] LS Gaz R 476; in *Dixit v Dixit* (23 June 1988, unreported), CA the court appointed one of the parties' solicitors as a trustee of a post-nuptial settlement which was varied. In *Re F* (1965) 109 Sol Jo 212 Cumming-Bruce J revoked a grant of letters of administration to the principal beneficiary and granted letters of administration to the applicant's solicitors.
4. Although the transcript states that the parties' *counsel* were appointed as trustees, I am informed by Mr J Jopling of counsel that this is a mistake for their *solicitors*.
5. Under s 114(2) of the Supreme Court Act 1981, it is no longer mandatory for letters of administration to be granted to a trust corporation or two administrators where a life interest or minority subsists, as it was under s160(1) Supreme Court of Judicature (Consolidation) Act 1925. The power to add a second administrator if a minority or life interest arises is discretionary – s 114(4) of the Supreme Court Act 1981.
6. Note, (1951) 70 Law Notes 92.
7. In *Re F* (1965) 109 Sol Jo 212 Cumming-Bruce J revoked a grant of letters of administration and made a fresh grant consequent upon an award of provision. The report in The Times, 25 February 1965 makes it clear that Cumming-Bruce J made this order under s 162 of the Supreme Court of Judicature (Consolidation) Act 1925 (now s 116 of the Supreme Court Act 1981).
8. Emphasis added.

because the directions will not then be for the purpose of 'giving effect to the order', but there is nothing improper in the consequential directions being the most important part of the provision ordered.[9]

The Incidence of Any Provision Ordered

If the court makes no direction as to how the burden of any provision ordered is to be borne the order of application set out in section 34 and Part II of the First Schedule to the Administration of Estates Act 1925 will apply. Section 2(4), re-enacting the position under the 1938 Act[10] and the 1965 Act,[11] gives the court power to direct which parts of the net estate shall bear the burden of any order, by making consequential directions:

> ... for the purpose of securing that the order operates fairly as between one beneficiary[12] of the estate of the deceased and another.

This power enables the court to apportion the incidence not only between different classes of beneficiary in the net estate but also unequally between the same class exonerating one or some at the expense of the other.[13] A court is not *strictly* bound by express declarations of the deceased as to how an award should be borne.[14] Although most awards are made out of residue, it is a fallacy to assume that an award will normally or primarily be made out of the residuary estate.[15] The court has apportioned the burden of provision between an annuitant and the residuary legatee,[16] between pecuniary and residuary legatees,[17] and rateably over the whole estate.[18] In practice small pecuniary legacies and bequests to friends

9. *Re Mason* (1975) 5 Fam Law 124.
10. S 3(2).
11. S 28(3).
12. 'Beneficiary' is defined by s 25(1). This definition does not cover a survivor of a joint tenancy where an order has been made under s 9, persons interested in dispositions intended to defeat applications for financial provision under s 10, contracts to leave property by will affected by s 11 or under an ante- or post-nuptial settlement, but it is suggested that the same principles apply to these people as they apply to beneficiaries.
13. *Re Preston* [1969] 1 WLR 317, [1969] 2 All ER 961.
14. *Re Preston* [1969] 1 WLR 317, [1969] 2 All ER 961 and see p 414, *post*.
15. *Re Simson* [1950] Ch 38, at 40, [1949] 2 All ER 826, at 827G–H (per Vaisey J).
16. *Re Westby* [1946] WN 141.
17. *Re Jackson* [1952] 2 TLR 90.
18. *Re Simson* [1950] Ch 38, [1949] 2 All ER 826.

of the deceased rarely suffer the burden of an award.[19] In exercising its wide discretion as to the apportionment of the burden the court should first of all have regard to the claim of beneficiaries who could be applicants under the Act.[20] Firstly, for instance, provision in favour of an infant child by an earlier marriage of the deceased should not be ordered at the expense of a second wife who has a substantial claim under the Act, if there are other beneficiaries without such claims in the estate. Secondly, regard should be had to the matters which influence the court in deciding whether or not the deceased has made reasonable provision for the applicant, but which are not sufficient in themselves to enable the beneficiary to apply successfully himself.[1] For instance a court should hesitate before ordering provision at the expense of a mistress of the deceased[2] or a relative who cared greatly for the deceased, but who does not come within section 1(1)(e) or where the deceased is under a 'moral obligation' to hand property derived from another to particular beneficiaries.[3] Thirdly, it is suggested that the court should order the burden to be borne in accordance with the presumed intention of the deceased and that it should have regard to any express declaration of the deceased.

The provisions of section 34 and Part II of the First Schedule to the Administration of Estates Act 1925 are to a considerable extent based upon the presumed intentions of the deceased and regard should be had to them. However, in many cases an award under the 1975 Act will be unforeseen and other approaches based

19. For example in *Re Bunning* [1984] Ch 480, [1984] 3 All ER 1 the estate of the deceased was worth £220,000, the deceased's will provided for legacies to individuals totalling £26,000 and to charities and the residue was divided as to 80% to the charities and as to 20% to the individuals. The Plaintiff did not join the individual legatees as defendants and the charities did not join them either with a view to making them share the burden of any award. In *Re Jennings* [1994] Ch 286, at 293F–G, [1994] 3 All ER 27, at 31j-32b where the net estate was £300,000, individual pecuniary legatees received £170,000 and the residue passed to charities, it was agreed between the beneficiaries that the burden of an award of £40,000 should be borne entirely by the residuary beneficiaries.
20. See in particular *Re Campbell* [1983] NI 10. An example of this is *Rajabally v Rajabally* [1987] 2 FLR 390 where the three beneficiaries were adult sons, one of which was mentally ill and unemployed, whereas the other two were self-supporting. The Court of Appeal extinguished the interests of the self-supporting children, but effectively preserved the interest of the mentally ill child.
1. See pp 149–150, 157–159, *ante*.
2. See per Vaisey J in *Re Simson* [1950] Ch 38, at 40, [1949] 2 All ER 826, at 825H-828A; per Hollings J in *Malone v Harrison* [1979] 1 WLR 1353, at 1363H.
3. See pp 157–159, *ante*.

on the presumed intention of the deceased should be adopted.[4] It is submitted that it is wrong for the court to use the power to order the incidence of an award to prefer one type of beneficiary against another, where neither have any claim under the Act, in the absence of any indication of the deceased's intentions to that effect. In particular it is submitted that it is wrong to prefer adult children of the deceased who have no possible claim under the Act to charities or non-relatives.

A wrong exercise of the court's powers was *Re Preston*.[5] In this case the deceased bequeathed half his residuary estate to a lady friend of his who was not his mistress and half to infant relatives of his all of whom were being cared for by their parents and none of whom had any possible claim recognisable by the Act upon the deceased. He further directed that any provision ordered to be made by a court in favour of his estranged wife should be at the expense of the part of the residue bequeathed to two of the four infant beneficiaries. Burgess V-C made an order for provision in favour of the deceased's estranged wife and ignoring the deceased's express declaration ordered that all the infants should be treated equally and ordered that the deceased's lady friend bear twice the rateable proportion of the award. In this case Burgess V-C was applying his own ideas as to the devolution of property within a family in defiance of the deceased's express intentions and acting beyond any objective of Inheritance Act legislation.

A better approach was adopted by Roxburgh J in *Re Jackson*.[6] In this case the deceased bequeathed certain pecuniary legacies which he directed to be paid in priority, certain other pecuniary legacies and a residuary gift. The provision ordered would have swallowed up the residue entirely and Roxburgh J, having regard to 'the general nature of the testamentary dispositions', ordered that

4. See the facts in *Re Simson* [1950] Ch 38, [1949] 2 All ER 826 and *Re Jackson* [1952] 2 TLR 90. Australasian legislation generally provides that the burden is to be borne by beneficiaries rateably, subject to the court's discretion – DE GROOT AND NICKEL para 707.1–707.3; DICKEY, 161–163.
5. [1969] 1 WLR 317, [1969] 2 All ER 961. Burgess V-C had been Counsel in *Re Simson*.
6. [1952]2 TLR 90; a not dissimilar overall result was reached in *Re Simson* [1950] Ch 38, [1949] 2 All ER 826 and in *Moody v Haselgrove* (16 November 1987, unreported), CA. In *Re Bunning* [1984] Ch 480, at 500A–B, [1984] 3 All ER 1, at 12c-g Vinelott J ordered that the burden of the award should be borne by the charitable residuary beneficiary and then by the charitable legatees rateably. The question whether any of the burden should be borne by the individual beneficiaries did not arise as they had not been made parties to the action. The statement of Eastham J in *Re Crawford* (1982) 4 FLR 273, at 281G that once an order under s 9 has been made a severable share is to be treated differently from any other part of the net estate is *in itself* undoubtedly correct.

the burden of the award should be borne rateably by the residue and the pecuniary legacies, but exonerated the legacies which were to be paid in priority to the others. This approach paid full regard to the deceased's presumed intentions in his direction as to the priority of certain legacies, and the unlikelihood that the residuary gift should be completely extinguished.

The provisions of section 2(4) can not be used to increase the share of a beneficiary in the estate who is neither an applicant nor has applied for provision.[7]

Recording of the Order

Section 19(3), re-enacting previous legislation,[8] requires that a copy of every order 'made under this Act', other than an order made under section 15,[9] shall be sent to the Principal Registry of the Family Division for entry and filing and that a memorandum of the order shall be endorsed on the grant of representation to the estate of the deceased. Rules of Court dealing with this requirement have been made.[10] This requirement does not cover an order dismissing an application,[11] but, whether or not the order is technically made 'under this Act', it does cover any kind of order compromising an application.[12] The Rules of Court provide for the grant of representation to be retained by the court until the memorandum is endorsed thereon and for the sending of a copy of the order to the Principal Registry of the Family Division.[13]

7. *Re Campbell* [1983] NI 10. But see *Moody v Haselgrove* (16 November 1987, unreported), CA where the Court of Appeal altered the priority of pecuniary legatees so as to ensure that the fund designated for their payment had been exhausted by costs – the case can be justified upon the basis of attaching a condition to the award in favour of the applicant.
8. 1938 Act, s 3(3); 1965 Act, s 28(3).
9. S 52 of the Administration of Justice Act 1982.
10. RSC Ord 99, r 7; CCR 1981 Ord 48, r 8.
11. Both the 1938 Act and the 1975 Act use the expression 'made under this Act'. In a *Practice Note* [1941] WN 185 the judges of the Chancery Division directed that this wording applies to orders dismissing an application. However, both RSC Ord 99, r 7 (made in 1976) and CCR Ord 48, r 8 use the expression 'and if an order is made under the Act' which would not cover a dismissal of an application. It is submitted that the meaning of the expression 'made under this Act' is a question of statutory interpretation and that this can not be altered by Rules of Court or Practice Directions, but that the interpretation of the current rules is correct.
12. *Practice Direction (Chancery Division): 16B(i)*
13. RSC Ord 99, r 7; CCR Ord 48, r 8 – curiously there is no express provision in the Rules of the Supreme Court for a copy of the order to be sent to the Principal Registry of the Family Division.

Variation of Maintenance Orders and Agreements

Most orders for periodical payments imposed by the divorce courts and most maintenance agreements cease upon the death of the payer. However, an order for secured periodical payments survives against the payer's estate and a maintenance agreement may be expressed to continue after the death of the payer. Sections 31(6) and 36 of the Matrimonial Causes Act 1973 respectively give the court power to vary such orders and agreements after the death of the payer on an application by the deceased's personal representatives or the payee.

When an application is made by a payee, who will almost always be qualified as an applicant under the 1975 Act, in most cases it will be better to make an application under the 1975 Act which gives the court a wider perspective and wider powers. The Law Commission considered whether these powers of post-mortem variation should be retained when the jurisdiction considerably overlapped with that for family provision. The Law Commission recommended that the powers of variation be retained because proceedings under the 1975 Act would not permit an application for a variation by the deceased's personal representatives, some applications for variation would be simple enough to be dealt with purely as variations and former spouses in respect of whom orders had been made under section 15 could not apply under the 1975 Act.[14] It is submitted that this reasoning is correct, but in practice there will be very few cases indeed in which a payee will find it more convenient to seek a post-mortem variation rather than to make a full application under the 1975 Act. One such case is an application by a former spouse who has made a final settlement of her claims against the deceased which has not been incorporated in an order under section 15 but which includes an order for secured periodical payments. A full application under the 1975 Act by such a former spouse would fail,[15] but it might well be proper to accede to an application for a variation of the order for secured periodical payments.

The Law Commission did recommend that various measures be adopted to integrate the operation of the powers of post-mortem variation and the 1975 Act and these were incorporated in sections 16–18 of the 1975 Act. The actual operation of section 31(6) and

14. LAW COM, paras 263–276.
15. *Re Fullard* [1982] Fam 42, [1981] 2 All ER 796.

section 36 of the Matrimonial Causes Act 1973 is not dealt with in this book and the reader is referred to books on matrimonial law.[16] When an application is made for provision under section 2 of the 1975 Act by a person who was at the time of the death of the deceased entitled to payments from the deceased under a secured periodical payments order made under the Matrimonial Causes Act 1973,[17] the payee or the personal representatives of the deceased may apply for an order under which the order for periodical payments is varied, discharged or if suspended then revived.[18] There is no time-limit upon such an application, but the application for provision under section 2 must have been made within six months of the taking out of a grant of representation or the court must have extended time under section 4. This power extends to any instrument executed in pursuance of the order for secured periodical payments.[19] In deciding whether to exercise the power the court shall have regard to all the circumstances of the case, including any order which the court proposes to make under section 2 or section 5 and any change (whether resulting from the death of the deceased or otherwise) in any of the matters to which the court was required to have regard when making the secured periodical payments order.[20]

An almost exactly comparable power exists in relation to 'maintenance agreements' by virtue of section 17. The power extends to varying or revoking the agreement[1] and a variation by the court under this section has all the like consequences as if the variation had been made immediately before the death of the deceased by agreement between the parties for valuable consideration.[2] The power of variation includes the power to make an order of retrospective effect remitting any accrued liability under the agreement.[3] In deciding whether to exercise this power the court shall have regard to all the circumstances of the case, including any order which the court proposes to make under section 2 or section 5 and any change (whether resulting from the death of the deceased

16. See JACKSON AND DAVIES, 152–153, 357; RAYDEN, paras 29.94–29.102.
17. This includes the predecessors of the Matrimonial Causes Act 1973, s 25(6).
18. S 16(1)
19. S 16(2)
20. S 16(3), derived from Matrimonial Causes Act 1973, s 31(7).
1. S 17(1).
2. S 17(3). The original legislation was s 2 of the Maintenance Agreements Act 1957. For the historical background to the Maitenance Agreements Act 1957 and commentary on the usefulness of the legislation, see Cretney, '*From Status to Contract?*' in Rose, *Consensus Ad Idem: Essays in Honour of Guenter Treitel*, 270–273.
3. *Warden v Warden* [1982] Fam 10, [1981] 3 All ER 193.

or otherwise) in any of the circumstances in the light of which the agreement was made.[4]

To come within section 17 the maintenance agreement must provide 'for the continuation of payments under the agreement after the death of the deceased'.[5] 'Maintenance Agreement' for section 17 is defined in a similar, but slightly different, way to the definition in section 34(2) of the Matrimonial Causes Act 1973, as an agreement:

> ... made, whether in writing or not and whether before or after the commencement of this Act, by the deceased with any person with whom he entered into a marriage, being an agreement which contained provisions governing the rights and liabilities toward one another *when living separately*[6] of the parties to that marriage (whether or not the marriage has been dissolved or annulled) in respect of the making or securing of payments or the disposition[7] or use of any property, including such rights and liabilities with respect to the maintenance or education of any child, whether or not a child of the deceased or a person who was treated by the deceased as a child of the family in relation to that marriage.[8,9]

Unlike the definition in section 34(2), an agreement need not be in writing in order to come within section 17. A 'maintenance agreement' can only be made between parties to the marriage and may not involve third parties.[10]

While the policy and drafting of section 17 and section 18 cannot be criticised, it may be argued that both sections are unnecessary since the same result could be achieved by a robust exercise of the court's power to give consequential directions under section 2(4).

The corollary of section 16 and section 17 which allows the court to treat an application for family provision as including an application to vary an order for secured periodical payments or a maintenance agreement is section 18 which allows the court to treat an application under section 31(6) of the Matrimonial Causes Act

4. S 17(2).
5. S 17(1).
6. Emphasis added. The financial arrangements must be for the *situation* when the parties are living separately, but the *entire* agreement need not be for the purpose of living separately – see JACKSON AND DAVIES, para 13.11, fn 5; compare *Ewart v Ewart* [1959] P 23, [1958] 3 All ER 561 construing Maintenance Agreements Act 1957.
7. 'Disposition' is construed widely – *D v D* (1974)5 Fam Law 61, 118 Sol Jo 715.
8. For the definition of 'child of the family', see s 1(1)(d) and pp 74–77, *ante*.
9. S 17(4).
10. *Young v Young* (1973) 117 Sol Jo 204, sed quaere.

1973 for the variation of an order for secured periodical payments and an application under section 36(1) of the Matrimonial Causes Act 1973 for the variation of a maintenance agreement[11] as accompanied by an application for provision under section 2.[12] The application to vary must be made by the payee,[13] who cannot be a former spouse in respect of whom an order under section 15 has been made,[14] and the court has a discretion whether or not to 'deem' that an application for provision under section 2 has been made.[15] For instance it is submitted that a court would not exercise its powers under section 18(1), where the time limit for applications under section 2 has expired or where a former spouse applying for a variation had made a final settlement of her claims against the deceased but which had not been made the subject of an order under section 15.[16] The main purpose of section 18 is to enable an applicant for a variation to have the benefit of the enhanced definition of the 'net estate', particularly the power to set aside dispositions designed to defeat applications for financial provision[17] and this is expressly provided for by section 18(2) together with a power to give consequential directions.

Although the same time-limit applies to applications under section 31(6) and section 36(1) of the Matrimonial Causes Act 1973[18] as applies under the 1975 Act, the power to deem that an application for family provision has been made can create substantial uncertainty for persons who are interested in the 'net estate' but are not a beneficiary of the estate, such as the survivor of a joint tenancy. The failure of an applicant to apply directly under section 2 is an indication to such a person that his rights will not be challenged, but the court can give the applicant all the benefits of an application under section 2 long after the time-limit has expired. It is suggested that courts should be reluctant to use their powers under section 18 unless some good reason is shown why an applicant did not initially apply under section 2 directly and should have particular regard to any change of position by any person interested in the 'net estate' who is not a beneficiary of the estate between the expiration of the time limit and the making of the order under section 18. It is

11. As defined by Matrimonial Causes Act 1973, s 34(2) and not by s 17(4) of the 1975 Act.
12. S 18(1).
13. S 18(1).
14. S 18(3).
15. S 18(1) uses the word 'power'.
16. Compare *Re Fullard* [1982] Fam 42, [1981] 2 All ER 796.
17. LAW COM, para 275.
18. S 31(7), (9), s 36(2), (6) of the Matrimonial Causes Act 1973.

suggested that any applicant who intends to apply under section 18 should if at all possible apply directly under section 2. It is submitted that section 18 is an unnecessary piece of legislation – in almost all circumstances it is of no real practical use and capable of producing hardship to persons interested in the 'net estate'.

The First Schedule to the Children Act 1989 contains provisions comparable to sections 31(6) and 36 of the Matrimonial Causes Act 1973 whereby secured orders for periodical payments in favour of children[19] and maintenance agreements which provide for the maintenance of children and continue after the death of the payee[20] can be varied after the death of the payee. Somewhat curiously the provisions of sections 16, 17 and 18 of the 1975 Act have not been amended to apply to such amendments.[1]

19. Para 7.
20. Para 11.
1. The provisions of paras 7 and 11 of the First Schedule to the Children Act 1989 are derived from s 12 and s 14 of the Family Law Reform Act 1987 which was enacted as a result of Law Commission Report No 118: Family Law: Illegitimacy. This report contains no discussion as to whether ss 16, 17 and 18 of the 1975 Act should apply to orders and agreements made in favour of children (paras 6.35–6.39, 6.42–6.46).

Chapter 10

THE EFFECT OF THE ACT ON THE ADMINISTRATION OF THE ESTATE

PART 1: GENERALLY

An order for provision under the Act varies the dispositions of the deceased's will or intestacy *as from the date of death*. This is the effect of section 19(1) which provides:

> When an order is made under section 2 of this Act then *for all purposes* ... the will or the law relating to intestacy ... shall have effect and *be deemed to have had effect* as from the deceased's death *subject to the provisions of the order*.[1]

Accordingly a successful applicant will have, subject to any express provision in the order to the contrary, exactly the same rights, no more and no less, as if he were a beneficiary under the deceased's will or interested in the deceased's intestacy. The full effect of this provision was stated by Wynn-Parry J in *Re Pointer*:

> It is clear from the provisions of [the 1938 Act] that a dependant in whose favour an order is made under the Act is placed for all purposes in the position of a beneficiary. Secondly, it is clear that the effect of any such order is to vary the will in question. [Section 3(1)][2] is in wide terms... The reference to the enactments relating to death duties shows that the section proceeds on the footing that the provision made by the order is to be treated as a legacy. In my judgment the scheme of the Act involves first, that, assuming the necessary conditions obtain, the court may by order make provision for the dependant applying to it; secondly, if it makes such an order the provision made thereby is to be treated for all purposes as a legacy; and thirdly, the will is for all purposes to have effect as if that legacy had been contained in it when it was made.[3]

1. Emphasis added. The last phrase was originally introduced by the Intestates' Estates Act 1952.
2. The predecessor of s 19(1).
3. [1946] Ch 324, at 326, [1946] 2 All ER 409, at 411B–C, approved by Russell LJ in *Re Jennery* [1967] Ch 280, at 285C–D, [1967] 1 All ER 691, at 694B–C.

This relation back of the order can cause problems in the administration of the estate, with matters such as interest,[4] and it is often advisable to make some or all of the order's provisions take effect from a date after the date of death, such as the date of the order or the end of the executor's year.[5]

On a very literal reading of section 19(1), it would apply section 15 of the Wills Act 1837 to any order and thus prevent provision being made for a person who witnessed the will of the deceased. It is suggested that a court will not so construe section 19(1) since to do so will defeat the policy of the 1975 Act and no way advance the policy of section 15 of the Wills Act 1837.[6] Possibly the order itself would direct that section 15 of the Wills Act 1837 should not apply.

The Enforcement of an Order

Because an order under section 2 has the effect of a variation of the dispositions of the deceased's will or intestacy, it is enforced in exactly the same way as a gift in a will or an interest in an intestacy is enforced.[7] An order under section 2(1)(b) for the payment of a lump sum is not enforceable as an ordinary judgment or an order to pay money[8] and an order for the transfer of specific property under section 2(1)(c) is enforced as if it were a specific gift in a will. While the 1975 Act substantially assimilated the court's powers on an application for family provision with those under the Matrimonial Causes Act 1973, it did not in any way assimilate the method of enforcing orders made under the two jurisdictions. An order creating a settlement under section 2(1)(d) or varying an ante-nuptial or post-nuptial settlement may by itself effect the settlement or the variation or it may require other documents to be executed. The failure to execute a document required to be executed by an order of the court can be enforced directly by committal, if necessary, or by the court executing the necessary documents on behalf of the recalcitrant personal representative.[9] Once such a settlement has come into effect, it is enforced by the usual remedies for the execution of trusts.

4. See p 384, *ante*.
5. ROSS MARTYN, 77; pp 408–412, *ante*.
6. ALBERY, 35; REM, (Note), (1946) 64 LQR 19.
7. *Re Jennery* [1967] Ch 280, [1967] 1 All ER 691.
8. Ibid.
9. Supreme Court Act 1981, s 39, applied to the County Court by s 38 of the County Courts Act 1984 as amended: *Danchevsky v Danchevsky* [1975] Fam 17, [1974] 3 All ER 934.

If difficulties of enforcement are anticipated, applicants should onsider making use of the substantive hearing to aid the nforcement of the order. Use might be made of the power to give onsequential directions to the appointment of new trustees.[10] At a ubstantive hearing of an application the court can make there and hen an order for the administration of the estate,[11] or any lesser rder relating to administration of the estate.[12]

The Liability of Personal Representatives

Because section 19(1) treats a successful applicant as if he were a erson interested in the deceased's will or intestacy, an applicant's ight of action against a personal representative is the same as a eneficiary's right of action, namely an action for devastavit or reach of trust.[13]

The 1975 Act does not impose any special new form of liability n a personal representative, but causes the existing duties to be wed to a new class of persons. With some limited exceptions,[14] the 975 Act does not deprive a personal representative of any defence o an action brought against him. In particular, a personal epresentative (or a trustee) can apply for relief under section 61 of he Trustee Act 1925.[15] A case for the fairly automatic grant of relief y the court would be where the personal representatives have made n interim distribution of the estate without a court order of the kind dvocated by Cross J in *Re Ralphs*.[16]

The 1975 Act does modify the position of a personal epresentative in relation to a successful applicant or other eneficiaries in the estate in two ways. Firstly, the Act affords certain efences to personal representatives. These are in relation to the istribution of the estate after six months from the date on which epresentation was first taken out in case the court extends the time

0. *Re Haig*, Browne-Wilkinson J [1979] LS Gaz R 476; *Dixit v Dixit* (23 June 1988, unreported), CA; Note, (1951) 70 Law Notes 92 and see p 411, *ante*.
1. *Re Lofts* [1968] 1 WLR 1949, [1969] 1 All ER 7.
2. Under RSC Ord 85, r 2; applied to the County Court by s 76 of the County Courts Act 1984.
3. On the general liability of personal representatives see Williams, Mortimer & Sunnucks, *Executors, Administrators and Probate* (17th edn), Ch 55;
4. See p 424, *post*.
5. On Trustee Act 1925, s 61, generally, see Snell, *Principles of Equity* (29th edn), pp 290-1; Wolstenholme and Cherry, *Conveyancing Statutes* (13th edn), Vol 4, pp 87–89.
6. [1968] 1 WLR 1522, [1968] 3 All ER 28 and see pp 356–357, *ante*.

for making an application,[17] in relation to the distribution of th estate without anticipating an application for a variation of an orde for periodical payments,[18] in relation to complying with an interin order for provision under section 5 'by reason of that (net) estat not being sufficient to make the payment, unless at the time o making payment he has reasonable cause to believe that the estat is not sufficient',[19] in relation to meeting the liability of the estat under a contract to make a will[20] or in relation to distributing th estate without having taken into account that an application woul be made under section 10 or section 11.[1] Secondly, the 1975 Ac impliedly alters a personal representative's duties in order to tak account of the general scheme of the Act. A personal representativ cannot claim the protection of an advertisement under section 2 of the Trustee Act 1925,[2] if an applicant applies after two month from the advertisement but before the six months allowed by sectio 4 has elapsed, because the general policy of the Act is to allow a applicant up to six months from the date on which representatio was first taken out in order to apply.[3]

Likewise it is submitted that a clause in the deceased's wil permitting a personal representative to distribute the estate withou regard to the provisions of the 1975 Act will not be enforced, eve in the absence of a consequential direction[4] in the order deleting it

If for any reason an applicant cannot enforce his rights agains a personal representative, he has the same rights as a beneficiary

17. S 20(1)(a).
18. S 20(1)(b).
19. S 20(2) – this covers a personal representative's liability to a creditor as well a to other beneficiaries. It is doubtful whether a creditor has any right of actio against a person in receipt of an interim payment under s 5, *sed quaere*.
20. S 20(3).
1. S 12(4).
2. On Trustee Act 1925, s 27 generally, see Wolstenholme and Cherry *Conveyancing Statutes* (13th edn) Vol 4, pp 35–37.
3. See fn 4, p 328, *ante*. The duty not to distribute to beneficiaries within si months of the date on which representation was first taken out is not expressl stated in the 1975 Act but was to some extent judicially recognised in *Re Simso* [1950] Ch 38, [1949] 2 All ER 826 and in *Re Ralphs* [1968] 1 WLR 1522 [1968] 3 All ER 285 and recognised implicitly by s 20(3). The failure of a applicant to give notice to a personal representative after s 27 of the Truste Act 1925 advertisement *about which he actually knows* may create an estoppe against the applicant and may cause a court to be reluctant to exercise discretionary power in his favour – compare *Escritt v Escritt*(1981) 3 FLR 280
4. Under s 2(4).
5. Such rights are specifically preserved by s 20(1) in the event of an applicatio out of time or a variation under s 6.

ı the estate to follow the assets wrongfully distributed to the eneficiaries of the estate[6] or to trace assets.[7]

'he Effect of an Order on Property which does ıot Pass to Personal Representatives

'he 1975 Act does not spell out with any great clarity the exact effect f an order made under section 2 on property which is part of the ıet estate', but which does not form part of the 'estate' passing to ıe personal representatives. The matter is not dealt with by section 9(1), which only deals with the deceased's will or intestacy; but ıe scheme of section 19(1) may be a guide to what is not otherwise learly stated by the Act. The 1975 Act uses three techniques to npose orders on property which comes within the extended efinition of the 'net estate'. Firstly, certain types of property are utomatically[8] or after a court order[9] declared to be part of the 'net state'. In such a case an order under section 2 takes effect as a eclaration of trust and is enforced by the normal remedies for the xecution of the trust. In addition an order under section 2(1)(d), :) can be enforced directly.[10] For example, where an order is made nder section 2(1)(a) for periodical payments, after an order has een made under section 9 making the deceased's severable share ı jointly held land part of the net estate, the effect is that the survivor olds the legal estate in the land on trust for himself absolutely as) half[11] and as to half for himself but charged with an annuity in ıvour of the applicant. Secondly, the court can make orders equiring the payment of money or the transfer of property for the

5. On following assets generally see *Ministry of Health v Simpson* [1951] AC 251, [1950] 2 All ER 1137; Williams, Mortimer & Sunnucks, *Executors, Administrators and Probate* (17th edn), pp 1076–1081.
7. On tracing generally see Williams, Mortimer & Sunnucks, *Executors, Administrators and Probate* (17th edn), pp 974–977; Goff and Jones, *The Law of Restitution* (4th edn), pp 75–93.
3. A general inter vivos power of appointment, s 25(1); property passing under a statutory nomination, s 8(1); property passing under a donatio mortis causa, s 8(2) and see pp 294–297, *ante*.
). The deceased's severable share in jointly held property s 9(1); see pp 297–303, *ante*.
). See p 422, *ante*.
1. As to the exact amount of property effected by an order under s 9, see s 9(1), (2) and pp 298–299, *ante*.

purpose of making an order for financial provision.[12] Such an order can be enforced directly, if necessary by an application for committal, but it also by itself creates a trust as does any order made under section 2 consequent on the first order. Thirdly, section 11(2)(ii) provides that a court can order a personal representative not to give effect to the rights of a person entitled to enforce a contract to make a will who is in some sense a creditor of the estate. Such an order can be enforced directly if necessary by committal or more usually by a devastavit against the personal representative.

Thus it is submitted that orders made affecting the 'net estate' which is not under control of the personal representatives generally have the effect of creating a trust and thereby imposing the liability of a trustee on the person holding such property. Such a person is not a personal representative,[13] but the principles governing the liability of a personal representative, such as the rules governing an interim distribution of the property,[14] may be a guide to the liability of such a trustee. It is submitted that an order made under the Act affecting property part of the 'net estate' not passing to the personal representatives in the absence of special statutory exceptions and express directions in the order, relates back to the date of death of the deceased. This appears to follow from section 9(3) which provides:

> Where an order is made under [section 9(1)], the provisions of [section 9] shall not render any person liable for anything done by him before the order,

which would be unnecessary if the order did not prima facie relate back to the date of death and by analogy with section 9(1).

12. In respect of dispositions intended to defeat an application for financial provision, s 10(2) and see pp 303–312, *ante*; in respect of a contract to make a will, s 11(2)(i) and see pp 313–320, *ante*.
13. It is suggested that the relevant limitation period is six years under s 21(3) of the Limitation Act 1980 and that an action only 'accrues' when an order is made rather than when an earlier breach of trust occurs. S 22(a) of the Limitation Act 1980 refers to an interest in 'any such estate ("whether under a will or an intestacy")'.
14. See *Re Ralphs* [1968] 1 WLR 1522, [1968] 3 All ER 285 and see pp 356–357 *ante*. It is suggested that the same limitations on the effectiveness of an advertisement under s 27 of the Trustee Act 1925 as apply to personal representatives (p 424, *ante*) apply to trustees or potential trustees in this situation.

PART 2: TAXATION

It is the general policy of the Act, like its predecessors, that capital taxes should be payable as if the Order for family provision were effective from the date of death of the deceased. To effect this general intention section 19(1) provides:

> Where an order is made under section 2 of this Act then for all purposes, including the purposes of the enactments relating to Inheritance Tax, the will or the law relating to intestacy ... shall have effect and be deemed to have had effect from the deceased's death subject to the provisions of the order.[15]

It is important to realise that section 19(1) applies only to orders made under section 2 and not to orders for interim provision made under section 5 and that any retrospective effect of the order is always 'subject to the provision of the order'.

Inheritance Tax

The general policy of section 19(1) as regards Inheritance Tax is carried into effect by the detailed provisions of section 146 of the Inheritance Tax Act 1984.

Firstly, section 146(1) provides that where an order is made out of the 'net estate' of the deceased Inheritance Tax will be payable as if the deceased's estate had devolved on death subject to the provisions of the order.

Secondly, section 146(4) deals with an order made out of property forming part of the 'net estate' by reason of section 8 (statutory nominations and donatio mortis causa) and by reason of an order made under section 9 (deceased's severable share in jointly held property). Such provision is limited to an amount net of any Inheritance Tax borne by the nominee, donee or survivor, and this net amount is calculated before any adjustment of Inheritance Tax liability consequent upon the order for family provision.[16] If such an order results in a repayment of Inheritance Tax, the tax is repayable to the personal representatives.[17] Any tax repaid to the

15. Essentially repeating the Inheritance (Family Provision) Act 1938.
16. S 8(3), s 9(2).
17. Inheritance Tax Act 1984, s 146(4).

personal representatives forms part of the 'net estate'[18] and can therefore itself be subject to an order for family provision.

Thirdly, section 146 has provisions dealing with orders under section 10 made against donees under dispositions designed to defeat an application for family provision. Section 146(2), which deals specifically with orders under section 10, only applies if the personal representatives elect that they should apply and only if the impugned disposition was a 'chargeable transfer'.[19] Thus if the impugned disposition were made to a spouse of the deceased (an exempt transfer), the value of the property or the amount of the money which the donee is ordered to provide will be chargeable to Inheritance Tax as part of the deceased's estate on death.[20] When a donee is ordered under section 10 to provide money or property, the personal representatives may elect to claim repayment of any Inheritance Tax paid upon the deceased's disposition.[1] The cumulative total of the deceased's transfers of value will be reduced by the amount of the transfer[2] and the property or money ordered to be provided by the donee will form part of the deceased's estate on death and be assessed to Inheritance Tax accordingly.[3] Any tax repaid to the personal representatives forms part of the deceased's estate and Inheritance Tax is payable thereon.[4] Where an order under section 10 requires the payment or transfer of less than the maximum amount permitted by section 10, the above provisions apply proportionately.[5]

An example may help to demonstrate the operation of this provision and the circumstances when the personal representatives will find it advisable to elect under section 146(2).

> On 1 April 1995 the deceased who had previously made transfers of value totalling £215,000 transferred £30,000 to his mistress. Because this was a Potentially Exempt Transfer[6] no Inheritance Tax was immediately payable. The deceased died two and a half years later leaving no estate on death. Because the Potentially Exempt Transfer had 'failed' the mistress was obliged to pay Inheritance Tax of £12,000 (£30,000 at 40%). If the court orders the mistress to

18. Inheritance Tax Act 1984, s 146(5).
19. Inheritance Tax Act 1984, s 146(2). 'Chargeable Transfer' is defined as 'any transfer of value made by an individual ... but is not an exempt transfer' – Inheritance Tax Act 1984, s 2(1).
20. By reason of s 19(1) and Inheritance Tax Act 1984, s 146(1).
1. Inheritance Tax Act 1984, s 146(2)(i).
2. Inheritance Tax Act 1984, s 146(2)(ii).
3. Inheritance Tax Act 1984, s 146(10).
4. Inheritance Tax Act 1984, s 146(5).
5. Inheritance Tax Act 1984, s 146(3).

disgorge the sum of £18,000 (£30,000 minus Inheritance Tax of £12,000) and the applicant is the wife of the deceased, the personal representatives would be well advised to claim repayment under section 146(2). They would receive £12,000, but would not have to pay inheritance tax on the full £30,000 because the applicant is the spouse of the deceased.[7]

Fourthly, section 146(6) provides that any variation of a settlement under section 2(1)(f) or section 10 will not give rise to any charge to Inheritance Tax solely by reason of the variation. If by reason of an order made under the 1975 Act an interest in possession comes to an end, no Inheritance Tax is payable in respect of such termination and an Order under the 1975 Act cannot be an occasion when an exit charge arises under a discretionary trust.[8]

When any Inheritance Tax has to be repaid in accordance with section 146, the tax repaid includes any interest *actually paid* thereon.[9] Where tax has been under- or over-paid in consequence of an order for family provision, interest is only payable on the under- or over-payment from the date of the order.[10]

Strictly s 146 only applies to actual orders made by the court. However, section 146(8) applies section 146 to a compromise of family provision litigation which is embodied in a Tomlin Order.[11] Section 146(8) only applies to terms 'which *could have been included in an order* under section 2 or section 10 of the Act'. This would exclude terms which are beyond the powers of the court under the Act, such as benefits to non-applicants and in cases where the applicant would not be able to satisfy the court that the will or intestacy did not make reasonable provision for the deceased, which is a pre-condition of any order under section 2.[12]

Where a family provision claim is compromised without a court order, the compromise may come within the provisions of section 142 of the Inheritance Tax Act 1984 which permit the parties to elect to treat a variation of the dispositions made by the operation

6. For Potentially Exempt Transfers see s 3A of the Inheritance Tax Act 1984.
7. Rates of tax introduced by Finance Act 1996. On the limits to which orders may be drawn to minimise the amount of tax payable, see *Re Goodchild* [1997] 3 All ER 63, at 76d–77f per Morritt LJ.
8. Inheritance Tax Act 1984, s 146(6).
9. Inheritance Tax Act 1984, s 146(7).
10. Inheritance Tax Act 1984, s 236(2).
11. For Tomlin Orders, see p 415, *ante*.
12. Dymond, *Capital Taxes*, Vol 1, paras 8.551–8.559. Another example of terms which could not be included would be an order affecting the deceased's severable share in jointly held property where the application was made after the six-month time limit.

of the deceased's will or intestacy made within two years of the death of the deceased as if the variation had been effected by the deceased.

In considering compromising claims under the 1975 Act, regard should be had to the provisions of section 29A of the Inheritance Tax Act 1984.[13] This section applies where:

(a) the transfer of value made on the death of any person is an exempt transfer and
(b) the exempt beneficiary, in settlement of the whole or part of any claim against the deceased's estate, effects a disposition of property not derived from the transfer.

This section only applies to transfers *on death* to exempt beneficiaries (such as spouses, charities, political parties). Where the section applies, the deceased is treated as having made a transfer of value in favour of the person whose claim is compromised.[14] In determining the amount of Inheritance Tax no account is taken of any liability of the claimant to pay the Inheritance Tax[15] or of the availability of Business or Agricultural Relief.[16] The section does not apply if the exempt beneficiary compromises the claim out of assets which were vested in the deceased immediately before his death. An example may help to illustrate the effect of the section:

> A deceased dies on 1 August 1997 leaving a widow and a child from an earlier marriage who is about to embark on a three year degree course and whom the deceased had maintained during his lifetime. The deceased had previously made transfers of value totalling £215,000. The only property passing on death was the deceased's severable share in a joint bank account containing £200,000 which passed by survivorship to the widow. If the widow compromises without a court order the claim of the child under the 1975 Act by paying £30,000 out of her own half share of the joint bank account, section 29A will apply and the deceased will be treated as having made a chargeable transfer of value of £30,000 which will result in a charge to Inheritance Tax of £12,000. If instead the sum of £12,000 is paid out of the deceased's severable share of the bank account, section 29A will not apply. At best the widow will not have made a transfer of value because there was no intention to confer

13. Originally introduced by s 172(1) of the Finance Act 1989 as part of a set of provisions concerning orders under the 1975 Act and deeds of variation, most of which were not actually enacted.
14. S 29A(2).
15. S 29A(4)(b)(i).
16. S 29A(4)(b)(ii).

gratuitous benefit[17] and at worst the widow will have made a Potentially Exempt Transfer.

Because both section 19(1) and section 146(1) refer only to orders made under section 2(1) of the 1975 Act, they do not apply to orders for costs. Thus in cases where the applicant is a spouse and inheritance tax is otherwise payable, it may be desirable to compromise the application on terms that a larger all inclusive sum is payable to the applicant than a lesser sum and costs.[18]

Capital Gains Tax

By virtue of section 19(1) an order of the court awarding family provision will be treated as having taken effect at the date of death of the deceased for the purpose of capital gains tax. Section 19(1) refers to 'the order', and it is not certain whether this includes a compromise embodied in a Tomlin Order.[19] Where a family provision claim is compromised without a court order, the compromise may come within the provisions of section 62(6) of the Taxation of Chargeable Gains Act 1992 which permit the parties to elect to treat a variation of the dispositions made by the operation of the deceased's will or intestacy made within *two years* of the death of the deceased as if the variation had been effected by the deceased.

Section 19(1) only applies to orders under section 2. Accordingly an order made in respect of a donatio mortis causa, the deceased's severable share in jointly held property or under section 10 will result in a disposal of the property subject to the order for the purpose of capital gains tax.[20] In respect of the deceased's former severable share in jointly held property advantage may be taken of the provisions of section 62(6) of the Taxation of Chargeable Gains Act 1992 on variations of the dispositions of the

17. S 10(1).
18. Any compromise contained in a Tomlin order must satisfy s 146(8).
19. Whiteman and Wheatcroft, *Capital Gains Tax* (4th edn), para 28-92 argue that a Tomlin order falls within s 19(1), but state that the current Revenue practice is not to treat a Tomlin Order as being made under s 19(1).
20. The limitations of s 19(1) were illustrated by the decision of the Court of Appeal in *Dixit v Dixit* (23 June 1988, unreported). At first instance Waite J purported to vary the trusts of a house which did not form part of the net estate under s 2(1)(f) or s 2(4). The variation was not within s 19(1) and gave rise to an immediate Capital Gains Tax charge of about £8,500. The Court of Appeal noted that Waite J had not taken any account of this liability and varied the order so as to lead to a result which did not involve any immediate charge to Capital Gains Tax.

deceased's estate which apply to any 'property of which [the deceased] was competent to dispose'.

The effect of section 19(1) and section 62(6) of the Taxation of Chargeable Gains Act 1992 is to make a successful applicant a 'legatee',[1] so that the transfer to him by the personal representatives of any asset is deemed to be a disposal at the asset's value at the date of death.[2]

Income Tax

Section 19(1) would appear to be applicable to Income Tax. This is relevant to the taxation of income arising between the date of death and the date of the court order and to ensure that the deceased as opposed to a beneficiary under the estate is treated as the 'settlor' of any disposition made under the 1975 Act.[3] It must be remembered that the provisions of section 142 of the Inheritance Tax Act 1984 and of section 62(6) of the Taxation of Chargeable Gains Act 1992 do not affect Income Tax and a deed of family arrangement has no retrospective effect for the purposes of Income Tax.

Tax Planning

It is important for practitioners to be aware of the fiscal implications of family provision orders, since taxation can substantially increase or decrease the real burden of an award of family provision to an applicant upon the persons interested in the deceased's estate. Careful appreciation of the fiscal implications can result in provision being ordered, in effect, substantially at the expense of the Exchequer.

For example:

> A deceased wills all his property to his son, leaving his widow without any provision. The widow makes a claim under the Act. If family provision were ordered giving the widow a life interest in half the

1. For the definition of 'legatee' see Taxation of Chargeable Gains Act 1992, s 64(2).
2. Taxation of Chargeable Gains Act 1992, s 62(4).
3. Eg Income and Corporation Taxes Act 1988, s 663 (settlement on children); s 673 (settlements in which settlor retains an interest); see *Harvey v Sivyer* [1986] Ch 119.

estate, the son's loss of immediate enjoyment of half the estate would be partially compensated by the reduced rates of Inheritance Tax borne by the son on the combined death of his father and the widow. Furthermore, if the widow's provision took the form of a purchase of a house, the son would probably have the benefit of a rise in value of the house free of capital gains tax.[4]

4. See Taxation of Chargeable Gains Act 1992, s 62(1), s 225.

Chapter 11

NORTHERN IRELAND

Family provision came late to Northern Ireland.[1] Attempts were made to introduce Bills which followed the scheme of the 1938 Act in 1937, 1938 and 1952 in the Northern Ireland Parliament but all of these failed.[2] As a result of the last abortive Bill a committee under the chairmanship of Judge Johnson QC was set up in 1953, which by a majority recommended that a scheme similar to the 1938 Act be introduced in Northern Ireland.[3] A minority, which included Professor FH Newark, dissented on the ground that the evidence adduced to the committee was insufficient to justify any limitation on freedom of testation. The conclusion of the Johnson Committee was eventually implemented by the Inheritance (Family Provision) Northern Ireland Act 1960, which followed the 1938 Act, as amended by the Intestates' Estates Act 1952, and the Matrimonial Causes (Property and Maintenance) Act 1958. The only important modification effected by the Northern Ireland legislation was a provision preventing the benefit of an order being charged or assigned without the sanction of the court.[4] In 1969 the changes made by the Family Provision Act 1966 were implemented by the Family Provision (Northern Ireland) Act 1969.

The entire legislation was repealed and replaced by the Inheritance (Provision for Family and Dependants) (Northern Ireland) Order 1979,[5] which applies to deaths of individuals domiciled in Northern Ireland[6] on or after 1 September 1979.[7] The Order almost entirely follows the 1975 Act. The Order provides that any statement made by the deceased shall be admissible in evidence to prove the truth of the statement, even though Northern Ireland has not enacted all the provisions of the Civil Evidence Act 1968.[8] The Order has been periodically amended to incorporate changes

1. On succession law generally in Northern Ireland, see Grattan, *Succession Law in Northern Ireland*.
2. Report of the Family Provision Committee (NI Cmd 330-1953), paras 14, 15.
3. Report of the Family Provision Committee (NI Cmd 330-1953).
4. S 7; this provision was not repeated in the 1979 Order.
5. SI 1979/924.
6. Art 3(1); on the effect of this and other conflict of laws implications, see Ch 3.
7. Art 1(2).
8. Art 9.

made in the English legislation, the most significant of which is the Succession Order 1996 which implements the provisions of the Law Reform (Succession) Act 1995.[9]

Reported case law shows an unjustified preference on the part of the Northern Irish judiciary for adult children[10] and for freely using the power to set aside transactions intended to defeat family provision claims.[11]The decisions on claims by surviving spouses[12] and infant children[13] have been exemplary and in some cases have shown a better approach than that adopted by the English judiciary.[14]

9. Succession (Northern Ireland) Order 1996, SI 1996/3163.
10. *Re McGarrell* [1983] 8 NIJB; *Re Creeney* [1984] NI 397.
11. *Re Weir* [1983] NIJB 45; *Morrow v Morrow*, Campbell J (5 April 1995, unreported).
12. *Re Weir* [1983] NIJB 45; *Morrow v Morrow*, Campbell J (5 April 1995, unreported); *McGuigan v McGuigan*, Kerr J (25 March 1996, unreported).
13. *Re Patton* [1986] NI 45; *Re Weir* [1983] NIJB 45.
14. See pp 185–186, ante.

Appendix A

Applications for Family Provision

PART 1

Year	HIGH COURT 1938 Act	HIGH COURT Matrimonial Causes Act[1]	HIGH COURT Variation of Maintenance Agreements[2]	COUNTY COURT Matrimonial Causes Act[1]	COUNTY COURT 1938 Act	COUNTY COURT Variation of Maintenance Agreements[2]	COUNTY COURT Grants of Representation[3]	Source
1939-51	2,500							4
1951	196							7
1960		31	0				248, 966	5
1961		39	2				266, 109	5
1962		37	1				285, 276	5
1963		45	0				290, 757	5
1964		35	2				289, 757	5
1965		39	1				273, 760	5
1966		51	6	County Court jurisdiction introduced			251, 921	5
1967		49	12	20	1		236, 251	5
1968		43	6	71	7	6	256, 019	5
1969		32	3	64	31	3	252, 148	5
1970		32	3	77	26	2	250, 804	5
1971			15	55	13	10	251, 748	5
1972			8	59	11	6	265, 958	5
1973			8	50	10	15	272, 095	5
1974	295	67	1	32	10	8	278, 005	6
1975	322	59	1	30	16		279, 311	6
1976			0		1	1	259, 183	6
1977					1	1	251, 703	6
1978					2		253, 868	6
1979					2		258, 011	6

PART 2

	HIGH COURT		*COUNTY COURT*		
Year	Chan Div 1975 Act, s 1	1975 Act, s 1	Matrimonial Causes Act 1973, s 36	Grants of Representation[3]	Source
1976	390	16	1	259, 183	
1977	409	51	1	251, 703	
1978	427	80		253, 868	6
1979	452	105		258, 011	6
1980	476	175	4	266, 914	6
1981	204	113	6	265, 838	6
1982	146	210	2	279, 127	6
1983	112			280, 832	6
1984	130			269, 171	6
1985	125			257, 074	6
1986	138			239, 027	6
1987	130			227, 682	6
1988	127			234, 475	6
1989	183			231, 883	6
1990	139			242, 654	6
1991	120	1 July 1991 County Courts given unlimited jurisdiction		258, 362	6
1992	109			247, 161	6
1993	59			246, 324	6
1994	56			252, 249	6
1995	99			248, 947	6

1. Matrimonial Causes (Property and Maintenance) Act 1958, s 3; Matrimonial Causes Act 1965, s 26.
2. Matrimonial Agreements Act 1957, s 2; Matrimonial Causes Act 1965, s 25; Matrimonial Proceedings and Property Act 1970, s 15; Matrimonial Causes Act 1973, s 36.
3. By way of comparison, in 1972 (a typical year), there were 591,900 deaths recorded in England and Wales (*Digest of Statistics*). In 1993 there were 162,679 divorces (*Judicial Statistics*).
4. Crane, 'Family Provision on Death in English Law', (1960) 35 NYUL Rev 984, at 1000.
5. *Civil Judicial Statistics* for the appropriate years.
6. *Judicial Statistics* for the appropriate years.
7. 498 Parl Deb HC, col 1090 (28 March 1952, Mr Hylton Foster).

For Part 2 of the Table, the High Court figures are for proceedings *commenced* in the Chancery Division. No figures are available for the Family Division. Until 1980 the figures are for both London and the Provinces, after 1980 the figures are for London only. The author would guess that roughly an equal number of proceedings are currently commenced in the Family Division as are commenced in the Chancery Division and that roughly an equal number of proceedings are commenced in the Provinces as are commenced in London.

The County Court figures in Part 2 of the Table are for *orders made*. No figures are available after 1982.

In 1995 there were recorded as having been made 1,775 Standing Searches, a figure that has remained fairly constant over the years. The principal use of a Standing Search is for 1975 Act applications. Taking into account that many applications under the 1975 Act are made without a Standing Search and that in many Standing searches no application under the 1975 Act is made, a total of 2,000 per annum for applications under the 1975 Act *in all courts* does not seem an unreasonable estimate.

Appendix B

Statutory Material

MATRIMONIAL CAUSES ACT 1973

(c 18)

An Act to consolidate certain enactments relating to matrimonial proceedings, maintenance agreements, and declarations of legitimacy, validity of marriage and British nationality, with amendments to give effect to recommendations of the Law Commission [23 May 1973]

PART II
FINANCIAL RELIEF FOR PARTIES TO MARRIAGE AND CHILDREN OF FAMILY

Variation, discharge and enforcement of certain orders, etc

31 Variation, discharge, etc, of certain orders for financial relief

* * *

(6) Where the person liable to make payments under a secured periodical payments order has died, an application under this section relating to that order [(and to any order made under section 24A(1) above which requires the proceeds of sale of property to be used for securing those payments) may be made by the person entitled to payments under the periodical payments order] or by the personal representatives of the deceased person, but no such application shall, except with the permission of the court, be made after the end of

the period of six months from the date on which representation in regard to the estate of that person is first taken out.

Note: Sub-s (6): words in square brackets substituted by the Matrimonial Homes and Property Act 1981, s 8(2)(b).

⋆ ⋆ ⋆

Maintenance agreements

36 Alteration of agreements by court after death of one party

(1) Where a maintenance agreement within the meaning of section 34 above provides for the continuation of payments under the agreement after the death of one of the parties and that party dies domiciled in England and Wales, the surviving party or the personal representatives of the deceased party may, subject to subsections (2) and (3) below, apply to the High Court or a county court for an order under section 35 above.

(2) An application under this section shall not, except with the permission of the High Court or a county court, be made after the end of the period of six months from the date on which representation in regard to the estate of the deceased is first taken out.

(3) A county court shall not entertain an application under this section, or an application for permission to make an application under this section, unless it would have jurisdiction by virtue of [section 22 of the Inheritance (Provision for Family and Dependants) Act 1975] (which confers jurisdiction on county courts in proceedings under [that Act if the value of the property mentioned in that section] does not exceed £5,000 or such larger sum as may be fixed by order of the Lord Chancellor) to hear and determine proceedings for an order under [section 2 of that Act] in relation to the deceased's estate.

(4) If a maintenance agreement is altered by a court on an application made in pursuance of subsection (1) above, the like consequences shall ensue as if the alteration had been made immediately before the death by agreement between the parties and for valuable consideration.

(5) The provisions of this section shall not render the personal representatives of the deceased liable for having distributed any part of the estate of the deceased after the expiration of the period of six months referred to in subsection (2) above on the ground that they ought to have taken into account the possibility that a court might permit an application by virtue of this section to be made by the surviving party after that period; but this subsection shall not prejudice any power to recover any part of the estate so distributed arising by virtue of the making of an order in pursuance of this section.

(6) Section 31(9) above shall apply for the purposes of subsection (2) above as it applies for the purposes of subsection (6) of section 31.

(7) Subsection (3) of [section 22 of the Inheritance (Provision for Family and Dependants) Act 1975 (which enables rules of court to provide for the transfer from a county court to the High Court or from the High Court to a county court of proceedings for an order under section 2 of that Act) and paragraphs (a) and (b) of subsection (4)] of that section (provisions relating to proceedings commenced in county court before coming into force of order of the Lord Chancellor under that section) shall apply in relation to proceedings consisting of any such application as is referred to in subsection (3) above as they apply in relation to [proceedings for an order under section 2 of that Act].

Note: Sub-ss (3), (7): words in square brackets substituted by the Inheritance (Provision for Family and Dependants) Act 1975, s 26(1).

INHERITANCE (PROVISION FOR FAMILY AND DEPENDANTS) ACT 1975

(c 63)

An Act to make fresh provisions for empowering the court to make orders for the making out of the estate of a deceased person of provision for the spouse, former spouse, child, child of the family or dependant of that person; and for matters connected therewith [12 November 1975]

Note: Capital transfer tax: except in relation to a liability to tax arising before 25 July 1986 capital transfer tax shall be known as inheritance tax and the Capital Transfer Tax Act 1984 may be cited as the Inheritance Tax Act 1984, by virtue of the Finance Act 1986, s 100.

Powers of court to order financial provision from deceased's estate

1 Application for financial provision from deceased's estate

(1) Where after the commencement of this Act a person dies domiciled in England and Wales and is survived by any of the following persons—

(a) the wife or husband of the deceased;

(b) a former wife or former husband of the deceased who has not remarried;

[(ba) any person (not being a person included in paragraph (a) or (b) above) to whom subsection (1A) below applies;]

(c) a child of the deceased;

(d) any person (not being a child of the deceased) who, in the case of any marriage to which the deceased was at any time a party, was treated by the deceased as a child of the family in relation to that marriage;

(e) any person (not being a person included in the foregoing paragraphs of this subsection) who immediately before the death of the deceased was being maintained, either wholly or partly, by the deceased;

that person may apply to the court for an order under section 2 of this Act on the ground that the disposition of the deceased's estate effected by his will or the law relating to intestacy, or the combination of his will and that law, is not such as to make reasonable financial provision for the applicant.

[(1A) This subsection applies to a person if the deceased died on or after 1st January 1996 and, during the whole of the period of two years ending immediately before the date when the deceased died, the person was living—

(a) in the same household as the deceased, and

(b) as the husband or wife of the deceased.]

(2) In this Act "reasonable financial provision"—

(a) in the case of an application made by virtue of subsection (1)(a) above by the husband or wife of the deceased (except where *the marriage with the deceased was the subject of a decree of judicial separation and at the date of death the decree was in force* and the separation was continuing), means such financial provision as it would be reasonable in all the circumstances of the case for a husband or wife to receive, whether or not that provision is required for his or her maintenance;

(b) in the case of any other application made by virtue of subsection (1) above, means such financial provision as it would be reasonable in all the circumstances of the case for the applicant to receive for his maintenance.

(3) For the purposes of subsection (1)(e) above, a person shall be treated as being maintained by the deceased, either wholly or partly, as the case may be, if the deceased, otherwise than for full valuable consideration, was making a substantial contribution in money or money's worth towards the reasonable needs of that person.

Notes: Sub-s (1): para (ba) inserted by the Law Reform (Succession) Act 1995, s 2(1), (2).

Sub-s (1A): inserted by the Law Reform (Succession) Act 1995, s 2(1), (3).

Sub-s (2): words in italics in para (a) substituted by the words ", at the date of death, a separation order under the Family Law Act 1996 was in force in relation to the marriage" by the Family Law Act 1996, s 66(1), Sch 8, Pt I, para 27(1), (2), subject to savings in s 66(2) of, and Sch 9, para 5 to, the 1996 Act, as from a day to be appointed.

2 Powers of court to make orders

(1) Subject to the provisions of this Act, where an application is made for an order under this section, the court may, if it is satisfied that the disposition of the deceased's estate effected by his will or

the law relating to intestacy, or the combination of his will and that law, is not such as to make reasonable financial provision for the applicant, make any one or more of the following orders—

(a) an order for the making to the applicant out of the net estate of the deceased of such periodical payments and for such term as may be specified in the order;
(b) an order for the payment to the applicant out of that estate of a lump sum of such amount as may be so specified;
(c) an order for the transfer to the applicant of such property comprised in that estate as may be so specified;
(d) an order for the settlement for the benefit of the applicant of such property comprised in that estate as may be so specified;
(e) an order for the acquisition out of property comprised in that estate of such property as may be so specified and for the transfer of the property so acquired to the applicant or for the settlement thereof for his benefit;
(f) an order varying any ante-nuptial or post-nuptial settlement (including such a settlement made by will) made on the parties to a marriage to which the deceased was one of the parties, the variation being for the benefit of the surviving party to that marriage, or any child of that marriage, or any person who was treated by the deceased as a child of the family in relation to that marriage.

(2) An order under subsection (1)(a) above providing for the making out of the net estate of the deceased of periodical payments may provide for—

(a) payments of such amount as may be specified in the order,
(b) payments equal to the whole of the income of the net estate or of such portion thereof as may be so specified,
(c) payments equal to the whole of the income of such part of the net estate as the court may direct to be set aside or appropriated for the making out of the income thereof of payments under this section,

or may provide for the amount of the payments or any of them to be determined in any other way the court thinks fit.

(3) Where an order under subsection (1)(a) above provides for the making of payments of an amount specified in the order, the order may direct that such part of the net estate as may be so specified shall be set aside or appropriated for the making out of the income thereof of those payments; but no larger part of the net estate shall be so set aside or appropriated than is sufficient, at the date of the order, to produce by the income thereof the amount required for the making of those payments.

(4) An order under this section may contain such consequential and supplemental provisions as the court thinks necessary or

expedient for the purpose of giving effect to the order or for the purpose of securing that the order operates fairly as between one beneficiary of the estate of the deceased and another and may, in particular, but without prejudice to the generality of this subsection—

(a) order any person who holds any property which forms part of the net estate of the deceased to make such payment or transfer such property as may be specified in the order;
(b) varying the disposition of the deceased's estate effected by the will or the law relating to intestacy, or by both the will and the law relating to intestacy, in such manner as the court thinks fair and reasonable having regard to the provisions of the order and all the circumstances of the case;
(c) confer on the trustees of any property which is the subject of an order under this section such powers as appear to the court to be necessary or expedient.

3 Matters to which court is to have regard in exercising powers under s 2

(1) Where an application is made for an order under section 2 of this Act, the court shall, in determining whether the disposition of the deceased's estate effected by his will or the law relating to intestacy, or the combination of his will and that law, is such as to make reasonable financial provision for the applicant and, if the court considers that reasonable financial provision has not been made, in determining whether and in what manner it shall exercise its powers under that section, have regard to the following matters, that is to say—

(a) the financial resources and financial needs which the applicant has or is likely to have in the foreseeable future;
(b) the financial resources and financial needs which any other applicant for an order under section 2 of this Act has or is likely to have in the foreseeable future;
(c) the financial resources and financial needs which any beneficiary of the estate of the deceased has or is likely to have in the foreseeable future;
(d) any obligations and responsibilities which the deceased had towards any applicant for an order under the said section 2 or towards any beneficiary of the estate of the deceased;
(e) the size and nature of the net estate of the deceased;
(f) any physical or mental disability of any applicant for an order under the said section 2 or any beneficiary of the estate of the deceased;
(g) any other matter, including the conduct of the applicant or any other person, which in the circumstances of the case the court may consider relevant.

(2) Without prejudice to the generality of paragraph (g) of subsection (1) above, where an application for an order under section 2 of this Act is made by virtue of section 1(1)(a) or 1(1)(b) of this Act, the court shall, in addition to the matters specifically mentioned in paragraphs (a) to (f) of that subsection, have regard to—

(a) the age of the applicant and the duration of the marriage;

(b) the contribution made by the applicant to the welfare of the family of the deceased, including any contribution made by looking after the home or caring for the family;

and, in the case of an application by the wife or husband of the deceased, the court shall also, unless at the date of death a *decree of judicial separation* was in force and the separation was continuing, have regard to the provision which the applicant might reasonably have expected to receive if on the day on which the deceased died the marriage, instead of being terminated by death, had been terminated by a *decree of divorce*.

[(2A) Without prejudice to the generality of paragraph (g) of subsection (1) above, where an application for an order under section 2 of this Act is made by virtue of section 1(1)(ba) of this Act, the court shall, in addition to the matters specifically mentioned in paragraphs (a) to (f) of that subsection, have regard to—

(a) the age of the applicant and the length of the period during which the applicant lived as the husband or wife of the deceased and in the same household as the deceased;

(b) the contribution made by the applicant to the welfare of the family of the deceased, including any contribution made by looking after the home or caring for the family.]

(3) Without prejudice to the generality of paragraph (g) of subsection (1) above, where an application for an order under section 2 of this Act is made by virtue of section 1(1)(c) or 1(1)(d) of this Act, the court shall, in addition to the matters specifically mentioned in paragraphs (a) to (f) of that subsection, have regard to the manner in which the applicant was being or in which he might expect to be educated or trained, and where the application is made by virtue of section 1(1)(d) the court shall also have regard—

(a) to whether the deceased had assumed any responsibility for the applicant's maintenance and, if so, to the extent to which and the basis upon which the deceased assumed that responsibility and to the length of time for which the deceased discharged that responsibility;

(b) to whether in assuming and discharging that responsibility the deceased did so knowing that the applicant was not his own child;

(c) to the liability of any other person to maintain the applicant.

(4) Without prejudice to the generality of paragraph (g) of subsection (1) above, where an application for an order under section 2 of this Act is made by virtue of section 1(1)(e) of this Act, the court shall, in addition to the matters specifically mentioned in paragraphs (a) to (f) of that subsection, have regard to the extent to which and the basis upon which the deceased assumed responsibility for the maintenance of the applicant, and to the length of time for which the deceased discharged that responsibility.

(5) In considering the matters to which the court is required to have regard under this section, the court shall take into account the facts as known to the court at the date of the hearing.

(6) In considering the financial resources of any person for the purposes of this section the court shall take into account his earning capacity and in considering the financial needs of any person for the purposes of this section the court shall take into account his financial obligations and responsibilities.

Notes: Sub-s (2): first words in italics substituted by the words "separation order under the Family Law Act 1996" and second words in italics substituted by the words "a divorce order" by the Family Law Act 1996, s 66(1), Sch 8, Pt I, para 27(1), (3), subject to savings in s 66(2) of, and Sch 9, para 5 to, the 1996 Act, as from a day to be appointed.

Sub-s (2A): inserted by the Law Reform (Succession) Act 1995, s 2(1), (4).

4 Time-limit for applications

An application for an order under section 2 of this Act shall not, except with the permission of the court, be made after the end of the period of six months from the date on which representation with respect to the estate of the deceased is first taken out.

5 Interim orders

(1) Where on an application for an order under section 3 of this Act it appears to the court—

(a) that the applicant is in immediate need of financial assistance, but it is not yet possible to determine what order (if any) should be made under that section; and

(b) that property forming part of the net estate of the deceased is or can be made available to meet the need of the applicant;

the court may order that, subject to such conditions or restrictions, if any, as the court may impose and to any further order of the court, there shall be paid to the applicant out of the net estate of the deceased such sum or sums and (if more than one) at such intervals as the court thinks reasonable; and the court may order that, subject to the provisions of this Act, such payments are to be made until such date as the court may specify, not being later than the date on which the court either makes an order under the said section 2 or decides not to exercise its powers under that section.

(2) Subsections (2), (3) and (4) of section 2 of this Act shall apply in relation to an order under this section as they apply in relation to an order under that section.

(3) In determining what order, if any, should be made under this section the court shall, so far as the urgency of the case admits, have regard to the same matters as those to which the court is required to have regard under section 3 of this Act.

(4) An order made under section 2 of this Act may provide that any sum paid to the applicant by virtue of this section shall be treated to such an extent and in such manner as may be provided by that order as having been paid on account of any payment provided for by that order.

6 Variation, discharge, etc of orders for periodical payments

(1) Subject to the provisions of this Act, where the court has made an order under section 2(1)(a) of this Act (in this section referred to as "the original order") for the making of periodical payments to any person (in this section referred to as "the original recipient"), the court, on an application under this section, shall have power by order to vary or discharge the original order or to suspend any provision of it temporarily and to revive the operation of any provision so suspended.

(2) Without prejudice to the generality of subsection (1) above, an order made on an application for the variation of the original order may—

(a) provide for the making out of any relevant property of such periodical payments and for such term as may be specified in the order to any person who has applied, or would but for section 4 of this Act be entitled to apply, for an order under section 2 of this Act (whether or not, in the case of any application, an order was made in favour of the applicant);

(b) provide for the payment out of any relevant property of a lump sum of such amount as may be so specified to the original recipient or to any such person as is mentioned in paragraph (a) above;

(c) provide for the transfer of the relevant property, or such part thereof as may be so specified, to the original recipient or to any such person as is so mentioned.

(3) Where the original order provides that any periodical payments payable thereunder to the original recipient are to cease on the occurrence of an event specified in the order (other than the remarriage of a former wife or former husband) or on the expiration of a period so specified, then, if, before the end of the period of six months from the date of the occurrence of that event or of the expiration of that period, an application is made for an order under

this section, the court shall have power to make any order which it would have had power to make if the application had been made before the date (whether in favour of the original recipient or any such person as is mentioned in subsection (2)(a) above and whether having effect from that date or from such later date as the court may specify).

(4) Any reference in this section to the original order shall include a reference to an order made under this section and any reference in this section to the original recipient shall include a reference to any person to whom periodical payments are required to be made by virtue of an order under this section.

(5) An application under this section may be made by any of the following persons, that is to say—

(a) any person who by virtue of section 1(1) of this Act has applied, or would but for section 4 of this Act be entitled to apply, for an order under section 2 of this Act,
(b) the personal representatives of the deceased,
(c) the trustees of any relevant property, and
(d) any beneficiary of the estate of the deceased.

(6) An order under this section may only affect—

(a) property the income of which is at the date of the order applicable wholly or in part for the making of periodical payments to any person who has applied for an order under this Act, or
(b) in the case of an application under subsection (3) above in respect of payments which have ceased to be payable on the occurrence of an event or the expiration of a period, property the income of which was so applicable immediately before the occurrence of that event or the expiration of that period, as the case may be,

and any such property as is mentioned in paragraph (a) or (b) above is in subsections (2) and (5) above referred to as "relevant property".

(7) In exercising the powers conferred by this section the court shall have regard to all circumstances of the case, including any change in any of the matters to which the court was required to have regard when making the order to which the application relates.

(8) Where the court makes an order under this section, it may give such consequential directions as it thinks necessary or expedient having regard to the provisions of the order.

(9) No such order as is mentioned in section 2(1)(d), (e) or (f), 9, 10 or 11 of this Act shall be made on an application under this section.

(10) For the avoidance of doubt it is hereby declared that, in relation to an order which provides for the making of periodical payments which are to cease on the occurrence of an event specified

in the order (other than the remarriage of a former wife or former husband) or on the expiration of a period so specified, the power to vary an order includes power to provide for the making of periodical payments after the expiration of that period or the occurrence of that event.

7 Payment of lump sums by instalments

(1) An order under section 2(1)(b) or 6(2)(b) of this Act for the payment of a lump sum may provide for the payment of that sum by instalments of such amount as may be specified in the order.

(2) Where an order is made by virtue of subsection (1) above, the court shall have power, on an application made by the person to whom the lump sum is payable, by the personal representatives of the deceased or by the trustees of the property out of which the lump sum is payable, to vary that order by varying the number of instalments payable, the amount of any instalment and the date on which any instalment becomes payable.

Property available for financial provision

8 Property treated as part of "net estate"

(1) Where a deceased person has in accordance with the provisions of any enactment nominated any person to receive any sum of money or other property on his death and that nomination is in force at the time of his death, that sum of money, after deducting therefrom any [inheritance tax] payable in respect thereof, or that other property, to the extent of the value thereof at the date of the death of the deceased after deducting therefrom any [inheritance tax] so payable, shall be treated for the purposes of this Act as part of the net estate of the deceased; but this subsection shall not render any person liable for having paid that sum or transferred that other property to the person named in the nomination in accordance with the directions given in the nomination.

(2) Where any sum of money or other property is received by any person as a donatio mortis causa made by a deceased person, that sum of money, after deducting therefrom any [inheritance tax] payable thereon, or that other property, to the extent of the value thereof at the date of the death of the deceased after deducting therefrom any [inheritance tax] so payable, shall be treated for the purposes of this Act as part of the net estate of the deceased; but this subsection shall not render any person liable for having paid that sum or transferred that other property in order to give effect to that donatio mortis causa.

(3) The amount of [inheritance tax] to be deducted for the purposes of this section shall not exceed the amount of that tax which has been borne by the person nominated by the deceased or, as the

case may be, the person who has received a sum of money or other property as a donatio mortis causa.

9 Property held on a joint tenancy

(1) Where a deceased person was immediately before his death beneficially entitled to a joint tenancy of any property, then, if, before the end of the period of six months from the date on which representation with respect to the estate of the deceased was first taken out, an application is made for an order under section 2 of this Act, the court for the purpose of facilitating the making of financial provision for the applicant under this Act may order that the deceased's severable share of that property, at the value thereof immediately before his death, shall, to such extent as appears to the court to be just in all the circumstances of the case, be treated for the purposes of this Act as part of the net estate of the deceased.

(2) In determining the extent to which any severable share is to be treated as part of the net estate of the deceased by virtue of an order under subsection (1) above, the court shall have regard to any [inheritance tax] payable in respect of that severable share.

(3) Where an order is made under subsection (1) above, the provisions of this section shall not render any person liable for anything done by him before the order was made.

(4) For the avoidance of doubt it is hereby declared that for the purposes of this section there may be a joint tenancy of a chose in action.

Powers of court in relation to transactions intended to defeat applications for financial provision

10 Dispositions intended to defeat applications for financial provision

(1) Where an application is made to the court for an order under section 2 of this Act, the applicant may, in the proceedings on that application, apply to the court for an order under subsection (2) below.

(2) Where on an application under subsection (1) above the court is satisfied—

(a) that, less than six years before the date of the death of the deceased, the deceased with the intention of defeating an application for financial provision under this Act made a disposition, and

(b) that full valuable consideration for that disposition was not given by the person to whom or for the benefit of whom the disposition was made (in this section referred to as "the donee") or by any other person, and

(c) that the exercise of the powers conferred by this section would facilitate the making of financial provision for the applicant under this Act,

then, subject to the provisions of this section and of sections 12 and 13 of this Act, the court may order the donee (whether or not at the date of the order he holds any interest in the property disposed of to him or for his benefit by the deceased) to provide, for the purpose of the making of that financial provision, such sum of money or other property as may be specified in the order.

(3) Where an order is made under subsection (2) above as respects any disposition made by the deceased which consisted of the payment of money to or for the benefit of the donee, the amount of any sum of money or the value of any property ordered to be provided under that subsection shall not exceed the amount of the payment made by the deceased after deducting therefrom any [inheritance tax] borne by the donee in respect of that payment.

(4) Where an order is made under subsection (2) above as respects any disposition made by the deceased which consisted of the transfer of property (other than a sum of money) to or for the benefit of the donee, the amount of any sum of money or the value of any property ordered to be provided under that subsection shall not exceed the value at the date of the death of the deceased of the property disposed of by him to or for the benefit of the donee (or if that property has been disposed of by the person to whom it was transferred by the deceased, the value at the date of that disposal thereof) after deducting therefrom any capital transfer tax borne by the donee in respect of the transfer of that property by the deceased.

(5) Where an application (in this subsection referred to as "the original application") is made for an order under subsection (2) above in relation to any disposition, then, if on an application under this subsection by the donee or by any applicant for an order under section 2 of this Act the court is satisfied—

(a) that, less than six years before the date of the death of the deceased, the deceased with the intention of defeating an application for financial provision under this Act made a disposition other than the disposition which is the subject of the original application, and

(b) that full valuable consideration for that other disposition was not given by the person to whom or for the benefit of whom that other disposition was made or by any other person,

the court may exercise in relation to the person to whom or for the benefit of whom that other disposition was made the powers which the court would have had under subsection (2) above if the original application had been made in respect of that other disposition and the court had been satisfied as to the matters set out in paragraphs (a), (b) and (c) of that subsection; and where any application is made under this subsection, any reference in this section (except in subsection (2)(b)) to the donee shall include a reference to the person to whom or for the benefit of whom that other disposition was made.

(6) In determining whether and in what manner to exercise its powers under this section, the court shall have regard to the circumstances in which any disposition was made and any valuable consideration which was given therefor, the relationship, if any, of the donee to the deceased, the conduct and financial resources of the donee and all the other circumstances of the case.

(7) In this section "disposition" does not include—

(a) any provision in a will, any such nomination as is mentioned in section 8(1) of this Act or any donatio mortis causa, or

(b) any appointment of property made, otherwise than by will, in the exercise of a special power of appointment,

but, subject to these exceptions, includes any payment of money (including the payment of a premium under a policy of assurance) and any conveyance, assurance, appointment or gift of property of any description, whether made by an instrument or otherwise.

(8) The provisions of this section do not apply to any disposition made before the commencement of this Act.

11 Contracts to leave property by will

(1) Where an application is made to a court for an order under section 2 of this Act, the applicant may, in the proceedings on that application, apply to the court for an order under this section.

(2) Where on an application under subsection (1) above the court is satisfied—

(a) that the deceased made a contract by which he agreed to leave by his will a sum of money or other property to any person or by which he agreed that a sum of money or other property would be paid or transferred to any person out of his estate, and

(b) that the deceased made that contract with the intention of defeating an application for financial provision under this Act, and

(c) that when the contract was made full valuable consideration for that contract was not given or promised by the person with whom or for the benefit of whom the contract was made (in this section referred to as "the donee") or by any other person, and

(d) that the exercise of the powers conferred by this section would facilitate the making of financial provision for the applicant under this Act,

then, subject to the provisions of this section and of sections 12 and 13 of this Act, the court may make any one or more of the following orders, that is to say—

(i) if any money has been paid or any other property has been transferred to or for the benefit of the donee in accordance with the contract, an order directing the donee to provide, for the purpose of the making of that financial provision, such sum of money or other property as may be specified in the order;

(ii) if the money or all the money has not been paid or the property or all the property has not been transferred in accordance with the contract, an order directing the personal representatives not to make any payment or transfer any property, or not to make any further payment or transfer any further property, as the case may be, in accordance therewith or directing the personal representatives only to make such payment or transfer such property as may be specified in the order.

(3) Notwithstanding anything in subsection (2) above, the court may exercise its powers thereunder in relation to any contract made by the deceased only to the extent that the court considers that the amount of any sum of money paid or to be paid or the value of any property transferred or to be transferred in accordance with the contract exceeds the value of any valuable consideration given or to be given for that contract, and for this purpose the court shall have regard to the value of property at the date of the hearing.

(4) In determining whether and in what manner to exercise its powers under this section, the court shall have regard to the circumstances in which the contract was made, the relationship, if any, of the donee to the deceased, the conduct and financial resources of the donee and all the other circumstances of the case.

(5) Where an order has been made under subsection (2) above in relation to any contract the rights of any person to enforce that contract or to recover damages or to obtain other relief for the breach thereof shall be subject to any adjustment made by the court under section 12(3) of this Act and shall survive to such extent only as is consistent with giving effect to the terms of that order.

(6) The provisions of this section do not apply to a contract made before the commencement of this Act.

12 Provisions supplementary to ss 10 and 11

(1) Where the exercise of any of the powers conferred by section 10 or 11 of this Act is conditional on the court being satisfied that a disposition or contract was made by a deceased person with the intention of defeating an application for financial provision under this Act, that condition shall be fulfilled if the court is of the opinion that, on a balance of probabilities, the intention of the deceased (though not necessarily his sole intention) in making the disposition

or contract was to prevent an order for financial provision being made under this Act or to reduce the amount of the provision which might otherwise be granted by an order thereunder.

(2) Where an application is made under section 11 of this Act with respect to any contract made by the deceased and no valuable consideration was given or promised by any person for that contract then, notwithstanding anything in subsection (1) above, it shall be presumed, unless the contrary is shown, that the deceased made that contract with the intention of defeating an application for financial provision under this Act.

(3) Where the court makes an order under section 10 or 11 of this Act it may give such consequential directions as it thinks fit (including directions requiring the making of any payment or the transfer of any property) for giving effect to the order or for securing a fair adjustment of the rights of the persons affected thereby.

(4) Any power conferred on the court by the said section 10 or 11 to order the donee, in relation to any disposition or contract, to provide any sum of money or other property shall be exercisable in like manner in relation to the personal representative of the donee, and—

(a) any reference in section 10(4) to the disposal of property by the donee shall include a reference to disposal by the personal representative of the donee, and

(b) any reference in section 10(5) to an application by the donee under that subsection shall include a reference to an application by the personal representative of the donee;

but the court shall not have power under the said section 10 or 11 to make an order in respect of any property forming part of the estate of the donee which has been distributed by the personal representative; and the personal representative shall not be liable for having distributed any such property before he has notice of the making of an application under the said section 10 or 11 on the ground that he ought to have taken into account the possibility that such an application would be made.

13 Provisions as to trustees in relation to ss 10 and 11

(1) Where an application is made for—

(a) an order under section 10 of this Act in respect of a disposition made by the deceased to any person as a trustee, or

(b) an order under section 11 of this Act in respect of any payment made or property transferred, in accordance with a contract made by the deceased, to any person as a trustee,

the powers of the court under the said section 10 or 11 to order that trustee to provide a sum of money or other property shall be subject to the following limitation (in addition, in a case of an application under section 10, to any provision regarding the deduction of [inheritance tax]) namely, that the amount of any sum of money or the value of any property ordered to be provided—

(i) in the case of an application in respect of a disposition which consisted of the payment of money or an application in respect of the payment of money in accordance with a contract, shall not exceed the aggregate of so much of that money as is at the date of the order in the hands of the trustee and the value at that date of any property which represents that money or is derived therefrom and is at that date in the hands of the trustee;

(ii) in the case of an application in respect of a disposition which consisted of the transfer of property (other than a sum of money) or an application in respect of the transfer of property (other than a sum of money) in accordance with a contract, shall not exceed the aggregate of the value at the date of the order of so much of that property as is at that date in the hands of the trustee and the value at that date of any property which represents the first mentioned property or is derived therefrom and is at that date in the hands of the trustee.

(2) Where any such application is made in respect of a disposition made to any person as a trustee or in respect of any payment made or property transferred in pursuance of a contract to any person as a trustee, the trustee shall not be liable for having distributed any money or other property on the ground that he ought to have taken into account the possibility that such an application would be made.

(3) Where any such application is made in respect of a disposition made to any person as a trustee or in respect of any payment made or property transferred in accordance with a contract to any person as a trustee, any reference in the said section 10 or 11 to the donee shall be construed as including a reference to the trustee or trustees for the time being of the trust in question and any reference in subsection (1) or (2) above to a trustee shall be construed in the same way.

Special provisions relating to cases of divorce, separation, etc

14 Provision as to cases where no financial relief was granted in divorce proceedings, etc

(1) Where, within twelve months from the date on which a decree of divorce or nullity of marriage has been made absolute or a decree of judicial separation has been granted, a party to the marriage dies and—

(a) an application for a financial provision order under *section 23* of the Matrimonial Causes Act 1973 or a property adjustment order under *section 24* of that Act has not been made by the other party to that marriage, or

(b) such an application has been made but the proceedings thereon have not been determined at the time of the death of the deceased,

then, if an application for an order under section 2 of this Act is made by that other party, the court shall, notwithstanding anything in section 1 or section 3 of this Act, have power, if it thinks it just to do so, to treat that party for the purposes of that application as if *the decree of divorce or nullity of marriage had not been made absolute or the decree of judicial separation had not been granted, as the case may be.*

(2) This section shall not apply in relation to a *decree of judicial separation* unless at the date of the death of the deceased *the decree* was in force and the separation was continuing.

Notes: Sub-s (1): first words in italics substituted by the words "a divorce order or separation order has been made under the Family Law Act 1996 in relation to a marriage or a decree of nullity of marriage has been made absolute", second words in italics substituted by the words "section 22A or 23", third words in italics substituted by the words "section 23A or 24", and words in italics after para (b) substituted by the words ", as the case may be, the divorce order or separation order had not been made or the decree of nullity had not been made absolute", by the Family Law Act 1996, s 66(1), Sch 8, Pt I, para 27(1), (4)(a)–(c), subject to savings in s 66(2) of, and Sch 9, para 5 to, the 1996 Act, as from a day to be appointed.

Sub-s (2): first words in italics substituted by the words "separation order" and second words in italics substituted by the words "the order" by the Family Law Act 1996, s 66(1), Sch 8, Pt I, para 27(1), (4)(d), subject to savings in s 66(2) of, and Sch 9, para 5 to, the 1996 Act, as from a day to be appointed.

15 Restriction imposed in divorce proceedings, etc on application under this Act

[(1) On the grant of a decree of divorce, a decree of nullity of marriage or a decree of judicial separation or at any time thereafter the court, if it considers it just to do so, may, on the application of either party to the marriage, order that the other party to the marriage shall not on the death of the applicant be entitled to apply for an order under section 2 of this Act.

In this subsection "the court" means the High Court or, where a county court has jurisdiction by virtue of Part V of the Matrimonial and Family Proceedings Act 1984, a county court.]

(2) In the case of a decree of divorce or nullity of marriage an order may be made under subsection (1) above before or after the decree is made absolute, but if it is made before the decree is made absolute it shall not take effect unless the decree is made absolute.

(3) Where an order made under subsection (1) above on the grant of a decree of divorce or nullity of marriage has come into force with respect to a party to a marriage, then, on the death of the other

party to that marriage, the court shall not entertain any application for an order under section 2 of this Act made by the first-mentioned party.

(4) Where an order made under subsection (1) above on the grant of a decree of judicial separation has come into force with respect to any party to a marriage, then, if the other party to that marriage dies while the decree is in force and the separation is continuing, the court shall not entertain any application for an order under section 2 of this Act made by the first-mentioned party.

Notes: Sub-s (1): substituted by the Matrimonial and Family Proceedings Act 1984, s 8; words in italics substituted by the Family Law Act 1996, s 66(1), Sch 8, Pt I, para 27(1), (5), subject to savings in s 66(2) of, and Sch 9, para 5 to, the 1996 Act, as from a day to be appointed, as follows—

"At any time when the court—

(a) has jurisdiction under section 23A or 24 of the Matrimonial Causes Act 1973 to make a property adjustment order in relation to a marriage; or

(b) would have such jurisdiction if either the jurisdiction had not already been exercised or an application for such an order were made with the leave of the court,".

Sub-ss (2)–(4): substituted by the Family Law Act 1996, s 66(1), Sch 8, Pt I, para 27(1), (6), subject to savings in s 66(2) of, and Sch 9, para 5 to, the 1996 Act, as follows—

"(2) An order made under subsection (1) above with respect to any party to a marriage has effect in accordance with subsection (3) below at any time—

(a) after the marriage has been dissolved;

(b) after a decree of nullity has been made absolute in relation to the marriage; and

(c) while a separation order under the Family Law Act 1996 is in force in relation to the marriage and the separation is continuing.

(3) If at any time when an order made under subsection (1) above with respect to any party to a marriage has effect the other party to the marriage dies, the court shall not entertain any application made by the surviving party to the marriage for an order under section 2 of this Act.".

[15A Restriction imposed in proceedings under Matrimonial and Family Proceedings Act 1984 on application under this Act

(1) On making an order under section 17 of the Matrimonial and Family Proceedings Act 1984 (orders for financial provision and property adjustment following overseas divorces, etc) the court, if it considers it just to do so, may, on the application of either party to the marriage, order that the other party to the marriage shall not on the death of the applicant be entitled to apply for an order under section 2 of this Act.

In this subsection "the court" means the High Court or, where a county court has jurisdiction by virtue of Part V of the Matrimonial and Family Proceedings Act 1984, a county court.

(2) Where an order under subsection (1) above has been made with respect to a party to a marriage which has been dissolved or

annulled, then, on the death of the other party to that marriage, the court shall not entertain an application under section 2 of this Act made by the first-mentioned party.

(3) Where an order under subsection (1) above has been made with respect to a party to a marriage the parties to which have been legally separated, then, if the other party to the marriage dies while the legal separation is in force, the court shall not entertain an application under section 2 of this Act made by the first-mentioned party.]

Note: Inserted by the Matrimonial and Family Proceedings Act 1984, s 25.

16 Variation and discharge of secured periodical payments orders made under Matrimonial Causes Act 1973

(1) Where an application for an order under section 2 of this Act is made to the court by any person who was at the time of the death of the deceased entitled to payments from the deceased under a secured periodical payments order made under the Matrimonial Causes Act 1973, then, in the proceedings on that application, the court shall have power, if an application is made under this section by that person or by the personal representative of the deceased, to vary or discharge that periodical payments order or to revive the operation of any provision thereof which has been suspended under section 31 of that Act.

(2) In exercising the powers conferred by this section the court shall have regard to all the circumstances of the case, including any order which the court proposes to make under section 2 or section 5 of this Act and any change (whether resulting from the death of the deceased or otherwise) in any of the matters to which the court was required to have regard when making the secured periodical payments order.

(3) The powers exercisable by the court under this section in relation to an order shall be exercisable also in relation to any instrument executed in pursuance of the order.

17 Variation and revocation of maintenance agreements

(1) Where an application for an order under section 2 of this Act is made to the court by any person who was at the time of the death of the deceased entitled to payments from the deceased under a maintenance agreement which provided for the continuation of payments under the agreement after the death of the deceased, then, in the proceedings on that application, the court shall have power, if an application is made under this section by that person or by the personal representative of the deceased, to vary or revoke that agreement.

(2) In exercising the powers conferred by this section the court shall have regard to all the circumstances of the case, including any order which the court proposes to make under section 2 or section 5 of this Act and any change (whether resulting from the death of the deceased or otherwise) in any of the circumstances in the light of which the agreement was made.

(3) If a maintenance agreement is varied by the court under this section the like consequences shall ensue as if the variation had been made immediately before the death of the deceased by agreement between the parties and for valuable consideration.

(4) In this section "maintenance agreement", in relation to a deceased person, means any agreement made, whether in writing or not and whether before or after the commencement of this Act, by the deceased with any person with whom he entered into a marriage, being an agreement which contained provisions governing the rights and liabilities towards one another when living separately of the parties to that marriage (whether or not the marriage has been dissolved or annulled) in respect of the making or securing of payments or the disposition or use of any property, including such rights and liabilities with respect to the maintenance or education of any child, whether or not a child of the deceased or a person who was treated by the deceased as a child of the family in relation to that marriage.

18 Availability of court's powers under this Act in applications under ss 31 and 36 of the Matrimonial Causes Act 1973

(1) Where—

(a) a person against whom a secured periodical payments order was made under the Matrimonial Causes Act 1973 has died and an application is made under section 31(6) of that Act for the variation or discharge of that order or for the revival of the operation of any provision thereof which has been suspended, or

(b) a party to a maintenance agreement within the meaning of section 34 of that Act has died, the agreement being one which provides for the continuation of payments thereunder after the death of one of the parties, and an application is made under section 36(1) of that Act for the alteration of the agreement under section 35 thereof,

the court shall have power to direct that the application made under the said section 31(6) or 36(1) shall be deemed to have been accompanied by an application for an order under section 2 of this Act.

(2) Where the court gives a direction under subsection (1) above it shall have power, in the proceedings on the application under the said section 31(6) or 36(1), to make any order which the court would have had power to make under the provisions of this Act if the application under the said section 31(6) or 36(1), as the case may be, had been made jointly with an application for an order under the said section 2; and the court shall have power to give such consequential directions as may be necessary for enabling the court to exercise any of the powers available to the court under this Act in the case of an application for an order under section 2.

(3) Where an order made under section 15(1) of this Act is in force with respect to a party to a marriage, the court shall not give a direction under subsection (1) above with respect to any application made under the said section 31(6) or 36(1) by that party on the death of the other party.

Miscellaneous and supplementary provisions

19 Effect, duration and form of orders

(1) Where an order is made under section 2 of this Act then for all purposes, including the purposes of the enactments relating to [inheritance tax], the will or the law relating to intestacy, or both the will and the law relating to intestacy, as the case may be, shall have effect and be deemed to have had effect as from the deceased's death subject to the provisions of the order.

(2) Any order made under section 2 or 5 of this Act in favour of—

(a) an applicant who was the former husband or former wife of the deceased, or

(b) an applicant who was the husband or wife of the deceased in a case where the marriage with the deceased was the subject of a decree of judicial separation and at the date of death the decree was in force and the separation was continuing,

shall, in so far as it provides for the making of periodical payments, cease to have effect on the remarriage of the applicant, except in relation to any arrears due under the order on the date of the remarriage.

(3) A copy of every order made under this Act [other than an order made under section 15(1) of this Act] shall be sent to the principal registry of the Family Division for entry and filing, and a memorandum of the order shall be endorsed on, or permanently annexed to, the probate or letters of administration under which the estate is being administered.

Notes: Sub-s (2): words in italics in para (b) substituted by the words ", at the date of death, a separation order under the Family Law Act 1996 was in force in relation to the marriage with the deceased" by the Family Law Act 1996, s 66(1), Sch 8, Pt I, para 27(1), (7), subject to savings in s 66(2) of, and Sch 9, para 5 to, the 1996 Act, as from a day to be appointed.

Sub-s (3): words in square brackets inserted by the Administration of Justice Act 1982, s 52.

20 Provisions as to personal representatives

(1) The provisions of this Act shall not render the personal representative of a deceased person liable for having distributed any part of the estate of the deceased, after the end of the period of six months from the date on which representation with respect to the estate of the deceased is first taken out, on the ground that he ought to have taken into account the possibility—

(a) that the court might permit the making of an application for an order under section 2 of this Act after the end of that period, or

(b) that, where an order has been made under the said section 2, the court might exercise in relation thereto the powers conferred on it by section 6 of this Act,

but this subsection shall not prejudice any power to recover, by reason of the making of an order under this Act, any part of the estate so distributed.

(2) Where the personal representative of a deceased person pays any sum directed by an order under section 5 of this Act to be paid out of the deceased's net estate, he shall not be under any liability by reason of that estate not being sufficient to make the payment, unless at the time of making the payment he has reasonable cause to believe that the estate is not sufficient.

(3) Where a deceased person entered into a contract by which he agreed to leave by his will any sum of money or other property to any person or by which he agreed that a sum of money or other property would be paid or transferred to any person out of his estate, then, if the personal representative of the deceased has reason to believe that the deceased entered into the contract with the intention of defeating an application for financial provision under this Act, he may, notwithstanding anything in that contract, postpone the payment of that sum of money or the transfer of that property until the expiration of the period of six months from the date on which representation with respect to the estate of the deceased is first taken out or, if during that period an application is made for an order under section 2 of this Act, until the determination of the proceedings on that application.

21, 22 *(S 21 repealed by the Civil Evidence Act 1995, s 15(2), Sch 2; s 22 repealed by the Administration of Justice Act 1982, s 75, Sch 9, Pt I.)*

23 Determination of date on which representation was first taken out

In considering for the purposes of this Act when representation with respect to the estate of a deceased person was first taken out, a grant limited to settled land or to trust property shall be left out of account, and a grant limited to real estate or to personal estate shall be left out of account unless a grant limited to the remainder of the estate has previously been made or is made at the same time.

24 Effect of this Act on s 46(1)(vi) of Administration of Estates Act 1925

Section 46(1)(vi) of the Administration of Estates Act 1925, in so far as it provides for the devolution of property on the Crown, the Duchy of Lancaster or the Duke of Cornwall as bona vacantia, shall have effect subject to the provisions of this Act.

25 Interpretation

(1) In this Act—

"beneficiary", in relation to the estate of a deceased person, means—

- (a) a person who under the will of the deceased or under the law relating to intestacy is beneficially interested in the estate or would be so interested if an order had not been made under this Act, and
- (b) a person who has received any sum of money or other property which by virtue of section 8(1) or 8(2) of this Act is treated as part of the net estate of the deceased or would have received that sum or other property if an order had not been made under this Act;

"child" includes an illegitimate child and a child en ventre sa mère at the death of the deceased;

"the court" [unless the context otherwise requires] means the High Court, or where a county court has jurisdiction by virtue of section 22 of this Act, a county court;

["former wife" or "former husband" means a person whose marriage with the deceased was during the lifetime of the deceased either—

- (a) dissolved or annulled by *a decree* of divorce or a decree of nullity of marriage granted under the law of any part of the British Islands, or
- (b) dissolved or annulled in any country or territory outside the British Islands by a divorce or annulment which is entitled to be recognised as valid by the law of England and Wales;]

"net estate", in relation to a deceased person, means—

- (a) all property of which the deceased had power to dispose by his will (otherwise than by virtue of a special power of appointment) less the amount of his funeral, testamentary and administration expenses, debts and liabilities, including any [inheritance tax] payable out of his estate on his death;
- (b) any property in respect of which the deceased held a general power of appointment (not being a power exercisable by will)

which has not been exercised;

(c) any sum of money or other property which is treated for the purposes of this Act as part of the net estate of the deceased by virtue of section 8(1) or (2) of this Act;

(d) any property which is treated for the purposes of this Act as part of the net estate of the deceased by virtue of an order made under section 9 of the Act;

(e) any sum of money or other property which is, by reason of a disposition or contract made by the deceased, ordered under section 10 or 11 of this Act to be provided for the purpose of the making of financial provision under this Act;

"property" includes any chose in action;

"reasonable financial provision" has the meaning assigned to it by section 1 of this Act;

"valuable consideration" does not include marriage or a promise of marriage;

"will" includes codicil.

(2) For the purposes of paragraph (a) of the definition of "net estate" in subsection (1) above a person who is not of full age and capacity shall be treated as having power to dispose by will of all property of which he would have had power to dispose by will if he had been of full age and capacity.

(3) Any reference in this Act to provision out of the net estate of a deceased person includes a reference to provision extending to the whole of that estate.

(4) For the purposes of this Act any reference to a wife or husband shall be treated as including a reference to a person who in good faith entered into a void marriage with the deceased unless either—

(a) the marriage of the deceased and that person was dissolved or annulled during the lifetime of the deceased and the dissolution or annulment is recognised by the law of England and Wales, or

(b) that person has during the lifetime of the deceased entered into a later marriage.

(5) Any reference in this Act to remarriage or to a person who has remarried includes a reference to a marriage which is by law void or voidable or to a person who has entered into such a marriage, as the case may be, and a marriage shall be treated for the purposes of this Act as a remarriage, in relation to any party thereto, notwithstanding that the previous marriage of that party was void or voidable.

(6) Any reference in this Act to an order or decree made under the Matrimonial Causes Act 1973 or under any section of that Act shall be construed as including a reference to an order or decree

which is deemed to have been made under that Act or under that section thereof, as the case may be.

(7) Any reference in this Act to any enactment is a reference to that enactment as amended by or under any subsequent enactment.

Notes: Sub-s (1): in definition "court" words in square brackets inserted by the Matrimonial and Family Proceedings Act 1984, s 8; definitions "former wife" and "former husband" substituted by the Matrimonial and Family Proceedings Act 1984, s 25, words in italics therein substituted by the words "an order or decree" by the Family Law Act 1996, s 66(1), Sch 8, Pt I, para 27(1), (8), subject to savings in s 66(2) of, and Sch 9, para 5 to, the 1996 Act, as from a day to be appointed.

27 Short title, commencement and extent

(1) This Act may be cited as the Inheritance (Provision for Family and Dependants) Act 1975.

(2) This Act does not extend to Scotland or Northern Ireland.

(3) This Act shall come into force on 1st April 1976.

SCHEDULE

SECTION 26

ENACTMENTS REPEALED		
Chapter	Short title	Extent of repeal
1938 c 72	The Inheritance (Family Provision) Act 1938	The whole Act.
1952 c 64	The Intestates' Estates Act 1952	Section 7 and Schedule 3.
1965 c 72	The Matrimonial Causes Act 1965	Sections 26 to 28A and section 25(4) and (5) as applied by section 28(2).
1966 c 35	The Family Provision Act 1966	The whole Act except section 1 and subsections (1) and (3) of section 10.
1969 c 46	The Family Law Reform Act 1969	Sections 5(1) and 18.
1970 c 31	The Administration of Justice Act 1970	In schedule 2, paragraph 16.
1970 c 33	The Law Reform (Miscellaneous Provisions) Act 1970	Section 6.
1970 c 45	The Matrimonial Proceedings and Property Act 1970	Section 36.
1971 c 23	The Courts Act 1971	Section 45(1)(a).
1973 c 18	The Matrimonial Causes Act 1973	In section 50, in subsection (1)(a) the words from 'and sections 26' to the end of the paragraph, in subsection (1)(d) the words 'or sections 26 to 28A of the

		Matrimonial Causes Act 1965' and in subsection (2)(a) the words 'or under section 26 or 27 of the Matrimonial Causes Act 1965'.
1975 c 7	The Finance Act 1975	In schedule 12, paragraph 6.

FORFEITURE ACT 1982

(1982 c 34)

An Act to provide for relief for persons guilty of unlawful killing from forfeiture of inheritance and other rights; to enable such persons to apply for financial provision out of the deceased's estate; to provide for the question whether pension and social security benefits have been forfeited to be determined by the Social Security commissioners; and for connected purposes. [13th July 1982]

BE IT ENACTED by the Queen's most Excellent Majesty, by and with the advice and consent of the Lords Spiritual and Temporal, and Commons, in this present Parliament assembled, and by the authority of the same, as follows:–

1 The "forfeiture rule"

(1) In this Act, the "forfeiture rule" means the rule of public policy which in certain circumstances precludes a person who has unlawfully killed another from acquiring a benefit in consequence of the killing.

(2) References in this Act to a person who has unlawfully killed another include a reference to a person who has unlawfully aided, abetted, counselled or procured the death of that other and references in this Act to unlawful killing shall be interpreted accordingly.

2 Power to modify the rule

(1) Where a court determines that the forfeiture rule has precluded a person (in this section referred to as "the offender") who has unlawfully killed another from acquiring any interest in property mentioned in subsection (4) below, the court may make an order under this section modifying the effect of that rule.

(2) The court shall not make an order under this section

modifying the effect of the forfeiture rule in any case unless it is satisfied that, having regard to the conduct of the offender and of the deceased and to such other circumstances as appear to the court to be material, the justice of the case requires the effect of the rule to be so modified in that case.

(3) In any case where a person stands convicted of an offence of which unlawful killing is an element, the court shall not make an order under this section modifying the effect of the forfeiture rule in that case unless proceedings for the purpose are brought before the expiry of the period of three months beginning with his conviction.

(4) The interests in property referred to in subsection (1) above are—

(a) any beneficial interest in property which (apart from the forfeiture rule) the offender would have acquired—
   (i) under the deceased's will (including, as respects Scotland, any writing having testamentary effect) or the law relating to intestacy or by way of ius relicti, ius relictae or legitim;
   (ii) on the nomination of the deceased in accordance with the provisions of any enactment;
   (iii) as a donatio mortis causa made by the deceased; or
   (iv) under a special destination (whether relating to heritable or moveable property); or

(b) any beneficial interest in property which (apart from the forfeiture rule) the offender would have acquired in consequence of the death of the deceased, being property which, before the death, was held on trust for any person.

(5) An order under this section may modify the effect of the forfeiture rule in respect of any interest in property to which the determination referred to in subsection (1) above relates and may do so in either or both of the following ways, that is—

(a) where there is more than one such interest, by excluding the application of the rule in respect of any (but not all) of those interests; and

(b) in the case of any such interest in property, by excluding the application of the rule in respect of part of the property.

(6) On the making of an order under this section, the forfeiture rule shall have effect for all purposes (including purposes relating to anything done before the order is made) subject to the modifications made by the order.

(7) The court shall not make an order under this section modifying the effect of the forfeiture rule in respect of any interest in property which, in consequence of the rule, has been acquired before the coming into force of this section by a person other than

the offender or a person claiming through him.

(8) In this section—

"property" includes any chose in action or incorporeal moveable property; and

"will" includes codicil.

3 Application for financial provision not affected by the rule

(1) The forfeiture rule shall not be taken to preclude any person from making any application under a provision mentioned in subsection (2) below or the making of any order on the application.

(2) The provisions referred to in subsection (1) above are—

(a) any provision of the Inheritance (Provision for Family and Dependants) Act 1975; and

(b) sections 31(6) (variation etc. of periodical payments orders) and 36(1) (variation of maintenance agreements) of the Matrimonial Causes Act 1973 and section 5(4) of the Divorce (Scotland) Act 1976 (variation etc. of periodical allowances).

4 Commissioner to decide whether rule applies to social security benefits

(1) Where a question arises as to whether, if a person were otherwise entitled to or eligible for any benefit or advantage under a relevant enactment, he would be precluded by virtue of the forfeiture rule from receiving the whole or part of the benefit or advantage, that question shall (notwithstanding anything in any relevant enactment) be determined by a Commissioner.

[(1A) Where a Commissioner determines that the forfeiture rule has precluded a person (in this section referred to as "the offender") who has unlawfully killed another from receiving the whole or part of any such benefit or advantage, the Commissioner may make a decision under this subsection modifying the effect of that rule and may do so whether the unlawful killing occurred before or after the coming into force of this subsection.

(1B) The Commission shall not make a decision under subsection (1A) above modifying the effect of the forfeiture rule in any case unless he is satisfied that, having regard to the conduct of the offender and of the deceased and to such other circumstances as appear to the Commissioner to be material, the justice of the case requires the effect of the rule to be so modified in that case.

(1C) Subject to subsection (1D) below, a decision under subsection (1A) above may modify the effect of the forfeiture rule in either or both of the following ways—

(a) so that it applies only in respect of a specified proportion of the benefit or advantage;

(b) so that it applies in respect of the benefit or advantage only for a specified period of time.

(1D) Such a decision may not modify the effect of the forfeiture rule so as to allow any person to receive the whole or any part of a benefit or advantage in respect of any period before the commencement of this subsection.

(1E) If the Commissioner thinks it expedient to do so, he may direct that his decision shall apply to any future claim for a benefit or advantage under a relevant enactment, on which a question such as is mentioned in subsection (1) above arises by reason of the same unlawful killing.

(1F) It is immaterial for the purposes of subsection (1E) above whether the claim is in respect of the same or a different benefit or advantage.

(1G) For the purpose of obtaining a decision whether the forfeiture rule should be modified the Secretary of State may refer to a Commissioner for review any determination of a question such as is mentioned in subsection (1) above that was made before the commencement of subsections (1A) to (1F) above (whether by a Commissioner or not) and shall do so if the offender requests him to refer such a determination.

(1H) Subsections (1A) to (1F) above shall have effect on a reference under subsection (1G) above as if in subsection (1A) the words "it has been determined" were substituted for the words "a Commissioner determines".]

(2) Regulations under this section may make such provision as appears to [the Lord Chancellor] to be necessary or expedient for carrying this section into effect; and (without prejudice to the generality of that) the regulations may, in relation to the question mentioned in subsection (1) above or any determination under that subsection [or any decision under subsection (1A) above]—

(a) apply any provision of any relevant enactment, with or without modifications, or exclude or contain provision corresponding to any such provision; and

(b) make provision for purposes corresponding to those for which provision may be made by regulations under [section 59 of the Social Security Administration Act 1992] (matters relating to adjudication).

(3) The power to make regulations under this section shall be exercisable by statutory instrument which shall be subject to annulment in pursuance of a resolution of either House of Parliament.

(4) [Section 175(3) to (5) of the Social Security Contributions and Benefits Act 1992] (provision about extent of power to make regulations) shall apply to the power to make regulations conferred by this section as it applies to the power to make regulations conferred by that Act, but as if for references to that Act there were substituted references to this section.

(5) In this section—

"Commissioner" has the same meaning as in the [Social Security Administration Act 1992]; and

"relevant enactment" means any provision of the following and any instrument made by virtue of such a provision:

the Personal Injuries (Emergency Provisions) Act 1939,

the Pensions (Navy, Army, Air Force and Mercantile Marine) Act 1939,

the Polish Resettlement Act 1947,

[the Child Benefit Act 1975,

[the Social Security Acts 1975 to 1991]],

[the Social Security Contributions and Benefits Act 1992],

[the Pension Schemes Act 1993],

and any other enactment relating to pensions or social security prescribed by regulations under this section.

Notes: Commencement order: SI 1982 No 1731.

Sub-ss (1A)–(1H): added by the Social Security Act 1986, s 76(2).

Sub-s (2): first words in square brackets substituted by SI 1984 No 1818, art 3; second words in square brackets added by the Social Security Act 1986, s 76(3); final words in square brackets substituted by the Social Security (Consequential Provisions) Act 1992, s 4, Sch 2, para 63(1).

Sub-s (4): words in square brackets substituted by the Social Security (Consequential Provisions) Act 1992, s 4, Sch 2, para 63(2).

Sub-s (5): words in square brackets in definition "Commissioner" substituted by the Social Security (Consequential Provisions) Act 1992, s 4, Sch 2, para 63(3); in definition "relevant enactment", first words in square brackets substituted by the Social Security Act 1986, s 86, Sch 10, Part VI, para 108(b), words in square brackets therein substituted by the Statutory Sick Pay Act 1991, s 3(1), reference to "the Social Security Contributions and Benefits Act 1992" added by the Social Security (Consequential Provisions) Act 1992, s 4, Sch 2, para 63(3), reference to "the Pension Schemes Act 1993" added by the Pension Schemes Act 1993, s 190, Sch 8, para 15.

Functions of Secretary of State transferred to the Lord Chancellor for certain purposes by SI 1984 No 1818, art 2, Schedule; functions of the Secretary of State for Social Services transferred to the Secretary of State for Social Security by the Transfer of Functions (Health and Social Security) Order 1988 (SI 1988 No 1843), art 1(2), Sch 1.

5 Exclusion of murderers

Nothing in this Act or in any order made under section 2 or referred to in section 3(1) of this Act [or in any decision made under section 4(1A) of this Act] shall affect the application of the forfeiture rule in the case of a person who stands convicted of murder.

Notes: Words in square brackets added by the Social Security Act 1986, s 76(4).

6 Corresponding provision for Northern Ireland

An Order in Council under paragraph 1(1)(b) of Schedule 1 to the Northern Ireland Act 1974 (legislation for Northern Ireland in the interim period) which contains a statement that it is made only for purposes corresponding to the purposes of this Act—

(a) shall not be subject to paragraph 1(4) and (5) of that Schedule (affirmative resolution of both Houses of Parliament); but

(b) shall be subject to annulment in pursuance of a resolution of either House.

7 Short title, etc.

(1) This Act may be cited as the Forfeiture Act 1982.

(2) Section 4 of this Act shall come into force on such day as the Secretary of State may appoint by order made by statutory instrument; and sections 1 to 3 and 5 of this Act shall come into force on the expiry of the period of three months beginning with the day on which it is passed.

(3) This Act, except section 6, does not extend to Northern Ireland.

(4) Subject to section 2(7) of this Act, an order under section 2 of this Act or an order referred to in section 3(1) of this Act and made in respect of a person who has unlawfully killed another may be made whether the unlawful killing occurred before or after the coming into force of those sections.

Notes: Functions of the Secretary of State for Social Services transferred to the Secretary of State for Social Security, by the Transfer of Functions (Health and Social Security) Order 1988 (SI 1988 No 1843), art 1(2), Sch 1.

INHERITANCE TAX ACT 1984

(1984 c 51)

An Act to consolidate provisions of Part III of the Finance Act 1975 and other enactments relating to inheritance tax [31st July 1984]

BE IT ENACTED by the Queen's most Excellent Majesty, by and with the advice and consent of the Lords Spiritual and Temporal, and Commons, in this present Parliament assembled, and by the authority of the same, as follows:–

* * *

PART II
EXEMPT TRANSFERS

CHAPTER I GENERAL

[29A Abatement of exemption where claim settled out of beneficiary's own resources]

[(1) This section applies where—

(a) apart from this section the transfer of value made on the death of any person is an exempt transfer to the extent that the value transferred by it is attributable to an exempt gift, and

(b) the exempt beneficiary, in settlement of the whole or part of any claim against the deceased's estate, effects a disposition of property not derived from the transfer.

(2) The provisions of this Act shall have effect in relation to the transfer as if—

(a) so much of the relevant value as is equal to the following amount, namely the amount by which the value of the exempt beneficiary's estate immediately after the disposition is less than it would be but for the disposition, or

(b) where the amount exceeds the relevant value, the whole of the relevant value,

were attributable to such a gift to the exempt beneficiary as is mentioned in subsection (3) below (instead of being attributable to a gift with respect to which the transfer is exempt).

(3) The gift referred to in subsection (2) above is a specific gift with respect to which the transfer is chargeable, being a gift which satisfies the conditions set out in paragraphs (a) and (b) of section 38(1) below.

(4) In determining the value of the exempt beneficiary's estate for the purposes of subsection (2) above—

(a) no deduction shall be made in respect of the claim referred to in subsection (1)(b) above, and

(b) where the disposition referred to in that provision constitutes a transfer of value—

(i) no account shall be taken of any liability of the beneficiary for any tax on the value transferred, and

(ii) sections 104 and 116 below shall be disregarded.

(5) Subsection (1)(b) above does not apply in relation to any claim against the deceased's estate in respect of so much of any liability as is, in accordance with this Act, to be taken into account in determining the value of the estate.

(6) In this section—
"exempt gift", in relation to a transfer of value falling within subsection (1)(a) above, means—

(a) a gift with respect to which the transfer is (apart from this section) exempt by virtue of the provisions of any of sections 18 and 23 to 28 above, or
(b) where (apart from this section) the transfer is so exempt with respect to a gift up to a limit, so much of the gift as is within that limit;

"the exempt beneficiary", in relation to an exempt gift, means any of the following, namely—

(a) where the gift is exempt by virtue of section 18 above, the deceased's spouse,
(b) where the gift is exempt by virtue of section 23 above, any person or body—
   (i) whose property the property falling within subsection (1) of that section becomes, or
   (ii) by whom that property is held on trust for charitable purposes,
(c) where the gift is exempt by virtue of section 24, 25 or 26 above, any body whose property the property falling within subsection (1) of that section becomes,
(d) where the gift is exempt by virtue of section 24A above, any body to whom the land falling within subsection (1) of that section is given, and
(e) where the gift is exempt by virtue of section 27 or 28 above, the trustees of any settlement in which the property falling within subsection (1) of that section becomes comprised;

"gift" and "specific gift"' have the same meaning as in Chapter III of this Part; and
"the relevant value", in relation to a transfer of value falling within subsection (1)(a) above, means so much of the value transferred by the transfer as is attributable to the gift referred to in that provision.]

Notes: This section was added by the Finance Act 1989, s 172, in relation to deaths occurring on or after 27 July 1989.

Inheritance Tax: except in relation to a liability to tax arising before 25 July 1986 capital transfer tax shall be known as inheritance tax and the Capital Transfer Tax Act 1984 may be cited as the Inheritance Tax Act 1984, by virtue of the Finance Act 1986, s 100. Accordingly references to capital transfer tax have been changed to references to inheritance tax throughout this Act.

* * *

PART V
MISCELLANEOUS RELIEFS

CHAPTER V MISCELLANEOUS

Changes in distribution of deceased's estate, etc

146 Inheritance (Provision for Family and Dependants) Act 1975

(1) Where an order is made under section 2 of the Inheritance (Provision for Family and Dependants) Act 1975 ("the 1975 Act") in relation to any property forming part of the net estate of a deceased person, then, without prejudice to section 19(1) of that Act, the property shall for the purposes of this Act be treated as if it had on his death devolved subject to the provisions of the order.

(2) Where an order is made under section 10 of the 1975 Act requiring a person to provide any money or other property by reason of a disposition made by the deceased, then—

(a) if that disposition was a chargeable transfer and the personal representatives of the deceased make a claim for the purpose—

(i) tax paid or payable on the value transferred by that chargeable transfer (whether or not by the claimants) shall be repaid to them by the Board or, as the case may be, shall not be payable, and

(ii) the rate or rates of tax applicable to the transfer of value made by the deceased on his death shall be determined as if the values previously transferred by chargeable transfers made by him were reduced by that value;

(b) the money or property shall be included in the deceased's estate for the purpose of the transfer of value made by him on his death.

(3) Where the money or other property ordered to be provided under section 10 of the 1975 Act is less than the maximum permitted by that section, subsection (2)(a) above shall have effect in relation to such part of the value there mentioned as is appropriate.

(4) The adjustment in consequence of the provisions of this section or of section 19(1) of the 1975 Act of the tax payable in respect of the transfer of value made by the deceased on his death shall not affect—

(a) the amount of any deduction to be made under section 8 of that Act in respect of tax borne by the person mentioned in subsection (3) of that section, or

(b) the amount of tax to which regard is to be had under section 9(2) of that Act;

and where a person is ordered under that Act to make a payment or transfer property by reason of his holding property treated as part of the deceased's net estate under section 8 or 9 and tax borne by him is taken into account for the purposes of the order, any repayment of that tax shall be made to the personal representatives of the deceased and not to that person.

(5) Tax repaid under paragraph (a)(i) of subsection (2) above shall be included in the deceased's estate for the purposes of the transfer of value made by him on his death; and tax repaid under that paragraph or under subsection (4) above shall form part of the deceased's net estate for the purposes of the 1975 Act.

(6) Anything which is done in compliance with an order under the 1975 Act or occurs on the coming into force of such an order, and which would (apart from this subsection) constitute an occasion on which tax is chargeable under any provision, other than section 79, of Chapter III of Part III of this Act, shall not constitute such an occasion; and where an order under the 1975 Act provides for property to be settled or for the variation of a settlement, and (apart from this subsection) tax would be charged under section 52(1) above on the coming into force of the order, section 52(1) shall not apply.

(7) In subsections (2)(a) and (5) above references to tax include references to interest on tax.

(8) Where an order is made staying or dismissing proceedings under the 1975 Act on terms set out in or scheduled to the order, this section shall have effect as if any of those terms which could have been included in an order under section 2 or 10 of that Act were provisions of such an order.

(9) In this section any reference to, or to any provision of, the 1975 Act includes a reference to, or to the corresponding provision of, the Inheritance (Provision for Family and Dependants) (Northern Ireland) Order 1979.

Notes: Sub-ss (1)–(5), (7) derived from the Finance Act 1976, s 122(1)–(5), (7); sub-s (6) derived from the Finance Act 1976, s 122(6), and the Finance Act 1982, Sch 17, para 29; sub-s (8) derived from the Finance Act 1976, s 122(7A), and the Finance Act 1980, s 92; sub-s (9) derived from the Finance Act 1976, s 122(8A), and SI 1979 No 927.

Inheritance Tax: except in relation to a liability to tax arising before 25 July 1986 capital transfer tax shall be known as inheritance tax and the Capital Transfer Tax Act 1984 may be cited as the Inheritance Tax Act 1984, by virtue of the Finance Act 1986, s 100. Accordingly references to capital transfer tax have been changed to references to inheritance tax throughout this Act.

CHILDREN ACT 1989

(c 41)
An Act to reform the law relating to children; to provide for local authority services for children in need and others; to amend the law with respect to children's homes, community homes, voluntary homes and voluntary organisations; to make provision with respect to fostering, child minding and day care for young children and adoption; and for connected purposes.
[16 November 1989]

* * *

SCHEDULE 1
FINANCIAL PROVISION FOR CHILDREN
SECTION 15(1)

Variation of orders for secured periodical payments after death of parent

7.—(1) Where the parent liable to make payments under a secured periodical payments order has died, the persons who may apply for the variation or discharge of the order shall include the personal representatives of the deceased parent.

(2) No application for the variation of the order shall, except with the permission of the court, be made after the end of the period of six months from the date on which representation in regard to the estate of that parent is first taken out.

(3) The personal representatives of a deceased person against whom a secured periodical payments order was made shall not be liable for having distributed any part of the estate of the deceased after the end of the period of six months referred to in sub-paragraph (2) on the ground that they ought to have taken into account the possibility that the court might permit an application for variation to be made after that period by the person entitled to payments under the order.

(4) Sub-paragraph (3) shall not prejudice any power to recover any part of the estate so distributed arising by virtue of the variation of an order in accordance with this paragraph.

(5) Where an application to vary a secured periodical payments order is made after the death of the parent liable to make payments under the order, the circumstances to which the court is required to have regard under paragraph 6(1) shall include the changed circumstances resulting from the death of the parent.

(6) In considering for the purposes of sub-paragraph (2) the question when representation was first taken out, a grant limited to settled land or to trust property shall be left out of account and a grant limited to real estate or to personal estate shall be left out of

account unless a grant limited to the remainder of the estate has previously been made or is made at the same time.

(7) In this paragraph "secured periodical payments order" means an order for secured periodical payments under paragraph 1(2)(b).

* * *

Alteration of maintenance agreements

10.—(1) In this paragraph and in paragraph 11 "maintenance agreement" means any agreement in writing made with respect to a child, whether before or after the commencement of this paragraph, which—

(a) is or was made between the father and mother of the child; and

(b) contains provision with respect to the making or securing of payments, or the disposition or use of any property, for the maintenance or education of the child,

and any such provisions are in this paragraph, and paragraph 11, referred to as "financial arrangements".

(2) Where a maintenance agreement is for the time being subsisting and each of the parties to the agreement is for the time being either domiciled or resident in England and Wales, then, either party may apply to the court for an order under this paragraph.

(3) If the court to which the application is made is satisfied either—

(a) that, by reason of a change in the circumstances in the light of which any financial arrangements contained in the agreement were made (including a change foreseen by the parties when making the agreement), the agreement should be altered so as to make different financial arrangements; or

(b) that the agreement does not contain proper financial arrangements with respect to the child,

then that court may by order make such alterations in the agreement by varying or revoking any financial arrangements contained in it as may appear to it to be just having regard to all the circumstances.

(4) If the maintenance agreement is altered by an order under this paragraph, the agreement shall have effect thereafter as if the alteration had been made by agreement between the parties and for valuable consideration.

(5) Where a court decides to make an order under this paragraph altering the maintenance agreement—

(a) by inserting provision for the making or securing by one of the parties to the agreement of periodical payments for the maintenance of the child; or

(b) by increasing the rate of periodical payments required to be made or secured by one of the parties for the maintenance of the child,

then, in deciding the term for which under the agreement as altered by the order the payments or (as the case may be) the additional payments attributable to the increase are to be made or secured for the benefit of the child, the court shall apply the provisions of sub-paragraphs (1) and (2) of paragraph 3 as if the order were an order under paragraph 1(2)(a) or (b).

(6) A magistrates' court shall not entertain an application under sub-paragraph (2) unless both the parties to the agreement are resident in England and Wales and at least one of the parties is resident in the commission area (within the meaning of the Justices of the Peace Act 1979) for which the court is appointed, and shall not have power to make any order on such an application except—

(a) in a case where the agreement contains no provision for periodical payments by either of the parties, an order inserting provision for the making by one of the parties of periodical payments for the maintenance of the child;

(b) in a case where the agreement includes provision for the making by one of the parties of periodical payments, an order increasing or reducing the rate of, or terminating, any of those payments.

(7) For the avoidance of doubt it is hereby declared that nothing in this paragraph affects any power of a court before which any proceedings between the parties to a maintenance agreement are brought under any other enactment to make an order containing financial arrangements or any right of either party to apply for such an order in such proceedings.

11.—(1) Where a maintenance agreement provides for the continuation, after the death of one of the parties, of payments for the maintenance of a child and that party dies domiciled in England and Wales, the surviving party or the personal representatives of the deceased party may apply to the High Court or a county court for an order under paragraph 10.

(2) If a maintenance agreement is altered by a court on an application under this paragraph, the agreement shall have effect thereafter as if the alteration had been made, immediately before the death, by agreement between the parties and for valuable consideration.

(3) An application under this paragraph shall not, except with leave of the High Court or a county court, be made after the end of the period of six months beginning with the day on which representation in regard to the estate of the deceased is first taken out.

(4) In considering for the purposes of sub-paragraph (3) the question when representation was first taken out, a grant limited to settled land or to trust property shall be left out of account and a grant limited to real estate or to personal estate shall be left out of account unless a grant limited to the remainder of the estate has previously been made or is made at the same time.

(5) A county court shall not entertain an application under this paragraph, or an application for leave to make an application under this paragraph, unless it would have jurisdiction to hear and determine proceedings for an order under section 2 of the Inheritance (Provision for Family and Dependants) Act 1975 in relation to the deceased's estate by virtue of section 25 of the County Courts Act 1984 (jurisdiction under the Act of 1975).

(6) The provisions of this paragraph shall not render the personal representatives of the deceased liable for having distributed any part of the estate of the deceased after the expiry of the period of six months referred to in sub-paragraph (3) on the ground that they ought to have taken into account the possibility that a court might grant leave for an application by virtue of this paragraph to be made by the surviving party after that period.

(7) Sub-paragraph (6) shall not prejudice any power to recover any part of the estate so distributed arising by virtue of the making of an order in pursuance of this paragraph.

Notes: Commencement: 1 April 1992 (para 6A); 14 October 1991 (remainder).

The Inheritance (Provision for Family and Dependants) (Northern Ireland) Order 1979, SI 1979/924

Laid before Parliament in draft
Made 26th July 1979
Coming into Operation 1st September 1979

ARRANGEMENT OF ORDER

Whereas Her Majesty, in pursuance of the Regency Acts 1937 to 1953, was pleased, by Letters Patent dated the 16th day of July 1979, to delegate to the six Counsellors of State therein named or any two or more of them full power and authority during the period of Her Majesty's absence from the United Kingdom to summon and hold on Her Majesty's behalf Her Privy Council and to signify thereat Her Majesty's approval for anything for which Her Majesty's approval in Council is required:

And whereas a draft of this Order has been approved by a resolution of each House of Parliament:

Now, therefore, Her Majesty Queen Elizabeth The Queen Mother and His Royal Highness The Prince Charles, Prince of Wales, being authorised thereto by the said Letters Patent, and in exercise of the powers conferred by paragraph 1 of Schedule 1 to the Northern Ireland Act 1974, and of all other powers enabling Her Majesty in that behalf, and by and with the advice of Her Majesty's Privy Council, do on Her Majesty's behalf order, and it is hereby ordered, as follows:—

Introductory

Title and commencement

1.—(1) This Order may be cited as the Inheritance (Provision for Family and Dependants) (Northern Ireland) Order 1979.

(2) This Order shall come into operation on 1st September 1979.

Interpretation

2.—(1) The Interpretation Act (Northern Ireland) 1954 shall apply to Article 1 and the following provisions of this Order as it applies to a Measure of the Northern Ireland Assembly.

(2) In this Order—

'adopted' means adopted in pursuance of an adoption order made in any part of the United Kingdom, the Isle of Man or any of the Channel Islands or, subject to sections 5 and 6 of the Adoption (Hague Convention) Act (Northern Ireland) 1969, a foreign adoption as defined by section 4(3) of that Act;

'beneficiary', in relation to the estate of a deceased person, means—

(*a*) a person who under the will of the deceased or under the law relating to intestacy is beneficially interested in the estate or would be so interested if an order had not been made under this Order, and

(*b*) a person who has received any sum of money or other property which by virtue of Article 10(1) or (2) is treated as part of the net estate of the deceased or would have received that sum or other property if an order had not been made under this Order;

'child' includes an illegitimate or adopted child and a child en ventre sa mère at the death of the deceased;

'the court' means the High Court, or where a county court has jurisdiction by virtue of Article 24, a county court;

'divorce county court' has the same meaning as in the Matrimonial Causes (Northern Ireland) Order 1978;

'former wife' or 'former husband' means a person whose marriage with the deceased was during the deceased's lifetime dissolved or annulled by a decree of divorce or of nullity of marriage granted under the Matrimonial Causes (Northern Ireland) Order 1978 or the statutory provisions repealed by that Order;

'full valuable consideration' means such valuable consideration as amounts or approximates to the value of that for which it is given;

'net estate', in relation to a deceased person, means—

(*a*) all property of which the deceased had power to dispose by his will (otherwise than by virtue of a special power of appointment) less the amount of his funeral, testamentary and administration expenses, debts and liabilities, including any capital transfer tax payable out of his estate on his death;

(*b*) any property in respect of which the deceased held a general power of appointment (not being a power exercisable by will) which has not been exercised;

(*c*) any sum of money or other property which is treated for the purposes of this Order as part of the net estate of the deceased by virtue of Article 10(1) or (2);

(*d*) any property which is treated for the purposes of this Order as part of the net estate of the deceased by virtue of an order made under Article 11;

(*e*) any sum of money or other property which is, by reason of a disposition or contract made by the deceased, ordered under Article 12 or 13 to be provided for the purpose of the making of financial provision under this Order;

'property' includes any chose in action;

'reasonable financial provision'—

(*a*) in the case of an application made by virtue of Article 3(1)(*a*) by the husband or wife of the deceased (except where the marriage with the deceased was the subject of a decree of judicial separation and at the date of death the decree was in force and the separation was continuing), means such financial provision as it would be reasonable in all the circumstances of the case for a husband or wife to receive, whether or not that provision is required for his or her maintenance;

(*b*) in the case of any other application made by virtue of Article 3(1), means such financial provision as it would be reasonable in all the circumstances of the case for the applicant to receive for his maintenance;

'statutory provision' has the meaning given by section 1(*f*) of the Interpretation Act (Northern Ireland) 1954;

'valuable consideration' does not include marriage or a promise of marriage;

'will' includes codicil.

(3) For the purposes of paragraph (*a*) of the definition of 'net estate' in paragraph (2) a person who is not of full age and capacity shall be treated

as having power to dispose by will of all property of which he would have had power to dispose by will if he had been of full age and capacity.

(4) Any reference in this Order to provision out of the net estate of a deceased person includes a reference to provision extending to the whole of that estate.

(5) For the purposes of this Order any reference to a wife or husband shall be treated as including a reference to a person who in good faith entered into a void marriage with the deceased unless either—

(*a*) the marriage of the deceased and that person was dissolved or annulled during the lifetime of the deceased and the dissolution or annulment is recognised by the law of Northern Ireland, or

(*b*) that person has during the lifetime of the deceased entered into a later marriage.

(6) Any reference in this Order to remarriage or to a person who has remarried includes a reference to a marriage which is by law void or voidable or to a person who has entered into such a marriage, as the case may be, and a marriage shall be treated for the purposes of this Order as a remarriage, in relation to any party thereto, notwithstanding that the previous marriage of that party was void or voidable.

Powers of court to order financial provision from deceased's estate

Application for financial provision from deceased's estate

3.—(1) Where after the commencement of this Order a person dies domiciled in Northern Ireland and is survived by any of the following persons:—

(*a*) the wife or husband of the deceased;

(*b*) a former wife or former husband of the deceased who has not remarried;

[(*ba*)any person (not being a person included in sub-paragraph (a) or (b)) to whom paragraph (1A) applies;]

(*c*) a child of the deceased;

(*d*) any person (not being a child of the deceased) who, in the case of any marriage to which the deceased was at any time a party, was treated by the deceased as a child of the family in relation to that marriage;

(*e*) any person (not being a person included in sub-paragraphs (*a*) to (*d*)) who immediately before the death of the deceased was being maintained, either wholly or partly, by the deceased;

that person may apply to the court for an order under Article 4 on the ground that the disposition of the deceased's estate effected by his will or the law relating to intestacy, or the combination of his will and that law, is not such as to make reasonable financial provision for the applicant.

[(1A) This paragraph applies to a person if the deceased died after the coming into operation of the Succession (Northern Ireland) Order 1996 and, during the whole of the period of two years ending immediately before the date when the deceased died, the person was living—

(*a*) in the same household as the deceased; and

(*b*) as the husband or wife of the deceased.]

(2) For the purposes of paragraph (1)(*e*), a person shall be treated as being maintained by the deceased, either wholly or partly, as the case may be, if the deceased, otherwise than for full valuable consideration, was making a substantial contribution in money or money's worth towards the reasonable needs of that person.

Powers of court to make orders

4.—(1) Subject to the provisions of this Order, where an application is made for an order under this Article, the court may, if it is satisfied that the disposition of the deceased's estate effected by his will or the law relating to intestacy, or the combination of his will and that law, is not such as to make reasonable financial provision for the applicant, make any one or more of the following orders:—

(*a*) an order for the making to the applicant out of the net estate of the deceased of such periodical payments and for such term as may be specified in the order;

(*b*) an order for the payment to the applicant out of that estate of a lump sum of such amount as may be so specified;

(*c*) an order for the transfer to the applicant of such property comprised in that estate as may be so specified;

(*d*) an order for the settlement for the benefit of the applicant of such property comprised in that estate as may be so specified;

(*e*) an order for the acquisition out of property comprised in that estate of such property as may be so specified and for the transfer of the property so acquired to the applicant or for the settlement thereof for his benefit;

(*f*) an order varying any ante-nuptial or post-nuptial settlement (including such a settlement made by will) made on the parties to a marriage to which the deceased was one of the parties, the variation being for the benefit of the surviving party to that marriage, or any child of that marriage, or any person who was treated by the deceased as a child of the family in relation to that marriage.

(2) An order under paragraph (1)(*a*) providing for the making out of the net estate of the deceased of periodical payments may provide for—

(*a*) payments of such amount as may be specified in the order,

(*b*) payments equal to the whole of the income of the net estate or of such portion thereof as may be so specified,

(*c*) payments equal to the whole of the income of such part of the net estate as the court may direct to be set aside or appropriated for the making out of the income thereof of payments under this Article,

or may provide for the amount of the payments or any of them to be determined in any other way the court thinks fit.

(3) Where an order under paragraph (1)(*a*) provides for the making of payments of an amount specified in the order, the order may direct that such part of the net estate as may be so specified shall be set aside or appropriated for the making out of the income thereof of those payments; but no larger part of the net estate shall be so set aside or appropriated than is sufficient, at the date of the order, to produce by the income thereof the amount required for the making of those payments.

(4) An order under this Article may contain such consequential and supplementary provisions as the court thinks necessary or expedient for the purpose of giving effect to the order or for the purpose of securing that the order operates fairly as between one beneficiary of the estate of the deceased and another and may, in particular, but without prejudice to the generality of this paragraph—

(*a*) order any person who holds any property which forms part of the net estate of the deceased to make such payment or transfer such property as may be specified in the order;

(*b*) vary the disposition of the deceased's estate effected by the will or the law relating to intestacy, or by both the will and the law relating to intestacy, in such manner as the court thinks fair and reasonable having regard to the provisions of the order and all the circumstances of the case;

(*c*) confer on the trustees of any property which is the subject of an order under this Article such powers as appear to the court to be necessary or expedient.

(5) Where—

(*a*) the deceased is survived by a wife or husband ('the surviving spouse') and is also survived by children who are either issue of the deceased and the surviving spouse or children adopted by the deceased and the surviving spouse jointly; and

(*b*) the surviving spouse becomes entitled under the deceased's will or the law relating to intestacy, or a combination of his will and that law, to the net estate of the deceased or to an interest in the estate which amounts to reasonable financial provision for both the surviving spouse and the children,

the court shall not make an order under this Article on the application of any of the children who is a minor.

Matters to which court is to have regard in exercising powers under Article 4

5.—(1) Where an application is made for an order under Article 4, the court shall, in determining whether the disposition of the deceased's estate effected by his will or the law relating to intestacy, or the combination of his will and that law, is such as to make reasonable financial provision for the applicant and, if the court considers that reasonable financial provision has not been made, in determining whether and in what manner it shall exercise its powers under that Article, have regard to the following matters:—

(*a*) the financial resources and financial needs which the applicant has or is likely to have in the foreseeable future;

(*b*) the financial resources and financial needs which any other applicant for an order under Article 4 has or is likely to have in the foreseeable future;

(*c*) the financial resources and financial needs which any beneficiary of the estate of the deceased has or is likely to have in the foreseeable future;

(*d*) any obligations and responsibilities which the deceased had towards any applicant for an order under Article 4 or towards any beneficiary of the estate of the deceased;

(*e*) the size and nature of the net estate of the deceased and the likely effect on any business undertaking included in the estate of an order resulting in the division of property;

(*f*) any physical or mental disability of any applicant for an order under Article 4 or any beneficiary of the estate of the deceased;

(*g*) any other matter, including the conduct of the applicant or any other person, which in the circumstances of the case the court may consider relevant.

(2) Without prejudice to the generality of sub-paragraph (*g*) of paragraph (1), where an application for an order under Article 4 is made by virtue of Article 3(1)(*a*) or (*b*), the court shall, in addition to the matters specifically

mentioned in sub-paragraphs (*a*) *to* (*f*) of that paragraph, have regard to—

(*a*) the age of the applicant and the duration of the marriage;

(*b*) the contribution made by the applicant to the welfare of the family of the deceased, including any contribution made by looking after the home or caring for the family;

and, in the case of an application by the wife or husband of the deceased, the court shall also, unless at the date of death a decree of judicial separation was in force and the separation was continuing, have regard to the provision which the applicant might reasonably have expected to receive if on the day on which the deceased died the marriage, instead of being terminated by death, had been terminated by a decree of divorce.

[(2A) Without prejudice to the generality of sub-paragraph (*g*) of paragraph (1), where an application for an order under Article 4 is made by virtue of Article 3(1)(*ba*), the court shall, in addition to the matters specifically mentioned in sub-paragraphs (*a*) to (*f*) of that paragraph, have regard to—

(*a*) the age of the applicant and the length of the period during which the applicant lived as the husband or wife of the deceased and in the same household as the deceased; and

(*b*) the contribution made by the applicant to the welfare of the family of the deceased, including any contribution made by looking after the home or caring for the family.]

(3) Without prejudice to the generality of sub-paragraph (*g*) of paragraph (1), where an application for an order under Article 4 is made by virtue of Article 3(1)(*c*) or (*d*), the court shall, in addition to the matters specifically mentioned in sub-paragraphs (*a*) to (*f*) of that paragraph, have regard to the manner in which the applicant was being or in which he might expect to be educated or trained, and where the application is made by virtue of Article 3(1)(*d*) the court shall also have regard—

(*a*) to whether the deceased had assumed any responsibility for the applicant's maintenance and, if so, to the extent to which and the basis upon which the deceased assumed that responsibility and to the length of time for which the deceased discharged that responsibility;

(*b*) to whether in assuming and discharging that responsibility the deceased did so knowing that the applicant was not his own child;

(*c*) to the liability of any other person to maintain the applicant.

(4) Without prejudice to the generality of sub-paragraph (*g*) of paragraph (1), where an application for an order under Article 4 is made by virtue of Article 3(1)(*e*), the court shall, in addition to the matters specifically mentioned in sub-paragraphs (*a*) to (*f*) of that paragraph, have regard to the extent to which and the basis upon which the deceased assumed responsibility for the maintenance of the applicant and to the length of time for which the deceased discharged that responsibility.

(5) In considering the matters to which the court is required to have regard under this Article, the court shall take into account the facts as known to the court at the date of the hearing.

(6) In considering the financial resources of any person for the purposes of this Article the court shall take into account his earning capacity and in considering the financial needs of any person for the purposes of this Article the court shall take into account his financial obligations and responsibilities.

Time-limit for applications

6. An application for an order under Article 4 shall not, except with the permission of the court, be made after the end of the period of six months from the date on which representation with respect to the estate of the deceased is first taken out.

Interim orders

7.—(1) Where on an application for an order under Article 4 it appears to the court—

(*a*) that the applicant is in immediate need of financial assistance, but it is not yet possible to determine what order (if any) should be made under that Article; and

(*b*) that property forming part of the net estate of the deceased is or can be made available to meet the need of the applicant;

the court may order that, subject to such conditions or restrictions, if any, as the court may impose and to any further order of the court, there shall be paid to the applicant out of the net estate of the deceased such sum or sums and (if more than one) at such intervals as the court thinks reasonable; and the court may order that, subject to the provisions of this Order, such payments are to be made until such date as the court may specify, not being later than the date on which the court either makes an order under Article 4 or decides not to exercise its powers under that Article.

(2) Paragraphs (2), (3) and (4) of Article 4 shall apply in relation to an order under this Article as they apply in relation to an order under that Article.

(3) In determining what order, if any, should be made under this Article the court shall, so far as the urgency of the case admits, have regard to the same matters as those to which the court is required to have regard under Article 5.

(4) An order under Article 4 may provide that any sum paid to the applicant by virtue of this Article shall be treated to such an extent and in such manner as may be provided by that order as having been paid on account of any payment provided for by that order.

Variation, discharge, etc., of orders for periodical payments

8.—(1) Subject to the provisions of this Order, where the court has made an order under Article 4(1)(*a*) (in this Article referred to as 'the original order') for the making of periodical payments to any person (in this Article referred to as 'the original recipient'), the court, on an application under this Article, shall have power by order to vary or discharge the original order or to suspend any provision of it temporarily and to revive the operation of any provision so suspended.

(2) Without prejudice to the generality of paragraph (1), an order made on an application for the variation of the original order may—

(*a*) provide for the making out of any relevant property of such periodical payments and for such term as may be specified in the order to any person who has applied, or would but for Article 6 be entitled to apply, for an order under Article 4 (whether or not, in the case of any application, an order was made in favour of the applicant);

(*b*) provide for the payment out of any relevant property of a lump sum of such amount as may be so specified to the original recipient or to any such person as is mentioned in sub-paragraph (*a*);

c) provide for the transfer of the relevant property, or such part thereof as may be so specified, to the original recipient or to any such person as is so mentioned.

(3) Where the original order provides that any periodical payments payable thereunder to the original recipient are to cease on the occurrence of an event specified in the order (other than the remarriage of a former wife or former husband) or on the expiration of a period so specified, then, if, before the end of the period of six months from the date of the occurrence of that event or of the expiration of that period, an application is made for an order under this Article, the court shall have power to make any order which it would have had power to make if the application had been made before that date (whether in favour of the original recipient or any such person as is mentioned in paragraph (2)(*a*) and whether having effect from that date or from such later date as the court may specify).

(4) Any reference in this Article to the original order shall include a reference to an order made under this Article and any reference in this Article to the original recipient shall include a reference to any person to whom periodical payments are required to be made by virtue of an order under this Article.

(5) An application under this Article may be made by any of the following persons, that it so say—

a) any person who by virtue of Article 3(1) has applied, or would but for Article 6 be entitled to apply, for an order under Article 4,

b) the personal representative of the deceased,

c) the trustees of any relevant property, and

d) any beneficiary of the estate of the deceased.

(6) An order under this Article may only affect—

a) property the income of which is at the date of the order applicable wholly or in part for the making of periodical payments to any person who has applied for an order under this Order, or

b) in the case of an application under paragraph (3) in respect of payments which have ceased to be payable on the occurrence of an event or the expiration of a period, property the income of which was so applicable immediately before the occurrence of that event or the expiration of that period, as the case may be,

and any such property as is mentioned in sub-paragraph (*a*) or (*b*) is in paragraphs (2) and (5) referred to as 'relevant property'.

(7) In exercising the powers conferred by this Article the court shall have regard to all the circumstances of the case, including any change in any of the matters to which the court was required to have regard when making the order to which the application relates.

(8) Where the court makes an order under this Article, it may give such consequential directions as it thinks necessary or expedient having regard to the provisions of the order.

(9) No such order as is mentioned in Article 4(1)(*d*), (*e*) or (*f*), 11, 12 or 13 shall be made on an application under this Article.

(10) For the avoidance of doubt it is hereby declared that, in relation to an order which provides for the making of periodical payments which are to cease on the occurrence of an event specified in the order (other than the remarriage of a former wife or former husband) or on the expiration

of a period so specified, the power to vary an order includes power to provide for the making of periodical payments after the expiration of that period or the occurrence of that event.

Payment of lump sums by instalments

9.—(1) An order under Article 4(1)(*b*) or 8(2)(*b*) for the payment of a lump sum may provide for the payment of that sum by instalments of such amount as may be specified in the order.

(2) Where an order is made by virtue of paragraph (1), the court shall have power, on an application made by the person to whom the lump sum is payable, by the personal representative of the deceased or by the trustees of the property out of which the lump sum is payable, to vary that order by varying the number of instalments payable, the amount of any instalment and the date on which any instalment becomes payable.

Property available for financial provision

Property treated as part of 'net estate'

10.—(1) Where a deceased person has in accordance with any statutory provision nominated any person to receive any sum of money or other property on his death and that nomination is in force at the time of his death, that sum of money, after deducting therefrom any capital transfer tax payable in respect thereof, or that other property, to the extent of the value thereof at the date of the death of the deceased after deducting therefrom any capital transfer tax so payable, shall be treated for the purposes of this Order as part of the net estate of the deceased; but this paragraph shall not render any person liable for having paid that sum or transferred that other property to the person named in the nomination in accordance with the directions given in the nomination.

(2) Where any sum of money or other property is received by any person as a donatio mortis causa made by a deceased person, that sum of money, after deducting therefrom any capital transfer tax payable thereon, or that other property, to the extent of the value thereof at the date of the death of the deceased after deducting therefrom any capital transfer tax so payable, shall be treated for the purposes of this Order as part of the net estate of the deceased; but this paragraph shall not render any person liable for having paid that sum or transferred that other property in order to give effect to that donatio mortis causa.

(3) The amount of capital transfer tax to be deducted for the purposes of this Article shall not exceed the amount of that tax which has been borne by the person nominated by the deceased or, as the case may be, the person who has received a sum of money or other property as a donatio mortis causa.

Property held on a joint tenancy

11.—(1) Where a deceased person was immediately before his death beneficially entitled to a joint tenancy of any property, then, if, before the end of the period of six months from the date on which representation with respect to the estate of the deceased was first taken out or 18 months from the date of the death (whichever first occurs), an application is made for an order under Article 4, the court for the purpose of facilitating the making of financial provision for the applicant under this Order may order that the deceased's severable share of that property, at the value thereof immediately before his death, shall, to such extent as appears to the court to be just in all the circumstances of the case, be treated for the purposes of this Order as part of the net estate of the deceased.

(2) In determining the extent to which any severable share is to be treated as part of the net estate of the deceased by virtue of an order under paragraph (1), the court shall have regard to any capital transfer tax payable in respect of that severable share.

(3) Where an order is made under paragraph (1), the provisions of this Article shall not render any person (other than a surviving joint tenant) liable for anything done by him before the order was made.

(4) For the avoidance of doubt it is hereby declared that for the purposes of this Article there may be a joint tenancy of a chose in action.

Powers of court in relation to transactions intended to defeat applications for financial provision

Dispositions intended to defeat applications for financial provision

12.—(1) Where an application is made to the court for an order under Article 4, the applicant may, in the proceedings on that application, apply to the court for an order under paragraph (2).

(2) Where on an application under paragraph (1) the court is satisfied—

(*a*) that, less than six years before the date of the death of the deceased, the deceased with the intention of defeating an application for financial provision under this Order made a disposition, and

(*b*) that full valuable consideration for that disposition was not given by the person to whom or for the benefit of whom the disposition was made (in this Article referred to as 'the donee') or by any other person, and

(*c*) that the exercise of the powers conferred by this Article would facilitate the making of financial provision for the applicant under this Order,

then, subject to the provisions of this Article and of Articles 14 and 15, the court may order the donee (whether or not at the date of the order he holds any interest in the property disposed of to him or for his benefit by the deceased) to provide, for the purpose of the making of that financial provision, such sum of money or other property as may be specified in the order.

(3) Where an order is made under paragraph (2) as respects any disposition made by the deceased which consisted of the payment of money to or for the benefit of the donee, the amount of any sum of money or the value of any property ordered to be provided under that paragraph shall not exceed the amount of the payment made by the deceased after deducting therefrom any capital transfer tax borne by the donee in respect of that payment.

(4) Where an order is made under paragraph (2) as respects any disposition made by the deceased which consisted of the transfer of property (other than a sum of money) to or for the benefit of the donee, the amount of any sum of money or the value of any property ordered to be provided under that paragraph shall not exceed the value at the date of the death of the deceased of the property disposed of by him to or for the benefit of the donee (or if that property has been disposed of by the person to whom it

was transferred by the deceased, the value at the date of that disposal thereof) after deducting therefrom any capital transfer tax borne by the donee in respect of the transfer of that property by the deceased.

(5) Where an application (in this paragraph referred to as 'the original application') is made for an order under paragraph (2) in relation to any disposition, then, if on an application under this paragraph by the donee or by any applicant for an order under Article 4 the court is satisfied—

(*a*) that, less than six years before the date of the death of the deceased, the deceased with the intention of defeating an application for financial provision under this Order made a disposition other than the disposition which is the subject of the original application, and

(*b*) that full valuable consideration for that other disposition was not given by the person to whom or for the benefit of whom that other disposition was made or by any other person,

the court may exercise in relation to the person to whom or for the benefit of whom that other disposition was made the powers which the court would have had under paragraph (2) if the original application had been made in respect of that other disposition and the court had been satisfied as to the matters set out in sub-paragraphs (*a*), (*b*) and (*c*) of that paragraph: and where any application is made under this paragraph, any reference in this Article (except in paragraph (2)(*b*)) to the donee shall include a reference to the person to whom or for the benefit of whom that other disposition was made.

(6) In determining whether and in what manner to exercise its powers under this Article, the court shall have regard to the circumstances in which any disposition was made and any valuable consideration which was given therefor, the relationship, if any, of the donee to the deceased, the conduct and financial resources of the donee and all the other circumstances of the case.

(7) In this Article 'disposition' does not include—

(*a*) any provision in a will, any such nomination as is mentioned in Article 10(1) or any donatio mortis causa, or

(*b*) any appointment of property made, otherwise than by will, in the exercise of a special power of appointment,

but, subject to these exceptions, includes any payment of money (including the payment of a premium under a policy of assurance) and any conveyance, assurance, appointment or gift of property of any description, whether made by an instrument or otherwise.

(8) The provisions of this Article do not apply to any disposition made before the commencement of this Order.

Contracts to leave property by will

13.—(1) Where an application is made to the court for an order under Article 4, the applicant may, in the proceedings on that application, apply to the court for an order under this Article.

(2) Where on an application under paragraph (1) the court is satisfied—

(*a*) that the deceased made a contract by which he agreed to leave by his will a sum of money or other property to any person or by which he agreed that a sum of money or other property would be paid or transferred to any person out of his estate, and (*b*) that the deceased made that contract with the intention of defeating an application for financial provision under this Order, and

(*c*) that when the contract was made full valuable consideration for that contract was not given or promised by the person with whom or for the benefit of whom the contract was made (in this Article referred to as 'the donee') or by any other person, and

(*d*) that the exercise of the powers conferred by this Article would facilitate the making of financial provision for the applicant under this Order,

then, subject to the provisions of this Article and of Articles 14 and 15, the court may make any one or more of the following orders:—

(i) if any money has been paid or any other property has been transferred to or for the benefit of the donee in accordance with the contract, an order directing the donee to provide, for the purpose of the making of that financial provision, such sum of money or other property as may be specified in the order;

(ii) if the money or all the money has not been paid or the property or all the property has not been transferred in accordance with the contract, an order directing the personal representative of the deceased not to make any payment or transfer any property, or not to make any further payment or transfer any further property, as the case may be, in accordance therewith or directing the personal representative only to make such payment or transfer such property as may be specified in the order.

(3) Notwithstanding anything in paragraph (2), the court may exercise its powers thereunder in relation to any contract made by the deceased only to the extent that the court considers that the amount of any sum of money paid or to be paid or the value of any property transferred or to be transferred in accordance with the contract exceeds the value of any valuable consideration given or to be given for that contract, and for this purpose the court shall have regard to the value of property at the date of the hearing.

(4) In determining whether and in what manner to exercise its powers under this Article, the court shall have regard to the circumstances in which the contract was made, the relationship, if any, of the donee to the deceased, the conduct and financial resources of the donee and all the other circumstances of the case.

(5) Where an order has been made under paragraph (2) in relation to any contract, the rights of any person to enforce that contract or to recover damages or to obtain other relief for the breach thereof shall be subject to any adjustment made by the court under Article 14(3) and shall survive to such extent only as is consistent with giving effect to the terms of that order.

(6) The provisions of this Article do not apply to a contract made before the commencement of this Order.

Provisions supplementary to Articles 12 and 13

14.—(1) Where the exercise of any of the powers conferred by Article 12 or 13 is conditional on the court being satisfied that a disposition or contract was made by a deceased person with the intention of defeating an application for financial provision under this Order, that condition shall be fulfilled if the court is of the opinion that, on a balance of probabilities, the intention of the deceased (though not necessarily his sole intention) in making the disposition or contract was to prevent an order for financial provision being made under this Order or to reduce the amount of the provision which might otherwise be granted by an order thereunder.

(2) Where an application is made under Article 13 with respect to any contract made by the deceased and no valuable consideration was given or promised by any person for that contract then, notwithstanding anything in paragraph (1), it shall be presumed, unless the contrary is shown, that the deceased made that contract with the intention of defeating an application for financial provision under this Order.

(3) Where the court makes an order under Article 12 or 13 it may give such consequential directions as it thinks fit (including directions requiring the making of any payment or the transfer of any property) for giving effect to the order or for securing a fair adjustment of the rights of the persons affected thereby.

(4) Any power conferred on the court by Article 12 or 13 to order the donee, in relation to any disposition or contract, to provide any sum of money or other property shall be exercisable in like manner in relation to the personal representative of the donee, and—

(*a*) any reference in paragraph (4) of Article 12 to the disposal of property by the donee shall include a reference to disposal by the personal representative of the donee, and

(*b*) any reference in paragraph (5) of Article 12 to an application by the donee under that paragraph shall include a reference to an application by the personal representative of the donee;

but the court shall not have power under Article 12 or 13 to make an order in respect of any property forming part of the estate of the donee which has been distributed by the personal representative; and the personal representative shall not be liable for having distributed any such property before he has notice of the making of an application under Article 12 or 13 on the ground that he ought to have taken into account the possibility that such an application would be made.

Provisions as to trustees in relation to Articles 12 and 13

15.—(1) Where an application is made for—

(*a*) an order under Article 12 in respect of a disposition made by the deceased to any person as a trustee, or

(*b*) an order under Article 13 in respect of any payment made or property transferred, in accordance with a contract made by the deceased, to any person as a trustee,

the powers of the court under Article 12 or 13 to order that trustee to provide a sum of money or other property shall be subject to the following limitation (in addition, in a case of an application under Article 12, to any provision regarding the deduction of capital transfer tax) namely, that the amount of any sum of money or the value of any property ordered to be provided—

(i) in the case of an application in respect of a disposition which consisted of the payment of money or an application in respect of the payment of money in accordance with a contract, shall not exceed the aggregate of so much of that money as is at the date of the order in the hands of the trustee and the value at that date of any property which represents that money or is derived therefrom and is at that date in the hands of the trustee;

(ii) in the case of an application in respect of a disposition which consisted of the transfer of property (other than a sum of money) or an application in respect of the transfer of property (other than a sum of money) in accordance with a contract, shall not exceed the aggregate of the value at the date of the order of so much of that property as is at that date in the hands of the trustee and the value at that date of any property which represents the first-mentioned property or is derived therefrom and is at that date in the hands of the trustee.

(2) Where any application such as is mentioned in paragraph (1) is made in respect of a disposition made to any person as a trustee or in respect of any payment made or property transferred in accordance with a contract to any person as a trustee, the trustee shall not be liable for having distributed any money or other property on the ground that he ought to have taken into account the possibility that such an application would be made.

(3) Where any application such as is mentioned in paragraph (1) is made in respect of a disposition made to any person as a trustee or in respect of any payment made or property transferred in accordance with a contract to any person as a trustee, any reference in Article 12 or 13 to the donee shall be construed as including a reference to the trustee or trustees for the time being of the trust in question and any reference in paragraph (1) or (2) to a trustee shall be construed in the same way.

Special provisions relating to cases of divorce, separation, etc.

Provision as to cases where no financial relief was granted in divorce proceedings, etc.

16.—(1) Where, within twelve months from the date on which a decree of divorce or nullity of marriage has been made absolute or a decree of judicial separation has been granted, a party to the marriage dies and—

(*a*) an application for a financial provision order under Article 25 of the Matrimonial Causes (Northern Ireland) Order 1978 or a property adjustment order under Article 26 of that Order has not been made by the other party to that marriage, or

(*b*) such an application has been made but the proceedings thereon have not been determined at the date of the death of the deceased,

then, if an application for an order under Article 4 is made by that other party, the court shall, notwithstanding anything in Article 3 or 5 have power, if it thinks it just to do so, to treat that party for the purposes of that application as if the decree of divorce or nullity of marriage had not been made absolute or the decree of judicial separation had not been granted, as the case may be.

(2) This Article shall not apply in relation to a decree of judicial separation unless at the date of the death of the deceased the decree was in force and the separation was continuing.

Restriction imposed in divorce proceedings, etc., on application under this Order

17.—(1) On granting a decree of divorce, a decree of nullity of marriage or a decree of judicial separation or at any time thereafter, the High Court or a divorce county court may, if that court considers it just to do so and the parties to the marriage agree, order that either party to the marriage shall not be entitled on the death of the other party to apply for an order under Article 4.

(2) In the case of a decree of divorce or nullity of marriage an order may be made under paragraph (1) before or after the decree is made absolute, but if it is made before the decree is made absolute it shall not take effect unless the decree is made absolute.

(3) Where an order made under paragraph (1) on the grant of a decree of divorce or nullity of marriage has come into force with respect to a party to a marriage, then, on the death of the other party to that marriage, the court shall not entertain any application for an order under Article 4 made by the first-mentioned party.

(4) Where an order made under paragraph (1) on the grant of a decree of judicial separation has come into force with respect to any party to a marriage, then, if the other party to that marriage dies while the decree is in force and the separation is continuing, the court shall not entertain any application for an order under Article 4 made by the first-mentioned party.

Variation and discharge of secured periodical payments orders

18.—(1) Where an application for an order under Article 4 is made to the court by any person who was at the time of the death of the deceased entitled to payments from the deceased under a secured periodical payments order made under the Matrimonial Causes (Northern Ireland) Order 1978, then, in the proceedings on that application, the court shall have power, if an application is made under this Article by that person or by the personal representative of the deceased, to vary or discharge that periodical payments order or to revive the operation of any provision thereof which has been suspended under Article 33 of that Order.

(2) In exercising the powers conferred by this Article the court shall have regard to all the circumstances of the case, including any order which the court proposes to make under Article 4 or Article 7, and any change (whether resulting from the death of the deceased or otherwise) in any of the matters to which the court which made the secured periodical payments order was required to have regard when making it.

(3) The powers exercisable by the court under this Article in relation to an order shall be exercisable also in relation to any instrument executed in pursuance of the order.

Variation and revocation of maintenance agreements

19.—(1) Where an application for an order under Article 4 is made to the court by any person who was at the date of the death of the deceased entitled to payments from the deceased under a maintenance agreement which provided for the continuation of payments under the agreement after the death of the deceased, then, in the proceedings on that application, the court shall have power, if an application is made under this Article by that person or by the personal representative of the deceased, to vary or revoke that agreement.

(2) In exercising the powers conferred by this Article the court shall

have regard to all the circumstances of the case, including any order which the court proposes to make under Article 4 or 7 and any change (whether resulting from the death of the deceased or otherwise) in any of the circumstances in the light of which the agreement was made.

(3) If a maintenance agreement is varied by the court under this Article the like consequences shall ensue as if the variation had been made immediately before the death of the deceased by agreement between the parties and for valuable consideration.

(4) In this Article 'maintenance agreement', in relation to a deceased person, means any agreement made, whether in writing or not and whether before or after the commencement of this Order by the deceased with any person with whom he entered into a marriage, being an agreement which contained provisions governing the rights and liabilities towards one another when living separately of the parties to that marriage (whether or not the marriage has been dissolved or annulled) in respect of the making or securing of payments or the disposition or use of any property, including such rights and liabilities with respect to the maintenance or education of any child, whether or not a child of the deceased or a person who was treated by the deceased as a child of the family in relation to that marriage.

Availability of court's powers under this Order in certain applications

20.—(1) Where—

(*a*) a person against whom a secured periodical payments order was made under the Matrimonial Causes (Northern Ireland) Order 1978 has died and an application is made under Article 33(6) of that Order for the variation or discharge of that order or for the revival of the operation of any provision thereof which has been suspended, or

(*b*) a party to a maintenance agreement within the meaning of Article 36 of that Order has died, the agreement being one which provides for the continuation of payments thereunder after the death of one of the parties, and an application is made under Article 38(1) of that Order for the alteration of the agreement under Article 37 of that Order;

the court to which the application is made under the said Article 33(6) or 38(1) shall have power to direct that the application shall be deemed to have been accompanied by an application for an order under Article 4.

(2) Where the court to which an application is made under the said Article 33(6) or 38(1) gives a direction under paragraph (1), that court shall have power—

(*a*) to make any order which it would have had power to make under the provisions of this Order if the application under the said Article 33(6) or 38(1) as the case may be, had been made jointly with an application for an order under Article 4; and

(*b*) to give such consequential directions as may be necessary for enabling it to exercise any of the powers available to it under this Order in the case of an application for an order under Article 4.

(3) Where an order made under Article 17(1) is in force with respect to a party to a marriage, a direction shall not be given under paragraph (1) with respect to any application made under the said Article 33(6) or 38(1) by that party on the death of the other party.

Miscellaneous and supplementary provisions

Effect, duration and form of orders

21.—(1) Where an order is made under Article 4 then, for all purposes, the will or the law relating to intestacy, or both the will and the law relating to intestacy, as the case may be, shall have effect and be deemed to have had effect as from the deceased's death subject to the provisions of the order.

(2) Any order made under Article 4 or 7 in favour of—

(a) an applicant who was the former husband or former wife of the deceased, or

(b) an applicant who was the husband or wife of the deceased in a case where the marriage with the deceased was the subject of a decree of judicial separation and at the date of death the decree was in force and the separation was continuing,

shall, in so far as it provides for the making of periodical payments, cease to have effect on the remarriage of the applicant, except in relation to any arrears due under the order on the date of the remarriage.

(3) A copy of every order made under this Order shall be sent to the Probate and Matrimonial Office of the Supreme Court for entry and filing, and a memorandum of the order shall be endorsed on, or permanently annexed to, the probate or letters of administration under which the estate is being administered.

Provisions as to personal representatives, etc.

22.—(1) The provisions of this Order shall not render the personal representative of a deceased person liable for having distributed any part of the estate of the deceased, after the end of the period of six months from the date on which representation with respect to the estate of the deceased is first taken out, on the ground that he ought to have taken into account the possibility—

(*a*) that the court might permit the making of an application for an order under Article 4 after the end of that period, or

(b) that, where an order has been made under Article 4 the court might exercise in relation thereto the powers conferred on it by Article 8,

but this paragraph shall not prejudice any power to recover, by reason of the making of an order under this Order, any part of the estate so distributed.

(2) Where the personal representative of a deceased person pays any sum directed by an order under Article 7 to be paid out of the deceased's net estate, he shall not be under any liability by reason of that estate not being sufficient to make the payment, unless at the time of making the payment he has reasonable cause to believe that the estate is not sufficient.

(3) Where a deceased person entered into a contract by which he agreed to leave by his will any sum of money or other property to any person or by which he agreed that a sum of money or other property would be paid or transferred to any person out of his estate, then, if the personal representative of the deceased has reason to believe that the deceased entered into the contract with the intention of defeating an application for financial provision under this Order, he may, notwithstanding anything in

that contract, postpone the payment of that sum of money or the transfer of that property until the expiration of the period of six months from the date on which representation with respect to the estate of the deceased is first taken out or, if during that period an application is made for an order under Article 4, until the determination of the proceedings on that application.

(4) For the purposes of this Order, where—

(*a*) an assent or transfer by a personal representative relating to registered land, or

(*b*) an application by a surviving joint tenant for his registration as owner of registered land,

is presented to the Registrar of Titles for registration, the Registrar shall, notwithstanding any provision of this Order, be entitled to assume that, as the case may be,—

(i) the personal representative is acting correctly and within his powers, or

(ii) the surviving joint tenant is entitled to be registered as owner of the land.

Admissibility as evidence of statements made by deceased

23.—(1) Without prejudice to the Evidence Act (Northern Ireland) 1939 (admissibility of documentary evidence), in any proceedings under this Order a statement made by the deceased, whether orally or in a document or otherwise, shall, subject to this Article and to any rules of court, be admissible as evidence of any fact stated therein of which direct oral evidence by the deceased, if he could have been called as a witness, would have been admissible.

(2) Where a statement which was made otherwise than in a document is admissible by virtue of this Article, no evidence other than direct oral evidence by a person who heard or otherwise perceived the statement being made shall be admissible for the purpose of proving it; but if the statement was made by a person while giving oral evidence in some other legal proceedings (whether civil or criminal), it may be proved in any manner authorised by the court.

(3) Where a statement contained in a document is proposed to be given in evidence by virtue of paragraph (1), it may, subject to any rules of court, be proved by the production of that document or (whether or not that document is still in existence) by the production of a copy of that document, or of the material part thereof, authenticated in such manner as the court may approve.

(4) For the purpose of deciding whether or not a statement is admissible in evidence by virtue of paragraph (1), the court may draw any reasonable inference from the circumstances in which the statement was made or otherwise came into being or from any other circumstances, including, in the case of a statement contained in a document, the form and contents of that document.

(5) In estimating the weight, if any, to be attached to a statement admissible in evidence by virtue of paragraph (1), regard shall be had to all the circumstances from which any inference can reasonably be drawn

as to the accuracy or otherwise of the statement and, in particular,—

(*a*) to the question whether or not the statement was made contemporaneously with the occurrence or existence of the facts stated, and

(*b*) to the question whether or not the maker of the statement had any incentive to conceal or misrepresent the facts.

(6) Subject to rules of court, where a statement is given in evidence by virtue of paragraph (1)—

(*a*) any evidence which, if the deceased could have been called as a witness would have been admissible for the purpose of destroying or supporting his credibility as a witness shall be admissible for that purpose; and

(*b*) evidence tending to prove that, whether before or after he made that statement, the deceased made (whether orally or in a document or otherwise) another statement inconsistent therewith shall be admissible for the purpose of showing that the deceased had contradicted himself;

but nothing in this paragraph shall enable evidence to be given of any matter of which, if the deceased had been called as a witness and had denied that matter in cross-examination, evidence could not have been adduced by the cross-examining party.

(7) Section 5 (rules of court) of the Civil Evidence Act (Northern Ireland) 1971 shall apply for the purposes of this Article as if any reference in that section to section 1 or 2 of that Act or to subsection (1) of either of those sections (except the reference in subsection (2)(*a*) to section 2(1)) included a reference to paragraph (1), and as if, in subsection (3)(*b*), for the words 'which is contained in a record of any direct oral evidence given' there were substituted the words 'which was made by a person, whether orally or in a document, in the course of giving evidence'.

(8) References in this Article to rules of court include, in relation to a county court, references to county court rules; and expressions used in this Article which are defined in the Civil Evidence Act (Northern Ireland) 1971 have the same meanings in this Article as in that Act.

Jurisdiction of county courts

24.—(1) A county court shall have jurisdiction to hear and determine any application for an order under Article 4 (including any application for permission to apply for such an order and any application made, in the proceedings on an application for an order under Article 4, for an order under any other provision of this Order) where it is shown to the satisfaction of the court that, at the date of the death of the deceased, the property included in his net estate for the purposes of this Order by virtue of paragraph (*a*) of the definition thereof in Article 2(2) did not exceed £15,000 in value.

(2) Where a county court makes an order under Article 4, the court shall have all the jurisdiction of the High Court for the purpose of any further proceedings in relation thereto under Article 8.

(3) A person dissatisfied with an order made by a county court in the exercise of the jurisdiction conferred by paragraph (1) or (2) or with the dismissal of any application instituted by him under the provisions of this Order shall be entitled to appeal from the order or dismissal as if the order or dismissal had been made in exercise of the jurisdiction conferred by Part III of the County Courts Act (Northern Ireland) 1959 and the appeal brought under the County Court Appeals Act (Northern Ireland) 1964,

and sections 2 (cases stated by county court judge) and 3 (cases stated by High Court on appeal from county court) of the last-mentioned Act shall apply accordingly.

Determination of date on which representation was first taken out

25. In considering for the purposes of this Order when representation with respect to the estate of a deceased person was first taken out, a grant limited to part of the estate shall be left out of account unless a grant limited to the remainder of the estate has previously been made or is made at the same time.

Effect of this Order on rights of Crown

26. Section 16(1) of the Administration of Estates Act (Northern Ireland) 1955 (passing of intestate's estate, in certain circumstances, to Crown as bona vacantia) shall have effect subject to the provisions of this Order.

Increase in county court jurisdiction under Article 38(3) of the Matrimonial Causes (Northern Ireland) Order 1978

27. In Article 38(3) of the Matrimonial Causes (Northern Ireland) Order 1978 (which gives a county court jurisdiction in certain matters affecting the estate of a deceased person where his net estate does not exceed £5,000 in value) for '£5,000' there shall be substituted '£15,000'.

Repeals, savings and transitional provisions

28.—(1) Subject to the provisions of this Article, the statutory provisions specified in the Schedule are hereby repealed to the extent specified in the third column of the Schedule.

(2) The repeal of those statutory provisions shall not affect their operation in relation to any application made thereunder (whether before or after the commencement of this Order) with reference to the death of any person who died before the commencement of this Order.

(3) Nothing in any repeal made by this Order shall affect any order made or direction given under any statutory provision repealed by this Order, and, subject to the provisions of this Order every such order or direction (other than an order made under section 3A of the Inheritance (Family Provision) Act (Northern Ireland) 1960 shall, if it is in force at the commencement of this Order or is made by virtue of paragraph (2), continue in force as if it had been made under Article 4(1)(*a*), and for the purposes of Article 8(7) the court in exercising its powers under that Article in relation to an order continued in force by this paragraph shall be required to have regard to any change in any of the circumstances to which the court would have been required to have regard when making that order if the order had been made with reference to the death of any person who died after the commencement of this Order.

(4) In the application of this Order to a former wife or former husband whose marriage with the deceased was dissolved or annulled, or to a wife or husband who was subject to a decree of judicial separation, under the Matrimonial Causes Act (Northern Ireland) 1939 before the commencement of Part III of the Matrimonial Causes (Northern Ireland) Order 1978—

(a) the references in Article 16(1)(*a*) to a financial provision order under Article 25 and a property adjustment order under Article 26 of that Order shall include references to an order under section 19(1) or (2) (or under either of those subsections as applied by section 19(7)), or under section 19(4), 20 or 21, of that Act of 1939;
(b) the references in Article 18 to a secured periodical payments order under that Order shall include references to an order entitling the former wife or former husband to an annual sum of money from the deceased secured under an order made under subsection (1), or subsections (1) and (7), of section 19 of that Act of 1939 and an order in favour of a child under section 22(3) of that Act, and the reference in Article 18(1) to Article 33 of that Order shall include a reference to subsection (6) of the said section 19 as extended by section 5 of the Law Reform (Miscellaneous Provisions) Act (Northern Ireland) 1951;
(*c*) the references in Article 20 to a secured periodical payments order under that Order shall include references to an order made under subsection (1), or subsections (1) and (7), of section 19 or under section 22(3) of that Act of 1939.

SCHEDULE

Repeals

Chapter or Number	Short title	Extent of Repeal
1960 c 15.	Inheritance (Family Provision) Act (Northern Ireland) 1960.	The whole Act.
1969 c 28.	Age of Majority Act (Northern Ireland) 1969.	Section 3(1).
1969 c 38.	Family Provision Act (Northern Ireland) 1969.	Sections 2 to 6. Section 7(3).
1975 c. 7.	Finance Act 1975.	In Schedule 12, paragraph 20.
S.R. 1976 No. 22.	Revaluation (Consequential Provisions) Order (Northern Ireland) 1976.	In the Schedule, the entry relating to the Inheritance (Family Provision) Act (Northern Ireland) 1960.
SI 1977/1250 (NI 17).	Family Law Reform (Northern Ireland) Order 1977.	Article 7.
SI 1978/1045 (NI 15).	Matrimonial Causes (Northern Ireland) Order 1978.	In Schedule 4, paragraphs 8 and 9.

RULES OF THE SUPREME COURT

ORDER 99

INHERITANCE (PROVISION FOR FAMILY AND DEPENDANTS) ACT 1975

Interpretation

1.—In this Order "the Act" means the Inheritance (Provision for Family and Dependants) Act 1975 and a section referred to by number means the section so numbered in that Act.

Notes: Order 99 substituted by SI 1976/337, r 19(1).

Assignment to Chancery or Family Division

2.—Proceedings in the High Court under the Act may be assigned to the Chancery Division or to the Family Division.

Notes: Substituted as noted to Order 99, r 1.

Application for financial provision

3.—(1) Any originating summons by which an application under section 1 is made may be issued out of [Chancery Chambers], the principal registry of the Family Division or any district registry.

[(2) The summons shall be in Form No 10 in Appendix A.]

(3) There shall be lodged with the Court an affidavit by the applicant in support of the summons, exhibiting an official copy of the grant of representation to the deceased's estate and of every testamentary document admitted to proof, and a copy of the affidavit shall be served on every defendant with the summons.

Notes: Substituted as noted to Order 99, r 1.

Para (1): words in square brackets substituted by SI 1982/1111, r 90.

Para (2): substituted by SI 1979/1716, r 48, Schedule, Pt 2.

Powers of Court as to parties

4.—(1) Without prejudice to its powers under Order 15, the Court may at any stage of proceedings under the Act direct that any person be added as a party to the proceedings or that notice of the proceedings be served on any person.

(2) Order 15, rule 13, shall apply to proceedings under the Act as it applies to the proceedings mentioned in paragraph (1) of that rule.

Notes: Substituted as noted to Order 99, r 1.

Affidavit in answer

5.—(1) A defendant to an application under section 1 who is a personal representative of the deceased shall and any other defendant may, within 21 days after service of the summons on him, inclusive of the day of service, lodge with the Court an affidavit in answer to the application.

(2) The affidavit lodged by a personal representative pursuant to paragraph (1) shall state to the best of the deponent's ability—

(a) full particulars of the value of the deceased's net estate, as defined by section 25(1);
(b) the person or classes of persons beneficially interested in the estate, giving the names and (in the case of those who are not already parties) the addresses of all living beneficiaries, and the value of their interests so far as ascertained;
(c) if such be the case, that any living beneficiary (naming him) is a minor or a patient within the meaning of Order 80, rule 1; and
(d) any facts known to the deponent which might affect the exercise of the Court's powers under the Act.

(3) Every defendant who lodges an affidavit shall at the same time serve a copy on the plaintiff and on every other defendant who is not represented by the same solicitor.

Notes: Substituted as noted to Order 99, r 1.

Separate representation

6.—Where an application under section 1 is made jointly by two or more applicants and the originating summons is accordingly issued by one solicitor on behalf of all of them, they may, if they have conflicting interests, appear on any hearing of the summons by separate solicitors or counsel or in person; and where at any stage of the proceedings it appears to the Court that one of the applicants is not but ought to be separately represented, the Court may adjourn the proceedings until he is.

Notes: Substituted as noted to Order 99, r 1.

Endorsement of memorandum on grant

7.—On the hearing of an application under section 1 the personal representative shall produce to the Court the grant of representation to the deceased's estate and, if an order is made under the Act, the grant shall remain in the custody of the Court until a memorandum of the order has been endorsed on or permanently annexed to the grant in accordance with section 19(3).

Notes: Substituted as noted to Order 99, r 1.

Disposal of proceedings in chambers

8.—Any proceedings under the Act may, if the Court so directs, be disposed of in chambers and Order 32, rule 14(1), shall apply in relation to proceedings in the Family Division as if for the words

["The Masters of the Chancery Division shall"] there were substituted the words "A [district judge] of the Family Division shall".

Notes: Substituted as noted to Order 99, r 1.

Words in first pair of square brackets substituted by SI 1982/1111, r 91.

Subsequent applications in proceedings under section 1

9.—Where an order has been made on an application under section 1, any subsequent application under the Act, whether made by a party to the proceedings or by any other person, shall be made by summons in those proceedings.

Notes: Substituted as noted to Order 99, r 1.

Drawing up and service of orders

10.—The provisions of the [Family Proceedings Rules] relating to the drawing up and service of orders shall apply to proceedings in the Family Division under this Order as if they were proceedings under those Rules.

[In this rule "Family Proceedings Rules" means rules made under section 40 of the Matrimonial and Family Proceedings Act 1984.]

Notes: Substituted as noted to Order 99, r 1.

Words in first pair of square brackets substituted and words in second pair of square brackets added by SI 1991/1884, r 7.

Transfer to county court

11.—*(Revoked by SI 1992/638.)*

COUNTY COURT RULES

ORDER 48
Family Provision
GENERAL NOTE

Amendments.–The County Court (Amendment No 4) Rules 1991 (SI 1991/1882) amended Ord 48 by removing references to s 36 of the Matrimonial causes Act 1973 (application for alteration of maintenance agreement after death of a party); applications under s 36 are now dealt with under r 3.3 of the Family Proceedings Rules 1991 (SI 1991/1247). The County Court (Amendment) Rules 1992 (SI 1992/793) amended Ord 48 by omitting r 2(1)(d) and substituting a revised r 9.

Interpretation

1.—In this Order—

"the Act of 1975" means the Inheritance (Provision for Family and Dependants) Act 1975;

"the deceased" means, . . . in the case of an application under section 1 of the Act of 1975, the person to whose estate the application relates.

Mode of application

2.—An application to a county court under section 1 of the Act of 1975 for provision to be made out of the estate of a deceased person shall be made by originating application stating—

(a) the name of the deceased, the date of his death and his country of domicile at that date;
(b) the relationship of the applicant to the deceased or other qualification of the applicant for making the application;
(c) the date on which representation with respect to the deceased's estate was first taken out and the names and addresses of the personal representatives;
(d) . . . . .
(e) whether the disposition of the deceased's estate effected by his will or the law relating to intestacy was such as to make any provision for the applicant and, if it was, the nature of the provision;
(f) to the best of the applicant's knowledge and belief, the persons or classes of persons interested in the deceased's estate and the nature of their interests;
(g) particulars of the applicant's present and foreseeable financial resources and financial needs and any other information which he desires to place before the court on the matters to which the court is required to have regard under section 3 of the Act of 1975;
(h) where appropriate, a request for the court's permission to make the application notwithstanding that the period of six months has expired from the date on which representation in regard to the estate of the deceased was first taken out, and the grounds of the request; and
(i) the nature of the provision applied for.

. . . . .

Notes: Originally paras (1), (2): para (2) evoked by and numbering of para (1) revoked by virtue of SI 1991/1882, r 3(2)(ii); sub-para (d) revoked by SI 1992/793, r 14

Filing of application

3.—(1) An application to which rule 2 relates shall be filed—

(a) in the court for the district in which the deceased resided at the date of his death, or
(b) if the deceased did not then reside in England or Wales, in the court for the district in which the respondent or one of

the respondents resides or carries on business or the estate or part of the estate is situate, or

(c) if neither of the foregoing sub-paragraphs is applicable, in the court for the district in which the applicant resides or carries on business.

(2) The applicant shall file with his originating application . . . an official copy of the grant of representation to the deceased's estate and of every testamentary document admitted to proof.

(3) Unless the court otherwise directs, the return day of the originating application shall be a day fixed for the pre-trial review of the proceedings.

Notes: Paras (1), (2): words omitted revoked by SI 1991/1882, r 3(d)(iii), (iv).

Parties

4.—(1) Without prejudice to its powers under Orders 5 and 15, the court may, at any stage of the proceedings, direct that any person be added as a party to the proceedings or that notice of the proceedings be served on any person.

(2) Order 5, rule 6, shall apply to an application under section 1 of the Act of 1975 . . . as it applies to the proceedings mentioned in that rule.

Notes: Para (2): words omitted revoked by SI 1991/1882, r 3(d)(v).

Answer

5.—Every respondent shall, within 21 days after service of the originating application on him, file an answer, which, if the respondent is a personal representative, shall state to the best of his ability—

(a) full particulars of the value of the deceased's net estate, as defined by section 25(1) of the Act of 1975;

(b) the persons or classes of persons beneficially interested in the estate, giving the names and (in the case of those who are not already parties) the addresses of all living beneficiaries, and the value of their interests so far as ascertained;

(c) if such be the case, that any living beneficiary (naming him) is a minor or a mental patient; and

(d) in the case of an application under section 1 of the Act of 1975, any facts known to the personal representative which might affect the exercise of the court's powers under that Act.

Subsequent application

6.—Where an order has been made on an application under section 1 of the Act of 1975, any subsequent application, whether made by a party to the proceedings or by any other person, shall be made in those proceedings in accordance with Order 13, rule 1.

Hearing
7.—Any application under section 1 of the Act of 1975 . . . may be heard and determined by the [district judge] and may, if the court thinks fit, be dealt with in chambers.

Notes: Words omitted revoked by SI 1991/1882, r 3(d)(v).

Endorsement of memorandum on grant
8.—On the hearing of an application under section 1 of the Act of 1975, the personal representative shall produce to the court the grant of representation to the deceased's estate and, if an order is made under the Act, the proper officer shall send a sealed copy thereof, together with the grant of representation, to the principal registry of the Family Division for a memorandum of the order to be endorsed on, or permanently annexed to, the grant in accordance with section 19(3) of the Act of 1975.

Transfer to High Court
9.—An order transferring an application under section 1 of the Act of 1975 to the High Court shall state whether it is desired that the proceedings be assigned to the Chancery Division or to the Family Division of the High Court.

Notes: Substituted by SI 1992/793, r 15.

Appendix C

NOTES OF CASES

Note: This Appendix contains notes of cases not to be found in the Law Report, nor otherwise reported or noted in journals readily accessible to lawyers, such as the New Law Journal, Solicitors' Journal and Law Society's Gazette, or in newspapers like *The Times* and *The Daily Telegraph*. In some cases the transcript has been included and in other cases there is simply a note based on information supplied by a barrister acting in the case. In some cases the decision relates to a procedural point. Decisions under the 1938 Act, the Matrimonial Causes (Property and Maintenance) Act 1958, s 26 of the Matrimonial Causes Act 1965 and the 1975 Act have been included.

Adams and Adams v Schofield and Adams

Court of Appeal (on appeal from Reeve J Family Division) Ormrod, Dunn LJJ and Sir Stanley Rees, 22 July 1981.
DK Rattee QC and *RE Pearce* for the Appellants (Plaintiffs)
M Mann for the Respondents (Defendants).
A Norris for the Insurance Company.
[The subsequent hearing on costs is noted at (1981) 131 NLJ 342.]

LORD JUSTICE ORMROD: I will ask Lord Justice Dunn to give the first Judgment.

LORD JUSTICE DUNN: We grant leave to appeal in this case and treat the hearing of the application as the hearing of the appeal.

This is an appeal from an order of Mr Justice Reeve which he made on 23 June of this year, dismissing an appeal from the District Registrar who had refused to extend the time for bringing proceedings under the Inheritance (Provision for Family and Dependants) Act 1975. Section 4 of that Act provides:

> An application for an order under section 2 of the Act' (which is the section giving the court power to make orders) 'shall not, except with the permission of the court, be made after the end of the period of six months from the date on which representation with respect to the estate of the deceased is first taken out.

The application in this case was made 19 days after the six months period had elapsed.

The background to the case is that the plaintiff is the widow of the testator. They had both been previously married. She had a son, Peter, by her previous marriage who she alleges in these proceedings was accepted by the testator as a child of the family and is accordingly himself a dependant and entitled to claim under the provisions of the Act. They were married in December 1976. It was plainly a stormy marriage, although, in fact, they were living together and still married when the testator died on 25 June 1980. They had one child of their union, a girl called Sarah, who was born in January 1978. At the date of his death the testator was 63 and the plaintiff was 33 years old. The testator had three adult children by a previous marriage.

Two thirds of the estate was represented by the value of what had been the matrimonial home in which, at the date of the death, the plaintiff, Peter and Sarah were living and where they are all three still living.

The will was made on 20 June 1980, five days before the death. It contained pecuniary legacies to the value of something under £7,000. All the personal chattels were left to Paul, a son of the testator by a previous marriage and also an executor, and the residuary estate was left to Paul, Gillian who was a daughter of the previous marriage, and Sarah, in equal shares. Probate of the will was granted on 22 August 1980, so that the limitation period ended six months after that date. But the will contained no provision for the plaintiff, nor for her son Peter. If she has to leave the matrimonial home the plaintiff will have nowhere else to go. Possession proceedings by the personal representatives are presently pending.

The originating summons under the Act was issued on 12 March 1981 which, as I have said, was 19 days after the end of the limitation period. A form of process had been issued on 3 March but it had been the wrong process. In fact, within two days of the death of the testator, on 27 June, a claim in general terms had been notified by the plaintiff's solicitors to the executors' solicitors, although at that time it was a claim to contest the will, but there had never been any doubt in the minds of the executors or the executors' solicitors that the plaintiff was intending to claim under this Act. Indeed in the course of correspondence an ex gratia offer was made on behalf of the executors.

It is right to say that two and a half months before the expiry of the limitation period the executors' solicitors gave the plaintiffs solicitors express notice that an application should be made within the six months' period and that any application for an extension of time would be strenuously resisted.

It is accepted, and was accepted by the learned judge, that no blame whatever for the delay attaches to the plaintiff herself. She was throughout represented by solicitors; she was pressing her solicitor to make the claim (of course she knew nothing of the technicalities of making a claim under this Act) and it was accepted that the failure to claim within the six months' period was due entirely to a mistake by her solicitor. The mistake was that he made the wrong entry in his diary. It is also plain from a perusal of the affidavit and the correspondence that, throughout the period when he was first instructed, he was 'lamentably remiss', as counsel for the plaintiff has put it. He failed to answer letters and he actively misled both his client, the plaintiff, and the personal representatives in regard to the date on which he had instructed counsel.

The learned judge, in refusing leave to make the application out of time, relied wholly on the fact that in his view the plaintiff had a clear case in negligence against her solicitor. He founded himself on a decision of the Vice Chancellor in *In re Salmon, decd* [1980] 3 WLR 748.

In that case the Vice Chancellor had this very section to consider and he laid down six guidelines for the consideration of judges who were required to construe the section. The sixth and last guideline was that it was relevant to consider whether a refusal to extend the time would leave the claimant without redress against anybody. In this case the learned judge went through all the guidelines and found, in effect, in favour of the plaintiff on five of them. He said in his judgment:

> Those consideration, so far, for what they are worth are in favour of the applicants.
>
> But I also have to consider why there was the delay in this case. Although I am prepared to accept that Mrs Adams is personally free from blame, relying entirely on her solicitors, nevertheless the acts of her solicitors must be imputed to her.

The learned judge then says that the delay was quite inexplicable and concluded his judgment in these words:

> In this case the Executors through their solicitors have done all they could to have the matter brought on in the proper way; and even after time expired they were trying by making an ex gratia offer to protect and preserve the estate being anxious to avoid proceedings and costs. They have not put a foot wrong, as opposed to the solicitors representing – I use the word almost in inverted commas – the applicants.
>
> In trying to keep the balance between these two parties, I have come clearly to the conclusion that I should exercise my discretion in favour of the Defendants and dismiss this application.
>
> In doing so I am in a sense doing an injustice to the applicants, but I remind myself of the sixth consideration.

(That is the sixth consideration laid down by the Vice Chancellor in *In re Salmon*). Then the learned judge concluded the judgment in these words:

> Mrs Adams has a clear case in negligence against her former solicitors, and I bear in mind that she may duly become able to recover damages from them. The injustice she suffers will to that extent be mitigated.

Mr Rattee, in a very helpful argument, has submitted quite shortly that, in basing his judgment on that one ground, the judge erred in principle, because he regarded the fact that the plaintiff had a clear case in negligence against her former solicitor as decisive of the matter and failed to take into account in reaching his decision, any other consideration, although all those considerations were found by the judge to come down in favour of the plaintiff.

In considering that submission it is necessary to look shortly at some of the cases which have been cited to us and first of all to look at *In re Salmon* itself, in particular the passage at page 755 where the Vice Chancellor deals with this point:

> Although the subject matter is different, there seems to me to be considerable force in the approach to be found in the line of cases

associated with the name of *Allen v Sir Alfred McAlpine & Sons Ltd* [1968] 2 QB 229, on dismissing actions for want of prosecution. Even if the plaintiff personally is completely blameless, the delays of his or her solicitors must be treated as the delays of the plaintiff, though injustice to the plaintiff will often be avoided by the existence of the plaintiff's right to sue the solicitors for negligence: see particularly – per Diplock LJ at pp 256-7. There may appear to be some logical difficulty in making the decision whether the defendants should escape liability under the Act of 1975 depend in any degree on whether the responsibility for the delay was that of the plaintiff personally or was that of the plaintiff's solicitors: the liability of the defendants, it may be said, ought not to depend upon the distribution of fault between the plaintiff and his or her solicitors. Nevertheless, however logic may affect the defendants' position, there is a real and plain difference to a plaintiff having a claim against his or her solicitors instead of against the defendants and having no claim against anybody.

In the passage in *Allen v Sir Alfred McAlpine & Sons Ltd* which was referred to, Diplock LJ (as he then was) had made observations which supported the view expressed by the Vice Chancellor in *In re Salmon*. However, in *Birkett v James* [1978] AC 324, Lord Diplock expressly resiled from what he had said in *Allen v McAlpine*. He put it this way:

(3) The relevance of the plaintiff's remedies against his solicitor

Where an action is dismissed for want of prosecution the fault must lie either with the plaintiff or with his solicitors or with both. Which of them is to blame for the inordinate and inexcusable delay does not affect the prejudice caused to the defendant, which is the justification for the dismissal of the action; nor should it, in principle, affect his remedy. If it were a matter which the judge ought to take into account in deciding whether to dismiss the action, the court upon an interlocutory application in an action between different parties would have to embark upon what in effect would be the trial of an action by the plaintiff against his actual or former solicitor for professional negligence. That, clearly, is impossible, and apart from an initial hesitation by Sachs LJ in *Sayle v Cooksey* … there has been a consensus of judicial opinion in the Court of Appeal that the question of what remedy, if any, the plaintiff will have against his solicitors if his action is dismissed is an irrelevant consideration: *Paxton v Allsop*.

Sachs LJ's hesitation was based upon some observations in my own judgment in *Allen v McAlpine* made in the context of a case where there was no question that the sole blame lay with the plaintiff's solicitor and that the only reason why her remedy against him would be ineffective was his impecuniosity. My Lords, on further consideration of the difficulties which would be involved if the court may take into account the prospects of the plaintiff having an effective remedy against his solicitors I think that I was wrong in saying that this was a relevant consideration. Upon the facts of the case to which my mind was then directed those difficulties were not apparent.

At page 335 Lord Edmund-Davies said:

> *(3) The relevance of an alternative remedy*
> Regarding the question whether the plaintiff in the instant case might be able to recover damages for negligence against his erstwhile solicitors, Cobb J sagely observed: 'It is only very rarely that a district registrar, or a master or a judge...can form a safe conclusion on such a matter.' Neither he nor the Court of Appeal appear to have paid any regard to this possibility. In this they were, in my judgement, correct.

And Lord Russell of Killowen agreed with both Lord Diplock and Lord Edmund-Davies that an alternative remedy against a solicitor was an irrelevant consideration in the context of an application to strike out for want of prosecution. Mr Rattee submitted to us that the considerations under section 4 of the Inheritance (Provisions for Family and Dependants) Act 1975 were akin to the considerations which arose on an application to strike out for want of prosecution.

However, a different view has been taken in relation to applications for extension of time under section 2D of the Limitation Act 1975. That section provides:

> In considering such an application the court shall have regard to all the circumstances of the case;

although the section itself sets out six matters to which the court is specifically required to have regard.

In *Firman v Ellis* [1978] QB 886, this court held that the prospect of a remedy against a solicitor was a relevant consideration. The Master of the Rolls, at page 909, put it this way:

> The question was much discussed whether, in exercising discretion, the court should have regard to the plaintiff's remedy against his own solicitor. In *Birkett v James...* Lord Diplock said that, in cases of dismissal for want of prosecution, it was not a relevant consideration; but Lord Salmon, at p 330, said that it might have some weight. But those cases are different. In cases under the Limitation Act 1975, I think that the negligence of the plaintiff's solicitor – and a remedy against him – is an admissible consideration. It is one of 'the circumstances of the case' and one of 'the reasons for the delay'. It may tip the scale where the defendant has been substantially prejudiced by the delay.

At page 912 Ormrod LJ said that:

> The defendants, however, argued that the plaintiffs will suffer no prejudice if their actions are statute-barred because in each case they have an unanswerable claim against their solicitors for damages for negligence. The plaintiffs, relying on *Birkett v James* [1978] AC 297, contended that this was an irrelevant consideration. I do not think that Lord Diplock's observations in that case can be applied to cases arising under section 2D, because under that section, the court is required to have regard to all the circumstances of the case, and this

> is certainly one of them. I do not think, however, that it carries much weight in these cases. The court is not concerned solely with financial prejudice to the plaintiff. It is prejudicial to be forced to start another set of proceedings and against a party whom one does not particularly wish to sue and to be deprived of a good cause of action against the original tortfeasor. This may not amount to serious prejudice, but it has to be balanced against no prejudice to the defendant at all. He, personally, has lost nothing, since no loss falls on him in either event; one or other insurance company will pay the damages and costs and his insurers have lost nothing but a fortuitous bonus arising from a harmless error by the plaintiff's solicitor.

At page 916 Lane LJ said:

> (1) In considering whether or not to relieve the plaintiff under section 2D, is it permissible to have regard to the question whether the plaintiff has a valid claim against his solicitor in negligence if he is statute-barred in the original action? The majority of their Lordships in *Birkett v James* ... held that in the circumstances of that case, which was an application to dismiss for want of prosecution not involving the Act of 1975, the existence or non-existence of a remedy against the plaintiff's solicitor was not a material consideration. But section 2D(3) enjoins the court to have regard to all the circumstances of the case, and I find it impossible to say that the insurance position of the plaintiff or of the defendant is not one of those circumstances, when the primary object of the inquiry is to discover the respective degrees of prejudice. What weight should be given to the point is another matter.

It is true that *Firman v Ellis* was subsequently overruled by *Walkley and Precision Forgings Ltd* [1979] I WLR 606; but, as Lord Diplock said in *Thompson v Brown* [1981] I WLR 744:

> I agree with what was said about the unfettered nature of the discretion by the court of Appeal in *Firman v Ellis*, although the actual decision in that case must be regarded as having been overruled.

Thompson v Brown was also a case under the Limitation Act and at page 750 Lord Diplock dealt with the alternative remedy against a solicitor. He said:

> The degree to which the plaintiff would be prejudiced by being prevented from proceeding with his action will be affected by how good or bad would have been his prospects of success; so too it will be affected by the extent to which the plaintiff will be able to recover in an action for negligence against his own solicitor the value of his lost prospects of success. But even where, as in the instant case, and as in *Browes*, if the action were not allowed to proceed the plaintiff would have a cast-iron case against his solicitor in which the measure of damages will be no less than those that he would be able to recover against the defendant if the action were allowed to proceed, some prejudice, although it may be only minor, will have been suffered by

> him. He will be obliged to find and to instruct new and strange solicitors; there is bound to be a delay; he will incur a personal liability for costs of the action up to the date of the court's refusal to give a direction under section 2D; he may prefer to sue a stranger who is a tortfeasor with the possible consequences that may have on the tortfeasor's insurance premiums rather than to sue his former solicitors with corresponding consequences on their premiums. It was suggested that it might be more advantageous to a plaintiff to sue his own solicitor rather than the original tortfeasor since he could recover in an action against the solicitor interest on damages from the date on which the writ against the tortfeasor would have been issued if reasonable diligence had been shown, whereas against the tortfeasor he could only recover interest on damages from the later date, after the expiry of the primary limitation period, at which the writ was actually issued. This, however, is fallacious; he can recover the difference in the interest on damages between the earlier and the later date in a separate action against his solicitor for negligence even if the action against the first tortfeasor is allowed to proceed.

At page 752 Lord Diplock said:

> ....when weighing what degree of prejudice the plaintiff has suffered, the fact that if no direction is made under section 2D he will have a claim over against his solicitor for the full damages that he could have received against the defendant if the action had proceeded must be a highly relevant consideration.

Mr Rattee submitted that, firstly, on the analogy of *Birkett v James*, a remedy against a solicitor, or the likelihood of it, was not a relevant consideration at all for the judge in considering section 4 of the 1975 Act because an application to strike out for want of prosecution was a closer analogy than an application for an extension of time under the Limitation Act 1975 because of the wording of section 2D of that Act. But, in the alternative, he submitted that the cases since *Allen v McAlpine*, which were not cited by the Vice Chancellor in *In re Salmon*, showed that the weight to be attached to a possible remedy against a solicitor depended upon the prejudice to be suffered by the plaintiff on the one hand, and the defendant on the other; and he submitted that, in this case, no prejudice would be suffered by the defendant, whereas considerable prejudice would be suffered by the plaintiff, or might be suffered by the plaintiff, if she were left to her remedy against the solicitor. Mr Rattee pointed out that the cases to which I have referred in the common law jurisdiction relate to actions for personal injuries, where the question of the computation of damages in an action against a solicitor for negligence arising out of his conduct of personal injuries litigation would be comparatively simple for the court to assess, once liability for negligence was established against the solicitor. But, he submitted, very different considerations would apply in an action against solicitors for negligence in the conduct of proceedings under the 1975 Act. He drew our attention in particular to section 2 of the Act, which gives the court powers to make no fewer than six different types of order. One of those is an order for a settlement, which might well be an appropriate form of order in this case. I say that without in any way seeking to tie the hands of any judge who may subsequently hear this application. But it is a good example of the difficulties with which the court would be faced in deciding the quantum of damages for negligence in an action against a solicitor. The court would have to try to ascertain which of the six orders the court considering the 1975 Act would have made, and if an order for a settlement were most likely then the court would have to do its best to put a value on the settlement. And Mr Rattee emphasised not only the financial prejudice likely to be suffered by the plaintiff if she were left to her remedy against the solicitor, but also the other less material matters which are referred to by Lord Diplock in his speech in *Thomas v Brown Contractors* and also by Ormrod LJ in his judgment in *Firman v Ellis*. Mr Rattee finally submitted that, in any event, the judge here was wholly wrong and plainly wrong to regard the fact that the plaintiff had a cast iron claim for negligence against her solicitor as decisive of the matter.

For the executors Mr Mann has sought to persuade us that the beneficiaries would suffer prejudice if the time were extended because any delay in the distribution of the estate is prejudicial. He pointed out, in reliance on *Chappell v Cooper* [1980] 1 WLR 958, that limitation periods are made to be obeyed and that they should not be lightly extended.

Speaking for myself, I am not prepared to go so far as to say that the chance of a plaintiff having a remedy against his or her solicitor is a wholly irrelevant consideration under section 4. I would prefer to put it that section 4 gives the judge considering the application an unfettered discretion. Parliament has not given any indication or any pre-conceived ideas as to the way in which the discretion is to be exercised. Unlike section 2D of the 1975 Act there is no attempt to lay down guidelines. It is left quite generally to the discretion of the court, subject only to the overriding consideration which affects the exercise of all discretion, that the discretion must be exercised judicially. In the circumstances of a particular case it may be that the fact that the plaintiff has a cast iron and easily computable remedy against her solicitor, may be a factor to which some weight could be attached. But in the circumstances of this case where we have a 19 day delay, the estate has not been distributed, the executors and their solicitors have always known that the plaintiff intended to make a claim, and where very serious prejudice will be suffered by the plaintiff if she is wholly barred from making a claim under the Act, I have no doubt in my mind that the judge was plainly wrong in principle when he attached decisive importance to the fact that she would have a cast iron claim against her solicitor.

Accordingly, for those reasons, I would allow the appeal and give leave to bring an application under the Act, notwithstanding that the limitation period has elapsed.

SIR STANLEY REES: I agree with the decision and the reasons for it, stated by Lord Justice Dunn and would refer only to one matter. That is that the learned judge, whose order is the subject of the present appeal, did not have the advantage of the citation to him of a number of authorities cited to us which clearly affected the weight to be given to the possible remedy which a plaintiff might have against his solicitor.

Lord Justice Ormrod: I agree with both judgments and would only add this. There is obviously, from the cases which have been cited to us, a certain amount of confusion about the relevance and importance of the existence of a claim for damages for negligence against a solicitor in this class of case. I think we should start from the principle that all limitation periods are intended to promote justice and not injustice, and where there is a discretion, or where Parliament has created a discretion to adjust the limitation period, the object of Parliament is to give the court power to adjust the balance of interest between the parties so as to avoid, so far as possible, the totally artificial situations which all time limits sooner or later give rise to. We have seen that throughout the history of the Limitation Acts themselves, with constant attempts to amend them in order to avoid the obvious injustice which arises from rigid rules. A similar process has been gone through in this particular branch of litigation, as Mr Rattee pointed out.

Here we have reached the state – and it is common ground – that under section 4 there is an unfettered discretion in the court to extend the time. That is relevant when it comes to assessing the weight of the argument which is often put forward in these cases, that the defendant has suffered prejudice by being deprived of the limitation period, but logically one must look at that in this way, that the value of the defence is no better than the limitation provision itself, so that, if the limitation period is qualified, the defence is proportionately qualified.

When it comes to considering what is the weight to be given to the existence of a claim for damages against solicitors in these cases, it seems to me that the right approach is to consider the justice of the case as between the parties, first of all, and to take into account all the matters set out very helpfully by the Vice Chancellor in *In re Salmon*. It is only, if, having done that computation, one finds that the plaintiff on the one hand has suffered severe prejudice, and the defendant on the other hand has suffered severe prejudice, or will if the limitation period is extended, that the claim for damages against the plaintiff's solicitors becomes relevant. In other words if, as in this case, all the indications are on the plaintiff's side and all point to extending time, and prejudice on the defendant's side is what I would call purely formal in the sense that they have lost the benefit of such protection as section 4 gives them, then the claim for damages against solicitors is of little weight. It is of little weight for this reason, that in a case of this kind it would be a bonus for the defendants. They would be relieved of a possibly substantial claim, which would be transferred to the shoulders of the solicitor's insurers, quite unnecessarily and contrary to the justice of the case. But quite a different situation would arise if the defendants were in a position to show that they had suffered, or would suffer real prejudice in one way or another if the time period was extended. Then, at that point, the alternative remedy in the plaintiff becomes highly relevant.

I, therefore, take the view that the learned judge in this case misdirected himself. I agree that he was not referred to the various cases that we have been referred to, but he did misdirect himself and he misdirected himself fundamentally in taking the view that it was proper for him to assess the conduct of the solicitors on either side in relation to one another. His criticism of the plaintiff's former solicitor is plainly justified, but this is not an exercise of comparing good and bad solicitors and awarding pluses for being competent and minuses for being incompetent. A remedy in damages, particularly, in this case would be most difficult to assess and not only that, it would lead to a very confusing situation in relation to the child, Sarah's interest under the will; so everything points to the time being extended, subject, of course, to such questions as costs and so on. I would therefore allow the appeal.

Appeal allowed with costs.

Barnsley v Ward

Court of Appeal (on appeal from Vinelott J Chancery Division), Orr, Ormrod and Templeman LJJ, 18 January 1980
R. Wakefield for the Appellant (Defendant)
JH Weeks for the Respondent (Plaintiff)

LORD JUSTICE TEMPLEMAN: This is an appeal against the order of Mr Justice Vinelott dated 31 August 1979 whereby he decided that the plaintiff, Mrs Barnsley, was in immediate need of financial assistance and exercised his powers under section 5 of the Inheritance Act 1975, to the extent of ordering the defendant, who is the sole executor of the will of George Pitkin, deceased, to pay to Mrs Barnsley £50 a week from 8 August 1979 until 31 December 1979 and £400 towards the costs of certain repairs. Nothing turns on the costs of the repairs. The conflict is about maintenance.

The powers given by the Act are that:

> Where...it appears to the court -
> (a) that the applicant is in immediate need of financial assistance, but it is not yet possible to determine what order (if any) should be made under that section; and
> (b) that property forming part of the net estate of the deceased is or can be made available to meet the need of the applicant;
> the court may order that, subject to such conditions, or restrictions, if any, as the court may impose and to any further order of the court, there shall be paid to the applicant out of the net estate of the deceased such sum or sums and (if more than one) at such intervals as the court thinks reasonable.

Mr Wakefield, who has appeared for the defendant, has rightly pointed out that raises three hurdles in the path of Mrs Barnsley. First, she must show that she is in immediate need; secondly, that there is property forming part of the estate which is or can be made available to meet that need and, thirdly, she must satisfy the court that it is right in the circumstances to exercise the court's discretion and make an order in the manner sought.

So far as the immediate need of financial assistance is concerned, it is quite plain on the evidence – and I may say that the evidence was not only given in writing but involved the taking of oral evidence – I think at the instigation of the learned judge, from Mrs Barnsley – that she was in need. She was then, and is now getting something in the region of £20 a week, or perhaps a little more, and her outgoings are £75 a week. That was the reason the learned judge made an order for £50 a week. What is taken against her is the same rather mean point taken before the learned judge, namely, that she did have a job and resigned from it. For reasons which the learned judge deals with in his judgment, life became impossible for her in that job. Life was made very difficult and she left; the learned judge found that she was reasonable in so doing. In any event, this power is not exercised to punish a person who loses a job. Of course, if there is evidence that an applicant is deliberately not taking advantage of employment opportunity, different considerations may prevail, but in the present case the matter was clear to the learned judge. Mrs Barnsley gave an undertaking that she would use her best endeavours to obtain reasonable employment and the judge was satisfied that she had done so to date. There is no evidence that she has failed in that ever since. There can be no doubt in my judgement that the learned judge had ample evidence on which to take the view that Mrs Barnsley was in immediate need of financial assistance.

Then it is said that there is no property which is or can be made available. I should say that the deceased died on 25 March 1978. He left his entire estate to his daughter, the defendant, who, the learned judge said, was herself 30, married and comfortably circumstanced. The real question to be decided at the trial, having regard to all the evidence including that of the testator's intentions before he died, is how the estate should be divided between his daughter and Mrs Barnsley – and possibly Mrs Barnsley's daughter, to whom the testator acted towards the end of his life, at any rate, in some form of loco parentis. In the meantime, against the background that, according to present information, the defendant is herself comfortably circumstanced, we examine the question of whether there is property which is or can be made available to meet these requirements of £50 per week.

First of all, there is a house in which Mrs Barnsley has been living and is allowed to live. That is worth somewhere between £40,000 and £56,000. There was evidence before the judge that Mrs Barnsley herself takes a realistic view and would be willing for the house to be sold if she could be found a suitable smaller house. However that may be, although there is up to £56,000 wrapped up there, there is also a mortgage of some £8,000 which is £4,000 in arrears. There is a minority company shareholding and, taking new evidence which we have been asked to look at by Mr Wakefield on behalf of the defendant, it would appear, if that evidence is correct, and without seeing balance sheets we must for the present purposes accept that it is correct, there will not be much money coming from that source.

More importantly, there is a property at Charlotte Street, Leamington Spa, in which the deceased had a half share, now worth about £35,000. The property is let and there is a rent review clause in the lease. If the rent review clause is operated, the value of the half share may climb. Of course the defendant is naturally reluctant to sell. She says, 'If we wait a little, we may get more than £35,000.' That is a very prudent and proper attitude to take but it is impossible, it seems to me, for the defendant at one and the same time to say 'I prefer to keep Charlotte Street because there will be more money in it for me and possible Mrs Barnsley if we do' and at the same time to wring her hands and say that there is no property available to meet the very pressing needs of the plaintiff who is living at the moment in circumstances of great difficulty – and in my judgement unnecessarily so. The testator has been dead for two years. No doubt there is a certain amount of bad feeling, but the defendant must recognise that there is some obligation to Mrs Barnsley and some sensible result must be reached.

Speaking for myself, I deprecate appeals against orders made under section 5, because where a judge comes to the conclusion that an applicant is in immediate need of financial assistance, his conclusion and his order can be almost completely frustrated by an appeal. It is essentially a matter for the judge of first instance on hearing the evidence and seeing the parties. Mr Justice Vinelott, as one would expect, approached the case with great care. He gave a very full, fair and lucid judgment. He made an order that £50 a week should be paid from 6 August to 31 December 1979. Here we are in January 1980 and the unfortunate Mrs Barnsley has not received a penny, simply because of an appeal which, in my judgement, never had any chance of success. I hope that in matters of this kind – notwithstanding the inevitable bad feeling – people will have regard to the object of the section and be more willing to accept what is after all a finding of fact by the judge of first instance that a particular applicant has immediate need of financial assistance.

It seems to me to be quite plain that all three requirements of the section have been satisfied and this appeal should be dismissed.

That, as I have said, would only give the lady money between August and December 1979. It seems that the learned judge fixed the December date in order to see by then whether there had been any change in circumstances one way or the other which might make any difference. Mrs Barnsley, through her counsel, has asked for the order to be varied to delete the words 'until December 31 1979' and substitute the words 'until judgment in the action or further order'. It seems to me that we ought to make that variation. We are told, and it can be put on oath if necessary, that Mrs Barnsley's finances have, if anything, deteriorated. If the defendant wishes to waste more money she can apply again. In the circumstances outlined to us, and having regard to the facts, this lady has been kept out of the money between August and December 1979 and on the information received as to her existing circumstances, it seems to me to be a waste of time to cut off the £50 a week on 31 December, so I would dismiss the appeal and allow the cross-notice for variation, deleting the words 'until 31 December 1979' and substituting the words 'until judgment in the action or further order'.

LORD JUSTICE ORMROD: I agree. I have only one thing to say and that is that I entirely endorse what my Lord has said about the undesirability of appeals from interim orders made by judges of first instance in cases of this kind. On a number of occasions in recent weeks this court has said, in relation to appeals from interim orders concerning custody in the Family Division, that it is very unlikely indeed that this court will interfere. It will certainly only do so in the most extreme circumstances. The whole purpose of an interim order is to hold the situation as reasonably as possible pending final determination. If people come to this court wasting all the time inevitably involved and wasting money, they should do so with every expectation of having their appeals dismissed.

Lord Justice Orr: I agree with both judgments.

Order: Appeal dismissed with costs
Cross-notice allowed
Legal aid taxation

Re Bayliss, Bayliss v Lloyds Bank Ltd

Court of Appeal (on appeal from Deputy Judge RCS Ellison, Worcester County Court) Stamp, Ormrod and Geoffrey Lane LJJ 9 December 1977.
A Boyle for the Appellant (Plaintiff)
A Ward for the second, third and fourth Respondents (Defendants)
D Jackson for the eighth Respondent (Defendant)

Lord Justice Stamp: This appeal, if I may say so, has been extremely well argued and I should like to express my gratitude to both counsel for the assistance which they have given us in this rather difficult situation.

This is an appeal by Mrs Jean Hilary Bayliss, a widow, against an order by His Honour Deputy Judge RCS Ellison made in Worcester County Court on 20 February of this year, whereby he in effect dismissed the widow's application for reasonable provision for her maintenance by way of a lump sum payment out of the estate of her late husband. The application was of course made under the Inheritance (Family Provision) Act 1938.

The husband died as long ago as 5 December 1970, after twenty-two years of happy marriage. No one suggests that it was anything other than a happy marriage or that the widow was in any way failing in her wifely duties. It was the deceased's second marriage. At the date of the marriage the deceased had three children by his first wife who had died, namely a son Hubert, who is the second defendant in these proceedings, a daughter June who is now Mrs Morris and a daughter Aileen, who is now Mrs Piggott. At the date of the second marriage the family was living on a farm and the ages of the three children of the first marriage ranged from fourteen to nine years, the boy Hubert being the youngest. The plaintiff in effect took the place of the first Mrs Bayliss in relation to the completion of the upbringing of the children of that first marriage. There were four children of the second marriage: a son named Peter born on 31 March 1950, Gillian who was born on 23 March 1955, Yvonne born on 28 August 1958 and Isabel who was born on 4 July 1962. It is to be noted that Isabel was born after the date of the deceased's will and is still a minor. None of the three elder children of the second marriage oppose their mother's claim, but Isabel, being a minor, is in a particular position to which I shall have to refer towards the end of this judgment. So the situation was, at the time of the husband's death in 1970, that the widow and four children were living together in the matrimonial home which was a farm.

Before reading the relevant parts of the deceased's will, dated as long ago as 12 February 1960, it is convenient to observe that the family was at one time wealthy, but the deceased accumulated debts towards the end of his life. Excluding the matrimonial home, which is a house called Rosebank still occupied by the widow and I think the two youngest children, and excluding some insurance policies to the value of not more than about £2,800, the assets of the estate, all of which have been realised since the death of the deceased, fetched upwards of £47,000, whereas the liabilities in respect of the deceased's business alone were upwards of £34,000.

As I have indicated, the marriage was a long one, a happy one, and there is no reason whatsoever to suppose that the deceased intended to leave his widow otherwise than well provided for, it being manifest that the financial situation at the time of his death was quite different from that which he had supposed that it would be when he made his will.

With that introduction, I shall read the relevant parts of the will. As I have said, it was dated 12 February 1960 and it appointed Lloyds Bank Ltd as executors and trustees. There were some small pecuniary legacies to employees, which did not in fact take effect. There was a specific bequest to the son Hubert of an oak chest. There was a bequest to the widow absolutely of all personal chattels and then the will proceeded as follows:

> 5. I bequeath to each of my daughters June Margaret Morris and Aileen Rosemary Piggott the sum of One Thousand Five Hundred Pounds provided if either of my said daughters shall die in my lifetime leaving a child or children living at my death who shall attain the age of twenty-one years then I bequeath the said sum of One Thousand Five Hundred Pounds to such child or children of the deceased daughter.

Then he bequeaths to the son Hubert the freehold house and shop known as number 11, The Square, Bromyard and the slaughterhouse and the leasehold premises known as number 36 High Street, Bromyard. He then goes on to bequeath the business of butcher and slaughterhouse carried on by him at the two addresses which I have mentioned. Then there are some declarations regarding properties to which I need not refer. I pause to observe that the properties dealt with by clause 6 have been sold, and the net amount available for division between the two daughters of the first marriage and the son is, or was, £3,605, that is to say enough to satisfy the pecuniary legacies and £605 for Hubert. It is however also to be observed that the legacies remain unpaid and if they are now to be paid, they would bear interest from the end of the executors' year, so that a very substantial sum of interest would be payable which would exhaust the £605 which Hubert would otherwise claim.

There then follows the gift of the testators' residuary estate which he directed, subject of course to the payment of his debts, funeral and testamentary expenses, etc., should be invested and held in trust for his widow during her widowhood, with the provision that after her death or remarriage the estate was to be divided into four equal shares; as to two such shares for the son Peter, as to one such share for the daughters Gillian and Yvonne. In each case if and when they attain the age of twenty-one.

Then there is a substantial clause in the event of any of them dying under the age of twenty-one. It is to be noted that there is of course no provision for Isabel, who was not born at the time of making the will. There are certain declarations, to some of which I think I must refer. There was a declaration that:

> ...no sale shall be effected of my freehold property 'Rosebank' New Road, Bromyard aforesaid in which I now reside or any other house in which I shall be residing with my wife at the date of my death during the widowhood of my wife without her consent in writing and that until the sale thereof the Bank shall permit my wife to occupy the same as long as she shall so desire.

Then there was a provision that if his wife desired to carry on the business of a Ladies' and Gentleman's hairdresser at 5, The Square, Bromyard, or the business of a butcher at 70, Commercial Road, Hereford, or the business of cafe proprietor at the Danube Cafe, Hereford, or any other business or businesses carried on by him at the date of his death, then he made certain directions regarding the stock in trade. It is sufficient to say that in effect the widow, if she elected to carry on any one or more of these businesses, was to have free use of the stock in trade, but on giving up the business she would be required to pay into the estate the value of the stock in trade at the time she took the business over. Those are the only provisions of the will to which I need refer, emphasising that the testator clearly had the future welfare of his widow very much in his mind.

It appears that at no time since the date of the death of the deceased have the assets been sufficient to meet the debts, funeral expenses and legacies of £3,000 and the £605 payable to Hubert without resort to Rosebank. After the time for applying for relief under the Act had expired, when she discovered that this was the situation, the widow applied to the Chancery Division to extend that time. The application came before Mr Justice Ungoed-Thomas who on 13 December 1972 extended the time and remitted the cause to the County Court. There, I am sorry to say, it remained for far too long, no one apparently doing much about it, except perhaps to discuss it, until September 1975. When the matter came before the learned judge, he heard it for three days. Now the executors had an overdraft at the bank amounting to £1,650. They have administered the whole estate except for Rosebank. The legacies of £1,500 and the balance of the property given to Hubert, an aggregate amount of £3,605, remain unpaid. This means that before taking any account of costs in the Court below, Rosebank would, if matters took their normal course, have to be sold in the due course of administration, and out of the proceeds of that sale there would have to have been paid £1,650 borrowed by the executors from the bank and £3,605 to which I have referred, an aggregate amount of £5,255. At this point, therefore, the situation was that all the widow, against whom no finger has been pointed and who had lived happily with her husband for 22 years, all she would have, was a life interest in the matrimonial home which would have to be sold in order to pay out of the proceeds around £5,255, of which £3,605 would be payable to the children of the deceased's first marriage. There were two valuations on Rosebank made in November 1976. One valuer put it at £16,000 and the other at £19,000. I do not think that it matters which of these valuations is the right one. If Rosebank were sold and the net proceeds of the sale, after paying the £3,255, were invested the widow could not expect to receive a sum amounting to more than £11,000 or £14,000, less any expenses of the sale which counsel accepted would amount to something approaching £1,000. Even at ten percent, not more than £1,400 a year would be received by her under the trust of the residue.

But it is worse than this. We are told that the costs alone in the Court below, directed to be paid out of the estate, amounted to some £3,000, although it may come to less than that. If to that sum we were to add £500, which it is suggested will be the cost of this appeal, the income of the widow would be reduced accordingly. Nor would she have any roof over her head, unless practically the whole of the balance of the proceeds of the sale were invested in purchasing another property for her, and it would have, I would think, to be a very small one; but that would depend upon whether Rosebank is valued at £16,000 or £19,000.

I would say that unless the widow is otherwise well-endowed the deceased, who is described by his wife as a hard-working and generous man, erroneously and lamentably in the words of the Act 'failed to make reasonable provision' for the maintenance of the widow. Looking at the matter as fairly as I can at the date of the deceased's death a reasonable testator with the relevant facts before him would not, in my view, have made any provisions for the grown-up children of the first marriage, but would have given the whole of his estate to his wife absolutely. In my view this testator failed to make reasonable provision. The widow is not otherwise well-endowed. She has a widow's pension which at the time of the hearing was £22 a week. Shortly before the death of her husband she set up in a butcher's business which unfortunately has not turned out to be a success and has had to be sold to pay debts. It was sold for £3,000 plus £10 a week for four years. The debts that had to be paid amounted to some £4,000. £1,000 is still owing. She had and has a small business of a toyshop. In the year ended 31 December 1974 that business suffered a nett loss of £342.60. In the year ended 31 December 1975 the business made a nett profit of £752. There is a flat above the shop which can be let at some £22 a week. Apparently it is not always let at that figure. The widow makes a little money by breeding dogs and cats. In a good year she made £734 out of that. She is about 50 years of age and must, I think, have been working rather hard. One thing appears to be abundantly plain, she cannot save for her old age. She has virtually no capital and, as I have said, she owes the sum of £1,000. The meagre income which she has plus her meagre savings do not in my judgement make the provision made for her by the deceased a reasonable one.

The judge in the course of his judgment dealt with some questions of construction of the Statute which we are told were not discussed before him, counsel taking the view that, at least for the purposes of this particular case, the law was quite clear and that no question of construction of the Act fell to be determined. Plainly you look at the situation as you find it after and not before the death of the deceased and you approach the question whereby reasonable provision is made as an objective and not a subjective matter. The learned judge appears to have accepted the objective approach in the hearing, but dealt with the matter as though the correct approach was a subjective one. Without stating the facts or giving the figures which led to that conclusion, he concluded that the deceased had made reasonable provision for his widow. I confess that I am totally at a loss to understand how he arrived at that conclusion. There being nothing else to give, the widow ought in my judgement to have absolutely the matrimonial home, and that ought to take effect in priority to any interests of the grown-up, well-established children of the first marriage.

I am satisfied that in this case reasonable provision was not made and that reasonable provision would be nothing less than a sum equal to the value of the nett estate of the deceased.

There was a slight complication in the Court below, in that there was a claim by Isabel, acting by the Official Solicitor, for maintenance. The judge acceded to that claim and ordered that the £605 and the legacy of £1,500 given to Mrs Piggott, should be held in trust until the girl had completed her school education, to use the income for that education. That was of course on the footing that the widow failed in her application. In this Court, on the footing that the widow's claim has succeeded, counsel on behalf of Isabel very properly conceded that Isabel's claim should not be maintained. Her mother will look after her.

I would allow this appeal in the sense that I have indicated.

Lord Justice Ormrod: I agree. There is nothing I can usefully add to the judgment which my Lord has given.

Lord Justice Geoffrey Lane: I also agree.

Re Chatterton

Court of Appeal (on appeal from Reeve J Family Division), Ormrod, Waller and Brandon LJJ 1 November 1978.
PJ Fox for the Appellant (Plaintiff)
JS Trenhaille for the Respondents (Defendants)

Lord Justice Ormrod: Lord Justice Brandon will give the first judgment in this case.

Lord Justice Brandon: This is an appeal against an Order made by Mr Justice Reeve on 11 July 1978, upon an application under the Inheritance (Provision for Family and Dependants) Act, 1975. The application related to the estate of a man called Walter James Ernest Chatterton. The applicants were firstly the widow, Mrs Jennifer Mary Chatterton, and secondly the child of the deceased and the widow, Katrina Louise Bedford Chatterton, who I take it was suing through her mother as next friend. The Judge dealt with both the applications and made provision out of the deceased's estate for the benefit of both the applicants; that is, the mother and the child. The appeal, however, concerns only so much of his Order as relates to the child, and it is only the child who is the appellant before us.

The history of the matter is this. In November 1971, the mother married the deceased after a seven-month courtship. She was then aged 23, the deceased was aged 47. He had been married before, but there had been no children of that marriage. The mother already had a child from a previous marriage, then aged about 6, a girl. It was the intention that the deceased should take on this child of the mother as a child of the family. Unfortunately, right from the beginning, the mother and the deceased quarrelled and, after only a very short time – namely about four months – the mother left the deceased, after which they never lived together again. Shortly after leaving the deceased, at the end of March 1972, the mother sought a Matrimonial Order in the Magistrates' Court, on the ground of the deceased's persistent cruelty; but that application was dismissed and she came away empty-handed.

In May 1972 the child, who is the appellant before this court, Katrina, was born. It is apparent from what I have already said that she was the only child of the deceased. After the child was born, for a period which is not clear on the evidence but which we have been told is to be measured in months rather than years, the deceased made voluntary payments to the mother for the maintenance of Katrina at the rate of £5 a week; but he never saw the child and the evidence is that he did not even know her name at any time. It does not appear whether that was by his wish or the mother's wish or by their combined wish, but that at any rate is what happened.

On 23 October 1972, the deceased made a will, after receiving advice from his solicitors. He had been minded to leave all his estate to certain charities. The solicitor told him that that would not really do and that he ought to make some provision for the child Katrina. He suggested to him that it would be a fair and reasonable thing to leave half his estate to that child. The deceased paid some regard to that advice, but could not swallow the whole of it. In the upshot, in his will he left his estate on trust in four parts. One part – that is a quarter – was to go to Katrina when she should attain the age of 18, and the other three parts, three quarters, were to go to some seven different charities, all catering for animals. The will further provided that, if Katrina should fail to reach the age of 18, then her share should also go to the charities. Under the will, the trustees were given wide powers to advance capital to Katrina during her minority, and they were also given very wide powers of investment so far as the estate as a whole was concerned. Just as a matter of history, in November 1972 an appeal by the mother from the Magistrates' decision discussing the summons was dismissed by the Divisional Court of the Family Division.

The deceased left a note, which he signed on 23 October, the same time as his will, explaining why his will was in the form it was. He said this: 'I have made no provision in my will for my second wife because we were married and lived together for a period of less than four months and parted in such circumstances that I do not feel under any obligation to make any financial provision for her. I have made some financial provision for the daughter of my marriage. I have never seen my daughter and I do not anticipate seeing her. I do not even know her name. I consider therefore that in the circumstances the provision made for her by this will gives sufficient.' It seems that by this time or about this time any payments of a voluntary character the deceased made for the benefit of Katrina had ceased to be paid and a number of years went by during which the mother and Katrina were dependent for their support on Social Security Benefits.

On 2 March 1977, the deceased was found dead, and no doubt the contents of his will were made known to the mother. She no doubt took advice; and on 5 December 1977, an application was issued under the Act to which I have referred, in which both the mother and Katrina sought some provision to be made for them out of the estate. What the learned judge did, after hearing the evidence and considering the arguments on both sides, appears from a transcript we have of the proceedings before him. He did not give a lengthy judgment. He asked counsel for the parties whether they wanted him to do more than give what he called a 'verdict'. He was told that they did not. He then said this: 'Well, my verdict is that the mother ought to receive £1,000 out of the estate. And perhaps I go a little beyond a verdict; she is the mother of the deceased's child – that is a most important matter. I think there's to be further provision also for the daughter. I think she should have one half of the residue thereafter on the same terms of the will.' The judge, in saying 'thereafter', meant clearly after the £1,000 had been provided for the mother. Having expressed his view in that way, he made an order accordingly.

The mother, as I have said, is content with his Order so far as she is concerned. This appeal is brought on behalf of Katrina; and what counsel for Katrina has said is that the judge's Order ought to be varied in two ways. First of all he says that it is not right that Katrina should only take under this will if and when she reaches the age of 18, which is what the will provides. He says that that limitation on her right ought to be deleted altogether, so that she has a vested interest from now on. That he regards as a secondary matter. His main application to this court is that a very much larger part of the estate should be allotted to Katrina than the half which the judge thought fit.

I have already mentioned the Act under which this application was made. I do not desire to read large sections of it, because I do not think that would serve any useful purpose. What the Court has to consider is whether the deceased by his will made reasonable provision for Katrina, and if it is of opinion that he did not, then it has power in its discretion to alter the will, in effect, so as to make reasonable provision. Under section 2 of the Act there are various ways in which the court can produce that result. Among other things, it can make 'an order for the settlement for the benefit of the applicant of such property comprised in that estate as may be so specified'. The judge, therefore, clearly had power, if he thought the provision made was inadequate, to alter the settlement on the child so as to make a larger part of the estate available for her. Equally, we have power, if we think fit, to vary the will further by making a still larger part of the estate available to her.

[His Lordship then referred to s 3(1)(a), (d), (e), (g).]

One of the matters which the Court has to have regard to is, of course, the net amount of the estate. We have been told that the net estate, after the £1,000 has been paid to the mother, comes to something like £17,000. It has been agreed that, if that were invested in a normal and reasonable way by the trustees, it might be expected to produce an income of something of the order of £700 a year. It could, of course, be invested to produce either more or less, the trustees having the very wide powers of investment to which I have already referred.

If the matter is left as it is, this child will have an income of something like £14 per week for the foreseeable future; perhaps a larger income if the trustees are successful in the investment policy. It may be that they cannot keep pace with inflation. It may be that they will succeed in keeping pace with it to some extent at any rate. Further, this child, when she reaches the age of 18, will come into the whole of the half share under the judge's Order – that is, £8,500 – unless in the meantime the trustees have used their powers of advancement. It is not suggested that the judge was wrong in concluding that the deceased had not made reasonable provision. We are not asked to reconsider that decision, though I for my part entirely agree with it. As to the provision which he thought was reasonable, I can see nothing wrong at all with what the learned judge did. It seems to me that for this child to be provided with an income of £14 a week, give or take a pound or two either way, depending on the nature of the investment, until she is 18 and then come into a sum of £8,500, is ample provision for her. Of course, the deceased might have adopted a different attitude and left the whole of his money to her. In that case, it would have been a very generous act and going far beyond what it seems to me is comprised in the expression 'reasonable provision'. In considering these matters, the court must have some regard to the walk of life in which these people were and are and the sort of life which the child would have if the father had continued to live until she was 18. The fact is that while the father was alive, the mother did not claim anything from him in respect of the child and although he had obligations towards the child over a period of some years, he did not discharge them and no-one sought to compel him to discharge them. I do not think that ought to colour the result one way or the other, but it is fair to say that, if this child gets the benefit which she will get under the Order of Mr Justice Reeve, there is every reason to suppose that she will be as well off or indeed better off than if the father had lived; one might say even if the father had lived and the marriage had remained alive.

In all these circumstances, I cannot see that there is any reason why this order should interfere with the discretion exercised by the learned judge. I cannot say that if I had been trying the case I should necessarily have reached precisely the same conclusion, but I think that his conclusion is an entirely fair and just one, and I think it should stand. For these reasons, I would dismiss the appeal.

LORD JUSTICE WALLER: I agree. I would add only this, that the solicitor who represented the deceased and who was advising the deceased at the time of making his will not only advised him that in his view it would be a suitable proportion to leave to the child a half, but when the testator considered that advice, as described in the affidavit, 'he was extremely reluctant to leave any part of his estate to either of the applicants'. So he went away having had that conference with his solicitor, but nevertheless the solicitor sent to the testator a draft of the will in almost precisely the form which the learned judge found, namely, that one half of the estate should be left to this applicant and the balance to the charities. The testator apparently considered that for some three months and then amended the draft in the form in which it ultimately was. It shows that an objective view at the time of the making of the will was very similar to that which the learned judge found.

LORD JUSTICE ORMROD: I agree with all that has been said by both my Lords and that this appeal should be dismissed.

Order: Appeal dismissed; no Order as to costs.

Clark v Jones and Another

Court of Appeal (Civil Division), 2 December 1985
J Quirke for the First Applicant.
A Hotham for the Respondent.

DILLON LJ: This is an appeal by Mrs Lily Bett, who was the respondent in the lower court, against an order made by His Honour Judge Mott in the Wolverhampton County Court on 8 July 1985 in proceedings under the Inheritance (Provision for Family and Dependants) Act 1975 in relation to the estate of George Denis Jones, deceased.

George Denis Jones died on 7 January 1981. He was employed by the Post Office Telephone Department (as it then was) at a salary of some £8,000 or £8,500 a year. He died intestate, and his next of kin under the laws of intestacy were his four married sisters, who like him, live in Bilston in the West Midlands. One of these is Mrs Betts, the respondent below and present appellant, and she obtained letters of administration to the deceased's estate and is his sole personal representative.

However, there were two other people who made applications for provision out of the deceased's estate under the 1975 Act. One of those was his former wife, Mrs Alice Jones. The deceased had married her in 1954, and the marriage had lasted for over 25 years and had been dissolved by decree absolute in August 1980. There were no children of the marriage. The other applicant was the present respondent, Mrs Clark. She is now in her late 50s. She is a widow with four married daughters, one, at any rate, in New Zealand.

The deceased came as a lodger to her house in Bilston in 1979. They went on holiday together; and some six months after the deceased had first come to her house as a lodger they began living together, as it were, as man and wife, and that state of affairs continued until the deceased's death. Mrs Clark expected the deceased to marry her; and although it does not appear that he was in any great hurry to do so, his marriage having been dissolved in 1980, the judge formed the view that it was more likely than not that they would have got married if the deceased had not unfortunately died. The relevance of that, of course, is that it points to the relationship between the deceased and Mrs Clark as one which, although only of some three years' duration, was potentially long-lasting.

The deceased left an estate which the learned judge took at the figure of £33,245 as at 31 May 1985. We are told that with further accrual of income the estate now is some £34,544, of which some £3,600 fails to be paid out in respect of the costs of the proceedings at first instance. The principal asset of the estate was a large death grant which became payable on his death in service under the terms of his employers' pension scheme. In addition, there was some £3,000 for a motor car and some remnants of money from other sources, possibly including his share of the matrimonial home, the proceeds of which had been split equally between Mrs Jones and himself on the divorce.

In the court below it was accepted that Mrs Alice Jones, as the former wife of the deceased had locus standi to make application for financial provision from his estate under the Act. It was disputed whether Mrs Clark had any locus standi to make such an application. She claimed as a person who immediately before the death of the deceased was being maintained wholly or partly by the deceased.

The judge in his order awarded Mrs Jones a lump sum of £11,000 out of the estate and awarded Mrs Clark a lump sum of £6,000 out of the estate. The basis of Mrs Betts' appeal to this court is that the judge gave Mrs Clark too much; the award should not have exceeded £2,500. Accordingly, on the appeal it is conceded by Mrs Betts that Mrs Clark, on the facts of this case, did have locus standi to apply under section 1(1)(e) of the Act.

The Act lays down the factors which the court should have regard to in exercising its power to make orders for financial provision under the Act. These are listed under sub-heads (a) to (g) in subsection (1) of section 3 of the Act, sub-paragraph (g) including the words 'and other matter, including the conduct of the applicant or any other person, which in the circumstances of the case the court may consider relevant'. In addition, in the case of an applicant such as Mrs Clark claiming as a person who was being maintained either wholly or partly by the deceased, the court was to have regard to the extent to which and the basis upon which the deceased assumed responsibility for the maintenance of the applicant and to the length of time during which the deceased discharged that responsibility.

So far as the facts are concerned, Mrs Jones' circumstances are not relevant to this appeal, as the award in her favour is not challenged. Mrs Clark's circumstances, as put in evidence by her, were to the effect that she had a widow's pension as a result of her former husband's death of £35.80 a week; she had wages of £40 a week gross, £27 a week net, as a general hand in a shoe shop, and she had a small amount of savings.

Mrs Betts put in evidence showing that she herself is not well off. She is on social security without any job of her own and with a husband who is unemployed, unwell and unlikely ever to be able to work again. But no evidence was put in as to the means and needs of her three sisters who are the other beneficiaries under the intestacy. The evidence as to them merely indicates that they are or have been married and live in the area of Bilston.

We are told that their husbands are still working, and therefore presumably they are better off than Mrs Betts. It seems to me that if any case is to be made as to the needs of the next of kin relative to the needs of the applicant, the personal representative – in the present case, Mrs Betts – ought to put in evidence setting out the financial resources and requirements of the relevant beneficiaries.

The learned judge considered the means of the various parties. He calculated that Mrs Clark was better off while the deceased was living with her than she had been before because of the expenditure which he undertook. He paid originally £20 but later £40 a week for his lodgings and food, which she provided, and she looked after him, as one would expect having regard to the relationship. On the other side, he paid various expenses in relation to holidays. He had a car, which she did not, and therefore took her to visit a married daughter in London, and took her around generally and out into the country on pleasant expeditions together. He gave her clothing from time to time – dresses and such like. He gave money for her grandchildren in small yearly presents. He had given her an eternity ring as a form of engagement ring. He had contributed to the cost of new bedroom furniture and kitchen units in the house and to improve the bathroom and lavatory. Also, because of his employment, there was a telephone in the house, and he paid all the costs of that although presumably Mrs Clark had the benefit of being able to use it, and he did jobs around the house which are generally described as 'do-it-yourself'.

The judge took the view that it was appropriate to regard him as contributing something over £1,000 a year. It seems from the figure of £5,000 that he arrived at that he took a figure of £1,000 and a five-year multiplier.

Mr Hotham, for Mrs Betts, says that the award should not have been greater than £2,500, which he justifies by a similar approach of a dependency of £500 a year and a five-year multiplier, although Mr Hotham candidly says that there is no hard and fast rule. You could take a higher figure for dependency and a smaller multiplier as the association had not lasted so very long.

Mr Quirke, for Mrs Clark, has put forward a calculation which is in part based on the figures given in evidence and in part on his, for the most part as he claimed, relatively conservative estimates of what might have been covered by a general description such as the value of outgoings on the car and clothing. He arrived at a dependence of £2,004 a year. I am bound to say that Mr Quirke's figures are in various respects too high, but I do not think that very greatly matters. The approach of calculating a figure for dependency and a multiplier may be a convenient approach in some cases such as this. It is certainly not a hard and fast approach, because the essence of the discretion of the court under the 1975 Act is that it is a very general discretion. The most relevant citation from authority which has been offered to us, in a case in which counsel wisely abstained from relying too much on other decisions on other facts, is the statement of Sir Reginald Goff in *In re Coventry, decd* (1979) 3 All ER 815, [1979] 3 WLR 802 at page 808:

> What is proper maintenance must in all cases depend upon all the facts and circumstances of the particular case being considered at

> the time, but I think it is clear on the one hand that one must not put too limited a meaning on it; it does not mean just enough to enable a person to get by; on the other hand, it does not mean anything which may be regarded as reasonably desirable for his general benefit or welfare.

Considering all the facts of this case and abstaining from any precise calculations or adding a little more on one head and taking a little more off another head, I see no basis on which this court should interfere with the conclusion at which the judge arrived at the end of a very careful judgment, and I would accordingly dismiss this appeal.

ROBERT GOFF LJ: I agree.

Order: Appeal dismissed with costs to be paid out of the estate. Legal aid taxation of respondent's costs.

Clifford v Tanner and another

Court of Appeal (Civil Division), 10 June 1986
RW Egleton for the Appellant.
ME Brabin for the Respondents.

NICHOLLS LJ: This is an appeal from an order made by Mr Recorder Boothman sitting in the Barnstable County Court on 21 February 1986, whereby he refused to grant to the applicant, Mrs Doris Clifford, permission to make an application under the Inheritance (Provision for Family and Dependants) Act 1975 after the expiry of the statutory period of six months from the date on which probate was first granted to the estate of her late husband, Thomas Clifford.

The facts in short are these. Mr and Mrs Clifford married on 22 May 1963. He was then aged 60 and she was 45. For each it was a second marriage. The deceased had one daughter by his first marriage, Mrs June Tanner. She is the first respondent in these proceedings. The deceased and Mrs Clifford lived together at No 15, Pulchrass Street, Barnstaple. That was a house which had been bought by the deceased in May 1950 for about £1,000. It is with this house that the present proceedings are concerned.

On 12 April 1977 the deceased made a will under which he gave his wife the right to live in the house until remarriage. Subject to that, he gave the house to his daughter and divided the rest of his property between his wife and daughter. Two months later, in circumstances which do not appear from the evidence, on 15 June 1977, the deceased executed a deed of gift in favour of Mrs Tanner. By that deed, expressed to be made in consideration of his natural love and affection for his daughter and in consideration of the covenant on her part contained in the deed, the deceased conveyed the house to Mrs Tanner, and she entered into a covenant to permit her father and Mrs Clifford, her step-mother, and the survivor of them to live in the property, provided they paid the outgoings and kept the property in repair, the daughter being expressed to be released from this covenant in the event of Mrs Clifford remarrying after the death of the deceased.

Two years later, by a further deed dated 5 October 1979, the 1977 deed was varied in that Mrs Tanner was in effect released from her covenant as regards Mrs Clifford, not only if Mrs Clifford remarried, but also in the further events of Mrs Clifford letting or sharing possession of the property.

I now come to the events of 1983, which are crucial on this appeal. The marriage had run into difficulties, and in June 1983 the deceased presented a divorce petition founded on his wife's alleged unreasonable behaviour. We have been shown some correspondence between the parties' solicitors. Suffice it to say that on 5 July 1983 Mrs Clifford's solicitors, Messrs Jeremy Fergusson & Co wrote to the deceased's solicitors, Messrs Slee, Blackwell and Slee, asserting the financial contribution made by their client to repairs and renewals and expressing the hope that discussions between solicitors would bring about a settlement on their client's claim to the house.

What at that stage they understood the position to be regarding the house is not altogether clear, because, on the one hand, they mentioned that Messrs Slee, Blackwell & Slee had told them that the deceased had made a gift of the property to Mrs Tanner, and, on the other hand, they referred to a tenancy for life of Mrs Clifford which they understood to be contained in the deceased's will. That was on 5 July.

On 6 July the deceased made a new home-made will, under which he appointed his daughter, Mrs Tanner, and her husband, Mr William Tanner, who is the second respondent in these proceedings, to be his executors and he left everything he should die possessed of to his daughter.

On 14 July Mr Clifford's solicitors wrote to him concerning his divorce petition and a legal aid application, and in the penultimate paragraph of the letter they said this:

> I think it would be right that you should now release your daughter of her Covenant to allow Mrs Clifford to live in your house after you die and for this purpose have prepared a deed of Release of Covenant for you and Mrs Tanner to sign.

A deed to that effect was duly executed and dated the following day, 15 July 1983. The deceased died on 21 September 1983. Leaving aside any interest he may have had in the house, the evidence is that his estate comprised only a small sum of money and the proceeds of some modest life policies. This money was wholly spent in discharging certain legal costs and defraying in part the funeral expenses. Probate was granted to the two named executors on 9 January 1984, but the originating application was not issued until 19 March 1985, which is some eight months or so outside the statutory six-month period.

By the originating application Mrs Clifford seeks primarily an order that she be allowed to remain in the house for the rest of her life. The question of whether leave should be granted under section 4 of the Inheritance (Provision for Family and Dependants) Act 1975 to make the application out of time was heard as a preliminary issue on 21 February 1986. In his full and careful judgment the learned recorder followed the guidelines summarised in the judgment of Mr Justice Browne-Wilkinson (as he then was) in *Re Dennis* [1981] 2 All ER 140. He considered first the guidelines that the application should only be granted if there were an arguable case. His conclusion was that it might be too strong to say that the application was hopeless, but he did not think it was very far off. His reason was this. The position of the deceased's estate being as I have summarised, Mrs Clifford's application for financial provision cannot get anywhere unless the court makes an order under section 10 of the 1975 Act arising out of the deceased's execution of the 1983 deed variation. In passing I observe that Mrs Clifford seeks to make a claim under this section also in respect of the 1979 deed of variation.

[His Lordship read out section 10(1), (2), (7)].

The initial gift of the house was made more than six years before the deceased's death and hence is outside the scope of that section; but the release of the covenant to permit Mrs Clifford to live in the house was made only some months before the deceased died. The learned recorder was very dubious whether this release was a disposition. Further, basing himself on the letter of 14 July 1983, he was of the view that Mrs Clifford would have grave difficulty in establishing that the 1983 deed of variation was executed by the deceased with the requisite intention. The recorder then considered the other guidelines, but I think it is clear that ultimately the basis on which he decided the matter and refused leave was that the substantive application was near hopeless.

I need not consider further the other matters referred to by the recorder in his judgment, of which the principal one was delay (the recorder found that there had been some, but not inordinate, delay from January to August 1984 and that the application had been pursued promptly thereafter), because in this court Mr Brabin accepted that, if the court were satisfied that Mrs Clifford had succeeded in showing that she had an arguable case and that, delay apart, this would be an appropriate case for leave to be given to her to make her application, leave should not be refused solely on the ground of delay.

So I turn to the question of whether an arguable case has been shown. As I have said, this is an application where, in order to succeed, Mrs Clifford must succeed in obtaining an order under section 10 of the Inheritance (Provision for Family and Dependants) Act 1975. There is no estate. Accordingly, in considering whether leave should be given under section 4, in my view in this case the court is concerned to see whether Mrs Clifford has an arguable case for obtaining relief under section 10. If she has not, it would be pointless to grant leave to her to proceed with her application.

Mr Brabin's first point was that nowhere in the Originating Application is there any assertion that the 1983 deed of variation was executed with the intention of defeating an application for financial provision under the 1975 Act; nor was there any assertion to this effect in the evidence; nor was there any evidence on this point. I am unable to accept this argument. The Originating Application refers to the 1983 deed of variation, and in paragraph 9 Mrs Clifford seeks reasonable financial provision for herself 'out of the Deceased's Estate by way of an Order For Section 10 of the said 1975 Act reviewing the transactions made in the six years prior to the Deceased's death and making an order allowing me to remain in the property, 15 Pulchrass Street, for the rest of my life'. There may be shortcomings and deficiencies in this wording. But I would not be disposed to dismiss Mrs Clifford's application for that reason. Those shortcomings and deficiencies are curable without causing prejudice to the respondents.

As to the evidence, the undisputed surrounding circumstances are that the deceased was aged about 78 when he executed the 1983 deed of variation. He was not well. He was confined to a wheelchair and living in a nursing home. The deed had the effect (and presumably was executed with the intention of achieving the effect) that Mrs Tanner was thenceforth under no obligation under her covenant to permit Mrs Clifford to live in the house after the deceased's death. In the event the deceased died some two months later. In my view those circumstances are sufficient to give rise to a triable issue on this point of intention. Moreover, the letter of 14 July 1983 does not provide a conclusive answer on the point. The letter can indeed be read as supporting a contention that the 1983 deed of variation came into being as part of a normal arrangement made in the context of a pending hostile divorce suit. But those are all matters which need to be investigated properly. The letter of 14 July at the moment stands in isolation and it needs to be set in context of all that had passed between the deceased and his solicitor on this subject. At present, I observe there is no evidence from the solicitor.

Mr Brabin's next point was that there was here no 'disposition' within the meaning of section 10. He pointed out that under section 1 of the Inheritance (Provision for Family and Dependants) Act 1975 an application may be made on the ground that the disposition of the deceased's estate, effected by his will or the law relating to intestacy or the combination of his will and that law, was not such as to make reasonable financial provision for the applicant. Here, he submitted, the right released by the deceased had no value, or at any rate no substantial value, to the deceased, so that the release of that right by the deceased in his lifetime did not take out of his estate property which otherwise would have been available for making reasonable financial provision for Mrs Clifford. I feel unable to accept this. I am in no doubt that the 1983 deed of variation was a disposition within section 10. Immediately prior to execution of that deed the deceased was possessed of the benefit of the covenant given by his daughter under the original deed of gift. He, and after his death, his personal representatives, had the right to enforce, or, if he and they chose, to release that covenant. I am in no doubt that, unless and until released, the covenant was capable of being made the subject of an order for specific performance, in respect both of the deceased's occupation of Mrs Clifford's occupation, on the application of the deceased or, after his death, his personal representatives. That right was an asset belonging to the deceased. In the event he chose to give up that right, to release it, in favour of his daughter. Subsection (7) is not a comprehensive definition of a 'disposition', but, even if it were, I think that the deed of release was a gift of property of any description within that subsection, although the property given in this case was of a very unusual nature.

Indeed, in the course of argument Mr Brabin was prepared to accept that the benefit of Mrs Tanner's covenant was capable of being an asset of the deceased's estate, but he submitted that on the facts of this case it would not be of any value. I do not agree. The existence of this covenant was a serious fetter on Mrs Tanner's rights in and enjoyment of the house, and it substantially depreciated the property in her hands. The release of that covenant would be of considerable value to her: prima facie she could be expected to be willing to pay for the release of her obligations under that covenant. The person to whom such payment would need to be made by her would be the person alone entitled to enforce the covenant: the deceased, or, after his death, his personal representatives. In this way he and they had an asset which had a realisable value.

For these reasons in my view the execution of the 1983 deed of variation was a disposition. Accordingly, I consider Mrs Clifford has an arguable case for an order under section 10. In my view, therefore, the recorder misdirected himself in law when exercising his discretion and it falls to this court to exercise for itself the discretion conferred by section 4 of the Inheritance (Provision for Family and Dependants) Act 1975. In my view the applicant, Mrs Clifford, should be permitted to make her application out of time. This is a case in which Mrs Tanner has always known that Mrs Clifford was claiming the house, or at least the right to continue to live there. No distribution had been made in reliance on the absence of proceedings within the six-month period. A copy of the 1983 deed of variation, which is crucial in this matter, was not provided by Mrs Tanner's solicitors until October 1984, which was itself outside the six-month period. Once Mrs Clifford's advisers had seen this deed, they proceeded with reasonable expedition to institute the applicant. Whether Mrs Clifford will succeed in obtaining an order under section 10, either in relation to the 1979 deed or the 1983 deed, can only be decided at the trial, but I think Mrs Clifford has discharged the burden of showing that it would be just in this case to permit her to proceed.

For these reasons I would allow the appeal and substitute for the order made by the learned recorder in answer to the preliminary issue, an order permitting Mrs Clifford to make her application out of time.

NEILL LJ: I agree that this appeal should be allowed for the reasons given by my Lord. I also agree that this court, in the exercise of its own independent discretion, should give permission that the applicant may apply for an order under section 2 of the 1975 Act, which will involve and include an application for an order under section 10.

Therefore for these reasons, this appeal will be allowed and an order made in those terms.

Order: Appeal allowed to the extent that there be substituted for the order below an order permitting the appellant to make application out of time; costs here and below to be costs in the proceedings.

Cumming Burns v Burns

Court of Appeal (Civil Division), 4 July 1985

Leolin Price QC and *R Sterling* for the Appellants.

Michael Mark for the Respondent.

PURCHAS LJ: This is an appeal from an order made by Mr EG Nugee QC, sitting as a deputy judge of the High Court on 24 May 1983, dismissing an application by the appellant, Helen Cheyne Cumming Burns (to whom I shall refer as 'Mrs Helen Burns') under the Inheritance (Provision for Family and Dependants) Act 1975, (to which I shall refer hereafter as 'the Act'). The respondent, Margaret Duncan Burns (to whom I shall refer as 'Mrs Margaret Burns') is the executrix and sole beneficiary under the will of John Edward Burns, to whom she was married at the date of his death. The will was made on 24 July 1979, the year of John Burns' death, which was on 17 December 1979. The application was under s 1(1)(b) of the Act.

Mrs Helen Burns was formerly married to Mr John Burns and has not since re-married. The learned judge dismissed the application on the ground that Mrs Helen Burns had failed to establish that the disposition of John Burns' estate was not such as to make reasonable financial provision for her or, to transpose the provisions of the Act, she had failed to show that it was unreasonable that no provision had in fact been made for her.

The history relevant to the application is set out with admirable clarity in the judgment. It is necessary for me only to refer to some of the salient dates and facts derived from that judgment.

The deceased, John Burns, was born on 28 October 1907. He married Mrs Helen Burns on 11 July 1929, when he was 21 and she was 18. He was a lance-corporal in the army, and between then and 1939 he and Mrs Helen Burns lived together in army married quarters in circumstances which can properly be described as modest.

Between 1930 and 1935 they had four children. In 1939 and 1940 they lived together, first with John Burns' parents, and later in rented accommodation in Folkestone, subsequently moving to Edinburgh, where the deceased was stationed during the early part of the war. He took a commission in 1940 and volunteered for overseas service in North Africa. He went to North Africa and to the Middle East, where his army career prospered and he rose to the rank of major.

At an early date in his service overseas he met Mrs Margaret Burns, then Margaret Standfast; this was in Egypt, and it is clear that from an early stage they formed a close affection for each other.

In the meanwhile John Burns had been remitting appropriate maintenance to Mrs Helen Burns and the children, but did not, like many people – through no fault of his, I am sure – achieve a return to this country until the end of the war.

Before that had happened, however, he had discussed with Mrs Margaret Burns the question of their marrying when and if he was free to marry her, and it was on that basis that they continued.

In about June 1945 John Burns returned on leave to this country and paid a brief visit to his home in Edinburgh. He saw his wife and children; they had been living there during the war years, continuing in a modest way of life. The deceased stayed only a few days and Mrs Helen Burns, clearly with some justification in my judgement, formed the view that John Burns had deserted her because he had tired of his family responsibilities; he was perhaps one of those who enjoyed army life and, unknown of course to Mrs Helen Burns, he had formed the relationship with Mrs Margaret Burns.

He eventually left the army in 1947 with the rank of Lieutenant-Colonel; he paid another short visit to his family in Edinburgh and from that point onwards, believing that he would not obtain a divorce, he told Mrs Margaret Burns that he probably would not be able to marry her and that she should choose whether to continue living with him as his wife or pass out of his life altogether. Mrs Margaret Burns chose the former course and on 2 August 1945 she changed her name by deed poll to Burns.

She herself had been serving with the nursing service and was demobilised in January 1946. After a short interlude she went to live with John Burns, who had bought himself a fishing boat with their joint savings and had converted it into a home.

The conditions in which they were living at that time were still clearly modest, notwithstanding a gratuity, I take it, from his military service. They started a business of trawling for fish; this was not a success and after a year or two it was abandoned.

It was at this time that Mrs Margaret Burns received the first of a number of sums of money by way of inheritance. Speaking very generally, the various sums of money were all devoted either to meeting indebtedness arising from their joint enterprise (at a later stage they were running a farm) or was diverted to the support of John Burns and, of course, Mrs Margaret Burns, with whom he was then living.

The first inheritance was £7,000, then, in 1960, there was another inheritance of £15,000 and later, shortly afterwards, she inherited a further £15,000 as a result of the deaths of her parents.

Towards the end of 1963 John Burns decided to try and achieve the dissolution of his marriage; by 1965 this was done. From the documents before the court, the matter was dealt with perfectly formally, with professional assistance on both sides. A decree nisi was pronounced on 2 November 1965 and that was made absolute early in 1966. Two days after the decree absolute John Burns entered into a maintenance agreement with Mrs Helen Burns; that agreement is dated 15 February 1966. It is a formally executed document, providing for maintenance for Mrs Helen Burns, rising in stages over a period of years, culminating on 28 October 1972, after which date the sums ceased to increase.

It is to be noted in passing that this document provides that

> The wife will out of the said monthly sums or otherwise support and maintain herself and will indemnify the husband against all debts to be incurred by her and will not in any way at any time pledge the husband's credit.

And then:

> In the event of the failure of the husband to make the said payments as and when the same become due the wife shall be at full liberty at her election to pursue all and every remedy in this regard either by enforcement of the provisions hereof as if this agreement had not been made.

The payments under that agreement were faithfully observed and continued until the death of John Burns. At the same time Mrs Helen Burns, with the consent and co-operation of John Burns, effected a life policy, the premiums for which she shouldered the responsibility; but he co-operated to the extent of submitting himself to a medical examination. Unfortunately, that policy was written without profits and suffered heavily as a result of inflation. It was originally for the sum of £500, but by 1974 Mrs Helen Burns decided, I am sure wisely, to surrender the policy and she obtained the modest yield of £113.80. The significance of taking out that policy, to my mind, is that the parties had in contemplation the future support of Mrs Helen Burns should anything untimely happen to John Burns.

After the agreement in 1966 there was no direct contact between Helen Burns and John Burns, although the latter kept in touch with the children, with the knowledge and encouragement of their mother; but the mother, as she put it in evidence before the learned judge, 'kept right out of the way'.

The learned judge has summed up the life of Mrs Helen Burns in these words:

> Mrs Helen Burns seemed to me to have had a hard life, which she has borne uncomplainingly, and it is understandable that when she learnt that Colonel Burns had left an estate valued at over £60,000 she should feel that it would have been reasonable that she should have had some benefit from it, particularly as the quite modest payments she had been receiving from him stopped at his death.

Meanwhile, it is necessary to record how this state of affairs came about. John Burns married Mrs Margaret Burns within two months or so of the making absolute of the decree nisi, on 22 April 1966. With the money that Mrs Margaret Burns had inherited they bought a farm but that was sold shortly afterwards in 1967 for the sum of £13,000. There is no evidence in this case of John Burns' either having capital or receiving, after his service with the army, any substantial income. The learned judge has considered this in his judgment in relation to the possibility of orders being made upon the dissolution of the first marriage even if the statutory provisions now available in such circumstances had existed then.

With the proceeds from the sale of the farm, the last matrimonial home in effect, The Priory at Totnes, Devon, was bought. It was an old house; it needed considerable work to be done upon it and this was carried out by John Burns and Mrs Margaret Burns. His income at that time was modest. His army pension was roughly £265, of which he paid £208 a year to Mrs Helen Burns under the maintenance agreement. Mrs Margaret Burns shouldered all the expenses; John Burns worked from a bank account which was permitted to move into an overdrawn position and which, when it was necessary from time to time, Mrs Margaret Burns topped up with money of her own. It is not necessary in this judgment to go into details; the overall picture is perfectly clear, namely that the provider of finance throughout this period was basically Mrs Margaret Burns.

She was, and is, a lady of admirable sensibility. Amongst other things she felt, in the traditional way, that the master of the house should be the person who had control of the finances and the money. So it was that on

14 February 1969 she executed a formal deed of gift of The Priory. It was given to John Burns to hold in fee simple, and my Lord pointed out during the course of argument the value of the transfer assessed for stamp duty indicates that at that time the property had already achieved a substantial value.

Mrs Margaret Burns said in evidence that the reason for doing this (and I quote from the judgment) was because she wanted him to have something of his own; he had worked very hard during their time together; he had never had anything; all their assets had belonged to her and she wanted him to have as much as she had. She reckoned that the house was worth about the same as her investments, so by giving the house to him she was making an equal division of her property between them. She had to go on paying the bills, however, as he had no money. She appreciated that by giving him the house she was putting it in his power to leave it to his children, or even to his former wife; but she trusted him and was content to accept this possibility.

We have been referred to a transcript of part of the evidence of Mrs Margaret Burns. Again it is not necessary in this judgment to rehearse it in detail; it is quite clear that Mrs Margaret Burns never seriously contemplated the possibility of that property, or even part of the proceeds thereof, finding their way to Mrs Helen Burns. She said frankly in evidence that she considered that she had no moral obligation to make any payment to Mrs Helen Burns, but she said that she was a generous person. Reading the transcript it is clear, however, that she would not accept any claim of right against any of the proceeds of that property resting in Mrs Helen Burns.

In 1973 they raised some money by selling part of the garden of The Priory. Again this was used, as had been much of the previous inherited sums, in paying off the overdraft, which at that stage stood around £4,000. The learned judge has considered in detail the advisability of having an overdraft up to 1973, and has reviewed the position of their investments; I do not think it is necessary to consider these matters.

As I have said, John Burns died on 12 December 1979, In addition to The Priory, which was his, he had some Premium Bonds and Loan Stock. His estate was sworn at probate at the net value of £64,616; that was on 7 March 1980.

The will was in the simplest of terms. It left the whole of the estate to Mrs Margaret Burns and appointed her sole executrix and trustee of the will.

Before his death Mrs Margaret Burns and John Burns had discussed the possibility of selling The Priory. They knew that if he died, Mrs Margaret Burns would not be able to afford to stay there and, so it is fairly said by Mr Price, who has appeared for the appellant, there was in contemplation before the death the sale of this one major asset. At the time of the death it was valued for probate at £65,000, which gives a reflection upon the negative value of the other assets, or debits, of the estate.

However, about four months after the death, Mrs Margaret Burns received an offer of £85,000, which was above any offer that she had obtained, so she sold The Priory and with part of the proceeds bought a smaller house in Totnes for £50,000. The learned judge found that:

> Her total gross income, including state pension, is about £7,000 on which she pays a tax of about £1,700, leaving a net income of about £5,300. She put in evidence a statement of her annual outgoings, which amount to about £5,200, but part of this was accounted for by £750 repairs to her house...In her evidence the defendant accepted that she did not at present have an actual need of all her capital, but she is 69 years old and has no close family on whom she can rely for assistance, and she foresees a time when she may need someone to look after her if she is ill. She has a niece whom she would very much like to help with the schooling of her children.

The learned judge also dealt, clearly and in detail, with the financial position of Mrs Helen Burns; it is convenient at this stage for me to give the essentials of that. Mrs Helen Burns' income was found to be about £1,890, derived wholly from state pension or social security, which paid her rates and a contribution to her expenses for fuel and repairs. I quote from the judgment:

> She lives rent free in the flat in Edinburgh which her son and one of his daughters had bought for her, but she pays for minor repairs, decorations and other outgoings so far as they are not met by social security. After allowing for regular expenditure on a fairly modest scale, she is left with between £3 and £4 a week for extras such as birthday cards and presents.

It is clear from the findings of the learned judge that there is an imbalance between the standard of living available to Mrs Helen Burns and that available to Mrs Margaret Burns; that is a matter which the learned judge clearly had in mind.

It is now convenient to refer to the statutory provisions of the Act against which this application was brought.

[His Lordship quoted extensively from sections 1-3(1)(d)]

In rehearsing the general history, the learned judge clearly had regard to those matters. I must return later in this judgment to one particular aspect under sub-paragraph (d) in relation to the disposition of the property, The Priory.

Sub-paragraph (e) refers to the size and nature of the estate of the deceased; again the learned judge clearly had regard to that.

Sub-paragraph (f) is not relevant; sub-paragraph (g) has been described as a sweeping-up section:

> Any other matter, including the conduct of the applicant or any other person which in the circumstances of the case the court may consider relevant.

I pause only to comment that in this case there has been no evidence or allegation adversely either to the applicant or any other person. But of course, under this sub-paragraph it is open to the learned judge to have regard, if he wishes to do so, and he may well have done so, to the fact that it was due to the financial support of Mrs Margaret Burns that the family was viable financially in the latter years at all. On the other hand there was the contribution made by Mrs Helen Burns in bringing up the family during the early years.

I can pass now to subsection (2) of s 3:

Again the learned judge had regard, and certainly has referred to them in his judgment, to the matters raised specifically under subsection (2).

I can now pass to subsection (5). That merely clarifies the position that the court must take in considering the evidence:

> In considering the matters to which the court is required to have regard under this section, the court shall take into account the facts as known to the court at the date of the hearing.

The learned judge referred to these provisions; he referred also to a decision in the case of *In re Fullard deceased* [1981] 2 All ER 796, [1982] Fam 42, which was a decision of this court. Mr Price has submitted that there are distinctions to be drawn from the facts in that case, and relies on part of the judgments of Lord Justice Ormrod and myself, in which indication was given in particular circumstances the course approved by the court in *In Re Fullard* would not be the appropriate course. I can deal with it fairly shortly.

The facts of that case were that after a long marriage of 40 years the plaintiff and the deceased were divorced. The deceased re-married and died within a comparatively short period of time. The basic proposition in the decision of the court was that after prolonged negotiations over the dissolution of the first marriage, the parties had come to a financial settlement of the ancillary applications; and that it would seem extremely unlikely in the time context in that case that anything would have occurred which could strike at the presumption that when the assets and financial provisions were considered on the dissolution of the marriage, a different position would be achieved under the Inheritance (Provision for Family and Dependants) Act 1975. But Lord Justice Ormrod did suggest that where there had been periodical payment continuing for a long time, that was an acknowledgement of a continuing responsibility, and where the effect of the death was to unlock substantial capital, or where substantial capital had been acquired subsequently to the divorce, things might well be different. Mr Price submitted that circumstances were different in this case; there was acknowledged a formal agreement for maintenance which was carried out over a period of a considerable number of years, from 1966 to the date of the death; but in my judgement the death does not appear to have unlocked substantial capital, though Mr Price submitted that substantial capital might have been, and has been acquired, or could have been made available, on the sale of the property.

I pause only to make this comment, that in my own judgment in *In Re Fullard* I expressed a doubt as to whether a substantial accretion of capital after the death would have any effect. That was not intended in any way to be a statement of law; it was merely a consideration of the difficulties that would arise and a necessity to look at the details under which the capital accretion had occurred.

So Mr Price submits that his case can be distinguished from *In Re Fullard* [1982] Fam 42, [1981] All ER 796, and with that submission I agree. There are features in this case which are quite different from the circumstances in which the court reached the conclusion that it did in *In Re Fullard*.

But that does not mean to say that the result is necessarily different. The same considerations and criteria must be applied. The learned judge clearly had regard to the various features, and I come now to the point on which Mr Price submits that he fell into error.

If I can adopt an expression of Mr Price, it can be summarised in the proposition that the learned judge acted upon a quasi resulting trust when, in his will, Mr John Burns left the whole of his property to Mrs Margaret Burns because she had in effect given it to him, and he felt obliged, so it is suggested, to return it without using any of the possible proceeds, were it to be sold – a sale which was in contemplation at the time of making the will or thereabouts – to fulfil his obligations to Mrs Helen Burns.

I quote from the judgment:

> In the present case, of course, the marriage between Colonel Burns and the plaintiff had been dissolved before the court acquired its wide powers under the Act of 1970, and it may be that in some situations in which that is the case the views expressed by the Court of Appeal would not apply with full force' – that is referring to *In Re Fullard*. 'But in the present case, if the court had possessed the widest possible powers in 1966, it could not have ordered Colonel Burns to transfer capital to the plaintiff because he did not possess any at that time. The fact that he had been making regular payment of maintenance for nearly 14 years before his death under the maintenance agreement and for many years before that voluntarily in recognition of his obligations to the plaintiff, and that there was a reasonable amount of capital in his estate at the date of his death, brings the present case in terms within the first of the two situations envisaged by Lord Justice Ormrod; and when one balances the financial resources and needs of the plaintiff against those of the defendant, which are two of the matters to which the court is directed to have regard to section 3(1)(a) and (c) of the Act of 1975, there can be little doubt that other things being equal, the balance on this point would come down in favour of the plaintiff, even when one takes into account the fact that her children have given her generous support and may be expected to continue to do so. But when one looks into the balance of the obligation and responsibilities which Colonel Burns had towards the plaintiff and the defendant respectively, which are the matters referred to in section 3(1)(d), the scales turn strongly – and in my view decisively – in favour of the defendant. She lived with him for over 30 years, and after the failure of his fishing business and loss of his job he was dependent upon her for virtually everything that he had – the farm on which for 14 years they made a living (not a very handsome one), the home they made in The Priory and the money with which to renovate it and to pay their ordinary living expenses, even the small holding of investments which stood in his name. On the other side no criticism has been made of the plaintiff. It was said on her behalf that the fact that she was content to accept a modest amount of maintenance in an inflationary time, instead of applying for an increase which she could have done, gives rise to a moral obligation

> on Colonel Burns and that, as he was free to deal with The Priory as part of his estate, and he and the defendant were thinking of selling it during his lifetime, he could have given effect to that moral obligation out of the proceeds of sale.
>
> In other circumstances there might be force in such an argument, but the circumstances of this case are unusual and I think it right to take into account the way in which The Priory came to form part of his estate. It was not put in his name with any intention that he should dispose of it to anyone other than the defendant, although he was legally free to do so, and it was certainly not put in his name to enable him to make provision for the plaintiff. The defendant had complete trust in him and he did not fail her. It would, in my view, be quite wrong for the court to say that he was under a moral obligation to make provision for the plaintiff out of the proceeds of sale of The Priory or out of any other part of his estate.

In his very able and attractive argument Mr Price submits – and I hope I do not do his argument an injustice – that although the learned judge, by mentioning the various matters under sub-paragraphs (a) to (g) of s 3(1) of the Inheritance (Provision for Family and Dependants) Act 1975 in his judgment, may be said to have paid regard to those matters, in effect what he has done is to have regard and to take into account to an extent exclusive of the other features the matters under sub-paragraph (d), namely the motive and moral duty relating to the disposal of The Priory; and Mr Price submits that in doing so the learned judge has erred in a matter of principle; or, I suppose, must be plainly wrong. It has (and I now transpose the submission) in effect distorted the learned judge's approach to these matters to which it was mandatory for him to have regard, albeit that I think it is conceded by Mr Price that the degree of weight to be put on any one or other of those factors must be a matter of discretion for the judge in executing the balancing exercise. In this case, however, Mr Price had submitted that it went beyond that and amounted to an error which would leave it open to this court to exercise its own discretion de novo, and once that position was reached, Mr Price submitted, this court ought to exercise its discretion in favour of the appellant and award a modest lump sum to make reasonable provision for the maintenance of the appellant, which had been an omission in the dispositions effected by the will. The test to be applied had been stated in many various ways. I find it convenient to refer to an extract from the judgment of Lord Justice Asquith in *Bellenden (formerly Satterthwaite v Satterthwaite* [1948] 1 All ER, 343 at p 345, which finds itself adopted in the speech of Lord Fraser of Tullybelton in the recent decision of the House of Lords in *Gregory v Gregory* [1985] 2 All ER 225, (1985) 1 FLR 647.

The case of *Satterthwaite* was an appeal against an order for maintenance payable to the divorced wife; the quotation from the judgment is:

> It is of course not enough for the wife to establish that this court might or would have made a different order. We are here concerned with a judicial discretion and it is of the essence of such a discretion that

> on the same evidence two different minds might reach widely different decisions without either being appealable. It is only where the decision exceeds the generous ambit within which reasonable disagreement is possible, and is in fact plainly wrong, that an appellate body is entitled to interfere.

For my part, I have listened very carefully to the submission so ably made in support of this appeal. But in the end, as I hope appears from the parts of the judgment to which I have already refereed, the learned judge sets out all the relevant matters to which he ought to have had regard under the provision of s 3 of the Inheritance (Provision for Family and Dependants) Act 1975. It may be a matter of speculation, into which this court should not be privileged to enquire, the individual weight, or weights, which the learned judge saw fit to attach to each or any of the criteria to which he had to have regard. That he had them in mind is clear from the words of this detailed and, if I may respectfully say so, admirably expressed judgment, and it is quite impossible to follow Mr Price's submission that it can be said that his concentration, if it was concentration, on the matters under s 3(1)(d) was so out of balance as to pass beyond the wide range of discretion envisaged in that short extract from the judgment of Lord Justice Asquith to which I have referred.

For those reasons I find it quite impossible to say that the learned judge was plainly wrong and I look without any success, for any aspect in which he has erred in principle.

Accordingly this appeal must fail.

OLIVER LJ: I agree.

I add only this; I think it is really only an echo of what my Lord has already said. Mr Price, in attacking the learned judge's decision, grasped at the outset, with his usual frankness and good sense, the nettle that this appeal necessarily involves seeking to persuade this court that it ought to interfere with the exercise of what is, and what is intended to be, essentially a discretionary exercise by the judge of the first instance. He had, therefore, either to show that the conclusion reached by the learned judge was one which a reasonable judge could have come to, or which was plainly and clearly wrong; or that the discretion had been exercised on some wrong principle; that is to say either by taking into account something that the judge out not to have taken into account, or failing to take into account some consideration that he ought to have taken into account.

To attack the decision in the first of those is in my judgement plainly not possible in this case, as indeed I think Mr Price has recognised. His argument has therefore necessarily had to concentrate upon demonstrating some point which the learned judge failed to take into account which he should have taken into account, or that he entertained something that he ought not to have done. That has led to a close, careful, detailed and, if I may say so, thoroughly fair analysis of the relevant parts of the judgment, in order to see, not only whether the learned judge had regard to every single one of the relevant considerations to which he is directed to have regard by s 3(1)(a) and (g) of the Inheritance (Provision for Family and Dependants) Act 1975, but also what regard he had to those factors.

In substance the submission has been, as indeed it had to be, that the learned judge, although he mentioned all the factors, was so overpowered by the factor in s 3(1)(d) – what Mr Price describes as 'the moral resulting trust' – that he failed, to use the statutory words, to 'have regard' to the other factors mentioned, and this exercise has been done, if I may say so, with Mr Price's usual charm and skill. But for my part, like my Lord, I have found myself unpersuaded that the learned judge failed to take into account anything that he should have taken into account or that he took into account things that he should not have taken into account.

It is true that it is not always sufficient merely to mention the factors; the judge has to 'have regard' to them. Equally, it is never necessarily a fair assumption that because a judge does not stress and mention every factor that he has had in his mind, his decision is necessarily one which is open to attack; and I do think in these cases, particularly in this jurisdiction, we are in danger in this court of being invited only too often to make an over-analysis of what is, in essence, a fairly commonsense exercise. I only say that because I think attention ought to be concentrated on what was said by Lord Justice Ormrod in *In Re Fullard* [1981] 2 All ER 796, to which my brother has already referred.

At [1981] 2 All ER 796, p 47 of the report, Lord Justice Ormrod says this:

> Lord Justice Buckley put it even more succinctly at p 494' – he is referring there to the report in *In Re Coventry* – 'where he formulated the question thus: 'was it, or was it not, reasonable in the circumstances of the present case that the deceased made no financial provision for the plaintiff?'
>
> I hope that it will now be possible to apply these statutory provisions in a way in which I am sure they were intended to be applied – which is sensibly and simply. It is very easy to over-complicate the analysis of words like 'reasonable' which are used in legislation. The court should decide what is reasonable in the circumstances. It is complicated, of course, by discussion of 'objective tests' and 'subjective tests' but, when all is said and done, it comes back to the same question. 'In the circumstances is it or is it not reasonable?'

If I may say so respectfully, that states succinctly and clearly a general commonsense approach, which I feel is the right approach in cases of this sort. I say this only because, as I have said, I do feel that we are sometimes in danger of being led to an over-analysis of decisions of judges of first instance in this discretionary jurisdiction. I hope that in saying that it will not be thought for a moment that I am in any way criticising Mr Price's conduct of this case, which as I have said, has been conducted throughout with his usual charm, courtesy and frankness.

For the reasons which my Lord has given, I too am unpersuaded that the learned judge came to the wrong conclusion and I too would dismiss this appeal.

Order: Appeal dismissed with costs; appellant's liability under such order to be nil; usual order for costs of respondent in the appeal to be met by legal aid fund, unless within ten weeks the Law Society shows cause.

Dixit & Others v Dixit & Others

Court of Appeal (Civil Division), 23 June 1988

Q Iwi for the Appellants.

JMF Parker for the Respondent; *P Scriven* for the Respondent (Rita Dixit); *L Henderson* for the Respondent (Nita Nicole Dixit)

SIR NICOLAS BROWN-WILKINSON V-C: This is an appeal from an order made by Waite J under the Inheritance (Provision for Family and Dependants) Act 1975 in the estate of Mr Vamanbhai Mastubhai Dixit ('the deceased').

The facts are fully stated in the judgment of the learned judge, and all of them are relevant to our decision in this case. I have them well in mind but I will endeavour to summarise them as best I can in order to keep this judgment to a reasonable length.

The deceased was of Indian extraction, born in India. His first wife was also of Indian extraction and born in India. By his first marriage he had five daughters, the eldest, Pallavi, Norma, Toral, Rekha and finally Janet. His first wife died in 1965 and his eldest daughter, Pallavi, died in 1971.

The deceased remarried on 1 January 1968 to the plaintiff in these proceedings, Saroj Dixit, who was also of Indian extraction. I will refer to her as 'the widow'.

There were two children of the second marriage, Rita, born on 2 February 1972 (who is now 16 years of age) and Nita Nicole (normally referred to as Nicky) born on 28 October 1973.

By his will, dated 11 January 1972, so far as relevant, the deceased specifically bequeathed his house, 78 Bulstrode Road, Hounslow, to his daughters by his first marriage, Toral and Rekha, upon the youngest of them attaining the age of 18. They have both attained that age.

The deceased left his residuary estate to the four surviving children of the first marriage in equal shares.

His will makes no provision either for the widow or for the two children of the second marriage. His net estate consisted of the house, 78 Bulstrode Road, and approximately £4,000 in cash.

He died on 31 May 1982 aged 63, or thereabouts. On 1 March 1983 Letters of Administration with Will annexed were granted to the four children of the first marriage, the bank which had been appointed executor having renounced probate.

These proceedings under the 1975 Act were commenced on 14 April 1983. The plaintiffs are the widow and the two children of the second marriage. The defendants are the four children of the first marriage.

The deceased came to this country with his first wife in 1957 and took a job, which he thereafter retained, as a civil servant. He purchased a house in Bath Road, Hounslow, in the joint names of himself and his first wife as the family home. Further, in 1964 he purchased another house, 63 Cecil Road in the same names. That house was bought as an investment and was let to tenants. In June 1965 his first wife died and the deceased's mother (the children's grandmother) came from India in order to look after the children.

Following the death of his first wife, the investment property at 63 Cecil Road was put into the joint names of Pallavi and Norma.

The second marriage was an arranged marriage, the nuptials having apparently taken place over the telephone to India. The deceased had not met the widow prior to her arrival in this country. There was then a civil ceremony of marriage in this country on 1 January 1968. The marriage was throughout, as the Judge found, an extremely unhappy one. It was marked by continuous quarrels, separations and conflict between the parties and between the widow on the one hand and her step-daughters and the grandmother (so long as she was there) on the other. I shall expand on that later in this judgment, but the background to this case is one of perpetual quarrelling both during the second marriage and after the death of the deceased.

In 1969 a further investment property was purchased, 4 Temple Road, Hounslow. It was in the joint names of the deceased and the widow. Again it was let. Soon after her arrival in this country the widow took employment and the evidence is that she contributed, in part, to the costs of maintaining the family out of her earnings.

In 1970 both the deceased and the widow visited India. There was a regrettable incident. Because the conflicts between the widow and the deceased were so acute the deceased returned to this country without the widow, but bringing the widow's return ticket with him. The Judge said that on any basis that was a regrettable piece of behaviour on the part of the deceased.

Not put off by this, the widow returned to this country and on her return, presumably in an effort to avoid the continued conflict in the home, the deceased arranged for the widow to live in the investment property, 63 Cecil Road, where she continued to reside for a considerable period. During that period the deceased split his time between the main family home in Bath Road and 63 Cecil Road.

Pallavi having died in March 1971, the family home in Bath Road was sold, and the property 78 Bulstrode Road, was purchased in the sole name of the deceased. On 11 January 1972 the deceased made his will, the content of which I have mentioned. Following the making of that Will, the eldest child of the second marriage, Rita, was born on 2 February 1972. Shortly thereafter, on 26 April 1972, the deceased caused himself and the widow to execute a Declaration of Trust concerning the investment property in Temple Road. The Declaration of Trust was not well framed. A great deal turns on it in this case. The Declaration is as follows:

> 1. During our joint lives for ourselves in equal shares
> 2. On the death of either of us and during the life-time of the survivor as to one solely in favour of the said survivor and as to the other solely on the trusts hereafter expressed
> 3. On the death of the said survivor as to both capital and income for such of our children as are then living who attain the age of 18 years absolutely and if there be more than one in equal shares...

There was a final remainder for the four surviving children of the first marriage.

Although the precise operation of the Declaration of Trust might give rise to considerable doubts in certain circumstances, for practical purposes it is clear that after the death of the deceased the interest of the widow is limited to an interest in one half of Temple Road; the other half is held on trust during the lifetime of the widow for the two children of the second marriage, contingent upon their attaining the age of eighteen, and after her death they will take the capital if they both have attained the age of 18.

That Declaration of Trust for Temple Road having been made, the family condition changed again in the autumn of 1972. The grandmother who had remained in the household after the remarriage, and with whom the widow had quarrelled bitterly, returned to India. It was at that stage that the widow, with her daughter Rita, went to live in 78 Bulstrode Road for the first time as a home. Throughout this period the widow was working at various forms of employment.

The second child, Nicky, was born on 28 October 1973. The trusts of Cecil Road had been adversely affected by death of Pallavi and as a result, in 1973, there was a new Declaration of Trust which the deceased caused to be executed, declaring that Cecil Road was to be held in trust for Norma and Janet absolutely.

In August 1974, the widow, who had been employed with BOAC, lost her job. It was at that stage that the idea of going to America first surfaced. The widow had a sister in New York, and the project was formed that the family might consider emigrating there. As a result late in 1974 the deceased, the widow, Rita and Nicky all went to New York to investigate the position. The deceased did not stay long, but the widow and the two children remained there, the widow and Rita for some three years, Nicky having suffered health problems returned to this country late in 1975.

Late in 1976 the deceased returned to New York, having taken leave from his job, in order to join the widow. Whilst he was there the widow confessed to him that she had had an adulterous affair with a Mr Singh. The Judge found that the deceased forgave her for that. However, the deceased did not find life in the United States palatable and after a period of five months he returned to this country, in February 1977. The widow followed him back to this country initially to live in the house in Temple Road for some two months but shortly thereafter she returned to the main home at 78 Bulstrode Road.

In 1978 Rekha left home and she was followed, in 1979, by the youngest daughter of the first marriage, Janet. It is plain that the state of the marriage remained extremely unhappy – on an occasion the Police had to be called, as a result of what was occurring. The conditions of the youngest children were, as the Judge found, extremely unhappy and unsatisfactory. One of the bones of contention was that the widow had not given up her hope of making a home in the United States. In order to keep her Green Card valid against the wishes of the deceased she returned to New York on at least three occasions.

In February 1982 the widow again expressed a wish to go to the United States, this time to visit San Francisco. She went, without the approval of the deceased – indeed he expressed a clear wish that she should not visit New York.

Notwithstanding his wishes the widow went to New York where Mr Singh was living – although there is no evidence that the relationship which had previously existed between them was at that stage resumed. While the widow was in New York, approximately three months after she had returned to the United States, the deceased died on 31 May 1982. The widow returned in time for the end of the funeral ceremonies.

After the death of the deceased, Norma and Janet sold the Cecil Road property, and distributed the proceeds amongst themselves. The widow, Rita, Nicky, Norma and Toral were all living at 78 Bulstrode Road. The conditions must have been appalling as the quarrels remained acute. The Judge was extremely concerned as to the impact which that atmosphere had on the younger children. Wardship proceedings were commenced in 1982. An order was made in that year which sought to regulate the joint occupation of the Bulstrode Road house by the warring factions, but it is common ground that that regulatory order did not solve the problem.

As a result in 1986 the wardship was eventually discharged. Conditions remained as I have described them when the matter came before Waite J.

It is clear from the learned Judge's judgment that the conditions under which the two younger children, Rita and Nicky, were living, was having an adverse effect upon the children.

Before coming to the decision of the Judge in the matter, I seek to summarise the various family assets as they existed and which have to be considered in any application under the Inheritance (Provision for Family and Dependants) Act 1975. First, the Cecil Road investment property. As I have said it had been sold for some £22,000 net. Janet, who was planning to be married, put her share of the proceeds into buying a property, which is now reflected in her own home. Norma, perhaps less prudently, did not do so. It is not clear what happened to her share, but the Judge found that there is some £8,500 available to her. She is not married.

Second, the Temple Road property is held on the terms of the Declaration of Trust, from which it is clear, that, at best, the widow has a life interest in one half of it during her life. The value of Temple Road at the date of the deceased's death was some £15,000. At that time it was occupied by a tenant and in a very bad state of repair. Part of that bad state of repair was due to subsidence damage, which was covered by insurance. Since the death of the deceased, the widow has improved its value. First, she has obtained possession of Temple Road from the tenant. Second, she has arranged to recover the insurance monies required to remedy the subsistence damage. Third, she has obtained a local authority grant to improve the property.

At the time the matter was before the learned Judge, he found that Temple Road had increased in value to some £45,000 as it stood. However, that was before much of the work had been carried out, and some £27,000 required to be spent on the property. Of that figure of £27,000 all, save some £6,500 or £7,000 was, he thought, covered by insurance or by the local authority grant. If and when the necessary work had been done, the Temple Road property he accepted would have an open market value of some £70,000.

Finally, there was 78 Bulstrode Road – the matrimonial home, if that be the correct word. That is the only property which passed under the Will of the deceased. And it is bequeathed specifically to Toral and Rekha. It was occupied by these 'warring factions'. Its value at the date of the deceased's death was some £27,500. At the date when the matter was before the Judge he found its value to be £65,000 as it stood, and that if a further £8,000 was expended on it by way of repair and improvement, it would have an open market value at that time of £75,000.

In addition to the proceeds of sale from these properties, the only other asset was the sum of £4,000 in cash which passed under the residuary gift.

The family circumstances are as follows; The widow is approximately 46. In addition to whatever interest she has in Temple Road, she has a regular employment producing a gross salary of £7,360. Further, she has a pension from the Civil Service in respect of the deceased's service of £1,216 per annum, which is index-linked. She also has a State pension of nearly £2,900 per annum. Therefore, in total, her income is about £11,500. She also receives child benefit for Rita and Nicky amounting to £750 per annum.

Rita and Nicky have an independent pension from the Civil Service amounting to £973 per annum for the two of them. However, that pension only lasts until they attain the age of 17, or conclude their full-time further education.

Turning to the children of the first marriage: Norma is now 36 years old and unmarried. She is an actress who, like many of her kind, is not always able to secure engagements, and during such periods she sometimes works as a temporary typist, and sometimes is in receipt of unemployment supplementary benefit. She has the proceeds of her share in Cecil Road to the value of £8,500. With Rekha's approval, she lives in the Bulstrode Road house with Toral.

Toral is 32 and unmarried. She has a job at a salary of £900 per month gross – or £575 per month net.

Rekha is married, her married name being Breach.

She has a child of her own. At the time when the matter was before the Judge, she had given up her work, but while she was working, the joint income of herself and her husband was £18,000 per annum. Her husband's salary is apparently about £12,000 per annum.

Janet, the youngest daughter is married, and both she and her husband are employed. Her share of the Cecil Road property was, as I have said, invested directly or indirectly in her present home.

Those are the assets of the estate and the circumstances of the various claimants upon it.

Before the learned Judge the two minor children of the second marriage, Rita and Nicky, were not separately represented. They appeared by the same Counsel as their mother, and in his judgment the learned Judge commented adversely on that fact. As will emerge, but for the separate representation in this Court, the position would have become acute in this Court.

The evidence before the Judge was that both the widow and the two children, Rita and Nicky, both preferred the Bulstrode Road property to the Temple Road property. It was said that they were all very attached to it, and they wanted to go on living there. Bulstrode Road and Temple Road basically appear to be very similar properties. They are very close to each other in Hounslow.

However, the Judge apparently accepted that if the children were to move to Temple Road from Bulstrode Road there would be a somewhat more complicated bus journey for them to get to school. He also said that the Bulstrode Road property has a good sized garden, which Temple Road does not.

I must now turn to the Judge's finding as to the widow's conduct which features in this case. I quote from his assessment of her personality:

> She is strong-willed, assertive, garrulous, and (I fear it is necessary to add from my own observations of her) self-centred. No doubt there were also attributes of the deceased's personality which clashed with hers. However that may be, it is the sad fact that the marriage, though consummated and fruitful in the sense that the parties had sexual intercourse and eventually bore children, was never successful. The widow became involved, almost from the very beginning, in loud and persistent quarrels, with her mother-in-law, and with her step-daughters.

I have referred to her adulterous affair with Mr Singh in New York and repeat that the Judge found that the deceased forgave her for that.

The Judge also found that it was against the express wishes of the deceased (although without any actual prohibition of his part), that the widow went back to the United States early in 1979 and again in 1983. He also found that by going from San Francisco to New York in 1982, the widow was acting entirely contrary to her understanding with the deceased.

The Judge found that when the widow returned from New York in March 1979, there was an open row between her and the deceased and the step-daughters which was so serious that the Police had to be called in. He found that in September 1981 the marital disharmony had advanced to the point that the widow and the deceased were planning a permanent separation.

Finally, the Judge summed up the widow's attitude to returning to the United States in this way:

> Her stubborn insistence upon maintaining her employment prospects in the United States long after the deceased had abandoned his own plans for moving there, and her insensitive insistence upon remaining there during the months preceding his death in circumstances which she must have known would be upsetting for him, is something that I ought to take into account against her claim.

Those I think are the totality of the findings made by the Judge as to her conduct. It is fair to say (and I will return to it) that the Judge on the other hand found that she had, in part, contributed to the family welfare, not only out of her earnings but also in terms of her care for the members of the family.

The conclusion of the Judge flowing from these facts was to this effect: first he found that the Will did not make any reasonable provision either for the widow or for Rita and Nicky. Having done so, he set out his objectives in a passage which I must now read:

> Common sense and justice both appear to me to require that any provision should be directed principally towards putting to an end

the five-year impasse over the occupation of 78 Bulstrode Road. The devising of an appropriate means to that end, and one which takes due account of all the statutory criteria laid down by the Act, would in my judgement require the Court to aim, if they are achievable in law, for the following three objectives:

(1) The widow, so long as she wishes to remain in England, should have secure and suitable accommodation for herself and (while they remain in her care) Rita and Nicky.

(2) Principally for the children's sake, though this is a matter in which her own preferences are also entitled to consideration, that home should, if possible, be 78 Bulstrode Road.

(3) The accommodation problem generally should be solved in a manner which – so far as it is possible to do so – strikes a fair balance between the claims of the widow and the minors as the deceased's sole dependants within the meaning of the Act on the one hand, and the moral claims on his estate on the other hand of the adult daughters for whom he felt an understandable wish to provide.'

The Judge said that as to the first of those objectives there was no difficulty and he varied the trust affecting the Temple Road property – that is to say the investment property in which the widow already had an interest – so as to give her a full life interest in it, and giving Rita and Nicky vested interest in the remainder, instead of interests which were dependent upon their surviving their mother.

In his judgment, he sought to attain the second objective in this way. He held that under Section 2(4) of the 1975 Act, he could, as he called it 'switch the assets' so as to produce the result that the full life interest with remainder to Rita and Nicky, which he had just produced by varying the trust of the Temple Road property, were to be made to apply to Bulstrode Road, and the trust formerly affecting Bulstrode Road, namely for Toral and Rekha, would be made to apply to Temple Road, the result being, if that could be done, that the widow, Nicky and Rita got their rights of occupation in the property in which they desired to have them, namely, Bulstrode Road.

The order as drawn did not reflect what was said in the judgment. Although it produced the same result it was not done in the way the Judge anticipated. The order, as drawn, first varied the will so as to give the widow a life interest in Bulstrode Road, with the remainder to the two children; and then, under Section 2(1)(f) of the Inheritance (Provision for Family and Dependants) Act 1975 varied the trusts affecting Temple Road so as to leave that property in trust for Toral and Rekha absolutely.

The judgment of the learned Judge does not disclose any reference to the tax repercussions of what he was proposing to do. However, the order as drawn does provide that if any party 'shall be assessed to any liability for capital gains tax arising out of the terms of this order' there should be liberty to apply. The position is this, that Counsel say that the suggestion of 'switching' the properties had come from the learned Judge, and that at the hearing leading up to his judgment, the repercussions of it for tax purposes had not been appreciated.

When the matter came back before the Judge to settle the exact terms of the order, the possible liability for capital gains tax was raised, but of course by that stage the Judge had reached his decision as to what was the correct order to make, and the matter was dealt with simply by the insertion in the order of the provision which I have mentioned.

It is common ground before this Court that the effect of the Judge's order will inevitably be to give rise to a substantial immediate liability for capital gains tax in respect of the Temple Road property. On any footing the order of the learned Judge produces a termination of the existing trusts affecting Temple Road, and substitutes wholly new trusts.

The amount of the capital gains tax liability is not common ground, but it appears to be in the region of £8,500. That is not a substantial sum in some contexts, but in the context of this family where cash is extremely short is a burden which the parties do not think it is appropriate to incur.

We heard submissions as to whether the Judge had jurisdiction to do what he purported to do under Section 2(1)(f) of the 1975 Act. The Judge, in effect, revoked the trusts of the Temple Road property and resettled that property on new trusts. It was submitted that such an operation did not constitute a variation of the trusts but a revocation and resettlement and that, as such, the Judge had no power to do what he purported to do.

I find it unnecessary to decide that point because it is common ground that the Judge's decision in this case, as an exercise of discretion, cannot stand in its entirety since the tax implications of his order were not present to his mind and were not, for the reasons already stated, pointed out to him by Counsel. He therefore exercised his discretion in this case on a basis which overlooked a material factor which should have affected it.

Although Miss Parker for the widow, kept it open as a 'last ditch' argument, otherwise I think it was common ground between the parties that given the very minor advantages that would accrue by giving the widow, Rita and Nicky interests in Bulstrode Road rather than in Temple Road, to produce such a switch of beneficial interest could not be in the interests of a family who were short of capital to the extent that this family is. The tax burden far outweighed the remote benefits obtained by the switch. The interests in the property are sentimental, not real.

In those circumstances in this Court we have to reconsider the matter, not in my judgement de novo, but bearing in mind that the final assessment of the Judge cannot stand. The first matter which has to be considered before any question of discretion arises is whether the Court is satisfied that the Will, as drawn by the testator in the circumstances of the case, failed to make proper provision for his defendants.

There was a further dispute whether, for this purpose, one has to look at the values and circumstances as they existed at the death of the deceased, or whether the effect of Section 3(5) of the Inheritance (Provision for Family and Dependants) Act 1975 is to require the Court to look at the circumstances at the time of the hearing.

Again, it is not necessary to decide that point since, in my judgement, on either footing, it is clear that the Will failed to make reasonable provision for the widow and the two children of the second marriage. In my judgement, unhappy as the conduct of the widow was in certain respects, it is not such as wholly to disqualify her from any provision being made under the Act. If she was entitled to any provision at all, the very minimum to which she must have been entitled was somewhere to live during her lifetime. And the same goes for the minor children. The only place provided for the widow and for Nicky was Temple Road, which was not the matrimonial home. The position of Temple Road as at the date of the deceased's death was that it was tenanted, and therefore could not be occupied, and in any event the widow was only entitled to a half interest in it during her lifetime. That might have been alright during the minority of Rita and Nicky, but once they grew up, where was she to live thereafter in default of agreement with her children? At the date of the hearing, vacant possession had been obtained by the widow by her own efforts, but there still remained the difficulty that she had no assured right of residence in Temple Road once the children were of full age.

For those reasons I have no doubt that the Judge was correct that the Will failed to make reasonable provision. This Court therefore has to decide what is reasonable provision to make for the widow and the two children. Since the hearing before the Judge there had been another major development. In May 1988 – that is to say about a month ago – the younger daughter, Nicky, aged 14, decided to leave her mother and the house at Bulstrode Road where they have all been living, and go to live with her sister, Rekha, Mrs Breach. That has given rise to further wardship proceedings as to her future. The lack of separate representation before the Judge is brought into sharp relief by this new development, since it is now clear that the interest of at least Nicky and her mother are far from being the same. As a result, the Official Solicitor has been brought in as Next Friend of both Rita and Nicky. Since Rita is still at home with her mother, the interests of Rita and Nicky are not identical.

As a result, they have been represented before us by separate Counsel. The position of these two children is roughly this: first of all the Judge held, as I have said, that they have both suffered very great damage from the warring conditions in which they have spent their lives and are continuing to spend their lives. As to Rita, she is still with her mother. She has in the past – although the present position may be different – got on very well with her half-sisters. She is academically bright, but not outstanding; it is hoped that she will go to Godolphin and Latymer School to do her 'A' levels next September. The evidence is that her present examination performance is being affected by conditions at home. Her long-term wish is to go to University. If she goes to Godolphin and Latymer School, she will have an aided place, but it may be that given the family resources she will require about £1,000 per annum for two years to pay the fees to the extent that they are not paid by the State. The younger child, Nicky, is not so bright academically, and the possibility is that there will be no further education for her after she has reached the normal school-leaving age. But given her departure from home to live with Mrs Breach, there must be doubt as to where she will be living in the months and years ahead.

The widow's proposal is on the following lines: first of all, she proposes that she should give up her interest in Temple Road so that her two children, Rita and Nicky, should take that property absolutely. In return she says that Bulstrode Road should be vested in her absolutely, but on the terms that she raises a mortgage and pays something in the region of £20,000 to those who, under the Will, are entitled to the Bulstrode Road property – namely Toral and Rekha – in compensation for their loss.

In making that submission on behalf of the widow, Miss Parker in her able argument stresses the terms of Section 3(2) of the Inheritance (Provision for Family and Dependants) Act 1975. Section 3(2) sets out a number of well-known matters to which the Court must have regard.

[His Lordship read out Section 3(2)]

Miss Parker submits that if an order had been made under Section 24 of the Matrimonial Causes Act 1973, on a divorce, in the circumstances of the present case the widow would certainly have received a substantial capital payment and that her conduct (though not that of an ideal wife) would not have been such as, under Family Division practice, to disentitle her to such capital payment.

Miss Parker also stressed that the Judge had found that the widow had made contributions to the welfare of the family; she went out to work between 1968 and 1974, and paid at least part of her earnings to the deceased. Whilst she was in the United States between 1974 and 1977 the widow maintained herself and Rita – and indeed Nicky until she returned to this country by reason of her ill health. In addition, the widow did work in the home, although it is not clear to what extent.

Whilst accepting the force of those factual statements, in my judgement Miss Parker is over-stressing the status of the provisions of Section 3(2). The requirement is to 'have regard to' what provision the applicant might reasonably have expected to receive. I agree with the submission that the widow's conduct probably would not of itself be sufficient to disqualify her from capital provision in divorce proceedings, but that does not mean that under the 1975 Act the Court has to make the same provision as if there had been a divorce. In my judgement the choice of words is not accidental; the two jurisdictions are materially different. The provision made under divorce is not a final disposition of the property by one parent for the benefit of himself and his spouse and children; the ultimate destination is not regulated by the divorce order. Whereas under the 1975 Act the Court has the extremely delicate function of weighting the obligations by one spouse to another against the deceased's ordinary right to regulate the ultimate destination of his property by his Will, and in particular the obvious desire of the deceased in this case to provide for the children of both marriages equally by giving each of them a half share in one house or another.

In *Re Besterman (Deceased)* [1984] Ch 458, [1984] FLR 503, at page 513 of the latter report Oliver LJ said:

> In an application under the 1975 Act, however, the figure resulting from the section 25 exercise is merely one of the factors to which the court is to 'have regard' and the overriding consideration is what is 'reasonable' in all the circumstances.

I agree, and in a case such as the present where there are complex factors to be taken into account, both on a divorce and in the case before us, it does not seem to me possible to postulate clearly and irrevocably that the widow would certainly have received a capital provision on a divorce.

Taking that factor and all the other factors into account, and having regard to all the other factors mentioned in Section 3 of the Inheritance (Provision for Family and Dependants) Act 1975 for myself I would not be able to fault the approach of the Judge had it not been for the capital gains tax factor. The basic problem in this case is not one of money and property, but of homes for people to live in. The deceased having provided Cecil Road for two of his daughters, had two houses, Temple Road and Bulstrode Road. By the Declaration of Trust he had already provided Temple Road for the benefit of the widow and her two children, Bulstrode Road, in his mind, was for the benefit of the two other children by his first marriage, Toral and Rekha. Moreover, it was Norma's home as I understand it. The basic need in this case was to separate the combatants who are crowded together in one house quarrelling with each other, which is extremely detrimental to the younger children. Since it is not possible to swap the houses and therefore give effect to the children's sentimental attachment to Bulstrode Road, in my judgement there is no alternative in this case but to leave matters basically as they are, namely, to give the widow and her two children the interest which they currently have under the Declaration of Trust in Temple Road, and to leave Toral and Rekha with the house at Bulstrode Road where they can, if they wish, permit Norma to live.

In those circumstances I have no doubt that the right course is to vary the trusts of the Temple Road property so as to ensure that the widow has a certain right in the whole of it during her lifetime. Therefore those trusts should be varied so as to give her a full life interest with remainder after her life interest for the two children of the second marriage, Rita and Nicky, if they attain the age of eighteen years.

Finally, in order to separate Temple Road wholly from the other side of the family the ultimate trust should be for the widow. The suggestion that the widow should have capital does not appeal to me. I am not staisfied weighing all the difficult factors in this case, that it is right to provide her with captial at the expense of cutting down the interest which two out of the six daughters would have. The proposed fund to compensate Toral and and Rekha would leave them substantially worse off than their two full sisters and their two half sisters. No case has been made to show that the widow immediately requires capital. In those circumstances, bearing in mind but not attaching too much importance to the conduct of the widow in this case, I can see no reason for giving her capital at the expense of the other children of the deceased. However, in my judgement reasonable provision does require that if the widow and her children are to have Temple Road as their house and Bulstrode Road is to be the house of Toral and Rekha, Temple Road should be put into a state fully suitable to be lived in – which it is far from being at the present time. There are no accurate figures available as to the cost of doing this once the insurance monies and the local authority grants ahave been used to the full. However, the estimate appears to be in the region of between £7,000 to £8,000.

In my judgement, therefore, it is right to raise from the estate of the deceased, that is to say by a charge on the Bulstrode Road property (which is the only effective asset) a sum of £7,000 to be paid over to the trustees of the Temple Road property to be employed in the renovation and repair of that property.

In addition, there is evidence that the widow has been put to very substantial expense and has incurred liabilities in getting the Temple Road property to its present state.

For example, she has incurred the costs of obtaining possession and she has laid out money to carry out work which is not covered by insurance or grant. The amount of her expenditure is not clear, but it is approximately £2,500. For myself, therefore, I would provide the sum of £2,500 to the widow to make good, insofar as it is possible, the money she has had to expend to get Temple Road into its present state.

The Official Solicitor, and Counsel appearing for Rita and Nicky, whilst accepting that the provision of Temple Road in good condition would be beneficial for them, asked for more for those two children. The first points out, quite correctly, that by giving the widow a full life interest in the Temple Road property in place of her interest in one half of it, the Court is cutting Rita and Nicky out of any income during the life of their mother. Moreover, there is need, so it is submitted, to cover the costs of Rita's education at the Godolphin Latymer School, for which £2,000 or more may be required.

Finally, it is said that the deceased's estate had a liability to maintain these children, as does their mother, and that there should be weekly payments for them amounting to £40 a week, £20 of which it is said should come from the widow and £20 a week from the adult children. In an ideal world that might be a good idea, but in my judgement one cannot get a quart out of a pint pot, which is what that suggestion is seeking to do. There is no immediate need for any maintenance payment at all. Both children are being maintained. The elder children have limited means, and quite apart from the monies which I propose should be raised to pay for past and future renovation of Temple Road, they have what will be an extremely heavy burden, namely their costs of these proceedings.

In my judgement it is appropriate that Rita and Nicky should receive some compensation for their loss of income interest, and I also think it is appropriate that Rita's educational opportunity should not be lost for want of funds. But for myself I am against making any order for regular maintenance payments in their favour. In my judgement the best that can be done is to direct that there should be raised out of the Bulstrode Road property two further sums of £2,500 to be used for Rita and Nicky. I would propose that those sums should be paid to the trustees of the Temple Road property, that is to say the widow's trustees, to be held in trust for Rita and Nicky respectively, and that the trustees should have the widest power to apply both capital and income for their benefit. If that were to be done, there would be a fund available to meet Rita's educational expense and equality would be maintained between Rita and Nicky.

The order which I think appropriate is this:

First, as to Temple Road, the existing trust is to be varied to give the widow a full life interest;

Subject thereto, such of Rita and Nicky who attain the age of 18 takes the capital equally with the ultimate remainder if both die at the age of 18 to the widow absolutely.

I also propose, with Mr McCormick's kind agreement, that he should be appointed co-trustee of the Temple Road property to act with the widow.

Second, as to Bulstrode Road, I propose that the Will should be varied so as to direct that there should be raised the sum of £15,000 to be paid, first, as to the £7,500 to the trustees of Temple Road to be laid out in repairing and renovating the Temple Road house; secondly, as to £7,500 to the widow in repayment of her expenditure; thirdly, as to the remaining £5,000 to be paid to the trustee of Temple Road in trust as to £2,500 each for Rita and Nicky absolutely with the widest powers to use income and capital for their benefit.

The costs of these proceedings are totally disproportionate to the sums at stake, and it is most regrettable that these parties have continued litigation at such length in what is a comparatively small estate. In the circumstances I do not think there is any way in which the costs can be fairly dealt with other than by leaving the parties to discharge their own costs, which I fear will be a major burden on the properties that they are taking.

Finally, as to the residue of £4,000 which was bequeathed to all four children of the first marriage, I would not propose any variation, but, like the Judge, would leave the trusts of residue undisturbed on the basis that that £4,000 will almost certainly be the first source of costs of these proceedings incurred by the four children of the first marriage.

I would allow the appeal and substitute that order, subject to agreeing terms of Minutes of order with Counsel.

NOURSE LJ: I agree and have very little to add.

Had it not been for the immediate change to capital gains tax on 4 Temple Road which it is now realised will be occasioned by paragraph 4 of Waite J's order, and assuming always that he had a jurisdiction to make the order contained in that paragraph, I too would have found it impossible to disagree with the solution propounded in his very clear and convincing judgment.

Broadly speaking, that solution achieved the twin advantages of producing a clean break between the two sides of the family and giving a house to each of them. In my judgement those advantages remain as desirable of attainment as they have ever been. But given the necessity of avoiding the charge to capital gains tax, estimated at more than £8,000, the room for manoeuvre is very limited. Thus, although the Judge stated that 78 Bulstrode Road should if possible be the widow's home, principally for the younger daughters' sake, and although Miss Parker has told us that staying there is the only thing which the widow now cares about, that is no longer a practical possibility – unless, which would in my view be wholly unreasonable and therefore unacceptable, Toral and Rekha, or Norma in her place were to be deprived of a house for themselves. So the only practical solution is for the widow and the younger children to move to 4 Temple Road, but on terms which, so far as they may be, ensure that that house can be made reasonably fit for habitation as a home.

I agree that those terms should be as stated by my Lord. The only respect in which they may be said to depart from the approach of Waite J is in the provision of a sum of £2,500 for each of the younger daughters.

His view was that the order he had made provided by indirect means the best way of ensuring that they were properly maintained. However, that was when the widow and the younger children were going to remain in 78 Bulstrode Road. I am sure that the Judge would have thought that those capital sums were no more than reasonable compensation for having to leave that house and go to 4 Temple Road.

For these reasons, as well as for those stated by my Lord, I agree that this appeal should be allowed. I concur in the order proposed by him.

STUART-SMITH LJ: I agree that this appeal should be allowed and I agree with the order proposed by my Lord, for the reasons which have been given.

Order: Appeal allowed. Each party to pay their costs of the appeal.
Draft Minute to be prepared and submitted for approval.

Re Dymott, Spooner v Carroll

Court of Appeal (application for leave to appeal out of time from Purchas J, Family Division, reported in Daily Mirror 26/7/80), Ormrod, Dunn LJJ, and Wood J, 15 December 1980
Paynter-Reece for the Applicant (Plaintiff).
W Blackburne for the Respondent (Defendant).

LORD JUSTICE ORMROD: This is an application for leave to appeal by the plaintiff in an application under the Inheritance Act 1975.

The position is this. The plaintiff and the deceased were both people of considerable age and in 1975 they formed an association together and lived together in a sense, in that they each had their own homes but spent a great deal of time together. They were both working in the same employment and it is quite clear on the evidence of the plaintiff in her affidavit that, up to March 1978, they were living together as what one might call 'independent contractors' each maintaining themselves out of their earnings but sharing holidays and sharing in various ways – no doubt housekeeping and so on – but there is no suggestion whatever that up to March 1978 the plaintiff was in any way at all dependent on the deceased.

In March 1978 the plaintiff ceased to work. Thereafter, for a period of five months until August 1978, the deceased paid £10 per week to the plaintiff. In August he had a heart attack and ceased to be employed thereafter. From August until he died in June 1979 – that is nearly a year later – they continued to live together in this way, each of them living on their sickness benefit or whatever it was that they received. On the deceased's death his will appeared and from his will it is clear that he left his assets to a lady who now lives in Italy and for what was obviously a very good reason. (It is not necessary to say more than that.)

The learned registrar, we are told, came to the conclusion that £10 per week, in the circumstances of this case, was not a substantial contribution to the maintenance of the plaintiff. On appeal to the learned judge, however, the learned judge took the view that it was a substantial contribution within the meaning of the Act but the crucial question was whether or not the plaintiff could bring herself within the terms of section 1(1)(e) of the Inheritance Act which reads:

> Any person who immediately before the death of the deceased was being maintained, either wholly or partly, by the deceased....

It is perfectly plain that the plaintiff was not being maintained by the deceased at all from the time of his illness in August 1978 until his death in July 1979. The question which Mr Paynter-Reece has urged upon us is whether or not the judge was wrong in taking the view that it was that period (August to July) that he ought to look at rather than the period March to August 1978. Mr Paynter-Reece submits that the plaintiff has an arguable case, applying the reasoning in *In re Beaumont* [1979] 3 WLR 818, for saying that the state of affairs between March and August 1978 should be the basis on which the court proceeds to judge whether or not the plaintiff was being maintained immediately before the death.

The learned judge at page 9 of the judgment said this at G:

> I am of the opinion that £10 per week was paid in acknowledgement of a responsibility to maintain the plaintiff, and that that amount of money was a substantial contribution towards her reasonable needs.

That is the foundation of Mr Paynter-Reece's submission

He went on then to consider the period August to July. He said – and it is not disputed – that looked at alone, so far as that period was concerned the plaintiff would not have any case whatever for saying that she was maintained in whole or part by the deceased during that period. The judge's conclusion is my view is to be found at D where he says:

> Reluctantly I have come to the conclusion that phase IV cannot be considered as an extension of a heart attack in August 1978 leading to death. Taking the facts as established by the plaintiff's affidavits, after three weeks in hospital the deceased and the plaintiff established a settled way of life which lasted for nearly a year, during which neither party financially supported the other, and that, therefore, neither was financially dependent on the other. In these circumstances phase IV represented a settled state of affairs or a regime, which had been established immediately before the death within the meaning of that expression described in the learned Vice-Chancellor's judgment in *In re Beaumont* deceased. In my judgement the regime which existed during phase III had been replaced by the regime of phase IV immediately before the death.

All this is the most extraordinarily involved and complicated way of deciding whether or not a plaintiff should have a claim as against the estate of a deceased person, but it is all due to the use of this phraseology in the Act which certainly creates great difficulty in construction and interpretation.

The view I have come to is that it is not arguable in this case, looking at the evidence, that the norm of this relationship was one of dependence on the part of the plaintiff. The whole relationship from 1975 onwards was on the basis of two people with independent means living together and sharing their lives in whatever way they chose to do so. It would seem to me, that the period March to August should be regarded as an exceptional period in their lives, whereas the continuing of mutual independence is the way in which these people chose to live. Consequently the only thing I would be in some doubt about in the learned judge's judgment below is his conclusion at the bottom of page 9 where he said:

> I am of the opinion that £10 per week was paid in acknowledgement of a responsibility to maintain the plaintiff.

The evidence which was before the learned judge is before us, so we are entitled to look at it. When one looks at the plaintiff's evidence on this crucial aspect of the case, this is all she says at paragraph 6 of her first affidavit:

> (6) When I stayed with Mr Dymott I naturally did everything for him which I would have done had I been his wife. We had started to have intercourse when we went to Jersey in 1976, and continued to do, so long as his health allowed it.
>
> Since we were both working there was no arrangement for money to pass between us.
>
> (7) That in or about March 1978 I ceased working. He thereafter gave me the sum of £10 per week out of which I met the expenses so far as I could.
>
> (8) That in or about August 1978 Mr Dymott was taken ill and had a heart attack. He was admitted to hospital. I was with him constantly while he was in hospital. He was allowed to return home after about three weeks, and went back to his home at 20 Dockwell Close, Bedfont.

In paragraph 9 she says that after she looked after him and when he was in hospital there was not enough money to pay his own expenses and she contributed to that and thereafter each of them lived on their respective Social Security benefits.

I find it difficult to extract from that evidence – and it is the only evidence on the point – anything to support the learned judge's conclusion that £10 a week was paid in acknowledgement of a responsibility to maintain the plaintiff. In those circumstances I think that the appeal would be unarguable if we gave leave. I would refuse leave to appeal for that reason.

Before parting with it, I would like to say one thing. It is very tempting in these Inheritance Act cases to move to strike out these applications on the ground that they disclose no reasonable cause of action. The only result of doing that is to land these cases in this court on purely technical argument as to whether or not the plaintiff has an arguable case – and the merits are lost sight of completely in the process. Whether in fact this is a way of saving money or not, I do not know. It would be very much better if these matters were tried before the learned registrar on the merits and on the evidence, because all we are debating is whether or not Mr Paynter-Reece could (and I think perhaps only theoretically) make a case, and having decided that theoretically he may be able to make a case, the whole matter goes back to the registrar to decide on the merits on precisely the same evidence. That does not strike me as being a reasonable way of dealing with these cases. It is a great pity that they are not dealt with immediately on their merits.

Having said that, I would refuse leave to appeal.

LORD JUSTICE DUNN: I agree.

MR JUSTICE WOOD: I agree.

Order: Leave to appeal refused.
Respondent's costs including costs reserved against plaintiff and Law Society.
Plaintiff's contribution assessed at nil.
Order nisi against Law Society.

Eeles v Evans & Others

Court of Appeal (Civil Division), 4 July 1989
J Cherryman QC and *J Rodgers* for the Appellant.
J Weeks QC and *J Dixon* for the Respondent.
The first and second Defendants did not appear and were not represented

DILLON LJ: This is an appeal by Mrs Violet Eeles, the plaintiff in the proceedings, against an order made by His Honour Judge Boothman at the trial in the Gloucester County Court on 25 October 1988, whereby the Judge ordered that certain provision be made for the plaintiff under the Inheritance (Provision for Family and Dependants) Act 1975 out of the estate of her late husband.

The plaintiff claims that the provision which the judge ordered to be made for her is inadequate and should be increased by the court. The proceedings were originally instituted in the Family Division of the High Court in the Gloucester District Registry, but were remitted to the Gloucester County Court.

The plaintiff was born on 9 February 1914, so she is now aged 75. She was 74 at the time of the hearing in the court below, though the judge in his judgment treated her as being 73. She married the deceased, Ormond Henry Eeles in May 1933. It was a long marriage. There was one child, a daughter, Ruby Violet Eeles, the third defendant. She was born in December 1934. She herself married in 1955 and had one child, a son Charles, who is referred to in the evidence but is not otherwise relevant, and her marriage was dissolved in May 1981.

The plaintiff left the deceased in 1978 after 45 years of marriage and petitioned for judicial separation and financial provision. There was shortly after a consent order to maintenance in the judicial separation proceedings, but in March 1979 her petition was amended to pray for a divorce while still claiming full financial provision and by consent she was given leave to file the amended petition. The petition for divorce was not defended and so a decree nisi was obtained in August 1979, which was made absolute on 14 May 1981. However, the deceased had been taken ill in 1980. He died on 16 January 1982 and since that was such a short time after the decree absolute the judge exercised the power conferred by section 14 of the Inheritance (Provision for Family and Dependants) Act 1975 to treat the plaintiff as if her decree of divorce had not been made absolute during the deceased's lifetime.

After the separation the deceased made a will on 20 May 1980 whereby he left his entire estate to the third defendant, his daughter Ruby, and that was proved by the executors, two solicitors, on 11 May 1982. The estate was sworn at that stage at £164,699 gross, £159,715 net.

The judge referred to the deceased as having been a successful businessman. He was not during his lifetime a very rich man. He was a horse slaughterer (or a Knacker, as it is otherwise called) who carried on that business in partnership with a brother. He and his brother had formerly carried on the business in a partnership with their mother since shortly after the war. It appears that the land where the business was carried on was treated as an asset of the partnership. Formerly a tenancy of the land had been an asset of the partnership.

The deceased lived with the plaintiff, until she left him, in the house called 'The Firs' at Church Road, Longlevens, Gloucester, which was valued for probate at £48,000. The style of life of the deceased and the plaintiff seems to have been comfortable. They had all they wanted, but the house was not elaborate and the drawings of the deceased from the partnership were not very great.

What has considerably changed the position is that some of the land on which the partnership was carried on had, as was known before the deceased's death, developmental potential. Consequently in the realisation of the deceased's estate, the executors, on suitable advice, applied for and obtained planning permission. The sales of the land were not ultimately completed until 1986 and the amount of the estate was in the result very much greater than was supposed at the time of the grant of probate. The judge referred in his judgment to a figure of £420,000 as the net value of the estate (£578,000 gross). The estate accounts showing a figure of £420,000 and reconciling it with the present state of affairs are not however available. It looks as if the £420,000 was an interim figure.

Since the death of the deceased there have been various interim distributions of capital. The plaintiff received a sum of £10,000 which was used to pay her own costs of the divorce proceedings. The daughter Ruby received the property, The Firs, which was vested in her. It was subsequently sold and the proceeds went into the house where she now lives. The exact proceeds may have been £55,000, but I do not think it greatly matters. Apart from The Firs Ruby had received capital advances from the estate amounting to some £129,500, including a sum of £9,567 paid to her in respect of her own legal costs. Taking everything into account one can say that Ruby has received some £177,500 and the plaintiff £10,000. If those figures are added back to what is now left, namely £150,000, the result is a net estate of around some £330,000. I say £150,000 is now left. There is also £30,000 earmarked for the paying the costs of these proceedings which were directed to be paid out of the estate. That has to be met before there can be any payment to the plaintiff or to Ruby.

The circumstances of the parties are as follows. Ruby on her divorce became entitled to her previous matrimonial home, which has long since been sold because she went to live in The Firs, but to no other provision from her husband. She has no earning capacity, because of a bad back, and no other assets – apart from her entitlement to this estate and what she has received by way of the interim distributions – other than the house at Portland where she now lives.

So far as the plaintiff is concerned, at one stage in 1983 the executors bought a property called Jaythorpe as a residence for the plaintiff, but it remained vested in the executors and did not become an asset of the plaintiff. Subsequently in 1985 she decided that she was unable to cope with living on her own at Jaythorpe. Accordingly it was sold and the proceeds were received by the executors and are held as part of the balance of the estate included in the figures that I have mentioned. Since then the plaintiff has been living at an old peoples' home in Gloucester. It is not in doubt that she was a loyal wife to the deceased throughout the 45 years they had lived together and kept his house in spotless condition. She was considered by the judge not to be a lady of high intelligence. The judge said he was satisfied that the deceased was the stronger personality. The plaintiff suffers from anxiety and is not capable of living on her own and managing her own affairs. I do not suggest that she is need of the care of the Court of Protection, but she is going to spend the rest of her life in some old peoples' home, or in a nursing home or a hospital being looked after by others. She is, on the medical evidence, generally in good health, or she was at the time of the trial.

Ruby was regarded by the judge, and he so found, as extravagant, having regard to the amount she had received and spent. In her defence it is fair to say that from the death of the deceased until January 1987 she had no income whatsoever. She met her living expenses by borrowing from the bank and rolling over the indebtedness and the interest on the borrowings. Therefore she had at various times, and despite the sums paid to her to help her in keeping down her responsibilities to the bank, very high overdrafts, because bank interest makes that way of living very expensive. She has the idea that with further capital she could extend her house at Portland and get an income from using it as a guest house or for providing bed and breakfast. Those are broadly the circumstances of the parties.

It was common ground that as the deceased had made no provision for the plaintiff, it was right that provision should be made for her under the 1975 Act. That Act provides for reasonable financial provision. In the case of an application by a wife of the deceased, or for that matter a husband (and the plaintiff is to be regarded as a wife in view of the application of section 14) the term 'reasonable financial provision' means such financial provision as it would be reasonable in all the circumstances of the case for the wife to receive, whether or not that provision is required for her maintenance. The Act then sets out in section 3 various matters which the court is to take into account in considering an application for reasonable financial provision. These include, under section 3(1)(a), the financial resources and financial needs which the applicant has or is likely to have in the foreseeable future, '(c) the financial resources and financial needs which any beneficiary of the estate of the deceased has or is to have in the foreseeable future', and '(d) any obligations and responsibilities which the deceased had towards any applicant for an order or towards any beneficiary of the estate of the deceased'. (Here I interject that from the time of the deceased's illness, and possibly from the time the plaintiff left him, Ruby was acting as housekeeper for the deceased and looking after him, though he also had full time nursing.)

Paragraph (e) provides for the size and nature of the net estate of the deceased, and (g) is 'any other matter, including the conduct of the applicant or any other person which in the circumstances of the case the court may consider relevant', it is also specifically directed by subsection (2) of section 3 that 'without prejudice to the generality of paragraph (g) in subsection (1) where an application for an order under section 2 is made by a wife or husband, or former wife or former husband of the deceased, the court is, in addition to the matters specifically mentioned, to have regard to the age of the applicant and the duration of the marriage, the contribution made by the applicant for the welfare of the family of the deceased and in addition, in the case of an application by the wife or husband of the deceased, the court shall (with an immaterial exception) have regard to the provision which the applicant might reasonably have expected to receive if on the day on which the deceased died the marriage, instead of being terminated by death, had been terminated by a decree of divorce. It is also provided in subsection (5) of section 3 that 'In considering the matters to which the court is required to have regard under the section the court is to take into account the facts as known to the court at the date of the hearing.'

The plaintiff puts her case on appeal on a number of grounds, the principal ones of which seem to be tailored by reference to the decision of this court in *Re Besterman deceased* [1984] Ch 458, [1984] 2 All ER 456. The plaintiff prays in aid in particular the aspects on which in *Re Besterman* this court felt that the judge at first instance had failed to take relevant matters into account and so had not exercised his discretion properly, leaving it open to this court to exercise its own fresh discretions. It is important, however, to have in mind the words of Oliver LJ in *Re Besterman* at [1984] Ch page 479 G-H, where he said this:

> I desire to emphasise what has been said no doubt many times before that each case in this jurisdiction depends upon its own particular facts and I think that it would be a pity if this case should be used as a basis for drawing general deduction of principles to be applied in other, and probably quite different, cases whether of large or small estates.

The deceased in *Re Besterman* was a very wealthy man. The net estate was much larger than in the present case and the residuary beneficiary there was a university, not a close member of the deceased's own family who had no other source of support.

The grounds of the appeal are as follows. First (in the order in which it has been stressed in this appeal), it was said that the judge failed to have regard to the size of the net estate, but he misdirected himself that his function was merely to divide the monies left in the hands of the executors between the plaintiff and the daughter Ruby. As to that, in my judgement, as a practical matter, what the judge had to do was to divide the monies left between the plaintiff, for whom provision had to be made, and Ruby, who was the only beneficiary under the will. There was no source of provision for the plaintiff other than what was left and would otherwise go to Ruby. But on the judge's judgment, in dealing with the monies left, he plainly had fully in mind the whole context of the case, including the distributions which had been made out of the estate to Ruby and what had become of them. He had the whole picture in mind and was therefore considering the estate as a whole and not just the distribution of the monies left in the hands of the executors, though in practice it comes to the same thing in the amount of pounds, shillings and pence available.

Secondly it is said that the judge failed to have regard to the provision of section 1(2)(a) of the Inheritance Act under which reasonable financial provision for a wife is not necessarily limited to such provision only as is required for her maintenance. As to that, in my judgement, in a case such as this the wife must get at least what is required for her maintenance. To ascertain that may therefore fairly be a starting point. It is hardly possible to consider a case without considering what the wife's needs are. But section 1(2)(a) does not mean that the court is bound to give her more than is required for her maintenance. Apart from anything else, the court also has to consider the financial resources and needs which the third defendant, as a beneficiary of the estate, had or was likely to have in the foreseeable future. I do not take the view that the judge failed properly to consider section 1(2)(a), or that he felt constrained to give the plaintiff more than she required for maintenance.

Then it is said that the judge failed to have proper regard to the provisions of section 3(2) of the Act, which require the court to have regard to the provision which the plaintiff might reasonably have expected to receive if the marriage had been terminated by a decree of divorce on the day on which the deceased died. He said in his judgment that he had that factor in mind, but he did not explain how he took it into account.

The difficulty is that the question, in the circumstances of the present case, becomes a highly artificial question. One has to assume that there was a divorce on the date of the deceased's death and that the deceased was at that stage somehow alive. One has nonetheless to take into account the development value of the land realised later, although so long as the partnership continued, being a partnership during joint lives, the deceased's brother could object to any sale of the land. One also has to take into account that the plaintiff's own needs and requirements, whether for maintenance or beyond have changed since the date of death. In the upshot it seems to me that the question what provision would the plaintiff reasonably have been expected to receive if there had been such a divorce as is mentioned in the section merely asks substantially the same question as the Inheritance Act itself asks, and does not help to provide the answer.

It is argued for the plaintiff that there is a rule of thumb in matrimonial cases that, at any rate where there has been a long marriage and the wife has no capital of her own, she should receive between one third and one half of the husband's capital. We have been referred to recent authority where it was said that a judge at first instance, who applied that one third rule, was not misdirecting himself, but we have also been referred to authorities which establish that there is no binding rule that the wife should receive one third, or one third to one half; each case must depend on its own facts. Here the facts are difficult, whether considered from the matrimonial angle or from the Inheritance Act angle. I think that the judge's consideration of what the plaintiff might reasonably have been expected to receive if the marriage had been terminated by a decree of divorce came down to this, that he felt that what he was awarding her, having regard to all the other factors of the case, was in line with what she would, or could reasonably have expected to, receive if there had been a divorce. I do not take the view therefore that there is any material misdirection of himself on that heading.

Another point taken for the plaintiff was that the judge failed to give sufficient effect to the extravagance of Ruby. '[The Judge] failed to have any or any proper regard to the evidence that the Third Defendant had squandered the substantial sums already advanced to her out of the estate, which showed that any further monies coming to the Third defendant out of the estate would not be for her lasting benefit.' As I have said, the criticism of the extravagance of Ruby has to recognise that she was in the difficulty of having to live for a number of years without income or other means. But laying that apart, I cannot for my part form the view that the judge was under any duty to give any more weight to the extravagance of Ruby than he did in his judgment.

The crux of the matter as I see it is the remaining ground of appeal. It is said that '[The Judge] failed to have any or proper regard to...the Plaintiff's financial needs in the foreseeable future in the shape of the cost of nursing care and/or nursing home accommodation which she would necessarily need in her advancing years and state of health.' That involves taking into account imponderables. What expenses will she have to meet and how soon? What nursing or medical attention will she need and where will she be able to get it? How long will she live? It is said that we should take a somewhat random view of her expectation of life, which has been variously suggested as from 11 to 14 years. The judge thought that she was a rather old 73. It does not follow that she will not live for much longer than that. Has the judge given her sufficient provision, or should it be more? But that is not the correct question. I refer to a passage in the judgment of Asquith LJ in *Bellenden v Satterthwaite* [1948] 1 All ER 343, which was approved by Lord Fraser in *G v G* [1985] 2 All ER 225, [1985] 1 WLR 647. *Bellenden v Satterthwaite* was an appeal against an order for maintenance payable to a divorced wife. Asquith LJ said:

> It is, of course, not enough for the wife to establish that this court might, or would, have made a different order. We are here concerned with a judicial discretion, and it is of the essence of such a discretion that on the same evidence two different minds might reach widely different decisions without either being appealable. It is only where the decision exceeds the generous ambit within which reasonable

> disagreement is possible, and is, in fact, plainly wrong, that an appellate body is entitled to interfere.

The question then is, should the amount she receives be so much more than the judge awarded her, that we can say that what he has given her is plainly wrong? The judge gave her a lump sum of £5,000 and the income for her life of the sum of £85,000, which was to be settled and held by trustees, with power to the trustees to advance to her up to one half of the capital. We do not know how the judge arrived at his figures, except by endeavouring to take into account the factors mentioned in his judgment, which are the factors which under the Act he should have taken into account. The £85,000 which is to be held by the trustees he suggested might be invested in a building society, but he did not seek to fetter what the trustees did in the exercise of their powers and in this court it has been conveniently taken that the £85,000 would yield her an income of 10 percent clear of tax, ie £8,500. £5,000 was given to her for spending and holidays and in argument no income has been attributed to it. She also has a state widow's pension. At the time of the trial that was £2,280 which with the £8,500 from the settled sum would give her an annual income of £10,780. That had to meet her fees at the old peoples' home, which is privately owned and not a local authority home. These were running at the rate of £180 a week, which produces a total of £9,360 a year. Therefore the judge's figures gave her at that stage a cushion of some £1,420 a year above the fees of the old peoples' home. Out of that she would have to meet any expenditure outside the home, such as on clothing or travel into or around Gloucester, presents and other miscellaneous expenses. There would also be a surplus which might, but not necessarily would, build up towards meeting further future expenses. We have been told that since then the fees of the old peoples' home have increased to £190 a week, but her pension has also gone up to £2,614 a year which, with the £8,500 would give her an annual income of £11,116. The higher fees at the old peoples' home come to £9,880 so the cushion has fallen to £1,236. It is likely that that pension will to some extent continue to rise and the fees will also continue to rise. Whether the income on the £8,500 rises we do not know. There may be a possibility that it falls. That is one of the other imponderables in the case, though it seems unlikely to fall unless costs also fall.

Can one say that the judge's figures are so short of what he ought to have awarded her that he was plainly wrong? If capital is used, of course it will reduce the future income from the £85,000, but there is over £40,000 of capital available to be used and there is the fact that she has a generally limited expectation of life, though one cannot put a time on it. Also the court is concerned to take into account the position of Ruby. including the fact of all the advances she has had and what has become of them. But the fact that she has had these advances does not mean that she is now to be put out of mind.

I think that perhaps the judges' order was perhaps not generous to the plaintiff, but I cannot say in my view that it was so inadequate as to be plainly wrong. Therefore on principles this court should not interfere and I would dismiss this appeal.

Woolf LJ: I would also dismiss this appeal for the reasons given by my Lord. There is nothing I can usefully add to those reasons.

Sir John Megaw: I also agree.

Order: Appeal dismissed with costs. Order nisi. Legal aid taxation of the Appellant's costs.

Re Fergusson, Fergusson v McDonald

Chancery Division, Foster J, 16 June 1980

An application by an adult daughter of the deceased

Foster J: The plaintiff Valerie Fergusson applied under the 1975 Act for provision out of the estate of her mother who died intestate in 1978. Letters of administration had been granted to the defendant (the deceased's husband).

The defendant met the deceased in 1947. At that time the deceased (who was married to James Fergusson) had two children Sylvia and Valerie (the plaintiff). From 1954 the deceased and the defendant lived together at Corby, Northampton. In 1957 they moved to Hartley Green. In 1958 they purchased a house in Watford ('the house') for £2,500. They raised £2,125 on mortgage, £100 was lent to the defendant by his employer and £275 came from the sale of his racing pigeons. The house was conveyed to them in equal shares. In 1974 the deceased was made redundant and did not work again. Shortly afterward the deceased married the defendant.

In March 1980 the defendant, who is 65, received a lump sum superannuation payment from his employer. After July this year when the defendant retires he will get a pension of £36 per week. He says that he thinks he will be able to live on this. He has taken a mortgage of £3,000 for improvements to his house and he has nearly paid this off. Otherwise he has capital of £1,500 at the moment in the National Westminster Bank. The house at the moment is in urgent need of repair and it has woodworm.

The deceased's estate was sworn at £24,100. The house was said to be worth £25,000 and is now not much more. It is a common ground that the deceased and the defendant are beneficially entitled to the house.

Thus this is a claim against an effective estate of £12,000-£12,500.

The plaintiff was born in 1946 and is now aged 34. When she left school she learned how to prepare poodles. She is mad about dogs and calls them her children. She finds it very difficult to get work and has never had a permanent job. She now works Mondays, Tuesdays and Wednesdays at Woolworths for 12 hours and gets £16.18 per week. On Thursdays and Fridays she grooms dogs. She has contributed very little to the household expenses and looks after her own 6 dogs. Her mother, while she was alive, helped by acting as a kennel worker. The plaintiff is intelligent but totally unwilling to stand on her own two feet. She has had many rows with her step-father over the years.

The house has three bedrooms, a bathroom/lavatory, a sitting room/diner and a kitchen. Valerie and her step-father live there at the moment. There are three bedrooms of which Valerie has one, her step-father has the second and the third is occupied by six dogs.

From July 1980 the step-father will be there for all of the day during his retirement. He will be living in a glorified kennel. He may wish to re-marry, and he cannot have any relatives to stay at the moment because of these dogs. The plaintiff asked to be able to continue to live in the house. She has got savings of £15. She does cook and do odd jobs for her step-father. Finally she suggested that the house should be sold and that she should be paid £10,000 but there was no evidence as to what price the house could be sold for.

The plaintiff also relies on two documents which were found among the papers of the deceased. The first is a letter dated 10 September 1972 commencing with the words 'I will the house to Valerie'. This was not a will and even if it was it would soon have been revoked by the deceased's marriage. Secondly, the plaintiff relies on a letter dated 6 August 1974 to Sylvia containing the sentence, 'I don't know how many years I can put up with living with these rows.' The letter cannot be read as meaning that the deceased proposed to leave her husband. It is far better for Valerie to leave to stop the rows with her step-father.

The law. The Judge cited *Re Coventry* [1979] 3 All ER 815 especially the passage by Lord Justice Goff at page 820 and following. He noted that applications in small estates were to be discouraged and that the question to be decided was not simply how could the available assets be fairly divided. There were two stages to go through. First of all has the deceased failed to make reasonable provision for Valerie? In all the circumstances the plaintiff fails to get over the first hurdle. On that ground the application fails and I dismiss it. Even if I had thought that the plaintiff did not fail on the first stage, in the exercise of my discretion I think that the suggestion that the Plaintiff and the defendant continue to live together is unreal. Anything else involves having to sell the house. Valerie is a strong and intelligent girl; it is time for her to face life, if necessary without her dogs. I hope that the defendant will give her adequate time to go.

Order: i Application dismissed;
ii Defendant's costs to be paid by the plaintiff, but not to be enforced without leave of the court;
iii Order nisi against the Legal Aid Fund for payment of Defendant's costs. (The Law Society did not oppose this order being made absolute)
[ex rel James Behrens, Barrister.*]*

Re Haig

Browne-Wilkinson J, 22 February 1989
DC Unwin for the Plaintiff.
JL Jopling for the Defendant.

MR JUSTICE BROWNE-WILKINSON: In this case the Plaintiff, Mrs Powers is making a claim under the Inheritance (Provision for Family and Dependants) Act 1975 that provision should be made for her maintenance out of the estate of Michael Haig who died on 20 May 1977. Mrs Powers in now seventy three years old and at the death of Mr Haig he and Mrs

Powers were living together as man and wife at 43 Caernarvon Road, Stratford, London E15. Mr Haig by his will left his whole estate to his only son, who is the sole Defendant. He is also the executor of the will. The value of Mr Haig's estate net after capital transfer tax is probably in the region of £57,000 but it is not possible to be wholly accurate as to the value.

Before dealing with the facts of the case I must say something about the evidence which the Court has had to consider. The Plaintiff gave evidence on her own behalf on affidavit and in cross-examination. I am afraid she was a very unsatisfactory witness. She was certainly muddled in her thinking and that may well account for a number of contradictions which occurred in her evidence. But I am satisfied that on some points she was not really trying to tell the truth. I feel unable to rely on her evidence unless it is supported by other evidence or by the probabilities of the case. Mrs Powers' evidence was supported by that of her daughter, Mrs Guy, and of a neighbour, Mrs Moodnick. I think that they were doing their best to give their evidence honestly, but it is plain that these matters have been mulled over in the witnesses' minds and that feeling between the Plaintiff camp and the Defendant camp runs fairly high; I think there may be some element of reconstruction in their evidence. I think the same is probably true of Mrs Woolvett who is an old friend of Mrs Powers: there is an element of exaggeration and reconstruction in her evidence.

On the other side the son, Mr Terry Haig, the Defendant, also gave evidence on affidavit and under cross-examination. Again his evidence was often confused. But on a considerable number of occasions the answers which he gave in cross-examination actually contradicted what he had previously said in his affidavit evidence. No satisfactory explanation was given by him of those conflicts. At times I wondered whether he really understood the difference between stating what facts had occurred and what he thought might have occurred or ought to have occurred. I also think that on occasion he was aware that the evidence he was giving was not accurate. I find his evidence, if anything, even less reliable than that of Mrs Powers. However his evidence was supported by Mr Green and Mr Nichols who seemed to me to be reliable witnesses, making some allowance for their clearly apparent desire to support the son against Mrs Powers. Finally evidence was given by a Mrs Lloyd whose evidence was wholly unreliable and I totally disregard it.

There is another feature of this case which has not made it easy. As will appear, both during Mr Haig's lifetime and possibly after it, there have been some complicated dealings with cash in notes and jewellery. I was not provided with any explanation why these very substantial sums in cash were being dealt with in a rather unconventional manner, though it is of course easy to speculate as to the reason. I believe that unexplained difficulties about this cash may have caused some of the evidence given in this Court to be less frank than it otherwise might have been.

On the basis of this rather unsatisfactory evidence I will do my best to state the facts as I find them to be.

Mr Haig and Mrs Powers first met in 1972 or 1973. He was then fifty-nine years old and his wife had died some five years before. She was then sixty seven and had been widowed for some fifteen years. He was living alone at a flat in Townley Court, E15 and in addition he had a chalet at West Mersey. He was engaged in the wholesale fish business at Billingsgate Market which he carried on with his son through the medium of a company, Michael Haig Ltd. Mr Haig Sn owned all but five of the 1,000 issued shares, the remaining five shares belonging to his son. I should make it clear that it would be quite wrong to draw the conclusion that they were company directors or anything of that kind. They were basically carrying on a business selling fish at Billingsgate. Such bookkeeping as there was was done I think primarily on their behalf by bookkeepers and accountants. The company even so was in quite a large scale of business; the audited accounts show that in the year to November 1976 it had a turnover of some £620,000 which produced a book profit of £2,500 odd after directors' remuneration of £12,000, there being only two directors, Mr Haig and his son. In the following year, the year to November 1977, the turnover was up to £750,000. After directors' remuneration of some £9,960 there was a loss of £2,400.

At the time that Mrs Powers and Mr Haig met, she was running a cafe at 18 Ordell Road, Bow, and she lived at the same address. She then owned and still owns this property. It is common ground that Mrs Powers and Mr Haig became very fond of each other. Mrs Powers says, and I accept, that they used to spend weekends at her house in Ordell Road. Although I think she probably exaggerates the position, I also accept that she would on occasion stay with him at his flat. He was a lonely man, at least during the winter, and wanted Mrs Powers to give up her cafe and set up house with him. He told her that he would maintain her if she came and lived with him, but she was unwilling initially to do so because that involved closing down the cafe.

However, in December 1974 there was a robbery at the cafe and the cafe thereafter never reopened. At approximately the same time, whether before or after the robbery I am not certain, she eventually did agree that she would set up house with Mr Haig. They agreed that they should look for a house which he would buy where they would live together. It is one of the features of this case that it was very much at the same time, that is to say on 7 March 1975, that Mr Haig chose to make his will leaving everything to his son. After looking for a house they eventually found one at 43 Caernarvon Road, Stratford, E15 which was just a few doors away from the house owned and occupied by the son, his wife and children. That property was acquired in the middle of 1975, but substantial work including installing central heating and certain other improvements had to be done, and in fact Mrs Powers and Mr Haig moved in the Caernarvon Road house early in 1976. Some furniture was brought from Mr Haig's flat and he bought carpets for the new house. Mrs Powers removed most of her furniture from Ordell Road and used it to furnish the new house. In addition she has told us that she bought a washing machine and a refrigerator out of her own money. All the evidence before me is that they lived happily there together, the relationship striking Mr Nichols, Mr Haig's best friend, as being one of an ordinary couple living as man and wife. There is no evidence before us that there was at that stage or indeed at any stage during Mr Haig's lifetime any friction between Mrs Powers on the one hand and the son on the other. Mr Haig paid all living expenses and as Mrs Powers said treated her generously.

In November 1976 most unfortunately the deceased became seriously ill. That was less than a year after they had moved in to Caernarvon Road house. He was in hospital from 27 November 1976 until 10 December 1976 when he returned to the Caernarvon Road house. However on 20 December he went back into hospital for two days for tests, and at that stage it was diagnosed that he had a brain tumour which was incurable and that he was in the ordinary course of medical experience bound to die within the next few months. The doctors did not tell Mr Haig these facts. However they did tell Mrs Powers and the son. Neither Mrs Powers nor the son thought it right to tell Mr Haig himself what the facts were. However, Mr Nichols' evidence shows that Mr Haig did ask to be told the truth by Mr Nichols and Mr Nichols told him that he had a brain tumour. When Mr Haig was told that by Mr Nichols, he in turn asked Mr Nichols not to tell his son or Mrs Powers. One therefore has the extraordinary position whereby everybody involved knew that Mr Haig had a terminal illness, but Mr Haig apparently thought that Mrs Powers did not know and Mrs Powers thought that Mr Haig did not know. That strange position seems to have existed until either the end or very shortly before the end.

Mr Haig after that two day stay in hospital returned to Caernarvon Road where he was looked after by Mrs Powers. Apart from the evidence of Mrs Lloyd which I wholly discount there is no suggestion that during this time Mrs Powers did not look after Mr Haig in his last illness entirely properly. There is a conflict of evidence as to Mr Haig's physical condition at the time, that is to say from Christmas 1976 onwards. He was obviously a very sick man. However he was capable of going to a party which he attended in January 1977 and apparently another party in February 1977. The Plaintiff's evidence suggests that he was on occasion in quite robust health. The Defendant's evidence suggests that he was very weak indeed. Doing the best I can I think probably both sides' evidence is exaggerated. He was a sick man; on occasion he was capable of being quite active, but he was ill and was not at work. He was eventually readmitted to hospital on 28 March 1977 where he remained until his death on 20 May 1977.

Shortly after his death there appears to have been a row between Mrs Powers and the son. The reasons for that row have not been investigated before us. It obviously was very shortly after the death because it was before the date of the funeral. Thereafter Mrs Powers insisted that she was going to stay on at the house at 43 Caernarvon Road, and the son appears to have been equally insistent that she should get out. In fact she is still there today. The relationship between them has become very embittered. That is a feature which I will have to consider later on.

Section 5(4) as I have said requires me to consider the extent to which and the basis upon which the deceased assumed responsibility for the maintenance of the applicant. It is to be remembered that it is not only people in the position of Mrs Powers, that is to say, a woman living with a man as man and wife without being married, who are covered by paragraph (e) in subsection (1) of section 1. There may be other people who are being maintained other than quasi-spouses. It seems to me that under subsection

(4) I have to have regard to the whole relationship between the parties. To the extent that there is any express agreement as the basis on which the two were to live together, then that is something to which I must have regard. But I think I must have regard to the basis on which they actually lived together as indicating the nature of the responsibility which the deceased assumed. However, the Act gives very little guidance as to the way in which the Court should approach the problem.

Doing the best I can on the evidence it is clear that Mrs Powers wanted Mr Haig to marry her. However I am satisfied on the evidence that he often broadcast the view that he was never going to marry again. I think Mrs Powers was well aware of this. Mrs Powers said, and I accept, that Mr Haig had said he would provide for her and maintain her. But I do not think there is any evidence of any express agreement between Mrs Powers and Mr Haig that he would maintain her financially after his death. It will be remembered that he was nine years younger than Mrs Power, and in the ordinary course of nature if they stayed together it was probably she that would die first. Mrs Powers says that Mr Haig assured her that she could live in the new house, the Caernarvon Road house, for the rest of her life. I do not accept this evidence of any express agreement to that fact. I think it is right that they moved in on the basis that the relationship was a permanent one and that they would live together in the foreseeable circumstances for the rest of their joint lives. But I do not accept any evidence to the effect that he expressly said that. I think the only reliable evidence as to the basis on which responsibility for maintenance was assumed was that at his bequest she had left her house and that they had together chosen and furnished a house for them both to live in where they lived happily as man and wife, he maintaining her.

All that has to be considered against the background that he was not prepared to marry her. I think it is quite possible, as Mr Nichols suggested, that Mr Haig thought that Mrs Powers would not be averse to acquiring some of his wealth and he was not prepared to marry her so as to give her rights in priority to those of his son and grandchildren. The relationship, as indicated in the evidence, was one in which they enjoyed each other's company; she was good fun, he enjoyed her company. But there is certainly some indication that Mrs Powers was not immune to a perfectly natural desire for security and to receive the advantage of Mr Haig's considerable financial means. However I do not accept the suggestion that Mrs Powers went into this relationship only as a money grubber. All the evidence suggests that they were fond of each other.

I now have to consider one of the most extraordinary features of this case. Mrs Powers says that in February 1977 Mr Haig gave her a valuable ring which had belonged to his former wife. Her evidence was that they became engaged to be married. She says that a party was given as a party to celebrate her birthday and their engagement. I accept that she was given this ring, and I think she may have taken this as being an engagement ring. But I cannot on the evidence accept that he thought he had proposed marriage or been accepted. He knew he was dying and in the circumstances might conceivably have married her quickly. But to become engaged in those circumstances, without any talk, because there was no talk, of any date for marriage seems improbable. Moreover, I accept that he did not mention any engagement either to his son or to his brother-in-law or to his oldest friend Mr Nichols. The Plaintiff was unable to point to anyone to whom he did in fact say that he was engaged. As to the so-called engagement party, the witnesses on behalf of the Plaintiff are extremely vague. They say little more than it was an engagement party: there is no evidence of any announcement of an engagement, and the most Mr Haig is said to have done is to ask people whether they liked the ring he had given her. In those circumstances I cannot accept that there was in fact an engagement between Mr Haig and Mrs Powers. I think, as I say, Mrs Powers may have persuaded herself that an engagement was intended.

I must now consider what provision in fact Mr Haig did make for Mrs Powers. It is common ground that he in fact gave her £6,000 in notes. But there is a most acute conflict of evidence between Mrs Powers on the one hand and the son on the other as to when this took place and for what purpose the money was given. All I can do is to find that £6,000 was in fact given to Mrs Powers by Mr Haig and that at the time he died that money was still intact. I think it was reasonable for Mr Haig to take the view that at the time he died that he had provided her with £6,000 which would be available for her maintenance. In addition to the £6,000 Mrs Powers had the ring which he had given her and which was said to have a value of £5,750 (if one is buying it) or £2,750 (if one is selling it). She had the property at Ordell Road which was in a very bad state of repair and not fit to live in without substantial uneconomic repairs being carried out on it. Its value as it stood was some £8,000. She had a car which I find had been purchased partly with money provided by her but I think probably with money also provided by Mr Haig. And she had some jewellery of her own, the exact amount of which is not proved or known. In addition she had a widow's pension of £17.50 per week.

Turning to the son's position, it is accepted that he has no financial need of any acute kind. The estate which Mr Haig had to dispose of consisted of these main assets: first, the 995 shares in the company which were put in for probate purposes as having a value of just under £13,000 but which have since been agreed at a rather higher figure with the estate duty office. He had £1,800 cash at the bank; some money with building societies, and a life policy which produced £1,186. He had the house at 43 Caernarvon Road which was put in for probate purposes at £8,000 though that is substantially less than the real value; another freehold property which went in at £2,000 and the chalet at West Mersey which was put in for probate at £800. There is no need for us to go into the matter in great detail, because it will be seen that there is a very large amount of cash available. More than sufficient to meet any award of a kind which it is suggested I should make in this case. In addition to those assets, if the Plaintiff's evidence were correct, there is a substantial sum in Krueger Rand and extra cash which has not been accounted for. It is not necessary, even if it were possible, for me to decide as to whether there were any such additional assets.

The first matter I have to decide is whether the Will itself failed to make reasonable provision. In other words, in this case was it reasonable for Mr Haig to make no provision in his Will for Mrs Powers? I find this a difficult question because the Act gives no guidance as what it is reasonable for a man to provide for a woman with whom he is living after his death, there being no legal obligation between them at all. Moreover, he had declined to marry her. I do not think there can be any general test. I think all that the Court can do is look at the circumstances of each particular case and see what in those circumstances the Court thinks to be a morally reasonable thing for a man to have done. Here he persuaded a lady of over 70 to establish a new home with him. Their relative ages were such that if the relationship between them lasted, he would be the survivor and she would in fact have been provided with a home during the rest of her life. I think this may explain the remark which Mr Haig made to Mr Moodnick soon after they moved into Caernarvon Road to the effect that this was to be Alice's home for the rest of her life. He had agreed to maintain her while they were living together. I think that in those circumstances there was a moral responsibility on him to provide her with a home for her life if the unexpected happened and he were the first to die, provided of course that at that time the relationship between them was still on foot. I think he also had a responsibility, having said he would maintain her, to see that she would not be left in any great need.

I turn then to consider whether in fact he did provide reasonable maintenance. First as to income, I think he behaved very reasonably. I do not think he was under any obligation to provide more than the £6,000 he in fact gave her. At the time he died she had substantial other assets which could be sold and her widow's pension. The £6,000 that he had given her could be used to supplement her income either by buying an annuity or by drawing from time to time on capital. She was over 70 years old, and that was a good sum to enable her, not simply to live on the basis of the State pension, but to supplement it and supplement it substantially. I think the financial provision was very reasonable provided she had a home to live in. It may be (though I certainly cannot find it as a fact) that Mr Haig thought that Mrs Powers would in fact stay at 43 Caernarvon Road for the rest of her life. Mr Haig was not aware of any friction between the son and her. The son gave evidence of a conversation in which Mr Haig said it was up to him, the son, how long Mrs Powers stayed there. That seems to me to indicate the view that she was probably going to stay there but had no legal right to do so. However her certainly failed to ensure that she had a right to stay there, and I think in the circumstances of this case, bearing in mind particularly the move to the new house and her age, that he was under an obligation to provide her with that house during her life. In the circumstances I think the Will does fail to make provision for this lady.

What is the reasonable provision that I should order to be made? Mrs Powers has put in a statement of her needs which are calculated, if I may say so, on a generous scale. First of all it assumes that she will continue to run the motor car and secondly she is allowing no less than £17.50 a week for food alone. I am not satisfied that she is entitled to look for a standard of living on such a generous scale as that. There are further facts that I ought to look at, because in considering whether Mr Haig behaved reasonably I have attributed great importance to the £6,000. Unfortunately practically none of that is now left, some twenty one months after the death. Mrs Powers has chosen to spend £2,100 of that on buying the chalet at West Mersey. The evidence before me suggests that the son asked for, and received, a wholly excessive price for that chalet. However he has offered to buy it back from her for £2,100 and she has declined to accept that. So there has gone £2,100. Apart from that she has spent money on the legal costs of this case which if she gets an order for costs she will recover. But she has also on any footing been living in a fairly generous way. She has spent some £350 on having her car resprayed. She has in fact gone through the rest of the money already. I am not saying that she has been wildly extravagant; but I think she has been spending money on the basis, not of providing for her future right through to her death, but simply until she gets something more out of the estate. I do not think it would be right for the Court to provide her with extra income simply because she has chosen to spend the money which Mr Haig provided in the way that she has.

I think the assets she is left with (including the proceeds of sale of Ordell Road if she sells it) are fully sufficient to enable her to live, provided she lives rent free. I do not mean live in terms of merely subsist; I mean live reasonably bearing in mind all the circumstances.

As to the living accommodation, were it not for the embittered relationship between Mrs Powers and the son, the obvious course would be to give her the right to stay in Caernarvon Road. But everybody accepts that in the state of human relations which exist, that would be an impossible position with the son living virtually next door. I think the right course is to direct a sale of the 43 Caernarvon Road property and that the proceeds be used to purchase another house. Another house should be purchased costing not more than the proceeds of sale of Caernarvon Road. Mrs Powers should have the right to reside in Caernarvon Road until it is sold and in the new house when purchased rent free during her life or until she remarries, but her right should be conditional on her keeping that property in good repair. I should indicate that in my view the moral obligation on the estate to provide for Mrs Powers lasts only as long as she is not maintained by anybody else. If that were to come about, which seems very unlikely, in my judgement the defendant would have good grounds to apply to vary that order. I will discuss with Counsel the mechanics of giving effect to my order.

(Counsel[1] appointed as trustee, the Plaintiff awarded her costs out of the estate)

1. Counsel is a typing error for solicitor.

Re J (a Minor)

Court of Appeal (Civil Division), 9 December 1991

J Rosford-Tanner for the Appellant.

B Roller for the Respondent.

BALCOMBE LJ: This is an appeal from an order of His Honour Judge Mathewman QC given in the Nottingham County Court on 16 December 1990. The case before him was an application under the Inheritance (Provision for Family and Dependants) Act 1975 for provision out of the estate of Peter William Johnson (deceased).

The applicant was Lisa, the deceased's daughter by his first marriage, who was born on 8 February 1974. The deceased and Lisa's mother were divorced in 1976 and Lisa has since lived with her mother. She retained contact with her father and was very close to him. The deceased remarried in 1977 to Barbara June Johnson, whom I will call 'the widow'. By her he had one child, Sophie, who is now aged five. The deceased died on 11 March 1989. The widow is his executrix and the sole beneficiary of his estate.

The deceased and the widow lived in a house in their joint names. This passed to the widow on his death by survivorship and is not part of his estate. The widow continues to live in it with Sophie. There was a mortgage on the house which was paid off by an endowment policy on the deceased's life with the Prudential Assurance Company.

There was also a life policy for the sum of £40,000. This represented the estate. After payments of debts, the judge took the net estate at the sum of £30,000.

On 13 May 1987 the Magistrates' Court had made an order by consent, ordering the deceased to pay Lisa maintenance in the sum of £10 per week.

The deceased was employed as a plater. At his death he was earning a sum of £140 per week. He was sole supporter of his widow and Sophie.

Lisa was much upset by her father's death. She left school earlier than she might otherwise have done. At the date of the hearing she was earning £35 per week working part time in a chip shop.

I turn now to consider the provisions of the Act. Lisa was qualified to make an application as a child on the basis that the disposition of the deceased's estate was not such as to make reasonable financial provision for her. That is section 1(1) of the Act. In her case, reasonable financial provision is under section 1(2)(b):

> ...such financial provision as it would be reasonable in all the circumstances of the case for the applicant to receive for his maintenance.

It is here conceded that the disposition of the deceased's estate was not such as to make reasonable financial provision for Lisa, since he left her nothing. Where the court is satisfied that the disposition of the deceased's estate is not such as to make reasonable financial provision for the applicant, then under section 2 it can make a range of orders including, under section 2(1)(b), a lump sum payment. Thus there is a two-stage process.

In *In re Coventry, dec'd* [1980] Ch 461, [1979] 3 All ER 815 at page 486G of the former report Lord Justice Goff referred to the judgment at first instance by Mr Justice Oliver in the following terms:

> Oliver J directed himself as follows, ante, p 469G:
>
> So these matters have to be considered in two stages – first in determining the reasonableness of such provision (if any) as has been made by the deceased for the applicant's maintenance and, secondly, in determining the extent to which the court should exercise its powers under the Act if, but only if, it is satisfied that reasonable provision for the applicant's maintenance has not been made.

> In my judgement, in so saying the judge was perfectly correctly giving effect to the provisions of section 2(1) of the Act. There are these two stages....

However, although there are two stages, the same factors have to be taken into account in deciding, first, whether the disposition of the deceased's estate is such as to make the reasonable financial provision for the applicant and, if not, secondly, in what manner the court should exercise its powers under section 2. That appears from the opening words of subsection 3(1). Thus, although in any given case there may be no single figure which it can be said represents a reasonable financial provision for the applicant, there will be a bracket below which it can be said that the disposition of the estate does not make reasonable financial provision for the applicant and above which it can be said that the disposition makes financial provision for the applicant which exceeds that which is reasonable. The court, in exercising its powers to make an order, cannot exceed the upper limit.

The factors which the court has to take into account under section 3(1) which are relevant to this case appear in the following sub-paragraphs:

[His Lordship read out sub-paragraphs (a) – (g)]

There is one further point I would make. What is reasonable financial provision for Lisa is not limited to the period of her infancy. On the other hand, she is of an age when she is soon likely to be able to maintain herself.

With these considerations in mind, I turn to the note of the judgment in this case. The judge said he was grateful for the authorities which had been cited to him, and that he bore in mind those authorities and the whole of sections 2 and 3 of the Act. Those authorities were cited to us and I have to say that I did not find them of any great assistance. A little later he said:

> I take into consideration, as I am bound to, the earning capacity of each party, the finances of each party, what it is that each ought to get and what it is that each is capable of getting for herself.

Later still:

> I have to look at the possibility of inflation rising. I look at the fact that Lisa was close to her father, they had a close relationship, he bought her things which quite plainly her mother couldn't have bought for her. I take account of the fact that the defendant [widow] has limited earning capacity and further has a dependant child who is only 5 years of age. I do take account of the fact that Lisa was close to her father and was plainly devastated by his death...[which has] destroyed her school life if no other part of her life...She earns £35 a week in a chip shop part time, she may go to college, I don't know...in any event that is merely one of the matters that I take into consideration.

Having given the net estate figure of £30,000, he said this:

> Having regard to the authorities and to the matters that I have taken into consideration I take the view that whichever way one does it there ought to be something like a seven-fold increase in the

> maintenance that was being paid and I have therefore come to the conclusion that one quarter of the net estate is the appropriate figure to award to Lisa and that will be an award of a lump sum of £7,500.

I have to say that I do not understand what the judge meant when he referred to a seven-fold increase in maintenance. If he meant a figure of £70 a week, to me that makes no kind of sense. Nor do I understand how that leads him to the conclusion that Lisa should be entitled to one quarter of the net estate.

Although this court is always reluctant to interfere with the discretion of a judge of first instance, it must do so where it is satisfied that he has reached a decision outside permitted bounds, and more especially so when the processes of reasoning by which he reached that conclusion cannot readily be followed. In so far as he did so by multiplying £10 per week by seven and then making some calculation from that, he was clearly wrong. £10 per week, which is by any standard a low sum for maintenance, came to an end on the deceased's death. At the same time, the deceased's income ceased but was replaced by the proceeds of the insurance policy. I can find no necessary connection between the level of the lifetime maintenance payable to Lisa under the magistrates' order and the lump sum to be ordered under the 1975 Act.

Here then we have a 16 year old girl, badly affected by her father's death. She has a home with her mother and is entitled to maintenance until she can be self-supporting. On the other side of the scales is the widow with a young child aged five. She has the support of the deceased's income, which she enjoyed during his lifetime, but has now by survivorship a house free of mortgage in which to live and a net estate of £30,000 for the support of both her and Sophie. The widow also has an earning capacity which she may be able to exploit when Sophie is old enough.

I say in parenthesis that it appears that the widow has dissipated much of the estate in breach of an undertaking to the court, but that seems to me irrelevant for present considerations. Giving the matter the best consideration I can and taking into account the matters which I have mentioned, it seems to me that the maximum reasonable financial provision for Lisa is the sum of £5,000.

I would therefor allow this appeal, and substitute a sum of £5,000 for the £7,500 ordered by the judge.

STAUGHTON LJ: I agree. The late Mr Johnson had prudently taken out two insurance policies. One paid off the mortgage on the house, the other provided a lump sum of £40,000. After what the judge found to be legitimate expenses, the net estate was £30,000. It was left by him to the widow. She has lost the support of her husband's earnings amounting to £140 a week. She has no other resources. At the time of the trial she was looking after a young child aged five years, and had no earning capacity. She did contemplate taking a course and obtaining work at some time in the fairly distant future when the child was grown up. She said in evidence: 'If I can get part-time work, I would, but it is like gold dust.' So, in effect, apart from state benefits, the estate is the support of her and the young child.

Lisa, on the other hand, is now nearly 16, embarking on adult life. The widow has, in my judgement, much the larger claim upon the estate. What is reasonable financial provision for Lisa must yield to that.

I agree with the order proposed by Lord Justice Balcombe.

LORD DONALDSON MR: I also agree with the order proposed. In my judgement, applying the lettered paragraphs (c) and (d) of section 3(1) of the Inheritance Act 1975 we are faced with the claims of the widow as the beneficiary of the estate, which I agree with my Lord, Lord Justice Staughton, have in any event to have priority over that of a teenage daughter. In addition, account must be taken of the obligations which the widow has towards the younger daughter, who will have to be maintained for quite a number of years to come.

But for the presence of the younger daughter in the equation, I would not have thought that the Judge's order could be faulted, even if his reasons may be a little obscure. But, given the presence of the younger daughter, I agree that £5,000 would be an appropriate figure to award the older.

Order: Appeal allowed: Respondent to contribute £500 towards the costs of the appeal; order for costs below to remain undisturbed; £4,500 of money in court to be paid out to the Respondent's solicitors and the balance to be paid out to the Appellant's solicitors; leave to appeal to the House of Lords refused.

Jevdjovic v Milenko and others; Jevdjovic v Jevdjovic and others

Court of Appeal (Civil Division), 12 March 1990

C Hutton for the Respondent.

B Weatherill for the Appellants.

DILLON LJ: This is an appeal by the first and third defendants, who are the administrators to the Estate of Milorad Jevdjovic, deceased, against an order made by Mr Francis Ferris, sitting as a deputy judge of the High Court in the Chancery Division on 7 October 1988. By that order, on an application by the plaintiff, Andelija Jevdjovic, the widow of the deceased, for provision under the Inheritance Act 1975 he ordered that the freehold of a property, 5 Beauclerc Road, Hammersmith, London W6, be transferred to the plaintiff absolutely.

The history of the matter is that the deceased and the plaintiff were both born in Serbia in 1904. They married in the Serbian part of Yugoslavia on 1 February 1942. They had both been married before and their first spouses were dead. The plaintiff by her first marriage had one son. The deceased had one son, Pavle, and two daughters.

At the time of the marriage in 1942 the deceased was with the nationalist forces in Yugoslavia. He later withdrew with them into Italy and then went to Germany at the end of the war. He came to the United Kingdom in 1948 as a farmworker and stayed here. His wife remained in Yugoslavia bringing up her own son and the three children of the deceased's first marriage. There were no children of her marriage to the deceased. She remained in Yugoslavia until just after 1960, when she came to this country. By that time the deceased had ceased being an agricultural worker and had bought 5 Beauclerc Road in his sole name. It was the house where he and his wife lived. They also let rooms to lodgers. The deceased had a job in this country and was unquestionably domiciled here by the time of his death on 14 November 1982. In 1975 he bought the adjoining house, 3 Beauclerc Road, in the joint names of himself and his son by his first marriage, Pavle, as joint tenants at law and in equity. Pavle's son Milenko came to England in 1974 to study and has remained in England ever since.

On the death of the deceased the property, 3 Beauclerc Road, accrued to Pavle as surviving joint tenant. He died in Yugoslavia in March 1984 (it does not appear that he ever lived in this country) being survived by his widow and one son in Yugoslavia and the son Milenko in England, and Milenko has in effect succeeded to 3 Beauclerc Road.

The deceased left a home-made will, which was made on 17 May 1976. He appointed executors, who renounced probate. He then provided:

> I DEVISE AND BEQUEATH my house situated on 3 Beauclerc Road Hammersmith. ..to my grandson...Milenko (who at present living here with me) with the furnitures, and the other my house situated on 5 Beauclerc Road Hammersmith...to my son....Pavle (who is father to my grandson Milenko and who residing in Yugoslavia) with the furnitures and also my saved money to my son Pavle but, after made necessary payments by the executors as stated below under the point 3.
>
> 3. I DESIRE THAT MY wife Andja may stay in the house where she is now for the lifetime and enjoy my house and furnitures free by her wish but, not to sell anythings at all, and after her death the house and furnitures will duly belong to said my son Pavle. The executors may withdraw necessary sum of money of my save from Bank in order to pay costs of my funeral and grave, and to erect monument for me, and to each executor £100 my grants in order to cover their own costs for these services. I have two daughters there in Yugoslavia and I granted £500 to each of them but, to the first one I gave it already, and if I will not give it to the other while I am alive, the executors must give £500 to the other my daughter from my saved money in Bank.

A grant of Letters of Administration was made to the deceased's estate on 11 April 1984, with the Will annexed. It was granted to attorneys for Pavle and a fresh grant with the Will annexed de bonis was granted much later, after Pavle's death, as the attorneys ceased to have authority on his death.

The present application by the widow, for relief under the 1975 Act, was issued out of time for reasons that do not need to be examined. It was issued out of time by leave of the court. However, one consequence of having been issued out of time is that the court has no power to make any provision for the widow out of the property of which the deceased was beneficial joint tenant up to the date of his death. That follows from section 9 of the 1975 Act.

It is accepted by all that the Will is to be construed as giving the widow a life interest in the whole of 5 Beauclerc Road and the furniture there.

She has therefore been in receipt of the rents from the lettings from time to time since the date of the deceased's death. Unfortunately relationships between the widow and Milenko have deteriorated since that date.

5 Beauclerc Road is freehold and it was valued for the purposes of the Inland Revenue affidavit on the deceased's death at £23,000. 3 Beauclerc Road was then valued at £26,000. There was a further report on 5 Beauclerc Road in February 1986. It was then valued, subject to the existing tenancies, at £76,000. It appeared that there had been no maintenance done on it since the deceased's death. It was further valued in October or early November 1987 at £112,000 in its condition without having had any further maintenance done on it. That was the latest figure which the judge had when the matter came to trial before him.

We have been supplied with a further agreed valuation dated 7 March 1990 where the valuers, Messrs Collingwoods, comment, 'the general condition of the interior is very poor and in our opinion major works of repair and modernisation need to be carried out in order to bring the property up to modern day standards'. They consider that the value of the property with full vacant possession as at September 1988 would have been £155,000 and as at March 1990 £140,000. Alternatively with part vacant possession, subject to the existing tenancies, the value as at September 1988 would have been £135,000 and as at March 1990 £120,000. There is another valuation stating somewhat baldly that at March 1990 the value 'is in the region of £140,000'. It is of course well-known that for a year or more there has been a very dull property market in this country.

There is evidence that the local authority has required works to be done on No 5 if it is to continue to be let to lodgers, but so far those works have not been done.

So far as other assets of the estate are concerned, the position is nebulous. The Inland Revenue affidavit showed cash of £6,450 and a sum in a Halifax Building Society account of £7,200. It also showed £63 odd in the National Savings Bank and £1,030.95 paid as funeral expenses. There are other complications as to moneys due to the estate and it appears that a further sum of £4,400 was ultimately recovered. But what happened to some of the cash shown in the Inland Revenue affidavit is a matter of dispute between the widow and the grandson Milenko, which the deputy judge did not find it necessary to resolve. In effect the cash was no longer there. For practical purposes the other assets, such as they are, are likely to be absorbed in payment of administration expenses and costs. The deceased's daughter's legacy has not been paid by the time of the hearing.

It was accepted in those circumstances that the provision made by the deceased's Will did not in the event make reasonable provision for the deceased. It is important to bear in mind that in the case of a widow, reasonable financial provision is not limited to provision to be received for maintenance, but is such financial provision as it would be reasonable in all the circumstances of the case for a husband or wife to receive, whether or not that provision is required for his or her maintenance. There are further directions in the Act as to the matters to be taken into account in awarding provision and the court is given extensive powers under section 2 as to the orders it can make, including power to order a lump sum or to make an order for the transfer to the applicant of a particular property comprised in the estate. There are also powers to order a settlement and there are ancillary powers to confer on the trustees of any property which is the subject of an order such powers as appear to the court to be necessary or expedient for giving effect to the order, or for the purposes of securing that the order operates fairly as between one beneficiary of the estate and another.

One of the questions that was raised at the hearing below was whether the widow would continue to live in London in No 5 Beauclerc Road, so far as she could, or whether she would go to live in Yugoslavia. Her son there has died, but she has a grandson who is married. There was evidence that she had been ill and had gone before the hearing, for a while at any rate, to stay with her grandson in Yugoslavia. She was asked certain questions about what she would do if she had extra money. She gave her evidence through an interpreter. She said that if she had any extra money she would save it so that she could fix the house. She had in fact since the deceased's death apparently saved up some £5,000 of extra income. During his lifetime she had generally done the cleaning and housekeeping of both houses looking after the tenanted parts as well as the parts which the deceased and herself occupied. She was asked what she would like to be able to do if she were free to do exactly what she wanted and could afford it, and she said 'Fix up the house'. She was asked: 'Do you like living in England?' She answered: 'If I didn't like it, I wouldn't be coming back.' 'Q. Do you like living in Yugoslavia?' 'A. Yes, I like to go to see the family.' 'If you could have a new house or a new flat, would you like that?' 'A. Yes, of course.'

The judge dealt with that aspect at page 8 of his judgment. He said this:

> The Plaintiff says that she is happy in this country and would like to stay here, presumably envisaging that she will stay indefinitely at 5 Beauclerc Road, although, not surprisingly, she also said in evidence that she would be happy if she could have a new house or flat. It was suggested on behalf of the Defendants that her real intention is to return to Yugoslavia and to live there with her grandson. I accept the Plaintiff's evidence that that is not her present intention. However, with all the uncertainties which have existed as to the extent of her interest in the estate and the absence of any ability to put her hands on a significant sum of cash and the fact that her benefit under the will or a substantial part of it consisted of her right to reside at 5 Beauclerc Road, she has not really had any genuine freedom of choice since her husband died and I think it quite possible that once these proceedings are out of the way she may change her mind about going back to Yugoslavia. I take that into account, but, doing so, it does not appear to me to make any real difference to her position.

We have admitted further evidence on this appeal to show what the up-to-date position is. That evidence falls into two parts. The first evidence obtained from the Social Security Department which shows that her retirement pension from the Department of Social Security has been paid to her in Yugoslavia since 5 May 1988. That was earlier in the year in which the matter came on for trial, when she went to Yugoslavia to stay with her grandson.

There is also an affidavit, sworn by a Mr Jevdjovic residing in Yugoslavia, which records, when translated into English from Serbo-Croat, that the widow has resided at the address of her grandson Milo Savid in the village of Gorjani, Sevojno, Yugoslavia during the past twenty months. The deponent's village and the village of the grandson are neighbouring villages and are quite small. He then confirms that she arrived in Gorjani in May 1988. He says in his affidavit:

> My house is situated close to her grandson's house and [her] arrival was immediately made known to me...I have frequently [seen her there]. I am also familiar with the fact that Andjelija Jevdjovic went back to England for a court hearing in October 1988, and did not remain there, but, approximately 3 weeks later, returned to her grandson's address in the village of Gorjani in Yugoslavia where she resides to this very day. Andjelija Jevdjovic told me and many other villagers who live in the neighbouring area that she has returned to Yugoslavia for good and does not intend to go back to England. In conversation she also remarked that she could be well-off living here in Yugoslavia from the two pensions that she is receiving in Yugoslavia and that she would sell the house which was granted to her by the court in England as soon as possible, and would give the money from the sale to her grandson and two grand-daughters.

Then there are references to the amount that she thought she might get.

The judge, considering the matter on the basis that she had no present intention of returning to Yugoslavia but might do so, said this (after the passage which I have read):

> If she were to give up living at 5 Beauclerc Road, she would need alternative accommodation either in this country or in Yugoslavia. I am not prepared to assume that she could or would go to Yugoslavia and live with her grandson or some other member of her family without making any contribution to her accommodation and maintenance. If, on the other had, she were to move to a self-contained flat in Hammersmith, she would need a very considerable sum if she were to purchase a flat, or if she were to rent one (assuming that rental is possible) the rent would no doubt also be very substantial and could only be produced by the investment of a very substantial amount of capital.

Mr Weatherill, for the appellants, has submitted to us, and I accept, that the judge has misdirected himself there in that he appears to have assumed that if she were to rent a flat she would need a capital sum sufficient to pay the rent out of the income it yielded and that there should be no question of her having recourse to capital to pay the rent. Mr Weatherill has also pointed out that the purchase of an alternative property as a residence for her did not necessitate giving her the amount of capital required to purchase the property. It could have been done by the purchase of a property to continue to be held by trustees.

The judge then went through the circumstances of the parties and said this (at page 11):

> Another way in which (the submission of the widow) appeared to me not to be acceptable is that, insofar as emphasis was laid upon the Plaintiff's frugal standards of life, that did not recognise what seems to me to be a pressing need for a lady of the Plaintiff's age to have cash available to meet emergencies and to have the economic freedom, if it can be provided for her, to move to some accommodation more suited to her needs than the room which she occupies at 5 Beauclerc Road, coupled, as it seems inevitably to me, with a need to manage the rest of 5 Beauclerc Road and to ensure that the tenants of other parts of house have the rent collected and that the house itself is cleaned and so forth.

Obviously it is right that she should have capital available to meet financial needs and emergencies, but it does not automatically follow that she should have the whole of the only valuable asset in the estate absolutely for that reason.

The judge referred to the need to raise money to deal with the house or for raising lump sum provision for her. He said:

> If it was raised out of the estate, a sale of 5 Beauclerc Road would appear to be essential, but that would deprive the Plaintiff of her present living quarters, and if that were to happen then the provision, whether by way of lump sum or by way of income provision, would need to provide not only for maintenance, a supplement to her existing pension income and some for emergencies but also, as I have already indicated, for an alternative place to live...

Then he said as against that, Miss Hutton (who was appearing for the plaintiff) submitted that nothing less than the award of the entire estate would suffice for the plaintiff's needs and Miss Hutton drew attention to the fact that among the matters which had to be considered in the case of a wife of the deceased was the provision which the applicant might reasonably have expected to receive if on the day on which the deceased died the marriage, instead of being terminated by death, had been terminated by a decree of divorce. That is in section 3(2) of the Act. The judge pointed out that 'one difficulty about that analogy is that it is difficult to know what the divorce court would have done: it would have had to have regard to the fact that the Deceased was not the absolute owner of number 3' , and the fact that the deceased would, on a divorce hypothesis, have been still living. Miss Hutton nonetheless suggested that if what had happened had been divorce on the date of the deceased's death, the obvious order for the divorce court to make would have been to require the deceased to transfer number 5 to the plaintiff, keeping number 3 as his own residence. That is what the judge did in the event do, ordering the transfer of number 5 to the deceased.

I find the divorce analogy no more than a cross-check on the calculations and not compelling in the circumstances of this case, and I find considerable difficulty in seeing that the divorce court would have ordered the transfer of number 5 outright to the plaintiff, leaving the deceased merely with his half interest in number 3 owned jointly with his son Pavle.

Looking at the case as it was at the time when the judge decided it, I have no doubt that he went wrong in the exercise of his judicial discretion in giving the plaintiff as much as he gave her. It is far more than she should, in the circumstances of this case, have been given. That is underlined, now that it is apparent that the widow went almost immediately to Yugoslavia and has settled there. We were told that she went to Yugoslavia as soon as the notice of appeal was given and might yet come back here if the appeal were to be dismissed, but that is not in line with the further evidence which we have received. That makes it plain, fitting in with the arrangements she has made over her pension, that she has settled in Yugoslavia.

I take the view that the order which the judge ought to have made, and the order which we should now make, is that there be raised and paid to the widow out of the capital of the estate by a sale of 5 Beauclerc Road the sum of £50,000. She will also have a life interest in the balance of the proceeds of sale of 5 Beauclerc Road and the furniture.

Accordingly I would allow this appeal, discharge the order of the judge and make the provision for the widow which I have indicated.

BALCOMBE LJ: I agree, and although we are differing from the judgment of the judge below, there is nothing I would wish to add.

BELDAM LJ: I agree.

Order: Appeal allowed. No order as to costs of the appeal, save that the appellants are entitled to their costs out of the estate in due course of administration. Legal aid taxation on both sides.

Legat v Ryder and Ors Re Legat Dec'd

Chancery Division, 2 May 1980

DILLON J: I have before me an application under the Inheritance (Provision for Family and Dependants) Act 1975, whereby the Plaintiff, Mrs Joyce Legat, seeks reasonable provision for her maintenance out of the estate of her deceased husband, Peter Legat. The Plaintiff and the deceased were married at Taiping in Malaya on 8 April 1955. At that time he was aged 27, she was some 8 years older aged 35. She had been married before – nothing turns on that, and they were both employed as Government Officers. He had been to school in York and then to Cambridge University, where he did not take a degree, and he was employed as a Police Officer.

In 1957 the deceased and the Plaintiff returned to England from Malaya. They purchased in joint names a shop in a village in Somerset. Although the purchase was in joint names, the price was provided by the deceased out of money received by him from an aunt. The Plaintiff made no capital contribution to the purchase, except that she bought a small motor car with money which she had received as a gratuity when she gave up her employment in Malaya.

The Plaintiff did a good deal of work with the deceased in running that business, which was continued until 1962 when it was sold for a little over £8,000. In 1962 when the business was sold The Plaintiff and the deceased moved from Somerset to Buckinghamshire, and out of the proceeds of the business in Somerset, a house at Stone, near Aylesbury was bought, free of mortgage for £4,500 and another £1,000 was spent on modernising it. The house at Stone was conveyed into the deceased's sole name and no claim to a beneficial interest in that house was ever made by the Plaintiff. The balance of the proceeds of the shop in Somerset, about £2,500, was spent by the deceased in buying in his own name a minority shareholding in a company which ran a chicken farm, and the deceased's principal job from then onwards was helping his fellow directors in that company in running the chicken farm.

The Plaintiff got a job after moving to Stone; part of the time it was part-time only, and she worked full-time for about a year. She also, shortly before leaving Somerset, received about £10,500 from her mother's estate.

The marriage, however, did not thrive – at any rate after the move to Stone, There were no children, and in December 1966 the Plaintiff left the deceased. It appears that she had arranged to buy for herself a house nearby and on completion of the acquisition of that house she moved out. leaving certain furniture for the deceased but taking her own possessions with her. This may well have been prompted in part by the deceased having brought people to see the Stone house on the footing that that was going to have to be sold. It is unnecessary to go far into the history before the Plaintiff left.

The Plaintiff then presented a divorce petition seeking a decree nisi on the ground of alleged cruelty. The petition was not contested by the deceased, and it appears that his attitude was that after all he was glad to be free from his marriage. A decree nisi of divorce was granted on 8 March 1968 and it was made absolute in June 1968. The Plaintiff never claimed maintenance from the deceased. An order for a token sum was made but never drawn up during the deceased's lifetime.

The marriage having thus been dissolved, the plaintiff in 1970 sold her house near Aylesbury and bought a hotel in Kings Lynn to which she then moved. She ran this hotel for some 6 years until 1976, working no doubt very hard and running the hotel successfully. The deceased sold the house in Aylesbury for some £9,000 in 1973, and spent about a year after that staying in the Plaintiff's hotel in Kings Lynn. He did not do any work there, he did not make any payment, but was provided with free accommodation and maintenance by the Plaintiff. They did not live together as man and wife, but the year passed without discord. At the end of the year the deceased returned to the Aylesbury area so that he could devote more attention to the chicken farm, and thereafter the Plaintiff did not see him again except for one day when he came to Kings Lynn to collect some furniture which she had been storing in her hotel for him.

In 1967, after the Plaintiff had left him, the deceased met Mrs Attenborough, the Third Defendant, who was then living with her husband at Weston Turville, near Aylesbury. The deceased became a friend of Mrs

Attenborough and her husband. Unfortunately, around 1970 Mrs Attenborough and her husband separated and their marriage was ultimately dissolved on Mrs Attenborough's petition in December 1973. The evidence indicates that though the deceased was a friend of Mrs Attenborough prior to the dissolution of Mrs Attenborough's marriage there had been no sexual relations between them. After the deceased left the Kings Lynn hotel, however, he went to stay with Mrs Attenborough around Christmas 1973, and stayed on after the dissolution of her marriage, and after a time they started to live together as man and wife.

The deceased made his will on 9 August 1977. By it he appointed Mr Ryder (who was an old friend) and a Mr Boyle (a solicitor of Aylesbury) to be his executors; and he directed that after payment of all debts, funeral expenses and testamentary expenses the residue of his estate should be held for the sole benefit of Mrs Attenborough and should be paid and transferred to her as soon as conveniently possible after his death. This will replaced an earlier holograph will in Mrs Attenborough's favour which he had made in 1976.

The deceased died of cancer on 20 August 1977. He was only 50 years old. He had been ill for the last 2 years of his life, and during that period Mrs Attenborough had been concerned to nurse him, to take him to the hospital and to do all she could to help him. The will was proved on 31 October 1977 by the two executors named in the will, and the present application by the Plaintiff was issued in due time on 17 April 1978.

The deceased's net estate for the purposes of the Act is of a value (it is agreed between the parties) of £20,000, consisting of £6,000 in a building society, £2,000 household effects, £2,000 quoted securities and £10,000 being the agreed net value of his shareholding in the chicken farm company of Prime Broilers Ltd. That company no longer carries on the business of chicken farming and has entered into a contract, with the details of which I am not concerned, for the sale of certain land for development, on terms to which I need not refer as the value of the asset is agreed.

The Plaintiff is now 60 years of age. She will be 61 in June. She owns free of mortgage her own house, 18 Deena Close in Ealing. This has suffered recently from subsidence and she has had to have it underpinned. The main cost of this, as I understand it, is covered by insurance and claims against the National House Builders Registration Council, but the fact of the subsidence and underpinning may affect the resale value of the house. I am told that if there had been no subsidence and underpinning the value of the house would be around £35,000. She has also investments of her own of some £20,000, which give her an income of £2,000 as year. Since she attained the age of 60 she has been in receipt of a state pension of £1,124 a year. This is not quite the full amount of a State pension for a woman of 60, since she spent some years of her life overseas; it is, however, nearly the full amount and it is the figure presently payable without regard to increases forecast for next November. In addition, at present she also works as an assistant housekeeper in a hotel, and for this she receives an income of £2,700 a year. It is a responsible position and she works 35 hours a week and a five day week, and of course as a result of her years in Kings Lynn she has considerable experience now of hotel management; she had worked, when living at Stone, as domestic supervisor in a hospital. But as she is now 60 it is obvious that the time will come when she will be unable to continue her present job. It is her understanding that her employers are currently interviewing a possible replacement for her, although it does not appear that there has been any particular intimation that she is as yet required to leave the job.

Mrs Attenborough is 44. She owns her own home in Weston Turville free of mortgage. She has two sons of her marriage who make their home with her; they are now aged 13 and 14 and go to private schools. She has investments of about £12,000; a deposit in a building society of £4,000. The income from her investments come to about £1,800 a year, and she has a small additional income of some £250 a year from a family trust. She receives maintenance from her former husband for herself at the rate of £1,400 a year. This was the rate fixed at the time of the divorce and she has not applied for any increase. Her husband has remarried and has two further children, and her attitude to money matters with him, as she explained in evidence, is that she prefers the attitude between them to remain moderately friendly as it is. She receives a further £600 maintenance from her former husband in respect of the children, and he pays the children's school fees and has paid extra expenses – such as special tuition or 'kitting up' the older boy to go to Public School. She receives also a child allowance for the children. She works in a shop part-time for one day a week, for which she receives £9.60 per day, but is not in a position to take any job which would require her to work in the school holidays; she has no training or experience for any job, except perhaps work in a shop, which is what she did before her marriage.

There is no doubt, of course, that as a former wife of the deceased who has not remarried the Plaintiff is entitled to present this application seeking provision out of his estate. This is a case in which no provision at all has been made for the Plaintiff by the deceased, and the first question that arises is whether the deceased's disposition or lack of disposition has produced an unreasonable result? The second question which arises is, if so, what provision ought to be made?

The law is conveniently summed up by Oliver J in his judgment in *Re Coventry Decd* [1979] 2 All ER 99, [1979] 2 WLR 853 in a passage which starts at p 864. Oliver J has just cited from a judgment of Buckley J in *In Re Ducksbury Decd* [1966] 2 All ER 374, [1966] 1 WLR 1226, and Oliver J continued:

[His Lordship read out the well known passage from *Re Coventry*]

Now many things seem to me to follow from that passage. Firstly, it is not enough to say that it the deceased had paid a sum by way of legacy to the Plaintiff that would have been a reasonable thing for the deceased to have done. Secondly, the Court is not concerned simply to reward the Plaintiff for meritorious conduct in that she was the deceased's wife for 11 years, she worked for the business in Somerset for 5 years and she contributed from her own marriage and the income from her inheritance from her mother towards the household expenses while they were living at Stone. Thirdly, the object is to provide reasonable provision – which does not just mean subsistence – and is not to provide legacies.

Provision for maintenance can be made by way of a lump sum, and it is suggested in this case that if provision is to be made the provision should be by way of a lump sum, so that the deceased's estate can be wound up, and not by way of income provision for maintenance over the years. It is suggested on behalf of the Plaintiff that there should be provision of a lump sum of £4,00 or £5,000. Conversely, it is submitted on behalf of Mrs Attenborough that if there is to be any provision at all, contrary to the primary submission, it should be by way of a lump sum of perhaps £2,000.

But the real question at the first stage is whether the disposition which the deceased has made by his will, or lack of disposition, has produced an unreasonable result in that it does not make any provision for the Plaintiff in respect of her maintenance? Now, in 1966 the Plaintiff, who had bought herself another house, left the deceased and thereafter she lived independently of him. She supported herself until she moved to Kings Lynn. She then bought and developed her own business, and so far from relying on the deceased she provided for him for the period while he was staying in her hotel. She sold the Kings Lynn hotel profitably, and so was able to buy her own house where she now lives, and to have a not insubstantial capital sum – some £20,000 – over to invest.

Accepting in full that her earning capacity cannot last long, even though it may be that she could achieve a part-time job when she can no longer hold a full-time job, and that her income will fall when she has to give up her job, she will still have a marginal income over her expenditure, with no problem of finding accommodation.

On the whole, therefore, it seems to me that she fails to get over the first hurdle under the Inheritance (Provision for Family and Dependants) Act 1975 in that the deceased's disposition has not produced an unreasonable result. I do not think he was, in all the circumstances, under an obligation to provide for her by his will. The object of the Act is not to award her a legacy, even though it may be that if the deceased had awarded her a legacy that would have seemed a not unreasonable thing for the deceased to have done. Therefore, I dismiss this application.

Order: Application dismissed.

Re Lewis, Lewis v Lynch

Court of Appeal (on appeal from Blackett-Ord VC, sitting as a deputy judge of the Chancery Division), Buckley, Shaw and Brightman LJJ, 13 March 1980.

JM Price QC and *JAD Gilliland* for the Appellant (Plaintiff).
Derek Mallard for the first and second Respondents (Defendants).
David Purry for the fourth and fifth Respondents (Defendants).
William George for the sixth Respondent (Defendant).

Lord Justice Buckley: I have asked Lord Justice Brightman to deliver the first judgment in this appeal.

Lord Justice Brightman: This is an appeal from a decision of His Honour Judge Blackett-Ord on an application by the deceased's widow under the

Inheritance Act of 1938, the Act which was in force, subject to certain amendments, at the date when the deceased died. The learned judge came to the view that the deceased had not made reasonable provision for his widow. There is no appeal from that part of the decision. The judge then made an award in favour of the widow. The widow now appeals, submitting that the judge's order was inadequate. The widow seeks a lump sum of £10,000 in addition to the provision which the learned judge gave.

The deceased died in March 1974. The hearing took place at Manchester in February of 1979. The reason for the long delay was that negotiations took place over a considerable period in an attempt to reach a compromise solution.

I will sketch in the family. Both the deceased and his widow had been previously married. There was issue of each of the three marriages. The deceased was first married to Mrs Phyllis Lewis, who died in 1966. There were three children of that marriage, the first defendant, Mrs Phyllis Lynch, the third defendant, Mr Raymond Lewis and a son, Alan, who died in 1977. Alan left two children, Paul and Debra, who are the fourth and fifth defendants; they are both under age, Paul being aged 15 and Debra aged 13.

The marriage of the deceased to the widow took place in 1968. The deceased died in 1974, leaving one child of that marriage, Stephanie, the sixth defendant, who is aged 11. Of the widow's previous marriage there was one child, Kay, not of course a party to these proceedings, who is aged a little under 16. The widow herself is approaching 50.

The last will of the deceased was made in March of 1971, that is to say, three years after the marriage was solemnised and about three years before he died. He appointed his daughter, Phyllis, and her husband to be executors and trustees. He gave his two motor cars and other personal effects to his widow absolutely. He then gave her an annuity of £2,000 during her life. He empowered his trustees, in their absolute discretion, to spend the sum of £10,000 in the purchase of a house for his widow during her widowhood, she paying all the outgoings. He then disposed of his residue among his issue. In broad effect he gave his residuary estate to his four children per stirpes, on the footing that the three stirpes, the children of his first marriage, should each bring into the hotchpot the sum of £20,000, which apparently he had given during his lifetime to his daughter and to each of his two sons. The effect of the hotchpot provision is to give the bulk of the immediately distributable residuary estate to the deceased's daughter Stephanie.

After the death of the deceased the executors sold the matrimonial home. They were then faced with a problem, because they were authorised, and desired, to buy a house for the widow, but they had only £10,000 available to that purpose under the terms of the will. This sum of money was not adequate to enable them to buy anything appropriate for the widow. They solved their problem by spending £18,000 on the purchase of a five-roomed bungalow for the widow. That purchase was not authorised by the terms of the will. It was probably one of those judicious breaches of trust which Lord Justice Selwyn is reputed to have said was the greatest use of a trustee.

The evidence before the Vice-Chancellor was that the widow's other income, apart from the annuity, was virtually confined to her state pension of just under £2,000 a year. Counsel told us that the widow's net income today, including the annuity but leaving out of account the child allowance in respect of Stephanie and a maintenance payment which the widow receives for the time being in respect of Kay, amounts to about £3,400 a year net of tax. The child allowance and the maintenance payment together amount to a little over £600 a year.

If one looks just at the cash figures in the estate, the available liquid assets amount to about £50,000; that is, a sum of about £48,000 which is shown in certain figures which have been supplied to us, plus an additional £2,000 of which we were told yesterday and which I need not explain. An annuity fund has already been purchased, at a cost of £18,000, so that the estimated balance, representing residue, can be taken as about £32,000; to be accurate, on the figures presented to us yesterday, it is £31,400. That balance would go as follows under the will varied by the learned judge's order: Stephanie would take £22,850, each of the other stirpes would take £2,850.

I will leave the figures for the time being and say a word about the statute. I need not read it. It is sufficient to say that the first issue to be decided by the learned judge was whether or not the will made reasonable provision for the maintenance of the widow. He answered that question in favour of the widow. He then had jurisdiction to exercise the discretion given to him by the Act, and to order that such reasonable provision as he thought fit should be made out of the deceased's net estate for the maintenance of the widow during her widowhood. Such maintenance can, under a provision in the statute, include a lump sum.

The learned judge exercised his discretion as follows. He confirmed the widow in her occupation of the bungalow during widowhood and, as in ancillary provision, directed that she should be the tenant for life thereof for the purposes of the Settled Land Act, with all the advantages appertaining to that status. The effect of this, in terms of money, was to give her a life-interest during widowhood in an extra £8,000, converted into the house, but of course it did not provide her with any more money than that which was given to her by the will.

Mr Price, who appears for the widow, is faced with this problem, that once the judge has found that reasonable provision has not been made for the maintenance of a dependant, the Act entrusts to him a discretion to determine what provision ought to be made out of the net estate. An appellate court has no jurisdiction to interfere with an exercise of the discretion unless the judge has made an error of principle. Included, I think, as an error of principle would be a fundamental mistake on quantum as distinct from what could be described as an arguable conclusion on quantum – I think that is the difference; a fundamental mistake on quantum can be corrected, but not an arguable conclusion on quantum. It is never for this court to impose its own discretion unless it has first come to a decision that the judge's exercise of his discretion is insupportable.

Mr Price addressed himself to that difficult problem. He submitted a number of grounds upon which he said the judge had erred in principle.

His main submission – and if I may say so with respect, it is the only one which I think has any cogency – was that there were two defects in the will in the context of the maintenance of the widow, and only one was remedied by the learned judge. One deficit in the will was the impracticable provision of the purchase of a suitable house at a cost of £10,000. No doubt that was a reasonable provision in 1971 when the will was made, but it had become unrealistic after the death of the testator. The other defect in the will, Mr Price submitted, was the bequest of a fixed annuity of £2,000. That again was no doubt reasonable provision for a widow in the circumstances of the plaintiff at the time when the will was penned, but Mr Price submitted that it had become unrealistic as a result of the inroads of inflation by the time the matter came before the learned judge.

The criticism of the decision which Mr Price suggested was that the judge was at pains to remedy the first of these defects, but overlooked the necessity of remedying the second defect, namely the fall in the purchasing power of the fixed annuity, so that the widow would not have enough money to live in the house.

Figures were in evidence, and were read to us, which indicate that even if the widow manages to make ends meet for the time being, she certainly will be hard put to do so in the near future. Indeed, I think it was not seriously challenged that she might have to go out to work in order to maintain the living standards which she is entitled to expect; that, I would think, is not an agreeable solution for a lady aged nearly 50 who has a young child of 11 years to look after.

Various solutions were suggested by Mr Price for dealing with the problem. The solution which he said would be the most practical and the least damaging to the interests of the other beneficiaries, was one under which each of the four stirpes should contribute £2,500 out of his or her capital entitlement, so as to produce a lump sum of £10,000 for the widow as additional provision for her maintenance.

That solution is not opposed by the first defendant, Mrs Phyllis Lynch, who is content to leave the matter to the court. Nor is it opposed by Mr Raymond Lewis, who appeared in person in the court below but who has not appeared before us. Nor is it opposed by Stephanie's guardian ad litem; his attitude, under the very proper advice of counsel, is that it is in the interest of Stephanie that her mother should be relieved of future financial embarrassment.

The only opposition (and it is perfectly proper opposition) comes from the guardian ad litem of Paul and Debra. Their counsel, Mr Parry, has confined his able submissions to the real point at issue, namely, whether this court is justified in imposing at its own discretion, thereby supplanting the discretion of the learned judge. In an address of well-studied moderation, but none the less cogent, Mr Parry has submitted that the judge's exercise of his discretion reflects a supportable view of the justice of the case and should not be disturbed.

I confess that my own attitude to the case has fluctuated during the course of argument, because I recognise that the over-riding by an appellate court of a carefully considered exercise of discretion on the part of the trial judge in this type of case is a step not lightly to be taken. But I have come to the conclusion on balance, that this court should, exceptionally, exercise its own discretion in the matter. I do so on the basis of my acceptance of Mr Price's main argument, that having reached a conclusion that reasonable provision had not been made by the will for the maintenance of the widow, and having surmounted the difficulty arising over the inadequate financial facilities for the purchase of the house, the judge did not reach a correct conclusion as to the adequacy of the annuity. On the basis that the sum of £10,000 provided for the house was woefully inadequate when the time came, I take the view on the figures which are in evidence that the judge should have reached a somewhat similar conclusion in relation to the annuity and should have increased it to take account of the ravages of inflation.

The method of finding additional maintenance for the widow proposed by Mr Price seems to me eminently reasonable. It will make a big difference to the widow. It will make, as counsel concedes, an insignificant difference to Stephanie and only a small difference to the other beneficiaries. It seems to me to be an excellent way of resolving the problem.

For my part, I would allow the appeal and I would add to the order the provision of a capital sum of £10,000 for the benefit of the widow. We have not yet heard argument as to when that sum ought to be treated as set aside and whether it carries interest from some earlier date than today, and therefore at this stage I express no view upon it, although I have some private thoughts.

[In the event, the sum was to be paid at once, but interest was not sought.]

LORD JUSTICE SHAW: I agree and adopt the views expressed by my Lord as to the proper approach of this court to questions of the nature which have arisen in this appeal.

Like Lord Justice Brightman, I am of the opinion that the learned judge failed to take account of the fact that corresponding to the acknowledged increase in the capital expenditure involved in the acquisition of an appropriate house, there would inevitably also arise an increase in current household expenditure and outgoings. For this no provision was made in the decision of Vice-Chancellor Blackett-Ord. In ignoring this aspect of the matter, it appears to me that the learned judge erred in principle.

Accordingly, I would allow the appeal and make the order proposed by my Lord.

LORD JUSTICE BUCKLEY: I also agree.

This court will not disturb an exercise of judicial discretion by a judge of first instance merely because the appellate court, if it had been dealing with the matter of first instance itself, would have been inclined to make some different order. If the judge at first instance is shown to have erred on some point or principle, this court can of course correct his error. Or if the appellate court is clearly of the opinion that the order which the judge has made was wrong in all the circumstances of the case, this court can correct the learned judge's error. The order made may, for instance, be so clearly inadequate that the judge either must have failed properly to appreciate the effect of the facts of the case, or must have misdirected himself as to what would reasonably be necessary to remedy the inadequacy of the testamentary disposition made by the testator in the case of an application under this particular jurisdiction.

In the present case it appears to me that the testator's testamentary dispositions, which were made now a good many years ago and indeed some three years before he died, and have been overtaken by very rapid inflation, are inadequate in two respects; first, it was found that the provision of the sum of £10,000 to provide a house for his widow was an inadequate sum to provide any house of a suitable kind. Secondly, it is in my opinion now demonstrably clear that the annuity of £2,000 a year is an inadequate income provision to enable her to maintain a proper standard of living suitable for herself, the child of her first marriage, for whom she is still responsible for caring, and her child by the testator, who is at present only 11 years of age.

As has been pointed out in the judgment delivered by Lord Justice Brightman, the learned judge dealt with the first problem. The trustees had in fact applied a greater sum than £10,000 in buying a house; they had bought a house for £18,000 and the learned judge had regularised that transaction, and indeed improved the position of the widow in some respects by putting her into the position of being a Settled Land Act tenant for life of the house. But it does not appear from his judgment that the learned judge gave any thought to the question of whether sufficient income had been provided for the lady. In that respect I think, on the facts of the case, that it is shown that the learned judge failed to take into account one aspect of the matter that he should have taken into account. On that ground I think it is open to this court to modify his order.

For the reasons which have been given by my brethren, I fully concur in the view that an appropriate modification would be to make a further provision for the testator's widow in a capital sum of £10,000.

Accordingly, I would also allow this appeal and I concur in the order proposed by Lord Justice Brightman

Order: Appeal allowed; Order of Vice-Chancellor Blackett-Ord varied by introducing a provision of £10,000 to be provided for the widow, such sum to be paid with interest only from Friday, 14 March 1980; Order as to costs before Vice-Chancellor Blackett-Ord not to be disturbed; legal aid taxation, if required.

McGuigan v McGuigan

Chancery Division – Northern Ireland, 25 March 1996

KERR J: Patrick McGuigan died on 4 December 1994. He was 93 years old. He is survived by his widow, Alice Veronica, his two sons, Brian and Gerald, and a daughter, Anna. Mr and Mrs McGuigan had married in 1930 and they lived throughout their married life at Brackalislea, Draperstown, County Londonderry. They built a house there, 'Ave Maria', in the 1950s. It replaced an older dwelling. Mr McGuigan was a farmer as his father had been. In 1938 he became the owner of the family farm, known as Crockanroa, and another farm of roughly equivalent size known as 'Deeny's place'. The farms are separated by the Crocknamohill Road. To the north of the road is Deeny's place, Folio 10471, County Londonderry, comprising 10 Acres 1 rood and 3 perches. The Crockanroa or home farm, Folio 10384, County Londonderry comprises 9.59 acres.

Mr McGuigan made several wills during his lifetime, the first apparently in January 1963. No fewer than nine wills followed between May 1963 and July 1989. By his first will he bequeathed his estate to his wife for life. She was also given a power of appointment over the estate; in the event that this was not exercised, after her death, his son Brian was to inherit the entire estate subject to the payment of legacies to the other children, Gerald and Anna. Mrs McGuigan was aware of this will. She has said that she believed that it was her husband's intention to divide the land between her two sons. She was unaware of all subsequent wills until after her husband's death.

That Mr McGuigan had active and frequently changing testamentary intentions is clear from a consideration of the dispositions he provided for in these wills over the years to 1989. From 1981 onwards, his grandson, Eugene, son of Brian, featured as a beneficiary in all but one of Mr McGuigan's wills. In his final will, Mr McGuigan bequeathed to his wife the dwelling house and the farm at Crockanroa for life and, on her death, to his grandson Eugene absolutely. Eugene was to be entitled to the 'take' of the lands in the farm on payment to Mrs McGuigan of an annual amount of £500. He was also to receive the outhouses on the home farm and Deeny's place absolutely.

Dissatisfied with the provision made for her under her husband's final will, Mrs McGuigan has applied under Article 4 of the Inheritance (Provision for Family and Dependants) (Northern Ireland) Order 1979 for an order that reasonable financial provision be made for her from the deceased's estate. Before turning to the factors to be taken into account in deciding whether such an order should be made, I should say something more of the background of Mrs McGuigan, her current circumstances, and the value of the deceased's estate.

Mrs McGuigan is now aged 81. She married the deceased when she was very young and they lived together for almost sixty-five years. She has given evidence (and I have no difficulty in accepting) that theirs was a frugal existence in the early years of their marriage. She was required to work long hours and help out, when required, on the farm. She kept hens and saved money from the sale of eggs. Her thrift enabled her to buy a new Fiat car in 1980. She considered that she and her husband ran the farms between them; it was, in her words, 'a partnership throughout'. At the moment she lives alone in the family home. She receives £52.04 widow's pension and £54.66 income support per week. She has savings of £3,448.23. She uses her car to go to church and to do her shopping. She estimates the annual running costs of the car to be approximately £2,000. She considers that her car should be replaced and she believes that this will require the expenditure of some £6,000.

Valuers acting on behalf of the estate and for Mrs McGuigan have agreed that the lands at Crockanroa and Deeny's place have a value of £3,000 per acre and that the dwelling house is worth £35,000. The estate has a value of approximately £95,000 therefore. There is a dispute about the letting value of the lands, however. Mr Burke, on behalf of Mrs McGuigan, described them as good, arable lands and considered that the minimum letting price which he could obtain was £160 per acre. A maximum of £220 per acre might be possible. Mr Burns for the estate considered that the probable letting value was £100 but would be prepared to agree £120 per acre. He referred to similar lettings which his agency had handled to support his valuation. Having heard and carefully considered the competing claims as to the letting value of the lands I have concluded that £150 per acre represents the most likely level at which these lands could be let.

In considering whether to make an order under Article 4, the court is obliged to have regard to a number of matters. The first of these is the financial resources and the financial needs which the applicant has or is likely to have in the foreseeable future. I have already set out the extent of the admitted income and capital of the applicant, Mrs McGuigan. I was invited by Mr McBrien (who appeared on behalf of the respondents Brian McGuigan and Eugene McGuigan) to reach the conclusion that Mrs McGuigan had greater resources than she had admitted to because, he suggested, she had been, at best, less than candid about her income and savings. In two affidavits of 24 May 1995 and 8 February 1996, the applicant claimed that her only income was £72 per week income support. It was not until the respondents pressed for discovery of the applicant's benefit books that it was belatedly revealed in a final affidavit of 11 March 1996 that the applicant was in receipt of a total weekly income of £106.70 comprised of State pension and income support. The applicant in that affidavit apologised for 'putting forward a figure which was mistaken'. She stated that she did not intend to mislead but neither in the affidavit nor in her evidence did Mrs McGuigan put forward any acceptable explanation for this inaccuracy. Furthermore, in her first affidavit she made no reference to the savings of some £3,500 in the Bank of Ireland. In evidence Mrs McGuigan appeared to suggest that this was only revealed because inquiry had been made by the respondents about its existence.

Regrettably, I feel obliged to conclude that Mrs McGuigan was less than forthcoming about her assets and income. I do not believe, however, that this reticence provides sufficient reason to accept the respondents' claim that she has other resources which she has concealed from the court. I cannot be certain that she does not but I do not feel justified in concluding that she has and I do not believe that the possibility of the existence of other funds should influence the decision in this case.

I turn then to consider Mrs McGuigan's financial needs. I must say immediately on this topic that the applicant's case was conspicuously lacking in precision. An estimate of £2,000 per annum was made by her in her second affidavit as representing the running costs of her car. The support offered for this was a sheaf of receipts from Diamond Service Station, a business formerly owned by her brother, some invoices from car repairers and a letter from an insurance broker about the renewal premium for car insurance. It emerged during the cross-examination of Mrs McGuigan that the receipts from Diamond Service Station were prepared by the current owner of the business in consultation with her for the purpose of this case. Many of the receipts fail to distinguish between petrol and other types of fuel supplied. Some bear obviously erroneous dates such as 31 April 1995, 31 June 1995 and 31 September 1995. Documents showing – or purporting to show – expenditure on cylinder gas and coal or coal products were lumped together with no attempt being made either in affidavit or oral evidence to analyse them in order to produce a reliable estimate of annual expenditure on these items. Other bills were haphazardly produced as a coverall exhibit to the second affidavit of the applicant and the court was given minimal assistance in evaluating them as a measure of the applicant's actual financial needs. Mr Denvir (who appeared for the applicant) suggested in his closing submissions that if one chose a weekly expenditure of £30 per week on food, the applicant's net basic annual requirement could be met by £4,985; alternatively, if one assumed £40 per week, the annual figure would be £5,505. No breakdown of these figures (beyond that for the weekly food bill) was suggested or attempted.

One must not underestimate the difficulty in making a reliable estimate of annual household expenditure; in this case the difficulty in putting forward such an estimate was, no doubt, enhanced by Mrs McGuigan's hearing problems but I feel bound to say that I would have welcomed a somewhat more specific and focused approach to the presentation of this part of the applicant's case. The quandary in which the court was placed by this lack of precision was compounded by the indefinite nature of the submissions as to the effect on the applicant's entitlement to income support if her income is supplemented from other sources such as from letting the lands.

Doing the best I can on the somewhat limited information available I have concluded that the likely level of actual financial needs of the applicant is £5,000/£5,500 per annum. Her current income from the State is £5,548. If her capital or income from letting exceeds £3,000 her income support will be reduced by £1 per week for each complete £250 by which the sum of £3,000 is exceeded. It is on this basis that my judgment on whether the testator has made reasonable financial provision for the applicant has been based.

The second statutory factor to which regard should be had (viz the financial resources and financial needs which any other applicant under Article 4 of the 1979 Order has or is likely to have in the foreseeable future) does not arise in this case. There is not – nor is there likely to be – any other applicant.

The third factor is the financial resources and financial needs which any beneficiary of the estate has or is likely to have in the foreseeable future. Apart from a somewhat oblique reference to Eugene McGuigan's financial status by the statement in his father's affidavit that he now lives in a mobile home with his wife and two young children, there is no evidence as to his current financial situation. Eugene McGuigan elected not to file an affidavit or to give oral evidence. It was accepted, therefore, by Mr McBrien on his behalf that he could not advance a case that he was needy. In the future it is likely that his financial position will improve. His father gave evidence that he was in the process of transferring three farms to Eugene. These comprise a total of 45 or 46 acres. By the same token, however, there is no reason to suppose that Mr Eugene McGuigan is or is likely to be a man of conspicuous wealth. On the whole, therefore, the third factor is essentially neutral in one's assessment of the respective merits of the applicant's and respondent's cases.

The fourth matter to be taken into account by the court is the requirement to consider any obligations and responsibilities which the deceased had towards any applicant for an order under Article 4 or towards any beneficiary of the estate of the deceased. The latter of these considerations can be dealt with succinctly. No evidence was led before this court to suggest that the deceased owed any obligation or had any responsibility towards the principal beneficiary under his will, Eugene McGuigan, beyond that of a grandfather to a grandson. I have derived from the terms of earlier wills of the testator that he had other grandchildren. Nothing was advanced on behalf of Eugene McGuigan to suggest that he enjoyed a better claim on his grandfather's bounty than they.

By contrast, the obligations and responsibilities which the deceased had to his wife were both obvious and undeniable. She had been his faithful spouse for more than 64 years, she had borne his three children and she had, on her own unchallenged account, supported and assisted him in his farming activities throughout his life. The obligations and responsibility owed by the testator to the applicant were beyond question, therefore.

It is clear, however, that Mr McGuigan was alive to these obligations and responsibilities. A consistent theme of all his wills was the grant of at least a life interest in part or all of the estate to his wife. That implicit acknowledgement of his responsibility for his wife and his obligation to her over the years of their marriage must be viewed against the statutory provision which decrees that reasonable financial provision in the case of a spouse is not confined to such as is required to support that spouse but is such as 'it would be reasonable in all the circumstances of the case' for her to receive (Article 2(2) of the 1979 Order). One must also bear in mind the enjoinder contained in Article 5(2) of the Order which provides:

[His Lordship read Article 5(2).]

On one view, the age of the applicant may be regarded as a factor weighing against making substantial provision for her. As against this however, the view may be taken that throughout her long marriage she contributed significantly to the success of the farming enterprise and made it possible for the deceased to preserve his ownership of the lands which now form the bulk of the estate. I do not believe that these competing factors can be set against each other in any qualitative way. They are factors to be taken into account individually for whatever intrinsic influence they may have on the court's overall judgment rather than as offsetting each other. I consider it important that the applicant was married to the deceased for such a long time and plainly made a major contribution to the family income in terms of looking after the house, caring for her husband and children and helping with farm work. I must also have in mind, however, that the need for capital provision for the applicant is obviously not as great as would have been the case for a young widow.

The assistance to be derived from that part of Article 5(2) which requires the court to have regard to the provision which the applicant might reasonably have expected to receive had her marriage been brought to an end by divorce is perhaps of limited value in the case of a marriage which had lasted as long as Mr and Mrs McGuigan's but this part of the legislation reinforces the reminder to the court that an applicant spouse is entitled to seek provision beyond that which is required to maintain her. The length of the applicant's marriage to the deceased and the daily contribution which she made must not be lost sight of in making one's assessment of what is reasonable provision for her. These factors are not to be discounted by an undue emphasis on her relatively modest needs.

The next factor to be taken into account is the size and nature of the net estate of the deceased and the likely effect on any business undertaking included in the estate of an order resulting in the division of property. In this context, Mr McBrien submitted that I should bear closely in mind that the estate essentially consists of farm lands and the dwelling house and that it was obvious that the deceased wanted to buy the farms together as a farming unit. To the latter point the ready answer is available that such an intention was not evinced by the testator in earlier wills. In 1965, Mr McGuigan left to his son Brian the meadow known as 'Matthew's meadow' and the office housing known as 'Deeny's offices'. He gave his wife a life interest in the residue of the estate and after her death to his son Gerald absolutely. That was altered in 1976 to leave the residue to his wife and Gerald absolutely. It was altered again in 1978 to delete the bequest to Brian of Matthew's meadow. That bequest was reinstated in the will of March 1981 but the beneficiary on this occasion was Eugene McGuigan. In 1983 the lands were to be divided between his two sons.

Even on this incomplete review of the deceased's testamentary dispositions it is clear that there is no warrant for believing that he had a settled wish to keep the farms together as one farming unit. I do not consider, therefore, that the case of *Re Rowlands* [1984] Family Law 280 (cited by Mr McBrien as support for the proposition that regard should be had to the desirability of preserving all the testator's lands as a single farming unit) has in fact any relevance to the present circumstances. Unlike the situation in the *Rowlands* case, there was simply no acceptable evidence before me that it was the desire of the testator to try to keep the farms together as farming units for the benefit of future generations. Nor was there evidence that, if the lands were not preserved as a single unit, that this would have an unduly adverse effect on the business undertaking of the farm. Indeed there was no evidence whatever on this topic. I do not consider, therefore, that I should be inhibited from making any order by the need to preserve intact the landholding of the testator.

It was not suggested that any physical or mental disability of the applicant should operate to influence the decision of the court under Article 5 1)(f).

The final factor to which the court should have regard is (by virtue of Article 5(1)(g)):

> ... any other matter, including the conduct of the applicant or any other person, which in the circumstances of the case the court may consider relevant.

On behalf of the respondents it was suggested that the applicant's lack of candour should tell against her. The applicant was less than candid in my view. I cannot believe, however, that, in the overall scheme of things, this should or could cause her any disadvantage. It must be viewed in the context of her age and her presumed lack of familiarity with court proceedings and against the background of long, devoted support of her husband which she feels has been betrayed by his failure to make reasonable provision for her in his will. This factor does not signify, therefore, in my assessment of the applicant's entitlement. By the same token, I do not consider that I should accede to the applicant's invitation to penalise the respondents for the somewhat veiled suggestions made on their behalf (but which they were unable to make good by evidence) that the applicant had greater resources than she was prepared to admit to; in view of the applicant's tardy and less than forthright disclosures of the full extent of her assets and income, suspicion of further means was justified and inquiry by cross-examination warranted.

It was submitted by Mr McBrien that the factors outlined in Article 5 (insofar as they are relevant to the instant case) should be considered by the court in two stages, in line with such authorities as *Re Moody* [1992] 2 WLR 640 and *Re Weir* [1991] 2 NIJB 45. The first stage, he suggested, involved the objective judgment as to whether reasonable provision had been made for the applicant. The second stage was reached only if it was concluded that reasonable provision had not been made; it involved the subjective assessment by the court of what, in all the circumstances of the case, was required by way of modification of the deceased's testamentary dispositions to make reasonable provision for the applicant.

For my part, while accepting that there is a two-stage exercise, I do not consider that it is of particular assistance to label either as objective or subjective. It appears to me that there are objective and subjective elements in both stages. Furthermore, I have difficulty in accepting the supplementary suggestion made by Mr McBrien that a different weighting should be given to various factors for the purpose of each stage of the exercise. It seems to me that if, for instance, the contribution made by a wife to the success of her husband's business is a strong factor influencing the court's decision that he has failed to make reasonable provision for her, it should be an equally potent factor in the court's assessment of what is required to ensure that reasonable provision is made for her. In any event, it appears to me that a strictly theoretical approach to this inquiry, involving as it does an evaluation of a unique set of circumstances and human factors, is inappropriate. I consider that the court should have in mind all relevant matters, particularly those, adumbrated in the statutory provision and should make its decision against a general appreciation of those matters rather than seek to attribute to each of them an individual weight or importance.

Using this approach I have unhesitatingly concluded that the deceased failed to make reasonable provision for the applicant in his will. Her current financial requirements and the contribution which she has made to their family and the farm were not sufficiently recognised, in my opinion.

In deciding what provision should be made for the applicant, three further matters deserve mention and consideration. The first of these is the testamentary freedom of the deceased. It is to be remembered that the 1979 Order and its predecessors were not designed to rob testators of all freedom to dispose of their estate as they chose. The need to ensure that reasonable provision be made for spouses and dependants must be balanced against the right (albeit the qualified right) of a testator to bequeath his property as he wishes.

Secondly, in making an assessment of what provision to make for the applicant, I should bear in mind the effect that an alteration in the terms of the deceased's will might have on the applicant's entitlement to income support. I have already adverted to the unsatisfactory state of the evidence on this topic which renders judgment on it less than easy. It was accepted by Mr Denvir for the applicant, however, that it was a matter to which I could have regard, although he reminded me of the policy exemplified in such cases as *Re Collins* [1990] 2 All ER 47 which discourages testators from relying on state benefit to supplement the provision which they ought to make for their spouses and dependants.

The contrast in the submissions made to me as to how this potential problem should be dealt with could not have been more stark. Mr McBrien suggested that I should make no Order which would imperil Mrs McGuigan's full entitlement to income support. Mr Denvir argued that I should remove her entirely from the realm of income support by ordering that she be entitled absolutely to the entire estate of the deceased. I found neither argument attractive. It appeared to be implicit in Mr McBrien's submission that I should adjust my concept of what amounted to reasonable provision for the testator to make for Mrs McGuigan by assuming that she would continue indefinitely to receive from the State the full amount of income support of which she is currently in receipt. On the other hand, to give effect to Mr Denvir's suggestion would be to extinguish all testamentary freedom on the part of Mr McGuigan. As will appear, I have chosen a path between these two extremes. My order may well have an effect on Mrs McGuigan's entitlement to income support; if it does this is an unfortunate but inevitable consequence of requiring that reasonable provision be made for her out of the estate of her husband.

The third matter to which I should refer is the question of costs. To my considerable surprise, I was informed that costs in this matter to date are estimated at some £20,000. When one takes into account the value of the dwelling house, it is evident that this represents a very substantial depletion of the value of the estate. It is greatly to be regretted that this matter could not be resolved between the various members of this family without incurring such substantial costs. I cannot make any reliable judgment as to whether costs will reach this level, but it appears to me that I must have regard to the high probability that the value of the estate will be substantially reduced by the payment of legal costs and expenses.

Having taken all these matters into account I have decided that the terms of the deceased's will should be varied so that the applicant, Mrs McGuigan, should have a life interest in all the deceased's lands and the buildings thereon including the dwelling house, Ave Maria, with remainder to Eugene McGuigan absolutely. I do not consider, however, that her stake in the family home and the farms, earned by her years of work and caring for the deceased and their family, is adequately reflected by a life interest in the deceased's estate and I order, therefore, that she should further receive out of the estate the sum of £5,000 absolutely, to be realised, if necessary, by the sale of part of the lands.

I order that her costs be recovered from the estate and I will hear counsel for the respondents as to whether their costs should likewise be recovered for the estate.

Order: Judgment Accordingly.

Moody v Haselgrove & Others

Court of Appeal (Civil Division), 16 November 1987
The Appellant appeared in person.
M King for the Respondent.

NOURSE LJ: This is an appeal from a decision of Falconer J given on 7 May 1987 on an application under the Inheritance (Provision for Family and Dependants Act) 1975. The deceased was Mr Robert John Moody. He was married to the plaintiff, Anna Moody, on 14 March 1974. He made his will on 29 January 1981 and died on 28 May 1983.

After his death Mrs Moody initiated a series of actions aimed to prevent probate of the deceased's will from being obtained by the executors named therein. There were three such actions. In the third and conclusive one His Honour Judge Finlay gave judgment pronouncing for the deceased's will on 30 October 1983. Pursuant to that order probate was duly granted to two of the executors named in the will, Mr DK Haselgrove and Mr AR Jones, on 25 June 1986. The third executor so named was one of the deceased's sisters, Susan Elizabeth Evelyn Musgrave. She survived him but has since died.

The material provisions of the Will are as follows. Clause 1 contained the appointment of the executors. By clause 5 the deceased devised his freehold property, No 133 Hampton Road, Chingford, London E4, on trust for sale and with a direction that his trustees should allow Mrs Moody to occupy the property as a residence free of rent for as long as she wish 'upon condition that she shall pay all rates taxes and other outgoings payable in respect thereof and shall keep the same in good repair and condition (but without impeachment for waste) and insured in the names of my Trustees against such risks and in such amounts as my Trustees shall from time to time require'. In later provisions of clause 5, the deceased dealt with the possibility of a sale of the property and the purchase of another freehold or leasehold dwelling-house or flat to be selected by Mrs Moody and to be held on the same trusts. By clause 5(c) he directed that when Mrs Moody notify his trustees in writing that she no longer desired to reside in the original or replacement property, the property was to be sold and the income of the freehold proceeds to be paid to Mrs Moody during her lifetime. After her death there was an ultimate trust for such of the deceased's three cousins, Percy Griffin, Mervyn Griffin and Arthur Griffin, as should survive him, and if more than one equally between them. By a second clause numbered 5 the deceased gave his residuary estate to his trustees upon trust to pay his funeral and testamentary expenses and debts and to hold the residue upon trust to pay three legacies of £1,000; one to the Parish Priest of a church in Ireland, and one to each of his sisters, Mrs Musgrave and Mrs Greta Peacock. Subject thereto he directed the residue, in the events which have happened, to be held on trust for Mrs Moody absolutely.

Mrs Moody was of the opinion that the Will did not make reasonable financial provision for her within section 1 of the Inheritance (Provision for Family and Dependants) Act 1975. Accordingly, after the grant of probate she pursued another course and issued an originating summons on 8 November 1986. That was the application which came before Falconer J on 7 May 1987.

All three of the deceased cousins, the Griffins, survived him. When the matter came before the learned judge the position was that the estate was held for the benefit of Mrs Moody, the three cousins and the three legatees. The cousins were joined as parties to the proceedings, but the legatees were not. The attitude which has apparently been adopted by the legatees is that they did not wish to participate in the proceedings. On the other hand they have not in any way relinquished their claim to the legacies.

The matter came before the learned judge on the basis of two affidavits by Mrs Moody as to the merits of her application and one short affidavit by Mr Arthur Griffin, which simply said that he and his brothers opposed the application. Mrs Moody appeared in person, as did Mr Arthur Griffin. The two executors appeared by Mr King. The appearances have been the same in this court.

The learned judge, having considered the assets of the estate, observed that, in addition to the freehold house, there had at the deceased's death been some £8,000 or £9,000 cash with building societies. By the time the matter came before him that sum, together with the accrued interest on it, was liable to be virtually exhausted by the costs of Mrs Moody's unsuccessful probate proceedings, in respect of which the executors were entitled to take their costs out of the estate by reason of their having been incurred in upholding the Will for which the court pronounced. In fact Mrs Moody had been ordered to pay some costs personally, but those costs have not been paid and they also must be taken out of the estate.

Accordingly, when the matter came before the judge it was clear to him that he was effectively dealing only with the house at 133 Hampton Road. He stated his conclusion as to the merits of Mrs Moody's claim at page 4B of the transcript:

> I am satisfied that on that regard the Applicant, Mrs Moody, has established unreasonableness of the provisions of the will for the purposes of the statute and that some further provision ought to be made particularly to enable her to maintain the property. The question is what is the best way of achieving that objective.
>
> I am satisfied that the best way of achieving the objective is to make provision by raising money on the freehold interest which under the Will goes to the three Griffins. I am very anxious that, as far as possible, I should not entirely defeat the intentions of the testator

> but at the same time to make reasonable provision to meet the unreasonableness to which I have just referred.

He then discussed two alternative ways in which that end could be achieved and pointed out that the remaining question was as to what sum he should direct to be raised in order to cover both the outstanding balance of costs and also the sums of money which he had determined ought to be paid here and now to the three Griffins by way of acceleration of their interests in the house after Mrs Moody's death. He was of the opinion that his order, to the details of which I shall soon come, should preserve the house for Mrs Moody subject to payment of those sums. At page 4H he said:

> I have to think therefore what would be a reasonable sum to raise against the freehold to be divisible in three parts, one to go to each of the three Griffin cousins, because it is their interest of course which must be abated to provide Mrs Moody with the freehold interest subject of course to such charge as necessary to raise the money for that purpose. I have come to the conclusion, doing the best I can, that if a sum of £9,000 be raised so far as the Griffins are concerned, that is to say which will allow each of them to get a capital sum of £3,000 – their ultimate interest is to be abated to that extent but of course they will get the money reasonably quickly....

What it came to was that the judge made an order preserving the house for Mrs Moody, but making provision for payment out to the Griffins of all outstanding costs here and now, so that the administration of this estate – and indeed the whole sorry story – could be brought to an end as soon as possible and Mrs Moody left with the house.

The form which the judge's order took was this. It was ordered, pursuant to section 2 of the Inheritance (Provision for Family and Dependants) Act 1975 that the disposition of the estate of the deceased effected by his Will should be varied in the manner shown in the schedule. By paragraph (1) of the schedule No 133 Hampton Road was directed to 'be held upon...the following terms and conditions in lieu of the trusts and provisions [set out in the Will]'.

Paragraph (2) is in these terms:

> The First and Second Defendants as personal representatives of the said deceased shall borrow the sum of £12,000 upon such terms as they shall determine (but to the intent that no periodic payment of interest or other periodic payment shall be payable thereunder) upon the security of the said freehold property and shall use such sum in the following manner:
>
> (a) as to £9,000 thereof to divide the same equally between the Third, Fourth and Fifth Defendants hereto
>
> (b) as to the remainder upon trust to pay thereof all testamentary and other administration costs charges and expenses to the extent that the residuary estate of the said deceased is insufficient to bear the same and subject thereto upon trust for the plaintiff absolutely.

Paragraph (3) provides that subject to the provisions of paragraph (2) the house shall be held upon trust for Mrs Moody absolutely.

Thus the judge's order was to enable the executors to obtain if they could a mortgage under which the interest would be rolled up, the sum so raised being sufficient to pay off the Griffins and the outstanding costs. The body of the order contained a liberty to apply, no doubt in case the executors found that the scheme would not work.

The position today, as it has been put before us by Mr King, is this. The executors sought a revaluation of the property in May of this year. Their valuer was prevented by Mrs Moody from going inside. He was able only to inspect the property from the outside. He was of the opinion that it was in need of some external redecoration and he put a value on it of approximately £65,000, subject to survey. Mrs Moody has told us today that she thinks that that figure is too high. However, it is the best figure we have and, if the valuer was unable to get into the property, it was hardly possible for him to make a more accurate valuation.

The other assets of the estate consists of cash with building societies of about £13,800. That is the sum which now represents the original £8,000 or £9,000 held by the deceased together with interest to date. Against those assets there are outstanding liabilities for, first, the costs of the three probate actions, including the costs which were ordered to be paid personally by Mrs Moody. They add up to £9,957.67. Then there are the normal costs of administration to date, which amount to £1,581.25. Finally, the executors estimate that their costs of these proceedings, including the costs of this appeal, are approximately £3,500. The total of those three items is about £15,000. That exceeds the £13,800 in hand by about £1,200. There is then the £9,000 to be raised to pay out the Griffins if the learned judge's order stands. The executors' total requirement would be about £10,000 and would be adequately covered by the £12,000 which is directed to be raised by the order.

In support of her appeal before us today, Mrs Moody has taken two main points. First, she has said that it is unjust that the Griffins should receive between them £9,000, or indeed any sum at all. Her case has throughout been that she should have the whole of the beneficial interest in the house. As to that, and having listened carefully to everything which Mrs Moody has said, I have to say that the course which the judge took was well within his discretion. He was entitled to take a course which did not entirely defeat the deceased's intentions. It seems to me that he made an order which was favourable to Mrs Moody, because the Griffins, instead of having a reversion in a house which was to be worth up to £65,000, although postponed in practice until Mrs Moody's death, were reduced to an accelerated interest in only £9,000. Mr Arthur Griffin has made it clear to us today that he would have liked to have had more than £9,000 for himself and his brothers. I can understand that. But he has not formally cross-appealed against the learned judge's order and I think that he was wise not to do so because again, as against him and his brothers, the order was well within the judge's discretion. I would only advise Mrs Moody to try to understand that on that score alone she obtained something of a victory at the hands of the learned judge.

Mrs Moody's second complaint has centred on the fact that the executors have now to be paid a total of around £15,000 in respect of their costs of the various proceedings and administration expenses. She appreciates that in normal circumstances they would be entitled to those costs and expenses, but she says that they have been guilty of wilful misconduct, neglect and unreasonable delay. I would emphasise that we are not on this appeal concerned with any precise question of quantum, as would be a court which was considering some question of taxation. We are only concerned to see that the amount which is to be raised pursuant to the judge's order is one which can properly be raised on the evidence which is before us. Again, having listened very carefully to everything that Mrs Moody has said and having very carefully read paragraphs 7 and 8 of her supplementary notice of appeal, I have to say that she has not established that we could interfere with the judge's order on this ground. There is no evidence to support any of the charges of misconduct.

In the circumstances, and subject to one final comment, I think that this appeal should be dismissed. However, there is, it seems to me, an omission in the learned judge's order, and that is in regard to provision for the three legatees. As I have said, they have not in any way relinquished their claims. The position is that if this matter had followed its normal course, there would have been a fund of some £8,000 or £9,000 available to satisfy the legacies, which were expressly charged on the residuary estate before payment of the balance to Mrs Moody. However, as a result of Mrs Moody's unsuccessful proceedings, that fund is no longer available and in my view it is right and proper that the legacies should accordingly attach to the house. I was initially in some doubt as to whether that was an order which the court could make, but under the guidance of Mr King I find that section 2(4) of the 1975 Act is sufficiently wide to empower us to order that the legacies, instead of being charged on residue, shall be charged on the house. I see no reason why they should not be charged and paid accordingly.

In the result I would vary the learned judge's order by amending the sum to be raised under paragraph (2) of the schedule to £15,000 by inserting as a new sub-paragraph (a) a provision (in terms to be settled by Mr King) for payment of the legacies of £3,000 and by relettering the existing sub-paragraphs (a) and (b) as (b) and (c) respectively. With that variation, to deal with a point which I do not think was put before the learned judge, I would affirm his order and dismiss this appeal.

LLOYD J: I agree with the judgment which has just been delivered and the order which my Lord proposes.

PURCHAS LJ: I also agree.

Order: Appeal dismissed. Costs to be paid out of the estate.

Morrow v Morrow and Another

Chancery Division – Northern Ireland, 5 April 1995

CAMPBELL J: Mary Morrow has brought these proceedings under the Inheritance (Provision for Family and Dependants) (Northern Ireland)

Order 1979 ('the 1979 Order') because she claims that the disposition of the estate of her late husband John Orr Morrow effected by his will dated 30 November 1992 is not such as to make reasonable financial provision for her.

The first defendant, John Leslie Morrow, is her son. The second defendant, Reverend John Braithwaite, is the executor of the will which was proved on 27 April 1994, power being reserved to the two other executors named in the will, May Morrow and John Leslie Morrow.

Mrs Morrow, who is now aged 75, was married to John Orr Morrow for 52 years. Throughout their marriage they lived together on the family farm of some 52 acres at 12 Tullymakill Road, Ballydrain, Comber, County Down until the death of Mr Morrow on 26 November 1993.

They had three children. John Leslie, their only son, who is now aged 52, is married and he and his wife have two grown up children. They live at 11 Tullymakill Road in a house built in 1970 on land which was given to him by his father and originally formed part of the family farm. He obtained a degree in Agriculture at The Queen's University of Belfast and he is a qualified company secretary. Between 1964 and 1967 he worked in Armagh and in 1967 he moved to the Department of Agriculture in Belfast and he married in the same year. He became redundant in 1988 and began working as a labourer with the Co-operative Wholesale Society. After doing this work for three years he held another post with the Society until 1991. While he was with the Society, in the Autumn of 1988, he formed a company which is engaged in the export of seed potatoes. It is a seasonal business and takes up a small proportion of his time. He has an income from this source of £700 per month net.

In 1992 his father transferred the farm to his son and since then he has farmed the lands other than 10 acres in front of his house which he has let in conacre.

Mr and Mrs Morrow's elder daughter Jennifer who is now 49, joined the Civil Service in 1963. She married in 1967 and she lives with her husband and family in County Antrim. She was given £25,000 as gift by her father during his lifetime.

The Morrow's younger daughter, Gillian, is aged 41. In 1971 she became an undergraduate at The Queen's University of Belfast. She married in 1981 but her marriage broke down in 1989 and she has lived in a cottage on the family farm since that time. This cottage which is now her property was sold to her by her father at a figure considerably below market value.

In the early days of their marriage Mr Morrow ran the farm with the assistance of farm labourers and one of Mrs Morrow's duties was to provide food for them in addition to doing other tasks on the farm and looking after her family. By 1964 the number of labourers had been reduced to one and as the farm could no longer sustain that expense they were forced to dispense with his services. Mr Morrow continued to work the farm on his own with the assistance of machinery such as a tractor and some additional help from Mrs Morrow. She gave evidence that she worked on the farm planting potatoes and bunching vegetables and taking them to market. She said that she also helped her husband when he was moving cattle and that she looked after the calves. I have no doubt that their son helped also on the farm when he could both at weekends and on summer evenings. I accept that he bought some items of machinery for the farm from time to time not only to help his father but also because, as the only son, he expected that one day he would inherit the farm. It was therefore in his own interest to help his father to keep the farm in good working order.

In April 1980 Mr Morrow was badly injured when he fell out of a loft on the farm and as a result of his injuries he was in receipt of invalidity benefit until his 65th birthday of that year when he became entitled to a pension. After his accident a number of cows and calves on the farm were sold and cash was realised. He engaged a contractor to bale hay for him and to harvest the barley and as he had more or less retired from farming he let some of his land. His wife suggested to him that they should sell the farm but he was not prepared to consider doing so.

Until the late 1980s the Morrow family appear to have been perfectly happy. The evidence suggests that Mrs Morrow had the more dominant personality and that her husband was more interested in a quiet life. In 1989 the marriage of the younger daughter Gillian broke down and it has been suggested that from about that time the relationship between Mr and Mrs Morrow began to deteriorate.

As things got worse between Mr and Mrs Morrow, Gillian sided with her mother and Jennifer and John Leslie with Mr Morrow. This continued to be the position until the death of Mr Morrow in November 1993 and the family remains divided.

According to Mrs Morrow from about 1989 her husband began to suffer from a change of personality and became aggressive. She said that his memory began to fail and she illustrated this by describing how he would ask her the route along roads that he knew well and had driven along frequently over the years. Mrs Morrow had acted as the book-keeper for the farm over the years and some of the bank and building society accounts were in their joint names. After her husband retired they pooled their pensions to allow Mrs Morrow to pay small bills, however she claimed that from September 1992 onwards Mr Morrow refused to give his pension to her and this appears was another source of friction between them.

Her son offered a different explanation for the differences that existed between his parents. He said that has father had discovered in September or October 1992 that substantial sums of money had disappeared from one of the joint accounts and that his father felt that having started out in life with nothing he was going to end it with nothing. He alleged that his mother had declared that she was going to run the farm into debt so that it would not be worth anything. John Leslie Morrow said that it was this that led to the transfer of the farm from father to son in November 1992.

The differences between Mr and Mrs Morrow grew although they continued to live under the same roof and money was only one of the subjects for dispute. Mrs Morrow felt that her husband was unwell and that he was suffering from senile dementia or Alzheimer's disease though she had no medical support for this opinion. Her husband's general practitioner, Dr Donaldson, who gave evidence said that Mr Morrow had been examined by him, by his partner and by a Consultant Dr Mathai and that none of them had found any evidence of mental deterioration.

Mr Morrow's general health was not good as he had a carcinoma of the face and suffered from cardiac failure. Dr Donaldson said that he visited him frequently as he was keeping both of these conditions under review. On one occasion in 1991 Mrs Morrow told him that she hated her husband so much that she could stick a knife in him. The doctor said that he took this threat seriously though he accepted that he did not report it to the police. The doctor gave evidence of seeing marks on Mr Morrow in May 1991 when he complained to him that he had been attacked by his wife and asked the doctor to record his findings. Dr Donaldson saw him in December 1992 when he complained of having been assaulted by his wife and daughter and there were signs of bruising to his hand and he complained of pains in one of the joints of his left index finger.

In February 1993 Mrs Morrow issued a summons against her husband for a financial provision order and an exclusion and personal protection order. Her husband issued a cross-order against her seeking a personal protection order. The parties attended Newtownards Magistrates' Court and the cases did not proceed as Mrs Morrow indicated that she would issue a petition for judicial separation. Such a petition was issued in May 1993 but it did not reach trial.

On 25 November 1993, which was the day before Mr Morrow died, Dr Donaldson went to the farm to see him. He found Mrs Morrow baking in the kitchen and she pointed out to the doctor the direction to her husbands' room. Before the doctor reached the room Mr Morrow emerged wearing only a vest and looking cold and miserable. Mrs Morrow proceeded to give the doctor a lecture on wills. On the advice of the doctor arrangements were made for Mr Morrow to be taken to his son Leslie's house and it was there that he died on the following day.

Mr Morrow had made a will on 8 December 1974 which has not been introduced in evidence. He made his next will on 9 August 1990 in which he left his entire estate to his wife for life and on her death or re-marriage to his son absolutely.

On 17 October 1990 he made another will by which he gave his daughter Jennifer £25,000 to be paid out of the proceeds of the transfer of the cottage to Gillian at half value during his lifetime. He devised the remainder of his estate to the trustees to hold for the benefit of his wife during her lifetime and to pay her 90% of the income and the balance to his son, together with a right of residence for his wife.

Under the terms of his next will, made on 24 May 1991, he gave his wife a right of residence, his motor car and his herd of cattle and 90% of the income. He gave his daughter Gillian the right to graze a pony without charge on the farm and a gift to Jennifer of £25,000 was also included. On the following day he made another will giving his wife 90% of the income but not mentioning the gift of the motor car and cattle to her, the gift to Jennifer or the right to graze a pony previously given to Gillian. He explained in a letter dated 25 May 1991 that he had made the will on 24 May in the presence of his wife and that she had demanded that he change his earlier will and he believed that this was as a result of pressure from his daughter Gillian who, he said, had been ill-treating him and pressuring his wife to do likewise. He said that he had left out the gift of £25,000 to Jennifer as it had already been paid to her.

A will was made on 31 May 1991 which is in identical terms save for the fact that Mrs Morrow was made an executor. On 25 November Mr Morrow made another will giving his livestock and his car and two fields comprising approximately 11 acres and 95% of the income from the rest of the land and a right of residence and his daughter Gillian the right to graze a pony on the land adjoining her cottage. If his wife wished to sell the two fields his son was to be given an option to purchase them at market value.

By his last will dated 30 November 1992 which was proved on 27 April 1994, Mr Morrow left some small items to his son and to his daughter Jennifer and he left his motor car and the residue of his estate to his wife absolutely. In this will Mr Morrow referred to the provision he had made for his wife in the agreement of the same date by which he had transferred the farm to his son and to substantial sums of money that she had received during his lifetime. He referred in particular to £8,200 which she had withdrawn during the year 1991-92 from a joint account with the Alliance and Leicester Building Society. The value of his estate did not exceed £10,000.

The agreement of 30 November 1992, which is referred to in the will of the same date, was made between John Orr Morrow and his son John Leslie Morrow. It is recited that JO Morrow has agreed to transfer to JL Morrow all his lands comprised in Folios 2734 and 2735 County Down and all his livestock, machinery and tools in consideration of the undertakings and payment to be made by JL Morrow. Mr and Mrs Morrow are to be entitled to live in the dwelling house on the farm for their joint lives free of rent and their son is made responsible for the structural repair of the dwelling house but not for the internal decoration. He is required to make an annual payment of £2,000 to JO Morrow for himself and Mrs Morrow during their joint lives and to the survivor of them during the lifetime of the survivor. Provision is made for this sum to be reviewed at fixed intervals and in default of agreement the amount is to be fixed by the partners of Messrs McFarland MacCorkell and Graham solicitors. They are directed to have regard to the ratio which the proposed sum bears to the annual conacre lettings of the land in proportion to the sum which £2,000 bears towards the present letting value which is agreed by the parties at £3,300 per annum.

The agreement states that if the survivor of Mr Morrow and Mrs Morrow ceases to reside in the dwelling house the annual payment shall be suspended whilst that person resides elsewhere. I assume that provision is intended to avoid the impact of regulations made under the Health and Personal and Social Services (Northern Ireland) Order 1972 which make provision for the assessment by Health and Social Services Boards of the resources by way of capital and income of residents in accommodation arranged for them under the Order.

Since the death of her husband, Mrs Morrow has continued to live in the farm dwelling house which consists of a large kitchen, three bedrooms and two reception rooms. It fronts onto the farm yard and has an area of rough grass to the rear. Because she and her son are not on speaking terms she is not permitted to go into any of the fields and she is therefore confined to the house and garage. In the atmosphere that exists between them she is very much aware of a lack of privacy as the farm buildings and outhouses adjoin her home.

Her income consists of a pension of £57.60 per week and the received interest of £1,200 a year on a building society account and as long as she resides in the house she is entitled to receive an income of £2,000 a year under the agreement made between her husband and her son. She has a total of £32,951.68 on deposit in building societies, £200 of War Stock and £268.55 in a current account. She claims that the figure of £23,327.73 which is on deposit with the Halifax Building Society in her sole name was accumulated by her from sales of cattle in her name during her marriage. The sum of £6,084.15 in her name in the Leeds Permanent Building Society is the balance of £8,000 from a joint account with her late husband.

In this application under the Inheritance (Provision for Family and Dependants) (Northern Ireland) Order 1979 Mrs Morrow claims not only that reasonable financial provision has not been made for her but she seeks also an order pursuant to Article 12 of the 1979 Order setting aside the transfer of the farm by her husband to their son.

The first question to be answered is whether the dispositions of Mr Morrow's estate failed to make reasonable provision for Mrs Morrow. If the estate is to be taken as being confined to the property vesting in his personal representative under his will the answer must be in the negative because, after some specific legacies of goods and chattels, Mr Morrow left the residue of his estate to his wife absolutely. If his estate is to be taken as consisting of his property before the disposition of 30 November 1992 by which he transferred his farm to his son the question requires further consideration before it can be answered.

In *Re Moody* [1982] 2 All ER 524 Waite J in delivering the judgment of the Court of Appeal in an appeal from a decision under the Inheritance (Provision for Family and Dependants) Act 1975 noted, at page 534, that the 1975 Act (like the 1979 Order) does not, in laying down the lengthy catalogue of matters to which the judge is bound to have regard, specify the order in which he should tackle them. He suggested that the logical starting point would be appraisal of the notional entitlement assuming that there had been a decree of divorce and that with this yardstick the judge should then take into account any other matter in Article 5 to which he is required to have regard which has not been considered by him in the appraising process. This is the approach which I intend to follow.

Mr and Mrs Morrow were married for 52 years and she is now aged 75. During their married life, when they were working the farm, she played her part and she brought up the children. The main family asset was the farm and it has been agreed that on 30 November 1992 the value of the land and dwelling house was £165,000. This figure does not include the value of the cattle and other items transferred to their son at that time.

Mrs Morrow's capital is, in round figures £33,219. Her income, as long as she lives in the dwelling house provided for her on the farm, is approximately £5,916 per annum after tax. If she decides to move on to live elsewhere her income will be reduced by £2,000 a year under the terms of the agreement made between her husband and her son. Although she said in an affidavit that she wanted to continue to live in the dwelling house, by the time of the trial it was clear that because of the poor relationship which she has with her son she now wished to consider living elsewhere. If she chooses to move out she will need sufficient capital to provide her with a house and an income on which she can live.

Other matters under Article 5 to which I am required to have regard include the financial needs present and future of her son John Leslie Morrow. It is his intention to work the whole farm and it is his wish that in due course the farm will pass to his son. He has given notice to his conacre tenant, a Mr McDowell, of his intention to farm all the lands himself. If he is to continue to work the farm he will require a proper financial reward for his endeavours. The average conacre letting value of the farm is between £3,640 and £4,160 per year. The evidence suggests that there is no reason why he should not farm this land successfully himself and earn considerably more than the letting value of it by growing crops, which could include vegetables and second early potatoes, and by rearing cattle. It would be open to him to take more land in conacre. He owns the house in which he lives subject to a mortgage, the amount of which has not been disclosed.

I am obliged to have regard to the likely effect on any business undertaking included in the estate of an order resulting in the division of that property. In Northern Ireland, which is largely an agricultural economy, people have an attachment to the land and to family farms in particular. Many farms have been in the same family name for generations because the claim of a son to succeed his father in the ownership of a farm has always been very strong. As many farms are small this has avoided them being sub-divided into even smaller units which would be uneconomic. Whether in due course the change that has already occurred in the wider community will allow the daughters of farmers to be entitled to expect equal treatment to their brothers remains to be seen. In the present case Mrs Morrow has said that she does not disagree with her son getting the farm.

In the will he made on 31 May 1991 Mr Morrow gave his wife the two fields and 90% of the letting income from the remainder of the land. He had long experience of working this farm and at that time he does not seem to have considered that the loss of these two fields would have caused the farm to cease to be an economic unit although he did give his son an option to purchase them if Mrs Morrow decided to sell. I consider that a reduction in the size of this farm by around 10 to 12 acres would not have a serious effect on the remainder as a business undertaking.

Under Article 5(1)(g), the court may have regard to any other matter, including the conduct of the applicant or any other person which it considers relevant. The relationship between Mr and Mrs Morrow had reached a very low ebb before his death. This was towards the conclusion of a marriage that had lasted over 50 years and during all the years that her family was growing up Mrs Morrow appears to have been a good mother who looked after the home and cared for her family. She also played her part in the work of the farm. Whatever may have been the true cause of the breakdown in relations between Mr and Mrs Morrow in more recent years the period of such disagreement, however distressing it may have been to their children, represents but a small fraction of the terms of their long marriage. It occurred at a time when they were both of advanced years and the health of one of them was in a terminal state. In those circumstances I consider that it would be wrong to attach blame to either of them and I regard therefore as irrelevant to my consideration the conduct that was alleged against Mrs Morrow.

Having completed this exercise I conclude that viewed objectively the dispositions of the estate were unreasonable. The share of the capital with which she has been left is too small having regard to the length of the marriage and her contribution to the life of her family and to the farm. Secondly, the income which has been given to her from the farm is only of limited value to her because it ties her to living in the dwelling house on the farm and restricts her freedom to live where she wishes. I am unable to accept that a judge would have ignored such a restriction in making an order on the breakdown of marriage.

Normally having arrived at this second stage I would go on to determine what order should be made in the exercise of my discretion. In this case the dispositions are only inadequate if the application under Article 12(2) is successful. Accordingly I now turn to consider that application. The agreement of 30 November 1992 was made less than a year before the death of Mr Morrow on 26 November 1993. Was it made with the intention of defeating an application for financial provision under the 1979 Order? John Leslie Morrow said that his father decided to make the transfer after he had discovered that his wife had moved money out of an account in their joint names into an account in her sole name. According to him his father said that he was going to sign the farm over otherwise there would be nothing left. Mrs Morrow said that when she asked her husband why he had done this to her he replied because he was afraid that he was going to lose everything. In his will in clause 8 he said:

> In making provision for my wife in this my will I am taking into account the provision made for her in an Agreement dated the 30th day of November 1992 made with my son John Leslie Morrow when I transferred my farm to him whereby she shall be entitled to reside in the dwelling house on the farm free of rent and shall receive an annual sum. I am also taking into account that she has received substantial sums of money during my lifetime and withdrew from a joint account in the Alliance & Leicester Building Society sums totalling £8,200 during the year 1991-1992.

I am satisfied on a balance of probabilities and applying a subjective approach that while Mr Morrow may well have had the intention of making sure that everything would not be lost by transferring the farm to his son, this was not his sole intention because it was his intention also to make the transfer in such a way as would defeat an application for financial provision by his wife under the Order. Full valuable consideration was not given for the disposition and I am satisfied that the exercise of the powers under Article 12 would facilitate the making of financial provision for Mrs

Morrow under the Order. Having considered the circumstances in which the disposition was made, the relationship of Mr Morrow to his son and the conduct and financial resources of John Leslie Morrow, I conclude that this is a case in which I should be prepared to exercise my discretion under Article 12 of the Order.

The order which is to be made has to provide her with the capital and income which she requires for the remainder of her life in the absence of any evidence to suggest that she should be treated as having anything less than a normal life expectancy. Being a spouse's case I must have regard to what she would have expected to receive if her marriage had been terminated by a decree of divorce.

The current value of the entire farm including the dwelling house is £200,000 and the current value of the 10.5 acres in the two fields which adjoin the side of the Ringneill Road opposite to the rest of the farm, is £35,000. A figure of £35,000 would increase her capital to £68,000 in round figures which would represent 34% of the current value of the entire farm without taking account of any stock or implements transferred by Mr Morrow to his son. I consider this represents the capital sum to which she is entitled whether she lives in the house on the farm or not. The order will provide that if Mrs Morrow decides to sell all or part of these 10.5 acres her son John Leslie Morrow is to have an option to purchase at market value.

As to income, Mr John Charles McDowell gave evidence that he was taking this land at £70 per acre per year and he put the average of such land at £70 to £80 per acre. Taking an average of £75 per acre then 41.5 acres would produce £3,112.50 per year. If Mrs Morrow was given 75% of this sum (not conditional on her living in the dwelling) she would receive £2,334,37. By rounding it up to £2,500 per year and in return making no provision for any increases in conacre rents in the future, she would have a total net income after tax of £6,316 or £121.46 per week from the interest on her existing building society account, her pension and her income from the farm. She could then use capital generated from sale of the two fields to buy a home for herself. If on the other hand she chooses to continue to live in the dwelling house on the farm she will not have this additional capital sum of £35,000 available to generate more income. In a building society account, keeping her capital intact, she might expect to increase her total income – after tax in this way to about £7,758.75 or £150 per week. In my judgement it is for her to decide whether she wishes to use her additional capital to increase her income or to buy a house for herself. The annuity of £2,500 for her life, will be secured by charging it on the remaining 41.5 acres.

As the dwelling house is on the farm and it is in the interest of John Leslie Morrow as well as of his mother that is should be kept structurally sound I shall not remove from him the responsibility which he assumed under the agreement of 30 November 1992 for the structural repairs while his mother continue to be responsible for its internal decoration. This responsibility will continue so long as Mrs Morrow continues to use it as her main dwelling.

Order: Judgment accordingly.

O'Reilly and Another v Mallon and Others

Chancery Division – Northern Ireland, 10 March 1995

CAMPBELL J: In these proceedings which were issued on 25 May 1990 the late Mrs Eileen O'Reilly, the widow of Robert O'Reilly and their elder son Robert Eugene O'Reilly claim that the disposition of the estate of Robert O'Reilly effected by his will is not such as to make proper provision for them

Robert O'Reilly died on 20 November 1987 and his will, which is dated 22 May 1981, was proved on 9 January 1990 by John Mallon and Patrick Mallon. Patrick Mallon has since died and John Mallon as the sole surviving executor is the first defendant. The second and third defendants are the two remaining children of Robert and Eileen O'Reilly and they are the main beneficiaries under his will.

When the matter came before this Court on 12 June 1991 it appeared to the satisfaction of the Court that Mrs Eileen O'Reilly was in immediate need of financial assistance but it was not then possible to determine what order (if any) should be made on the application. An interim order was made under Article 7 of the Inheritance (Provision for Family and Dependants) Order 1979 ('the 1979 Order') by which it was ordered that John Mallon as executor pay Eileen O'Reilly (in addition to the annuity of £5,000 per annum, to which she was entitled under the will) such sums as appeared reasonable in respect of accounts for rates, telephone, home help, a night nurse and oil.

Eileen O'Reilly died on 1 January 1992 and her son Robert Eugene, the second plaintiff, is her sole executor. In this application the preliminary point raised is whether her claim under the 1979 Order survives her death.

By section 14(1) of the Law Reform (Miscellaneous Provisions) Act (Northern Ireland) 1937 it is provided that subject to the provisions of the section,

> ...on the death of any person after the commencement of this Act all causes of action subsisting against or vested in him shall survive or as the case may be for the benefit of, his estate...

In *Sugden v Sugden* [1957] 1 All ER 300 a husband had been ordered to pay maintenance of one shilling a year for his wife during their joint lives and to pay or cause to be paid to his wife the sum of £300 a year less tax for each child. The question arose whether the husband's estate after his death was liable to pay the maintenance of £300 a year for the children until they were 21. Denning LJ (as he then was) held that it was an obligation which was personal to him and ended with his death. At page 134 he said:

> The judge was much influenced by section 1 of the Law Reform (Miscellaneous Provisions) Act 1934 which he thought applied so as to make the sums for maintenance continue after the father's death. I do not agree with that view. The section only applies to causes of action which subsist against the deceased at the time of his death. The legislature had particularly in mind causes of action in tort which used to fail with the death to either party under the old

> common law maxis action personalis moritur cum persona. 'Causes of action' in the section, means, I think, rights which can be enforced – or liabilities which can be redressed – by legal proceedings in the Queen's courts. These now survive against the estate of the deceased person. Causes of action are not, however, confined to rights enforceable by action, strictly so called – that is, by action at law or in equity. They extend also to rights enforceable by proceedings in the Divorce Court, provided that they really are rights and not mere hopes or contingencies. They include, for instance, a sum payable for costs under an order of the Divorce Court, or a right to a secured provision under an order already made against a man before his death; see *Ryde v Ryde* and *Mosey v Mosey and Barker*.
>
> It must be noticed, however, that the section only applies to causes of action subsisting against the deceased on his death. This means that the right or liability must have accrued at the time of his death.
>
> In an action in the Queen's Bench there is usually no difficulty in determining when the right or liability accrued due; but there is more difficulty in proceedings in the Divorce Court. In that court there is no right to maintenance, or to a secured provision, or the like, until the court makes an order directing it. There is, therefore, no cause of action for such matters until an order is made.

In *Whyte v Ticehurst* [1986] 2 All ER 158 the question was raised whether a claim made by a widow against her deceased husband's estate upon which no order was made during her lifetime survived her death for the benefit of her estate. The claim had been made under Section 1 of the Inheritance (Provision for Family and Dependants) Act 1975 (the 1975 Act) of which the 1979 Order is the Northern Ireland counterpart. The husband had made a will bequeathing the matrimonial home, which had been conveyed in his sole name, to a charitable institution subject to his wife's right to remain there during her lifetime. In February 1984 he died and his widow made a claim on the ground that the will did not make reasonable provision for her. In December 1984 the widow died and her personal representatives sought leave to proceed with her claim on behalf of the estate under Section 1(1) of the Law Reform (Miscellaneous Provisions) Act 1934. Mr Registrar Guest held that there was no enforceable cause of action and dismissed the application. On the appeal Booth J said at page 69 that to her mind the purpose of the 1975 Act

> ...was to enable the court to place the surviving spouse in the financial position he or she would have been in had a matrimonial decree been granted during the lifetime of the other. The foundation of the jurisdiction is, as in matrimonial legislation, the relationship of the two parties to the marriage, and the only right that the statute gives is the right of the survivor to apply for relief against the estate of the deceased Spouse.

Booth J went on to hold that the principles in *Sugden v Sugden* [1957] 1 All ER 300 continued to apply and that it was still the case that no enforceable right existed until the order was actually made. The claim was personal to the survivor and upon the death of both parties to the marriage the claim ceased to exist and it was only when an order had been made upon a claim that an enforceable cause of action subsisted for the benefit of one estate against the other.

A similar question arose for consideration in *Re Bramwell (deceased), Camobel v Tobin and Another* [1988] 2 FLR 263 where a widow, Mrs O'Malley, had married a widower, Mr Bramwell, in 1975. The marriage was unsuccessful and on 25 January 1970 they parted company. In July 1986 Mr Bramwell died and his widow (Mrs O'Malley) survived him by six months until February 1987.

Prior to her death she had instructed her solicitor to make a claim under the 1975 Act. The defendants applied to have the application, made after her death, struck out on the ground that her inchoate right under the Act to apply to the court for financial provision was not a 'cause of action' which was presented for the benefit of her estate by Section 1(1) of the Law Reform (Miscellaneous Provisions) Act 1934. Sheldon J, agreeing with the reasoning of Booth J in *Whyte v Ticehurst* (supra) as to the purpose of the legislation, added that in his opinion this conclusion was supported by the express provisions to such an effect in the Act.

In Article 5 of the 1979 Order the matters are stated to which the court is to have regard in exercising the powers under Article 4. These include: 'the financial resources and financial needs which the applicant has or is likely to have in the foreseeable future': 'any physical or mental disability of any applicant for an order'; and, 'in the case of an application by the wife or husband of the deceased the provision which the applicant might reasonably have expected to receive if on the day on which the deceased died the marriage instead of being terminated by death had been terminated by a decree of divorce'. It is clear that these are all matters can only apply to a surviving spouse. I find myself in agreement with the view expressed by Booth J in *Whyte v Ticehurst* [1986] 2 All ER 158 and by Sheldon J in *Re Bramwell (deceased)* under the equivalent legislation in England and Wales.

When the interim order was made by this Court on 12 June 1991 it was stated that it was not at that time possible to determine what order (if any) should be made. The only cause of action which the estate of Mrs Eileen O'Reilly has is in respect of any payments, due under the terms of that order, which may have been outstanding at the time of her death on 1 January 1992. Her claim under Article 4 of the 1979 Order was personal to her and it did not survive her.

Order: Judgment accordingly.

Perry v Horlick

Court of Appeal (Civil Division), 18 November 1987

R Percival for the Appellant.
E Weaver for the Respondent.

SIR JOHN DONALDSON MR: This is an appeal against the refusal of His Honour Judge Batterbury on 17 March 1987 to grant permission under

Section 4 of the Inheritance (Provision for Family and Dependants) Act 1975 to bring proceedings to make a claim under the Act.

Section 4 , under which the application was made, is in these terms:

[His Lordship read out Section 4]

There was some discussion as to exactly what the approach should be to this time limit; whether this was a limitation period of six months which could be extended in the discretion of the court or whether this was something different. For my part I would regard this as a declaration by Parliament that a would-be applicant was entitled to bring his application within the six month period stated in the section as of right but that, after the expiration of that period, it required the leave of the court, and no more than that.

Unfortunately, the Act does not indicate on what principles the court should grant or refuse permission. It has been left to the court to fill in that gap. It is obviously a decision which has to be reached on judicial principles. However, for my part I have been very greatly assisted by the judgment of Sir Robert Megarry, V-C (as he then was) in *Re Salmon, deceased* [1981] 1 Ch 167, [1980] 3 All ER 532. I can take it sufficiently from the headnote, where it is said:

[His Lordship read out the headnote in [1981] Ch 167.]

I think a word has to be added about that part of the guidelines which refers to the distribution of the estate, because under Section 20 of the Act provision is made whereby if a personal representative distributes the estate after the end of the six month period, he is not personally to be under any liability solely on the ground that he ought to have taken into account the possibility that the court would permit the making of an application under Section 2 after the end of the six month period or that, where an order has been made, the court might exercise powers under Section 4, which relates to the variation or discharge of orders for periodical payments. However, the section goes on to make it clear that, although that protects the personal representatives, it does not protect the beneficiaries. If the beneficiaries have received benefits of any kind from the estate they are at risk of having to return them.

Against that background I can turn briefly to the facts. The applicant had been living with the deceased, Mrs Gertrude Ellen Horlick, for some twenty-four years before her death as a lodger. His case was that that relationship changed imperceptibly over the years until he became more in the nature of an adopted son. That of course is something which would have to be investigated in any proceedings. I merely record it as his allegation. He says that in the last four years of Mrs Horlick's life he lived in the property rent free, she having gone to hospital, where she remained until her death. He says, however, that during that period he maintained the house and had to meet the outgoings. His case is that being allowed to live rent free on those terms nevertheless made him a person who, immediately before the death of the deceased, was being maintained either wholly or partly by the deceased within the meaning of Section 1(a), (g) of the Act.

Mrs Horlick died on 12 March 1984. Mr Perry, the applicant, moved with reasonable promptitude to inquire what was to be his future. He consulted solicitors, and on 11 April 1984 they wrote to Mr Horlick, the son, saying:

> We have been consulted by Mr EF Perry...following the death of your mother on 12 March, 1984.
>
> Our client is concerned to know your intentions with regard to the house and we understand that you may have instructed solicitors to act in the Estate. If so, we would be obliged if you would forward this letter to them and ask them to reply direct to us.

That produced the very prompt reply, on 10 April, from solicitors acting for Mr Horlick, saying:

> We confirm that we are acting for Mr Victor William Frank Horlick of the estate of his late mother.
>
> Our client has yet to come to a decision in relation to 48 Cavendish Road, Rochester.

I should perhaps have added that that property virtually constitutes the whole of the estate.

In that situation, and bearing in mind that Mr Perry was in occupation and living in the house rent free, it is perhaps not surprising that, when an application for legal aid in support of a claim for an equitable interest in the property was turned down in or about that month, he decided to do nothing and wait and see what happened. If he had thought about the matter – which I venture to think he probably had not – he would have realised that the six month period certainly had not started to run then, because the solicitors' letter refers to Mr Horlick merely as 'the proposed administrator'.

In fact the matter remained like that until 18 January 1985, nine months or so later, when Mr Horlick's solicitors wrote to the solicitors acting for Mr Perry, saying:

> We act for Mr VWF Horlick who is the administrator of the Estate of the late Mrs GE Horlick.
>
> Mr Horlick has now decided to dispose of 48 Cavendish Road and wishes to place the same on the market for sale with vacant possession, and we should therefore be grateful if you would accept this letter as notice terminating, on the 28 February 1985, Mr Perry's Licence to occupy the property.

That did of course give the information that Mr Horlick must somehow have obtained a grant of administration, but whether it had been obtained on 17 January or some earlier date was not disclosed. We now know that the grant of administration had been obtained on 3 September 1984, over four months before. So in that state of ignorance Mr Perry's solicitors wrote back saying:

> Our client will not be vacating the property...and will be making an immediate application to the Court for a Declaration of Trust in relation to the property.

I should have said that the original application for legal aid made in April 1984 had been turned down on financial grounds. Matters having come to a head in this way, Mr Perry applied again for legal aid. But, as we all know, these things do take time. The next letter was a letter from the solicitors acting for Mr Horlick dated 11 February simply saying:

> ...we...are prepared to accept service of proceedings...

and dealing with an enquiry made by Mr Perry's solicitors as to whether there was a will. Again there was no mention of when the grant had been made.

In fairness to Mr Horlick's solicitors it should be said that it may be that it never occurred to them that any question would arise of an application under the 1975 Act, either on the grounds that they had never thought about it at all or because they thought that, whatever else might be said about Mr Perry's claims, they were not likely to succeed under that Act if they would not succeed on the broad basis of having an equitable interest in the property. But, however it may be, they gave him no clue that his time had at that stage expired. That information was only provided on 15 April 1985, when they sent a photocopy of the grant of letters of administration.

Up to that time there had been no mention of any application under the Act, but legal aid was in the process of being granted in the sense that it was granted to take counsel's opinion. It is a fair inference that counsel's opinion for the first time raised this question of a claim under the 1975 Act. The fact that there might be such a claim was passed on to Mr Horlick's solicitors on 31 May. Thereafter there was a delay owing to the fact that it was necessary to get the limitation of the legal aid, which principally was limited to obtaining counsel's opinion, removed. The proceedings themselves were not begun until 6 September 1985.

The learned judge referred himself to the Act and to the case of in *Re Salmon, deceased* [1981] 1 Ch 167, [1980] 3 All ER 532. He went through the history of the matter. He came to the conclusion that Mr Perry had a case which was fit for investigation, but he refused permission on the basis of his application of guidelines. I think that the best thing I can do is to refer to that part of the judgment which deals with that. The judge dealt, of course, with the extent to which legal aid had been the basis of the delay, and he also considered whether there was any possibility of Mr Perry having any redress against his solicitors, but he rejected, and rightly rejected, that as a possibility. He continued:

> ...The other guidelines referred in *Re Salmon* are not in point. First, negotiations were not in progress; and secondly, regarding distribution of the Estate, it is intact.
>
> In exercising a discretion judicially, it is always necessary to stand back and hold the balance between the parties. On the one hand the applicant says that he is only a few months out and what does it matter? – no prejudice has been suffered. That is true, in the sense that the Estate has not been administered, but for the personal representatives to be burdened with a second Action unnecessarily is a burden.' (The reference to the second action is of course to the fact that the application under the 1975 Act could run in parallel with an action for a declaration that he had an equitable interest in

> the property.) 'The house would need to be sold because there is no free money in the Estate and there is the question of prejudice. The Respondent says, I stand pat on the limit; circumstances have not been demonstrated which enable the applicant to escape the rigours of the limit which is there for a serious purpose.
>
> Against that is the fact of the second action which the Applicant brings, in which he asserts that he is beneficially entitled to an interest in the house. The impact of that is that if leave is refused, proceedings will not be at an end. The separate sets of proceedings have lives of their own and it might be convenient to hear one after the other, or together. However, Parliament has ordered time limits to the bringing of proceedings under the Inheritance Act for good reason, to which I must have regard.
>
> In my judgement, the substantial case required has not been shown, and the application must be dismissed.

I accept of course that this was a discretionary decision for the learned judge and that we ought not to intervene unless he has misdirected himself or he has reached a decision which is manifestly wrong. But I do sometimes find in these cases that such a compartmentalised approach is difficult. The decision itself may seem to be on the borders of being wrong, and, looking at the reason, one may feel that the judge has not fully and completely directed himself aright, yet I personally sometimes have difficulty in labelling the matter as neatly as the academics would prefer. This is to some extent such a case.

But it does seem to me that the learned judge has attached very little importance to two facts which are related; first that the estate has not been administered; and secondly that the applicant is living in the estate. It is not a case of somebody who is outside laying a claim to the estate and somebody who has done nothing about it. He was there as an obstacle to the winding up of the estate throughout. There has been no possibility of the estate being administered as long as he was there. It is very much less unreasonable for him to have waited to see what the intentions of the administrator were, sitting there as he was, than it would have been an outsider standing by and not indicating a claim.

Secondly, I cannot accept that the learned judge is really right when he appears to regard the fact that there are potentially two actions as having very little weight. If the two actions were wholly unconnected I would agree with him. But they are really two ways of putting the same claim, and he does not seem to me to have contemplated the very unfortunate situation which could arise, even if may be unlikely, in which a judge, trying what I may describe as the trust action – the claim for an equitable interest – came to the conclusion that the applicant failed on that but came to the conclusion, which would of course be better in the circumstances, that he would have had a very good claim under the 1975 Act. That seems to be to be a highly unfortunate situation.

Of course the learned judge's approach would have weight if we were going to add greatly to the costs in any way by this second action, or if it was going to delay the administration of the estate. But as far as I can see it will do neither. Until the question of his equitable interest can be sorted out one way or the other it is difficult to see how this estate can be administered. Equally, many of the facts which have to be investigated in the context of that claim will go to any claim under the 1975 Act, and it is difficult to see what further facts will have to be investigated.

For all those reasons it seems to me that the learned judge erred and did misapply the approach which should be applied under the Act in deciding whether or not to give permission for an application to be made after the expiration of the six month period. For those reasons I would allow the appeal and grant the application.

MUSTILL LJ: I agree with the order proposed by my Lord. I confess that, had it not been for the second of the matters to which my Lord the Master of the Rolls has referred, I would have hesitated before holding that there could be detected any such error in approach by the learned judge as would justify the intervention of this court. That factor, does, however, seem to me to make all the difference.

In the broadest terms the dispute between the parties is whether the applicant has any right to the house which is the subject-matter of the dispute or to a share in the estate of which the house is the only asset. This dispute is in any event going to be before the court. Whatever the outcome of the present application, the respondent is going to be in the unfortunate position of resisting proceedings by a legally aided opponent. I cannot for my part see that his position is going to be made appreciably worse if the instant proceedings are allowed to go ahead. One must therefore ask whether it is in the interests of justice that only half of the dispute should be before the court, so that, even if facts emerge in the proceedings which are undeniably going to take place which show that the applicant would have had a good claim under the act if he had been allowed to prosecute it, he should be disbarred from having the benefit of the right which the facts disclose.

I do not think that it would be in the interests of justice to arrive at such a position. I would agree with my Lord that this is a consideration to which the learned judge below did not attach sufficient, and perhaps, any, importance. Accordingly I do think it legitimate to review the matter afresh, and, having done so, arrive at the same conclusion as the one just expressed by my Lord.

NICHOLLS LJ: I agree that, for the reasons given by my Lords, this appeal should be allowed.

Order: Appeal allowed; application granted, costs below to be costs in cause subject to a caveat that, insofar as the cause results in somebody who was at the time broadly aided being under any liability, that should not be enforced without further order of the court; appellant to have his costs out of the appeal.

Kvetoslava Polackova v Jan Sobolewski (Executor of Antoni Pichlak deceased) & Others

Court of Appeal (Civil Division), 28 October 1985

R Ferm for the Appellants.

JM Collins for the Respondent.

ANTHONY LINCOLN J: This is an appeal from the order of His Honour Judge Fitzhugh, Deputy Vice-Chancellor, made on 21 February 1985, by which he granted leave to the plaintiff, the former wife of the deceased in this matter under s 4 of the Inheritance (Provision for Family and Dependants) Act 1975, enabling her to bring proceedings against the estate of the deceased notwithstanding that she was out of time, six months having expired since the representation had been taken up with regard to this estate; by that order the learned deputy vice-chancellor reversed an earlier order made by Mr Registrar Bowyer, refusing leave.

The facts of the case all turn about an estate which is worth roughly £100,000. The parties were married on 4 August 1951. There were three children of the family; two of them were children of the marriage and the third was taken into the family by the deceased, and is the child of the applicant, the former wife. This lady, who is the step-daughter of the plaintiff, and is the fourth defendant in these proceedings, plays no part in them whatsoever, not having any interest in either their success or their failure.

In July of 1963, the marriage having become a difficult one there was a separation between the parties. In January of 1965 the deceased made a will, in which he left nothing whatsoever to the former wife, the respondent to this appeal. On 27 May 1965 proceedings were launched by the deceased in the divorce court, alleging among other things cruelty. In the acknowledgement of service put in on behalf of the respondent to this appeal, who was also the respondent in the divorce petition, it was indicated that no alimony, as it was then called, and no maintenance would be sought. In the ensuing pleadings the respondent to this appeal (whom I shall now call 'the former wife') cross-prayed for dissolution, but in her prayer there was included no element either of alimony or maintenance and in a subsequent amendment of those pleadings there was equally no prayer for such relief.

In the event the proceedings were conducted on the basis of the deceased's petition, on his allegation of cruelty; a decree nisi was granted to him and subsequently, on 1 July 1968 that decree was made absolute. There having been no claim for ancillary relief by the former wife it was then open to her, if she had so chosen, to apply for leave to make such an application if she thought it right to do so.

A consequence of the decree absolute was that an order had to be made with regard to the children, who are all now adults but were then under 16. Custody was granted to the deceased and it is alleged – and we will proceed upon these allegations for the purpose of this hearing – that the former wife was in no position to look after the children at that stage; she had suffered from depression and she was a full working wife.

The deceased died on 10 December 1982; he was 69 and she was 57. She and he had therefore been separated, on the face of it, for some 19 years. However, in the affidavit which she swore in support of the originating summons applying for a share in the estate, she deposed to the fact that there had been a resumption of association between the deceased and herself very shortly before his death. This is disputed by the defendants, and evidence was put in to the effect that there were surrounding circumstances and conversations showing the improbability of this allegation. But again, in the hearing of an application for leave to apply out of time, it is impossible for the court to resolve such interlocutory disputes and therefore the court must proceed on the basis of the allegations of the former wife unless there are obvious reasons for believing them to be wholly without foundation.

On 6 January 1983, it having come to the notice of the former wife that her former husband had died, she sought advice from solicitors, Messrs Lee and Priestley, as to her position. In turn those solicitors wrote to the solicitors for the defendant, being the solicitors concerned with the distribution of the estate, asking what the position was. They received no reply.

Nothing much was done until 9 August, when the former wife consulted a different firm, Messrs Henry Hyams & Co. They wrote on that day to the solicitors for the personal representatives, saying that they understood that those solicitors were acting in respect of the estate, and they said this:

> Our client instructs us that as part of the estate of the above named, there is a considerable area of property, to which she contributed one half of the purchase monies in the early 1960s. Our client also claims that she is entitled to a share in the estate, as a potential dependent of the deceased.
>
> We would be most grateful if you could contact us, firstly to confirm that you are acting in relation to the estate, and secondly to confirm whether the situation with regard to the land, full details of which we can in due course supply to you-

that sentence was not in fact grammatically completed, but at all events it made clear that they wanted to know the position.

On 22 August Messrs Henry Hyams & Co wrote to the former wife, asking to make an appointment so that they could talk to her and discuss the legal position with regard to her potential application against the estate. They also wrote to the solicitors for the personal representatives, pointing out that they were still awaiting a reply to their letter in which they had asked for information about representation.

Those solicitors wrote to the former wife's solicitors on 12 August, confirming that they did act in the administration of the estate, but saying that the collection of the assets had not then been completed and that it was not proposed to make a distribution at that stage. 12 August can therefore be considered to be a date on which it would be reasonable to suppose that action would be taken by the advisers of the former wife to institute proceedings in this matter.

On 13 September the Solicitors, Messrs Henry Hyams, pointed out that they had never received the original letter which had been sent much earlier, an indication that sometimes the post is in default. The solicitors for the former wife wrote on 13 September 1983, saying:

> Please make a further appointment to see the writer bearing in mind that we have only six months after the Grant of Probate of the will to make our application under the Inheritance Act,

and they say that they require documentary evidence and so on.

Nothing was done thereafter until 13 March 1984, some seven months afterwards.

The former wife asserts today that she never received that letter written on 13 September. It is a little surprising that she did not make the slightest enquiry of her solicitors to find out what was going on, for irrespective of the requirements of the statute as to limitations on bringing action, she must have been more than interested in moving her application forward if she had one, or at least of discussing it with her solicitors. However, she relies on the default of the postal authorities and says that she never received that letter.

The date at which probate was taken out was 8 June 1983; the six month period permitted by statute expired on 8 December 1983.

Accordingly, when the solicitors wrote on 13 March, indicating that they intended to apply under the Inheritance (Provision for Family and Dependants) Act 1975 for financial provision, they were some three months out of time. The learned judge held that that was not a very great delay, and as I understand it, it is conceded that the delay is in all the circumstances not very significant.

The correspondence moved on and proceedings were in fact put in hand, to be supported by an affidavit sworn on 30 July 1984 by the former wife. This affidavit set out first of all something of the history which I have already recited, with references to the children, it also gave an incorrect account of the dates on which she sought legal advice. As I understand it, that mistake was put right at the hearing, either before the learned registrar or before the learned vice-chancellor; nothing turns upon that mistake. The rest of paragraph 6 relates to this delay; I need not dwell on that here. Some little time was taken up in applying for a legal aid certificate, first to enable her to obtain advice; subsequently that certificate was widened in order to enable her to pursue the proceedings themselves.

As to the history of the marriage, the affidavit can be summarised quite briefly in this way; first, that by modern standards it was a long marriage, having lasted from 1951 to 1963, some 12 years, and longer than that if one takes into account the period until the decree absolute. During the course of the marriage, so the allegation runs, both the deceased and the former wife purchased various properties. They purchased 175 Burley Road Leeds in 1973. It was purchased in the name of the deceased out of his savings and on a mortgage. That property was used, not merely to house the couple but also to house lodgers, who paid the former wife £3.50 per week for full board. In 1956 the couple purchased a second property, an 8 bedroomed property, at Clarendon Place, Leeds. In that case it is alleged – and I emphasise that these are allegations and no more – that the deceased had saved £450 and the former wife the same figure, in her case from payments made to her by the lodgers. That enabled them to purchase this property. So they were now in a position to retain Burley Road and let it as lodgings for students, and the former wife provided accommodation for students at Clarendon Place.

It was in about 1956 that the former wife says that she suffered from a severe depression and had to go into hospital for a quite considerable period. When she emerged in 1957, she rented a garage near the Clarendon

Place property and used it buy, store and sell secondhand furniture, making a modest profit from these transactions. So that now she was receiving cash, both from the furniture trade and also from the lodgers, and she used some of that cash to support the family.

She says that from 1958 on, the deceased became unemployed and remained so for the rest of his life, except for a short interval in 1960, until 1963. Throughout that period of five years she was the one who supported the family from the earnings that she was making.

In 1959 they both purchased Brandon Grove, and subsequently it was agreed between her and the deceased that she could buy out that interest for a small sum of money. Then she took lodgers and installed them in Brandon Grove, making money from that trade. In 1962 the couple purchased the freehold land and buildings known as School Farm, Selby, which she purchased at an auction at a price of £3,150; the deceased had produced £650 and she contributed £2,500 cash which, as she says, represented savings from her earnings. The property was transferred into the name of the deceased.

It is right to break off at this point to say that the former wife is claiming that there is some form of trust in that property held by the personal representatives on behalf of the deceased, and she is claiming a declaration that such a trust exists in separate actions which are due to come on in due course in the Chancery Division.

To resume the history, she alleges that she gave the deceased £500 for equipment on the farm and that the couple were now, in 1963, involved in quarrels, the marriage beginning to founder, and they increasingly lived apart: she lived with the children at 10 Brandon Grove, but she continued her work. She worked as a cook and as a cashier/supervisor at a bingo hall, so she was a working wife.

That brings the history, briefly, to 1963, when the deceased began the divorce proceedings. The former wife became seriously ill; she received treatment in hospital over many months in the course of the proceedings and, as I have already said, in the result the deceased was granted the custody of the two children of the marriage, Lavina and Carol, the former wife obtaining no financial provision.

All that remains is to recite the fact that the deceased sold Clarendon Place in 1975 and part of the land at School Farm. As to the circumstances of the former wife herself, she is now unemployed; she receives supplementary benefit which, at the time of the affidavit, amounted to £26.50. Brandon Grove is the subject of an order for compulsory purchase and she expects to receive some £2,000 in respect of her interest in that property. Meanwhile she alleges that she has been compelled to borrow money from friends and relatives, and has a debt in excess of £1,000. In the closing paragraph of her affidavit she claims that she is in need of financial provision and that the disposition of the deceased's estate is not such as to make reasonable financial provision for her. So it is clear that she is claiming provision in the form and nature of maintenance, and not a lump sum.

The affidavit in response puts many of these facts in issue. It is disputed that she was about to resume the relationship with her husband before his death, and much else is put in issue, raising issues of fact for the court which will have to try this matter.

There are two arguments put before this court by the applicant. The first is grounded upon the delay itself, though it was conceded very frankly by Mr Ferm on behalf of the appellant that that was the weaker of the two arguments he proposed to put before the court.

So far as the delay is concerned, he says, in a word, that there was a total failure on the part of the former wife to get in touch with her legal advisers during the period I have indicated; that no sufficient reason has been produced to justify that failure, and that the prejudice that it has occasioned amounts to the personal representatives being unable to distribute the estate. These do not appear to the court to be reasons for holding that such a delay is prejudicial in any normal sense of the word, and apart from the second argument, this seems not to be a valid ground for refusing relief in the circumstances here.

The fact of the delay is argued upon us as one that can be taken into account in conjunction with the alternative argument, namely that the former wife has no arguable case that can be put before the trial judge and that accordingly she should be refused relief now. The permission required under section 4 of the 1975 Act is granted in cases in which it can be shown by the applicant for such permission that he or she has an arguable case, and the onus lies upon the applicant. But what is said here is that, in all the circumstances as they are disclosed, there is no possibility at all of a serious argument being launched. In particular it is said that the former wife failed to make any application in her cross-prayer for relief, or in the amended cross-prayer or in the acknowledgement of service – and of course these are factually correct submissions – and that when the decree was granted there was an opportunity under the Matrimonial Causes Rules1977, rule 68(2) to apply to the court for leave to claim ancillary relief notwithstanding the absence of any such item in the cross-prayer; that if such an application had been made during the lifetime of the deceased, it would have simply had no chance whatsoever of succeeding. It is said that the length of the separation, 19 years; the fact that the children were brought up by the deceased and not by the former wife; the delay itself and the failure to make these claims, all show that there was no possibility of the former wife establishing that there has been a failure to make reasonable provision in the deceased's will for her.

In my view r 68(2) has nothing whatever to do with this application. The circumstances which this court has to take into account, as required by s 3(5) of the Inheritance (Provision for Family and Dependants) Act 1975 are the circumstances which prevail at the time of the hearing. Those circumstances may be the same as, or they may be different from, those which would have prevailed had the former wife made an application during the lifetime of the deceased.

At this stage of the hearing if the former wife is granted leave she will have the right to adduce evidence of all the circumstances as they obtain today. Moreover, the assets which are to be found in the estate were probably – and it would appear from the facts that this is right – not available for any application which the wife could have made during the lifetime of the deceased. He was unemployed for a good deal of the time and she was employed, whereas there are quite different and separate factors to be taken into account today. What are her present resources? If the facts alleged in the supporting affidavit are proved to be correct, then her resources today are a very great deal worse than they were during the lifetime of the deceased. But in any event the affidavit relies upon factors which undeniably the court has to take into account. The contribution of the wife during the marriage now lies historically very far in the past, but the court has to take such a factor into account. Equally, the length of the marriage; equally the resources of the wife today and the amount of the assets in the estate. None of these matters could have been taken into account at any earlier time.

I therefore find it difficult to see that this court is in any way assisted by a consideration of the fact, if it be fact, that the former wife failed to make an application and failed with good grounds to make an application. One gets no assistance from those circumstances.

One is driven back, therefore, to the considerations which apply in the case of an order under Rules of the Supreme Court, Order 14: Has this applicant, the former wife, an arguable case? In my judgement it is quite clear that she has an arguable case if she establishes the facts set out in her affidavit. She may fail to do so, but if they are found by the learned judge to be correct, then there are factors there which he will have to balance against the contrary factors, and the latter may be thought very weighty, in order to reach the conclusion required by the Act, namely the objective assessment as to whether reasonable provision has been made by the will of the deceased in this case.

For these reasons I would hold that the best course for the future would be for this matter to be tried, as a triable issue, alongside the issue which has already been raised in the Chancery proceedings with regard to the declaration of a trust and that the matter be heard and determined accordingly.

For those reasons I would dismiss this appeal.

RALPH GIBSON LJ: I agree.

For the reasons which my Lord has given it is plain to me that this appeal must be dismissed.

OLIVER LJ: I also agree.

Order: Appeal dismissed, with costs against appellants as executors; legal aid taxation of respondent's costs.

Re Portt, Allcorn v Harvey

Court of Appeal (on appeal from Judge Clover, Oxford County Court), Roskill, Brandon and Ackner, LJJ, 25 March 1980
DGA Jackson for the Appellant (Plaintiff).
DC Gerrey for the Respondents (Defendants).

LORD JUSTICE ROSKILL: I shall ask Lord Justice Ackner to deliver the first judgment.

LORD JUSTICE ACKNER: This is an appeal by Mrs Allcorn against the dismissal on 25 April 1979 by His Honour Judge Clover of her application under the Inheritance (Provision for Family and Dependants) Act 1975. It arises in these circumstances. The applicant is the daughter of the deceased, who died at the age of just over 90. She herself is now approaching 71. The respondents in this appeal are, firstly, the executor, her brother, who was left by the mother the modest sum of £100, but the main respondent, the second respondent, is Mrs Carolyn Ann Woodcock, who is the only daughter of the brother, the first respondent, the only grandchild of the deceased and the niece of the appellant.

The will was made in 1969 and the deceased died on 24 March 1977. Probate was granted on 8 July 1977, and we regret to say that the value of the estate is only some £12,000; a value which makes appeals to the Court of Appeal undesirable, as this court has only recently said in the case which was strongly relied upon by the appellant, namely the case of *In re Coventry* [1979] 3 WLR 803. The application, as I have said, was made under the Inheritance (Provision for Family and Dependants) Act 1975, and the only section to which I need draw attention are, first of all, section 1, which gives a child of the deceased – hence the appellant in this case – the right to apply to the court for an order on the ground that the disposition of the deceased's estate effected by her will is not such as to make reasonable financial provision for the applicant.

[His Lordship then referred to s 1(2)(b), s 3(1)(a), (b), (c).]

In a very careful and well reasoned judgment His Honour Judge Clover set out the relevant facts concerning the applicant and the second respondent. As to the applicant he said this:

'The Applicant is 70 years old. She lives in an old and attractive cottage in Wallingford, but it is in need of quite substantial repair and renovation. It is valued at £11,000 and is not subject to any charge. In addition to owning her own house she has available in cash or immediately realisable securities some £10,698. She has an unearned income from pensions and investments of £2,200, so with her house worth £11,000 and with £11,000 in cash she does not, on the face of things, appear to be in any great need. She is not in a position of luxury and could do very well with having a little more than she has got.' We have been shown figures relating to her outgoings and it is quite clear that these are less than her income, although the margin is not great and, in dealing with those figures, I have not taken into account possible expenditure of some size on the maintenance of the house. The learned judge goes on:

'The position is complicated by litigation with the Local Authority in respect of subsidence. She is claiming £6,000 and the costs of redecoration. There are some indications that she could justify the sum of £6,000; the Surveyor says she should spend at least £1,700 to do' – the judge wrongly refers to underpinning. It should be – 'roof repairs, but the only cloud that hangs over her is this High Court action.' Reference to that litigation is of some importance because he goes on to say this: 'It is said she is a highly litigious woman, and I have heard evidence that she has made a succession of claims without any prospect of success. She thinks her husband died due to the overflowing of a sewer; she made a claim against one of the local doctors.' Mr Jackson has in fact told us that the claim was made against a group of doctors. 'She is a highly litigious person, on her own evidence. She gave evidence in a vehement and combative style. Her disposition to make claims is relevant; it had something to do with the fact that when her mother had made her will she didn't change it. The litigious nature of the applicant was a major reason for that. I have heard evidence that the mother cut her daughter out of her will because of a blazing row. They had many such rows. After one, the mother made her will in 1969 and that will was later proved. Not long after, the mother told her son that she wasn't going to alter it because her daughter would waste it on litigation. I prefer the evidence of Mr Harvey to that of Mrs Allcorn. The deceased found the talk of litigation very upsetting; it reduced the mother to a state of collapse. She asked Mr Harvey to keep her daughter away. The mother cut her daughter out of the will because of the row and refused to alter it because of her daughter's litigious activities and the effect that these activities had on the old lady.'

In the part which I have just quoted from the judgment the learned judge is in fact pointing out the testator's reason for rejecting the applicant and, to my mind, he is accepting that reason as being a perfectly intelligible one, and I take the view that that is very material.

The learned judge in regard to the granddaughter – no point is taken on the £100 left to the brother – says this: 'The granddaughter's situation is that she has no capital apart from the joint ownership of a house the equity in which is about £11,000; she has no free capital; she is earning £3,000 a year and is not likely to earn much more than that. Her husband is earning £9,300 a year with prospects of advancement. They are not in financial need with a joint income of over £12,000. They have no children, but apart from their home they have no capital at all. If they had a family, the granddaughter would have to stop work and there would be a drop in income. Although they are in no sense in need, they can't be described as being in a state of affluence. They don't need the money from the estate but then nor does the Applicant. In my judgement, having regard to the conduct of the Applicant towards her mother there was no failure by the mother to make reasonable financial provision for the Applicant. I don't think it was unreasonable for her to have made no provision.'

The learned judge concluded the substance of his judgment by saying this: 'Even if conduct had not been a live issue, when I consider the Applicant's financial position and the fact that the only cloud over her position is another law suit, I am not prepared to hold that there has been a failure to make reasonable financial provision because having regard to the comparative financial positions I can see nothing unreasonable in what the mother did. There was no failure to make reasonable provision. I see nothing really strange or aberrant in her taking that view. Looking at the daughter's capital position, she is all right, she does not need anything. The granddaughter is all right but she may have expectations in the future, one doesn't know when. She leaves the money where it is more likely to be needed. For these reasons I find the application must fail.'

The main basis of Mr Jackson's submissions, which were put clearly and forcibly and in considerable detail before us, is essentially that there was wide disparity – in the notice of appeal it is referred to as extreme disparity – between the financial position of the granddaughter as compared with that of the daughter; and he says for that reason we should essentially interfere.

I accept that there was a disparity. There was a disparity which was recognised by the learned judge. It was clearly a fact to be taken into account. There were also other factors to which the judge alluded. In my judgement the learned judge gave adequate consideration to the factors which he had to have in mind. He correctly weighed, as he was required to do by section 3, those three specific matters in sub-paragraphs (a), (c) and (d) and, in a judgment which was detailed, clear and concise, reached a right conclusion.

I would accordingly dismiss this appeal.

LORD JUSTICE BRANDON: I agree. In the case of *In re Coventry dec'd*, to which my Lord referred in his judgment, Lord Justice Buckley said at page 817:

> The decision which falls to be made by a court in a case of this kind is essentially a qualitative decision; that is to say, the decision whether the disposition which the deceased has made, if any, is such as to make reasonable financial provision for the applicant. It is a qualitative decision, or what is sometimes called a 'value judgment'. A decision of that kind is one which is particularly difficult to disturb on appeal, unless the judge of first instance has clearly proceeded on some error of principle. There is no indication that I can find in Oliver J's judgment that he failed to take account of any relevant circumstance that he ought to have taken account of, or that he paid attention to anything to which he ought not to have paid attention, or that he erred in principle in any way.

I would say precisely the same with regard to the judgment of His Honour Judge Clover in the present case. I cannot see that he failed to take into account any relevant circumstance that he ought to have taken into account, or that he paid attention to anything which he ought not to have paid attention, or that he erred in principle in any way.

That does not exhaust the grounds upon which this court might interfere with a decision because, if his decision nevertheless seemed plainly wrong, the authorities show that this court could and should substitute their own judgment. But, so far from the learned judge's judgment seeming to me to be plainly wrong, it seems to me to be a very sensible and wise judgment on the case as a whole.

I, too, would dismiss the appeal.

LORD JUSTICE ROSKILL: I agree with both judgments. In my view the judgment of the learned county court judge, which was a most full and careful one is quite unassailable.

All I would add to the judgments which have been delivered is a reference to the last sentence of the headnote in *In re Coventry, dec'd* [1979] 3 WLR 803:

> Litigation, and in particular appeals, in respect of such small estates as the present should be discouraged because the consequence was to dissipate the whole estate in costs and leave nothing for the claimants.

It is no fault of the respondents, who have had this unfortunate piece of litigation forced upon them by the wholly unreasonable conduct of the appellant; but one has again to say that this is another case where the family have become embroiled in disastrous litigation, out of which no-one are the beneficiaries except perhaps the lawyers.

I agree the appeal should be dismissed.

Order: Appeal dismissed with costs.

Rann v Jackson

Court of Appeal (on appeal from Judge Toyn sitting as a deputy judge of the Family Division), Roskill and Geoffrey Lane LJJ and Sir David Cairns, 6 November 1978
DA McConville for the Appellants (Plaintiff).
AB Taylor for the Respondent (Defendants).

LORD JUSTICE ROSKILL: We need not trouble you, Mr Taylor. I will ask Sir David Cairns to deliver the first judgment.

SIR DAVID CAIRNS: This is an appeal from a decision of His Honour Judge Toyn, sitting as a judge of the Family Division at Birmingham. He had before him a claim under the Inheritance (Provision for Family and Dependants) Act 1975, an Act which repeals the Inheritance (Family Provisions) Act 1938, and enables a provision to be made for persons who would not have any claim under the 1938 Act. Under the 1938 Act claims could be made by an unmarried child of a deceased or by a child suffering from some disability, but not by a married child who had no disability. The plaintiff in this case, Mrs Alice Berle Rann, was the daughter of the testator, James Ambrose Homer, a married woman with no disability. She claimed that the provision made for her in her father's will was inadequate and that she was entitled to some further provision at the hands of the court under the Act of 1975. The defendants to her action were the executors of the will, one of whom is Mrs Joyce Olwyn Homer, who was the residuary legatee under the will. The learned judge held that the plaintiff was not entitled to any further provision than was made for her by the will and accordingly dismissed her action, and she appeals to this court.

[His Lordship then referred to s 1(1)(c), (2)(b), s 2(1), s 3(1)(a), (b), (c), (d), (e), (g).]

The estate was of the approximate value of £23,000, about half of that value being represented by the house in which the testator lived, and he left £2,000 to Mrs Rann, the plaintiff, one or two other small legacies, and the residue to Miss Homer, his unmarried daughter.

The issues in this case are whether the learned judge made the right approach; and whether, if he was wrong in his approach, the right approach would have led to a more substantial provision for the plaintiff, and accordingly whether the court ought to order such provision to be made.

The plaintiff is a lady of 54. The defendant, Miss Homer, is a few years younger. The plaintiff, as I have said, is married, and Miss Homer unmarried. The learned judge found, in his judgment, that the plaintiff's husband has his own business. They have three children, who are grown up. The business, the learned judge said, was not a particularly prosperous one, it had been carried on by Mr Rann for some 7 or 8 years; he took a spirited view of the matter in that whatever the economic climate might be at the moment he had hopes for the future; he was self-supporting and thinks that he is going to pull through; he has not made a fortune but does not regard himself as being on the doorstep of destitution.

On the other side of the picture is the defendant Miss Homer. She has gone to work throughout her adult life, earning now a reasonable income, in the neighbourhood of £3,000, and she has been able to acquire some capital, amounting to £17,000. She had had an opportunity of marriage earlier in life, but had not married, and learned judge put it in this way. I am reading from the foot of page 6 of the transcript of his judgment:

> The fact remains that she gave up the prospect of marriage, and she has remained single, without a husband, without children, without all those things that people normally look forward to when they marry. On the other hand Mrs Rann says well what sort of sacrifice has she made. Life hasn't treated me all that well; it is part of the chances of life. Children grow up and go their ways, and it may have been in the testator's mind that a daughter who had the prospect of marriage with a man that obviously the testator approved of because he is a beneficiary to the will – and there is no doubt, it is common ground he did do things to help – it may be that the testator thought some specific recognition and compensation was due for a daughter who had given up the way she might have made for her life, with a family of her own in fact, to stay at home.

Having considered, as it appears to me, all the relevant circumstances of the case as they are set out in section 3 of the Act, the learned judge, at page 8D, said:

> Under section 1(2)(b) reasonable financial provision means such financial provision as it would be reasonable in all the circumstances of the case for the applicant to receive, being in this case her maintenance. Now how should one look at that in relation to a lady of 54 years of age, married still, with a husband running his own business, and a grown-up family. Those are the sort of matters that I have, I think, to take into account under section 3(1)(a), and I am invited to compare them, for example, with the situation of the second defendant under section 3(1)(c). Likewise I have to consider para (d) of section 3(1), particularly in relation to those matters, and also para (f). There are other matters as well but those are the principle matters.

> Is it reasonable to say on the one hand that a lady of 54, married and with a grown up family, would be looking for financial provision from her father or her father's estate against her background? Look at it the other way round: Is it reasonable that the testator, given those circumstances should be saying to himself, 'I have an obligation to make financial provision for a daughter who is married and who has a husband who is working and running his own business'?

That last sentence I have read is challenged by Mr McConville, on behalf of the plaintiff, the appellant in this court. He contends that the learned judge wrongly applied a subjective test instead of an objective test. That seems to me to be a misunderstanding of the learned judge's approach. He had to decide what was reasonable. It is true that he put it in the way, 'What would a reasonable testator have done?', but it seems to me that that is merely a matter of language. He was taking account, obviously, of all the various factors that the Act requires him to take into account insofar as there was evidence relating to any of those matters.

This being a new Act, there is no English authority upon it, and Mr McConville has not been able to assist the court by any reference to any decisions which might have been made under the Act of 1938. The only authority which he has brought to our notice is a judgment of the Privy Council in a case on appeal from New Zealand, where they have an Act corresponding to our Act of 1938, but they were thirty years ahead of us. Their Act was passed in 1908. The case is *Allardice v Allardice* [1911] AC 730. What happened there was that a claim was made by certain married daughters of the testator, and as it was put in the headnote:

> The court below having exercised its discretion in favour of three married daughters of the testator by a wife who had divorced him, his will disposing of all his estate in favour of his second wife and her children, their Lordships declined to interfere; and approved the general view taken by the court below as to the proper scope and application of the powers conferred by the Act.

That Act provided that the court might make such provision for the plaintiffs or some of them as to the court should seem fit out of the testator's estate, those general words. The learned judge of first instance in New Zealand, Mr Justice Chapman, had looked at the matter in this way. He said:

> This claim relates to children, but in what sense does the statute refer to children? I can only conceive that it refers to children for whose proper support there is at the time of the testator's death no adequate provision. ...Here however none of the daughters approach a condition that can properly be called want.

The New Zealand Court of Appeal said that that was the wrong approach, and that the whole of the circumstances of the child or children who made a claim should be considered. The decision of the New Zealand Court of Appeal was affirmed by the Privy Council. They said that Mr Justice Chapman had been wrong to approach it on the basis that a condition of want had to be established by the plaintiff, but that all the circumstances had to be taken into account.

It does not appear to me that the case assists the plaintiff here. The learned judge did not approach it on the basis that want or destitution had to be proved. He did approach it, as I have indicated, by a full consideration of the whole of the circumstances.

For my part I am satisfied that there was nothing which he took into account that he ought to have disregarded, and nothing that he failed to take into account which was relevant.

In those circumstances it seems to me that it would be quite impossible for this court to interfere with his decision and I would dismiss the appeal.

LORD JUSTICE LANE: I agree.

LORD JUSTICE ROSKILL: I entirely agree with the admirable judgment of the learned deputy Judge in the court below.

Appeal dismissed, with costs.

Riggs v Lloyds Bank Plc and Another

Court of Appeal (Civil Division), 27 November 1992
G Hamilton for the Respondent.
J Gordon for the Appellant.

DILLON LJ: This appeal involves a dispute between a brother and his sister. The appeal is an appeal by the second defendant in the proceedings, Mr Ronald Edward Darch, against an order made by His Honour Judge Weeks, QC, on 22 July 1991 when sitting as a deputy judge of the High Court of Bristol. The successful party, respondent to the appeal, is the plaintiff, Mrs Heather Ann Riggs, the sister of the second defendant. The first defendant, Lloyds Bank Plc, is joined as the personal representative of the deceased father of the plaintiff and the second defendant, Edward Albert Darch. He died on 2 April 1989. He left a will dated 20 November 1974, whereby in the event, which happened, of his wife predeceasing him he left his whole estate to his son, the second defendant, absolutely and made no provision for the plaintiff. The will was duly proved by Lloyds Bank.

The appeal raises two completely separate issues, which the judge had to decide at the same time, because two quite separate claims by Mrs Riggs against her father's estate were consolidated. One was a claim for provision under the Inheritance (Provision for Family and Dependants) Act 1975 and the other was a claim for a transfer on the basis of proprietary estoppel of a certain strip of garden ground adjoining the house where Mrs Riggs and her family live.

I propose, solely as a matter of convenience because it is the point which has most recently been argued, to deal first with the claim under the Inheritance Act.

I should mention that at the date of the trial the second defendant was aged 57. He was married and he had a married daughter. The plaintiff was aged 42. She had had one marriage which resulted in divorce, but then she had married her second husband, Mr Riggs, in 1978 and she had two children by the second marriage, who were aged 14 and ten at the time of the hearing.

The Inheritance Act provides by section 1(1):

> 'Where after the commencement of this Act a person dies domiciled in England and Wales and is survived by any of the following persons...'

Then there are categories (a) to (e), and the section continues:

> ...that person may apply to the court for an order under section 2 of this Act on the ground that the disposition of the deceased's estate effected by his will or the law relating to intestacy, or the combination of his will and that law, is not such as to make reasonable financial provision for the applicant.

Of the several categories (a) is the wife or husband of the deceased; (b) is a former wife or former husband of the deceased who has not remarried; (c) is a child of the deceased; (d) is a person treated by the deceased as a child of the family (that does not arise in the present case), and (e) is 'any person (not being a person included in the foregoing paragraphs...) who immediately before the death of the deceased was being maintained, either wholly or partly, by the deceased'. Subsection (2) then defines what is meant by 'reasonable financial provision'. It is provided by subsection (2)(b) that in the case of an application other than by a husband or wife of the deceased the phrase means 'such financial provision as it would be reasonable in all the circumstances of the case for the applicant to receive as maintenance'.

An applicant, who is not a spouse or child of the deceased, seeking to come in under subhead (e) of subsection (1) would have to have shown that immediately before the death of the deceased he or she was being maintained wholly or partly by the deceased. A child (son or daughter) can rank under subhead (c) or subsection (1), whether or not being maintained, immediately before the death, by the deceased, but even so the reasonable financial provision is limited to such as it would be reasonable in all the circumstances of the case for the applicant to receive for his or her maintenance.

Section 3 of the Act provides:

[His Lordship read out the opening words of section 3(1).]

Then there are listed various subheads, of which (a) is the financial resources and financial needs which the applicant has or is likely to have in the foreseeable future; (b) is the financial resources and financial needs which any other applicant for an order under the section is likely to have in the foreseeable future; (c) is the same in relation to beneficiaries of the estate; (d) is obligations which the deceased had towards any applicants; (e) is the size and nature of the net estate; (f) is irrelevant; and (g) picks up anything else that the court may consider relevant.

Subsection (5) of section 3 provides:

> In considering the matters to which the court is required to have regard under this section, the court shall take into account the facts as known to the court at the date of the hearing.

It follows that it was necessary to consider the size and nature of the net estate of the deceased at the date of the hearing, and likewise to consider the financial resources and financial needs as at that time.

The principle asset of the deceased's estate was some property known as Summerclose Nursery, Dorchester Road, Broadway, Weymouth in Dorset. It seems that the deceased bought that land at the end of 1952 at a time when he owned another nursery at Templecombe, which was actually sold in 1954. The second defendant, the deceased's son, lived at Summerclose even after his marriage until about 1957, when he moved to Yeovil. The deceased had a bungalow built in Summerclose in 1958 where he lived up to the date of his death. The plaintiff was given a piece of land at the southern tip of the Summerclose Nursery in June 1971 to build a house on. There were certain restrictions which made it difficult for her to borrow money, and the deceased lent her, therefore, at that time £1,000 interest free to enable her to build the house.

The deceased had apparently carried on a poultry business for a time at Summerclose which was not very successful, and he then directed his activities back to horticulture on the land of the Summerclose Nursery at that stage. The plaintiff was very interested in flowers and gardens. She had started a florist business in 1972, which was sold in 1976 when the £1,000 was repaid and she divorced her first husband. She kept the house, which had by then been built, following the divorce, and married Mr Riggs, as I have mentioned, in 1978.

I need not, on this aspect of the case, go into certain other aspects of the land just by the plaintiff's house. There is a plan which shows the division of the land on which the plaintiff's house is shown edged in yellow. the land immediately adjoining it at the southern end of the Summerclose Nursery is shown edged in green. Above that there is the larger part of the nursery shown edged in red. On that part there are, as an aerial photograph shows, some derelict greenhouses and a number of what are called chalets. Above that there is another area shown edged in blue on which the bungalow where the deceased lived is to be found, plus a further derelict greenhouse and an access to the east above that.

The position is that there is apparently an element of hope value in the lands edged red and blue in the respect that there is quite a likelihood that planning permission for the erection of a number of dwellings on that land will be granted after the completion of what is referred to as the Dorchester Road bypass, which is not expected to happen for some four or five years at any rate. The valuation, therefore, of those properties (the land edged blue and the land edged red), was estimated at £65,000 for the one and £55,000 for the other, taking into account such prospects as there are of future development. But the position would be that if the land could be held until the development took place it would probably be vastly more valuable.

I have mentioned the deceased's horticultural business on the nursery. He had a heart attack in 1982 and his wife died in August 1984. From then onwards, at any rate, he gave up his horticultural activities and he derived income from summer lettings of a dozen small huts, referred to as chalets, which stood on the red and blue edged parts of the Summerclose Nursery.

The case put forward for the plaintiff under the Inheritance Act is that she helped the deceased really throughout her adult life because she had always been living so nearby, both caring for him and helping him, though he lived in the bungalow after his wife died, and again over that period cleaning out the chalets at the beginning and end of each letting season and taking a great deal of trouble over doing that. So it is said that it was unreasonable for the deceased not to make provision for her by his testamentary disposition, even though he had given the land on which her home had been built, had lent her, interest free for several years, the £1,000 I have mentioned, and had, to anticipate the other aspect of this case, agreed that she should have the land edged green on the plan I have mentioned as the garden and amenity land of the house she had built.

The judge considered in some detail the financial circumstances of the deceased and all the matters which he was specifically required to have regard to by section 3 of the Act. His conclusion in his judgment, after considering the circumstances of the plaintiff, was that Mr and Mrs Riggs were living at not much above subsistence level. As to that, it has to be said that Mr Hamilton had opened the case to the judge on the basis that they were not necessitous. They appear to have been people living within their means, and they had a small mortgage for an extension to their house, to which I will have to come on the other aspect of the case. There was a car provided for Mr Riggs' work as a hospital laboratory technician, which was a reasonably well paid and secure job, and apparently they had holidays from time to time, including holidays in France. Their house was of the value of some £80,000 or £85,000 if the land edged green is taken into account, at any rate free from any restriction, And the mortgage for the patio or extension was only for some £8,000. They had quite a lot of hire purchase commitments, including the car, but they were able to pay those and they were living comfortably.

The judge also considered Mr Darch's, the second defendant's financial circumstances. He owned his house in Yeovil and there is an estimate of its value. His income seems to have been somewhat smaller than that of Mr and Mrs Riggs, but nothing very much turns on that. He had substantial savings, including monies in a building society account and stocks and shares, the total value being about £42,000.

There is one aspect of the financial matter which I have not yet mentioned, and that is that there was a sum of cash (£10,000) kept by the deceased in the roofs of the chalets, which had not been disclosed to Lloyds Bank. But after the deceased's death the second defendant and the plaintiff split that. The second defendant took £4,000, of which £2,000 went to his daughter and £2,000 he retained. The plaintiff took £6,000, of which £2,000 was invested as savings by her, and the remaining £4,000 was invested equally for each of her two children. That is a sum which falls to be taken into account in the net estate. The judge directed that the £6,000 should be treated as on account of the sum that he awarded the plaintiff on this application, but the £6,000 is not money that is in way in issue in these proceedings. It was split between the brother and sister. There is no question of it being recoverable from the sister if this claim fails. It is merely a sum to be worked through in the calculations like the £4,000 which the second defendant took.

The judge, when he completed the calculations and he referred to the difficulties about realising the potential of the nursery land (the lands edged red and blue, which could have a gross value of as much as half a million pounds and a net value after development of as much as £300,000), then comes to consider the position. He says this:

> I have found this a borderline case, but in my judgement, in the light of the financial position and needs of his son and daughter respectively, the obligations he owed to them both and the size and nature of his estate, it was unreasonable for Mr Darch to make no provision at all for his daughter's maintenance in his will, particularly in the few years after his death when his grandchildren would be under age and his daughter's needs at their greatest. I have considered whether this should be in the form of an annual sum, because it is intended to meet current expenditure rather than make capital provision. It would, however, I think, be hard on Mr Darch to impose a continuing obligation as a charge on the estate. [Mr Darch is the second defendant.] I see no reason to believe that Mrs Riggs, who appears a sensible woman, not given to wasting money, will use the money other than to assist with everyday living expenses.
>
> The sum I propose to award is £20,000.00, payable in two instalments. The first will be payable in a month's time, the second in 13 months from today. From the first instalment Mr Darch will be entitled to deduct the £6,000 which Mrs Riggs or her children have already had from the estate. There will, therefore, be one payment of £4,000.00 in August 1991 and one payment of £10,000.00 in August 1992. The sums will not carry interest until the date on which they are payable. They are not intended as a legacy to Mrs Riggs, but as a commuted sum for maintenance while her children are still dependent.

Insofar as there are points of law as to the construction of the Inheritance Act raised in this case, it is only necessary to refer to the case of *In re Coventry* [1980] Ch 461, [1979] 3 All ER 815, and to the approval in that case of various passages in the judgment of Mr Justice Oliver (as he then was) in the court of first instance. I should refer first to page 185 in the judgment of Lord Justice Goff, where he said between letters C and D:

> What is proper maintenance must in all cases depend upon all the facts and circumstances of the particular case being considered at the time, but I think it is clear on the one hand that one must not put too limited a meaning on it; it does not mean just enough to enable a person to get by; on the other hand, it does not mean anything which may be regarded as reasonably desirable for his general benefit or welfare.

I note also that the view that maintenance does not mean 'mere subsistence' was expressed as long ago as *In re Borthwick* [1949] Ch 395, [1949] 1 All ER 472, under the original Inheritance Act, and there is a reference also (and I am referring to the notes in *Halsbury's Statutes* to section 1 of the current Act) that 'the expression usually denotes payments which directly or indirectly enable the applicant to discharge the recurrent costs of daily living'. Then in the judgment of Lord Justice Buckley in *In re Coventry* at 494 it is said at letter E:

> It has been common ground between counsel in this court that 'maintenance' in this context does not relate merely to subsistence, but must have a more generous construction than that.

Then at page 495 Lord Justice Buckley cites from the judgment of Mr Justice Oliver as follows:

> In my judgement Oliver J there correctly states the problem, and I think he states the appropriate test to be applied.

In the present case the burden of the case that was put before the court on behalf of the plaintiff under the Act was that she was a daughter who had helped her father and for whom it was therefore reasonable that her father should make provision by his will and it was unreasonable and unfair that this land, with its development potential, should be given entirely to the son, the second defendant. It was suggested, therefore, that there was a moral obligation to provide for the plaintiff and therefore there had been no reasonable provision. It was accepted that provision out of income would be difficult because it would be undesirable to sell the land to invest the proceeds, although there was currently some rent because the bungalow that the deceased had occupied had been let to a Mr Said, for the time being at any rate.

So the judge reaches his conclusion. But his conclusion is that the money which he was awarding – and I take it at £14,000 rather than £20,000 on the footing that the figure of £20,000 is to clear out of the calculation the £6,000 which she had already had from the net estate – was required for her needs at a time when they would be greatest because the plaintiff's children would be dependent on her and her husband and under age – that is to say, over the next ten years. There was no general need for maintenance for the plaintiff, as I have already briefly described her circumstances, and the claim for maintenance over the years when she would have the greatest need because her children were young (as I follow the course of events) was a claim which was not specifically put forward on behalf of the plaintiff at all, but devised by the judge. The only relevant reference to it in the evidence is in a passage in which the judge was asking questions of the plaintiff after the conclusion of her re-examination. He asks then the ages of the children and that they were at school and asks how long they are expecting to stay at school. She said:

> 'A. Well, my son is hoping to get a job with Customs and Excise, which means that he is going to have to study hard and probably

> stay on at school or college until he gets his qualifications, so probably some years yet.
>
> Q. Is that GCSE, or is that 'A' level?
>
> A. I haven't gone into exactly what he needs, as he is 14 and is just starting out. His teachers at an open evening recently suggested if he works hard now, they sort of streamline them into different studies according to what job they want to do. so they suggest that he goes into his streams, works hard for a couple of years, and then they will review where he goes from there.'

Then the judge asks about the daughter and whether she would change next year to a comprehensive school, and continues:

> 'Q. And would you expect her to stay until 16?
>
> A. Oh, at least. She is quite clever; she is probably more clever than her brother, and I think she will stay on and study for a good career.'

Then the judge goes on to ask a bit about the income of the plaintiff's husband.

As I see it, the judge had been very concerned at the fact that he was only entitled to provide for maintenance, and he has directed himself to a matter which was not fully explored (the need for the children over the immediate coming few years) because it was not the case that was being put forward by the plaintiff. The essential case that was being put forward by the plaintiff really to my mind falls foul of the words that I have quoted from the judgment of Lord Justice Goff in *Re Coventry* at page 485 as a sum of money reasonably desirable for her general benefit of welfare, or, to put it another way in the words quoted by Lord Justice Buckley, to give her a sum of money because the deceased was unreasonable in not giving it to her.

In my judgement, notwithstanding that Lord Justice Buckley ended by saying that the decision to be made was a qualitative decision, or what is sometimes called a 'value judgment', and that a decision of that kind is one which is particularly difficult to disturb on appeal, the judge here has proceeded on an error of principle in that he has taken something which is not maintenance and tried to turn it into maintenance by expressing a general view that it was for the period while the children were dependent, when that was not the case that was being put before him. Accordingly, I would, differing with all respect from the judge in his handling of this aspect of the matter, allow the appeal against the award of, in effect, the £14,000. I can see no circumstances in this case for awarding any sum for maintenance to the plaintiff on the basis of the case that was put forward, and it is not right to use the Act to award her a legacy.

[His Lordship then considered the proprietory estoppel claim.]

Accordingly I would dismiss the appeal in relation to the finding in respect of the land edged green and the case founded on proprietary estoppel.

BUTLER-SLOSS LJ: I agree with the judgment of my Lord, Lord Justice Dillon, and that the appeal should be allowed in respect of the point relating to inheritance and dismissed in respect of the proprietary estoppel.

Simon Brown LJ: I too agree.

Order: Appeal relating to the Inheritance Act claim allowed; appeal founded on proprietary estoppel dismissed; paragraph (4) of the judge's order set aside; no order for costs as between the plaintiff and the second defendant in this court or in the court below; legal aid taxation of the plaintiff's costs of the appeal; the direction for legal aid taxation of her costs in the judge's order not affected; the directions in paragraphs (6) and (7) of the judge's order as the first and second defendant costs being paid out of the estate not affected.

Rhodes v Dean and Others

Court of Appeal (Civil Division), 28 March 1996

D McConville for the Appellant.

J Quirke for the First and Second Defendants.

The Third and Fourth Respondents did not appear and were not represented.

Ward LJ: Aubrey Dean died on 1 May 1989. In about July 1985 he had begun to live with the plaintiff, who is the appellant, Mrs Rhodes. He had made his last will on 11 April 1986, leaving a quarter of his estate to each of his son and daughter, whom he named as his executors, and to his two grand-daughters, the four respondents in this appeal. He left the appellant nothing. She applied for an order under the Inheritance (Provision for Family and Dependants) Act 1975. On 13 September 1994 His Honour Judge Micklem, sitting as a judge of the High Court, dismissed that application with costs. He found that the plaintiff had established that she was partly being maintained by the deceased otherwise than for full valuable consideration because he was making a substantial contribution in money or money's worth towards her reasonable maintenance. She was accordingly, in his judgment, a person who fell within s 1(1)(e) of the Act. Against those findings the respondents would wish us to hear the submissions put forward by their respondent's notice, but it was not necessary to call upon them to develop those submissions. That was because the learned judge further found that it was reasonable for the testator to have made no financial provision for the appellant in his will.

The facts which give rise to this dispute are, shortly stated, these. The parties met some time in the summer of 1984, shortly after the deceased lost his wife. Their friendship developed and during 1984 the deceased was spending more and more time, particularly at the weekends, with the plaintiff. He was a man of 61 years of age. He had been a coal merchant. He had also dabbled in property, renovating and selling houses. He was living in his former matrimonial home but developing a property nearby with a view to moving in there. The plaintiff was 53 years old. She had been married much earlier, but that marriage had come to grief decades previously and she had lost touch with her husband. She had had a long and settled relationship with another man, which ended in 1980. She was living in a former council property, which had been purchased by herself but, effectively, by her daughter, who was a serving police officer.

In about July 1985 the deceased managed to sell his old home and he began to live with the plaintiff at her address. He lived there until February 1987, that is for about eighteen months. He had decided some time in 1985 to give up the coal merchant business; and he used the proceeds of the sale of his old house to buy three other properties, which he renovated and let to tenants. The plaintiff assisted him in that endeavour. He made his will in April 1986, which was therefore some nine months after he had begun to live with the plaintiff but whilst still living with her in her home. The work on the property which was destined to be their home was completed in February 1987, and they moved in and they remained there until his death.

The plaintiff's property was transferred to her daughter in April 1987. That had always been their intention, because it was the daughter, after all, who was paying for the property. The daughter said that in July 1988 she gave the plaintiff £5,000 out of the proceeds of sale. As to that money the judge found (p 100):

> Mrs Rhodes was not clear how much of this £5,000 she had spent by the time of the testator's death. In her first affidavit she deposed that she still had some £1,000 of it left, but in cross-examination her recollection was that the whole had been long gone by the time the testator died, spent on herself, on presents for her family, on buying meals out and other extras for herself and the testator.

In September 1988 the deceased sold the three investment properties and paid the proceeds into an account which he opened in the joint names of the plaintiff and himself. So far as this account is concerned, the judge made this finding:

> ...so far as day-to-day expenses of living of himself and Mrs Rhodes were concerned, those expenses must have come out of the joint account once that had been opened in June 1988.

As I have said he died on 1 May 1989. So this was a cohabitation of some four years in duration, partly in the home of the plaintiff and for just over two years in the home of the deceased. He left an estate which was valued for probate purposes at some £187,000 but, for the purposes of the hearing, having regard to capital transfer tax, the costs of the litigation and perhaps to falling property prices, it was accepted that the net value of the estate would be about £100,000.

It was for the plaintiff to prove her dependency and to bring herself within s 1(1)(e) of the Act. That she did. The judge was satisfied that (p 16):

> Looking at the matter in a common sense way it seems to me to be clear beyond doubt that the testator was making a substantial contribution in money or money's worth and money towards the reasonable needs of Mrs Rhodes and that there was in the words of Butler-Sloss LJ [in *Bishop v Plumley* [1991] 1 WLR 582] an 'obvious

> imbalance' in favour of Mrs Rhodes. I find that Mrs Rhodes was substantially dependent on the testator before he died.....I am satisfied that Mrs Rhodes is a dependant who may apply to the court under the Act.

I put aside for a moment the challenge to that finding which the respondents would wish to make.

The next question for the court to decide – the crucial question, and the one which raises itself in the appeal – is really this: is the disposition of the deceased's estate effected by his will such as to make reasonable financial provision for the plaintiff? Here no provision was made for her by the will, and so the question in reality is whether, in all the circumstances of this case, no provision is nonetheless reasonable financial provision. Reasonable financial provision is defined in s 1(2)(b) of the Act as:

> ...such financial provision as it would be reasonable in all the circumstances of the case for the applicant to receive for his maintenance.

The learned judge correctly directed himself in accordance with the well-known decision in *In re Coventry, dec'd* [1980] 1 Ch 461, [1979] 3 All ER 815 and cited the judgment of Goff LJ at p 485 to this effect:

> What is proper maintenance must in all cases depend upon all the facts and circumstances of the particular case being considered at the time, but I think it is clear on the one hand that one must not put too limited a meaning on it. It does not mean just enough to enable a person to get by; on the other hand, it does not mean anything which may be regarded as reasonably desirable for his general benefit or welfare.

My Lord, Lord Justice Nourse, in *In Re Jennings (dec'd), Harlow v National Westminster Bank PLC and Others* [1994] Ch 286, [1994] 3 All ER 27 emphasised at 297 of the former report, that:

> ....'maintenance' connotes only those payments which will directly or indirectly enable the applicant in the future to discharge the cost of his daily living at whatever standard of living is appropriate to him;...

In determining whether the applicant has been reasonably provided for, having regard to the disposition of the estate, the court is required by s 3(1) of the Act to take into account the several factors there listed, of which the material ones are these:

[His Lordship read out sub-sections (a), (d)-(g).]

In the case of an applicant who, like this one, makes the application by virtue of section 1(1)(e), there is the special provision in s 3(4) to this effect:

[His Lordship read out section 3(4).]

The Act goes on to direct the court to have regard to and to take into account the facts as they are known at the date of the hearing and to have regard to earning capacity.

The learned judge therefore correctly set about the task of making the necessary comparative findings which s 3(1) specifies. Dealing with the plaintiff's case, he found that her financial position and needs were as follows (p 22D):

> The financial resources of Mrs Rhodes at the testator's death consisted of a pension of £26.60 per week by way of income. As to capital she had some furniture, which she had brought from [her home] and, more importantly, she had the sum of £35,869.14 in the joint account. Her needs were for accommodation and a supplement to her pension by way of income. Mrs Rhodes was not in a position to earn her living when the testator died.

He properly took into account her health, and said (p 25E):

> Mrs Rhodes suffers somewhat from arthritis and this may, unhappily, get worse as she gets older. For this reason it is desirable that she should be accommodated on the ground floor, but it is not a requirement she has such accommodation. There is no suggestion, for example, that she has been living only on the ground floor at 11 Queen Street. Mrs Rhodes does not require a house rather than a flat to meet her needs.

In directing himself to her requirements, he was correctly addressing himself as to her maintenance needs.

He compared the position of the beneficiaries. I can summarise that quite shortly. The son and daughter were, fortunately, in the happy position that they had no needs which could not be met from their existing resources. The elder grandchild, who is now about 27, is married and she and her husband likewise can meet their outgoings from their income, to which she makes a contribution as a hairdresser. Her younger sister, who is now 21, is also a hairdresser and is also independent of her parents, which must be a consolation to them which some of us can envy. She too, therefore, has adequate resources to meet her needs. The judge was correct in taking account of promises that the deceased made to his grandchildren to set each of them up in business; and they gave evidence, which may have been vague but which was convincing enough, that £30,000 each would be required for that purpose. As I have indicated, the estate had some £100,000 net of expenses.

It was not enough to make this comparison. The crucial enquiry is the s 3(4) enquiry. That comprises the three elements; first, the extent to which the deceased assumed responsibility for the maintenance of the plaintiff; secondly, the basis upon which he assumed it; and thirdly, the length of time for which he discharged it. Maintenance here must bear the same meaning as it does elsewhere.

Turning, therefore, to the three elements; first, as to extent, the judge found (p 23D):

> As to the extent to which and the basis upon which the testator assumed responsibility for the maintenance of Mrs Rhodes, it is I think clear that the testator assumed responsibility for providing

> accommodation for Mrs Rhodes. But I think equally that he did not assume responsibility for meeting all her maintenance needs.

He had earlier found (p 16C):

> The mutual companionship they gave each other may be thought as cancelling out, but the testator was making a substantial contribution to Mrs Rhodes' maintenance by providing accommodation for her. The evidence does not enable the court to make any findings as to what proportion of the weekly household expenses was being provided by each....

In summary, therefore, he was finding, as it seems to me, (a) that the responsibility was for maintenance by way of accommodation only, but (b) the plaintiff had not succeeded in establishing that he had assumed responsibility for her day-to-day living expenses. As to the latter finding, though it may perhaps seem surprising (given the lifestyle being adopted by this couple, to which I shall return) that the deceased was not subsidising the plaintiff to some extent. It is nonetheless a finding to which the judge was perfectly entitled to come and one which was peculiarly within his province to make. He had listened to three days of evidence, whilst the minutiae of daily living were dissected, and he had the fullest opportunity to assess the plaintiff's evidence relating to it. I would not disturb that finding. As for the former finding, this seems to be confirmed by the view he took about the basis upon which the deceased had assumed that responsibility.

Secondly, as to that basis the judge had, at an early stage in the judgment, said (p 7E):

> There is no doubt that the testator was concerned that Mrs Rhodes should have a roof over her head and was so concerned both before and after he put the proceeds of the sale of the three partnership properties to which I have referred into the joint account in September 1988.

The evidence before him was, among other passages, that the deceased had said to the plaintiff on several occasions, 'I can't expect you to give up the security you have without my making proper provision for you.' But it appears that the discussions they were having mainly involved one or other property either being given to her or put into their joint names, and there is therefore a heavy emphasis, summarised by the evidence that she gave that, 'The deceased assured me I would be well provided for should anything happen to him and he always promised me I would have the house.'

Further insight into the basis upon which the parties were operating their lives is gained from other passages in the judgment. The judge said (p 23F):

> (The plaintiff) was, for financial purposes, treated as his housekeeper as long as that arrangement was financially advantageous to both of them; she worked in the little letting business, so long as that subsisted. When Mrs Rhodes received a pension she put that into a common pool.

He said further:

> In practice Mrs Rhodes appears to have been expected to get what she could from the State as a separate individual and the testator paid the rest. But the difference between the totality of Mrs Rhodes' need and what she herself supplied is uncertain. It is far from the familiar situation of man and wife.

He made that finding with due regard to the evidence she had given of their having spoken of marriage, which would have been difficult, given her matrimonial problems. These are important findings because they refute an essential plank of Mr McConville's attractive submission made to us today that this relationship was akin to marriage. The judge did not view it so, and I see no reason to disturb his finding.

Thirdly, as to the duration of this responsibility, the finding there was that:

> ... the testator discharged responsibility for providing accommodation for Mrs Rhodes only for some two years and two months.

These factors, under s 3(1) and s 3(4), are all to be held in balance by the judge who hears the matter. It is his judgment and the exercise of his discretion which determines eventually whether the financial provision, using the language of s 1(2)(b), 'would be reasonable in all the circumstances of the case for the applicant to receive for his maintenance'.

It is submitted that an error made by the learned judge was not to give any or sufficient weight to the standard of living that was enjoyed by this couple as the benchmark for what is reasonable. I do not agree with that criticism. It might be appropriate, where one is dealing with a widow's claim, to have express regard to the standard of living enjoyed during the marriage, but here the matter is at large. Here the standard of living is but a matter to which the court has overall regard, and it is a matter which more usually will lie within the decision that has to be made as to the extent of the responsibility, the basis of it and the duration of it. The judge made these findings about this matter. He observed:

> It seems that the testator was concerned about his health throughout the whole time he was living with Mrs Rhodes and was determined to enjoy himself while he could.

Her evidence was that they had as a result enjoyed a good standard of living; they had taken a number of holidays abroad, in Spain and in the United States; they kept a small motor home in Florida and a little motor home in England to enjoy the beauty of the countryside.

The findings that the learned judge made about Mrs Rhodes were (p 22G):

> There is no direct evidence of Mrs Rhodes ever having earned her own living. For many years before she met the testator she had lived in a council house apparently supported by the State. Her style of life was modest. Her style of life changed dramatically when in 1988 the testator gave up his business, but Mrs Rhodes could not

> reasonably expect to continue to travel and live off capital once the testator had died. The style of life they shared was not a style of life which the testator himself appears to have enjoyed before he met Mrs Rhodes. In substance, it seems that after his wife died and having met Mrs Rhodes, the testator decided to stop working and enjoy the benefits of the profit of boom and indeed enjoy himself while life lasted. I do not therefore regard Mrs Rhodes' standard of life with the testator as the measure of her need.

In my judgement, he was right so to rule. Reasonableness is the appropriate touchstone. He judged that to be (p 25B):

> I do not regard Mrs Rhodes' style of life as requiring that she owns this property in which she is accommodated. Much of her life, so far as the court is aware, has been spent in rented accommodation provided by the local council. Mrs Rhodes does not require accommodation having more than one bedroom to meet her need for accommodation, though it would be more advantageous to her to have a spare room in which she could receive members of her family as guests.

It seems to me, therefore, that in the result the learned judge was arriving at conclusions which may be summarised as follows. Though her need was for accommodation and some supplement to her pension, the deceased had, for but a short time, only maintained her by the provision of accommodation, and reasonable accommodation did not require the quality of residence to which she had hardly had time to grow accustomed.

So the learned judge turned to what is the crucial factor in this case, which is this. I have mentioned it but in passing. At the time of his death the joint account, which contained monies coming entirely from the deceased, held just under £36,000. That sum of money was largely expended, and the judge made a number of findings about that. The Plaintiff seems to have spent money partly on her living and meeting certain of the expensive costs of running the home before she obtained income support benefits to assist her. But she went on a number of holidays, which were quite costly; she bought a number of household items – a dishwasher and the like; and, more importantly, she made an improvident loan to her son of some £15,000 for him to invest in a company which collapsed. I do not read the judge to be excessively pejorative when he concluded (p 32P):

> Mrs Rhodes had dissipated £27,000 odd in the first thirteen months after the testator's death.

That is a statement of fact. What he also found is this (p 33b):

> ....she simply went on living in 11 Queen Street after the testator's death and, beyond obtaining a number of particulars of other houses, took no serious steps to find other accommodation throughout the period between the testator's death and the hearing of her application.

Consequently, the judge had this problem to resolve. That whereas a house such as the home in Moore Street which she and her daughter had occupied might have been valued at some £38,000 at the date of the trial, and whereas residential properties might be rented for anything between £35 and £55 weekly, the fact is that her old home could have been purchased for some £25,000 at the time of the untimely death of the deceased. So the judge made this crucial finding (p 34B):

> ...I find on the balance of probability that Mrs Rhodes could after the testator's death have bought herself suitable freehold accommodation with the £35,859 in the joint account and had several thousand pounds over had she chosen to do so.'

Against those findings he came to this conclusion (p 37):

> ...the testator had made provision in his lifetime which, having regard to all the matters I have set out, gave Mrs Rhodes on his death what it was reasonable for her to receive from him as being required for her maintenance. I bear in mind particularly, but certainly not exclusively, the extent and length of her dependency and the extent to which the testator assumed responsibility for her maintenance. The testator had made himself responsible for providing Mrs Rhodes with accommodation and, perhaps, some small contribution to her maintenance beyond that. By putting the monies in the joint account the testator provided Mrs Rhodes with ample money to purchase suitable accommodation, that is accommodation which was reasonably required by her, and provided her with some thousands of pounds beyond that. In my judgement it was, looking at the matter objectively, reasonable for the testator to make no provision for Mrs Rhodes in his will, having regard to the fact that he had provided for her by acting in his lifetime.
>
> The court has to have regard to what has happened since the testator's death and until the date of this hearing. The circumstances that Mrs Rhodes has now dissipated what she received from the testator should not in my judgement lead the court to impose a higher test or a different test, nor should it lead the court to take the view that what was reasonable at the time of the testator's death is at this stage of the enquiry no longer reasonable. To the extent that Mrs Rhodes has borne the burden of larger outgoings at 11 Queen Street than she would have done in a smaller house, that is something for which she can blame only herself. It is not something which can be laid at the door of the estate. If Mrs Rhodes now has to leave 11 Queen Street and cannot buy another house that is, again, a result of her own decisions and action.
>
> That Mrs Rhodes is now in her present unhappy position does not in my judgement lead to the conclusion that, objectively regarded, Mrs Rhodes ought now to have more maintenance by way of accommodation provided out of the estate.

That may, on a narrow view, from her perspective seem a harsh finding, but I can see nothing wrong in law with the approach and the way in which the judge has directed himself, and the conclusion is one to which he was perfectly entitled to come. In my judgement it is appropriate to look at what reasonably she might have been able to do at the point of death and to judge the matter in that light. I see no error in the judge's approach. Without, therefore, needing to call upon the respondents to develop their other grounds for supporting his conclusion, I would dismiss the appeal.

We have been told that since the judgment proceedings have been taken for possession and that there is a judgment for some £19,000 in respect of means profits. So far that has not been enforced. I doubt whether the plaintiff has the wherewithal to meet those monies. I can say no more about that, but I hope the matter might lie where it presently sits.

Apart from that, in my judgement the appeal must be dismissed.

SCHIEMANN LJ: I agree.

NOURSE LJ: I also agree.

Order: Appeal dismissed.

Smith v Loosley and others

Court of Appeal (Civil Division), 18 June 1986

BWT Leech for the Appellants.
AH Norris for the Respondent.
N Cameron for the Executors.

DILLON LJ: This is an appeal by the third, fourth, fifth and sixth defendants in these proceedings, Mr and Mrs Corrick and their daughters, against an order of Mr Justice Hollings made on 3 March 1986. By that order the learned judge dismissed an appeal by the present appellants against an order of Mr Registrar Rowe of 30 January 1986 which had granted the plaintiff in the proceedings, Mrs Jennie Smith, an extension of time for bringing the proceedings seeking relief out of the estate of her late husband, Horace Leonard Smith, under the Inheritance (Provision for Family and Dependants) Act 1975.

The plaintiff is, as I have indicated, the widow of the deceased. She was born in 1900 and is now aged 86. Their marriage was in 1930. There were no children. Contrary to usual experience in applications under the Act, the marriage was long and happy, and ended only with the death of the deceased on 7 February 1985. At the time of the marriage the deceased worked as a bricklayer for a local builder and the plaintiff had been working in shops in London, but she gave up work on her marriage. The deceased was a hard-working man who gradually built up his own successful business as a builder which was disposed of when he retired some ten years before he died, and he left a net estate of a gross value of some £276,000. It comprises the house in which he and the plaintiff were living, No 70, Oxford Road, Marlow, a number of other houses in Oxford Road, Marlow and Crown Road, Marlow, some of which were the subject of specific devises in his will and substantial amounts of cash in building societies. The deceased left his last will dated 28 January 1985, by which he appointed the first two defendants who are solicitors his executors. Their firm had prepared the will. The effect of the will is to give the widow a life interest in the chattels and in the residuary estate, including the house that was the matrimonial home and to provide that after her death pecuniary legacies of some £25,000 will be payable and the balance of the estate will go to Mr and Mrs Corrick or their children. Mr Corrick was a nephew of the deceased and the evidence is clear that up to some months after the deceased's death the plaintiff was on terms of close friendship and affection with the Corricks who had been very close to the deceased until he died.

The figures put in evidence show that the total estimated income from the estate which would be payable to the plaintiff is some £14,300. In addition, of course, she would be able to continue to occupy the matrimonial home. The capital value I have already mentioned as a gross value. It seems that the net value of the estate would be about £230,000–£240,000.

The deceased's will was proved on 19 April 1985. That is an important date because of the provisions of the Inheritance (Provision for Family and Dependants) Act 1975. That Act enables a surviving spouse to apply to the court for an order under section 2 of the Act on the ground that the disposition of the deceased's estate effected by his will is not such as to make reasonable financial provision for the applicant. But section 4 provides that 'an application for an order under s 2 of this Act shall not, except with the permission of the court, be made after the end of the period of six months from the date on which representation with respect to the estate of the deceased is first taken out'.

The six-month period expired on 19 October 1985, but the originating summons in these proceedings was not issued until 4 December 1985. In accordance with the practice, that summons therefore asked in paragraph 1 for an order that she may be granted permission to make application under the Act, notwithstanding that the six months period had expired; and it was on that application that the registrar, Mr Registrar Rowe, made the order giving her leave to make the application out of time.

The plaintiff puts forward in her fairly brief affidavit in support of the application a general explanation of why she did not apply earlier. She says that in fact when her husband died she was ill and upset and would let others get on with things. It is quite clear that during their joint lives the deceased had handled all business matters and looked after that side of their joint affairs entirely. The plaintiff had never had to trouble to direct her mind to any business or financial matter. She says in her affidavit that she began to wonder what would happen if she died, and thought that she 'would like to give away some odd bits and pieces around the house as 'thank yous' to people who had been good to [her] husband and [herself]' and as mementoes. But, when she told Mrs Corrick that, Mrs Corrick said that she must not give anything away because it did not belong to her, and that she then 'understood that it was all in [her] husband's will and was all going to [Mr and Mrs] Corrick', and this upset her. She said that 'the things in the house had either been bought by both of [them] or had been given to both of [them] and [she] did not think it right that they should be in [her] husband's will. [She could not] bear to think that after 55 years of marriage the things in the house [did] not belong to [her] and that [she was] using everything...with someone else's permission'. So she said she ultimately asked her doctor's husband, because her doctor was married to a solicitor, to come and advise her. She then discovered from him that the house in which she lives is not hers either. As to that, the evidence from the executors and one of their partners who prepared the will is very clear indeed. Of course the plaintiff knew of the death of her husband when it happened, and she was told the terms of the will. It appears that in fact when the will was executed there had been a discussion between the solicitor taking instruction and the deceased about what he wanted to do, and the deceased in the presence of the plaintiff had explained what he wanted to do and had given his reasons. He had said that, whilst desirous of making proper provision for his wife, he was conscious of the fact that during their long marriage he had attended to all the family business and financial matters, and he thought that after his death it was unlikely that the plaintiff would be able to deal properly with the financial side of her affairs because of her age and lack of experience. He wanted her to have an adequate income so that she could live comfortably, but should not be burdened with financial decisions regarding the capital of the estate, and he was also afraid that she might be persuaded to give things away unwisely because she had so little financial experience.

It also appears from the evidence of one of the solicitors that the plaintiff told the solicitor her fears about giving things away at a meeting they had at the house on 11 June 1985, and the solicitor then reassured her that she could give away anything that was hers or that had come to belong to her because it had been owned jointly by her husband and herself, but she could not give away anything that belonged to the estate, because that was on the trusts of the will. There is fairly strong evidence that she understood the terms of the will, but undoubtedly she is an old lady and it seems that she had difficulty in taking in all the implications about what is a life interest. Also it appears that she had a row with Mrs Corrick in August of this year. In the upshot, it was only in October that she got the solicitor, the doctor's husband, to come and advise her. Within a matter of days he wrote to the executors noting her interest and possible claim, but that was only the day before the six months from the grant of probate expired. Thereafter time was not wasted and the summons was issued on 4 December. As is obvious in view of the terms of the will, the estate has not been distributed.

The question then is one of the discretion of the court; under section 4 of the Act the court has a discretion to extend time, and the Act sets no fetters on the exercise of that discretion. What is said in the present case for the appellants is that the former Vice-Chancellor, Sir Robert Megarry, has laid down guidelines in the case of *Re Salmon* [1981] Ch 167, [1980] 3 All ER 532, which the court should observe in considering any application for an extension of time under the Act. The Vice-Chancellor set out some five or six points, of which the second is:

> I think that the onus lies on the plaintiff to establish sufficient grounds for taking the case out of the general rule, and depriving those who

> are protected by it of its benefits. Further, the time limit is a substantial provision laid down in the Act itself, and is not a mere procedural time limit imposed by the rules of the court which will be treated with the indulgence appropriate to procedural rules. The burden on the applicant is thus, I think, no triviality: the applicant must make out a substantial case for it being just and proper for the court to exercise its statutory discretion to extend the time.

One has to note, however, that the Vice-Chancellor made it very plain that he was not intending to lay down principles. He recognised, as one might expect, how dangerous it would be to endeavour to establish guiding principles anticipating the difference in facts between different cases. In the case of *Escritt v Escritt* [1982] 3 FLR 281, Lord Justice Ormrod cites *Re Salmon* pointing out that Sir Robert Megarry had shown that Parliament has left a discretion of the court in an entirely neutral way; it has given no indication as to what considerations should apply.

In the present case the learned judge, Mr Justice Hollings, who was of course exercising his own discretion although hearing an appeal from the registrar, did not go into great detail into the reasons why the application was made out of time, and therefore did not give any specific ruling on 'the substantial case for it being just and proper for the court to exercise its statutory discretion to extend the time', in the words of Sir Robert Megarry. What he did do, after examining all the facts, was to consider whether the plaintiff had shown an arguable case. He held, though he had had some hesitation about the whole application, that an arguable case was shown; that is not challenged on this appeal, though it will be if the case goes to trial, and therefore, notwithstanding the reasons given by the deceased himself as deposed to by the solicitor who took his instruction, it is not for us in this court to express any view on whether the plaintiff's case has strong or slight prospects of success at the trial. But the discretion is one discretion; it is not a hurdle race in the course of which an application whose application is out of time has to get over a succession of hurdles in the right order before he or she can get an extension of time under section 4. The importance of different factors will vary from case to case. Why the application is put out of time is obviously a relevant factor which will be much more relevant in some cases than in others. In the present case it seems obvious that the reason why it is out of time is that the plaintiff is an old lady; though she was told the terms and effect of the will and though she was told in June what she could or could not give away, it weighed on her mind; and, at any rate after she had had her row with Mrs Corrick, it seems to have worried her, but she did not get round in a hurry to seeking her own solicitor's advice and she had no idea about the Act or time limits until she received advice.

In the circumstances of this case, I take the view that the judge was absolutely entitled in his discretion to grant the extension of time or dismiss the appeal from the registrar. Whatever may be the outcome at the trial of the proceedings, it seems to me that the course he took was the just course in the circumstances.

I would dismiss this appeal.

Croom-Johnson LJ: I too consider that it is not possible for us to say here that Mr Justice Hollings misdirected himself in any way or was guilty of committing any error of principle in exercising his discretion in the way in which he did. It was submitted to us on behalf of the beneficiaries, the appellants, that the reason why the application is being brought is something which has to be satisfactorily explained before one proceeds further in order to see whether or not the application should be entertained. It was submitted that, if the explanation is missing or is in some way unsatisfactory, bound up as it may be with the length of the delay, that is something which in effect should conclude the matter. But in my view that is not the right approach. The discretion, which is in the court, as to whether it will extend the time under section 4 of the Inheritance (Provision for Family and Dependants) Act 1975 is a whole discretion as was submitted on behalf of the plaintiff.

In *Re Salmon* [1981] Ch 167 on page 174, also [1980] 3 All ER 532, Sir Robert Megarry, the Vice-Chancellor, did introduce the word 'guidelines' for the consideration of the court in exercising the discretion. That was picked up and used again in *Re Dennis* [1981] 2 All ER 140 by Mr Justice Browne-Wilkinson (as he then was) when he was dealing with the facts of that case. He himself recited (at page 143 of that report) the guidelines which the Vice-Chancellor had laid down in *Re Salmon*. They might just as well be called 'considerations', or 'factors', or 'facts' or some other suitable word, because they are all matters which had to be taken into account in the final exercise of the court's discretion. In addition to that, and what emerged from the case of *Re Dennis*, was whether at the end of the day the appellant in that particular case had an arguable case. Mr Justice Browne-Wilkinson held without hesitation that what was being asked for in that case did not amount to an arguable case on behalf of the applicant. What is an arguable case may of course vary; it may vary in strength; it may vary in nature; in particular it may vary according to whether or not the application which is brought under section 1 of the statute is brought on behalf of a husband or wife or whether it is brought on behalf of some other dependant or member of the family. The reason is that for members of the family other than husbands and wives the financial provision which has to be applied for is simply such sum as would be reasonable in all the circumstances of the case to the applicant to receive for his maintenance. In the case of a husband and wife, brought under section 1, subsection (2)(a) of the Inheritance (Provision for Family and Dependants) Act 1975, the financial provision should be such as would be reasonable in all the circumstances of the case for a husband or wife to receive, whether or not that provision is required for his or her maintenance. Therefore the grounds upon which reasonable financial provision may be ordered in respect of husbands or wives may well be a good deal wider than those grounds which are needed for other dependants. That is something which has to be taken into account in the assessment of the application when it comes to be made.

I agree with my Lord that one must not at this stage indicate whether there is a good chance or a bad chance of Mrs Smith, the plaintiff, succeeding in her application when it comes to be heard by the court. It may be that the court may have to consider whether in fact the application is for her own benefit at all, having regard to the provisions in the will and the considerations which guided her husband to make the will in the form in which he did. Those are all matters which will have to be decided hereafter, but for the present purposes in my view Mr Justice Hollings exercised his discretion in a manner in which he was entitled to do so, and I would agree that the appeal should be dismissed.

Order: Appeal dismissed; executors to have their costs of the appeal out of the estate in the due course of administration; respondent's costs of the appeal as between the appellants and the respondent to be hers in any event, but without immediate taxation.

Sobesto v Farren

Court of Appeal (on appeal from Judge Dow sitting as a deputy judge of the Family Division), Lord Denning MR and Donaldson LJ, 9 November 1979

A note of the hearing of the substantive application, *sub nom Re Dr Kozdrach*, follows immediately after this judgment
J Tatham for the Appellant (Plaintiff).
A Ward for the Respondent (Defendant).

THE MASTER OF THE ROLLS: Miss Sobesto is a young woman of 31 years of age. Her father and mother came from Poland 30 or more years ago, the father having been a judge there. They have been resident in England since that time. Also 30 or more years ago a Dr Kozdrach came from Poland. He was a medical doctor, and carried on his practice here.

It appears that some three or four years ago Miss Sobesto and Dr Kozdrach started living together as man and wife. They lived in his house at 27 Portland Rise, Finsbury Park. It was a large house, with a basement, ground floor, first floor and second floor. A good deal of it was devoted to the doctor's surgery and professional needs. But it was a large house where, on the evidence before us, they lived together as man and wife; and those who knew them well believed them to be man and wife. But they never married. Miss Sobesto gives one reason or another to explain why they never married, but says it was the intention of them both to marry. Meanwhile Miss Sobesto was studying at London University to obtain a degree in science, and has been receiving a grant in respect of her studies.

Dr Kozdrach was a good deal older than Miss Sobesto. He was in his 60s. It appears that he contracted an illness because he became infected by patients he was treating; and he died on 6 August 1978 – 16 months ago. It appears that he had made no will. Thereupon Miss Sobesto sought to have provision made for herself under the Inheritance (Provision for Family and Dependants) Act 1975, which does enable provision to be made for a woman who, although not married, is living with a man as his wife and is being maintained by him, so long as the man is domiciled in England – and I think we ought to assume for the moment that Dr Kozdrach was domiciled in England. That means that Miss Sobesto does have a claim under that Act for provision to be made for her, which would include the transfer of property, and may include the transfer of the house itself. At all events, she made a claim under that statute.

In applying that statute, regard has to be made as to any other persons who might have a claim on this bounty, or may be entitled to it in point of law. As far as we know, Dr Kozdrach had only one relative. That was a sister living in Poland – a Mrs Szczepanska. She is a woman in her 60s. She is a school-teacher in Poland, still at work, but no doubt she is going to retire soon. Certainly, as she is the only known relative of Dr Kozdrach, she herself would have a very considerable claim in respect of any property of his.

The position has now been reached where Mr Farren, a Solicitor of the Supreme Court, has been appointed attorney-administrator of the estate for the benefit of the sister. The question is, what is to be done? The various claims have to be sorted out at a full and proper hearing before the court. We are told that a provisional appointment has been made for February, although it might be possible to advance it to January, but not very far ahead – two or three months. But the crux of the matter is this: Mr Farren feels that this house ought to be sold straight away, and the money used for the gradual winding up of the estate. There are considerable other moneys left by the doctor, some in cash at the bank and some in stocks and shares, but in particular there is a bungalow or house in Spain. Mr Farren feels that the house at Portland Rise should be sold at once so that the assets can be got in. But Miss Sobesto says that it should not be sold now; because, if she succeeds in her application, the house might be transferred to her as being the most suitable way of dealing with the assets. With regard to the other money or assets, she says that it may be that some of them will go to the sister, but so far as the house is concerned she says she might have a considerable claim for it to be transferred to her.

It seems to me at the moment that that is quite a possible claim in which she might well succeed. It might well be found, on the full hearing, that the house should be transferred to her, and that the money and other assets should go to the sister. Against that, it could be said, 'It is too big a house for her. Let her go back and live with her parents meanwhile. She can carry on perfectly well with them.' But, inasmuch as the hearing may well be in February, it seems to me that it would be wrong to anticipate the final decision at this stage; and the right thing would be for the house not to be sold meanwhile but that it should remain as it is until the hearing. For that reason, I would be in favour of allowing the appeal and restraining the disposal of the house meanwhile in the expectation that the hearing will come on fairly soon. If this expectation is not fulfilled, then it should be open to Mr Farren to make an application if he thinks fit for the house then to be sold. Meanwhile it seems to me the right thing is for the house not to be sold, and that Miss Sobesto should remain there as she is. That is the main point of the case.

No doubt Mr Farren, as part of his duty, will do his best in collecting the other assets. He will do what is right in regard to the Spanish assets. But I would like to suggest that he ought not to remove the English assets from this country – from the ultimate jurisdiction of the court – because one does not know what the extent of Miss Sobesto's claim will be. Except for this: at the moment her claim is put at one-half; and it must be admitted that the sister will have quite a substantial claim to put forward. As we indicated in the course of the argument, something like £1,000 could easily be made available to her. She may want to come over and deal with the estate, and so forth. At all events, reasonable provision can be made by Mr Farren, who no doubt will administer all the assets very sensibly and reasonably in view of the competing claims upon them.

I would therefore allow the appeal to the extent of restraining the sale or disposal of the house until the full hearing before the court and final decision. If the hearing should be further delayed, it will be open to Mr Farren to make a further application to the court.

LORD JUSTICE DONALDSON: I agree. At the moment, and in contemplation of these applications to the court, each party has been persuading themselves of the strength of their own case. But my experience is that parties reach sensible settlements when instead they start considering the weakness of their own case and both reach the reasonable conclusion that they will lose. There is not a great deal of money in this estate. These proceedings, and indeed the winding up of the estate itself, is going to be very expensive. If they add to the expense, they will assuredly both lose, because there will be nothing left. It might be very much better if they both took thought to the weaknesses of their own cases – and they are considerable; both of them – and reached some sensible conclusion at the earliest possible moment and well before any hearing.

THE MASTER OF THE ROLLS: I endorse what my brother has said about that.

Order: Appeal allowed with costs in this court. Costs below reserved to trial judge. Liberty to apply.

Re Dr Kozdrach, Sobesto v Szczepanska and Farren

Family Division, Ewbank J, 7 April 1981.

This note is compiled from a Note in [1981] Conv 224 and a letter from the second defendant to the author. More information can be derived from the transcript of the interlocutory appeal, *sub nom Sobesto v Farren*, Court of Appeal, 9 November 1979.

Application by a mistress under s 1(1)(e).

The deceased died intestate, leaving an estate of about £52,000 before the payment of capital transfer tax. In addition to the facts which can be deduced from the Court of Appeal transcript, the applicant was young and capable of obtaining a good job and before the death of the deceased there was no impediment to marriage of the parties.

Order: i Lump sum of £19,000;

ii If the applicant paid a further sum of £9,000 to the estate within six months, the deceased's dwelling house (valued at £28,000 at the date of the hearing) was to be transferred to the applicant;

iii All parties' costs out of the estate up to £3,000 each side on a common fund basis, thereafter on a party and party basis.

Stephens v Stephens

Court of Appeal (Civil Division), 1 July 1985

J Hedgecoe for the Respondent.

N Wood for the Appellants.

BALCOMBE: This is an appeal against an order of His Honour Judge Micklem, sitting as a deputy High Court judge, made on 7 March 1985, on an application by a widow for provision out of her deceased husband's estate. The learned judge by the effect of his order, gave her the whole of the net estate absolutely.

The widow is a lady, now in her eightieth year. The deceased husband had been born in the year 1897, so that, when he died in 1982, he was 85. They were married on 30 July 1962. Both had been married before. The deceased had children by his first marriage, including a son, now aged 53, who is an executor of the deceased's will and, with his wife, is the appellant in this court; the wife is the other executor. The widow had also been married before. She had two children, a son and a daughter, by her first marriage. There were no children of the marriage between the widow and the deceased.

I turn to certain findings of fact, which will be found in the transcript of the learned judge's judgment at page 25F, where he says:

> I must go back and deal with the history of the marriage. The plaintiff first knew the deceased for a period of about three years from 1925 to 1928. He was an accompanist and she used to sing. But then in 1928 she moved away to a different part of the world, married and had children. She was, for her part, separated from her husband for some 20 years and in 1961 was living in a house of her own at Llanover, a freehold house, in which she was carrying on a small private school, she being a trained teacher.

He then sets out the circumstances which brought them together again, and says:

> She gave up her school and gave up living in her house. She gave up at the end of the term immediately before marrying the deceased and went to live, after the marriage, at his house Elsinore. Before the marriage there had been some discussion between them about both of them selling their houses and together buying a property, probably a bungalow because the deceased at that time was suffering from cataracts in his eyes and angina. However, though there were attempts on the part of the plaintiff and her daughter to find other premises, the deceased was in the event unwilling to move; the plaintiff sold her house at Llanover in December 1962 for £2,000 net of expenses. Some of the proceeds of sale were spent by her on a trip to Australia, but the bulk has been spent over the years supplementing the money of the deceased which was available for living expenses.
>
> The case that is put forward by the plaintiff is that the marriage endured for 20 years and was basically a happy one. She says (and I accept her evidence) that at the beginning things were difficult. It

> was a second marriage. She had been used to living alone and leading her own life for some 20 years and managing for herself. They had their ups and downs in the early days but basically it was a happy marriage, and I entirely accept that. They were both church-goers.
>
> Within two years of their marriage the deceased had a cataract operation and came back to his music, which was an interest he continued to share with the plaintiff. He came back to be the organist at the Methodist Church which they both attended and they had a life together which was in substance a happy married life for 20 years with some ups and downs at the beginning. That is broadly the situation with regard to the marriage.

The notice of appeal, among other things, asserts that the learned judge's findings as to the happiness of the marriage was against the weight of the evidence, but in any event that ground of appeal occupied no part of the case made before us, and for my part I would not wish in any way – I do not think I would be able – to dissent from what the learned judge said about the situation of the marriage.

The deceased made his will in 1982 not long before he died. In 1964 he had made a previous will by which he left nothing to the widow, but by the will, which was in the event his last will, dated 11 June 1982, he appointed his son, Malcolm Stephens, and his daughter-in-law, Margaret Joy Stephens, as executors. Then he gave the following directions to his executors concerning the property known as Elsinore, Church Road, Wrockwardine Wood, Oakengates, which he referred to as 'the house'.

> (a) my wife may live in the house as long as she wishes but without power for her to assign sub-let or part with the possession of the house or any part thereof
> (b) until my wife has in the opinion of the executors ceased to live in the house permanently it shall not be sold without her consent and my wife shall be responsible for all outgoings affecting it and for keeping it in repair and insured comprehensively on such terms as my executors require but my executors shall not be responsible for ensuring that my wife carries out her obligations in these respects
> (c) at the request of my wife my executors shall sell the house and buy another to which the same provisions as those expressed in the last clause shall apply
> (d) any cash balance arising from the sale and purchase shall form part of the residue of my estate
> (e) when my wife shall cease to live permanently in the house or in any new residence provided in substitution for the house then the house or the new residence shall form part of the residue of my estate
>
> 4. My executors shall hold the residue of my estate on trust to retain or sell it and:
> (a) pay debts capital transfer tax and executorship expenses
> (b) pay the income from the residue to my wife during her lifetime and after her death

(c) pay the residue to my son MALCOLM STEPHENS but if he shall die before me leaving issue then such issue shall take equally per stirpes the share their parent would otherwise have taken.

The last clause did not take effect. Then there was an investment clause.

It is common ground, and indeed was so conceded before the learned judge, that Mr Malcolm Stephens, the deceased's son, is financially secure and is in no way in need of the reversionary interest left to him by the will. Further, the learned judge found, at page 32 of the judgment, the motives which actuated the deceased in making provision in the way he did. The learned judge said this about the executors:

> ...the resistance is based on their understanding of the wishes of the deceased. His expressed wish was that there should be nothing coming from his estate which it should be possible for the plaintiff (the widow) to pass on to her son by a previous marriage. I have not expressed it exactly in the way in which it was expressed in the evidence, but that was the point and that is why the application is resisted.

The estate consisted almost entirely of the house Elsinore, which had been valued not long before the date of the judgment at £23,000. There was also as part of the estate a sum of the order of £4,000, mainly made up of National Savings Certificates, which were nominated to the first defendant, Mr Malcolm Stephens, which he had apparently cashed, the proceeds of which he had retained. So the net estate was of the order of £27,500, from which costs would probably have to be met at the end of the hearing.

The learned judge stated the widow's position as follows:

> Under the will it is common ground that the plaintiff has a right to live in the house and she can ask for another house to be bought, but both with regard to Elsinore and any subsequent house she is to meet all the outgoings to keep it in repair and to keep it insured. Her case is that she really has no money with which to do this. Her case is that the little she has from the State is not sufficient to meet the outgoings that she has. She has got a few pounds capital – perhaps £200 and no other means. She says she cannot afford to live in the house, that it is too big for her. She and her husband kept the substantial garden up very well, but she is now in her eightieth year and crippled with arthritis, she cannot cope with it. She has no help in the house and the house is too big for her. She would like to find somewhere else. She says that in all the circumstances she has a claim under the Act.

In evidence before the judge it became clear that the widow's means were some £2,137 a year from her pension, and at the time of the trial she had savings of about £200. Her evidence, as it eventually came out after cross-examination, was that her outgoings were some £1,346 a year, leaving a surplus between her income and her outgoings of some £791, but at least a third of that was attributable to the voluntary help which the executors – ie her stepson and daughter-in-law – afforded to her by paying quite a number of the expenses and outgoings of the house.

In those circumstances, the learned judge had two decisions to make: first, did the will make reasonable provision for the widow? Secondly, if it did not, what was the appropriate order to make?

I turn now to consider the relevant provisions of the Inheritance (Provision for Family and Dependants) Act 1975. Section 1(1)(a) makes it clear that a wife is a person who may make an application for provision. Section 1(2)(a) provides that in the case of an application made by a wife, 'reasonable financial provision' means 'such financial provision as it would be reasonable in all the circumstances of the case for a ...wife to receive, whether or not that provision is required for...her maintenance'. That, of course, was an expansion of what the old law had provided by way of the entitlement of a wife to make a claim. Section 2 deals with the type of orders that a court can make under the Act, and section 3(1) is in the following terms:

[His Lordship read out section 3(1).]

Then there are a number of matters listed in paragraphs (a) to (g), mainly of course dealing with financial matters – financial resources, the needs of the applicant, the size of the net estate – and concluding with paragraph (g):

> ... any other matter, including the conduct of the applicant or any other person, which in the circumstances of the case the court may consider relevant.

Then subsection (2) of section 3 of the Inheritance (Provision for Family and Dependants) Act 1975:

[His Lordship read out section 3(2).]

So, as I have said, the question which the learned judge had to decide was, first, did the will make reasonable provision for the widow? The learned judge dealt with that question at the bottom of page 31 of the transcript of the judgment, when he said:

> Taking those matters into account, I ask myself first of all, does the will make such financial provision as is reasonable in all the circumstances for the plaintiff to receive? I answer that question unhesitatingly, no; there is not enough here under the will. The limitation to an interest limited to her life in the house with a restriction on renting, assigning, subletting – that is of making any money out of the property and the total absence of any other income from the estate make it quite clear to me that there is not here, under this will, financial provision which is reasonable to the circumstances.

For my part I agree with what the learned judge said on this question. The will made no provision at all for supplementing out of capital any shortfall there might be in the life interest which the widow received; and in my judgement the learned judge was quite correct in saying that on this issue he could not take into account the voluntary provision which the stepson was making for his stepmother, because, of course, under the Act he was restricted to considering whether the combination of the will and the intestacy made reasonable provision for the widow.

So the second question arises: What order in the circumstances ought the court to have made? As I have said at the beginning of this judgment, the order which the learned judge in fact made was to give the widow the whole of the net estate, and the reasons he gave for making that order are as follows:

> I should say that factors that weigh most heavily with me in deciding on quantum are that there was a 20-year marriage, that there is no other person with a financial claim on the estate and that the plaintiff gave up her house and her job when she married on the understanding that they would find another house that was going to be in joint names but that never happened. It seems to me that in the circumstances the plaintiff is entitled to say she wants her independence, and the court should be slow to fix that quantum in a way which makes her dependent on the good will of the defendants for the rest of her life.
>
> There is one other factor to which I ought to refer, because it is relied on by the defendants. It may be wondered, from what I have said, why they are resisting the plaintiff's claim; the resistance is based on their understanding of the wishes of the deceased.

Then he sets out the passage which I have already read about the wish that there should not be anything for her to pass on to her son by a previous marriage. He continues:

> But bearing fully in mind that that was the intention of the deceased, it does not weigh heavily with me in the face of the case of the plaintiff, the fact remains that objectively regarded the will does not in my judgement make reasonable provision in all the circumstances, and reasonable provision for her is the prime object of any order the court makes.
>
> What is reasonable provision? Ought I to make any provision having regard to the generous offers made by Mr and Mrs Stephens? I think I should, because I must do the best I can with the net estate and because the offers are not secured. It would not be right in my judgement therefore to require the plaintiff to be dependent on the survival of the defendant Mr Stephens.
>
> It seems to me, there being no other financial claimants in this estate, the proper order is to say that the entire estate should be held on trust for the plaintiff. It will not give her very much room to manoeuvre, but at least she will be able to make her life. Whether she will be able to live in England and holiday abroad in the winter because of her arthritis, I cannot say. It seems, perhaps, unlikely, but at any rate the provision which I think it is reasonable to make for her is that the whole estate should be held on trust for her. That is the order I propose to make.

Mr Hedgecoe, who appeared for the respondent widow before this court, has submitted that the learned judge took into account all the factors which under the Act he was bound to take into account, and that therefore this court should not interfere with the exercise of what was undoubtedly a discretion on his part.

In my judgement, his exercise of the discretion on this aspect of the matter can be faulted in two particulars. First, it seems to me that he did not give full effect to that part of subsection (2) of section 3 of the Inheritance (Provision for Family and Dependants) Act 1975 about having regard to the provision which the widow might reasonably have expected to receive if on the day on which the deceased died the marriage had been terminated by a decree of divorce, bearing in mind that one would then have been dealing with two elderly people. What the learned judge said about that subsection was this (page 31B):

> Counsel on (the widow's) behalf relies on the provisions of section 3(2) of the Act and I accept, of course, that where the court is dealing with a plaintiff who is a widow it has to have regard to the provision which the applicant (the plaintiff) might have expected to receive if on the day on which the deceased died the marriage, instead of being terminated by death, had been terminated by a decree of divorce. Counsel argues that had there been a divorce the overwhelming probability is that, given the estate made up in this way and earlier sale by the plaintiff of her own house, there would have to have been a sale of the house and some capital provision would have been made for the plaintiff. I accept that, but note that on the hypothesis predicated there would have been two persons to provide for, while in the present case there is only one.

So what the learned judge appears to have done is to accept that the probable type of order on a divorce decree would have been a lump sum order – not necessarily in equal shares; it might have depended upon what income provision had been available – but certainly it is in the highest degree improbable in the circumstances of this case that an order on divorce would have given the whole of the available assets to one party (in this case the widow) and would not have divided them in any way. It does not seem right to me, with respect to the learned judge, to say that the answer to that is that on the hypothesis predicated there would have been two persons to provide for while in the present case there is only one, because in this context the other beneficiaries under the estate stand in the place of the husband in the event of a divorce.

Then again it seems to me that the learned judge's exercise of his discretion can be faulted, because, although he has stated what the deceased's reasons were, he said that they did not weigh heavily with him in the face of the case for the plaintiff. We have not in this country yet abolished the right of free testamentary disposition – the Inheritance (Provision for Family and Dependants) Act 1975 is of course an encroachment upon it – but, subject to a will not making reasonable provision for a dependant, the order which the court ought to make is to make proper provision for a dependant, bearing in mind the proper weight which should be given to the deceased's reasons for doing what he did. It seems to me, with respect, that the learned judge did not give any weight at all to the reasons why the deceased made the provision for his widow that he did, and, more particularly why he did not think it appropriate to give her the whole of his estate unencumbered.

Accordingly, if, as I have found, the learned judge did not exercise his discretion in a way which is not open to challenge, then it falls to this court to decide what is the proper order which he should have made and which we should now make. Essentially there are two courses open to us. As I have indicated, at the trial below the executors – also, of course, the residuary beneficiaries – made it clear that not merely were they prepared to continue to subvent the widow in the way in which they have already done, but were prepared to give undertakings to the court to that effect; and by their notice of appeal they have offered to repeat those undertakings to this court. The undertakings are basically to make good from their own funds the outgoings of Elsinore and also to pay the widow's fuel bills and television rental, and that would apply not only to Elsinore itself but to any property bought in substitution for it; to make up the shortfall in the cost of purchasing such substituted property, and to permit the plaintiff to take in such lodger or lodgers as they might reasonably approve; and in the course of argument, following a suggestion from the court, they agreed that they should secure those undertakings by giving a charge on their interest under the estate. But the widow continues to assert that what she requires most of all is her independence; and by analogy with the position on divorce, to which the court has to have regard, she asserts through her counsel that this is a case for a 'clean break'.

For my part I accept that submission that this is a case for a clean break, but nevertheless not a case for giving the widow the whole of the net estate. I would allow this appeal, direct that the house Elsinore be sold, and that out of the net proceeds of sale (and for this purpose treating the National Savings Certificates which were nominated to Mr Malcolm Stephens as part of the net estate) there be paid all the costs and expenses properly payable out of the estate, and what is left be divided between the widow and the residuary beneficiaries as to 60 per cent to the widow and 40 per cent to the residuary beneficiaries. That is the order which I would make.

PARKER LJ: I agree and have nothing to add.

SIR JOHN DONALDSON MR: I also agree.

Order: Appeal allowed. Order for costs below to stand. Costs in this court chargeable against estate on party and party basis. Legal aid taxation of respondent's costs.

Walker v Walker

Court of Appeal (Civil Division), 10 May 1988

The Appellant appeared in person.

M Blackett-Ord for the Respondent.

FOX LJ: This appeal relates to an application under the Inheritance (Provision for Family and Dependants) Act 1975 made by the former wife of Dr David Walker for provision out of his estate.

The plaintiff, Mrs Rosemary Myfanwy Eugenie Walker and Dr Walker were married in 1947. They had three children of the marriage. However, the marriage was dissolved by a Decree Absolute made in June 1975. Dr

Walker re-married the present defendant, Mrs Mary Irene Walker, in July 1975. By his Will, Dr Walker gave a few small legacies and the residue of his estate devolved to his second wife absolutely. The Will was made about 10 days before his death.

Consequent upon the dissolution of the marriage, the plaintiff made application to the court for ancillary relief, together with an application under the Married Women's Property Act in relation to certain chattels, the ownership of which is disputed by her.

At the time of the divorce, Dr Walker's main asset was his house, Lavender Cottage. In proceedings for ancillary relief an order was made in September 1976 for the house to be charged in favour of the plaintiff with an amount equal to one-third of its value. In addition the court ordered that Dr Walker should make to the plaintiff periodical payments during their joint lives at the rate of £10 per week. The one-third share in the property was ordered to be paid in effect as to two instalments of £1,500 each in March 1977 and June 1978. In fact they were not, but after Lavender Cottage was sold interest was ordered to be paid out of the proceeds of sale on the overdue instalments. In due course the amount of the instalments and interest which had accrued were paid.

In consequence of the order regarding the charging of an amount equal to one-third of the value of the house in favour of the plaintiff, in total, the plaintiff received approximately £7,899, which included all sums then outstanding under the earlier orders which were then due to her. £3,000 had to be paid to the Law Society in respect legal aid costs, and taking that deduction into account the Judge found that the plaintiff was entitled to £4,800 which was paid to her.

Dr Walker died in April 1983. Probate of his will was granted to the defendant as his sole personal representative. The estate consisted in the main of insurance policies.

Prior to his death, Dr Walker had ceased to carry on practice as a medical practitioner. He took up an appointment with the National Trust as a Warden of certain property in Cornwall. He and the defendant lived for some time at the National Trust property. When his employment with the Trust came to an end, he and the defendant lived in a flat in Poole which the defendant occupied as Warden of a hostel. After leaving Poole they moved to Norfolk where a house was purchased as joint tenants. Upon Dr Walker's death the house vested in the defendant absolutely by survivorship.

The total value of the net estate including chattels valued which the judge found (as he said, generously, at a figure of £5,000) was £29,998.

In September 1981 the Married Women's Property Act application relating to the chattels came before the Bournemouth County Court. In fact the plaintiff did not attend because she was ill. The court made an order that her application should be adjourned sine die, and the existing order for the periodical payment of £10 a week was ordered to be suspended. Dr Walker attended at that application.

The plaintiff says that she gave notice of an appeal against that decision, although Mr Blackett-Ord, who appears for the defendant, informs the court that those instructing him were unaware of the existence of such appeal. However, the plaintiff informed the court during the course of her address that she indicated to the County Court that her state of health did not permit of her proceeding with the matter, but that she would be pursuing her appeal when she was well enough to do so. In fact, she did not do so; nor did she make an application to lift the suspension upon the order suspending the periodical payments to her.

The plaintiff further informed the court that in the eighteen months which had elapsed between the September order and the death of Dr Walker she had not been well enough to proceed with any of the matters arising out of the orders of the County Court.

Judge Finlay found that after the marriage was dissolved the plaintiff had been the recipient of legacies involving sums which, together with £4,000 or so which she had received from the sale of Lavender Cottage, amounted to approximately £23,000. But from what the plaintiff told the court this morning there is some dispute as to that figure but I think such a dispute is not of consequence because she accepted that she received legacies of about £18,000 and as I understand what she said, there was included in the figure of £23,000 a sum of £4,000 which she received by order of the court in the ancillary proceedings. It would appear that after the marriage between her and Dr Walker was dissolved she received legacies amounting to £18,000.

The house in Norfolk in which the defendant lived with Dr Walker was sold after his death. The Judge found that the net proceeds of sale, after the discharge of a substantial mortgage, amounted to £5,000. The defendant used that £5,000 and other monies from the estate, to purchase a house in Poole for the sum of £22,000. We are told it was in a state of extreme disrepair and it was accepted by the Judge that the defendant spent a further £6,000 upon the property to put it in a satisfactory state of repair.

The plaintiff herself purchased a flat in Battersea for £14,000. It was a leasehold flat being held upon a term of 41 years from 1955. The lease therefore expires in 1996. She informed the court that the flat is in a bad state of repair and because of this she has been moved temporarily to other accommodation while repairs are carried out on the flat. She has received a grant towards those repairs so that when they are carried out she can return to the flat.

With regard to the question of the respective incomes of the parties, the plaintiff is on social security and, at the time of the hearing in July 1986 she was receiving from this source a total of £70.61p per week. It may be that the present figure of her income is higher, but that is not relevant for present purposes. Her flat in Battersea was valued at approximately £13,000.

The defendant has an income of some £4,960 a year, together with her earnings as an auxiliary nurse, which the Judge estimated at about £1,000 a year. Financially therefore, the defendant is in a better position than is the plaintiff.

As regards jurisdiction, however, the application was made under the Inheritance (Provision for Family and Dependants) Act 1975, to which I have referred.

[His Lordship read out Section 1(1), (2)(b).]

[His Lordship read out Section 3(1)]

The first question in issue in this case is: Was the disposition made by Dr Walker in his will such as to make reasonable financial provision for the plaintiff? That is to say such provision as would be reasonable in all the circumstances of the case for her to receive.

Consequent upon the break-up of the marriage, the court ordered what it regarded as a proper provision to make for the plaintiff by way of the one-third of the value of Lavender Cottage, together with the periodical payment of £10 per week during their joint lives. As I have said, Lavender Cottage was Dr Walker's main asset when the marriage ended.

Payment of the one-third share to the plaintiff was made together with the payment of £10 a week until, in consequence of the order of 9 September 1981, it was suspended.

If it be the case (as she tells the court) that the plaintiff appealed from that order, nothing was done in pursuance of that appeal by her in the eighteen months which elapsed between the making of the order and the death of Dr Walker. Indeed, she said she indicated to the County Court she would not proceed with it until she felt well enough to do so. She said she did not in fact feel well enough during that time. Equally, in the period of eighteen months, no step was taken by the plaintiff to make application to lift the suspension of the order in respect of the periodical payments of £10 a week.

The Judge said that when Dr Walker made his will ten days before his death in April 1983, he could reasonably have thought, first, that so far as capital was concerned, matters had been finalised when, in March 1989, following the sale of Lavender Cottage payment was made to the plaintiff of the one-third which was charged upon the proceeds of sale for the plaintiff's benefit by the order made in the Bournemouth County Court in pursuance of the plaintiff's application for ancillary relief in respect of a capital sum or a property adjustment order.

Secondly, so far as income is concerned, as I have said the order for periodical payments had been suspended in September 1981 and no application has been made to restore the periodical payments order. Even if Dr Walker was not aware of the legacies which the plaintiff received after their divorce, the Judge took the view (and in my view he was perfectly entitled so to do) that it was reasonable for Dr Walker, when making his will ten days before his death, to assume that financial matters between them had been finally disposed of.

I accept, of course, that Dr Walker and the plaintiff were married for a long time; they had three children. I am also prepared to accept when the plaintiff tells this court concerning the work she did for him and the family during the subsistence of the marriage and in that respect she had acted as a good wife. But this is a case in which it is necessary, first of all, to bear in mind that the net estate of Dr Walker consisted of the comparatively modest sum of £29,000, which was not sufficient to provide adequate maintenance for the two ladies concerned. Secondly, financial provision for the plaintiff had been made by the court in the manner I have indicated, and although it had in part been varied by the suspension of the periodical payments in 1981, nothing had occurred since that time to suggest that the plaintiff was seriously challenging that position.

The plaintiff told the court this morning that Dr Walker at the time he made his will was in a mental and physical state in which he was not capable of judging these matters, but there is no finding by the Judge of any mental incapacity, much less that Dr Walker's mental condition was such that he was not able to grasp simple facts regarding provision for the plaintiff. His will was proved in the ordinary way as a valid testamentary document.

Looking at the matter thus far, in my view when Dr Walker was considering the testamentary provisions ten days before his death, it was reasonable for him to conclude that, against the background which I have mentioned, it was not necessary for him to make further financial provision for the plaintiff in his will.

It is said that this was a case where assets were freed unlocked by his death. The main assets of the estate were the insurance policies, the largest of which, £15,000, was effected, not during the marriage of the plaintiff and Dr Walker, but during his marriage to the defendant. In total the monies from the policies did not provide enough by themselves, or indeed with any other assets, sufficient maintenance for both ladies. Dr Walker had to make a decision as to what was proper. Against the background to which I have referred, it seems to be it was reasonable for him to come to the conclusion which he did, and to make no provision for the plaintiff.

Looking at the whole matter therefore, and bearing in mind Dr Walker had re-married and had obligations to his second wife, even if one disregards (as I do for the present purposes) the fact that the plaintiff had received substantial sums from legacies prior to Dr Walker's death, I can see no reason to interfere with the conclusion to which the Judge came, in a careful judgment and after a review of all the circumstances of the case.

In those circumstances, I would dismiss this appeal.

MUSTILL LJ: I agree.

SIR RONALEYN CUMMING-BRUCE: I also agree.

Order: Appeal dismissed with costs. Legal aid taxation of defendant's costs.

Wallace v Thorburn

Court of Appeal (Civil Division), 9 October 1987

GM Jarand for the appellant.

The second applicant did not appear and was not represented.

H Swindells for the Respondent.

MAY LJ: This is an appeal from an order of His Honour Judge Morrison in the Mansfield County Court on 25 March 1987. He had before him on that occasion two applications by the first and second applicants, the first applicant being the appellant before us, for provision out of the estate of the first applicant's deceased husband. (I interpolate to say there had been a divorce before he died.) On those applications the learned judge ordered that provision to the extent of £7,200 should be made out of the estate in favour of the first applicant and to the extent of £800 in respect of the second applicant. There is no dispute about the provision for the second applicant, but the first applicant now appeals to this court asking that the order in her favour should be substantially increased.

It is convenient to refer to the relevant statutory provision at the outset. By section 1(1) of the Inheritance (Provision for Family and Dependants) Act 1975 it is provided that where a person dies domiciled in England and Wales and is survived by, amongst others, a former wife or children then these or any of them may apply to the court for an order under section 2 of the Act on the ground that the disposition of the deceased's estate effected by his will, which is the only relevant provision in the instant case, is not such as to make reasonable financial provision for the applicant. By subsection (2) a distinction is made in the meaning of the phrase 'reasonable financial provision' between the case of a surviving husband or wife on the one hand and a surviving person in any other of the classes referred to in subsection (1), amongst those, of course, being a former wife or a child of the deceased. In that latter case 'reasonable financial provision' by the subsection means such financial provision as it would be reasonable in all the circumstances of the case for the applicant to receive for his maintenance.

Section 2 of the Inheritance (Provision for Family and Dependants) Act 1975 gives the court power to make the appropriate provisions, referring to section 3 as containing matters to which the court ought to have regard in exercising its powers under section 2. It is unnecessary to go through the provisions of section 3. Suffice it to say that in general terms the court has to have regard to all the circumstances of the case to the extent that the court may consider it to be relevant. Thus it seems clear that the decision of a county court judge upon an application under section 2 of the Inheritance (Provision for Family and Dependants) Act 1975 in any particular case is pre-eminently a matter for the exercise of that judge's discretion. It follows that the Court of Appeal should be careful not to seek to supplant the judge's decision with a mere exercise of discretion on its part, unless it is demonstrated that the order of the court below was plainly wrong, or arrived at on a wrong basis, or, on the usual principles, if the court below has taken into account something which it ought not to have taken into account or has failed to take into account something which it ought to have taken into account. The jurisdiction of this court in appeals of this kind, particularly having regard to the specific provisions of sections 1, 2 and 3 of the Inheritance (Provision for Family and Dependants) Act 1975, is substantially restricted in that way and for those reasons.

Before coming to the facts of the case I wish briefly to refer to one of the two authorities to which our attention was helpfully directed, *Re Dennis (Deceased)* [1981] 2 All ER 140. In that case, in considering what was meant by the word 'maintenance' in sections 1, 2 and 3 of the Inheritance (Provision for Family and Dependants) Act 1975, Browne-Wilkinson J (as he then was) at page 145 said this:

> The word 'maintenance' is not as wide as that [ie a suggestion that it was the equivalent of providing for the well-being or benefit of the applicant]. The court, up until now, declined to define the exact meaning of the word 'maintenance' and I am certainly not going to

> depart from that approach. But in my judgement the word 'maintenance' connotes only payments which, directly or indirectly, enable the applicant in the future to discharge the cost of his daily living at whatever standard of living is appropriate to him. The provision that is to be made is to meet recurring expenses, being expenses of living of an income nature. This does not mean that the provision need be by way of income payments. The provision can be by way of a lump sum, for example, to buy a house in which the applicant can be housed...

On the facts of the instant case I would respectfully agree with that dictum. It may not be – and was never intended to be – a complete definition of the word 'maintenance' in the relevant statutory provision, but I think it has particular application in the present case.

Referring to the relevant facts in this case, in May 1950 the first applicant, the appellant before us, Mrs Wallace, was married to her husband ('the deceased'). She and her husband lived together for a period of some 33 years. In the course of that time five children were born to the couple and Mrs Wallace, with the help of her husband, brought them up. At any rate latterly, and it may be throughout the marriage, the latter was a miner. Difficulties arose in the marriage and upon a petition dated August 1982 a decree nisi was pronounced in September of that year and made absolute in February 1983. In the course of the marriage the matrimonial home at 26 Hardwick Drive, Ollerton was bought. After the decree nisi and at about the time of the decree absolute the deceased left that matrimonial home and it was subsequently sold for a net sum, to which I shall refer hereafter.

A final periodical payments order by way of ancillary relief was made in favour of the appellant against the deceased after divorce in the sum of £53 a week. That will give an indication of the level of earnings of the deceased and the standard of living that the parties were used to.

On 16 May 1985 the deceased executed a will by which he left his estate to the respondent. He died on 26 May 1985. Probate was granted to the respondent in July 1985.

The respondent is a lady who was herself also married. She worked with, or in the same place as, the deceased and they have known each other for some ten years. They became friendly and, as the learned judge said in the course of his judgment, 'There is not the slightest doubt he and she were seeing each other regularly and frequently and that she, having been herself divorced with a working son, gave to him very considerable help and solace. There is no suggestion of them living together as man and wife. She assisted him in obtaining new accommodation, with his laundry and feeding. No doubt as a result of all that, the deceased came to dispose of his estate to Mrs Thorburn [the respondent].' (I should add that the deceased was 58 years of age when he died. The appellant before us was herself 58, as it appears from the judgment at the time of the application before the judge. The respondent is 54 years of age.)

After the decree absolute the matrimonial home was sold in 1985 and realised £20,196 net of mortgage and other liabilities. In March 1985 £4,000 of those proceeds of sale was paid to the deceased and £4,000 to the appellant. The balance was subject to a further deduction for conveyancing costs and was held by a solicitor, because there remained a dispute between the deceased and the appellant about where a second mortgage liability of about £1,361 should lie. The question was whether that was a liability of both parties, or whether it was a liability solely of the deceased. In those circumstances on 9 March 1986 the balance held by the solicitor was just over £12,600 including interest. That was dealt with in this way. It was calculated that the appellant would be entitled to at least half of that, save for the disputed £1,361, and accordingly a payment was made to her solicitors of £5,645. The balance of £7,006 was retained in the names of the solicitors of both parties and was treated at the hearing of the application under the 1975 Act as an estate asset. The £5,645 initially held by the solicitors at this time for the appellant was then dealt with as follows, namely, £3,000 was retained by them in respect of potential costs as the appellant was legally aided and some £2,645 was paid out to her. It has subsequently been agreed that the costs of this matter, at any rate up to this appeal, should be dealt with out of the estate, and consequently that £3,000 inures to the benefit of the appellant. She dealt with the sum of £2,645 by spending £1,645 on furnishing her flat and on clothing and personal expenses for herself and the second applicant and retained the balance of £1,000. Thus, with the £3,000 which is now available to be released to her because of the agreement as to costs, she has capital of some £4,000.

Before coming to the estate itself, I deal with the two principal parties concerned and their circumstances, the appellant lives in a flat. It is not an expensive flat. She derives her income from supplementary benefit. She is not in the best of health and, as the learned judge found, she has no prospect of gainful employment because of her age and her health. 'It is unrealistic to suppose', said the learned judge, 'that she depends on anything other than benefit.'

So far as the respondent is concerned, she has her own house on mortgage, but it, too, is modest in the extreme, being a small prefabricated house of small value. She is in employment as a canteen assistant and has been such at all material times. Her evidence before the learned judge, which he accepted, was that she expected shortly to be made redundant.

Those were the circumstances of the relevant parties when the matter came before the learned judge.

In so far as the appellant's case was concerned, she was making no claim for periodical payments. Even if it were practical so to order, they would only be discounted against her supplementary benefit and be of little practical use to her. On the other hand she was seeking an award of capital, because she had made an informal arrangement to buy a small two bedroomed terrace house at a price of £15,750 which with costs would involve an investment of £16,000. For reasons which will be readily apparent from what I have already said, she was not a good candidate for a mortgage and the case put before the learned judge on her behalf was that she ought to have capital to realise her ambition of owning either that house to which I have referred, or something similar. However, as the learned judge commented, 'It seems that Mrs Wallace, [the appellant] has had no expert advice with regard to the purchase of this house, and there is many a slip between cup and lip.'

Against those circumstances I turn to the estate itself. As I have mentioned, the deceased was a miner and a substantial part of his estate comprised his entitlement under the National Coal Board Pension Scheme. That apparently amounted to £17,214 or thereabouts. There are still held to his credit the balance of the proceeds of sale of the matrimonial home amounting to £7,000 and when one added on interest of £1,131 there was a gross total for the estate of £25,352. There were estate liabilities of nearly £4,000 and consequently the net estate was £21,355, but of course that had to be reduced for the purposes of the present application by the aggregate of the costs of both sides, which it has been agreed should be paid out of the estate. We are told that they were estimated at an aggregate of £3,500, so the learned judge was dealing with an estate of £17,855.

Mindful of the restricted jurisdiction of this court to disturb an exercise by the learned judge below of his discretion in this matter, Mr Jarand's submissions on behalf of the appellant were twofold. First he submitted that when one looks at the relative circumstances of the appellant on the one hand and the respondent on the other, there may be little to choose between them, except that one must bear in mind the respondent is in employment, albeit subject to redundancy, and has a modest house of her own. But, he submits, one has also to bear in mind that this was a long marriage of 33 years and there were five children to the upbringing of which the appellant no doubt gave her time and attention for a substantial period and making a home for the deceased. In those circumstances, when one looks at a net estate of £18,000 and compares the long marriage on the one hand with the ten years friendship on the other, albeit one has no doubt that in the last years of his life the respondent was a great help and, as the learned judge said, solace to the deceased. The award of £7,200 in respect of the appellant was wholly inadequate.

Were that submission the only one made on behalf of the appellant in this case, I would have considerable doubts whether this appeal should succeed. However the learned judge concluded his judgment in this way:

> I have come to the conclusion that Mrs Wallace is entitled to financial provision in the sum of £7,200. I am satisfied that if made to her, together with her assets and capital, if she wishes to purchase a house, she will be in a financial position to do so.

The learned judge gave no explanation of that last sentence of his judgment, nor of how he had reached the figure of £7,200, or perhaps the figure of £8,000, when one takes into account the £800 which he awarded to the second appellant. With respect to him, and without such explanation, it is impossible to justify the conclusion which he expressed in the last sentence by the evidence that he had before him. The appellant only had capital to the extent of £4,000. If one adds that to the £7,200 which the judge awarded, one only reaches £11,200 which, on the evidence that the learned judge had before him, was not enough to buy a house, nor was it in any way sufficient to pursue a change of house.

I am therefore driven to the conclusion that the exercise of discretion of the learned judge below is susceptible to valid challenge in that the ultimate figure was arrived at either by an approach, the nature of which one cannot discern, or alternatively by an approach which on its face was wholly wrong. When one adds to that the further submission, which by itself would not have been enough, that out of an estate of some £18,000 an award of £8,000 to the appellant and the son is plainly wrong, I think Mr Jarand has made out his contention that the award of the judge below cannot stand.

In those circumstances it falls to this court to exercise its own discretion in reaching an appropriate figure. I start with the net estate of £17,800, from which I deduct the £800 awarded to the second appellant, leaving a net figure of £17,000. Leaving that figure for the moment, I turn to the £16,000 which on the evidence may be needed as the purchase price of a house for the appellant. I would not be minded to allow her the £7,000 which Mr Jarand suggested was necessary to cover the costs of moving. Against that £16,000 I set, first, £1,000 being an estimate of the amount that may come to her after the resolution of the dispute with regard to the second mortgage. Even if that figure is not to be taken into account, one has to bear in mind the £4,000 which she still has, which reduces the figure of £16,000 to £11,000. One can never be precise in the arithmetic, and if one takes £11,000 off an estate of £17,000, it leaves only £6,000 for the respondent. That, I think, is unjust in so far as the respondent is concerned.

Accordingly, approaching the matter on that basis, in my judgement, the proper figure for the learned judge to have awarded the appellant in the circumstances of the instant case would have been the sum of £10,000. I appreciate that figure, together with the free capital that she presently has, will not be enough to enable her to buy immediately the house, evidence in respect of which was given before the learned judge. On the other hand, I do not forget that there are four children in addition to the second applicant, into the circumstances of whom one need not go further, and such facilities as may be available to enable this lady to borrow whatever balance is necessary to enable her to acquire a modest house in which to live and which properly comes within the phrase in section 1(2)(b) of the Inheritance (Provision for Family and Dependants) Act 1975 as being a financial provision reasonable in all the circumstances for her to receive for her maintenance.

I would allow this appeal. I would set aside the order of £7,000 in the appellant's favour and substitute an order of £10,000, leaving the order in relation to the second applicant of £800 as it is.

WOOLF LJ: I entirely agree with the order proposed by my Lord and I also agree with the reasoning expressed by my Lord, though I will deal separately with the question of the sum which has been retained for the purposes of the second mortgage.

The learned judge in his judgment, apart from the portion of that judgment to which my Lord referred which appears at the end of his judgment, clearly sets out his process of reasoning. However, that reasoning, having regard to the assets available, produced a position where the net estate left by the deceased was not such as would meet the modest capital requirements of the applicant to enable her to purchase a home for herself out of the sum available as a consequence of the death of the deceased. Had there been a sufficient sum, then I would certainly have regarded it as a proper exercise of the jurisdiction under the Inheritance (Provision for Family and Dependants) Act 1975 to order the full sum sought by the applicant before the learned judge and before this court. However, in my view the court below was forced to accept that a lesser sum than that required by the applicant was the appropriate sum to award and in so far as the learned judge in the final paragraphs purported to be awarding a sum which in itself would enable the applicant to purchase a home, that was clearly wrong. In those circumstances, exercising our discretion afresh, the appropriate course is for the court to adopt such sum which is reasonable, having regard to the statutory provision, which will at least put the applicant in a position where she has a substantial springboard to enable her to do so. With regard to the figure of £10,000 which, like my Lord, I regard as being appropriate, I take the net estate as being £21,355.71. That sum was calculated on the basis that £1,361.36 was being treated as an asset of the estate. Accordingly that sum would come out of the estate and the calculations that thereafter followed were on that basis. In taking that view I am reflecting what is set out in the skeleton argument for the applicant at page 4, which indicates that the balancing sum of £7,006.61, which was retained in the names of the solicitors of both parties, was at the hearing treated as an estate asset. Accordingly, in reaching the sum of £10,000 as being appropriate, I recognise that out of the estate there has to come the sum required to pay the second mortgage, and that sum will not in any circumstances of the applicant. However, irrespective of the accuracy of my understanding of the position, I would still regard £10,000 as being the appropriate sum, though I would welcome the assistance of counsel as to whether my understanding of the situation is correct.

Accordingly I agree that this appeal must be allowed to the extent that the sum ordered by the learned judge should be increased to £10,00 in respect of the first applicant.

Order: Appeal allowed. No order as to costs. Legal aid taxation both sides.

Re Whittle

Court of Appeal (on appeal from Ungoed-Thomas J, Chancery Division) Lord Denning MR, Stamp and James LJJ 5 March 1983
Gerald Godfrey QC and *VR Chapman* for the Appellant (Defendant).
George Dillon QC and *T Cullen* for the Respondent (Plaintiff).

The Master of the Rolls: In this case a widow (who was cut out of the will of her husband) claims that a reasonable provision should be made for her under the Inheritance (Provision for Family and Dependants) Act 1975. Husband and wife married on 10 July 1926. She was older than he was. She was 25 and he was 21. They were both in humble circumstances in Shropshire. He was a miner; and her father was a miner. They had no children. After some 15 years, in 1941, they separated, when she was 40 and he was 36. It may have been his fault; we do not know; but, at all events, he formed an association with a younger woman and has lived with her continuously ever since. By this young woman he had a son Ronald, who was born in 1943, and a daughter who was born in 1957. From 1941 onwards the husband lived with the lady. She changed her name to his. She lived with him as his wife, whereas the true wife, from whom he separated in 1941, after a time went to a little house in Coventry. There was a deed of separation under which the husband paid his wife £2 a week from 1941 onwards. She occasionally had a little extra at Christmas – £10, it may be – and later somewhat more. On 16 April 1970 he died.

Meanwhile he and his family had prospered. They had a family business as travel operators and running coaches. He ran it with his brothers. Afterwards, when his son Ronald grew up, the son ran it with him. It prospered exceedingly. They took over other concerns and had shares in those companies. During this time, that is for 29 years, he was helped by the lady with whom he was living and his son. He made very considerable provision for them in his lifetime. There has been a good deal of discussion of the figures; but it does seem that, by way of shares, houses and so forth and shares in the business, he gave the lady with whom he was living anything from £34,000 to £50,000 or more. He gave his son Ronald large sums – at least £37,000. It might even have been a great deal more. He gave his daughter £37,000. It would look as if he made provision during his life for them in a sum of at least £200,000. Then, as I have said, he died on 16 April 1970.

By his will, apart from two small legacies of £350 to a niece and nephew, he left the whole of the residue of his estate to his son Ronald. The residue of that estate is certainly very considerable. Even after payment of duty, it would look as though it would be at least in the region of £60,000; but he cut out his wife completely. Now the question is, what is reasonable provision for her in all the circumstances. As I have said £2 a week was all the separation allowance she had. That is all the family offered her. Later on they offered £5. Counsel for the widow suggested that she should have £1,500 a year. The Judge accepted this figure and awarded it. Now there is an appeal saying it should be reduced to £750 or, at all events, no more than £1,000. As I see it, the position is this: the husband has made ample provision for the lady with whom he lived so long and for his son and daughter. His widow spent the best years of her life with him from the time she was 25 till she was 41. She saved enough to buy a little house in Coventry for £1,250. She has also managed to save a sum of £600. Apart from that she has nothing. She is living on an old age pension of £6 or £7 a week. The question is, what is the reasonable provision for her? The judge pointed out that £1,500 after tax would only be £900 a year; and that a reasonable expenditure to keep her out of penury would be £600 or £700 a year. That would be nothing on account of what is called 'jam on the bread.' On the circumstances of this case I must say that, having regard to the size of the estate and the years and years in which the widow has lived, as the Judge said, almost cheek by jowl with poverty, the Judge was entirely justified in saying that a reasonable provision in the circumstances would be £1,500 a year. I see nothing wrong with the Judge's judgment and would dismiss the appeal accordingly.

Lord Justice Stamp: I agree. Having regard to the size of the estate and the absence of any other moral obligation by this testator, I think he would have been acting unreasonably to have left his wife – his true wife – with less than £1,500 a year, and I would dismiss the appeal.

LORD JUSTICE JAMES: I also would dismiss the appeal for the reasons already given in the judgments.

Appeal dismissed with costs.

Winfield v Billington and another
Court of Appeal (Civil Division), 30 July 1990
D McConville for the Appellant.
J Cousins for the Respondents.

NOURSE LJ: This is an appeal from a decision of His Honour Judge Stuart-White given in the Redditch County Court as long ago as 21 July 1987 on an application under the Inheritance (Provision for Family and Dependants) Act 1975. The applicant is Mr Robert David Winfield. The application is made in respect of the estate of his deceased wife Gillian Ann Winfield. They were married in June 1977, he was at the age of 23 and she at the age of 21. In the same year they purchased a house, No 40 Cheswick Close, Winyates Green, Redditch. They purchased it in joint names for £9,500, of which £2,000 was paid as a deposit and the balance was raised on mortgage. £1,000 of the £2,000 deposit was provided by Mrs Winfield's parents, Mr and Mrs Billington.

There were two children of the marriage, Barry Graham Winfield born 20 August 1979, who is nearly 11 years old, and Paul John Winfield born on 13 June 1983, who is now seven years old. Very sadly, Mrs Winfield developed multiple sclerosis in 1979 and that had a progressive effect on her health. Relations between Mr and Mrs Winfield deteriorated and in March 1983, before Paul was born, they separated. In April 1983 Mrs Winfield petitioned for divorce on the grounds of Mr Winfield's unreasonable behaviour. He filed an answer denying the allegation, but there was no cross-petition. On 13 March 1984 Mrs Winfield was given leave to proceed by a supplemental petition alleging adultery. That petition was to proceed undefended and had it not been for Mrs Winfield's death on 31 March 1984 it would have resulted in a decree nisi. On her death the suit abated.

Immediately before her death the children, who had been living with Mrs Winfield at her parents' home, returned to Mr Winfield, with whom they have lived ever since. He has now remarried, his wife being Diane Margaret Winfield. They have a child, Amy Claire, who was born on 25 May 1986.

On 18 November 1983, after the commencement of the divorce proceedings, Mrs Winfield left her last will. Having appointed her parents, Mr and Mrs Billington, to be the executors and trustees thereof, she left the whole of her net estate to such of her two children as should survive her and attain the age of 18 years. If more than one in equal shares absolutely. Also in 1983 Mrs Winfield duly gave notice severing the beneficial joint tenancy in the matrimonial home, No 40 Cheswick Close, with the result that her half-share of the proceeds of sale passed under the terms of her will. She also owned investments worth about £9,000.

Probate of Mrs Winfield's will was granted to Mr and Mrs Billington on 18 June 1984. They were made the respondents in this application, which was instituted on 3 January 1985. In August 1986 an agreement was made between the parties for the sale of the former matrimonial home and the re-investment of the proceeds in a new property, 5 Boxnott Close, Webheath, Redditch, as a home for Mr and Mrs Winfield and the three children. That property was purchased in part with the assistance of a further mortgage, and Mr Winfield's new wife made a loan of £1,000.

In these proceedings Mr Winfield has not sought to disturb the dispositions of Mrs Winfield's will in regard of the £9,000 worth of investments. But he has at all times maintained that he ought to receive the whole of her one-half beneficial interest in the former matrimonial home. That plea was rejected by Judge Stuart-White. He came to the conclusion that the correct course was to reduce the presumptive share of the two children in the new house, which had been settled by agreement at one quarter, to one sixth and that the children should take their interests at age 21, instead of age at 18. He therefore made an order that Mrs Winfield's half share of the proceeds of sale of the former matrimonial home should be transferred to Mr Winfield absolutely, conditionally upon his charging the new home with payment of a sum equivalent to one sixth of its value to the children age at 21. In the result, Mr Winfield would remain the owner of the new home until the younger of the two boys attained the age of 21, at which stage he would have to raise one sixth of its then value, either by sale or by a further charge, and account for that one sixth to the two boys. Mr Winfield now appeals against that order.

Mr McConville, for Mr Winfield, has placed a particular reliance on section 1(2) and 3(2) of the 1975 Act. Section 1(2)(a) applies a special definition of 'reasonable financial provision' to the case of a surviving spouse and section 3(2) provides that, without prejudice to the generality of the other matters which the court must take into account on an application of this kind, the court must have regard to certain additional considerations in the case of a surviving spouse. In particular, the court has to have regard to the provision which the applicant might reasonably have expected to receive if, on the day on which the deceased died, the marriage, instead of being terminated by death, had been terminated by a decree of divorce.

Mr McConville's argument assumes, first, that if there had been a divorce custody of the two children would have been granted to Mr Winfield. He then submits that if this had been application in ancillary relief proceedings there is every likelihood – indeed he would say, a high probability – that an unconditional transfer of property order would have been made in Mr Winfield's favour in relation to the whole of Mrs Winfield's half-share of the beneficial interest in the former matrimonial home. What the judge said about that was this. Having regard to sections 1(2) and section 3(2), he continued:

> In fact there would have been a divorce had the deceased survived longer. However I do not derive much assistance from that. There

> is uncertainty regarding the children's custody that would have been crucial to any order being made as to the matrimonial home. It might have been that the children would have gone to the mother at their grandparents or it might be the father would have had custody of them at the former matrimonial home. It is impossible to make any assumptions. It no doubt depended on the course of the deceased's illness or otherwise if it improved.

Mr McConville accepts that all this is very much a matter of speculation at the worst or of reasonable assumption at the best. Clearly the judge for his part did not assume that custody would have been granted to Mr Winfield. I am bound to say that Mr McConville has failed to show that the learned judge acted on some error of principle or exercised his discretion in a manner which was plainly wrong. It is only if he can establish one or the other of those two things that Mr Winfield can ask this court to interfere with his order. It cannot be said that the judge was plainly wrong in not deriving very much assistance from the divorce analogy. Mr McConville was disposed to accept, I think, that if an unconditional transfer of property order had been made in respect of the whole of Mrs Winfield's share, Mr Winfield would certainly have been ordered to pay her maintenance. Equally, it seems to me to have been quite possible, depending on the situation of the parties at the time, that the court would have made some order to the same effect as the judge's order in this case. It would have been perfectly reasonable for the court to take the view that, even if custody was awarded to the husband, provision should nevertheless be made, by way of a deferred charge, for the wife to receive a share of the equity in the former matrimonial home when the children's up-bringing had been completed.

Whether that be right or wrong, I repeat that Mr McConville has failed to satisfy me that there is any ground on which this court can interfere with the order which the judge, in the exercise of his discretion and having taken all relevant considerations into account, thought that is was appropriate for him to make. I would therefore dismiss this appeal.

PARKER LJ: I agree. This was a matter of discretion and unless the learned judge could be shown to have misdirected himself in law or taken into account something that he should not have taken into account or vice versa or was plainly wrong this court will not interfere. It is not suggested that he misdirected himself and if it were he plainly did not. It appears to me that he took into account everything he should have taken into account, omitted nothing and his decision, far from being plainly wrong, was plainly right. I too would dismiss the appeal.

Order: Appeal dismissed with costs; order for costs not to be enforced without leave of the court; charge against the appellant's share of the property to stand; legal aid taxation of appellant's costs; if and insofar as the respondent is unable to recover her costs from other sources they should be paid out of the estate; application for costs against the Legal Aid Board adjourned for 10 weeks.

Re Wood

Chancery Division Mervyn Davies J, 2 April 1982
[also noted in (1982) LS Gaz 774]
C Heath for the Plaintiff.
R Pearce for the Defendants.

Mr Justice Mervyn Davies: This is a daughter's application under the Inheritance (Provision for Family and Dependants) Act 1975. The plaintiff is Miss Elizabeth Ann Wood, who is now 30 years of age. Miss Wood is the only child of Mrs Ann Wood, the deceased, who died intestate on 4 April 1980. Her father is the first defendant. Since 11 June 1969 Miss Wood has resided at Langdon Hospital in Dawlish. I have read an affidavit sworn on 3 July 1981 by Mr Lawrence Frederick William Rowe, who is a consultant psychiatrist and who works at Langdon Hospital. He is the medical officer professionally responsible for Miss Wood. The affidavit is distressing disclosing that Miss Wood is severely mentally subnormal, incapable of speech and with understanding of only the simplest and most basic matters. Mr Rowe states that there is no reason why Miss Wood should not live for another 30 years. I have also seen a copy of a previous affidavit by Mr Rowe sworn on 23 September 1980. There Mr Rowe states that the duration of Miss Wood's disorder has been since birth and that the prospects of mental recovery are nil. However, there he indicates that Miss Wood is capable of appreciating extra comforts and clothing. The affidavit just mentioned was sworn, as I understand, when an application was made to the Court of Protection for authority to make an application under the 1975 Act on Miss Wood's behalf. In consequence of the application, the Official Solicitor was on 4 November 1980 authorised by the Court of Protection to take and conduct such proceedings as he might be advised on Miss Wood's behalf against the estate of the deceased under the 1975 Act. In this way there is an application before me by Miss Wood, Miss Wood suing by the Official Solicitor as her next friend.

The deceased died, as I have said on 4 April 1980 and died intestate. On 4 July 1980 letters of administration to her estate were granted to her husband, William Edward John Wood, and his son Gerald Maxwell Wood, out of the Bristol District Probate Registry. Mr GM Wood was not a son of the deceased. He was a son of Mr WEJ Wood by Mr WEJ Wood's first marriage. The plaintiff's application under the Act is by the originating summons dated 22 December 1980. The defendants are named as the deceased's administrators, that is to say, Messrs WEJ and GM Wood. Mr WEJ Wood died on 18 January 1981. He left a will appointing his son, the second defendant, as sole executor and beneficiary. It appears that no order to carry on against the second defendant alone was made before the hearing before me, and so I have made such an order.

The consequence of the deceased's intestacy was that her husband took a statutory legacy of £25,000 and a life interest in half the residue of the deceased's estate. Subject to those benefits the plaintiff is entitled to the deceased's estate. Unfortunately the statutory legacy of £25,000 will account for nearly the whole of the deceased's estate, so that unless an order is made in the plaintiff's favour under the Act, she will receive very little indeed from her mother's estate. The letters of administration show the deceased's estate as being of a worth of £33,825 but it is common ground that that figure is not accurate. Before me counsel proceeded on the footing that the deceased's estate was worth £26,737.25 as disclosed in Exhibit GMW 1 to an affidavit of the second defendant sworn on 12 October 1981. Accordingly the plaintiff's benefit under the deceased's intestacy in the events which have happened is £1,737.25. As I have said, the first defendant's estate passes to the second defendant, so that any provision to be made for the plaintiff will have to be made at the expense of the second defendant. No other person appears to me to be concerned in the plaintiff's application.

Mr Heath appeared for the plaintiff. He referred to the Act and, in particular, to sections 1, 2, 3 and 25. Mr Heath submitted that two questions arise for consideration: (1) are the dispositions effected by the operation of the intestacy law such as to make reasonable financial provision for the applicant? (2) if not, what provision, if any, should be made pursuant to section 2 of the Act? Mr Pearce appeared for the defendant. I did not understand him to contend with any force that the first question should be answered in the affirmative. It was, I think, accepted, and rightly accepted, that the intestacy rule did not operate to make reasonable provision for the plaintiff. In this connection it is to be noted that the second defendant in his affidavit sworn on 12 October 1981 offers to pay to the plaintiff's receiver the sum of £5,000 in addition to the plaintiff's right under intestacy. In other words the second defendant is content to see £6,737.25 paid to the plaintiff.

I turn to the second question. It seems to me that this is a case where an order should be made. The appropriate order is, as I understand, 'for such financial provision as would be reasonable in all the circumstances of the case for the applicant to receive for her maintenance'. See section 1(2)(b) and *Re Coventry* [1980] Ch 461. *Re Coventry* suggests that maintenance in the context of the Act does not relate merely to subsistence but may have a more general construction: see pp 485 and 494.

It is section 2 of the Act which empowers the court to make an order, but certain guidelines respecting the exercise of that power are set out in section 3 of the Act. I propose now to consider the matters mentioned in section 3. First one has to have regard to the financial resources and financial needs which the applicant has or is likely to have in the foreseeable future. The terms, 'financial resources' and 'financial needs' are explained in section 3(6). In this case the applicant's financial resources are as follows. In the way of capital she has an absolute interest in the sum of £1,750 under a trust set up by her grandfather, the trust being called the James Whitwell Trust. As well the applicant has £801 in an account held at the hospital together with another £968 held for her in another account at the hospital, this other account being called her mobility account. So in all there is capital totalling £3,519. Mr Pearce said that that capital sum may well have increased since the time of the filing of the evidence in this case. I accept that that may be in some small degree. As well as this capital the applicant has certain state benefits. She receives an invalidity pension of £283.40 a year and a mobility allowance of £754 a year, so that she has an income of

£1,037 a year. I was told that these annual sums are or are about to be made tax free.

I now turn to the applicant's financial needs. I find it difficult to say what are the financial needs of a person in the applicant's unhappy situation, but I will mention the sums which, according to the evidence, are or could be usefully spent in making the applicant's life a little better. Taking para 7 of the first affidavit of the second defendant, it seems that £497 per year is spent on the applicant: clothing (£100), pocket money and presents (£41), and weekly hydrotherapy sessions (£356). These are modest sums. Then there is an annual sum required for the provision and maintenance of an electric wheelchair. Maintenance of the chair costs between £150 and £200 a year, and, if one is to buy a new chair every ten years, then a sinking fund of £140 a year is necessary, since a good new chair is likely to cost £1,400. So £290 or £340 a year is necessary in the way of chair provision and maintenance. Thus so far, one may say that financial needs amount to £497 plus £290 or £787 in total, or £497 plus £340 which would make £837 in total. There is then the matter of outings and holidays. I understand that Miss Wood is appreciative of outings and holidays. I refer in this connection to the two affidavits of Mrs GP Brocklehurst, an administrative assistant responsible for patient affairs at Langdon Hospital, and to an affidavit of Mrs Betty Eileen Jones, a state registered nurse at the Langdon Hospital. In her affidavit sworn on 30 June 1981, Mrs Brocklehurst says in para 8:

> Langdon Hospital is normally able to arrange for someone in Elizabeth's position to be taken out by Hospital staff on regular private trips on the terms that the Hospital is duly reimbursed both the amount of the direct costs of each outing and also for the time of the staff involved. In the case of nursing staff time is costed on the basis that there are 1,800 hours in a working year and that one hour therefore costs 1/1,800 of the basic annual salary of the person concerned. At current salary levels this formula produces hourly rates that vary from £1.75 to £2.24 in the case of a Nursing Assistant and from £2.23 to £2.69 in the case of a qualified Nurse (the exact amount depending in each case on the seniority of the person concerned).

Paragraph 9:

> At current rates therefore the cost to Elizabeth of a 6-hour round trip involving a mileage of (say) 50 miles on which she was accompanied by a Nurse would be of the order of £43 made up as follows: Cost of Nurse.....£13.92; Cost of Driver.....£13.01; Petrol.....£5; Subsistence for Nurse, £2.85; Subsistence for driver, £2.85; Pocket money for Elizabeth, £5; total £42.63.

Paragraph 10:

> This estimate is of course no more than an illustration. The total cost would naturally depend on the qualifications and the seniority of the Nurse, the distance covered, the amount of any entrance fees

incurred, etc, and the cumulative effect of variations in these different factors could be quite considerable.

Mrs Brocklehurst goes on:

> I am advised by the Senior Physiotherapist at Langdon Hospital, namely, Mrs M Caunter and I believe (a) that Elizabeth would benefit if the attendant controlled electric wheelchair recently purchased for her by the second defendant were to be fitted with a heavy duty battery which would enable the wheelchair to be operated over a greater distance before the battery needed to be recharged; (b) that Elizabeth enjoys hydrotherapy which at present she normally receives once a week and that she would benefit from two extra sessions a week. The cost of a heavy duty battery is at present about £70. Elizabeth will have to provide funds for the maintenance of the wheelchair, and these I estimate between £300.00 and £1,000.00. Additional hydrotherapy sessions can be supplied at Langdon Hospital at a cost of £3.42 each.

In her affidavit sworn on 22 January 1982 Mrs Brocklehurst says:

> In my affidavit of 13 June 1981 I referred to the cost of private trips for Elizabeth. The regularity of such trips would depend upon the availability of a nurse but they could easily be accommodated on at least a monthly basis. Elizabeth would benefit from as many trips as possible, ideally once a week when her mother was alive and it may be possible to arrange more frequently than once a month if a nurse was available.

She goes on:

> In addition to such trips on a regular basis Elizabeth, who greatly enjoys outings, would appreciate benefit from going on holiday. She used to spend holidays at home for up to two months a year when her mother was alive. The opportunity for patients such as Elizabeth to be taken on holiday increases each year as more specialised accommodation for the handicapped becomes available. The cost varies greatly, but as an illustration some of the patients of The Royal Western Counties Hospital stayed at a hotel in Blackpool run by the Mencap Society (the Society for the mentally handicapped) last year at the charge of £8.50 per person per day, for bed, breakfast and evening meal. Other patients went on a self-catering holiday at Butlins Holiday Camps where the costs of a four berth flatlet varies form £62.90 to £205.50 depending on the time of the year. If Elizabeth were to go on such a holiday she would in addition have to meet from her private funds, a proportion of the cost of nursing assistance and travelling expenses which would be shared equally between her and the other patients.

Then in paragraph 4 of this same affidavit, Mrs Brocklehurst says:

> New equipment is continually being designed and manufactured which improves and assists the handicapped person. For example,

> on behalf of one of the patients there has been recently purchased from his private funds a special bed/chair which enables a bedridden patient to 'sit' out from bed comfortably and for longer periods of time than was previously possible. The cost of such a piece of equipment is very high, in this case approximately £500 and while the National Health Service would like to provide specialised equipment and furniture for all the patients who need it, this is obviously impossible and so, in many cases, the patient's own personal piece of equipment is purchased from that patient's private funds. It is impossible to foresee what equipment Elizabeth will benefit from in the future and of course what new inventions there will be. However, if Elizabeth's physical condition deteriorates further then consideration would be given to purchasing any available equipment which would be of assistance to her.

Much to the same effect has been the affidavit of Mrs Betty Jones that I have mentioned. These extracts show that the applicant's needs, as I would understand them for a person in her situation, would extend to being provided with outings and holidays as well being provided with new aids that have been mentioned as and when such aids become available or found to be suitable for the applicant's use. If outings were to be provided, say, twice a month, then on Mrs Brocklehurst's figure about £1,200 a year would be required. Taken with a figure of £240 for holiday there would be a total figure for outings and holidays of £1,440. Adding that figure to the figures of £497 and £340 already mentioned, one gets a total 'needs' figure of £2,277. Bearing in mind that the applicant's state benefits at present provide an income of £1,037, one may consider that the applicant's 'maintenance' for the purpose of the Act requires at least the provision of the difference between those sums, that is, £1,243 per year.

I proceed to the other matters mentioned in section 3(1), (b) and (c), which do not apply. As to (d), the deceased had, in my view, compelling obligations and responsibilities toward the applicant and the more since it appears that the applicant's father (the deceased first defendant) was apparently without any resources from which he could be expected to make any provision for his daughter. As to (e) in section 3(1) the size of the net estate, as that term is defined in the Act, appears to be the £26,737 that I have mentioned. The error is readily realisable. One has, of course, well in mind (f) in the subsection. Then one comes to (g). In this connection it seems to me that it is a relevant consideration that the deceased's estate was derived from her own family and not in any way from her husband, the deceased first defendant. The effect of the intestacy law in this case is that the deceased's estate passes by way of her husband to her stepson, with her own daughter left with virtually nothing.

With these considerations in mind, it seems plain to me that a substantial order ought to be made in the applicant's favour for her maintenance. Her maintenance in hospital must be rendered more happy if she is afforded the outings and holidays she enjoys and as well, if possible, is able to be given some of the other comforts and pleasures which she appreciates in the way of a television set, tape recorders, extra new clothes and the like.

It seems to me that this is a case for an order in the way of a lump sum. The sum will be administered under the direction of the Court of Protection. I have in mind that a receiver could administer the fund, together with the applicant's other capital, and from time to time capital or income could be expended out of the whole fund as might be advised from time to time by the medical and nursing staff at Langdon Hospital. Mr Heath suggested that the whole of the deceased's estate ought to be made over for the applicant's benefit. I do not think that reasonable financial provision goes as far as that in this case. Mr Heath in the alternative view suggested a lump sum calculated in the figure of £15,126. The calculation was suggested by the course being taken by Hollings J in *Malone v Harrison* [1979] 1 WLR 1353. I found Mr Heath's suggestion for a mathematical calculation interesting and instructive. But in the particular circumstances of this case I think that what is required is to assess, having regard to the size of the deceased's net estate, what is the appropriate sum required for the applicant's maintenance, having regard to the applicant's other resources. I have in mind that there should be provided for the applicant such capital sum as will enable her to be maintained with the possibility of providing for her from time to time such benefits as I have already indicated.

Accordingly, I direct the sum of £15,000 to be paid out of the estate for the benefit of the plaintiff. That payment will be in satisfaction of the applicant's rights under the Act and of her rights under the intestacy. The remainder of the deceased's estate will pass by way of the first defendant's estate to the second defendant. The applicant's costs will be paid out of the estate, as will those of applicant's costs on a common fund basis. I desire to make it clear that the plaintiff's payment of £15,000 will be clear of all costs. The Official Solicitor may give a good receipt for the payment, and I desire that the Official Solicitor should consider with the Court of Protection how the money, together with the plaintiff's other assets, may be properly applied for her maintenance in conjunction with the medical and nursing staff at Langdon Hospital.

Index